HANDBOOK ON CONTINGENT VALUATION

Handbook on Contingent Valuation

Edited by

Anna Alberini

Associate Professor, Department of Agricultural and Resource Economics, University of Maryland, US and SIEV Coordinator, Fondazione Eni Enrico Mattei, Italy

James R. Kahn

John F. Hendon Professor of Economics and Director of Environmental Studies, Washington and Lee University, US and Collaborating Professor, Centro de Ciências do Ambiente, Universidade Federal do Amazonas

Edward Elgar
Cheltenham, UK • Northampton, MA, USA

Published by
Edward Elgar Publishing Limited
Glensanda House
Montpellier Parade
Cheltenham
Glos GL50 1UA
UK

Edward Elgar Publishing, Inc.
136 West Street
Suite 202
Northampton
Massachusetts 01060
USA

A catalogue record for this book
is available from the British Library

Library of Congress Cataloging-in-Publication Data
Handbook on contingent valuation / edited by Anna Alberini and James R. Kahn.
    p. cm. – (Elgar original reference)
  1. Contingent valuation. 2. Natural resources–Valuation. 3. Environmental policy. 4. Environmental economics. I. Alberini, Anna. II. Kahn, James R. III. Series.

HB846.55.H36 2006
33.7'01'51578–dc23   2005049466

ISBN-13: 978 1 84064 208 7
ISBN-10: 1 84064 208 4

Printed and bound by MPG Books Ltd, Bodmin, Cornwall

Contents

Contributors

Mary Clare Ahearn, Economic Research Service, US Department of Agriculture, USA

Anna Alberini, Department of Agricultural and Resource Economics, University of Maryland, USA

Dan Biller, World Bank, USA

Glenn C. Blomquist, Department of Economics, University of Kentucky, USA

Kevin J. Boyle, Department of Economics, University of Maine, USA

William S. Breffle, Stratus Consulting, USA

Richard T. Carson, Department of Economics, University of California, USA

James F. Casey, Department of Economics, Washington and Lee University, USA

Todd L. Cherry, Department of Economics, Applachian State University, USA

Gregory Cooper, Society and Professions Program, Washington and Lee University, USA

Maureen Cropper, World Bank and Department of Economics, University of Maryland, USA

J. Mark Fly, Department of Forestry, Wildlife, and Fisheries, University of Tennessee, USA

Peter Frykblom, Department of Economics, Applachian State University, USA

Brent Haddad, Department of Environmental Studies, University of California-Santa Cruz, USA

Mitiku Haile, Melelle University College, Ethiopia

Daniel R. Hellerstein, Economic Research Service, US Department of Agriculture, USA

Richard Howarth, Environmental Studies Program, Dartmouth College, USA

Paul M. Jakus, Department of Economics, Utah State University, USA

James R. Kahn, Environmental Studies Program and Department of Economics, Washington and Lee University, USA

Julian Lampietti, World Bank, USA

Carmelo J. Léon, Department of Applied Economic Analysis, University of Las Palmas, Spain

Roberto León, Department of Economics, University of Leicester, United Kingdom

John A. List, Agricultural and Resource Economics Department, University of Maryland, USA

John B. Loomis, Department of Agricultural and Resource Economics, Colorado State University, USA

Robert Cameron Mitchell, Clark University, USA

Edward R. Morey, Department of Economics, University of Colorado, USA

Christine Poulos, RTI International, USA

Karoline Rogge, Fraunhofer Institute for Systems and Innovation Research, Germany

Robert D. Rowe, Stratus Consulting, USA

Giovanni Ruta, World Bank, USA

Jason F. Shogren, Department of Economics and Finance, University of Wyoming, USA

V. Kerry Smith, Department of Agricultural and Resource Economics, North Carolina State University, USA

Becky Stephens, Department of Forestry, Wildlife, and Fisheries, University of Tennessee, USA

Steven Stewart, Department of Hydrology and Water Resources, University of Arizona, USA

Laura O. Taylor, Department of Economics, Georgia State University, USA

Hale W. Thurston, US Environmental Protection Agency, USA

Donald M. Waldman, Department of Economics, University of Colorado, USA

John C. Whitehead, Department of Economics, Appalachian State University, USA

Dale Whittington, University of North Carolina, USA

Acknowledgements

There are many people to thank in the writing, editing and publishing of this book. First and foremost, we would like to thank the authors for their hard work and incredible insights and for their patience, as this book was long delayed in coming together. Second, we would like to thank Elizabeth Creasey for her assistance in editing and producing the final manuscript. Finally we would like to thank Edward Elgar, Dymphna Evans, and Catherine Elgar for their editorial assistance and for their patience in staying with the book as it came together.

1 Introduction

Anna Alberini and James R. Kahn

1.1 Introduction

The process of valuing environmental resources has never been a straight-forward process. Although the valuation methodologies have been contributing to an understanding of the social benefits of environmental improvement (or costs of environmental change) for 50 years, the process of environmental valuation remains controversial, and in many ways divides the environmental economics profession. Additionally, the process of environmental valuation is questioned by any who approach the environmental decision-making process from the perspective of other academic disciplines, or from different stakeholder positions. Since the Exxon Valdez oil spill, and the resulting controversy over valuation methods, many eminent researchers have contributed to the process of developing a better understanding of valuation methods, how to reduce biases associated with their measurement, and how to better employ these estimates in the environmental decision-making process.[1]

This book represents a further attempt to contribute to the process of reducing these conflicts by improving valuation methods, reducing biases associated with estimates, and developing an improved understanding of the strengths and weaknesses of contingent valuation and associated methodologies. Despite the progress of others in recent years, this process of refinement and development must be continued. One important reason for this is that the valuation process has become more difficult at the same time it has become more crucial. The question of the times has shifted from the need to measure the damages associated with a specific environmental accident or specific impact on a local environmental resource to more of a focus on system-wide environmental change.

The Exxon Valdez spill generated a flurry of research in valuation methods and in contingent valuation specifically, which significantly contributed to the further development of these techniques. However, while we recognize that much progress was made, in some ways the process was analogous to a nation's military preparing to fight the last war rather than the war of the future. For the most part, research in the 1990s was focused on the development of better estimates for natural resource damage assessment, even though this decade saw system-wide change become more pronounced (or even alarming) with the increased awareness of atmospheric

change, loss of biodiversity, collapse of coral reefs, extensive tropical deforestation, desertification, and global climate change.

At the same time the parameters of environmental change increased the
difficulty of producing valid estimates of value, the need for valid estimates
also increased. Throughout the world, but particularly in the United
States, the political process has dismissed the results of scientific investigation with imprecise conjecture, pseudo-science, and political spin. If well-
established results such as the relationship between increased atmospheric
concentrations of greenhouse gases and mean global temperature, or the
impact of increased arsenic concentrations on human health are dismissed
by political spin, where does that leave value estimates based on hypothetical survey questions and statistical analysis of these responses? If the
results of contingent valuation and other valuation estimation techniques
are to have any possibility of influencing the policy process, they must be
sufficiently robust so that they will stand up to both scientific and political
contest.

This is the area in which this book tries to make its contribution. The
editors and the authors have worked hard to try to improve the understanding of contingent valuation so that it can be used in the decision-making
process and to further develop the techniques to improve the validity of the
estimates, thereby increasing the confidence by which we can use estimates
in the decision-making process.

The book is divided into three main sections. Part I is entitled 'Contingent
Valuation and Economic Theory', Part II is entitled 'Econometric and
Empirical Issues in Contingent Valuation', and Part III is entitled
'Applications'. Although we have organized the book this way, the chapters
tend to make contributions in more than one of these areas.

Part I leads off with Kerry Smith's 'Fifty years of contingent valuation'.
This comprehensive chapter summarizes the major developments and
contributions of contingent valuation since inception five decades ago.
Smith's contribution is followed by John Whitehead's chapter entitled
'Practitioner's primer on the contingent valuation method'. The Whitehead
chapter provides an excellent guide for the novice to implement his or her
first contingent valuation study. It is also an excellent source of tips and
insights for the more experienced contingent valuation practitioner. The
next chapter in this section is by John Whitehead and Glenn Blomquist and
examines how the results of contingent valuation studies can be used in conjunction with cost–benefit analysis. The next chapters examine contingent
valuation from non-neoclassical perspectives. Gregory Cooper looks at the
ethical implications of the use of contingent valuation, while Brent Haddad
and Richard Horworth examine contingent valuation from an ecological
economics perspective.

The second part focuses on statistical and methodological contributions of contingent valuation. The part begins with a discussion of the conjoint analysis methodology, by Steven Stewart and James Kahn. Laura O. Taylor examines how experimental economics can be used to better understand the nature of potential biases associated with contingent valuation. Mary Ahearn, Kevin Boyle, and Daniel Hellerstein examine design issues in the use of contingent valuation to inform a public policy decision, in this case the benefits of improved grassland bird populations due to the Conservation Reserve Program. The next chapter, by Carmelo J. León and Roberto León, discusses how Bayesian techniques can improve the process of hypothesis testing in contingent valuation. The part concludes with a chapter by Paul Jakus, which provides a discussion of ways to develop better value estimates when research budgets are restricted.

The third part focuses on applications, although many methodological insights are provided in these application chapters. The first chapter in this part is by Hale Thurston and looks at the application of contingent valuation methods using internet tools. Next, John Loomis uses contingent valuation to examine the value of wildlife and habitat preservation. Todd L. Cherry, Jason F. Shogren, Peter Frykblom, and John A. List are the authors of the next chapter, which focuses on the difficult task of measuring the value of endangered species. The next three chapters focus on the application of valuation methods in developing countries. Christine Poulos, Maureen Cropper, Julian Lampietti, Dale Whittington, and Mitiku Haile look at the use of contingent valuation to measure the benefits of a public health program, focusing on the provision of insecticide-treated mosquito nets. James Casey's chapter provides another example of conjoint analysis, using a case study that examines the value that subsistence farmers place on participation in agroforestry schemes. Dan Biller, Karoline Rogge and Giovanni Ruta provide a quantitative analysis of a set of contingent valuation studies in developing countries. The final group of chapters in this part look at contingent valuations studies of toxic substance problems. William Breffle, Edward Morey, Robert Rowe, and Donald Waldman look at the problem of PCBs and fish consumption advisories, while Richard Carson and Robert Cameron Mitchell look at trihalomethanes and public perceptions towards risk.

Note

1.   For a good summary of these contributions, see Smith's Chapter 2 of this book.

PART I

CONTINGENT VALUATION AND ECONOMIC THEORY

2 Fifty years of contingent valuation
V. Kerry Smith*, †

2.1 Introduction

Econometric analyses and testing of economic models began during the last 50 years. Contingent valuation (CV) developed over the same time period.[1] CV uses survey questions to elicit information that allows economic values for non-market resources to be estimated. Today contingent valuation occupies a strange position in economics. A significant component of the CV research, in both the USA and Europe, has been conducted to evaluate policy alternatives (see Carson, 2003). Little of this work has been associated with litigation. Yet in considering the relevance of CV estimates, the US Office of Management and Budget's (2003) draft guidance for preparing benefit–cost analysis as part of the evaluation of regulations reiterates several of the criteria for a reliable study that were recommended by the National Oceanic and Atmospheric Administration's (NOAA) Panel. The NOAA Panel was charged, in the early 1990s, with responsibility for evaluating contingent valuation for use in natural resource damage assessments.[2]

Current research on contingent valuation has pursued methodological issues in the structure of choice and open-ended valuation questions (Cameron et al., 2002), experimental design (Kanninen, 2002), interrelationships between public goods (Bateman et al., 2004), as well as numerous policy issues ranging from estimating the willingness to pay for reductions in risk of premature death (Krupnick et al., 2002 and Alberini et al., 2001) to managing waste from large-scale hog operations (Mansfield and Smith, 2002). Many of the issues raised in early contingent valuation surveys have been 'rediscovered' under the label of behavioral economics. Nonetheless, despite a spreading of survey methods to a wide range of applications (Blinder, 1991; Berry et al., 1998), there remains 'discomfort' among most economists about using the estimates from contingent valuation to measure consumers' willingness to pay for changes in non-market goods. This concern is especially pronounced in applications involving resources that might be associated with non-use values. In this respect, then, the empirical research sponsored by Exxon (see Hausman, 1993) continues to haunt CV researchers.

Fortunately, this anxiety has not impeded a robust research program from using CV, or CV-like, methods in at least four areas:

- refinement of econometric approaches for estimating parametric, semi-parametric, and non-parametric models using discrete and other types of censored responses to survey questions;
- application of repeated choice, preference scaling, or ranking questions with different sequences of hypothetical variations in the attributes of environmental resources;
- investigation of the incentive properties of different modes for eliciting respondents' preferences for market and non-market resources using theoretical, experimental, and survey techniques; and
- integration of revealed and stated preference data in the joint estimation of individual preferences where there exist opportunities to collect both types of information from a common group of individuals.

Moreover, in recent years the Association of Environmental and Resource Economists has recognized with their distinguished research awards several of the early research contributions relating to CV, including Randall et al. (1974), Bishop and Heberlein (1979), Hanemann (1984), and Mitchell and Carson (1989). Overall, then, the current activities in environmental economics are not consistent with the mainstream concerns. Clearly one motivation for the highly visible controversy in the United States – large-scale damage assessments – has been removed. A great deal of additional research has been developed, but CV and CV-like applications for the purpose of measuring economic values have reverted to a 'tolerated fringe' within environmental economics. There is not a strong presence in mainstream applications or among faculty in leading departments in the USA.[3]

This chapter has three objectives: (a) to describe what we actually know about the performance of survey approaches for inferring individuals' values for changes in non-market resources; (b) to outline several new, or under-recognized, reasons that assure, in my view, CV or CV-like methods will remain a significant part of efforts to understand consumer preferences for non-market (and new) goods; and (c) to suggest ways in which environmental economists can enhance acceptance for measures of the economic values of non-marketed goods in general and CV in particular by the mainstream body of the profession.

The chapter is developed in four sections after this introduction. Section 2.2 compares CV questions with others commonly used in economics and acknowledges the limitations in the information that is *actually* available for most revealed preference methods. Section 2.3 describes the evolution of CV research as well as the methodological and empirical issues the method helped to resolve. In the process it summarizes where we stand and why some economists in other fields remain skeptical about CV.

Section 2.4 describes reasons assuring that CV will not 'go away'. The last section discusses some practical steps that may help to increase confidence in the method.

2.2   Questions and economic data

A recent referee's report, commenting on some proposed travel cost recreation demand research, identifies a problem in much of empirical economics. The referee noted that data obtained from questions about a set of individuals' past fishing trips were not consistent with 'revealed preference methods'. *A market record had not provided them.* These comments reflect a difficulty in much of the empirical research in economics. There seems to be a belief that the information available from public sources is collected using a neutral external process that registers outcomes of people's market choices. This assumption is generally incorrect. The 2000 Census of the United States provides a tangible reminder that much of what we commonly accept as revealed preference data arises from surveys of individuals, describing their own (or their household's) activities or summarizing information developed from other sources (for example a firm's records) in response to a set of instructions.

Established US economic surveys, whether the Consumer Expenditure Survey, the Current Population Survey, Panel Study on Income Dynamics, or, more recently, the Health and Retirement Study, all result from interviews with samples of respondents. All require people to report information about their activities, financial circumstances, family, or health status. They often involve some type of judgment by the respondents involved. Using the implicit standards in the comment I cited at the outset of this section, none of the economic data in these sources would qualify as consistent with the 'revealed preference standard'. The reason is direct. There is no reason for public records of most market transactions. Only in situations where there are taxes or regulations does one find detailed economic data on prices and quantities.[4] Until recently the same statement would have applied to private records as well. However, the dramatic advances in micro-computers have enabled record keeping and expanded the prospects for maintaining and analysing private data that are the result of market transactions by individuals.[5]

While these new sources offer intriguing opportunities for research, they have not been the norm for revealed preference research to date. Instead, most economic data are derived from recall questions. These can include requests for information about the respondent's past behavior or about members of his/her household or extended family. The time spans involved can extend as long as a year or require periodic reports, through diaries or repeated interviews to form a panel.

At least two limitations in these types of questions are important to their role as a performance standard in evaluating the reliability of stated preference questions. First, there is an established literature on the effects of: time span, questioning mode, extent of aggregation of events by size or type, as well as the influence of demographic and cognitive factors on the recall bias in these responses. Westat, Inc.'s (1989) panel study of the effects of time span for the accuracy of responses to the US Fish and Wildlife Service's National Survey of Fishing, Hunting, and Wildlife Associated Recreation is one of the most widely recognized evaluations of these effects on data used in recreation models. This study found substantial overstatement of the proportion taking fishing trips as well as the average number of fishing trips, days, and trip-related expenditures using an annual recall question in comparison to shorter time periods. Earlier recall studies with surveys involving consumer expenditures and earnings confirm the presence of substantial biases with lengthening of the recall period and changes in the character of expenditures involved in the questions. Both over- and understatements have been reported.

Second, and equally important for panel databases, the process of collecting information from respondents should be considered an economic choice. Both the early recall studies and the more recent experience with the panel surveys used in damage assessment cases suggest respondents may well 'learn' that their answers can increase the time commitment expected of them. As a result, it has been suggested that observed declines in recreation participation in an ongoing panel are the result of survey incentives and *not* actual behavior (see Hanemann, 1995 and Desvousges et al., 1996 for further discussion).[6]

Conventional sources of microeconomic data can require tasks in addition to or instead of simple recall.[7] One especially important example involves the estimation of the rent and the home values for owner-occupied housing. Adjustment of this index to account for the rent attributed to owner-occupied housing has been an important component of the reforms made in recent years to the Consumer Price Index. What is used to meet this need is the home-owners' rent estimate? It is based on a hypothetical judgment responding to the following question:

> If you were to rent out your home today, how much do you think it would rent for monthly, unfurnished and without utilities?

The Census of Population uses a comparable question to estimate the property value. Owners are asked:

> What is the value of this property, that is, how much *do you think* this property would sell for if it were for sale?

Data derived from both of these questions have considerable impacts on economic policy. In non-market valuation the home value question continues to serve as a basis for estimating the marginal willingness to pay (WTP) for reducing air pollution (see Kahn, 1997 and Chay and Greenstone, 2000 as examples).[8]

The point of this overview of existing sources of micro-data is not one of discrediting all data describing individual consumption and prices (or other resource allocation choices associated with market exchanges). Rather, the lesson to be drawn from these examples is that data collection itself is an economic activity. What is collected is the outcome of an economic choice (for example a respondent allocates time, effort, and so on to provide the information requested). The debates over the reliability of contingent valuation have seemed to suggest that these issues are only relevant to stated preference data. I believe they are relevant in varying degrees to most commonly available public data sources.[9]

These concerns are the same as the first of the two questions often raised with CV – to what extent do respondents take the time and make the effort to seriously consider the hypothetical situation being posed? For most economic data the process of reporting the information imposes costs with few obvious benefits for the individual respondent. These disincentives provide a partial explanation for why survey research emphasizes the importance of making the context and framing of questions salient to those being surveyed.

Given this shared problem of creating incentives for respondents to expend time and effort, the key distinction between conventional surveys and CV surveys (on this issue) must be whether the hypothetical nature of the choice being offered (or the lack of experience in making these choices) makes it differentially more burdensome. When interpreted in this context, the efforts since the Carson et al. (1992) *Exxon Valdez* survey and the NOAA panel recommendations (as discussed in more detail below) can be seen as responsive to this concern. Unfortunately, despite the extensive research on the effects of information and other efforts to make CV choices tangible and salient, there have not been comparable efforts evaluating the sensitivity of reports provided about revealed preference behaviors as the character of the questions is altered. Thus, at this point all we know is that information can matter to CV responses (and we would expect that it should), but we cannot evaluate whether this effect is any different from what would happen if a comparable effort was made to evaluate the data about 'real' behavior or actual prices collected with more conventional economic surveys.

The second issue raised with stated choices stems from the role of financial incentives. It is argued that there is no reason to interpret tradeoffs reflected in stated choices as comparable to those where a choice cannot be made without an explicit financial commitment. This concern, in contrast to the first, has received attention and some of the findings are discussed below.

2.3 The evolution of CV

2.3.1 Early efforts and shared mistakes

After Davis's (1963) path-breaking research, initial applications of contingent valuation can be classified into three groups. Some discussion of each provides an important context for both the controversies that developed over CV's reliability and the lines of research present in the current literature. The first was a dominant initial component of the literature. The applications of CV in this group were interpreted at the time as 'experimental'. Interviews were often conducted by graduate students with convenience samples, and a key focus of the studies was to evaluate the influence of different ways the survey questions were asked, considering especially the importance of strategic responses.[10] A wide array of 'biases' was defined and questioning formats proposed to minimize their impact.[11]

The experimental flavor of the use of surveys may have stemmed from Davis's use of the term 'bidding games' to describe the iterative questioning of respondents, asking the maximum amount they would pay for some specified 'commodity'. The object of choice (or commodity) was a change in one or more dimensions of environmental resource that was described to each individual. The process involved a starting point and progressive adjustments by the interviewer up or down from it, based on the respondent's answers. Analogies to auctions and bidding were often used in the early literature (despite the fact that there was no interaction among consumers). The size of the increments, refinements to them, explanations for changes (once a response was given), and so on were vaguely described. In some cases, it was not clear whether individual interviewers (for example economics graduate students) adjusted survey scripts to try to make them more understandable to respondents. Questions were developed by researchers without apparent field testing in advance of the surveys involved. None of these comments is intended to be critical of this work. The research efforts were regarded by all involved as experimental and intended to evaluate the contingent valuation method in relatively small-scale applications.

The second group begins with Randall et al. (1974). This study is credited with doing the first, serious, professionally administered, population survey to collect CV responses.[12] It also used the so-called 'bidding game' framework, but adhered to the conventions of professional survey research with training of interviewers. The survey questionnaire was evaluated and revised in two pre-tests. This close adherence to the protocols of survey

research is the hallmark of the second line of research and is generally associated with all of the Mitchell–Carson surveys. While their work was conducted in several different stages (with a 1981 pilot survey), all of their
findings remained in unpublished EPA reports prior to their 1989 book. Bill
Desvousges and I had access to the early versions of their results and
worked cooperatively in exchanging results and questionnaires. Their final
water quality survey, conducted in November 1983, reflected both the experience of their pilot survey (conducted in 1981) and the findings of our
survey for the Monongahela study conducted in November–December
1981 (see Desvousges et al., 1983 and Smith and Desvousges, 1986).

That research, along with virtually all of the work conducted in the first
two groups, shared another attribute. Because they were generally funded
by mission agencies, projects intended to be primarily methodological had
to have a link to a specific policy issue. In many cases, they were never
envisioned to be ready for use in specific policy analyses. Rather the objective was to illustrate how the CV approach might offer estimates to meet
policy objectives, provided a more complete evaluation of the survey
alternatives was conducted. For example, the Monongahela study was
regarded as a methodological effort to evaluate CV questioning modes and
conduct a comparative study (following Brookshire et al., 1981, 1982) of
CV and revealed preference (for example travel cost recreation demand)
estimates of the value of water quality changes.[13] To my knowledge,
Randall et al. (1974) and Mitchell and Carson's final survey (1984) were
the primary exceptions. Nonetheless, after the fact, many of the studies'
results *have* been used in policy analyses. Later critiques of CV have
described the work *as if* those involved designed it to serve the policy
objectives identified in each study. This misunderstanding is unfortunate
and does not reflect the actual intentions of the researchers involved in
those early analyses.

A third group of research efforts seems to have been lost in discussion of
this early CV research. The first of these, predating Randall et al. (1974),
was the 1969 Hammack and Brown survey of hunters' willingness to pay for
hunting published in 1974 (see Brown and Hammack, 1973 and Hammack
and Brown, 1974). This group of studies focused on specific populations
(usually involved in some form of outdoor recreation) that were identified
through on-site surveys, licenses or, in Hammack and Brown's case, through
required federal waterfowl hunting stamps.

Following the Hammack and Brown lead in 1971–72, Charles Cicchetti
and I conducted the first (to my knowledge) CV survey to investigate what
was later described as the 'scope' of change in environmental quality using
a sample of wilderness recreationists.[14] The sample was derived from
an earlier record of their entry to the Spanish Peaks Primitive (later

Wilderness) Area in Montana (see Cicchetti and Smith, 1973). By varying the potential congestion it was suggested each respondent would experience during a proposed trip to the same area and then asking for their maximum willingness to pay for each trip, we estimated how different aspects of congestion affected their valuation of wilderness recreation trips at this site.

Research falling into either of the first two groups generally shared characteristics that I believe influenced both the development of subsequent applications and the degree of acceptance experienced later for the method. It appeared (to those doing it) that CV's ability to control the object of choice presented removed the need to impose prior restrictions (from economic theory) on how the results were interpreted. This statement is a complex way of saying the estimates were usually summarized with univariate statistics – sample means and variances – computed for the treatment groups comprising the sample. The treatments were usually attributes of the framing of the valuation question, the starting point used in the iterative bidding question, or the use of another question format. Several studies did report regression summaries of responses, and Desvousges and I (see Desvousges et al., 1983) attached considerable importance to the role of income as the only variable we hypothesized economic theory implied should be relevant. With the benefit of hindsight, more effort at linking the sources of use and non-use value would have provided a wider range of such variables to investigate. What was missing was a link between the functions estimated and the constrained preference models economic theory implied should be linked to economic tradeoffs.

Some years later Xiaolong Zhang and I (1997) proposed a framework that explicitly defined the structure of use and non-use values with an individual's preference function and then used travel cost and CV data to attempt to estimate the model. To illustrate the issues, we considered a specific functional form that conforms to Hanemann's (1988) proposed definition for non-use values. His suggestion requires separability between the resource(s) contributing to the non-use enhancement to well-being and the use-related motives. Consider an additively separable component with the quality of one of two types of beach resources providing the source of the benefits and the second providing the source for the non-use. Further, assume the use-related benefits arise from a trip to a recreation site, such as a beach. In the example here, we selected a specification for the indirect utility function that is consistent with a linear demand (and thus a finite choke price). The non-use contribution is assumed to stem from a CES function in the qualities (q_1 and q_2) for the use-related and the non-use resources. The latter might be an estuarine reserve, precluded from use to protect fragile habitat. Equation (2.1) illustrates the function. It would be consistent with a linear Marshallian demand (that is, $t = \text{trips} = \alpha + \beta p + \gamma m + \delta q_1$ with $\beta < 0$):

$$V = \exp(-\gamma p)\left(m + \frac{1}{\gamma}\left(\beta p + \alpha + \delta q_1 + \frac{\beta}{\gamma}\right) + d \cdot (q_1^{\eta} + q_2^{\eta})^{\frac{1}{\eta}}\right). \quad (2.1)$$

The point of our argument was to indicate that the specification of a preference structure allows an interrelationship between CV questions for non-use choices with either other non-use resources or with quality attributes that might be related to use of another resource. Thus, there should be cross-equation restrictions for the parameters associated with models for each data source. Table 2.1 illustrates these possibilities with the travel cost demand function and a variety of quality changes and payment mechanisms. Notice the shared parameters across the different willingness to pay definitions. These relationships become the source of the links I referred to earlier. We were unable to exploit fully this framework due to data limitations.

More recently, Herriges et al. (2004) have used structural logic to consider the importance of identification conditions in relating use and non-use values. With a modified Stone Geary specification, they use a Kuhn–Tucker corner solution model to explicitly introduce weak complementarity together with the prospect for corner solutions to attempt to estimate use and non-use values. They observe that tests of weak complementarity and the use/non-use value distinctions are conditional in an important way on the maintained assumptions associated with the preference specification. Moreover, they suggest, based on their analysis of this specification, that:

> The demand systems imply different welfare estimates depending upon what one assumes to be the underlying form of preferences, with no behavioral footprint available to distinguish among competing alternatives (p. 12).

However, as they conclude, this limitation arises when analysts are unwilling to use stated preference data to further discriminate among restrictions. This issue is one point of the algebra in Table 2.1. With multiple sets of choice information and a preference specification, we may be able to discriminate among some aspects of the alternative treatments of non-market goods. We will *not* escape all of the maintained restrictions associated with a parametric specification of preferences. They are what provide the linkages necessary to use multiple types of information in the tests of the role of non-market resources in preferences.

A second feature was the presumption that respondents *would* accept the hypothetical object of choice without asking how the implied change would be accomplished. The use of focus groups to evaluate CV wording

Table 2.1 Behavioral models linked by use and non-use motives

Travel cost demand	$trips = \alpha + \beta p + \gamma m + \delta q_1^0$ with $\beta < 0$
Willingness to pay for an improvement in q_1 from q_1^0 to q_1^1 (used-related)	$WTP = \delta(q_1^1 - q_1^0) + d \cdot (e^{\gamma p})[((q_1^1)^\eta + (q_2^0)^\eta)^{\frac{1}{\eta}} - ((q_1^0)^\eta + (q_2^0)^\eta)^{\frac{1}{\eta}}]$
Willingness to pay for an improvement in q_2 from q_2^0 to q_2^1 (non-use-related)	$WTP = d \cdot (e^{\gamma p})[((q_1^0)^\eta + (q_2^1)^\eta)^{\frac{1}{\eta}} - ((q_1^0)^\eta + (q_2^0)^\eta)^{\frac{1}{\eta}}]$
User fee (F) and improvement in use-related q from q_1^0 to q_1^1	$F = -\frac{1}{\gamma} \ln \left[\dfrac{m + \frac{1}{\gamma}\left(\beta p + \alpha + \delta q_1^0 + \frac{\beta}{\gamma}\right)}{m + \frac{1}{\gamma}\left(\beta p + \alpha + \delta q_1^1 + \frac{\beta}{\gamma}\right)} + \dfrac{((q_1^0)^\eta + (q_2^0)^\eta)^{\frac{1}{\eta}} - ((q_1^1)^\eta + (q_2^0)^\eta)^{\frac{1}{\eta}}}{m + \frac{1}{\gamma}\left(\beta p + \alpha + \delta q_1^1 + \frac{\beta}{\gamma}\right)} \right]$

came later in the evolution of CV practice (see Desvousges et al., 1984). As a result, some studies varied both the baseline condition of a resource and the new environmental conditions offered as part of the CV question without specific attention to the actual state of the resources involved.

Finally, the analysis rarely collected, and never (to my knowledge) used, information about the behavioral changes that an individual *would* make if the change in the resource was introduced. For example, when we asked about improvement in water quality conditions in the Monongahela River from its current (at the time) boatable conditions to swimmable conditions, we asked if those respondents would visit sites along the river more frequently. Unfortunately, we did not use their responses as integrated components of the analysis. Today, the responses to these follow-ups, asking about the number of additional trips and their location, would be integrated into the models and estimates used to analyse the data.[15]

The composite of the Bishop–Heberlein (1979) simulated market analysis, along with their introduction of discrete choice take-it-or-leave-it questions and Hanemann's (1984) explicit link between the econometric analysis and preference functions, set in motion changes that have brought the current analyses of CV data more directly into line with the practice of micro-econometric research in other applications. Now there is extensive use of restrictions from economic theory in the analysis of CV data.

What has not been appreciated in both the reviews of the CV literature and by critics of its findings is that the last category of the CV survey did not have the attributes of the first two. Beginning with Brown and Hammack, economic functions *were* specified to be consistent with the behavior being modeled. Changes in environmental resources *were* closely linked to existing conditions and behavioral responses were often assumed to take place. The result, I believe, is a less critical judgment on the findings from these studies on the part of mainstream economists.[16] This distinction has been interpreted as simply reflecting the experience of the respondents with the resource changes asked about and the focus on use values. However, it could equally well have been due to the distinctive differences in the CV questions and in the ways they were analysed.

2.3.2 *Discrete response CV*
Bishop and Heberlein's (1979) evaluation of CV versus travel cost methods introduced the discrete response CV question where a respondent states a purchase or voting decision. It is the intellectual 'parent' of most of the research focused on refining the econometric methods used with contingent valuation. In addition it motivated a specific focus on what economic theory implies can be learned about an individual's preferences from the answers given to discrete response questions. Hanemann's (1984) seminal

paper transformed the theory and the practice of CV for all single and multiple discrete response questions.[17]

An important byproduct of Hanemann's explicit use of theory in interpreting CV data was the need to be precise about the description of how people answer stated preference questions. All of this subsequent literature (including the research on the incentive properties of different types of CV questions, see Carson et al., 1999) assumes that they are equivalent in the incentives they create to actual choice questions.[18] Carson et al. describe this condition as a requirement of consequential choice. This requirement means not only must the objects of choice be presented in a way that they are believable, but respondents also must believe their answers have an impact on provision of the good.[19]

The attention given to linking the analysis of CV responses to the theory has not been uniform in all applications. There remains substantial confusion about the differences between discrete response and open-ended questions. Some of it arises from differences in maintained assumptions about consumer preferences for the open-ended and discrete response questions. Most estimates for mean or median willingness to pay with discrete response questions begin with a specification for preferences, including unobserved heterogeneity (that is, a distribution for the error). Comparisons of their results with other question modes cannot distinguish the effect of mode from these maintained assumptions, unless it is built into the design of the tests (see Huang and Smith, 1998, 2002 and Poe and Vossler, 2002). To my knowledge, Cameron et al. (2002) offer the first test of different question modes, including an 'actual' program that allows evaluation of the stated preference with a real solicitation for participation.[20] The program was a green energy plan offered by an electric utility that involved using renewable sources for energy and planting trees. Their study included: an actual choice using a dichotomous format, a hypothetical discrete choice with multiple prices, an open-ended question about willingness to pay (WTP), a payment card format, a multiple bounded elicitation, and a conjoint format.[21] They conclude that: 'The two methods which appear to be the least consistent with the others are the only two methods that attempt to elicit WTP directly, rather than inferring WTP from choices' (p. 422). In terms of pairwise tests of the mean willingness to pay, these two methods – open-ended and payment card – are distinctly different from the others.[22] Hypothetical dichotomous, with one price or with multiple prices, was not significantly different from the actual choice results. Conjoint and multiple bounded questions were also not significantly different from the actual. Of course, there were significantly different patterns in the variance of the estimate for WTP, with the one price hypothetical dichotomous choice exhibiting considerable variability. Once multiple prices were introduced, this spread was dramatically reduced.

2.3.3   *Pre-NOAA Panel damage assessments and CV*

The 1989 *Exxon Valdez* oil spill in Alaska changed the professional and public attention given to contingent valuation. Three studies conducted in support of the natural resource damage litigation associated with the spill have been especially influential on CV research. Two of these were intended to evaluate the plausibility of CV estimates of the non-use (or passive use) values people have for environmental resources.[23]

Desvousges et al. (1993) used a survey to elicit people's willingness to pay for avoiding the loss of wildlife (birds) in waste oil holding ponds. By varying the proposed number of birds that would be lost in the event action was not taken, their surveys investigated the sensitivity of CV estimates to the 'size' of the object of choice. The baseline population of birds, target population of respondents, and other dimensions of the CV survey were held constant across three different levels of bird losses. Their findings suggested no significant difference in the estimated mean (or median) willingness to pay for avoiding the different sized bird losses constructed with three independent samples.[24]

Diamond et al. (1993) also reported survey results testing several consistency features they argued were implied by well-behaved preferences. The two that have had the most impact on the subsequent literature were: their tests of CV estimates of the responsiveness to size of object of choice and of the adding-up conditions across different changes posed individually versus as a composite to independent samples.

Following the same practice as the early experimental and general population surveys, the primary reports of this research focused on univariate descriptive statistics for their tests. The clearest case (in terms of the object of choice) questioning consistency of *these* CV estimates with conventional theory seems to arise with the Desvousges et al. 'bird loss' surveys.[25] Diamond et al. (1993) considered different numbers of specific wilderness areas and these, as a result, are harder to reduce to a simple quantity metric.[26]

The last CV study in this litigation group is the Carson et al. (1992) effort to estimate the loss to US households as a result of the spill. In contrast to the earlier two studies, this CV survey *was* intended to develop an estimate of the welfare loss. While never published, the report to the State of Alaska has been widely available (http://www.oilspill.state.ak.us/pdf/econ5.pdf). I believe it had a dramatic effect on research practice. This was accomplished in at least three ways. First, the CV question is about a plan to change environmental resources, *not* a specified change. The plan describes what it is anticipated will happen and is quite specific about the process. As a result, people's choices are about the plan, not the resource. Use of the results to estimate people's willingness to pay for the resource change requires the analyst to consider whether respondents believed the plan would work (see Smith, 1997). Second, the survey was among the most detailed in terms of documenting the steps used in developing a framing of the object and circumstances of the choices posed.

Finally, the analysis distinguished the estimation of a mean willingness to pay from these censored responses from the multivariate analysis of the determinants of respondents' stated choices. As with the Desvousges et al. (1993) and Diamond et al. (1993) studies, the estimates minimized the maintained restrictions imposed on the stated responses in the process of estimating WTP.

2.3.4   NOAA Panel and CV

The *Exxon Valdez* case was settled before anyone learned how CV would fare in court.[27] However, the Superfund legislation and Oil Pollution Act required that regulations specify how the economic damages from natural resource injuries would be measured. Court rulings to challenges to draft rules suggested that CV could be used in this process. The concerns associated with future liabilities likely contributed to Exxon releasing a set of papers of the research it had sponsored in a highly visible conference in 1992. The Hausman (1993) edited volume includes those papers. It had a marked impact on rulemaking and the review panel chaired by Kenneth Arrow and Robert Solow was NOAA's General Counsel's response to the concerns about CV.[28]

The Panel's report provided an extensive set of guidelines for CV survey construction, administration, and analysis. In the Panel's view, 'the more closely the guidelines are followed, the more reliable the result will be' (Arrow et al., 1993, p. 4609). In addition, the Panel distinguished a subset of items from their guidelines for special emphasis and described them as *burden of proof* requirements. In describing the elements with this special focus, the Panel stated:

if a CV survey suffered from any of the following maladies, we would judge its findings 'unreliable':

- a high non-response rate to the entire survey or to the valuation question
- inadequate responsiveness to the scope of the environmental insult
- lack of understanding of the task by the respondents
- lack of belief in the full restoration scenario
- 'yes' or 'no' votes on the hypothetical referendums that are not followed up or explained by making reference to the cost and/or the value of the program. (Arrow et al., 1993, p. 4609)

The second item in this list, 'inadequate responsiveness to the scope of the environmental insult', or the scope test, attracted the most attention and was regarded at the time as an acid test for CV studies.

Given these guidelines and burden of proof requirements, the Arrow–Solow Panel concluded its report noting that:

> under those conditions (and others specified above), CV studies convey useful information. We think it is fair to describe such information as reliable by the standards that seem to be implicit in similar contexts, like market analysis for new and innovative products and the assessment of other damages normally allowed in court proceedings.
> . . . CV produces estimates reliable enough to be the starting point of a judicial process of damage assessment, including passive-use values [i.e., non-use values]. (Arrow et al., 1993, p. 4610)

Their recommendations focused attention on survey and questionnaire design. They also created expectations that there were some economic properties we should expect to observe in WTP estimates. Indeed, Diamond (1996) suggested that the scope test could be made more specific – offering a bound on the WTP estimates for different sized objects of choice. For example, using Δq_1 and Δq_2 as two different changes in an environmental resource q, with $\Delta q_1 > \Delta q_2$), Diamond's bound is given in equation (2.2):

$$WTP(\Delta q_1) \geq (\Delta q_1/\Delta q_2) \cdot WTP(\Delta q_2). \tag{2.2}$$

His result follows from three assumptions: (a) Δq_1 and Δq_2 represent losses in a base level of q to be avoided; (b) the utility function is quasi-linear, so the marginal utility of income is constant; and (c) the plan described as providing the means to avoid the losses is perceived to provide outcomes that are perfect substitutes for the environmental resource q. The first two assumptions influence the specific form of the WTP function and, as Diamond has argued, seem plausible as descriptions of a number of CV applications. The last is not as plausible and plays a central role in Diamond's specific bound for responsiveness to scope as well as in the adding-up test. That is, Hicksian WTP measures differences in the 'spacing' of indifference curves in monetary terms. This can be appreciated when the WTP to obtain the change is written as equation (2.3), (that is, with the initial income m_0, an unchanged price vector, and improved q_1, a higher utility level u_1 can be realized). This equation leads to the informal characterization of WTP as a monetization of the change in utility from u_0 to u_1:

$$WTP = e(p, q_1, u_1) - e(p, q_1, u_0). \tag{2.3}$$

Measures for WTP follow from how the utility function influences the derived relationship (given the effects of budget-constrained utility maximization) between changes in q, income, *and* the spacing in the feasible indifference curves. Normally we describe these distinctions as akin to substitution and income effects, but in fact they are interrelated. Unless we select specifications for preferences that impose specific constraints (for example quasi-linearity), we can expect that the curvature and spacing (or substitution and income) effects will appear to be separable only at a point. Their interrelationship changes as we change either the level of the environmental resource or the level of well-being. When the specification is simplified to permit us to abstract from the role of the income–utility link, it will also have implications for the effects of substitution. Without Diamond's perfect substitution assumption all we can expect from a scope test is that a large amount of the same object should have a greater measured WTP than a smaller amount (provided they are perceived this way by the respondents involved).

Closer scrutiny of the literature over the past five years has revealed in early CV studies that the estimates were in fact consistent with the properties implied by the scope test. Carson et al. (1997), Smith and Osborne (1996), Smith et al. (1997), and Takeuchi and Ueta (1996) (for Japan) among others report summaries of either past evidence or new small-scale surveys that satisfy the broad version of the NOAA Panel's scope test. Most of these studies relate to resources that support uses. As a result, it might be argued that responsiveness to scope effects would be more likely. That is, respondents evaluating changes in resources or their quality would respond to proposed alternatives considering both potential use and any non-use related reasons for their choices.

Overall, the NOAA Panel's report surprised the mainstream of the economics profession, who seemed at the time to have expected a complete repudiation of CV. By contrast, their summary appeared to endorse it. However, there is another interpretation that seems to have been overlooked. This view would hold that the panel's report established such stringent guidelines for CV surveys that it raised the 'price' for 'reliable CV' above the maximum willingness to pay for that information.[29] Thus, it did not have to mandate an end to CV, but instead 'priced the practice out of the market'.[30]

Some authors have argued the report had little overall merit. Rather than pricing 'reliable' CV surveys out of reach, they suggest it distracted practitioners' attention from the *real* problems of how to improve CV. For example, Harrison (2000) notes that:

> The NOAA report was a great disappointment. The CVM literature was slowly emerging from several decades of intellectual darkness, in which one conventional wisdom after another became established by mere repetition. The literature is full

of 'truth by assertion' in which opinions substitute for careful and scientific research; . . . Given the inability of CVM practitioners and consumers to weed out sense from nonsense in the extent literature, it is unlikely that there will be much progress as the result of the NOAA report (p. 2).

This observation is a strong criticism. As I noted earlier, Harrison also documents differences between the Panel's judgments and experimental or conceptual papers on related questions that had been completed at the time their work was undertaken. Nonetheless, it is important to return to the Panel's charge. It was specific to court cases involving damage assessments. Its guidance was to the legal community and potential experts as to the procedures to be used and issues to be addressed to satisfy a *burden of proof* judgment. This context is definitely not the same as should be used in outlining a research agenda or in developing guidance for 'best' research practices. An expert provides an opinion. To be sure, it should be informed by the relevant information, but it remains an opinion. As a result, it would seem to me that Harrison's criticism is not so much directed at the Panel, but rather at subsequent researchers who use the report as a litmus test or set of guidance principles for their research.

2.3.5 The Montrose study

To my knowledge, the only CV effort to meet the NOAA guidelines was undertaken as part of litigation. The analysis was associated with the alleged natural resource injuries due to PCB (polychlorinated biphenyl) and DDT releases in the Southern California Bight. Named for one of the chemical companies (Montrose) associated with some of the releases of these pollutants, the economic analysis for this case involved three components: (a) tests for three parts of the NOAA guidelines; (b) estimates of the willingness to pay for accelerated recovery of injuries assumed to be linked to the releases of the PCB and DDT; and (c) scope effects to evaluate whether willingness to pay measures were sensitive to the 'size' of the injuries. The tests of NOAA Panel recommendations used an exact replication of the Carson et al. (1992) *Exxon Valdez* questionnaire (updated to reflect the date of the new survey). Aspects of this work have been published (see Carson et al., 1997, 1998, as well as Krosnick et al., 2002). However, the distinguishing feature of the study – the scope test – while available as a government report in 1994, has never been published.

Table 2.2 summarizes the features of the three surveys used in the research in comparison to the characteristics of the original Alaska/*Exxon Valdez* analysis. All four surveys used discrete response (take-it-or-leave-it, voting-based) framing for the CV valuation questions as well as in-person interviews. The survey to test three NOAA Panel recommendations was conducted by the National Opinion Research Center at the University of

Table 2.2 A comparison of the features of four surveys

Attribute	Alaska	NORC	Southern California[a] base	Southern California[a] scope
Date of survey	1991	1993	1994	1994
Population	US	12 PSUs[b]	California	California
Object of choice	Plan to provide two Coast Guard ships to escort oil tankers in Prince William Sound to prevent future accidents and avoid future injuries due to oil spills	Same as Alaska	Plan to accelerate recovery of reproduction problems of four species by 45 years[c]	Plan to accelerate recovery of reproduction of two species by 10 years[d]
Sample size	1043	1182	1857	953
Nature of payment	One-time addition to federal income taxes	One-time addition to federal income taxes	One-time addition to California State income taxes	One-time addition to California State income taxes
Tax amounts	$10, $30 $60, $120	$10, $30 $60, $120	$10, $25, $80 $140, $215	$10, $25, $80 $140, $215
Focus groups	7	–	5	9

24

Pre-tests	2 (12, 18)	2[e] (64, 26)	4 (44, 57, 49, 116)	4 (44, 54, 40, 44)
Pilots	4 (105, 195, 244, 176)	–	4 (332, 460, 324, 473)	–
Response rate	75.2%	73.0%	72.1%	73.8%

Notes:

[a] Sample was intended to represent the population of English-speaking Californians, age 18 or older, living in private residences they own or rent (or whose rent or mortgage they contribute to). Thirteen primary sampling units were selected with probabilities proportional to their 1990 Census population counts, including: Del Norte and Humboldt; El Dorado, Placer, Sacramento and Yolo; Alameda, San Mateo, San Francisco, Marin and Contra Costa; San Joaquin; Santa Clara; Fresno; Santa Barbara; Ventura; Los Angeles County; Los Angeles City; Orange; Riverside and San Bernardino; and San Diego. Within the selected PSUs, 652 segments (city blocks, groups of blocks, or Census equivalents in rural areas) were selected with probabilities proportional to their 1990 Census counts of housing units.

[b] The 12 PSUs selected from NORC's master area probability sample were: Baltimore, MD; Birmingham, AL; Boston, MA; Charleston, SC; Harrisburg, PA; Ft. Wayne, IN; Manchester, NY; Nicholas County, KY; Portland, OR; Richmond, VA; Seattle, WA; and Tampa, FL.

[c] The four species include two birds: bald eagles, peregrine falcons; and two fish: white croaker and kelp bass. See Carson et al. (1994) for the description of the injuries. The time period for natural recovery was described as 50 years.

[d] For the scope scenario only the two fish species were described as injured, and the time period for natural recovery was reduced to 15 years.

[e] These pre-tests were conducted to evaluate the instructions used with the design variations, e.g. ballot box, and would-not-vote and composite versions of the questionnaire, not to evaluate framing.

Source: Carson et al. (1996c).

Chicago and is labeled here as the NORC study. It consisted of four separate questionnaires including: (1) a complete replication of the original Alaska instrument modified only slightly to reflect the timing of the new interviews in relation to the *Exxon Valdez* oil spill (termed the *replication* version); (2) a version in which the respondent votes on a paper ballot that is placed in a sealed box and the interviewer does not know the decision (the *ballot box* version); (3) a version where the respondent is told there are three options, 'for', 'against', and 'would not vote' (the *no-vote* version); and (4) a version with the three choice options and the ballot box (the *no-vote/ballot box* version).

Tests of the effect of including a would-not-vote option in a discrete choice/referendum CV question, as well as for the potential of a social desirability effect with in-person interviews (that is, respondents reporting support for a program to please the interviewer) suggest these possibilities were not concerns that require modifications to the framing or implementation of CV questions.[31]

The primary objective of the Montrose study was to estimate the damages associated with injuries to four species thought to have been impacted by DDT and PCB. As noted earlier, the final survey included a test for whether CV estimates of the willingness to pay for resource changes with little apparent use-related motivations would be responsive to the 'size' of the change. The objects of choice in the base and scope surveys were distinguished by the number of species that were identified as injured by the DDT and PCB deposits *and* the time span required for natural recovery to eliminate the source for these injuries. In the base scenario, four species – two birds (bald eagles and peregrine falcons) and two fish (white croaker and California sea bass) – were described as having reproductive problems in the areas affected by the DDT/PCB deposit. If the recovery was left to natural events, the base scenario suggested their recovery would require 50 years. The proposed plan being evaluated with the surveys assured an accelerated recovery of the species. Implementing the plan was to take five years. At the end of the implementation of the plan, the description associated with the CV question indicated that the recovery would be complete. Thus, in the base situation households were asked about a plan that would reduce the recovery time by 45 years. In the scope sample, the number of impacted species was reduced to two – the two fish – and the time for natural recovery was described as 15 years. The time described for the plan to be completed remained at five years.

Several aspects of the development of these scenarios and implementation of the scope test are not necessarily apparent from this summary. They arise because the survey design stressed the importance of logical consistency. It also recognized that when data collection involves 'in-person' interviews, variations in the conditions described in the interview must consider both the assignment of interviewers to versions of the survey and the task of explaining the reasons for these variations to those interviewers. Concerns for logical consistency arise because of the mechanism linking the deposit of DDT and PCB was off the coast of California (under 100 feet of water) to the injuries had to be detailed in a way the respondents could understand. The survey's explanation used the food chain, linking benthic organisms in direct contact with the deposits of DDT and PCB to larger organisms, small fish, and ultimately to the larger fish and then to the birds identified as having documented injuries. In the base scenario it was explained the birds became contaminated by eating contaminated fish. A smaller scenario could not confine the injury to the birds without also explaining how these birds were exposed to the substances that were described as the source of the problem. As a result, the scope was confined to the two fish species.[32] Both injuries were limited to the south coast of California.

To avoid confounding interviewer and version (base versus scope) effects, interviewers were randomly assigned to each version. This process implied each interviewer would be administering both questionnaires. While each respondent received one version, the interviewers administered the questionnaires in a random sequence. This process raised a separate issue. The training of interviewers was conducted to convince them the problem was real and the proposed plan feasible. This process assured they would be convincing in describing it to respondents. This strategy requires some explanation for the scope injury. It was described as reflecting potential scientific uncertainty about the injuries. This explanation was intended to avoid subtle differences in the interviewers' levels of confidence with each version of the survey.

Three separate tests of the responsiveness of WTP to the scope of the injuries presented in the Montrose survey were undertaken. The least restrictive tests are the simple contingency tests comparing the stated choices in the base and scope samples. Table 2.3 reproduces these tests at each of the tax amounts used in the discrete response CV questions (see Carson et al., 1994 for more details). There is a clear difference in stated choices between the two samples with more votes for the plan in the base (larger) injury description. Table 2.3 also reports two further tests. The first of these compares the Turnbull lower bound mean for WTP in both the base and scope samples (see Haab and McConnell, 1997). Both a simple test for differences in these means and a likelihood ratio test for differences in the non-parametric estimates of the distribution confirm significant differences in the base and scope distributions, with respondents willing to pay more for more significant programs.

Table 2.3   Tests for scope with Southern California survey

A. *Contingency tests tax amount*

		For	Against	χ^2	*p*-value[a]
$10	Base (%)	209 (55.9)	165 (44.1)	21.50	0.001 (R)
	Scope	72 (35.6)	130 (64.4)		
$25	Base	163 (46.3)	189 (53.7)	23.50	0.001 (R)
	Scope	45 (24.7)	137 (75.3)		
$80	Base	120 (32.9)	245 (67.1)	14.39	0.001 (R)
	Scope	35 (17.9)	161 (82.1)		
$140	Base	102 (26.5)	283 (73.5)	10.00	0.002 (R)
	Scope	29 (14.9)	166 (85.1)		
$215	Base	85 (22.3)	296 (77.7)	10.85	0.001 (R)
	Scope	19 (10.7)	159 (89.3)		

B. *Turnbull lower bound mean* (**LBM**)

	LBM	Std dev.
Base	$63.24	2.54
Scope	$34.02	2.82
Z-test	7.17	(reject null hypothesis of equality of **LBM** *p*-value <0.001)
Likelihood ratio	83.46	(reject null hypothesis of equality of distributions *p*-value <0.001)

C. *Survival model test results*
(1) Weibull

  Z-test for location parameter   (reject null hypothesis *p*-value <0.001)

  Likelihood ratio test for   (reject null hypothesis *p*-value <0.001)
    location and scale parameter

(2) Log normal

  Z-test for location parameter   (reject null hypothesis *p*-value <0.001)

  Likelihood ratio test for   (reject null hypothesis *p*-value <0.001)
    location and scale parameters

Note: [a]R – reject null hypothesis at most conventional levels for *p*-value.

Source: Carson et al. (1996c).

It is also possible to evaluate whether, following their stated 'votes', the respondents in the base and scope samples reported different perceptions of the seriousness of the injuries in each case. This difference is important because at the time of their vote, the respondents in each sample (that is, base and scope) were not aware of the alternative (larger or smaller) injury description. A severity evaluation was based on an attitude question asked after the CV choice. For the base questionnaire it was:

> All things considered, would you say the *fish* and *bird* reproduction problems I told you about in the South Coast were not serious at all, not too serious, somewhat serious, very serious, or extremely serious?

For the scope questionnaire this question replaced *fish* and *bird* with *fish*. A simple two-way chi square test indicated a significant difference in stated seriousness of the problem (that is, $\chi^2 = 148.90$ with a p value < 0.001).

There have been two types of responses to the Montrose findings. The first suggests that scope is not the 'real' hurdle for CV, but rather distinguishing different values for different types of environmental resources.[33] A second comment suggests the difference between the two estimates is not 'large enough'. The argument here implicitly calls for a decomposition of the injuries and an effort to evaluate whether respondents treat the difference in natural recovery time and the two versus four species as simple economic models might hypothesize. Most of this concern arises from a simple interpretation of the Diamond (1996) argument discussed earlier. In this case, two dimensions of the objective of choice vary between the base and scope surveys – the number of species affected and the time savings based on natural recovery. Judgments about the size of the difference in willingness to pay require assumptions about how each factor enters individual preferences. Conventional theory (as well as the empirical literature on how people evaluate the importance of different types of natural and environmental resources) offers little explicit guidance on how to address these types of questions.[34] Without exogenous information that allows the analyst to determine plausible restrictions to preferences there appears to be no straightforward resolution of these types of questions.

2.3.6 Joint estimation

In 1988, Trudy Cameron outlined how revealed and stated preference information, collected from a single sample, can be used in joint estimation of preferences.[35] Morikawa (1989) independently proposed stacking revealed and stated preference data to recover estimates of consumers' preferences for existing and 'new' features of transportation systems as part of using random utility models to describe consumers' decisions among different transportation modes.[36]

There are several important differences between the Cameron framework and the work by Ben-Akiva, Morikawa, and McFadden as well as the related activities of marketing researchers. The latter group has relied on a single response outcome – a choice of one type of program or policy from a set of different alternatives. It relies on extreme corner solution models whose behavioral foundation was described with simple (usually linear) preference functions. However, the earliest contributions did not attempt to impose the restrictions implied by constrained utility maximization. Cameron, by contrast, derived travel cost demand models from a quadratic utility function and then interpreted the CV question within the context of that constrained optimization framework, using the restrictions implied by theory.

This strategy has at least three important implications. First, and perhaps most important, it requires an explicit connection to be developed between the CV question and individual preferences. This description interprets how the object of choice posed in a CV question is introduced into an individual's utility function. The reason for being explicit arises because we wish to take advantage of the efficiency gains from estimating the same parameters with information from different choices. Models derived to describe the revealed preference and CV responses must share some structural parameters for the estimation to offer efficiency advantages. As a rule, the process requires selecting a specific functional form for the preference (or indirect utility) function and defining the observable outcomes from each approach in terms of that function (see Smith et al., 2002 for an example reversing that logic for preference calibration).

While it may not require defining a quantity metric for the environmental resource, the specification does imply the role of the resource for other types of behavioral outcomes must be described.[37] Thus, as Larson et al. (1993) demonstrated in later research, the specification of use and non-use values attributed to the change in environmental quality becomes explicit with the description of how 'q' (from earlier discussion of Diamond) enters the preference (or indirect utility) function. There is a potential 'downside' to this approach when a CV question has not been designed to consider explicitly how the choice that is posed to each respondent is to be linked to a behavioral model. Under such circumstances it may be possible, *ex post*, to offer several different connections. Each would impose different restrictions on the parameters to be estimated because each corresponds to a different interpretation of how people answered the questions. The Cameron (1992) and Englin and Cameron (1996) questions are in this category and thus different restrictions linking the stated and revealed preference models could be maintained. Without specifics about how respondents interpreted the questions, we cannot determine which interpretation is correct.

The second implication is that the analysis allows for evaluation of factors that influence the level of utility and those that influence how preferences are assumed to change with changes in the parameters of constraints (that is, prices or the levels of quasi-fixed goods). Take-it-or-leave-it choices are modeled as corner solutions (extreme or generalized) and to describe them we must deal explicitly with how the full choice set contributes to individual well-being.[38] The level of demand for a linked private commodity is a second-order response (that is, Roy's identity reveals features of the first derivatives of the indirect utility function). Without the stated choice information we would not be able to recover the separable contributions to well-being. This argument underlies Larson et al.'s measures of non-use values.

Third, there is, of course, no reason to require that joint estimation be confined to a single revealed and a single stated response, or that both always need to be present (see Zhang and Smith, 1997).[39] Indeed, as my discussion of conjoint analysis in the next section suggests, the primary innovation here is the stacking of multiple responses that requires a preference specification describing how attributes of the object of choice contribute to individual decisions. Eom and Smith (1994) illustrate some of the difficulties when multiple commodities convey the potential quality measure (or in their case a risk of cancer). Modeling can require development of consistent price and quantity indexes that reflect how the set of choices and amounts would change with the proposed policy.

Joint estimation has seen an increased number of applications. Many have adopted the basic logic proposed by Cameron (1992). The primary limitation seems to be the increased burden on data collection. It requires that the questionnaire carefully connect what is asked to a set of plausible behavioral responses.[40]

2.3.7   Conjoint analysis

Conjoint analysis (CJA) refers to a variety of different methods. Widely used in marketing research to evaluate consumer preferences for private goods, CJA has been proposed by a number of these researchers as providing 'the answer' to the problems posed by CV. These problems stem in part from the desire to evaluate the properties of willingness to pay functions. Calls for scope tests have increased interest in evaluating how the willingness to pay responds to the amount of the change in the object of choice offered and in how it is offered. When each respondent is only offered one alternative, the cost of investigating these issues becomes prohibitive.

The conjoint format seeks to decompose the object of choice into a set of attributes and to design choices (or rankings) in a framework that presents multiple alternatives to the same individual. Unfortunately, conjoint methods do not solve these problems. To understand why, some distinctions need to be drawn between the ways CJA is implemented. Two of the most common methods are ratings and choices.[41] I will discuss the issues that arise with each in turn.

Roe et al. (1997) illustrate the distinctions between CV and ratings by posing (in a very simplified form) a CJA question in comparison to their description of a CV question as follows:

CV: Would you pay an additional p to fish for salmon if fishing conditions were changed, from $\{q_1^0, q_2^0, \ldots, q_k^0\}$ to $\{q_1^1, q_2^1, \ldots, q_k^1\}$?

CJA: On a scale from 1 (very *un*desirable) to 10 (very desirable) how would you rate a salmon fishing trip with the attribute and price levels listed below?

Trip	$q_1^i, q_2^i, \ldots, q_k^i$	Price	Your rating
A	$q_1^0, q_2^0, \ldots, q_k^0$	p^0	—
B	$q_1^1, q_2^1, \ldots, q_k^1$	p^1	—

(Roe et al., 1997, p. 147).

They argue this comparison highlights the importance of asking each respondent to rate the baseline conditions. Moreover, they suggest that conventional Hicksian welfare measures can be recovered from models that estimate the ratings differences (that is, between each situation in comparison to the baseline).

There is a problem with their characterization of both the CV and the CJA cases. Conventional measures for WTP cannot be defined from either question. The problem arises because the default state if a respondent answers 'no' is *not* clear. One interpretation is that the number of trips is assumed to be invariant to the change in quality and prices. Another is that you could change the number of trips taken but only in the new condition. The specific models that are estimated in their analysis and in most conjoint studies assume that the demand for trips does not change. Each individual's demand is *always* one.[42]

Recently, Layton and Lee (2002) have suggested an innovative recoding of the ratings that would provide an interpretation consistent with a choice model. Using the random utility model, they convert the rating responses into a set of ranks. Basically, their logic follows from interpreting the ratings as a censored ranking. They recognize that the probability of any censored ranking can be represented as the sum of probabilities of some set of complete ranks. The information provided by creating the model of censored ranks based on three complete ranks depends on the number of alternatives evaluated by each respondent and the number of ties (which are endogenous in their description). Nonetheless, their strategy would seem to offer a promising way of using information previously considered inconsistent with conventional economic choice models.

A second issue arises with the rating issue itself. Even if the baseline condition is included in the listing (and each person's individual travel costs (per trip) were included in the prices), a request to provide a rating that ranges from 'undesirable' to 'desirable' asks that the respondent make a comparison to something that is not mentioned. Including the baseline condition in the list does not free the comparison from being associated with a specific standard. We can derive a net comparison but this process does not remove concerns about exactly what the 'price' is in that default condition. Only in the case of constant marginal utility of income (and thus no adjustment in desired trips) will CJA be able to estimate incremental WTP. It cannot recover WTP per day because the 'no-trip' alternative is not identified by the model.[43]

The second approach involves a description of a set of choice alternatives with specified attributes, including the cost as well as the non-consumption of any type alternative (Adamowicz et al., 1994, 1997 offer examples of this type of CJA).[44] In these applications the model used to analyse the CJA data relies on the IIA (independence of irrelevant alternatives) assumption. By offering a randomized set of alternatives, usually along with a constant, 'no-consumption' baseline, and pooling answers to these multiple questions across respondents, it is possible to estimate a conventional random utility model (RUM).[45] However, welfare measurement, including the per-trip measures commonly used with RUM applications involving revealed preference data, generally are *not* feasible. The reason follows directly from the expression for the unconditional indirect utility function – the choice set for each individual is not known.[46] Thus the conventional willingness to pay measures derived with RUM analyses from revealed preference responses are not available. Both of these conceptual issues ignore the econometric questions raised by pooling multiple responses across individuals. With the exception of Layton and Lee, much of the literature assumes responses are independent. This is probably incorrect given the experience with double-bounded CV questions.

Overall, then, CJA does not appear to have fully 'earned' the status claimed for it! The ability to collect larger amounts of information cannot be denied. It also seems reasonable to expect that the interactive process, with each respondent making repeated choices, does help them in evaluating situations where they may not have had experience. Nonetheless, the record to date seems to suggest the methods must face most of the questions posed with CV as well as some potentially difficult identification questions in recovering sufficient information to estimate the WTP with either the ratings or choice versions of CJA.[47]

2.3.8 'Homegrown values' and CV

As noted earlier, Bishop and Heberlein's research introduced the discrete responses approach to eliciting individuals' values and was the first to propose a simulated market approach for evaluating methods for non-market valuation. A simulated market refers to a situation where the investigator conducts real sales or purchases of commodities. Their research design was a purchase format and involved sending checks (in different amounts) to those recreationists who had received hunting permits. They asked the individuals to return the permit (and keep the check) or to return the check.[48] The primary objective was experimental – to implement 'real' transactions for an object of choice that matched what CV and travel cost methods were describing. This study also sought to use the results from the simulated market to evaluate the performance of both of these methods.

Their framework was imaginative and has generated a new type of experimental research to evaluate the reliability of CV. However, in many subsequent applications of the logic, results from simulated markets have been described as completely comparable to those from conventional experimental markets used in other types of economic applications. They are not.

When insights are derived about the performance of the economic institutions from experimental economics, they rest on three important assumptions: (1) the economic properties of rules governing exchanges between people are not affected by the size or character of the incentives people have to engage in those exchanges;[49] (2) these properties are not dependent on the specific individuals' attributes (for example experience, cognitive ability, and so on); and (3) the properties are insensitive to other aspects of the context in which they are undertaken.

Conventional laboratory experiments, as they are conducted for most economic applications, evaluate the properties of the rules governing transactions. Many applications rely on the fact that participants devote equivalent effort regardless of the size of the monetary incentive at stake. As Harrison (1989) has noted, sometimes the difference in rewards between an optimal response, requiring considerable effort to understand the incentive structure, and an approximately optimal one (but easier to understand) may be very small.

The second assumption arises because the participants are usually students, but the results are assumed relevant to other (potentially older and more experienced) individuals who might face the experimental manipulation in the 'real world.'

Simulated markets reverse the logic of the first assumption.[50] That is, instead of imposing controlled monetary incentives and changing the exchange rules to evaluate their properties, they select exchange rules *with known properties* and infer participants' underlying values. These studies then proceed to argue that, given the knowledge of one group's 'values', these measures can be used as a standard for evaluating another group's stated values, elicited with CV. Unfortunately, the logic relies on all people having the same values (or the same functions describing their values) and, perhaps more importantly, that people's attributes and the exchange context are unimportant to the insights derived for CV in general. Do people respond the same way to specific, small budget, private goods as to more public goods? While much of the most recent literature has sought to consider more public goods, these activities are recent and we have too limited experience to draw general conclusions

One notable example by Vossler and Kerkvliet (2003) exploits local referenda and follows the early proposals made by Carson et al. (1986). In these types of studies, CV survey is conducted in advance of an actual referendum and the results compared. In some situations where the action is financed with a change in local property tax rates, the tax 'price' experienced by each home-owner will depend on their assessed valuation. As a result, it is possible to observe a difference in anticipated prices for the proposed public action. The Vossler and Kerkvliet study reports the findings for one of the most careful and detailed of these efforts. It relates to a riverfront improvement project in Corvallis, Oregon. The authors find that survey votes and actual votes are not significantly different. They used actual precinct-level votes to estimate a probit, together with information from a post-election survey to collect demographic information. The estimated average for the actual and hypothetical willingness to pay measures were remarkably close – \$51.75 and \$52.27, respectively.

Moreover, tests of the common parameters of the respective choice models could not reject the null hypothesis that they were equal. Nonetheless, the authors do recognize the limitations in using these results for evaluating CV in other settings. They note that respondents to CV surveys may not be familiar with the policy and do not know they can vote in the future. Both conditions are different in their study. Equally important, as they note, the respondents to their hypothetical survey are unlikely to believe their responses will be consequential because they know 'the real referendum' is coming. Overall, then, while this research has certainly enhanced our understanding of the many influences on people's choices, we are nonetheless left with a collection of special cases that is difficult to use to evaluate CV (or conjoint) when there are not plausible mechanisms for observing how individuals 'choose' the environmental resources they wish.

To know how to use them requires answers to the same types of questions we had about CV. As a result, there is little point at this stage in providing a detailed review of all of the simulated market studies (see Schulze et al., 1996; Smith, 1997; Smith and Mansfield, 1998 for recent reviews and discussion of them). In some respects, the conclusion that the findings from simulated markets would be difficult to generalize was predetermined by the issues that motivated use of CV. CV is most useful where there is an absence of observed behavior that could be linked to variations in the amounts of the environmental resources whose economic values are to be measured. If homegrown value experiments (that is, relying on each participant's preferences as compared to induced preferences through a monetary incentive program) could be designed to provide the resources, then it should also be possible to offer something paralleling that mechanism for actual provision. We would then not need the valuation measure being sought. Thus, simulated markets can be designed for commodities that are always going to be questioned as more 'private' or 'use-oriented' than the CV application under study.[51]

2.4   A bottom line on CV

The majority of research on the reliability of CV seems to rest on the presumption that there exists a crucial experiment (or set of experiments) that, once conducted, will allow us to decide in favor of or against the method. I believe this is a strategy that can never succeed. Just as there is no single experiment that discredits the method, there is none that unambiguously supports it. In most science, the accumulated evidence of repeated and verifiable experiments testing (and failing to reject) some hypothesis corresponding to what might be described as a 'stationary theoretical principle' ultimately changes the beliefs of the scientific community. Accumulated evidence provides the basis for revisions in what are taken to be the principles governing the behavior that is observed. This strategy will not work with CV because the economic values to be measured (and even their relationship to observable characteristics of the background context) are unlikely to appear to be stationary.

One might ask if the economic values implied by the choices of non-market goods are less stationary than private goods. This question implicitly asks about individual preferences and the information set available as choices are made. It seems reasonable to expect that market goods and services with a large number of substitutes, as well as a reasonably large share of the individual budget, would be less stationary. Small price changes would induce large changes in the quantity demanded. By contrast, goods with few substitutes and small fractions of the budget have inelastic demands and would likely have relatively stationary choice patterns. These are basic concepts underlying the reasoning used to characterize price elastic and inelastic demands.

Converting them to judgments about economic values requires a more formal statement of the choice problem. For example, if we consider the lump-sum willingness to pay for a lower price of a marketed good, this measure of economic value likely follows the insights derived from elasticities. For example, consider the case of a constant elasticity demand function. Using Hausman's (1981) logic to derive the quasi-indirect utility function, equation (2.4) describes the Hicksian willingness to pay for such a price change (that is, $p_1 < p_0$):

$$WTP = m - \left(\frac{(1+\gamma)}{1+\beta} e^{-\alpha}(p_1^{1+\beta} - p_0^{1+\beta}) + m^{1-\gamma} \right)^{\frac{1}{1-\gamma}}, \qquad (2.4)$$

where m = income
       p = commodity price
       β, γ = price and income elasticities ($\beta < 0$)

In general cases, the degree of responsiveness of WTP to the price elasticity will depend on the other features of demand. Nonetheless, for this example they do follow the basic pattern described in terms of elasticities. As we move to non-market goods, the issues in answering the issue of stationarity concern how we define the choice giving rise to the measure of economic value.

Most definitions of non-use motives for environmental resources follow Hanemann's (1988) definition and treat them as arising because the resource makes a completely separable contribution to well-being. No private goods contribute to how it enhances individual utility. Under these circumstances, the willingness to pay for increases in such a resource should not be affected by the prices of other private goods and services. It would, of course, be bounded by available income.

Overall, then, stationarity of the economic values for environmental goods depends on the choices used to characterize the values and on what is assumed about how they contribute to individual preferences. As a rule, we do not know much about this second issue. Indeed, this issue is usually among the reasons analysis is undertaken.

Contingent valuation estimates are primarily questioned because those providing them never actually pay. While this is important, it misses a general characteristic of how valuation measures are actually used in all policy analyses. That is, when any set of benefit measures is used to evaluate the net gains realized from a new policy, *no one ever pays!* If they did, the measured gains would be different simply as a result of the availability of less income for other things.[52] Thus acceptance of CV may well be improved if the results from such studies were used to calibrate preference functions. The estimates of benefits for any policy could then be derived from these functions with the analytical restrictions implied by a budget constraint imposed through the maintained preference function.[53] This strategy shifts attention from the mechanism used to acquire information about people's preferences to how that information is used to compute the benefits attributed to specific policies.

There are several important precedents for this type of approach for policy analyses. Harberger's (1971) proposed approximate measures of the welfare gains or losses from price changes *imposed* a budget constraint on how these changes could be computed.[54] This restriction has been lost in the analyses of non-market changes. Such a 'Harbergerian calibration' would remove one aspect of the concerns raised with CV responses. That is, 'they are no longer payments that would never be made'. It is, as developed below, a logical consequence of the joint estimation strategy that has progressively developed from Cameron's important advance in the practices used to analyse CV information.

2.5 CV and the non-market economy

2.5.1 *Sources of continuing demands for CV*

A lack of alternatives provides the most compelling reason contingent valuation is unlikely to 'go away'. This motivation becomes especially important once we acknowledge that, even in situations where there is some prospect for revealed preference approaches, there may not exist a continuum of environmental resource alternatives. As a result, we may not observe any behavioral response to changes in environmental quality. As Bockstael and McConnell (1999) observed:

> Individuals will not change their behavior if they cannot adjust at the margin and if their next best alternative generates less utility than their current choice, even with environmental degradation. A localized water quality incident may not provoke a change in behavior if the next best alternative recreation site is still less desirable. . . . the individual may, instead suffer in (behavioral) silence (p. 26).

What this implies is that observed behavior (especially relying on models that assume marginal adjustments) may not capture losses (or gains) incurred by some individuals.

Combining this case with the primary ones that are usually cited for CV (that is, no available choice mechanisms to reveal behavior), we have three motivations for continued use of CV:

(a) provide people with the opportunity to make (state) choices for changes in environmental objects of choice not available on a discretionary basis;

(b) provide analysts greater resolution in the shape of benefit functions for different characteristics or components of environmental resources; and

(c) identify the heterogeneity in adjustment thresholds across people for different amounts of environmental resources.

None of these ideas is especially new. In some respects they bring us back to one of the motivations for public and environmental economics – the belief that there are some commodities people want (or want to avoid) that cannot be accommodated within conventional market exchanges. There may exist no means of making a choice (even among a limited number of alternatives). Nonetheless, all would agree that the commodity defining the choice could be extremely important. Under these conditions the commodity definition would seem to preclude (tautologically) revealed preference.

Most environmental resources do not fit this extreme case. There are ways people do make choices that *can* reveal something about their values. The trick remains to integrate these sources of choice information with what could be derived from stated preference surveys. The link between choice and economic value is clearest when people undertake activities that in some way rely on the services of the non-marketed resource. Improving the water flow rate in a river that supports whitewater rafting or the water level in a lake that provides boating and fishing opportunities should increase the likelihood that recreationists interested in these types of facilities would decide to use the improved resources. These increases in likelihood (or rate) of use provide information about the importance of the respective improvements to each type of uses.

Thus, if analysts search for choice information related to non-market resources, recognizing that it would need to be combined with contingent valuation information, we would then expect that stated preference findings would rarely be the exclusive basis for measuring people's values for improving environmental resources. Instead insights from these methods would be sources of complementary information.

2.5.2   CV as a source of complementary data

Ebert's (1998) overview of the conditions for consistently recovering welfare measures provides a general statement of the factors that underlie joint estimation of revealed and stated preference models. His synthesis suggests it is possible with incomplete conditional demand models to recover consistent welfare measures.[55] Given sufficient information about the conditional demands for private goods, along with the virtual price (or marginal willingness to pay) functions for non-market goods, he defines a set of weak integrability conditions. When these are satisfied, they assure that it is possible to construct welfare measures for changes in the observed goods' prices together with changes in the observed non-market goods. Joint estimation using revealed and stated preference data for unified models, especially in

cases where the process serves to isolate otherwise unobservable parameters, offers an example of how weak integrability would work. In these
cases the analysis has typically begun with a prespecified direct or indirect
utility function. His Proposition 2' implies that provided weak integrability
conditions are satisfied we could relax these assumptions as well. Thus,
parametric pricing is not a requirement for recovering sufficient information to develop consistent welfare measures. *Choice information is.*

Another way of interpreting professional objections to CV is to suggest
people's responses are at best motivated by a simple integral of one of the
stacked components of Ebert's incomplete conditional demand and should
not, on theoretical grounds alone, be expected to offer accurate welfare
measures. All prices and other public goods (or conditioning quantities) are
implicitly held constant.

Cameron's joint estimation addresses this concern, albeit to date the
applications have not been at the scale implied by Ebert's logic. While the
Cameron logic has attracted a number of comparable replications, it has not
been a 'transforming methodology' for non-market valuation. I believe the
reason is that it appears to imply all consumption choices (or at least a reasonably large number of the closely linked private goods with connections to
environmental resources) – market and non-market – must be collected
simultaneously in order to use the logic. The remainder of this section is a
suggestion that joint estimation does *not* require joint data collection. As a
result, we can recast the role of CV surveys. They can be treated as small-
scale *and complementary* data sources that are designed to search individual
preferences in regions not observed with ordinary market choices.

My proposal is for estimation of joint models with 'case-controlled' or
complementary independent samples. It is not a new practice in epidemiology, or even in some applications in economics, but to my knowledge has
not been recognized as a strategy for using CV in non-market valuation.[56]
The logic is straightforward. We begin analysis of consumer (or household)
choices using a framework that results from constrained optimization. The
outcomes we observe – whether the level of demand, a change in demand,
a bid, or a stated choice – are all defined explicitly in terms of that framework. This is the logic used by Cameron (1992) and is what underlies the
ability to define weak integrability conditions in Ebert (1998).

None of this requires samples from the same individuals for all the outcomes. It does require that they have the same preferences. Moreover, when
there is incomplete information in any one sample about the factors
influencing behavior they must be invariant across the individuals in that
sample. The framework used must also contain sufficient information to
identify the preference parameters to be estimated jointly with other
samples. Finally, when the samples are independent there must also be

shared parameters to assure any structural restrictions used in identifying parameters have an effect on the estimation.

Of course, it is important to acknowledge that the proposed ability to use complementary samples relies on the information an analyst is willing to add to the process. In this case, that corresponds to the detailed specifications for preference functions and constraints that underlie the parametric restrictions. As one reader has suggested, this approach seems to be the antithesis of using non-parametric strategies with a single, well-specified, change described in a survey. This limitation is certainly true. However, the information required is no more than is *already* required for the joint models where revealed and state preference information are collected from the same individuals.

To make this point more tangible, consider a simple example. Suppose the objective was to estimate the willingness to pay to avoid losses associated with an oil spill on recreational beaches. If we select California beaches as the location (recognizing the history of spills on the central coast of California, including the most recent associated with the *American Trader* case),[57] then we would have two sets of information available. The first includes travel cost data collected as part of NOAA's contribution to the Public Area Recreation Visitors' Survey (PARVS), an on-site survey of beach visitors.[58] The second is a large-scale contingent valuation survey sponsored by the State of California and the US Department of Justice. It was intended to serve as a basis for developing estimates of the per household '*ex ante* economic value for a program to prevent a specified set of natural resource injuries to those species of birds and inter-tidal life that are consistently affected by oil spills along California's central coast' (Carson et al., 1996b, p. iii).

The first data set reflects on-site use values from beach recreation. It seems reasonable to expect this behavior would be influenced by concern for injuries from oil to 'birds and inter-tidal life' impacted by oil spills along the central coast. Similarly it would seem respondents evaluating plans to avoid future oil spills would consider not only the injuries avoided, but also the avoided disruption to planned beach trips because of oil-spill-required beach closings.[59] One might also like to target the valuation estimates to specific beaches. The two studies were independently planned. The PARVS survey does not consider the values people might place on related species and the California Oil Spill (COS) study does not collect sufficient information to estimate travel cost recreation demand models. This situation is typical of most of the existing data sets available for non-market valuation.

Complementary analysis allows both to be used in estimating a single set of household preferences and the desired specific benefit measures developed. It requires explicit specification of how the object of choice enters consumer preferences. Because this exercise is intended to be an example, I will assume a linear travel cost demand with the implied gains from a plan to protect beaches from oil spills – both in assuring more consistent access and in avoiding injuries as an additive effect on the trip demand. This is designated as q in equation (2.5), with x the beach trips, tc the round-trip travel cost, and m income measured on a per household member basis:

$$x = \alpha_0 + \beta tc + \gamma m + \alpha_1 q. \tag{2.5}$$

Without loss of generality we can assume this function resulted (via Roy's identity) from an indirect utility function given in (2.6):[60]

$$v = \exp(-\gamma tc)\left(m + \frac{1}{\gamma}\left(\beta tc + \alpha_0 + \frac{\beta}{\gamma} + \alpha_1 q \right) \right). \tag{2.6}$$

The COS study presents a plan to escort oil tankers that could impact California's central coast paid for through a one-time income tax surcharge on California households.[61] For the purpose of this analysis, I assume the plan changes q from a baseline of q^0 to a new level of q^*. An individual's willingness to pay (WTP) for the plan can be derived using the definition in equation (2.6). A little algebra yields a simple expression in equation (2.7):

$$WTP = \left(\frac{\alpha_1}{\gamma} \right)(q^* - q^0). \tag{2.7}$$

Notice that all other aspects of the recreation behavior cannot be recovered from the choices about the plan, but they would affect the Marshallian consumer surplus measured for the plan based on the demand function given in equation (2.5).[62] Because there is only one variation in the plan we cannot recover estimates that isolate how changes in q^* influence an individual's value. Moreover, we cannot identify α_1 separately from γ with the CV data alone. As equation (2.7) suggests, it is the ratio of the two parameters that scales the increment of q. With variation in a fixed fee for each increment in q, we do not observe enough information to recover α_1 separately from γ. Likewise the travel cost information does not include variation in q – all individuals face the same level of protection for coastal resources from oil spills. As a result we cannot consider the value of changes in the plan.

This issue is one of the key problems posed with CV (and a motivation for the efforts to use an attribute-based format such as conjoint analysis). To make the CV question tangible, the proposed change in the resource (or the plan) is defined in specific terms. Without variation in the change $(q_1 - q_0)$ across people, we learn nothing about how WTP responds to q. Thus, the available literature rarely provides estimates that exactly correspond to the alternatives considered in policy evaluations using benefit information. As a consequence, analysts must adjust the available results to fit the features of each proposed resource change. This process is usually described as a benefits transfer. CV estimates for a single, well-defined, change in a specific resource provide very limited information to help guide this activity.

Efforts to develop these adjustments can be considered an identification problem. That is, does the available research offer sufficient information to allow those structural parameters relevant for describing people's choices to be identified? If the answer is yes, then they can be used to compute the required benefit measure (see Smith et al., 2002). This concern is the reason why I focus on what can be identified from the specific estimating framework. A limited benefit transfer would require that we have a measure of α_1.

Complementary sample analysis recognizes that joint estimation with the two samples allows recovery of $\alpha_1(q^* - q^0)$ because γ affects both decisions. More specifically, equations (2.5) and (2.7) can be used to define two choices.

Trip demand for a given q
$$x = (\alpha_0 + \alpha_1 q^0) + \beta tc + \gamma m. \tag{2.8a}$$

Vote for the COS plan at a one-time tax surcharge of T
$$WTP - T = \frac{\alpha_1}{\gamma}(q^* - q^0) - T. \tag{2.8b}$$

Joint estimation is accomplished (even with a take-it or leave-it CV question) by treating the score from the likelihood function for a respondent's vote as a moment condition. Stacking the moment implied by (2.8a) with this score, and applying a generalized method of moments estimator, it is possible to incorporate the cross-equation restrictions. More specifically, for my example using a logit framework to describe the take-it or leave-it discrete choices, the resulting first-order condition for the log-likelihood function, (L), is given in equation (2.9):

$$\left(\frac{\partial L}{\partial \theta}\right) = \sum_i \left[y_i - \frac{\exp(\frac{\alpha_1}{\gamma})(q^* - q^0)\theta - \theta T_i)}{(1 + \exp((\frac{\alpha_1}{\gamma})(q^* - q^0)\theta - \theta T_i))} \right] T_i. \tag{2.9}$$

In this framework θ is the reciprocal of the scale parameter and y_i is the discrete response variable for the choice each respondent makes. Combining (2.9) with (2.8a) we have a linear and a non-linear moment condition.

The discrete nature of the responses implies that we estimate the structural parameters up to the scale parameter, θ. Nonetheless logit or probit estimates of the model, as formulated by Cameron (1988), $y_i = a_0 + a_1 T$ yields an estimate for WTP. Equation (2.10a) defines a_0 and (2.10b) a_1 in terms of the structural parameters. Equation (2.10c) suggests that their ratio provides an estimate of WTP:

$$a_0 = \left(\frac{\alpha_1}{\gamma}\right)(q^* - q^0)\theta \qquad (2.10a)$$

$$a_1 = -\theta \qquad (2.10b)$$

$$WTP = -\left(\frac{\alpha_1}{\gamma}\right) = \left(\frac{\alpha_1}{\gamma}\right)(q^* - q^0). \qquad (2.10c)$$

With the joint estimator we can also identify the WTP *and* recover estimates for both $\alpha_1(q^* - q^0)$ and γ using the demand function. This would be important to the estimation of the willingness to pay to avoid an oil spill on the beaches of California's central coast if we had a more detailed set of design variations in the CV survey or some independent information allowing us to describe changes in q.

The joint estimator stacks data from two different surveys *as if* these responses were provided by the same person. In implementing the model, a variety of strategies can be used. In some cases the two samples would be used in the joint estimation. Alternatively, a random sample can be selected from the larger COS sample to 'match' one or more specified exogenous characteristics of the respondents that are assumed relevant to the model.[63] The COS sample includes individuals who use beaches as well as those who do not. The framework suggested here does not imply the structural parameters determining responses to the CV question for non-users will be different from users. The model implicitly assumes non-users have travel costs corresponding to their choke price.[64]

Table 2.4 provides some illustrative estimates for the model's parameters. Three sets of samples from the COS samples were considered. The first is a simple random sample from the full COS survey. The second matches the reported beach use distribution of the set of respondents to the COS survey from the central coast area of California to the distribution in the PARVS sample for the two beaches in the impact area for the spill. The last limits the random sample from the COS survey to households with members who traveled the coastal highway (Highway 1) in the last five years.[65] Two sets of estimates are reported with each set of samples. Separate estimates are given for the CV choice model with logit and the joint estimation with the complementary samples. The estimates of the travel cost demand model with the PARVS data (using OLS) do not change with the different samples from the COS survey and are reported in the first column. Independent logit analysis of the CV survey will change with the sample and the separate estimates with each sample are reported in the first column under each sample grouping. The logit choice model alone cannot identify the effect of beach quality and the oil spill plan. This limitation is indicated in the labeling of the parameters for each sample. Because PARVS and COS surveys

Table 2.4 Results for joint estimation with complementary samples

Parameter	Simple random		Use matched		Traveled Highway 1	
	OLS/LOGIT	JECS	LOGIT	JECS	LOGIT	JECS
α_0 (intercept)	26.413 (4.71)	26.413 (4.77)		26.422 (4.77)		26.412 (4.77)
β (travel cost)	−0.492 (−3.10)	−0.492 (−3.14)		−0.492 (−3.14)		−0.492 (−3.14)
γ (income)	0.081 (0.62)	0.081 (0.63)		0.080 (0.62)		0.081 (0.63)
$\bar{\alpha}_1$ (quality)		0.063 (0.61)		0.074 (0.61)		0.048 (0.60)
θ (reciprocal scale)	0.009 (3.48)	0.009 (3.21)	0.007 (2.87)	0.007 (2.82)	0.008 (2.89)	0.007 (2.70)
$\theta(\alpha_1/\gamma)$	0.789 (2.71)	–	0.928 (3.01)		0.605 (2.18)	
Proportion of yes responses	0.50		0.56		0.50	
Mean number of trips	18.44		18.44		18.44	
No. of observations	118	118	118		118	118
R^2	0.077	–	–		–	–

were undertaken five years apart, the Consumer Price Index (CPI) was used to adjust the travel cost and income levels reported in 1989 for PARVS to 1994 dollars. The second column in each 'sample-grouping' reports joint estimates with a generalized method of moments estimator, using as instruments the exogenous variables from each of the complementary samples.[66]

The estimates across the three samples are quite comparable, with a small increase in the size of the jointly estimated parameter (that is, 0.074 versus 0.063) for the quality/oil spill plan with the sample drawn from users in the central coast area. This difference is not statistically significant. Thus, at this stage, the best one can conclude is that there is suggestive evidence that the complementary analysis would help to target plausible individual effects. The primary advantage gained in this example is the ability to identify separate estimates for α_1. Such identification would allow benefit measures for a wide range of use and quality changes when it is applied to a CV survey with greater variation in the quality conditions included in the design variations presented to respondents.

More generally, the primary advantage of joint estimation is in the ability to recover an estimate of the effects of the plan (that is, $\alpha_1(q^* - q^0)$) on individual preferences. If the index people used to evaluate q were known, then we could estimate changes in q different from what was offered in the CV survey. Moreover, this ability is sustained without the need to have wide variation in q in the CV scenario.

I do not want to understate the difficulty in knowing the index or set of values people use to characterize q. In most realistic applications, q is likely to be multidimensional and to arise in bundles of different services or characteristic ties with technical restrictions on how the individual components can vary. My discussion of the issues associated with designing a scope test in the analysis conducted for the Montrose case is an example of those relationships. If the goal is to link the source of an injury to an impacted species, then the intervening connections must be established and changes must be plausible within that context. Technical measures of q are unlikely to be on the same scale as is used by people to make their own judgments about resources. All of these issues create significant challenges for any activity that proposes to parameterize a role for q in individual preferences.

Clearly, more work is needed on the impact of other types of sampling criteria. Nonetheless, the prospect of being able to investigate these alternatives with modest research resources highlights the potential importance of designing CV studies to serve as *complementary samples* that can be used to enhance the insights available with larger existing data sets. Under these circumstances, the structure of the CV object of choice and choice context can be designed to explore the role of q in preferences and its potential for interaction with priced commodities that may be linked to it.

6   Discussion

Contingent valuation has prompted the most serious investigation of individual preferences that has ever been undertaken in economics. These efforts have used teams of social scientists, drawing insights from cognitive and social psychologists, sociologists, and survey researchers into the approaches environmental economists now routinely use to elicit consumer choices. The success in this integration of research methods across these disciplines has, to some degree, been overlooked in the controversy about CV.

CV research has also transformed the framework used in experimental economics. Conventional experimental methods relied on using controlled incentives to study the effects of information and exchanges rules. Beginning with Bishop and Heberlein (1979) environmental economists changed the research framing to one that relies on known properties of exchange rules (and information sets) to study preferences and methods for eliciting them.

The framing of questions used in other economic surveys remains primitive by comparison to the methods designed by CV researchers. Borrowing from marketing research and psychology, a linked sequence of focus groups, cognitive interviews, and pre-tests is now routine practice in designing the key questions for CV surveys. The laboratory research under way at the Bureau of Labor Statistics and the Bureau of the Census, intended to improve conventional economic questions, is a decade or more behind standard practice in CV research.

These two activities, together with the insights derived from hundreds of applications, have offered a much better understanding of what is actually revealed about preferences from an individual's choices. Fifty years ago Houthakker (1950) demonstrated that Samuelson's (1938) argument that revealed preference analyses freed demand analysis from the need to specify a utility function was not correct. As Samuelson (1950) later acknowledged, the requirements for integrability are not so easily dismissed.

Unfortunately none of this work ever considered objects of choice that were not 'supported by' a budget constraint with constant (per unit) prices. Houthakker's proof demonstrated how we could vary prices and income so as to reveal non-integrable preference fields. This 'decade plus' sequence of research on what we really know about the properties of preferences from behavior has focused particular attention on the early theory associated with rationed goods. As Carson et al. (2001) suggest, intuition about what properties can be expected for income responsiveness or substitution that is formed based on insights using priced goods does not readily transfer to the case of rationed goods. Moreover, it is the rationed commodity case that is most directly relevant to non-market valuation. CV has provided both motivation for developing these insights and a methodology grounded in survey design and econometric analysis that allows economists to learn about consumer preferences without the separating hyperplane defined by income and prices.

As in the case of the revealed preference axiom, CV does not free the analyst from the use of assumptions. This recognition has been slow to come to CV applications. Restrictions from economic theory have been viewed as ways to discipline 'wayward' choices so they appear to be 'economic' decisions. This strategy is too narrow. Theory offers the opportunity for designing a constructive program where the economic model of choice can be used as an integral part of the design of understandable decisions for non-market resources. The primary limitation to a strategy that collects both CV questions and more conventional economic data has been the cost of data collection. However, the prospect of using complementary samples to estimate jointly preferences may relax this significant constraint.

The focus on using the theory of individual choice along with the insights from psychology and survey research in the design of stated preference surveys has another advantage. It offers the potential to 'build in' questions that elicit confirmatory behavioral responses. Measures of willingness to

48   *Contingent valuation and economic theory*

pay can *never* be confirmed but observable behavior can. By specifying explicitly the full dimensions of the economic choice process as a part of the design of CV questions it is possible to evaluate the performance of the maintained theory and the CV questions. This approach is the non-market equivalent of Varian's (1982, 1983) generalized axiom of revealed preference and may offer the opportunity, together with complementary sample analysis, to change the economic profession's view of stated preference research.[67]

Appendix A: Text of the California oil spill study's contingent valuation question

(*Source*: Carson et al., 1996b, Appendix A, pp. 8–14)

Recently, the federal government passed a new law to help reduce the number of oil spills. Ten years from now, all oil tankers and barges will be required to have two outer hulls instead of the single hull most of them have now. Double hulls provide much more protection against oil leaking after an accident.

However, it will take ten years before all single-hulled tankers and barges can be replaced. Until then, spills are expected to happen every few years along the central coast, just as they have in the past, unless something is done.

In the next ten years:

Scientists expect that a total of about 12 000 birds of various types will be killed by oil spills off the central coast. In addition, about 1000 more birds are expected to be injured, but survive. Also, many small animals and saltwater plants are likely to be killed along a total of about ten miles of shoreline.

The harm from an oil spill is not permanent. Over time, waves and other natural processes break down the oil in the water and on the shoreline.

Typically, within ten years or less after a spill, there will be as many of the affected birds as before the spill. The small animals and saltwater plants in the affected area recover somewhat faster, in about five years or less.

If taxpayers think it is worthwhile, the state could prevent this harm by setting up a prevention program for this part of the coast. This program would be similar to those successfully used by other states, such as the State of Washington. It would last for ten years, until all tankers and barges have double hulls.

This program would do two things.

First, it would help prevent oil spills from occurring. Second, if an oil spill does occur, it would prevent the oil from spreading and causing harm.

Here is how a central coast program would prevent spills from occurring. Oil spill prevention and response centers would be set up in three different locations along this part of the coast.

Specially designed ships, called escort ships, would be based at each center. An escort ship would travel alongside every tanker and barge as it sails along the central coast. This would help prevent spills in this area by keeping the tankers and barges from straying off course and running into underwater rocks, other ships, or pipelines.

If any oil were spilled, here is how the program would keep it from spreading and causing harm.

The crew of the escort ship would quickly put a large floating sea fence into the water to surround the oil. To keep it from spreading in rough seas, this fence would extend 6 feet above and 8 feet below the surface of the water.

Then skimmers would suck the oil from the surface of the water into storage tanks on the escort ship.

Other ships would be sent from the nearest prevention and response center to aid in the oil recovery and clean-up.

The money to pay for this program would come from both the tax-payers and the oil companies. Because individual oil companies cannot legally be required to pay the cost of setting up the program, all California households would pay a special one-time tax for this purpose.

This tax money would pay for providing the escort ships and setting up the three oil spill prevention and response centers along the central coast.

Once the prevention program is set up, all the expenses of running the program for the next ten years would be paid by the oil companies.

This money would come from a special fee the oil companies would be required to pay each time their tankers and barges were escorted along the central coast.

Once the federal law goes into effect ten years from now, all tankers and barges will have double hulls and this program would be closed down.

We are interviewing people to ask how they would vote on this central coast prevention program if it were put on the ballot in a California election.

There are reasons why you might vote for setting up this program and reasons why you might vote against it.

The program would prevent harm from oil spills in the central coast area during the next ten years. Specifically, the program would:

- Prevent the deaths of about 12 000 birds as well as the deaths of many small animals and saltwater plants along about 10 miles of shoreline, and
- Prevent 1000 more birds from being injured.

On the other hand,

- The number of birds and other wildlife it would protect is small in comparison to their total numbers, and none are endangered.
- Your household might prefer to spend the money to solve other social or environmental problems instead.
- Or, the program might cost more than your household wants to spend for this.

If the central coast prevention program were put into place, it would cost your household a total of $–. You would pay this as a special one-time tax added to your next year's California income tax.

If an election were being held today, and the total cost to your household for this program would be $–, would you vote for the program or would you vote against it?

The proposed tax amounts were randomly assigned as either $5, $25, $65, $120, or $220.

The study reports an estimate of the Turnbull lower-bound mean for the *ex ante* economic value of the oil spill prevention program of $76.45 (standard error of $3.78) in 1994 dollars.

Notes

*   An earlier draft of this chapter was presented at the Kobe Conference on Theory and Application of Environmental Valuation, organized by the Japan Forum of Environmental Valuation, 22–23 January 2000, at Kobe University, Rokkoudai Campus, Japan. Thanks are due to participants at that conference for helpful comments, to Richard Carson, Rick Dunford and Pierre du Vair for providing me with the two data sets used in the application described in section IV, and to Richard Carson, Bengt Kriström, and one anonymous referee for very detailed and constructive comments on a revised draft of the 2000 paper. Thanks are also due to Susan Hinton, who continues to make sense of my unending drafts. Partial support for this research was provided by the US Environmental Protection Agency under CR824861-01-0 and R-82950801 as well as from the NC Agricultural Research Service Project #NCO 5889.
†   This chapter was originally published in 'The International Yearbook of Environmental and Resource Economics 2004/2005' edited by Tom Tietenberg and Henk Folmer, Edward Elgar, 2004.
1.   Most economists attribute the first suggestion to use survey techniques to value non-market resources to Ciriacy-Wantrup (1947). In a market context with the objective of valuing attributes of fresh produce Waugh (1929) may well have been the first economist to use survey techniques. Often credited with the first application of hedonic price indexes, Waugh also conducted a survey to elicit valuation scales for these attributes and suggests values could be elicited directly. Robert Davis's famous Ph.D. thesis in 1963 marks the start of formal empirical efforts to use surveys to measure willingness to pay for non-market goods. Hanemann (1992) notes other less formal efforts as early as 1958, citing Mack and Meyers's (1965) contingent valuation survey.
2.   NOAA was designated a trustee for some types of natural resources under the Oil Pollution Act of 1990 and assigned the responsibility to develop regulations for natural

resource damages as part of the liability for these damages established in the United States by the Superfund legislation and the Oil Pollution Act. The Panel NOAA composed to assist in the rulemaking process included economists and other social scientists, including two Nobel Laureates. The Panel's report was published in the Federal Register in 1993, with follow-up comments in 1994 (see Arrow et al., 1994). The exact sequence of events leading to this panel and its activities is a complex story beyond the scope of this chapter. See Portney (1994), Diamond and Hausman (1994), and Hanemann (1994) for further perspectives on them. The Office of Management and Budget (OMB) guidance recommends that the NOAA Panel's scope test be conducted in an external or split sample format. It also calls for in-person interviews, ties judgments about reliability to response rates, and recommends reminders of substitutes and alternative expenditure possibilities as well as deflection of transaction values. Each of these elements is presumed to increase the reliability and quality of a CV study. However, as Harrison (2000) suggests, there is not a set of systematic tests of the effects of these choices that supports this recommendation. They certainly 'make sense'. The issue is documentation of the basis for suggesting them (OMB, 2003, p. 5519).

3. This judgment may be too extreme. Some reviewers of an earlier draft have suggested that the differences in economists' evaluations of contingent valuation are not as marked. It would be interesting to systematically compare the relative frequency of articles using laboratory experiments (also a new methodology) in the top economics journals to the same relative counts for those papers using contingent valuation or related survey methods in the top journals in the post-1992 period. My conjecture is that there would be a significant difference favoring applications of experimental methods.

4. Of course, a very detailed process is used to assemble the information necessary to construct the Consumer Price Index. But the price information must be collected. See Bureau of Labor Statistics (1997) for an overview.

5. Scanner data on sales in supermarkets have been available to marketing research firms for some time (see Cotterill, 1994). Because they are on privately held databases, these data are only recently becoming available to economists. Similarly, large-scale databases on housing sales are becoming available to economists and are transforming hedonic modeling. See Beron et al. (2001) and Sieg et al. (2002).

6. Without an experimental test evaluating the importance of these behavioral responses it is hard to judge the size of their effects. The logic for their existence parallels the concerns raised by Heckman (2001) about evaluating the general implications of policy interventions with social and natural experiments. One indirect set of information indicates the effects of incentives in a survey context do exist. Smith and Mansfield (1998) found differences with the time of the week a survey was conducted as part of an experimental evaluation of the reliability of CV. This analysis used a question offering to pay respondents to participate in a second interview. The sample was randomly assigned to different treatments – one offered 'real' payments and the other 'hypothetical' payments. The participation and implied opportunity cost of time depended on the timing of their initial interviews. The experimental question suggested the new interviews would be conducted under comparable conditions. It appears that respondents interpreted this framing to include the timing of the interviews. If we assume this interpretation of their expectations is correct, then they revealed a significantly different responsiveness to financial incentives depending on when the interviews would be conducted.

7. When the first systematic evaluation of contingent valuation was undertaken (see Cummings et al., 1986), I reviewed a range of economic surveys. It was possible to identify six tasks that were asked of respondents in economic surveys: recall, partitioning, judgment of a status, reports of sensitive information, evaluation of attitudes, and responses to hypothetical circumstances. See Smith (1986) for a report of the specific wording of some of the questions illustrating how these tasks were framed.

8. Early research by Kain and Quigley (1972) identified the biases in these reports when compared to market prices. While their analysis suggests that the averages from these reported values across people are reasonable as approximations of the average market prices, the individual values were found to be responsive to the census respondent

characteristics. Ideally, we might expect a new homebuyer to report accurately the market price he (or she) paid for the house involved. One referee for this chapter has suggested this is not obvious. My point is simply that I would not expect these reports to vary with the socioeconomic characteristics of the people providing them. Home sales prices are reported to county tax departments for assessing property taxes and these records are in the public domain. As a result, there does not appear to be a clear incentive to misrepresent the data. For many market goods, where there is no scope for bargaining, it would seem the same argument might apply.

9.   Even private databases developed from market transactions can involve a selection effect. These are likely to become increasingly important as consumers become aware that their choices are being saved and linked to other databases describing their demographic and financial characteristics. I do not have direct evidence that this recognition is growing. However, I do have several types of anecdotal information consistent with this conclusion. Recently, I attempted to obtain information from preferred customer cards from a large US retail grocery chain. The managers explained they could not cooperate because their customers expressed concerns about the record keeping and tracking of consumption. A small percentage of respondents to a recent mailed survey about the use of freshwater recreation sites in North Carolina also expressed similar concerns about the identification numbers on the surveys. About half the respondents who called to ask about the survey indicated they were aware of the tracking or asked how they were identified to be recruited for the survey. Finally, news accounts about tracking the usage of Internet sites by private consumers have caused many consumers to become increasingly sophisticated in the recognition of how their behavior is being recorded.

10. Some examples of studies in this category include: Brookshire et al. (1976), Rowe et al. (1980), and Schulze et al. (1981).

11. The biases initially identified included: strategic, starting point (for iterative 'bidding' elicitation questions), vehicle (for the payment mode), and information. Mitchell and Carson (1989) extended this framework to provide a fairly exhaustive description of the potential sources of bias in their 'Typology of Potential Response Effect Biases' (see Table 11.1, pp. 236–7).

12. In many respects this paper's descriptions of the key features of survey design closely parallel the subsequent guidelines attributed to the NOAA Panel almost two decades later:

> Some desirable characteristics of such surveys have been identified . . . The hypothetical situation presented should be realistic and credible to respondents. Realism and credibility can be achieved by satisfying the following criteria for survey instrument design: Test items must have properties similar to those in the actual situation; situations posited must be concrete rather than symbolic; and test items should involve institutionalized or routinized behavior, where role expectations of respondents are well defined (Randall et al., 1974, p. 136).

13. The work was originally intended to study water quality conditions at specific sites in North Carolina. Once the award for the research was made to the Research Triangle Institute, EPA staff indicated a preference for considering the Monongahela River as the study location. We learned much later after the research was completed that the Agency was involved in litigation concerning emission standards for steel firms in the area and there was some belief the results of the survey might have value in that case.

14. However there is an important distinction between the NOAA Panel's focus and our study. Scope was used as a gauge of the reliability of CV when it was used in natural resource damage assessments to estimate *non-use* values. In this study we were measuring changes in *use* values with the attributes of the conditions at the site involved in the recreation.

15. Indeed, in a recent conjoint analysis of smokers' responses to different types of hypothetical filters (to evaluate the importance of the health effects of cigarette smoking to smokers), a team including Reed Johnson and I asked about both the amount of filters after the choice *and* whether respondents would use them for every cigarette that they smoked. We conjectured that smokers might try to adapt to the price of these filters by adjusting the risks of health effects with less than a 100 per cent utilization pattern (for

example use filters with a subset of the cigarettes smoked to save money). Readers, I am sure, can appreciate the 'nightmare' we created for subsequent analysis.

16. I should add that I cannot cite specific evidence that this research had more influence on mainstream economists.

17. Taken together with Cameron (1988) and McConnell (1990), this research led to a much closer examination of the properties we should expect of Hicksian welfare measures. It was the large disparities between willingness to pay and willingness-to-accept measures and the subsequent speculation that they resulted from failures of CV that stimulated significant advances in economists' understanding of the properties of these measures. See Hanemann (1991, 1999) and Hanemann and Kanninen (1999).

18. The interest in incentive characteristics arises because the questions separate the individual's choice from the mechanism that describes how the collection of 'all' individuals choices is used to determine whether the stated offering would be provided. Thus the incentive analysis is really about provision mechanisms and *not* whether respondents take CV questions seriously. Taking them seriously is a maintained assumption that permits the subsequent analysis.

19. An issue raised independently by Shläpfer (2002) and Nicholas Flores concerns whether respondents adjusted the stated payment to reflect their personal circumstances – those in high income brackets *answering as if* the stated payment they would be required to make were lower than what they believe it would actually be. As Shläpfer notes, 'there clearly *is* a strategic reason for the respondent to do other than answer truthfully however, when payment levels do not correspond with the *actual cost* incurred by the respondent . . .'

20. A few recent related studies considering the form of the question include Balistreri et al. (2001), Poe et al. (2002), and Reaves et al. (1999).

21. The administration of the surveys across modes varied. The actual participation question was a telephone survey with a specific number of participants identified. The one price hypothetical discrete choice also identified the total number of desired participants for the program and was mailed. All other modes were mailed.

22. There is one potentially important limitation in their model. While the theoretical development of their joint model and estimator begins with a common preference function and error specification, their implementation introduces a subtle problem. One of the conditioning variables for their varying parameters across individuals is income. They explain this potential inconsistency as a reflection of eliciting income in classes and as an effort to use the mid-point of the class as discrete valued indicator of socio-demographic status to capture heterogeneity in preference parameters (p. 409). While this seems plausible, most sources of income from surveys convert interval responses to continuous measures using mid-points and adjustments for open-ended intervals. The expression for willingness to pay will be different with their non-linear form for preferences and this variable interpreted as the measure of income. Ideally, their comparisons would have reported other than income to provide the varying parameters. Given the importance of the functional form for preferences to their comparison across modes, their decision to use income as a proxy for demographics raises inevitable questions about whether they achieved the consistent comparison they sought.

23. As I have suggested throughout this discussion, the economic values can only be measured for a well-specified object of choice – which in this case is some change (positive or negative) in one or more environmental resources.

24. Their research also included consideration of discrete response versus open-ended questions and a second independent analysis of scenarios that evaluated plans to avoid injuries from different-sized oil spills.

25. There are a number of reasons, aside from the commodity, for questioning the relevance of the Desvousges et al. survey. What is important from the perspective of the evaluation of CV is the impact of the findings on the recommendations of the NOAA Panel and new research.

26. Indeed, in unpublished research Richard Carson and Nicholas Flores (1996) found that the estimates for different wilderness areas could be 'rationalized' by the sizes of the areas involved. That is, by simply regressing the mean WTP reported by Diamond et al. (1993)

on the number of acres preserved for each of the three areas, they reject the null hypothesis that WTP does not increase with size at a 0.01 level. Their results were based on summary statistics and not the original data, so the sample size was limited to the number of reported sample means.

27. The Exxon settlement for the oil spill called for $1 billion in natural resource damages. The Carson et al. (1992) estimated median was $30.91 (in 1991 dollars using the Weibull survival specification) per household.

28. The Panel also included Edward Leamer, Paul Portney, Roy Radner and Howard Schuman. For related discussion, see also Arrow et al. (1994).

29. One referee pointed out that perhaps the NOAA Panel sought to prevent the government from 'cutting corners'. That is, under the legal framework that the Panel was asked to take as guidance, the government gets reimbursed for all the costs of doing the research studies (including interest costs), provided that they were done in a cost-efficient manner, and that the government prevails on the claim. Under this framework, it may seem unlikely there would be disincentives to perform a state-of-the-art study. However, this is only part of the story. There are limits – in the time of public attorneys to bring cases and in the legal record of decisions to guide practice. So, state-of-the-art research does not necessarily assure success.

30. The final regulations for damage assessments changed completely in 1996, recommending a physical criteria 'habitat equivalency' (see Smith, 1999 for discussion), and CV research largely returned to the role of small-scale research studies. This change took place despite the fact that the rules do allow CV and other choice-based research to be used in these cases.

31. The NOAA Panel's concern about temporal reliability of CV responses seems to be more closely linked to highly visible damage assessment cases like the *Exxon Valdez*. Comparison of the 1991 and 1993 responses suggested it was not important for either the distributions of the discrete responses or the willingness to pay estimates derived from the *Exxon Valdez* survey. The details of each test are reported in Carson et al. (1997, 1998).

32. When I have described this research in workshops and to critics of CV, it has been suggested that more variations in species and time should have been pursued. This requirement for consistency in the linkages limited the design alternatives that could be undertaken.

33. Kahneman and Riktov (1994) rediscovered a critique of CV first raised by Cummings et al.'s (1986) evaluation – respondents seem to be willing to pay about $25 for anything. As a result, one might ask whether people's responses are simply reflections of a desire to 'do good things', or are specific efforts to improve the specific aspects of environmental resources that are posed in CV questions. See Carson et al. (1996a) and Smith (1996) for further discussion of this line of research.

34. Hanemann (1996) has made the same point quite forcefully in commenting on the earlier 'bird loss' experiments that began the line of research on scope tests. He observed that:

> My view is that economic theory *per se* provides no guidance about what people should care about or how much they should care. As in Diamond's case, one can always generate specific predictions by introducing some assumptions. But, those predictions are no more valid than the assumptions they rest on. As Simon [1986] has noted, 'almost all the action [in economics], all the ability to reach non-trivial conclusions, comes from the factual assumptions and very little from the assumptions of optimization. Hence, it becomes critically important to submit the factual assumptions to careful empirical test'. What I find disquieting is the apparent reluctance to do this. Thus, in the case of the birds or the wilderness areas, when CV data disconfirm his additivity assumption, Diamond chooses to reject the data and believe the assumption. I think that many of the assertions about what types of preferences are consistent with economic theory are merely expressions of personal opinion masquerading as statements of economic theory. The critics of CV are saying 'I don't feel that way about bird deaths, and I don't think that anybody else should' (Hanemann, 1996, p. 53).

35. Her unpublished paper circulated for several years before publication in 1992; see Cameron (1992) for the final version.

36. A number of applications followed in the early 1990s. See Morikawa et al. (1990), Ben-Akiva and Morikawa (1990), and Ben-Akiva (1992) as examples. Market researchers (see Swait and Louviere, 1993 and Swait et al., 1994) then used the frame-work to recover estimates of the ratio of the scale parameters for the errors assumed to be present for the two types of data – describing it as a type of calibration factor. See Louviere et al. (1999) for a fairly recent summary of the marketing applications in this literature.

37. The treatment of the amount of the environmental resource in functions linked to the responses provided by individuals depends both on whether scope effects are incorpor-ated in the CV design and on whether the form of preferences allows the effects of q to be identified. In some situations, we can also assume there are differences in the baseline conditions of q relevant to each respondent. In this situation, even if the CV question offers the same increment, it may be possible to identify the parameters of the resource measure with measures of the different baselines. A composite of early discussions of the modeling of responses from discrete response questions (especially McConnell's 1990 evaluation) and Cameron's paper triggered this line of research. I attempt to make this connection specific in Table 2.1 describing how behavior relates to WTP functions in Smith (1997).

38. This is a complex issue that offers the potential to relate the modeling of joint systems (revealed and stated preferences) to the Kuhn–Tucker approaches for modeling recrea-tion demand. It requires only the translation of questions into a format consistent with the preference specification being used.

39. Double-bounded questions offering interval estimates of willingness to pay are early reflections of the use of these interconnections.

40. As discussed below, the joint estimates do not have to involve responses from the same individuals. These types of applications have been prevalent in labor economics for some time (see Angrist and Krueger, 1992 and Arellano and Meghir, 1992), but have not found their way into environmental economics. There are several ways to implement these strategies and I illustrate one below. Others involving matching actual survey responses to pilot surveys or developing joint estimates are discussed in Sloan et al. (2003) and Smith and Pattanayak (2002), respectively.

41. Rankings have also been used in conjoint surveys. This questioning format corresponds more directly to a choice format comparable to the random utility model.

42. In the linear case they specify a ratings function as (omitting demographic effects)

$r(p, q, m) = f(v (p, q, m))$, where p = price, q = quality, and m = income.

They further specialize this in two cases:

$$(A)\, r (\ ) = f(v(q) + a\,(m - p))\text{ or}$$
$$(B)\, r (\ ) = f(v(q) + a \ln (m - p))$$

In both cases the Marshallian demand for trips is unity. There is a further issue in the comparisons. If we return to the case, they ask about quality change in the CV question, the specified 'p' is a price increment, *not* the price of the trip, and p^j in the conjoint version is presumably the price of a trip. Thus the price may not mean the same thing in both questions.

43. The form of the payment in Johnson and Desvousges (1997), as the percentage of a respondent's utility bill, poses even more serious problems when we attempt to link it to a Hicksian WTP.

44. One of the earliest applications of the multinomial choice framework in a CV/conjoint setting was undertaken in Carson et al. (1990). Respondents were offered the choice of purchasing a Kenai King salmon stamp that allows them to take different numbers of salmon in fishing trips. The number of salmon available in different types of stamps is controlled by the government so the choice set issue was avoided. A no-purchase alter-native was permitted using a nested logit framework. Thus, this early study avoided many of the criticisms of later conjoint research.

45. This conclusion relies on the properties of the type I extreme value distribution and simple nested logit models in allowing for random selections of choice alternatives in estimating the preferences underlying a RUM description of individual choice.

46. MacNair and Lutz (1998) have suggested a potentially important resolution of this problem. They call for using the initial choice set available to respondents and considering CJA as a supplement to a revealed preference analysis. In this context the revealed preference would be necessary to define the baseline choice set. An alternative is to use the estimated indirect utility function to evaluate baseline or status quo conditions as a single alternative relative to one new alternative (the policy option). This approach would not require an evaluation of the alternatives a person might consider and could be developed in a consistent way. However, this strategy abandons a central motivation for adopting a RUM in the first place, completely ignoring substitutes for the policy option.

47. The experience reported in Johnson et al. (2000) does indicate that there is learning and fatigue in a range of different conjoint analyses. Most of the studies in the literature have not incorporated these effects. Moreover, there has been very limited research evaluating whether these effects can be distinguished from the incentive and informational influences on respondent choices. For an alternative view on the potential strengths of conjoint methods, see Adamowicz and Boxall (2000).

48. Ninety-four per cent (22 people) returned either their check or the permit. Sixteen checks were not returned. The authors' discussion notes that when payment was stopped on the checks, five days after the deadline only one check had been cashed without returning a permit.

49. This assumption refers to attributes outside the confines of incentives defined by the optimization models used to describe behavior. For example, one participant may 'prefer' to deal with another – they enjoy the conversation that accompanies the exchange. *Ex post* we can rationalize that preference using conversation as a utility-enhancing jointly consumed 'product'. However, we could not have assumed it would be present based on the conventional optimization models used to describe individuals' choices.

50. A more detailed summary of their initial results as well as further experiments is provided in Bishop and Heberlein (1990).

51. One of the results from Carson et al. (1999) is relevant to those applications where individuals are asked to contribute voluntarily to the provision of a public good. There is a clear prediction about the expected results from 'real' and hypothetical applications of this approach. Their analysis suggests a real contributions format will lead to choices that *understate* WTP and the hypothetical consequential format in the sense that it is perceived as influencing a contributions program, should lead to choices that *overstate* WTP. Thanks are due to a referee for suggesting this connection to their work.

52. Of course we rely on having sufficient knowledge of preferences to compute a hypothetical case where the result is a gain with net benefits positive, even with such reallocations. My point is that this conclusion is a conceptual point and no more a 'revealed' outcome than CV is a revealed payment.

53. See Smith et al. (2002) for an example using this logic with results from contingent valuation, travel cost recreation demand, and hedonic methods.

54. See Hines (1999) for further discussion.

55. The primary contributions are Mäler (1974), Hausman (1981), LaFrance and Hanemann (1989), Willig (1978), and Bockstael and McConnell (1993).

56. In their use of independent macro- and micro-data sets in estimating labor supply responses, Imbens and Lancaster (1994) describe several analogies to the use of independent samples in jointly estimated models. In environmental economics, there are also a number of parallels including the use of the varying parameter model, regional recreation demand models, meta analyses, and others. Nonetheless, I could not find a discussion of using CV in ways that are analogous to the case-controlled or treatment samples used in epidemiology.

57. On 7 February 1990, a tanker, *American Trader*, spilled 416 598 gallons of oil off the coast of Huntington Beach, California. Some of the oil was washed ashore and approximately 14 miles of beach were closed for 34 days. This area closed extended from

Alanaitos Bay in Los Angles County to Crystal Cove State Beach in Orange County. Under the 1990 Oil Pollution Act, as well as California statutes, the trustees for resources injured as a result of the spill can seek damages for the injury, or loss of use of the affected resources. See Chapman et al. (1998) and Dunford (1999) for a discussion of the case from different perspectives. This example illustrates how existing data might be used to evaluate this type of loss.

58. This on-site survey was undertaken by NOAA for ten beaches in the summer of 1989. Five were in California, three in Oregon, and two in Washington. Two areas, San Onofre State Beach and Cabrillo-Long Beach, fall in an area close to the spill and were used for my example. See Leeworthy et al. (1990) for discussion. Independent analysis of these two along with Santa Monica beach was undertaken by Leeworthy and Wiley (1993).

59. My argument is somewhat similar to an early discussion by McConnell and Duff (1976). They considered the travel cost demand when there was uncertainty about entry. In this case their first-order condition adjusted the travel cost by the inverse of the probability of entry, because they could incur the cost and not be admitted. Here we might assume they know in advance about availability of the site so they do not have to incur the costs.

60. See Hausman (1981) for details and Bockstael et al. (1984) for other examples. Von Haefen (2002) provides a complete catalog of restrictions for the case of multiple equation applications.

61. The specific text of the COS contingent valuation question is given in Appendix A.

62. This format is the same specification Larson (1993) used to argue that q represented the effects of non-use or existence value because q did not appear in the Hicksian demand for recreation. This interpretation is arbitrary. My point here is to illustrate the use of complementary data sets in a straightforward way, not to consider the full implications of alternative linkages between q and x. Of course, that would be an important aspect of more detailed applications of the proposed methodology.

63. Examples of the basic logic proposed here can be found in Arellano and Meghir (1992) and Imbens and Lancaster (1994). There is an important addition to my proposal over theirs. It is the use of a formal structural model of choice that implies specific restrictions linking the individual models' parameters. It is also possible to consider matching to develop control samples for reduced form tests of treatments or manipulations to the information or context in stated preference analysis. This process requires a common set of questions across surveys. See Sloan et al. (2003) for an example.

64. The indirect utility function was derived from the travel cost demand model. As a result this is the only interpretation it allows for non-users. The general framework does not require this type of structure. We could select more complex treatments (see Table 2.1 above). This simply requires more common information from the samples being used in a complementary joint analysis.

65. The trips were reported in intervals with the COS study. The PARVS trip records were adjusted to conform to the COS format. The trip distribution with the numbers of respondents and the percentage of the sample for the three samples is given as:

Trips	PARVS	COS	COS/Central Coast
1 or 2	47 (39.8)	236 (21.7)	105 (26.4)
>3 and <=10	37 (31.4)	349 (32.2)	168 (42.3)
>10	34 (28.8)	283 (46.1)	124 (31.2)

For the other sample (that is, a household member boating or fishing in the past five years) there were only 500 households satisfying this criterion in the COS sample. To match the number of observations in the PARVS sample we selected randomly 23.6 per cent of this group.

66. The instruments for the first and second models included: the travel cost, income, age, amount of the one-time payment in the COS sample, whether an individual had traveled the coastal highway, lived in the central coast, and was familiar with birds likely to be

injured. The last model drops the variable associated with using Highway 1 because it was a part of the criterion defining the sample and adds a qualitative variable based on whether a respondent identifies himself (or herself) as an environmentalist.

67.   Crooker and Kling (2000) have taken a first step in this process in developing non-parametric bounds for CV estimates. My point is that once the objective of undertaking such behavioral 'tests' is built into the design of CV surveys we can expand the range of uses of revealed preference insights beyond the bounds they propose. As Houthakker proposed a sequence of price and quantity changes to uncover non-integrable preference fields, the CV research can also search the space of stated choices for consistent responses.

References

Adamowicz, V. and P. Boxall (2000), 'Future directions of stated choice methods for environmental valuation', paper presented at The Kobe Conference on the Theory and Application of Environmental Valuation, Kobe University, Rokkoudai Campus, Japan, 22–23 January.

Adamowicz, V., J. Louviere and M. Williams (1994), 'Combining revealed and stated preference methods for valuing environmental amenities', *Journal of Environmental Economics and Management*, **26**, 271–92.

Adamowicz, V., J. Swait, P. Boxall, J. Louviere and M. Williams (1997), 'Perceptions versus objective measures of environmental quality in combined revealed and stated preference models of environmental valuation', *Journal of Environmental Economics and Management*, **32** (January), 65–84.

Alberini, A., A. Krupnick, M. Cropper, N. Simon and J. Cook (2001), 'The willingness to pay for mortality risk reductions: a comparison of the United States and Canada', working paper, October.

Angrist, J.D. and A.B. Krueger (1992), 'The effect of age at school entry on educational attainment: an application of instrumental variables with moments from two samples', *Journal of the American Statistical Association*, **87** (418), 328–36.

Arellano, M. and C. Meghir (1992), 'Female labour supply and on-the-job search: an empirical model estimated using complementary data sets', *Review of Economic Studies*, **59** (3), 537–59.

Arrow, K., R. Solow, E.E. Leamer, R. Radner and H. Schuman (1994), 'Comment on NOAA proposed rule on natural resource damage assessments', ANPNM, comment no. 69, 7 January.

Arrow, K., R. Solow, P.R. Portney, E.E. Leamer, R. Radner and H. Schuman (1993), 'Report of the NOAA Panel on Contingent Valuation', *Federal Register*, **58** (10), 4601–14.

Balistreri, E., G. McClelland, G. Poe and W. Schulze (2001), 'Can hypothetical questions reveal true values? A laboratory comparison of dichotomous choice and open-ended contingent values with auction values', *Environmental and Resource Economics*, **18** (March), 275–92.

Bateman, I.J., M. Cole, P. Cooper, S. Georgiou, D. Hadley and G.L. Poe (2004), 'On visible choice sets and scope sensitivity', *Journal of Environmental Economics and Management*, **47** (January), 71–93.

Ben-Akiva, M.E. (1992), 'Incorporation of psychometric data in individual choice models', paper presented to American Marketing Association Advanced Research Techniques Forum, June.

Ben-Akiva, M.E. and T. Morikawa (1990), 'Estimation of switching models from revealed preferences and stated intentions', *Transportation Research* A, **24** (6), 485–95.

Beron, K., J. Murdock and M. Thayer (2001), 'The benefits of visibility improvements: new evidence from the Los Angeles metropolitan area', *The Journal of Real Estate Finance and Economics*, **22** (March/May), 319–38.

Berry, S., J. Levinsohn and A. Pakes (1998), 'Differentiated products demand systems from a combination of micro and macro data: the new car market', working paper 6481, National Bureau of Economic Research, March, Cambridge, MA.

Bishop, R.C. and T.A. Heberlein (1979), 'Measuring values of extra-market goods: are indirect measures biased?', *American Journal of Agricultural Economics*, **61** (8), 926–30.

Bishop, R.C. and T.A. Heberlein (1990), 'The contingent valuation method', in R.L. Johnson and G.V. Johnson (eds), *Economic Valuation of Natural Resources*, Boulder, CO: Westview Press.

Blinder, A.S. (1991), 'Why are prices sticky?: preliminary results from an interview study', *American Economic Review, Proceedings*, **81** (May), 89–100.

Bockstael, N.E. and K.E. McConnell (1993), 'Public goods as characteristics of non-market commodities', *Economic Journal*, **103** (3), 1244–57.

Bockstael, N.E. and K.E. McConnell (1999), 'The behavioral basis of non-market valuation', in J.A. Herriges and C.L. Kling (eds), *Valuing Recreation and the Environment*, Cheltenham, UK and Northampton, MA: Edward Elgar.

Bockstael, N.E., W.M. Hanemann and I.E. Strand, Jr. (1984), 'Measuring the benefits of water quality improvements using recreation demand models', Department of Agricultural and Resource Economics, University of Maryland, report to US Environmental Protection Agency.

Braden, J.B. and C.D. Kolstad (eds) (1991), *Measuring the Demand for Environmental Quality*, Amsterdam: North-Holland.

Brookshire, D.S., B.C. Ives and W.D. Schulze (1976), 'The valuation of aesthetic preferences', *Journal of Environmental Economics and Management*, **3** (4), 325–46.

Brookshire, D.S., R.C. d'Arge, W.D. Schulze and M.A. Thayer (1981), 'Experiments in valuing public goods', in V.K. Smith (ed.), *Advances in Applied Microeconomics*, Greenwich, CT: JAI Press.

Brookshire, D.S., M.A. Thayer, W.D. Schulze and R.C. d'Arge (1982), 'Valuing public goods: a comparison of survey and hedonic approaches', *American Economic Review*, **72** (1), 165–77.

Brown, G.M. and J. Hammack (1973), 'Dynamic economic management of migratory waterfowl', *The Review of Economics and Statistics*, **55** (February), 73–82.

Brown, T.C., P.A. Champ, R.C. Bishop and D.W. McCollum (1996), 'Response formats and public good donations', *Land Economics*, **72** (2), 152–66.

Bureau of Labor Statistics (1997), *BLS Handbook of Methods*, bulletin no. 2490, Washington, DC: US Department of Labor.

Cameron, T.A. (1988), 'A new paradigm for valuing non-market goods using referendum data: maximum likelihood estimation by censored logistic regression', *Journal of Environmental Economics and Management*, **15**, 355–79.

Cameron, T.A. (1992), 'Combining contingent valuation and travel cost data for the valuation of non-market goods', *Land Economics*, **68** (3), 302–17.

Cameron, T.A., G.L. Poe, R.G. Ethier and W.D. Schulze (2002), 'Alternative non-market value-elicitation methods: are the underlying preferences the same?', *Journal of Environmental Economics and Management*, **44** (November), 391–425.

Carson, R.T. (1997), 'Contingent valuation surveys and tests of insensitivity to scope', in R.J. Kopp, W.W. Pommerehne and N. Schwarz (eds), *Determining the Value of Non-Marketed Goods: Economic, Psychological, and Policy Relevant Aspects of Contingent Valuation Methods*, Boston: Kluwer Nijhoff.

Carson, R.T. (2003), *Contingent Valuation: A Comprehensive Bibliography and History*, Cheltenham, UK and Northampton, MA: Edward Elgar.

Carson, R.T. and N.E. Flores (1996), 'Another look at "Does contingent valuation measure preferences? Experimental evidence": How evident is the evidence?', discussion paper 96–31, Department of Economics, University of California, September.

Carson, R.T. and R.C. Mitchell (1993), 'The value of clean water: the public's willingness to pay for boatable, fishable, and swimmable quality water', *Water Resources Research*, **29** (July), 2445–54.

Carson, R.T., W.M. Hanemann and R.C. Mitchell (1986), 'The use of simulated political markets to value public goods', unpublished paper, Economics Department, University of California, San Diego.

Carson, R.T., W.M. Hanemann and D. Steinberg (1990), 'A discrete choice contingent valuation estimate of the value of Kenai King Salmon', *Journal of Behavioral Economics*, **19**, 53–67.

Carson, R.T., R.C. Mitchell, W.M. Hanemann, R.J. Kopp, S. Presser and P.A. Ruud (1992), 'A contingent valuation study of lost passive use values resulting from the Exxon Valdez oil spill', unpublished report to Attorney General of the State of Alaska, National Resource Damage Assessment Inc., La Jolla, CA, 10 November.

Carson, R.T., W.M. Hanemann, R.J. Kopp, J.A. Krosnick, R.C. Mitchell, S. Presser, P.A. Rudd and V.K. Smith (1994), 'Prospective interim lost use value due to DDT and PCB contamination in Southern California', report to National Oceanic and Atmospheric Administration, Natural Resource Damage Assessment Inc., La Jolla, CA, September.

Carson, R.T., N.E. Flores, K.M. Martin and J.L. Wright (1996a), 'Contingent valuation and revealed preference', *Land Economics*, **72** (February), 80–99.

Carson, R.T., M.B. Conaway, W.M. Hanemann, J.A. Krosnick, K.M. Martin, D.R. McCubbin, R.C. Mitchell and S. Presser (1996b), *The Value of Preventing Oil Spill Injuries to Natural Resources Along California's Central Coast*, Vol. I, Natural Resource Damage Assessment Inc., La Jolla, CA., 31 March.

Carson, R.T., W.M. Hanemann, R.J. Kopp, J.A. Krosnick, R.C. Mitchell, S. Presser, P.A. Rudd and V.K. Smith (1996c), 'Was the NOAA panel correct about contingent valuation?', discussion paper 96–20, Resources for the Future, May.

Carson, R.T., W.M. Hanemann, R.J. Kopp, J.A. Krosnick, R.C. Mitchell, S. Presser, P. Rudd and V.K. Smith (1997), 'Temporal reliability of estimates from contingent valuation', *Land Economics* (May), 151–63.

Carson, R.T., W.M. Hanemann, R.J. Kopp, J.A. Krosnick, R.C. Mitchell, S. Presser, P. Rudd and V.K. Smith (1998), 'Referendum design and contingent valuation: the NOAA Panel's no-vote recommendation', *Review of Economics and Statistics* (May), 335–7.

Carson, R.T., T. Groves and M. Machina (1999), 'Incentive and informational properties of preference questions', unpublished paper, Department of Economics, University of California, San Diego.

Carson, R.T., N.E. Flore and N.F. Meade (2001), 'Contingent valuation: controversies and evidence', *Environmental and Resource Economics*, **19** (June), 173–210.

Champ, P.A. and R.C. Bishop (2001), 'Donation payment mechanisms and contingent valuation: an empirical study of hypothetical bias', *Environmental and Resource Economics*, **19** (August), 383–402.

Champ, P.A., N.E. Flores, T.C. Brown and J. Chivers (2002), 'Contingent valuation and incentives', *Land Economics*, **78** (November), 591–604.

Chapman, D.J., W.M. Hanemann and P. Rudd (1998), 'The *American Trader* oil spill: a view from the beaches', *AERE Newsletter*, **18** (November), 12–25.

Chay, K. and M. Greenstone (2000), 'Does air quality matter? Evidence from housing markets', working paper, University of California, Berkeley.

Cicchetti, C.J. and V.K. Smith (1973), 'Congestion, quality deterioration, and optimal use: wilderness recreation in the Spanish Peaks Primitive Area', *Social Science Research*, **2**, 15–30.

Ciriacy-Wantrup, S.V. (1947), 'Capital returns from soil-conservation practices', *Journal of Farm Economics*, **29**, 1181–96.

Cotterill, R.W. (1994), 'Scanner data: new opportunities for demand and competitive strategy analysis', *Agricultural and Resource Economics Review* (October), 125–39.

Crooker, J. and C.L. Kling (2000), 'Nonparametric bounds on welfare measures: a new tool for nonmarket valuation', *Journal of Environmental Economics and Management*, **39** (March), 145–61.

Cummings, R.G., D.S. Brookshire and W.D. Schulze (eds) (1986), *Valuing Environmental Goods: An Assessment of the Contingent Valuation Method*, Totowa, NJ: Rowman & Littlefield.

Cummings, R.G., G.W. Harrison and E.E. Rutström (1995), 'Homegrown values and hypothetical surveys: is the dichotomous-choice approach incentive-compatible?', *American Economic Review*, **85** (1), 260–66.

Davis, R.K. (1963), 'The value of outdoor recreation: an economic study of the Maine woods', Ph.D. dissertation, Harvard University Department of Economics.

Desvousges, W.H., V.K. Smith and M. McGivney (1983), 'A comparison of alternative approaches for estimation of recreation and related benefits of water quality improvements', US Environmental Protection Agency report no. EPA-230-05-83-01, Washington, DC.

Desvousges, W.H., V.K. Smith, D.H. Brown and D.K Pate (1984), 'Detailed summary: the role of focus groups in designing a contingent valuation survey to measure the benefits of hazardous waste management regulations', EPA Contract No. 68-01-6595, June.

Desvousges, W.H., F.R. Johnson, R.W. Dunford, K.J. Boyle, S.P. Hudson and K.N. Wilson (1993), 'Measuring natural resource damages with contingent valuation tests of validity and reliability', in J.A. Hausman (ed.), *Contingent Valuation: A Critical Assessment*, Amsterdam: North-Holland.

Desvousges, W.H., S.M. Waters and K.E. Train (1996), 'Supplemental report on potential economic losses associated with recreation services in the Upper Clark Fork River Basin', unpublished paper, Triangle Economic Research, Durham, NC, 1 February.

Diamond, P.A. (1996), 'Testing the internal consistency of contingent valuation surveys', *Journal of Environmental Economics and Management*, **30** (3), 337–47.

Diamond, P.A. and J.A. Hausman (1994), 'Contingent valuation: is some number better than no number', *Journal of Economic Perspectives*, **8** (Fall), 45–64.

Diamond, P.A., J.A. Hausman, G.K. Leonard and M.A. Denning (1993), 'Does contingent valuation measure preferences? Experimental evidence', in J.A. Hausman (ed.), *Contingent Valuation: A Critical Assessment*, Amsterdam: North-Holland.

Duffield, J.W. and D.A. Patterson (1992), 'Field testing existence values: an instream flow trust fund for Montana rivers', working paper presented to W-133 Meetings, 14th Interim Report, R.B. Rettig (ed.), Department of Agricultural and Resource Economics, Oregon State University.

Dunford, R.W. (1999), 'The *American Trader* oil spill: an alternative view of recreation use damages', *AERE Newsletter*, **19** (May), 12–20.

Ebert, U. (1998), 'Evaluation of nonmarket goods: recovering unconditional preferences', *American Journal of Agricultural Economics*, **80** (May): 241–54.

Englin, J. and T.A. Cameron (1996), 'Augmenting travel cost models with contingent behavior data', *Environmental and Resource Economics*, **7** (2), 133–47.

Eom, Y.S. and V.K. Smith (1994), 'Calibrated non-market valuation', unpublished paper, Center for Environmental and Resource Economics, Duke University, August.

Freeman, A.M. III (1993), *The Measurement of Environmental and Resource Values: Theory and Methods*, Washington, DC: Resources for the Future.

Haab, T.C. and K.E. McConnell (1997), 'Referendum models and negative willingness to pay: alternative solutions', *Journal of Environmental Economics and Management*, **32** (February), 251–70.

Hammack, J. and G.M. Brown, Jr (1974), *Waterfowl and Wetlands: Toward Bioeconomic Analysis*, Baltimore: The Johns Hopkins University Press, for Resources for the Future.

Hanemann, W.M. (1984), 'Welfare evaluations in contingent valuation experiments with discrete responses', *American Journal of Agricultural Economics*, **66** (3), 332–41.

Hanemann, W.M. (1988), 'Three approaches to defining "existence" or nonuse values under certainty', working paper Department of Agricultural and Resource Economics, University of California, Berkeley, July.

Hanemann, W.M. (1991), 'Willingness to pay versus willingness to accept: how much can they differ?', *American Economic Review*, **81** (3), 635–47.

Hanemann, W.M. (1992), 'Preface', in Ståle Navrud (ed.), *Pricing the European Environment*, Oslo: Scandinavian University Press.

Hanemann, W.M. (1994), 'Valuing the environment through contingent valuation', *Journal of Economic Perspectives*, **8** (4), 19–44.

Hanemann, W.M. (1995), 'Review of Triangle Economic Research report on economic loss to recreational fishing in the Upper Clark Fork Basin', testimony in the Upper Clark Fork River case, 27 October.

Hanemann, W.M. (1996), 'Theory versus data in the contingent valuation debate', in D.J. Bjornstad and J.R. Kahn (eds), *The Contingent Valuation of Environmental Resources*, Cheltenham, UK and Brookfield, VT: Edward Elgar.

Hanemann, W.M. (1999), 'The economic theory of WTP and WTA', in I. Bateman and K. Willis (eds), *Valuing Environment Preferences: Theory and Practice of the Contingent Valuation Method in the US, EC and Developing Countries*, Oxford: Oxford University Press.

Hanemann, W.M. and B. Kanninen (1999), 'The statistical analysis of discrete-response CV data', in I. Batemen and K. Willis (eds), *Valuing Environmental Preferences: Theory and Practice of the Contingent Valuation Method in the US, EC and Developing Countries*, Oxford: Oxford University Press.

Harberger, A.C. (1971), 'Three basic postulates for applied welfare economics', *Journal of Economic Literature*, **9** (September), 785–97.

Harrison, G.W. (1989), 'Theory and misbehavior of first price auctions', *American Economic Review*, **79** (September), 749–62.

Harrison, G.W. (2000), 'Contingent valuation meets the experts: a critique of the NOAA Panel report', working paper, Department of Economics, University of South Carolina, Columbia, SC, October.

Hausman, J.A. (1981), 'Exact consumer's surplus and deadweight loss', *American Economic Review*, **71** (4), 662–76.

Hausman, J.A. (ed.) (1993), *Contingent Valuation: A Critical Assessment*, Amsterdam: North-Holland.

Heckman, J.J. (2001), 'Micro data, heterogeneity, and the evaluation of public policy: Nobel Lecture', *Journal of Political Economy*, **109** (4), 673–748.

Herriges, J.A., C.L. Kling and D.J. Phaneuf (2004), 'What's the use? Welfare estimates from revealed preference models when weak complementarity does not hold', *Journal of Environmental Economics and Management*, **47** (January), 55–70.

Hines, J.R., Jr (1999), 'Three sides of Harberger Triangles', *Journal of Economic Perspectives*, **13** (Spring), 167–88.

Houthakker, H.S. (1950), 'Revealed preference and the utility function', *Economica* **17**, 159–74.

Huang, J.C. and V.K. Smith (1998), 'Monte Carlo benchmarks for discrete response valuation methods', *Land Economics*, **74** (May), 186–202.

Huang, J.C. and V.K. Smith (2002), 'Monte Carlo benchmarks for discrete response valuation methods: reply', *Land Economics*, **78** (November), 617–23.

Imbens, G.W. and T. Lancaster (1994), 'Combining micro and macro data in micro-econometric models', *Review of Economic Studies*, **61**, 655–80.

Johnson, F.R. and W.H. Desvousges (1997), 'Estimating stated preferences with rated-pair data: environmental, health and employment effects of energy programs', *Journal of Environmental Economics and Management*, **34** (September), 79–99.

Johnson, F.R., K.E. Matthews and M.F. Bingham (2000), 'Evaluating welfare-theoretic consistency in multiple-response, stated-preference surveys', paper presented at the Kobe Conference on Theory and Application of Environmental Valuation, Kobe University, Rokkoudai Campus, Japan, 22–23 January.

Kahn, M. (1997), 'Are the social benefits for combating Los Angeles smog rising or falling?', working paper, Columbia University.

Kahneman, D. and I. Ritov (1994), 'Determinants of stated willingness to pay for public goods: a study in the headline method', *Journal of Risk and Uncertainty*, **9** (July), 5–38.

Kain, J.F. and J.M. Quigley (1972), 'Note on owner's estimate of housing value', *Journal of the American Statistical Association*, **67** (December), 803–6.

Kanninen, B.J. (2002), 'Optimal design for multinomial choice experiments', *Journal of Marketing Research*, **39** (May), 214–27.

Kopp, R.J. and V.K. Smith (1997), 'Constructing measures of economic value', in R.J. Kopp, W. Pommerhne and N. Schwarz (eds), *Determining the Value of Non-Marketed Goods: Economic, Psychological and Policy Relevant Aspects of Contingent Valuation Methods*, Boston: Kluwer Nijhoff.

Krosnick, J.A., A.L. Holbrook, M.K. Berent, R.T. Carson, W.M. Hanemann, R.J. Kopp, R.C. Mitchell, S. Presser, P.A. Ruud, V.K. Smith, W.R. Moody, M.C. Green and M. Conaway (2002), 'The impact of "no opinion" response options on data quality: non-attitude reduction or an invitation to satisfice?', *Public Opinion Quarterly*, **66** (Fall), 371–403.

Krupnick, A., A. Alberini, M. Cropper, N. Simon, B. O'Brien, R. Goeree, and M. Heintzelman (2002), 'Age, health and the willingness to pay for mortality risk reductions: a contingent valuation survey of Ontario residents', *The Journal of Risk and Uncertainty*, **24** (2), 161–86.

LaFrance, J.T. and W.M. Hanemann (1989), 'The dual structure of incomplete demand systems', *American Journal of Agricultural Economics*, **71** (May), 262–74.

Larson, D.M. (1993), 'On measuring existence value', *Land Economics*, **69** (November), 377–89.

Larson, D.M., J.B. Loomis and Y.L. Chien (1993), 'Combining behavioral and conversational approaches to value amenities: an application to gray whale population enhancement', paper presented to American Agricultural Economics Association, August.

Layton, D.F. and S.T. Lee (2002), 'From ratings to rankings: the econometric analysis of stated preference ratings data', unpublished paper, University of California, Davis.

Leeworthy, V.R., D. Schruefer and P.C. Wiley (1990), *A Socioeconomic Profile of Recreationists at Public Outdoor Recreation Sites in Coastal Areas*, Vol. 5, Washington, DC: National Oceanic and Atmospheric Administration.

Leeworthy, V.R. and P.C. Wiley (1993), 'Recreational use value for three Southern California beaches', unpublished paper, Strategic Environmental Assessments Division, National Oceanic and Atmospheric Administration, Rockville, MD, March.

Louviere, J.J. (1996), 'Relating stated preference measures and models to choices in real markets: calibration of CV responses', in D.J. Bjornstad and J.R. Kahn (eds), *The Contingent Valuation of Environmental Resources*, Cheltenham, UK and Brookfield, VT: Edward Elgar.

Louviere, J.J., R.J. Meyer, D. Bunch, R.T. Carson, B. Delleart, W.M. Hanemann, D. Hensher and J. Irwin (1999), 'Combining sources of preference data for modeling complex decision processes', *Marketing Letters*, **10**, 205–17.

Mack, R.P. and S. Myers (1965), 'Outdoor recreation', in R. Dorfman (ed.), *Measuring Benefits of Government Investments*, Washington, DC: The Brookings Institution.

MacNair, D. and J. Lutz (1998), 'Combining revealed and stated preferences to evaluate in-kind transfers for natural resource damages: an application to saltwater fishing', presented at the Center for Environmental and Resource Economics Camp Resources Workshop, Wilmington, NC, 13 August.

Mäler, K.G. (1974), *Environmental Economics: A Theoretical Inquiry*, Baltimore: The Johns Hopkins Press, for Resources for the Future.

Mansfield, C. and V.K. Smith (2002), 'Tradeoff at the trough: TMDLs and the evolving status of U.S. water quality policy', in J.A. List and A. de Zeeuw (eds), *Recent Advances in Environmental Economics*, Cheltenhen, UK and Northampton, MA: Edward Elgar.

McConnell, K.E. (1990), 'Models for referendum data: the structure of discrete choice models for contingent valuation', *Journal of Environmental Economics and Management*, **18** (January), 19–34.

McConnell, K.E. and V.A. Duff (1976), 'Estimating net benefits of recreation under conditions of excess demand', *Journal of Environmental Economics and Management*, **2** (February), 224–30.

McFadden, D. (1994), 'Contingent valuation and social choice', *American Journal of Agricultural Economics*, **76** (4), 689–708.

Mitchell, R.C. and R.T. Carson (1984), *A Contingent Valuation Estimate of National Freshwater Benefits: Technical Report to the U.S. Environmental Protection Agency*, Washington, DC: Resources for the Future.

Mitchell, R.C. and R.T. Carson (1989), *Using Surveys to Value Public Goods: The Contingent Valuation Method*, Washington, DC: Resources for the Future.

Morikawa, T. (1989), 'Incorporating stated preference data in travel demand analysis', unpublished Ph.D. thesis, Massachusetts Institute of Technology, Department of Civil Engineering.

Morikawa, T., M. Ben-Akiva and D. McFadden (1990), 'Incorporating psychometric data in econometric travel demand models', presented at Banff Symposium on Consumer Decision Making and Choice Behavior, May.

National Oceanic and Atmospheric Administration (1996), 'Natural resource damage assessments final rule for Oil Pollution Act of 1990', *Federal Register*, **61** (5 January), 440–510.

Office of Management and Budget (2003), 'Draft 2003 report to Congress on the costs and benefits of federal regulations: notice', *Federal Register*, **68** (February), 5492–527.

64   *Contingent valuation and economic theory*

Poe, G.L. and C.A. Vossler (2002), 'Monte Carlo benchmarks for discrete response valuation methods: a comment', *Land Economics*, **78** (November), 605–16.
Poe, G.L., J.E. Clark, D. Rondeau and W.D. Schulze (2002), 'Provision point mechanisms and field validity tests of contingent valuation', *Environmental and Resource Economics*, **23** (September), 105–31.
Portney, P.R. (1994), 'The contingent valuation debate: why economists should care', *Journal of Economic Perspectives*, **8** (Fall), 3–18.
Randall, A., B. Ives and C. Eastman (1974), 'Bidding games for valuation of aesthetic environmental improvements', *Journal of Environmental Economics and Management*, **1** (August), 132–49.
Reaves, D.W., R.A. Kramer and T.P. Holmes (1999), 'Does question format matter? Valuing an endangered species', *Environmental and Resource Economics*, **14** (October), 365–83.
Roe, B., K.J. Boyle and M.F. Teisl (1997), 'Using conjoint analysis to derive estimates of compensating variation', *Journal of Environmental Economics and Management*, **31** (September), 145–59.
Rowe, R.D., R.C. D'Arge and D.S. Brookshire (1980), 'An experiment on the economic value of visibility', *Journal of Environmental Economics and Management*, **7**, 1–19.
Samuelson, P.A. (1938), 'A note on the pure theory of consumer's behavior', *Economica*, **5** (February), 61–71.
Samuelson, P.A. (1950), 'The problem of integrability in utility theory', *Economica*, **17**, 355–85.
Schläpfer, F. (2002), 'A note on the issue of incentive compatibility in referendum-format CVM', unpublished paper, Institut für Umweltwissenschaften.
Schulze, W.D., D.S. Brookshire, E.G. Walther, K. Kelly, M.A. Thayer, R.L. Whitworth, S. Ben-David, W. Malm and J. Molenar (1981), 'The benefits of preserving visibility in the national parklands of the Southwest', *Methods Development for Environmental Control Benefits Assessment*, vol. VIII, final report to the USEPA Grant R805059010, Office of Exploratory Research, Office of Research and Development.
Schulze, W.D., G. McClelland, D. Waldman and J. Lazo (1996), 'Sources of bias in contingent valuation', in D.J. Bjornstad and J.R. Kahn (eds), *The Contingent Valuation of Environmental Resources: Methodological Issues and Research Needs*, Cheltenham, UK and Brookfield, VT: Edward Elgar.
Sieg, H., V.K. Smith, H.S. Banzhaf and R. Walsh (2002), 'Interjurisdictional housing prices in locational equilibrium', *Journal of Urban Economics*, **52** (July), 131–53.
Simon, H.A. (1986), 'Rationality in psychology and economics', in R. Hogarth and M.W. Reder (eds), *Rational Choice: The Contrast Between Economics and Psychology*, Chicago: University of Chicago Press.
Sloan, F.A., V.K. Smith and D.H. Taylor, Jr (2003), *The Smoking Puzzle: Information, Risk Perception, and Choice*, Cambridge, MA: Harvard University Press.
Smith, V.K. (1986), 'To keep or toss the contingent valuation method', in R.G. Cummings, D.S. Brookshire and W.D. Schulze (eds), *Valuing Environmental Goods: An Assessment of the Contingent Valuation Method*, Totowa, NJ: Rowman & Littlefield.
Smith, V.K. (1996), 'Can contingent valuation distinguish economic values for different public goods?', *Land Economics* (May), 139–51.
Smith, V.K. (1997), 'Pricing what is priceless: a status report on non-market valuation of environmental resources', in H. Folmer and T. Tietenberg (eds), *The International Yearbook of Environmental and Resource Economics*, Cheltenham, UK and Brookfield, VT: Edward Elgar.
Smith, V.K. (1999), 'Resource compensation and the restoration of injured natural resources: context and future research', unpublished paper, Center for Environmental and Resource Economics, Duke University, January.
Smith, V.K. and W.H. Desvousges (1986), *Measuring Water Quality Benefits*, Boston: Kluwer Nijhoff.
Smith, V.K. and L. Osborne (1996), 'Do contingent valuation estimates pass a "Scope" test? A meta analysis', *Journal of Environmental Economics and Management*, **31** (November), 287–301.

Smith, V.K. and C. Mansfield (1998), 'Buying time: real and contingent offers', *Journal of Environmental Economics and Management* (November), 209–24.

Smith, V.K. and S.K. Pattanayak (2002), 'Is meta analysis the Noah's ark for non-market valuation?', *Environmental and Resource Economics*, **22** (June), 271–96.

Smith, V.K., G. Van Houtven and S.K. Pattanayak (2002), 'Benefit transfer via preference calibration: "prudential algebra" for policy', *Land Economics*, **78** (February), 132–52.

Smith, V.K., X. Zhang and R.B. Palmquist (1997), 'Marine debris, beach quality, and non-market values', *Environmental and Resource Economics* (October), 223–47.

Swait, J. and J. Louviere (1993), 'The role of the scale parameter in the estimation and comparison of multinomial logit models', *Journal of Marketing Research*, **30** (August), 305–14.

Swait, J., J. Louviere and M. Williams (1994), 'A sequential approach to exploiting the combined strength of SP and RP data: application to freight shipper choice', *Transportation*, **21**, 135–52.

Takeuchi, K. and K. Ueta (1996), 'Another scope test on nonuse value of the Shimanto River, Japan', working paper, Kyoto University, Japan, April.

Varian, H.R. (1982), 'The nonparametric approach to demand analysis', *Econometrica*, **50**, 945–73.

Varian, H.R. (1983), 'Nonparametric tests of consumer behavior', *Review of Economic Studies*, **50**, 99–110.

Von Haefen, R.H. (2002), 'A complete characterization of the linear, log-linear, and semi-log incomplete demand system models', *Journal of Agricultural and Resource Economics*, **27** (December), 281–319.

Vossler, C.A. and J. Kerkvliet (2003), 'A criterion validity test of the contingent valuation method: comparing hypothetical and actual voting behavior for a public referendum', *Journal of Environmental Economics and Management*, **45** (May), 631–49.

Waugh, F.V. (1929), *Quality as a Determinant of Vegetable Prices: Studies in History, Economics and Public Law*, no 312, 1st AMS edn (from the Columbia University 1929 edition), ed. Faculty of Political Science, Columbia University, New York: AMS Press, 1968.

Westat, Inc. (1989), 'Investigation of possible recall/reference period bias in national surveys of fishing, hunting, and wildlife associated recreation', final report to US Department of Interior, Contract No. 14-16-009-87-008, December.

Whitehead, J.C., G.C. Blomquist, R.C. Ready and J.-C. Huang (1998), 'Construct validity of dichotomous and polychotomous choice contingent valuation questions', *Environmental and Resource Economics*, **11** (January), 107–16.

Willig, R.D. (1978), 'Incremental consumer's surplus and hedonic price adjustment', *Journal of Economic Theory*, **17** (2), 227–53.

Zhang, X. and V.K. Smith (1997), 'An integrated model of use and nonuse values', unpublished paper, Center for Environmental and Resource Economics, Duke University, July.

3 A practitioner's primer on the contingent valuation method

*John C. Whitehead**

3.1 Introduction

Consider the following hypothetical situation. You develop an intellectual interest in some good or service not typically traded in markets. It could be almost anything, such as adverse health effects from a hazardous waste disposal facility, a new sports arena, or preservation of a historic shipwreck. Its value could be important for efficiency reasons (e.g., a benefit–cost analysis of a management plan), for academic reasons (e.g., tests of economic theory), or for more important reasons (e.g., completion of a graduate thesis). Unfortunately, even though you may know the calculus of the consumer surplus triangle, you have no idea how to actually estimate the consumer surplus of anything in real life. Bummer.

You are industrious and dive right into the literature. You learn that there are several 'implicit market' methods that can be used to estimate economic value for non-market goods. You learn that the hedonic pricing method can be used to value location-related amenities, the travel cost method can be used to value recreational amenities, and the averting behavior method can be used to value health care and other services. But, these methodologies are not really what you are after. After all, your case study has pure public good attributes. It involves behavior beyond the range of historical experience. It may generate both use value and non-use (gasp!) value.

One lucky day you stumble across the contingent valuation method (CVM). You collect a bunch of journal articles from the *Journal of Environmental Economics and Management*, *Land Economics*, and *American Journal of Agricultural Economics* (to name a few), some books (e.g., Cummings, Brookshire, and Schultze, 1986; Mitchell and Carson, 1989; Bjornstad and Kahn, 1996), and begin to read. The good news is the literature is not difficult to understand (none of the articles are from the *Journal of Economic Theory*). The bad news is you find out that the contingent valuation method is a survey approach to valuation; you must collect your own primary data. Yikes! This topic wasn't covered in graduate school . . . not in Micro I or even Micro II. What are you going to do?

If you find yourself in this situation, don't lose sleep. The solution is almost pain free. You must simply figure out how to design and conduct a survey. People write books about this and you can read them. Three classic places to start are Sudman (1976), Dillman (1978), and Sudman and Bradburn (1982). Sudman tells you how to draw a sample, Dillman tells you how to conduct mail and telephone surveys, and Sudman and Bradburn tell you how to ask questions. More recent additions to this literature are Czaja and Blair (1996) with a focus on conducting telephone surveys, Maisel and Persell (1996) on sampling, and Mangione (1995) with a focus on mail surveys. If you read one or two of these books, then you should be in good shape.

What's that? You'd rather not ruin your spring break by reading one or two books? This chapter is an introduction to the collection of contingent valuation survey data. I go step-by-step through the survey design process with the assumptions that you have never conducted a survey before and your research budget is not especially large. After reading this chapter you won't be a survey expert, or look like one, but you will be able to design and conduct your own survey. You may even be able to fake it at professional meetings.

In the next section of this chapter I briefly review the benefits and costs of the various data collection approaches available. You can employ mail, telephone, in-person, and other methods of survey administration. Next I'll explore each step in the survey design process. This begins with questionnaire design and covers the nuts and bolts of collecting data. Then I'll cover what should be done with the data once you get it. I'll conclude with some flippant remarks and ideas for your second survey.

3.2 Mail, telephone, and in-person surveys

The issues to consider when choosing survey mode (mail, telephone, and in-person) are cost, time, and the amount of assistance available to you. Mail surveys are by far the least-expensive survey mode for the beginner. You can conduct a mail survey for anywhere from $5 to $10 per individual in the sample. So, a mail survey with a mail-out sample of 500 will cost about $2500 minimum (all values are in 2003 dollars). Mail surveys are labor intensive and, therefore, even cheaper if you don't include the opportunity costs of your own time. You could probably conduct a mail survey of a sample of 500 for $1500 if you do all the work. Note that the cost per completed interview will fall with increases in the response rate.

In contrast, you probably must hire professionals for telephone or in-person surveys. Cost-effective telephone surveys use computer-assisted telephone interview (CATI) software. The cost of telephone surveys greatly depends on the survey length due to long-distance phone charges. These costs might run from $15 to $40 for each 15 minute completed interview. In-person surveys will require mostly the travel and time costs of interviewers. Depending on who does the interviews, in-person surveys might cost $25–$50 per interview. Of course, all of these estimates rise with the quality of the survey research firm you might wish to employ.

Mail surveys require several months to conduct properly. Once the initial questionnaires are mailed, follow-up mailings should be conducted after about four and eight weeks. Responses will continue to trickle in even after you've developed preliminary willingness to pay estimates. Telephone and in-person surveys can possibly be conducted within a month or so of questionnaire design. If you are in a hurry and have plenty of interviewer help, you could try to conduct a telephone or in-person survey yourself. But, don't expect this to be a pleasant experience. Without the proper training, the interview process can be a painful process. Even worse, the data may end up more flawed than usual. If you wish to sample a large number of households (e.g., 500) in a short period of time (e.g., a few months) with a limited amount of assistance (e.g., one part-time research assistant) and you have other things to do, avoid conducting telephone and in-person interviews. Just think about talking to 500 strangers in addition to your normal professional activities, plus sleeping, eating, and having a little fun.

Other benefits of mail surveys are that you can provide visual aids (e.g., maps, bar charts, photos) and they allow some respondent privacy. Visual aids, which assist respondents with their answers, are impossible to include in a telephone survey. A willingness to pay question is considered by some to be a delicate subject. Mail surveys allow respondents some privacy and plenty of time when considering the amount of money they would give up that would leave them indifferent between having a government project or not. You may also get more honest income responses with mail surveys.

One of the costs of mail surveys is that they are self-administered. In any survey mode you can ask a single willingness to pay question without a serious problem. But, if you have a follow up willingness to pay question that depends on the answer to the first willingness to pay question, you can't trust your respondents to not peek ahead. This will limit your options. Another problem is that it is a bit easier for a potential respondent to throw a mail survey away than to rudely hang up on a persistent telephone interviewer. Low response rates have been reported in journal articles and you can imagine with horror the studies with very low response rates that never made it to a journal. Hopefully, with enough care and effort, this won't happen to you.

3.3 Questionnaire design
The first step in designing your mail questionnaire is to begin thinking about the questions you want to include. Start with the literature review.

Find contingent valuation studies of topics closely related to yours. If you can't find closely related studies, then find topics that are loosely related. The questionnaire design principles applied to these surveys will be similar to the principles you'll apply to your own survey. Once you find three or four survey instruments that you would like to read, beg the authors for a peek at their instruments. Write a letter, send an e-mail, or even call them on the phone. Most of these folks will pretend to be happy to forward you a copy of their instrument. Borrow the ideas that you like and revise them to your own situation. Make sure you cite the works that you borrowed questions from, at least once.

Once you have an idea of how survey questions look, consider the sections, or type of questions, in your questionnaire. A typical introductory section includes attitudinal questions. This asks for respondent knowledge and opinions about the survey topic. There is not much in economic theory to suggest these questions are important but they are for at least two reasons. First, these questions should be relatively easy, but interesting, to answer. You can also think of these as 'warm up' questions. This gets the respondent ready to answer some tougher and more thought-provoking questions. The second reason is that you might actually find a reason to use these variables when trying to explain your results (e.g., willingness to pay may not be a function of theoretically important variables until you control for respondents who do not have much knowledge about the matter).

The next section of the questionnaire could ask people about their behavior. How many days during the past year did you go outside and were exposed to air pollution? How many trips did you take to the beach during the past year? How often do you read newspapers about endangered species? These questions require more thought than the attitude questions. Trying to remember what you did last week can be a problem. Trying to remember what you did during the past 12 months can be a big problem. While you are thinking about behavioral questions, don't forget economic theory. Each behavior was engaged in because the benefits exceeded the costs. Find out something about the cost of the behavior. Do you have a respiratory condition? How far do you live from the beach? How much free time do you have to read the newspaper? With these questions you can estimate a behavioral model that might in some way be related to the hypothetical valuation questions. This relationship is crucial when trying to convince a narrow-minded skeptic (e.g., a labor economist) that your willingness to pay estimate is a valid measure of Hicksian compensating variation.

The valuation section should contain the primary valuation questions, additional valuation questions, and some debriefing questions. Unfortunately, in a contingent valuation survey you have about one chance to elicit an unbiased willingness to pay value. You have one chance because the answer to any other valuation question will be related in some way to the answer to the first question. So, think long and hard about the primary (i.e., first) valuation question and then consider follow-up valuation questions that could be useful. The follow-up questions could be designed to reduce the variance of willingness to pay or they could be designed to elicit willingness to pay values for variations in the scenario. Ask two or more questions, but don't ask 20; your respondents will tire of these quickly. Once you have all of your valuation questions sketched out, add some debriefing questions. Why are you willing to pay? Why aren't you willing to pay? Why don't you know whether you would be willing to pay or not? You'll also need a demographic section. Discover your respondents' race, age, marital status, education, number of children, and income. These are standard questions that can be borrowed from most surveys.

3.4   Writing questions: in general

You've decided that your questionnaire will have an attitudinal section, a behavioral section, a valuation section, and a demographic section. The next step is to begin writing your own questions. This can be a painful process. No one will understand what you are trying to ask when you first jot down a series of questions. The questions that you thought were only one question will actually be two questions combined into one. Your response categories will not cover the entire range of responses. The range of responses you provide will be ambiguous. It takes some time and effort to craft an effective questionnaire. Be patient.

The two types of questions are open-ended and closed-ended questions. Open-ended questions do not constrain respondents' answers because no response category is given: How many times during the past week did you walk your dog? Closed-ended questions constrain answers by specifying response categories: During the past week, did you walk your dog less than five times, between six and ten times, or more than ten times? The benefit of open-ended questions is that you end up with a point estimate of the response. If this is your dependent variable, you could use ordinary least squares to analyse it. If this is your independent variable, you could include the variable, as answered, on the right-hand side of your model. A closed-ended question might give you a yes/no response, an interval response (between $5 and $25), an ordinal scale response ('probably yes'), or some other monster that is more difficult to empirically analyse. If the closed-ended question is an independent variable, you usually must recode it into dummy variables. Open-ended questions are also easier to write. You only have to worry about writing the question; you don't have to worry about writing the response categories.

Although there are significant benefits to open-ended questions, most of your questions should be closed-ended for one simple reason. Closed-ended questions are much easier for respondents to answer. Closed-ended questions will be answered without as much worry about what the answer is supposed to look like (e.g., 'If I answer 93 will Dr Jones, Project Director, think I'm a silly fool?') or about unnecessary detail (e.g., 'Did I spend $152.36 last year on cheeseburgers or $152.46?'). With closed-ended questions respondents are able to focus on the question, answer it, and get to the next question. Using a simple rational choice model of answering questions with time constraints, the more difficult the question is, the less well developed the answer. The more time it takes to answer a single question, the fewer questions will be answered. You should plan on asking closed-ended questions in mail surveys unless it is difficult to do so. Some simple rules to follow when you write your questions are: (1) keep the questions (as) short (as possible), (2) make the questions clear, (3) each question should be only one question, and (4) response categories should be mutually exclusive and exhaustive. These rules might seem obvious but they are very easy to break. Try spending a long first day writing a draft of your questions. Go home, get something to eat, sleep eight hours, and go back to work. Then, read your questions carefully again and see how many rules you broke. Ouch!

Survey respondents usually have something else they would rather be doing than answering your questionnaire. Once they decide to tackle your questionnaire, they may only devote a certain amount of time to it. The more text you ask the respondent to read, the more text they will skip and the less accurate their answers will be. Try not to be too ambitious with each question. When writing questions, scratch out any unnecessary words or phrases, don't repeat things, and don't use big words. Unnecessary words and phrases are . . . unnecessary. You don't need them. When you repeat yourself in a question, the respondent gets irritated and may put the survey down. Big words are bad because they take longer to read and not everyone knows what they mean. If your respondent doesn't know what a word in the question means, then their answer to the question may not be what you intended it to be.

The survey question must be clear. Define your terms. If you need a precise measure of household income, don't simply ask: How much income did you make last year? The respondent will wonder what you really mean by income: Is it wages, dividends, and/or profits? If a term in the question might be ambiguous, then define it. Don't use jargon. It is especially tempting to use jargon in the valuation section of the questionnaire. If you want to estimate the benefits of reducing total suspended particulates by 25 per cent, you can't use the words 'total suspended particulates'.

One trap you may step into is to ask two questions at once. In the contingent valuation literature, the most common example of this problem is the open-ended willingness to pay question: 'What is the most money that you would be willing to pay for improved drinking water from the tap?' This single question is actually two questions. The first implicitly asks the respondent if they would be willing to pay anything at all. The second asks how much? These questions cause easily avoidable confusion among respondents. Split the single question into two questions: 'Are you willing to pay anything?' 'If yes, how much are you willing to pay?'

Response categories should be mutually exclusive and exhaustive. If you ask people how often they brush their teeth, give them more response categories than 'always' and 'never'. Make the categories exclusive. Don't provide '(a) never', '(b) once or twice a day', '(c) two to four times per day' as the three response categories. Some respondents overly deliberate about whether answer (b) or (c) is correct. Some respondents will want to answer 'more than four times per day'. Include this additional category and change the category (c) to 'three to four times per day'.

3.5   Writing the valuation scenario
The contingent valuation scenario must be (as) short (as possible), realistic, and simple. The components of a contingent valuation scenario include a description of the resource or policy context, a description of the policy or proposed change in resource allocation that will be valued, a payment vehicle, and a policy implementation rule. The description of the resource or policy context must be done in a paragraph or two, while explicitly describing exactly what is being discussed.

The description of the proposed policy should make explicit exactly what is being valued. Instead of phrases such as 'will improve drinking water' use phrases such as 'will improve tap water so that it tastes as good as bottled water and you will never get sick from it'. A concrete scenario allows each respondent to understand what, exactly, they are paying for. It also allows you to add different versions to your scenario. Each version can become an independent variable in your model of willingness to pay. Another version in the drinking water example could be constructed from the phrase 'will improve tap water so that it tastes as good as bottled water and you will not get sick more than one day a year from it'. Now you have a SICK variable equal to zero and one, depending on which survey version the respondent received.[1]

Respondents must have a way of paying for the change in resource allocation. In contingent valuation jargon this is the 'payment vehicle'. Typical payment vehicles include increases in water and/or utility bills, increases in state and/or federal taxes, increases in prices of related goods, fishing and hunting licenses, and contributions or donations to special funds. You must concern yourself with whether the payment vehicle is realistic, believable, and neutral. A local drinking water issue will not likely be financed with an increase in federal taxes or voluntary contributions. You should first consider whether an increase in the local water bill is realistic. In another example, a policy to limit the number of trawlers scraping the bottom of the local sound will not likely increase the market price of fish. Try using an increase in state taxes to fund enforcement. Some payment vehicles are natural. If you are analysing the benefits and costs of a red drum fishery management plan, a special red drum stamp that allows the catch of one (two, etc.) drum per trip might work. An example of a payment vehicle that may not be neutral is higher personal income taxes during a taxpayer revolt.

A closely related issue is the policy implementation or payment rule. The policy implementation rule can be explicit or implicit, but it must be enforceable. Otherwise, the contingent valuation question will not be incentive compatible. In the case of a special hunting license, a private good sold by government, the payment rule is implicitly understood by potential hunters. Pay for the stamp or don't go hunting. But, if the hunting regulation in the valuation scenario is not enforceable, many respondents might be happy to say that they would pay $10 for a duck stamp if it were easy to shoot a duck and not get caught doing it.

Respondents will believe that the state and federal government can raise taxes and enforce their payment. People will believe that a local government can raise utility bills and enforce their payment. The policy implementation rule in these cases is: if enough people are willing to pay enough money, then the government will implement the policy. Respondents have at least a weak incentive to tell the truth.

Voluntary contributions to special funds are more troublesome. The policy implementation rule is the same, but payment is not enforceable. If enough people say they will pay enough money, government may implement the policy. When government tries to collect money for the special fund, they would discover that people free ride. This may cause people who want the policy to overstate their willingness to pay. Voluntary contributions should only be used in valuation scenarios if other payment rules are exceptionally awkward (or if you are studying the economics of voluntary contributions). If the text of your valuation scenario is becoming long and you have no idea how it can be shortened and still maintain the integrity of the study, insert some questions in between the paragraphs. Ask people if they care about the policy: 'How concerned are you about the problem?' Ask people whether they believe what you are telling them: 'How effective do you think the management plan will be?' You might use these questions in your statistical analysis and you might not; but, they will break up the text so that respondents remain fresh and continue thinking about what you are telling them. They will also be less likely to skip big chunks of text to get to the next question because they'll be answering questions during the reading of the text.

3.6 Writing the valuation questions

The contingent valuation question is the most important question in the contingent valuation survey instrument. Since you are presenting a hypothetical situation to respondents, it is the most difficult question to write and the most difficult for respondents to answer. It is difficult to write because you must conjure up an imaginary scenario that is realistic, relatively short, and meets the objectives of the study. The question is difficult to answer because even the best contingent valuation scenarios are not realistic, they are long, and they tend to make people think about something they've never thought about before.

3.6.1   *Willingness to pay v. behavioral intentions*

A helpful suggestion might be to think of a contingent valuation question as a behavioral intention question, not as a willingness to pay question. A behavioral intention question asks people about behavior under hypothetical conditions: 'Would you donate $15 if that is how much it cost to protect sea turtle nesting habitat?' or 'How would you vote on the sewer bond if paying off the bonds cost you $125 per year?' or 'How many shellfish meals would you eat if they were safe and cost $12?' Many people can imagine how much money they would donate, how they would vote, and how much they would eat under different circumstances. Behavioral intentions are also easier to compare to actual behavior.

Willingness to pay questions ask people to speculate on how much they would be willing to pay for something, not what they would do in a certain situation: 'Would you be willing to pay $55 for an increase in water quality to the fishable level?' Most people aren't used to being asked about the size of their consumer surplus triangle. Also, hypothetical willingness to pay is not easy to compare with actual behavior. Even so, sometimes the willingness to pay question is unavoidable because a realistic scenario can't be constructed around a behavioral intention question. If this is the case, try to remember the difficulties that respondents have with hypothetical situations.

3.6.2   *Open-ended v. closed-ended*

Just like the typical survey question, there are two types of valuation questions: open-ended and closed-ended. Closed-ended questions include dichotomous choice (i.e., single-bound), and payment card questions. When follow-up questions are included, single-bound questions can become double or even multiple bounded. Even after a zillion journal articles comparing one version of the valuation question against another, many CVM researchers still don't agree about the appropriate form of the valuation question. If your survey budget allows it, try testing one of these against the others.

Many early CVM applications asked the open-ended question: 'What is the maximum amount of money that you would be willing to pay for the increase in ozone attainment days?' This question has several disadvantages. Being an open-ended question, it is relatively difficult to answer. You would really have to think hard about the size of your consumer surplus triangle. Instead, respondents may not think hard and simply say '$5' or '$25', the same amount they might write a check for when the neighbor kid asks for a school donation. Respondents will even skip the unfamiliar question entirely and go to the next question (they don't understand that this is the most important question to the CVM researcher!). Being not-so-incentive-compatible (do you tell the car salesperson your maximum willingness to pay?), the open-ended question is relatively easy to free ride on. Respondents might answer 'zero' or '$1', even if their other answers indicate they might have a much higher value for ozone attainment days.

An alternative to the open-ended question is the payment card question. The payment card question asks an open-ended question but provides dollar interval response categories to respondents. Respondents could be given the following response categories: 'Between $1 and $5', 'Between $5 and $10', 'Between $10 and $15', and 'More than $15'. Respondents would then indicate the response that most accurately reflects their maximum willingness to pay. You are left with a dependent variable that is almost continuous; for your preliminary models you can code the data at the mid-point of the intervals and model the responses with ordinary least squares regression. A problem is that payment card questions are prone to 'range bias'. In the example above, the average willingness to pay will likely be between $1 and $15. If another response category is included, say 'Between $15 and $20', the average willingness to pay may rise. The reason is that many survey respondents are very open to suggestion when answering unfamiliar questions. But, if your survey budget constrains you to use small samples, a payment card valuation question is an improvement over the open-ended valuation question.

The earliest version of the closed-ended question was the iterative bidding question. Everyone in the sample was asked: 'Would you be willing to pay $5 for the oil spill prevention program?' The $5 was the starting point. If the respondent answered 'yes', they would be asked the question again with a higher dollar amount (say $10). These questions would continue until the respondent answered 'no'. If the respondent answered 'no', they would be asked the question again with a lower dollar amount until the respondent answered 'yes'. You could keep iterating up and down until the respondent's willingness to pay was narrowed down to the dollar. The result was a continuous measure of willingness to pay obtained from relatively easy-to-answer questions that were more difficult to free ride on. Unfortunately, iterative bidding is prone to starting point bias. If your starting point is $5, the average willingness to pay amount ends up lower than if the starting point is $25.

The dichotomous choice question has been the dominant form of CV question since Bishop and Heberlien (1979). The dichotomous choice question is similar to the initial iterative bidding question with two differences: (1) the starting point is varied across survey respondents and (2) the starting point is the ending point (i.e., there is no follow-up willingness to pay). The advantage of the dichotomous choice question is that each respondent is asked a single valuation question that is relatively easy to answer. The major disadvantage is that you, the CVM researcher, only learn whether each respondent's willingness to pay is above or below the dollar amount threshold. More sophisticated econometric methods are necessary to develop an average willingness to pay amount. Even then, the variance on average willingness to pay tends to be large. Another disadvantage is that larger samples are necessary to implement the dichotomous choice approach. For each dollar amount version you include in your experimental design, you need a large sample (about a minimum of 30 or so) for statistical purposes. Hence, dichotomous choice contingent valuation costs more money to implement in the field.

The double-bound approach adds one follow-up question to the single-bound question. If the respondent answers 'yes' to the first question, then the dollar amount is increased, typically doubled, and the question is asked again. If the respondent answers 'no', then we are able to bound willingness to pay between the dollar amounts. If the respondent initially answers 'no', then the dollar amount might be halved and the question is asked again. Respondents end up in four groups: 'yes, yes', 'yes, no', 'no, yes', and 'no, no'. The benefit of the follow-up question is that analysis of these data substantially reduces the variance of the average willingness to pay estimate. A disadvantage of the double bound approach is that the responses to the follow-up questions might lead to willingness to pay estimates that differ from the willingness to pay estimates from the first valuation question. In other words, double-bound questions may also be prone to a form of starting point bias.

An extension of the double-bounded question is the multiple-bounded question. 'Yes, yes' and 'no, no' respondents are asked more follow-up questions until their willingness to pay value actually has upper and lower bounds. In effect, the multiple-bounded question approach is the same as the iterative bidding approach with a random starting point. The benefit of the multiple bounds is that you can even further reduce the variance of the willingness to pay estimate. The disadvantage is, again, the potential for starting point bias.

Contingent valuation researchers have also experimented with including more response categories to the closed-ended valuation question. The most practical category to include is 'don't know' in addition to the standard yes/no options – a trichotomous choice. After all, this is the most truthful response for many respondents. Polychotomous choice questions might include variations of the yes/no answer to indicate respondent uncertainty by adding categories such as 'definitely yes', 'probably yes', 'probably no', and 'definitely no'. These questions supply useful information about respondent preferences, but the appropriate use of these data in benefit estimation is still to be determined.

Dichotomous choice and payment card valuation questions are the easiest questions to implement in a mail survey. It is more difficult to ask double- and multiple-bounded valuation questions in a mail questionnaire but easy to do in a telephone survey. You must use complicated skip patterns that can be read by respondents before they answer the first question. In a telephone survey, payment card questions are difficult to implement and double- and multiple-bounded questions are easy to implement. Any of these questions are easy to implement in an in-person survey. Experimenting with the valuation question can be one of the more enjoyable components of doing contingent valuation research so don't let this quick review limit your range of choices. Develop your own incentive-compatible valuation questions, split your sample, and compare willingness to pay estimates from the alternative forms.

3.7 Get some feedback

Now you have a draft of contingent valuation survey questions. The next step in the process is to get some feedback. You'll need to talk with experts and real people about the questionnaire. Ideally, you'll have a research budget line for 'consultants'. If so, finding experts is not difficult. If your budget is smaller you need to be more creative. Ask advice from your graduate school cohort, your colleagues across the hall, and your friends and family members. Tell them that they will be contributing to science. Once they have stopped laughing, offer to buy them a cup of coffee. Eventually, and with the right incentive structure, you'll find plenty of experts and real people to help with your study. Once you have revised the questionnaire you should pre-test it in the field.

3.7.1   Experts

Potential experts include scientists from other disciplines who are familiar with the policy (e.g., biologists, toxicologists), those who are familiar with survey research (e.g., sociologists), and those who are familiar with economic values (e.g., economists). Talk with as many of these people as you can. Show them the survey. Ask them to read it and comment. At this point you should be concerned with whether your two paragraph policy scenario covers the facts of the situation and is truthful, whether the questions violate some survey norm that you don't know about, whether the valuation question is incentive compatible and whether it elicits the appropriate Hicksian valuation measure.

Don't be offended by the comments. Most of the experts are trying to help you. Carefully consider what the experts told you and revise the questionnaire accordingly. Only ignore a comment in extreme circumstances (e.g., too much coffee).

3.7.2   Real people

At this point your questionnaire is utility theoretic and scientifically sound. In fact, you are quite proud of it. You wish there was a *Journal of Questionnaires* that you could submit it to for publication. But, can your grandparents, neighbors, and students understand it? These are the real people who must understand what you are saying and asking. Otherwise, your survey project will be a failure. Making this determination is critical.

If your survey budget is big enough, you have enough money to hire a professional to conduct focus groups. Focus groups are tools used by marketers, politicians, and survey designers to understand how real people react to unfamiliar products, policy speeches, or survey questions. You've probably heard of these from television. You may even have participated in a focus group conducted by a textbook company at a professional conference.

Recruit people the same way you recruited experts. Offer them a token incentive, something besides their contribution to science. Make a donation to a church's special community fund. Make a donation to the local animal shelter. Try to talk to different age groups and don't rely totally on your students. Remember, students aren't always real people and they might be intimidated by the size of your cranium. If you use students, offer them a reward besides extra credit (e.g., a donation to the Kayak Club) and don't conduct the focus group during class time unless it is relevant to the course. You'll have students there who really don't want to participate and don't like what you are making them do. There are also opportunity costs – you really should cover international trade in micro principles.

The focus group can be as formal or informal as you'd like. It can include one real person or several. A typical focus group might involve you and several people where you ask them questions from the survey. If they make an ugly face, you know the question needs work. Find out which word(s) are causing the problem(s). Or, the focus group might involve one to three real people reading one page of your questionnaire at a time. Have them talk aloud when they have trouble understanding the contingent valuation scenario or a particular question. Make sure all your visual aids convey the information they are supposed to convey. The focus group shouldn't last much more than an hour. If you haven't covered everything that you want in an hour, let the nice people go home and arrange another focus group. If you are able and the real people are willing, videotape the session or have a research assistant take notes. You won't be able to remember everything that happens.

Don't be offended by the comments. The participants are trying to help you. Carefully consider what they told you and revise the questionnaire accordingly. Only ignore a comment in extreme circumstances (e.g., too much coffee).

3.7.3 Pre-test

Once you have gone through the second round of questionnaire revision it is time to pre-test the survey in the field. The pre-test is a small-scale survey where you follow most of the steps that you would follow in the big survey. The pre-test is your opportunity to make sure everything works the way it is intended, get an idea about your potential response rate, and identify any potential disasters. The pre-test should be as large as your survey budget and as time allows. If you have the resources, you can even conduct multiple pre-tests and even a large-scale pre-test: the pilot study.

Many researchers can only afford a single pre-test. If this is you, try to find a sample of between 30 and 100 real people. Conduct a mail survey pre-test following the same procedures that are outlined in the next section. Draw a random sample from a phone book (this won't cost anything), mail out your questionnaires, and hold your breath. If you have the time, conduct the follow-ups to the mail survey. The response rate obtained from the pre-test is an estimate of the response rate that you will obtain with the full survey. If the pre-test response rate is low, say between 20 per cent and 40 per cent, then this is an indication that something is wrong with the questionnaire. One of the main reasons that mail surveys are not returned is their length. If this is the case, chop some questions and increase your font size. The benefits of making the questionnaire shorter, e.g., a higher response rate, outweigh the costs of losing the variables from these questions. At some point, a low response rate makes your data worthless.

If 90 per cent of the respondents in the pre-test sample are female, or members of environmental organizations, or some other special population, then you have a biased sample. This may have occurred because your survey offended or disinterested members of the groups not adequately represented. The pre-test may also reveal problems with individual questions. If everyone in the pre-test skipped question number 4, then you know that question number 4 is a bad question. Rewrite it or drop it. If any of these problems occur and you don't know why, you'll need to go back to the focus group stage and find out what the problem is.

One of the most important questions you are pre-testing, of course, is the valuation question. If your survey contains a dichotomous choice valuation question, you'll need to pre-test the dollar amounts that are randomly assigned to respondents. You may have an idea of which values to insert after conducting the literature review. For example, if the economic literature indicates that all willingness to pay values for threatened and endangered species are between $1 and $75, then this is a reasonable range for your starting points. Still, you need to test these values. Suppose your dollar amounts are $1, $25, $50, and $100. If everyone answers 'no' to the $100 willingness to pay question, you aren't learning much from this dollar amount. Consider lowering the $100 amount to $75. If more than 40 per cent or 50 per cent of the sample says that they will pay $100, then add a higher dollar amount. A similar procedure could be used to pre-test payment card response categories. If no one says that they would pay more than $100 but 55 per cent say they would pay between $50 and $100, then you will learn more about willingness to pay by changing the response categories to 'between $50 and $75' and 'more than $75'. If you have no idea what a reasonable range is for your dichotomous choice dollar amounts or payment card response categories, try asking an open-ended valuation question in the pre-test. The range of willingness to pay values obtained give you an idea of the range of dollar amounts to use in the dichotomous choice question. In this case, a second pre-test may be necessary.

If, for some reason, you are not able to conduct a mail survey pre-test, consider a pre-test with convenience samples. Convenience samples include those obtained from intercept surveys. Go to a place where people hang out – the mall, the grocery store, or the boat ramp – and place the survey booklet with a postage paid return envelope on the car windshield. You'll get a lower response rate than if you mailed the survey to people at their home address, but you will distribute a large number of questionnaires quickly and cheaply. If you are bolder, you could 'intercept' people as they are leaving the mall, the grocery store, or getting their boat out of the water and ask them to take the questionnaire home, fill it out, and mail it back to you. You'll probably get a better response if you talk to them.

3.8 Survey design

Once you have completed your revisions and are satisfied with the question-naire it is time to draw a sample, print a large number of your survey instruments, and conduct the mail survey. Different groups on-campus (e.g., the print shop, the survey lab) or firms in the private sector are available to help you with these tasks. The rest of this section is a 'how to', if your research budget forces you to do these tasks yourself. Another consideration at this point is cost. Questionnaire design didn't really cost you anything, except time and any donations you felt compelled to make for focus groups participants. Constructing the survey and getting it in the mail will cost significant sums of money, even if you are on a shoestring budget.

3.8.1 The sample

A sample is a set of units from a population. In your case the population is the target group of people that you would like to reach. For example, if all individuals in Kansas is the population, a sample of individuals might be 200 individuals selected from all people in Kansas. There are several types of samples, convenience, quota, and probability samples are a few. You'll want to use a probability sample. A probability sample is one in which every member of the population has a known and non-zero chance of being selected. Units are selected randomly from the population. Probability sampling leads to the most representative samples of the population.

The first step in drawing a probability sample is to construct the sampling frame. A frame is a list of people in the population with contact information. One such list is a telephone book. Other frames include voter registration lists, drivers' license lists, fishing license holder lists, etc. Choose the sampling frame that best matches the population that you wish to survey. With mail surveys of special populations, this can be very difficult. Do the best you can. Even if your sampling frame is a close match to the population, your sample is already potentially biased. Your sample frame will not contain everyone in the population. For example, not everyone has a telephone and not every-one lists their telephone number in the phone book. People move. You have already missed your chance at questioning these people. The potential for bias increases as the size of the missing group grows.

Once you have your sampling frame, you must randomly choose units for your sample. Ideally, assign numbers to each unit in the sampling frame and then draw random numbers to select the individuals to be surveyed. If the sampling frame is large, this will be impractical. For example, assigning numbers to each individual in the phone book would be a long and tedious job. Another way to randomize the selection process is to develop simple rules. For example, if there are 250 pages in the local telephone book and you need 500 names and addresses, choose two names from each page.

Using your random number generator, pick a random number for the column on the page, and a random number for the names to skip before you find your selection. Or, pick a random number on your ruler and measure that far down the page to select the individual for the sample. If you need to sample a larger region or state, you can gather phone books from each city and town in the region and draw names from each phone book; or randomly select cities and towns to sample. Be careful here and use common sense. You may randomly select five rural areas and miss the largest city in the state. Your resulting sample will be biased. If you are sampling Georgia households, make sure a large number of individuals are from Atlanta. If you really don't care if the probability sample is representative of a larger region (e.g., you will be testing microtheory), you can select a couple of areas to sample from (e.g., a large city and a small town).

You can also purposely choose a biased sampling frame and weight the sample to reflect the true population. For example, suppose there are four urban areas in a region, each urban area has about 150 000 residents, and the region has 1 000 000 residents. The region is 40 per cent rural and 60 per cent urban. If you draw a sample of 500 with 100 names and addresses from each urban area and 100 names and addresses from a few randomly drawn rural towns, your sample will be biased. The sample will be 80 per cent urban and 20 per cent rural. If you weight the resulting data with weights equal to the proportion in the population divided by the proportion in the sample, the weighted sample will be representative of the population. In this case, rural households are under-represented and urban households are over-represented. The rural weight will be 40/20 = 2 and the urban weight will be 60/80 = 0.75. Make sure the sum of the weights equals the sample size.

Drawing the sample yourself will not cost you much. Telephone books are available in libraries. If you do have some money, survey sampling firms exist that will provide you specialized samples on demand. These samples will be better than the ones you draw yourself, but they cost money. A fairly recent price quote for a professionally drawn sample is $75 plus $.21 for each record (individual) in a computerized file of names and addresses.[2] For a sample of 1000 this will cost $285.

3.8.2   Gather materials

Now you have the questions to be included in the questionnaire and a list of names and addresses. You are also going to need a ball point pen or two, several reams of paper, some letterhead, some envelopes, some postage paid return envelopes, an extra long stapler, and some postcard stock. The amount of paper and envelopes you'll need depends on the number of contacts with respondents that you plan to make. The more contacts the greater the response rate and the greater the cost. A typical mail survey, with a good chance of obtaining response rates between 40 per cent and 70 per cent, as long as the survey topic is reasonably salient to respondents, might include three potential contacts: the original questionnaire booklet mailing, a post card follow up one week later, and a second questionnaire mailing two to three weeks later.[3] A conservative rule would be to get enough material for two complete mailings; that is, assume that the response to the first mailing is 0 per cent. You will definitely not run out of materials and you'll have plenty left over to supply eager journal referees, conference participants, job interviewers, students, and novice survey researchers who write to you asking for the finished product.

Let's assume you have a sample of 500 individuals. You will potentially send 1000 letters so go ahead and get 1000 sheets of letterhead. If you have letterhead left over, your college, school, division, or department may buy it back from you. Always use letterhead, it will increase the response rate. A blank sheet of paper doesn't look professional. If you can, get 1000 big envelopes with a return address pre-printed or stamped on it. A No. 10 regular white envelope may be too easy for respondents to misplace and it might be difficult to get all your survey materials stuffed into it. Get 1000 pre-printed metered return envelopes. Get 250 sheets of card stock. At the last minute you can get 500 second class postage stamps. You'll then need to get some more postage for the second mailing.

One more design element to consider at this stage is the cover page of the survey. Give your survey a title (e.g., 'Beach Use at the Jersey Shore') and a sub-title (e.g., 'A Survey of Public Opinion'). See other surveys for some ideas. Also find a graphic to put on the cover. If it is a drinking water survey, you might use an image of some grown up with a kid drinking a tall, cold glass of water. Make the cover eye-catching. You are hoping to turn innocent people into survey respondents with it. The logo of your funding agency or university might also be appropriate or required for the cover page. The cover page should also include a paragraph about the purpose of the survey and that all information supplied is confidential. The back page of the survey should thank respondents for completing the survey and give them a chance to tell you anything else that they would like. This text is standard so feel free to borrow it from others.

Construct the questionnaire booklet. Make sure the questions fit nicely on six or ten 7 inch (height) by 8.5 inch (width) pages with one inch margins or, if your research budget is not the minimum, make them fit on the standard 8.5 inch by 11 inch pages. Make sure you are using a font size (e.g., 12 point) and type (e.g., Arial) that is readable by people who aren't wearing their glasses. Real printing shops will make them on 8.5 inch by 11 inch paper with a nice cover.

If you are constructing the booklet yourself, get 2000 (3000) sheets of 8.5 inch by 11 (or 14) inch white paper for a six (ten) page survey. Take 2 (3) sheets of paper and hold them in 'landscape' mode. Fold them in half and you have a survey booklet. Open the booklet to what would be page 1. Now number the pages in the order that they would be read. Take the pages apart. You'll see that the questions need to be reordered in your word processor so that pages 1 and 6, 5 and 2, and 3 and 4 face each other. If you have different versions of the questionnaire (e.g., dichotomous choice), don't forget to make the different questionnaires different. Once the questions are on the page, fold in the middle and attach two staples with a regular stapler. Oops, the stapler isn't long enough. Now go back to the store and get an extra long stapler. Staple the pages and your survey booklet is ready to go.

The cover letter goes on letterhead. Address the letter to the individual: Dear John Smith, not Dear South Dakota Citizen. This is easy to do with the mail merge function on your word processor. Tell people the purpose of the survey ('the topic is very important to policy makers'), why you sent it to them ('one of only a few chosen'), why it is important that they send it back ('so that the results will represent accurately the opinions of South Dakota citizens'). Tell them it doesn't cost anything to mail it back and tell them to call you during the day or evening with any questions (at this point your potential respondents own your time). Now go get your ball point pen and sign all the letters yourself. If you are sending 1000 letters and questionnaires, sign them all. Sign the first 100. You'll get bored so take a break. Sign 200 more. Your hand will begin to hurt. Go home and sign the rest the next day. It is very important to individually sign all the letters.

Now you need to make the reminder postcards with the cardstock paper. Four postcards will fit on each 8.5 inch by 11 inch sheet. The postcards should remind people how important it is to send their questionnaires back and sincerely thank those who have already sent theirs back. You don't really need to sign these but go ahead and do it if you wish. Buy 500 post-card stamps.

3.8.3   In the field

Gather your research assistant or office mate or any other goofball willing to stuff envelopes in exchange for free pizza. Make sure that you have unob-trusively numbered each questionnaire so that you know who returns the survey and who doesn't. This is crucial. If you overlook this step, then you must hope your initial response rate exceeds some minimum threshold for policy analysis and/or publication. If you use a regular sized envelope, fold the questionnaire so that it will fit inside the return envelope, put the metered return envelope inside the questionnaire fold, and fold the letter so that it will be the first thing your potential respondent sees upon opening the envelope. Place a stamp on the envelope, place the envelope in the mail, and cross your fingers.

During the next few days, while the questionnaires are out in the mail, expect some questionnaires to be returned. Some will have bad addresses. This is unavoidable and not your fault. If you are 'sampling with replacement', send another questionnaire to the next person on your list. Also expect a few phone calls. Some people will want to be taken off the mailing list. Do it. Some will be so excited they'll want to send a check. Don't take the check. Tell them where their donation might be useful. Some might even have some questions about the survey. Respond to these the same way you respond to an undergraduate taking an exam – don't give the answer away but try to be as helpful as possible.

The returned questionnaires will hopefully begin to pour in. As each questionnaire is returned, record who returned it, and take this individual off your second mailing list. Put the postcards in the mail about one week after you sent the initial questionnaires. Questionnaires will continue to pour in. When the response has become a trickle, probably in about three to four weeks, send the second mailing out, which includes a second cover letter, questionnaire, and return envelope. The cover letter should be similar to the first cover letter but written more aggressively. Begin it with something like: 'A few weeks ago we sent you a survey on manatees in Florida. At this point we have not received your completed questionnaire'. Once you have signed all the cover letters again personally have another envelope stuffing party and put the second mailing in the mail.[4]

When you sit down to enter the data into a computer spreadsheet you'll encounter a few surprises. Respondents don't always follow your carefully explained directions. If given a choice between 'yes' and 'no', they will write 'maybe' beside the answers. If you ask them how many trips they took to the beach last year, they might write 'between 10 and 15' instead of a point estimate. When coding these responses use your best judgment. You don't want to lose an observation but you also don't want to answer the question for the respondent. If you code the 'maybe' response as a 'no' and the 'between 10 and 15' trip response as 12, make a note of this with an additional variable in your data for each applicable problem (e.g., JUDGE = 1 if a coding judgment call, 0 otherwise). When conducting your empirical analyses, determine if these judgment calls make a difference to your results. Are these people outliers? What happens to willingness to pay when you exclude them from the analysis? If a significant number of respondents require a coding judgment call on a key variable, make sure you have a footnote explaining what you did. Also during the questionnaire mailing process a significant event might occur that you feel may bias your overall results (e.g., an oil spill).[5] Create a new variable in your spreadsheet that is equal to 0 for questionnaires that were returned before the event and equal to 1 afterwards. Then you can test the effect of the event on the results. It will be impossible to test the effect of the event on the response rate, although you can tell a story if you think the event did affect the response rate. Try not to make the story sound like an excuse for a low response rate.

3.9 Reporting the results

Once the final responses stop trickling in you have your data. You'll be tempted to write out your likelihood function and begin testing your path-breaking models. Before you do, take a minute to conduct and write your research methods report. The methods report is that paragraph or two that you don't read in CVM papers that discuss the response rate and other things about data handling. Your initial methods report needs to be more detailed than this for several reasons. First, it is like eating oatmeal – it is the right thing to do. Second, at least one journal referee is going to want more detail about the sampling and survey procedures. Third, you'll learn much about the quality of your data if you explore it first before diving in with regression analysis. With this discovery you may be able to improve data quality. So, consider the following issues in the methods report.

3.9.1   The response rate

The survey response rate is calculated as the number of surveys returned divided by the number that reached their intended target. Some report the number of surveys returned divided by the number distributed. The former calculation will produce a higher response rate. It is also a more accurate measure of how well you developed your questionnaire. The latter response rate measures how well your questionnaire was developed and how well you sampled the population. If your sampling frame contains a number of bad addresses, then your response rate will be low. Professional sampling firms guarantee that only about 80 per cent of the names on their lists are still there. You should not be held to a higher standard so report the former response rate. If you mailed 1000 questionnaires and 200 of these were returned because of bad addresses, then 800 reached their intended target. If 400 of these were returned completed, then your response rate is 50 per cent. If you must, report both response rates.

3.9.2   Non-response and selection bias

You'll next need to see if your sample of 400 is representative of the population you sampled from. Look at the means of the demographic variables. Is the average income about the same as the population average income? Are there 52 per cent women and 48 per cent men as you expected? If not, you may have non-response bias. Non-response bias occurs when the respondents and non-respondents are different sorts of people for spurious reasons. Your non-respondents probably didn't look at the questionnaire before they threw it away. In other words, suppose you were able to collect contingent valuation data from non-respondents. When you estimate your willingness to pay model with a non-respondent dummy variable as a factor potentially affecting willingness to pay, the coefficient on this variable would not be significantly different from zero. You should treat a (non-response) biased sample the same way you treat a stratified sample. It doesn't matter whether you meant to collect a biased sample or not. Correct for non-response bias by constructing weights that make the weighted means of the data look like the population means.

A more serious problem is selection bias. Selection bias occurs when the respondents and non-respondents are different because of your survey topic. Suppose again that you were able to collect contingent valuation data from non-respondents. When you estimate your willingness to pay model, the coefficient on the non-respondent dummy variable would be significantly different from zero. Non-respondents might have a higher or lower willingness to pay for the policy problem your survey addresses. For example, individuals with relatively low incomes could not afford to pay higher taxes, so, instead of answering 'no' to your willingness to pay question, they did not return the questionnaire to you.

There is little to do about selection bias unless you know something about non-respondents. The best approach is to collect some information from non-respondents in a follow-up survey. Remember, non-respondents didn't reply in great numbers to your initial mail survey so they probably won't reply in great numbers to your follow-up survey, even if it is much shorter. You could, however, give them a call and obtain their gender, marital status, education, etc. Once you have data on non-respondents, test for selection bias with the standard sample selection econometric models. Estimate a probit model with response as the dependent variable and, if your independent variables explain the response behavior well, adjust willingness to pay statistically.

In practice your non-respondents will be of both types. In the absence of reliable weights or a follow-up survey of non-respondents, you should make some adjustments to your average willingness to pay value when aggregating benefits across the population. For example, if respondent income is much higher than the income of the population and income is a positive and significant predictor of willingness to pay, then your willingness to pay estimate may be biased upwards due to selection effects. To get a more accurate predicted measure of sample willingness to pay, you could plug population income into the willingness to pay function and aggregate the adjusted average. A more heavy handed solution to this problem is to set non-respondent willingness to pay equal to zero and aggregate. This gives you a lower-bound estimate of aggregate benefits. The aggregated average willingness to pay is an upper bound. A problem with this approach is that the width of the upper and lower bounds will be quite large and less useful for policy analysis if you have a relatively low response rate.

3.9.3   Item non-response bias and data imputation

Now begin to look at your variable summaries more closely. Your data suffer from item non-response. The sample sizes on each of your variables will be different. People skip some questions for some seemingly obscure reasons. The sample size on income will be the lowest of the demographic variables. One-fourth or more of the sample may refuse to reveal their income. Item non-response can lead to bias in the same ways that non-response and sample selection led to bias.

If you begin to estimate regression models with these data, your sample sizes will be different every time you include a different combination of demographic variables. You are engaged in what is called incomplete case analysis. The problem with incomplete case analysis is that when comparing regression models you are comparing apples and oranges. Some respondents drop out of Model 1 when you estimate Model 2. Even more respondents drop out when you estimate Model 3. Models 1, 2, and 3 are not comparable. If you conduct complete case analysis by deleting all observations with missing values, your useable response rate may fall significantly. In the response rate example above you may lose 100 additional observations from your sample of 400. Your useable response rate has fallen to 37.5 per cent. Your useable sample may be quite different from the original sample. This is no good. You have just deleted a lot of information provided by your respondents.

To increase your useable sample, you should consider data imputation. Imputation involves making up numbers, scientifically of course, for your missing values. You can impute with a measure of the central tendency of the distribution. If 50 people didn't report their education level, assign them the mean, median, or mode education level from the sample that reported income. More complicated imputation schemes are often desirable. Run frequencies on your variables with missing values against other variables. If the average education of women and men is significantly different, don't plug in the overall average for missing education values. If the average education level for women is 14 years, plug in 14 years of education for all women who did not report their education. The case of income is even more complex. If 100 people didn't report their income, estimate a regression model with income as the dependent variable using the 300 complete cases in your data. Predicting income for the 100 respondents is called conditional mean imputation. You are plugging in the average income conditional on other important variables such as education and work experience.

Make sure that you assess whether data imputation affects your willingness to pay results. There is a tradeoff. An increased sample size will lead to increased statistical efficiency. But, by imputing with the mean, median, or mode, the variability of the variable will fall. So, don't blindly impute values and estimate regression models. For each variable that has a significant number of imputed values, create a second variable (e.g., EDUC2). Run the regression models with both variables. If the results with the imputed data are no different than with the complete case data, then don't worry. Or, create a dummy variable (=1 if the case contains imputed values) and include it in your willingness to pay model. If the coefficient on the dummy variable is insignificant, then imputation does not significantly affect your results.

3.10   Conclusions

Once you have conducted your own survey, you'll never be the same economist again. You'll become aware that most economic data isn't generated by transactions in markets (cha-ching!), directly fed into a super computer, and electronically delivered to the economist. It is generated during surveys of the population, nicely cleaned and coded, and then electronically delivered to the economist. A contingent valuation survey is not much different from the surveys conducted by government agencies that economists use frequently.[6] The only difference is our obsession with valuation questions. Also, once you have conducted your own survey, your discussant comments and referee reports could become much more irritating to those who receive them as you incorporate your understanding of sampling, non-response bias, etc. Survey methodology is an important tool for economic research. Don't be ashamed of your new powers. Use them for the good of society. If your colleagues make fun of you in seminars or at lunch, just give them a smug smile. Not all super heroes with secret identities get a knowing pat on the back.

Once you have conducted your own contingent valuation survey, you'll probably want to conduct another. If you are fortunate enough to have an increased budget, consider other survey modes. If your research budget is a bit higher than that for a low budget mail survey but still relatively low, explore the possibility of 'piggybacking' on someone else's telephone survey. This involves writing a contingent valuation section and inserting it into another related survey. Some university survey research centers have institutionalized the piggyback survey with their annual, biannual, or quadrannual omnibus surveys. A typical survey research center might allow researchers to purchase space for a single question for $300 to $500 on an omnibus survey. A ten question contingent valuation scenario might cost between $3000 and $5000. By taking advantage of economies of scale, you'll get a large data set (e.g., $n = 1000$ or so) with your ten questions and standard demographics at relatively low cost.[7]

Your next big budget survey, conducted by the professionals, could employ state-of-the-art telephone–mail, telephone–mail–telephone, or in-person interviews. The telephone–mail survey employs an initial telephone survey to collect demographic data and recruit participants for the mail survey. You will obtain a high quality sample and information about the non-respondents to your mail survey. The telephone–mail–telephone survey is similar, but, instead of trusting respondents to answer the questions and mail the survey booklet back to you, you call them and ask them the questions. Hopefully, respondents have studied the information that you sent them in the mail and are able to refer to the survey booklet while the interviewer asks them questions. Finally, if you have the research budget that is the envy of all other contingent valuation researchers, hire some gee-whiz professional survey firm to conduct thousands of in-person interviews. May the force be with you.

Notes

*   The author would like to thank Jammie Price and Paul Chambers for numerous constructive comments.
1.   When adding scenario versions to your survey, be careful that the experimental design does not compromise the validity of your valuation scenario (see Leik, 1997).
2.   This price quote was obtained from Survey Sampling, Inc. (http://www.surveysampling.com), September 1999.
3.   A very thorough mail survey will contact respondents as little as three and as much as seven times. For respondents who send the survey back immediately, they'll get an introductory letter or postcard, the questionnaire itself, and a follow up postcard. Non-respondents (those who never answer your questions) will get the three contacts, a second and third survey instrument, an additional postcard and, finally, a telephone call.
4.   If you can afford it, send a second postcard reminder/thank you about a week after the second mailing. You can also follow-up with telephone calls if necessary to get a decent response rate.
5.   During the University of Kentucky basketball arena survey, Coach Rick Pitino resigned to take the head coaching job with the Boston Celtics (Johnson and Whitehead, 2000). In a surprise to the researchers (and probably Coach Pitino) willingness to pay for the new UK arena did not depend on Rick Pitino coaching the Wildcats.
6.   If you would rather use data gathered by the government, as most of our labor economist colleagues do, but still want to do contingent valuation research, take a look at the 'National Survey of Fishing, Hunting, and Wildlife-Associated Recreation'. The 1980, 1985, 1991, 1996, and 2001 surveys contain contingent valuation sections. The data are available on CD-ROM from the US Fish and Wildlife Service, Division of Federal Aid (http://fa.r9.fws.gov/surveys/surveys.html).
7.   Many of these centers have websites that will give you an idea of what is involved with a telephone survey.

References

Bishop, Richard C. and Thomas A. Heberlein (1979), 'Measuring values of extramarket goods: are indirect measures biased?', *American Journal of Agricultural Economics*, **61**: 926–30.

Bjornstad, David J. and James R. Kahn (1996), *The Contingent Valuation of Environmental Resources: Methodological Issues and Research Needs*, Cheltenham, UK and Brookfield, VT: Edward Elgar.

Cummings, Ronald G., David S. Brookshire, and William D. Schultze (1986), *Valuing Environmental Goods: An Assessment of the Contingent Valuation Method*, Totowa, NJ: Rowman & Allanheld.

Czaja, Ronald and Johnny Blair (1996), *Designing Surveys*, Thousand Oaks, CA: Pine Forge Press.

Dillman, Don A. (1978), *Mail and Telephone Surveys: The Total Design Method*, New York: Wiley.

Johnson, Bruce and John C. Whitehead (2000), 'Value of public goods from sports stadiums: the CVM approach', *Contemporary Economic Policy*, **18**: 48–58.

Leik, Robert K. (1997), *Experimental Design and the Analysis of Variance*, Thousand Oaks, CA: Pine Forge Press.

Maisel, Richard and Caroline Hodges Persell (1996), *How Sampling Works*, Thousand Oaks, CA: Pine Forge Press.

Mangione, Thomas W. (1995), *Mail Surveys: Improving the Quality*, Applied Social Research Methods Series, Volume 40, Thousand Oaks, CA: Sage.

Mitchell, Robert Cameron and Richard T. Carson (1989), *Using Surveys to Value Public Goods: The CVM Approach*, Washington, DC: Resources for the Future.

Sudman, Seymour (1976), *Applied Sampling*, New York: Academic Press.

Sudman, Seymour and Norman Bradburn (1982), *Asking Questions*, San Francisco: Jossey-Bass.

4 The use of contingent valuation in benefit–cost analysis

John C. Whitehead and Glenn C. Blomquist

4.1 Introduction

Benefit–cost analysis is policy analysis that identifies whether a government project or policy is efficient by estimating and examining the present value of the net benefits (PVNB) of the policy,

$$PVNB = \sum_{t=0}^{T} \frac{B_t - C_t}{(1 + r)^t},$$

where B_t are the social benefits of the policy in time t, C_t are the social costs of the policy in time t, r is the discount rate and T is the number of time periods that define the life of the policy. If the present value of net benefits is positive, then the program yields more gains than losses and the program is more efficient than the status quo. The contingent valuation method (CVM) is a stated preference approach for measuring the benefits, or, in the case of benefits lost, the costs of the policy. The purpose of this chapter is to provide an overview of the role the contingent valuation method plays in benefit–cost analysis.

We begin with a brief discussion about the role of benefit–cost analysis in policy making, the steps of a benefit–cost analysis, and how contingent valuation fits into this framework (see Boardman et al., 2001 and Johansson, 1993 for introductory and advanced treatments). Next, we discuss a range of issues for which the contingent valuation method is an appropriate tool for benefits measurement within the context of benefit–cost analysis. For the rest of this chapter we will consider contingent valuation as an approach to estimate the benefits of the policy, keeping in mind that it can also be used to estimate costs avoided. Then, we discuss some challenging methodological issues in the context of benefit–cost analysis. Aggregation issues are explored. Finally, we offer some conclusions, guidelines, and suggestions for future research that may lead to improvements in the application of contingent valuation in benefit–cost analysis.

4.2 The role of contingent valuation in benefit–cost analysis

Economists tend to think that markets work well most of the time. When we say that markets 'work well' we mean that they efficiently allocate resources. Resources that are allocated efficiently are employed in those uses where the marginal benefits are equal to the marginal costs. Efficiency exists when any further change in resource allocation causes someone to be worse off than before the change. Efficiency means that opportunities for 'win–win' changes no longer exist. When markets allocate resources efficiently within some basic constitutional framework, there is little reason for additional government intervention in an economy, unless the purpose is to make transfers to the advantage of a designated group at the expense of others not in the group. We are ignoring the calls for government intervention that are made by self-serving interest groups who use the power of the government for their own gain.

When markets fail to allocate resources efficiently there is reason to consider government intervention. Examples of government intervention that are considered to correct market failure include the Environmental Protection Agency's Acid Rain Program and the Justice Department's court proceedings against Microsoft. Benefit–cost analysis allows the demonstration of whether government intervention is superior to the existing market (and institutional) outcome in terms of allocative efficiency. Are the social benefits of a specific government intervention greater than the social costs and is the present value of net benefits as large as possible? The purpose of benefit–cost analysis is to inform social decision making and facilitate the more efficient allocation of resources.

The US government must conduct benefit–cost analysis for many policies. While previous presidential administrations required regulatory analysis and review, it was Executive Order 12291 'Federal Regulation' signed by President Reagan in 1981 that first required a regulatory impact analysis to be conducted for every government project with at least a $100 000 cost and that benefit–cost analysis be done whenever permissible by law (Smith, 1984). The executive order remained in effect until President Clinton signed Executive Order 12866 'Regulatory Planning and Review' in 1993. This executive order is similar to the earlier order in that it requires benefit–cost analysis of major regulations where permissible by law. Executive Order 13258 amended and replaced the previous executive order in February 2002 to make administrative changes, but the requirement for benefit–cost analysis still remains in effect during the current administration of President Bush. Another example of mandatory benefit–cost analysis is The Safe Drinking Water Act Amendments of 1996 that require 'cost–benefit analysis and research for new standards'.

A distinguishing characteristic among various benefit–cost studies is the timing of the analysis relative to the government intervention. *Ex ante* benefit–cost analysis is conducted before a government project or policy is implemented to determine expected net benefits. *Ex post* benefit–cost analysis is conducted after the government project or policy is implemented to determine whether the benefits realized exceeded the costs realized. There are several stages in a benefit–cost analysis. First, the benefit–cost analyst must determine standing. Whose benefits and costs count? Second, the scope of the project and various alternatives must be defined. Typically, policy makers make these decisions. Third, the physical impacts of the project must be defined and quantified. Since economists typically are not experts in medicine, ecology, geology, and other relevant disciplines, this task must often be conducted by others. At this stage economists can offer guidance to promote estimating the additional (marginal) effects of the proposed policy rather than average or total effects. The next few stages employ the abilities of the economist. Fourth, the physical impacts must be measured in monetary units such as year 2001 dollars, pesos, yen, or euros. Fifth, monetary values of impacts must be aggregated over the population with standing and those monetary values that accrue in the future must be discounted appropriately. Finally, benefit–cost analysts should perform sensitivity analysis, including various definitions of standing and scope, before making recommendations.

The social impacts of a project or policy include market and non-market impacts. The market impacts can be estimated using changes in market prices and quantities. Revealed preference and stated preference approaches can be used to estimate the monetary values of the non-market benefits. Revealed preference approaches infer non-market policy impacts with data from past individual behavior. The hedonic price method uses housing and labor market location decisions, the travel cost method uses participation, site choice, and frequency of recreation decisions, and the averting behavior method uses purchases of market goods related to the policy to infer non-market policy impacts.

Stated preference methods are implemented with hypothetical questions about future behavior. The CVM is a stated preference valuation method that asks willingness to pay, willingness to accept, or voting questions that directly estimate non-market benefits. The contingent valuation method is called 'contingent' valuation because it uses information on how people say they would behave given certain hypothetical situations, contingent on being in the real situation. Other stated preference methods are contingent behavior and conjoint analysis. Contingent behavior uses hypothetical recreation trips to implement the travel cost method, hypothetical location decisions to implement the hedonic price method or hypothetical purchases of market goods to implement the averting behavior method. Conjoint analysis is an approach where respondents are asked multiple questions about, for example, where they would take a recreation trip and which house or drug treatment they would purchase. The various alternatives offer different bundles of characteristics. Conjoint analysis allows the valuation of the attributes of the good.

While the usual role of the CVM in benefit–cost analysis is to estimate the monetary value of the non-market impacts of a project or policy, decisions made in other parts of the benefit–cost analysis will influence the decisions made in the CVM study. For example, the issue of standing will determine the geographic extent of the sample and aggregation rules. Questions about the scope of the project and various alternatives will influence the range of hypothetical questions that must be presented. The physical impacts of the project must be translated into terms that a survey respondent will understand. The appropriate discount rate will influence whether annual or one-shot willingness to pay questions will be used. Therefore, the economist conducting the CVM study should operate in conjunction with the other scientists on the research team and the public policy decision makers.

4.3   The advantages of the CVM
Compared to the revealed preference methods, the CVM and other stated preference methods clearly have advantages. Relative to the revealed preference methods, stated preference methods are most useful when an *ex ante* benefit–cost analysis must consider policy proposals that are beyond the range of historical experience. The stated preference methods are more flexible than the revealed preference methods, allowing the estimation of the impacts of a wide range of policies. Recently, stated preference data and revealed preference data have been combined to exploit the best characteristics of both. The stated preference data can be 'calibrated' (for example, grounded into reality) by the revealed preference data. The stated preference data can be used to more accurately estimate benefits beyond the range of experience. In addition to flexibility, stated preference methods can be used to estimate non-use values (for example, passive use values) and *ex ante* willingness to pay under demand and supply uncertainty. Before we turn to these issues, we first sketch an economic theory of value in order to place the discussion of the CVM in the appropriate applied welfare economic context.

4.3.1   *Theoretical background*
Respondents are assumed to answer contingent valuation questions based on the value they place on the policy or programs. To define this value consider a household utility function, $u(x,q)$, that depends on a vector of $i = 1, \ldots, m$ consumer goods, $x = [x_1, \ldots, x_m]$, and a vector of $j = 1, \ldots, n$ pure and quasi-public goods, $q = [q_1, \ldots, q_n]$. Utility is increasing in x and q and is twice differentiable. The maximization of utility subject to the

income constraint, $y = p'x$, yields the indirect utility function, $v(p, q, u)$, where p is a vector of $i = 1, \ldots, m$ market prices. The minimization of expenditures, $p'x$, subject to the utility constraint (at the pre-policy level), $u = u(x, q)$, leads to the expenditure function, $e(p, q, u)$. The expenditure function evaluated at the pre-policy indirect utility is equal to income, $y = e(p, q, v(p, q, y))$.

When faced with a change in the vector of public goods caused by a government project or policy, the willingness to pay for the change is the difference in expenditure functions. If the change in the public good is an increment, $q' > q$, the willingness to pay for the increment arises

$$WTP' = e(p, q, u) - e(p, q', u), \qquad (4.1)$$

where *WTP* is willingness to pay. Substitution of the indirect utility function into equation (4.1) yields the compensating surplus function in which willingness to pay is a function of observable variables

$$WTP' = y - e(p, q', v(p, q, y)). \qquad (4.2)$$

Since the expenditures necessary to reach the utility level with the increment are less than income, willingness to pay is positive. The corresponding willingness to pay value defined with the indirect utility function is

$$v(p, q, y) = v(p, q', y - WTP'). \qquad (4.3)$$

Willingness to pay is the dollar amount that makes the respondent indifferent between the status quo and the increment.

If the change in the public good is a decrement, $q > q''$, the willingness to pay is to avoid the decrement. When the indirect utility function is substituted into the expenditure functions, the compensating surplus function is

$$WTP'' = e(p, q'', v(p, q, y)) - y. \qquad (4.4)$$

Since the expenditures necessary to reach the utility level with the decrement are higher than income, willingness to pay is positive. The corresponding willingness to pay value defined with the indirect utility function is

$$v(p, q'', y) = v(p, q, y - WTP''). \qquad (4.5)$$

Willingness to pay is the dollar amount that makes the respondent indifferent between the status quo and the decrement.

4.3.2 Flexibility

Relative to the revealed preference methods, the contingent valuation method is the most flexible valuation approach available to policy analysts. The travel cost method is largely focused on the valuation of outdoor recreation trips and quality attributes of the sites. The hedonic pricing method is typically limited to analysis of labor, housing, and automobile markets because in other markets data are usually unobtainable for prices and observable characteristics that are useful for public policy analysis. The averting behavior approach is focused mainly on the health effects of air and water quality and safety effects of protection equipment. The other stated preference methods are limited by the necessity of framing the hypothetical question in the appropriate behavioral context.

In the theoretical framework sketched above, revealed preference methods are constrained to quasi-public goods. Quasi-public goods are those for which one or more elements of q is a characteristic of a market good. The Hicksian, or compensated, demand for the $i = 1$ market good is

$$\frac{\partial e}{\partial p_1} = x_1^h(p, q, u).$$
(4.6)

If q_1 is a quality characteristic of x_1, the demand for x_1 will move in the same direction as the change in q_1

$$\frac{\partial^2 e}{\partial p_1 \partial q_1} = \frac{\partial x_1^h(p, q, u)}{\partial q_1} > 0.$$
(4.7)

The use value, UV, for the increase in quality is

$$UV_1' = \int_{q_1}^{q_1'} x_1^h(p, q, u)dq.$$
(4.8)

Revealed preference methods require that the demand for the market good be estimated and then the effect of the quasi-public good on the market good must be isolated. If these two empirical conditions are satisfied, the implicit market method can be used to estimate a close approximation to use value, the uncompensated consumer surplus, resulting from the change in the quasi-public good.

In contrast, most any quasi-public good, for which there are implicit markets for comparison, and pure public goods, for which no implicit market exists, are within the domain of CVM applicability. Recently, applications of the CVM have appeared predominately in *Journal of Economic*

Literature category 'Q26: Recreation and the Contingent Valuation Method'. But they have appeared in numerous other *Journal of Economic Literature* subject categories as well. In the theoretical framework above, a CVM application can accommodate just about any pure or quasi-public good defined as characteristics of q. Willingness to pay for characteristics can be expressed as

$$WTP_1 = y - e(p, [q_1', q_2, \ldots, q_n], v(p, q, y)). \qquad (4.9)$$

The CVM might present survey respondents the dichotomous choice question: 'Would you be willing to pay $\$t$ for the policy that leads to Δq_1?' (where $\$t$ is a tax price and Δq_1 is the resource change). The only constraint that application of the CVM imposes is that a realistic valuation scenario must be constructed around $\$t$ and the delivery of q_1'.

This flexibility extends to valuation of projects of different scope. Multiple valuation questions can be used to estimate the value of the incremental benefits of a project to determine the scope at which the net benefits are maximized. Split-sample questions might ask about a doubling of the resource change: 'Would you be willing to pay $\$t$ for the policy that leads to $2 \times \Delta q_1$?' Or, follow-up questions might ask about a doubling of the policy change with a δ per cent increase in the tax price: 'Would you be willing to pay $\$t + \delta \times t$ for the policy that leads to $2 \times \Delta q_1$?' Most applications of the implicit market methods are limited to simulated changes in scope and the validity of these simulations for large changes are tenuous due to non-linearities and other complications.

The flexibility of the contingent valuation method is a meaningful advantage only if the willingness to pay estimates are valid. One test of validity is through a valuation comparison study. A comparison study is one in which theoretically similar valuation estimates from two or more methodologies are compared. Estimates that are statistically similar (i.e., overlapping confidence intervals) achieve a type of theoretical validity called convergent validity. The achievement of convergent validity is important for benefit–cost analysis because it increases the confidence in the valuation estimate. With increased confidence, less sensitivity analysis over the valuation estimates is necessary for benefit–cost analysis.

Much research has examined convergent validity of the CVM and implicit market methods. Carson et al. (1996) conduct a meta-analysis of over 100 studies that compare estimates from the CVM and revealed preference methods. They find that the estimates are positively correlated, suggesting the similarity of value estimates across valuation methodology. They also find that CVM estimates are about 30 per cent lower, on average, than those estimated from revealed preference methods.

Another approach to comparing stated and revealed preference data is joint estimation. As described previously, joint estimation can be used to estimate values beyond the range of historical experience, while grounding the estimates in actual behavior (Cameron, 1992; Adamowicz et al., 1994). For example, in the first joint estimation study, Cameron (1992) estimated the value of recreation trips using revealed preference data over the observed range of trip costs and identified the choke price through information from a CVM question.

There is still much debate over CVM estimates when they cannot be compared to estimates from implicit market methods. The irony in many of these cases is that the CVM is the only approach that can be used to estimate these values for benefit–cost analysis. One example is the estimation of non-use values to which we turn next.

4.3.3 Non-use values

Contingent valuation and conjoint analysis (see, Adamowicz et al., 1998) are the only methods available for measuring the economic value of policy for people who do not experience the changes resulting from policy directly. Direct changes might be experienced through on-site recreation, changes on the job, or changes in the neighborhood of residence, or through changes in one's own health. For some policies, non-use values may exist but their contribution to total value is not substantial. In these cases, revealed preference methods are sufficient. However, for some policies, ignoring the measurement of non-use values would lead to significant errors in policy analysis. For example, the benefits of the Endangered Species Act are dominated by non-use values. In these cases the use of the CVM is necessary. While some might argue that the measurement of non-use values should be included in our 'challenges' section, the potential for estimating non-use values is a strength of the CVM within the context of benefit–cost analysis. The alternative is greater reliance on a less-informed, imperfect political system of decision making.

The total value of a policy change (i.e., willingness to pay) can be decomposed into use and non-use values. For example, suppose that the change in q_1 is realized, while use of the market good related to q_1 is restricted to zero. The non-use value, NUV, of the policy change is

$$
\begin{aligned}
NUV_1 = {} & e([\bar{p}_1, p_2, \ldots, p_m], [q_1, q_2, \ldots, q_n], v(p, q, y)) \\
& - e([\bar{p}_1, p_2, \ldots, p_m], [q'_1, q_2, \ldots, q_n], v(p, q, y)), \quad (4.10)
\end{aligned}
$$

where $\bar{p}_1$ is the choke price for x_1. It is the price that is just high enough that the individual chooses to consume none of the good even though it is available. Non-use value is the difference in expenditure functions with and without the resource allocation change when use of the resource is zero. Subtraction of NUV from WTP yields the use value of the policy change

$$UV_1 = y - e([p_1, p_2, \ldots, p_m], [q'_1, q_2, \ldots, q_n], v(p, q, y))$$
$$- e([\bar{p}_1, p_2, \ldots, p_m], [q_1, q_2, \ldots, q_n], v(p, q, y))$$
$$+ e([\bar{p}_1, p_2, \ldots, p_m], [q'_1, q_2, \ldots, q_n], v(p, q, y)). \quad (4.11)$$

If, in the absence of policy, the use of the market good is zero, $x_1^h(p_1, q_1, \cdot) = 0$, the use value simplifies to

$$UV_1 = e([\bar{p}_1, p_2, \ldots, p_m], [q'_1, q_2, \ldots, q_n], v(p, q, y))$$
$$- e([p_1, p_2, \ldots, p_m], [q'_1, q_2, \ldots, q_n], v(p, q, y)). \quad (4.12)$$

In this simple case, the use value is the willingness to pay for the removal of the choke price with the increment in the resource.

Willingness to pay questions tend to elicit the total economic value. For some benefit–cost analyses, it may be important to empirically decompose the total value into use and non-use values (for example, with issues of standing). The non-use value can be elicited from survey respondents in several ways. The first, and the approach the early CVM literature adopted (Greenley et al., 1981), is with a counterfactual scenario: 'Would you be willing to pay t for the policy that leads to Δq_1 even if you are not allowed to consume Δx_1?' Counterfactual questions often are difficult for survey respondents to answer because they are placed in an even more unusual situation than a hypothetical situation. Another early approach asked respondents to divide their total willingness to pay into use and non-use percentages (Walsh et al., 1984). Respondents also find this counterfactual to be difficult.

Another approach is to focus on user groups instead of use and non-use values. The willingness to pay question would elicit total value as usual from current users and current non-users of the resource. Revealed and contingent behavior questions could be used to determine use of the resource with and without the policy. If use of the resource changes with the policy, use values can be estimated and then compared to the total value. The residual between total and use values is an estimate of the non-use value (for example, Huang et al., 1997). Some policies will not affect use of the resource. Then, the entire willingness to pay value is the non-use value.

Estimates of non-use value have drawn criticism because of a concern about theoretical validity. One theoretical validity test that has drawn much attention is the 'scope test'. The scope test is the requirement that non-use values, or willingness to pay for that matter, must be non-decreasing in the quantity or quality of the resource change

$$\frac{\partial NUV}{\partial q_1} = -\frac{\partial e}{\partial q_1} \geq 0. \tag{4.13}$$

While some research has failed to find that non-use values are sensitive to the scope of the policy change (Boyle et al., 1994), others have found sensitivity to scope (for example, Rollins and Lyke, 1998; Whitehead et al., 1998). These results do not imply that all non-use values estimated with the CVM are valid and useful for benefit–cost analysis. These results do imply, however, that in some important policy contexts non-use values estimated with the CVM are valid economic values for benefit–cost analysis. Whether non-use values should be included in the benefit–cost analysis is largely an issue of standing, not methodology (see Rosenthal and Nelson, 1992; Kopp, 1992).

4.3.4   Uncertainty

For policies and projects that involve significant uncertainty, as many do, the appropriate measure of the impacts of policy is an *ex ante* measure. *Ex post* measures of value can incorporate uncertainty by assigning probabilities to different outcomes. The sum of the probability weighted *ex post* willingness to pay amounts from revealed preference methods yields expected surplus. In contrast, the option price is the *ex ante* willingness to pay measured before the uncertainty is resolved. Any willingness to pay estimate elicited from CVM can be interpreted as an option price, regardless of whether the analyst explicitly incorporates uncertainty in the willingness to pay questions or theoretically or empirically models the uncertainty. This is so because contingent valuation respondents will answer willingness to pay questions after considering all of the uncertainties that they are aware of at the time.

In order to define willingness to pay under uncertainty, consider a policy that may yield an outcome of q'_{1a} with a probability of π_a or an outcome of q'_{1b} with a probability of π_b where $q'_{1a} > q'_{1b}$ and $\pi_a + \pi_b = 1$. Note that this is a situation of supply uncertainty. Similar definitions can be constructed for situations involving demand uncertainty (see Cameron and Englin, 1997). Under supply certainty, the corresponding willingness to pay values are WTP'_{1a} and WTP'_{1b}. The expected surplus of the policy is the sure payment regardless of which outcome occurs

$$E[S]_1 = \pi_a WTP'_{1a} + \pi_b WTP'_{1b}. \tag{4.14}$$

The expected surplus is an *ex post* measure of benefits and can be estimated with the revealed preference methods.

The option price, *OP*, is the *ex ante* willingness to pay for the increment before the uncertainty is resolved

$$v(p, q, y) = \pi_a v(p, [q'_{1a}, q_2, \ldots, q_n], y - OP_1)$$
$$+ \pi_b v(p, [q'_{1b}, q_2, \ldots, q_n], y - OP_1). \qquad (4.15)$$

It is the amount of money that must be subtracted from income so that the sum of the probability weighted utility functions are equal to utility under the status quo. In the case of supply uncertainty, willingness to pay questions could explicitly describe the various uncertainties before the valuation question is presented. Respondents would then incorporate the uncertainty into their response. Several studies show that respondents recognize the differences in probabilities. For example, Edwards (1988) elicits willingness to pay under various supply probabilities provided by the survey instrument and finds that the option price varies in the expected direction with the probabilities.

Subjective demand probabilities can be directly elicited from respondents before or after the valuation question is presented. Another approach is to estimate demand probabilities from revealed behavior. For example, Cameron and Englin (1997) provide an approach to compare option price and expected surplus estimates by using the demand probabilities of recreational fishing participation and fitted probabilities under different acid rain scenarios. While under certain restrictive conditions it is feasible to estimate the option price with revealed preference methods (Larson and Flacco, 1992; Kling, 1993), the CVM is the only approach that can estimate the option price with variation in demand and supply probabilities.

One problem that might be encountered in benefit–cost analysis under uncertainty is the failure of respondents to understand risk and probabilities. Understanding is especially challenging when probabilities are low. For example, Smith and Desvousges (1987) elicit values of reductions in the risk of death using CVM and find that, if the willingness to pay estimates are not related to the baseline risk in expected ways, estimates of the values of a statistical life are not plausible. While this is a potential problem, reviews and comparison studies indicate that the CVM estimates of the value of statistical life tend to fall in the range of the estimates from labor market studies (Blomquist, 2001; Viscusi and Aldy, 2003).

4.4   The challenges
Several issues indicate that the contingent valuation method is not a flawless approach to measuring policy impacts for benefit–cost analysis.

These issues include the difference between hypothetical and actual behavior, valuation of long-lived policy, valuation of multi-part policy, and the appropriate property rights.

4.4.1 Hypothetical bias

One of the more troubling empirical results in the CVM literature is the tendency for hypothetical willingness to pay values to overestimate real willingness to pay values in experimental settings (Cummings et al., 1995; Cummings et al., 1997; Blumenschein et al., 1997). In general, respondents in a laboratory market tend to state that they will pay for a good when in fact they will not, or they will actually pay less, when placed in a similar purchase decision. This result has been found in a variety of applications including private goods and public goods.

One simple illustration of a cause for this result is when the ceteris paribus condition does not hold between the actual and hypothetical scenarios. Respondents in the hypothetical scenario may expect that more income or time will be available in the future, and 'the future' is when the hypothetical scenario will occur. Then current income and time constraints are not binding in the survey setting, and hypothetical purchase behavior will be overstated relative to the current time period. Willingness to pay may be based on future expected income, $y + \Delta y$, instead of current income, y

$$WTP' = y + \Delta y - e(p, q', v(p, q, y + \Delta y)). \tag{4.16}$$

The effect of expected income growth on willingness to pay is

$$\frac{\partial WTP'}{\partial \Delta y} = 1 - \frac{\partial e}{\partial v} \frac{\partial v}{\partial \Delta y}. \tag{4.17}$$

Since the inverse of the marginal cost of utility is the marginal utility of income, $(\partial e/\partial v) = 1/(\partial v/\partial y)$, and, if the marginal utility of income is diminishing, $(\partial v/\partial y) > (\partial v/\partial \Delta y)$, the effect of an increase in expected income on willingness to pay is positive for normal goods

$$\frac{\partial WTP'}{\partial \Delta y} = 1 - \frac{\partial v/\partial \Delta y}{\partial v/\partial y} > 0. \tag{4.18}$$

In the real willingness to pay setting, when the growth in expected income is not realized, $\Delta y = 0$, the hypothetical behavior overstates the real behavior. While the divergence in hypothetical and actual willingness to pay has been challenged on empirical and methodological grounds (Smith and Mansfield, 1998; Haab et al., 1999; Smith, 1999), the willingness to pay estimates from the CVM must be considered upper bounds of benefits in the context of benefit–cost analysis unless steps are taken to mitigate hypothetical bias directly.

Research has attempted to empirically discover the source of the overstatement of willingness to pay and question formats that minimize the overstatement. Loomis et al. (1996) and Cummings and Taylor (1999) find that the divergence between hypothetical and actual willingness pay is mitigated or eliminated, respectively, by additional instructions about reporting true willingness to pay. Champ et al. (1997) and Blumenschein et al. (1998, 2001) find that hypothetical willingness to pay is similar to actual willingness to pay when adjusted by respondent certainty about payment. If the benefit category contains significant use values, calibration methods can also be used to adjust hypothetical behavior so that it is grounded in actual behavior.

Another approach to understanding this issue is an investigation of the incentive compatibility of different question formats. Carson et al. (2000) provide theoretical reasons why experimental market results tend to generate the divergence in hypothetical and actual willingness to pay. They argue that scenarios that involve the provision of public goods with a voluntary contribution format and the purchase of private goods should lead to overstatements of hypothetical willingness to pay. Hoehn and Randall (1987) and Carson et al. (2000) conclude that respondents, when considering a public good with individual policy costs and a referendum vote, will tend to truthfully reveal their willingness to pay. These formats too appear to mitigate against the divergence in hypothetical and actual willingness to pay.

4.4.2   Temporal bias

The choice of the appropriate social discount rate can be the most important decision in a benefit–cost analysis for long-lived projects. The same statement could be made about whether the willingness to pay question elicits annual or lump-sum amounts. Most contingent valuation applications elicit annual payments assuming the current period budget constrains the willingness to pay. Aggregation over time is then conducted by multiplying annual payments by the time period of the project after applying a discount rate. The present value of willingness to pay, $PVWTP_1$, is

$$PVWTP_1 = \sum_{t=0}^{T} \frac{WTP_{1t}^s}{(1+r)^t},\qquad (4.19)$$

where WTP_{1t}^s is the annual stated willingness to pay. This approach is problematic, and overstates the present value, if the respondent assumes they would only pay until the project is completely financed (paying their 'fair share'), say, $T = 5$, while the analyst aggregates over the life of the project, $T = 30$. Willingness to pay questions should explicitly state the time period if the benefit estimates are to be used in benefit–cost analysis.

An alternative is to assume that respondents are constrained by their lifetime wealth and elicit a lump-sum payment: 'Would you be willing to pay $\$t$, this year only as a one time payment, for the policy that leads to Δq_1?' In this case the respondent would apply his or her own rate of time preference to the project and state the present value of willingness to pay. The implicit annual willingness to pay amount is

$$LSWTP_1^s = \sum_{t=0}^{T} \frac{\overline{WTP}_{1t}}{(1+\rho)^t}, \tag{4.20}$$

where $LSWTP_1^s$ is the stated lump-sum willingness to pay, $\overline{WTP}_{1t}$ is the implicit annual willingness to pay of the policy, and ρ is the individual rate of time preference. This approach will tend toward an underestimate of willingness to pay if respondents do not have access to perfect capital markets in which to borrow or have difficulty with discounting.

If the average of the individual rates of time preferences is equal to the social discount rate, the two approaches should yield the same willingness to pay amount, $LSWTP_1^s = PVWTP_1$. However, there is some evidence that respondents answer lump-sum willingness to pay questions with an unrealistically high implicit discount rate. Comparison of lump-sum and annual willingness to pay amounts are used to estimate the rate of time preference. In the extreme case of an infinite rate of time preference, Kahneman and Knetsch (1992) find that a lump-sum payment and a series of five annual payments yield the same willingness to pay values. Stevens et al. (1997) and Stumborg et al. (2001), find that the lump-sum willingness to pay amount is larger than the annual amounts and the implicit discount rate is unrealistically high.

While evidence to the contrary exists, the annual willingness to pay question will generally yield larger estimates of the present value of willingness to pay. Define temporal bias as the upward bias in willingness to pay when annual willingness to pay questions are used when the lump-sum question format and individual rates of time preference are more appropriate. CVM researchers should consider whether lump-sum or annual willingness to pay amounts should be elicited for use in benefit–cost analysis in order to mitigate temporal bias.

4.4.3 Multi-part policy
Few government policies are independent of any other governmental policy. Most policies involve either substitute or complementary relationships with

others at either the same or different intergovernmental levels. For example, the protection of coastal water quality is a goal of both state and multiple federal agencies. The Clean Water Act, wetlands protection programs, and fisheries management plans all address coastal water quality. Depending on the ecological relationships, these policies may be substitutes or complements for each other. These relationships complicate the application of the CVM. The resulting problems that may be encountered have been called embedding, part–whole bias, and sequencing and nesting.

For example, consider two related projects that focus on improvement of q_1 and q_2. The willingness to pay for the improvement q_2' is

$$WTP_2 = y - e(p, [q_1, q_2', \ldots, q_n], v(p, q, y)). \tag{4.21}$$

The willingness to pay for the improvement $[q_1', q_2']$ is

$$WTP_{12} = y - e(p, [q_1', q_2', \ldots, q_n], v(p, q, y)). \tag{4.22}$$

Hoehn and Randall (1989) demonstrate theoretically that $WTP_1 + WTP_2 > WTP_{12}$ if $[q_1', q_2']$ are substitutes and $WTP_1 + WTP_2 < WTP_{12}$ if $[q_1', q_2']$ are complements. If projects q_1' or q_2' are valued independently, the willingness to pay amounts may not be different than willingness to pay for joint project, $WTP_1 = WTP_{12}$. Hoehn and Loomis (1993) empirically estimate an upward bias in independently valued substitute projects. This result is troubling if the projects are geographically related; for example, different wilderness areas (McFadden, 1994). Carson and Mitchell (1995) show that this result does not violate the non-satiation axiom of consumer theory if projects $[q_1', q_2']$ are perfect substitutes. Also, several applications using a variety of survey methods have found an absence of part–whole bias (Carson and Mitchell, 1995; Whitehead et al., 1998).

A related issue occurs with the sequential valuation of projects. Consider a three-part policy valued in two different sequences $A = [q_1', q_2', q_3']$ and $B = [q_2', q_3', q_1']$. The willingness to pay for q_1' in sequence A when placed at the beginning of a series of three willingness to pay questions typically will be larger than in sequence B when the question is placed at the end. Independent valuation, in effect valuing at the beginning of a sequence, will always lead to the largest of the possible willingness to pay estimates. This result is expected for the value of public goods estimated with the CVM due to substitution and income effects (Hoehn and Randall, 1989; Carson et al., 1998).

The unanswered question is: If a benefit–cost analysis requires the comparison of the benefits of q_1' to the costs of q_1', should the willingness to pay estimate at the beginning, in the middle, or at the end of a valuation sequence be used? This question is not unique to the application of the CVM in benefit–cost analysis. In fact, sequencing effects are common with market goods (Randall and Hoehn, 1996). The answer is likely to depend on the set of policies that is anticipated and their timing.

4.4.4 *Appropriate property rights*

For many public goods, the implicit property right of the good is held by society or the government; that is, someone other than the respondent. In this case, it is appropriate to ask a willingness to pay question, which is essentially: How much would you give up in order to obtain something that someone else currently owns? The willingness to pay question does not change the implicit property rights of the resource.

For some types of policy the respondent holds the implicit property right. A reallocation of fishing or hunting rights will take a resource away from a group that historically perceives that it owns the right to fish or hunt. In this case, the willingness to pay question essentially asks: How much would you give up in order to avoid losing something that you already own? The willingness to pay question changes the property rights. This complicates the valuation process if the change in the property rights has an effect on the estimated value of the good through, say, protest responses.

Another approach is to ask a willingness to accept question: 'Would you be willing to accept \$$t$ for the decrement Δq?' The willingness to accept question does not alter the implicit property rights. Consider a representative individual who gains utility from a public good (Q) with no good substitutes. The willingness to accept (WTA) the decrement with utility associated with property rights to the unchanged public good and the willingness to pay to avoid the decrement with utility associated with the reduced public good are

$$v(Q'', y + WTA) = v(Q, y)$$
$$v(Q'', y) = v(Q, y - WTP). \tag{4.23}$$

Randall and Stoll (1980) show that, when income effects are small (i.e., small WTA and WTP), willingness to pay will be a close approximation of willingness to accept. Considering the indifference curves implied by the comparison of the indirect utility functions in [y, Q] space, a sufficient amount of compensation of income (i.e., market goods) would leave the respondent no worse off than before the decrement in the public good. A number of empirical comparisons find, however, that willingness to accept significantly exceeds willingness to pay even with small income effects (e.g., Kahneman et al., 1990).

While the WTA–WTP divergence may be interpreted as an indication that the CVM is unsuitable for benefit–cost analysis under certain circumstances, the divergence can be explained. Hanemann (1991) shows that for a public good with no good substitutes, willingness to accept will exceed willingness to pay because willingness to accept is not income constrained. For a private good, for which there are good substitutes, willingness to accept and willingness to pay will not be different. Shogren et al. (1994) empirically demonstrate these results in a laboratory experiment. Other explanations exist for the WTA–WTP divergence. Carson et al. (1998) show that willingness to accept will be greater than willingness to pay when valued first in a sequence. Kolstad and Guzman (1999) argue that the divergence is due to the costs of information.

Although the WTA–WTP divergence can be theoretically understood, in application the willingness to accept question can be problematic. Willingness to accept questions often generate a large number of values that are not income constrained or with properties that do not conform to consumer theory. Primarily out of convenience, willingness to pay questions have been used when the willingness to accept question is theoretically more appropriate. In the context of benefit–cost analysis, using the willingness to pay to avoid the decrement in place of the willingness to accept question will provide a lower bound on willingness to accept (Carson et al., 1998).

4.5 Other issues
Next to discounting, questions of standing may be the most important to be decided in a benefit–cost analysis. Aggregating an average willingness to pay amount over two million instead of one million people will, obviously, double the aggregate benefits. Two examples highlight the problem. Most CVM applications choose to sample a narrow geographic or political region. If, in fact, the benefits of the project spill over regional boundaries, the narrowness will lead to an underestimate of benefits. Second, CVM survey response rates rarely achieve a level where extrapolation to the population of the sample average willingness to pay amount can be done without considering differences in respondent and non-respondent willingness to pay. Summing the sample average willingness to pay amount over the population, assuming respondent and non-respondent willingness to pay are equal, will tend to upwardly bias aggregate benefits for an improvement.

4.5.1 Geographic extent of the market
The geographic extent of the market may be the most overlooked issue in contingent valuation (Smith, 1993). Most CVM surveys sample local or regional areas such as states. The implicit assumption is that once a household is located on the other side of the border, its willingness to pay is zero.

A more plausible conjecture is that willingness to pay declines with distance from the resource. For example, the price of the recreation trip related to the policy-relevant quasi-public good is an increasing function of distance by construction: $p_1 = cd_1 + \phi w(d_1/mph)$, where c is the travel cost per mile, $0 > \phi > 1$, w is the wage rate, and mph is miles per hour. The effect of own-price (and distance from the resource) on willingness to pay is

$$\frac{\partial WTP_1}{\partial p_1} = \gamma x_1^m(\cdot, q_1) - x_1^m(\cdot, q_1') \tag{4.24}$$

where $x_1^m(\cdot)$ is the Marshallian demand function. The effect of the own-price on willingness to pay is the difference between Marshallian demands at different quality levels and is negative when $\gamma \to 1$, as expected (Whitehead, 1995).

The geographic extent of the market for the increment in q_1 is the distance such that $WTP_1 = 0$ and $x_1^m(\cdot, q_1) = x_1^m(\cdot, q_1')$. Whitehead et al. (1994) show how the effect of price on willingness to pay will change with the assumptions about the opportunity cost of time in the measurement of the price, and the omission of the prices of substitutes and complements in the empirical willingness to pay function. These results extend to the effects of price on the geographic definition of the market and suggest that the appropriate sample population for a CVM study that is focused on use values is one that includes all users and potential users of the resource. If q_1' is a quality improvement, the population to be sampled should extend beyond the range of current users of the resource to include potential future users with the quality improvement.

For non-use values, the own-price is irrelevant and distance may directly enter the expenditure function. Consider the non-use value for an endangered species of wildlife, say q_4, which is the willingness to pay to avoid the decrement, $q_4'' = 0$

$$NUV_4 = e([\cdot, \bar{p}_4], [\cdot, q''_4 = 0], [\cdot, d_4], v(p, q, y))$$
$$- e([\cdot, \bar{p}_4], [\cdot, q_4], [\cdot, d_4], v(p, q, y)). \tag{4.25}$$

The effect of distance on non-use value is negative

$$\frac{\partial NUV_4}{\partial d_4} = -\frac{\partial e}{\partial d_4} < 0 \tag{4.26}$$

if increasing distance from the resource increases expenditures necessary to reach the given utility. This result is plausible if information about the endangered species generates utility and the information is more costly to obtain the farther from the habitat or if consumers are parochial about species protection. Again, the geographical extent of the market is the distance such that $NUV_4 = 0$. In several empirical tests of this result, Loomis (2000) finds that non-use values decline with distance from the resource. For these public goods the sample should reflect that the geographic extent of the market is beyond *ad hoc* political boundaries.

4.5.2   Response rates and aggregation

Relatively few contingent valuation surveys achieve a response rate sufficient for aggregation over the population without major adjustments. While CVM surveys can achieve high response rates, these have fallen in recent years with the introduction of intensive telemarketing. Telephone survey samples routinely exclude the approximately 5 per cent of the population that do not own telephones or have unlisted numbers. In general, individuals who cannot afford phones may have lower willingness to pay for public goods. The non-response problem can be an even bigger issue with mail surveys, which tend to achieve response rates lower than telephone surveys, all else held constant. The relevant question for benefit–cost analysis is: 'Do survey non-respondents have standing?' Assigning full standing and aggregating over the entire population sampled when only, say, 50 per cent of the sample responded to the survey will lead to an overestimate of benefits if respondent willingness to pay is greater than non-respondent willingness to pay. Denying standing to non-respondents is sure to underestimate aggregate benefits. What value should be assigned to non-respondents?

Several empirical approaches for adjustment of sample average willingness to pay to non-respondents are available (Whitehead et al., 1993; Messonnier et al., 2000). If the sample suffers from non-response bias, the sample average willingness to pay values can be weighted on those observable characteristics for which the bias occurs. If the sample suffers from selection bias, the characteristics for which the bias occurs are unobservable. If demographic and other taste and preference information is available on non-respondents, econometric techniques can be used to adjust the sample average willingness to pay estimates to be representative of the population.

Unfortunately, information on non-respondents is typically not available and benefit–cost analysts are usually left with *ad hoc* adjustment procedures. An extreme adjustment procedure, offered by Mitchell and Carson (1989), is to alternatively assign non-respondents values of 0 per cent and 100 per cent of sample average willingness to pay to provide lower and upper bounds for true willingness to pay. This approach will lead to wide bounds at low response rates with diminishing bound widths as response rates rise (Dalecki, Whitehead, and Blomquist, 1993).

4.6 Conclusions

In this chapter we have argued that the contingent valuation method is a useful approach to estimating benefits or costs (lost benefits) for benefit–cost analysis. Relative to revealed preference methods, the CVM is more flexible, it can be used to estimate non-use values, and *ex ante* willingness to pay under demand and supply uncertainty. In many applications, the CVM is the only methodology that can be used due to the non-existence of related markets, large non-use values, or a significant amount of uncertainty about the outcome of the policy.

Researchers who adopt the CVM for their benefit–cost analysis should be aware of some of the methodological challenges. These include the potential for hypothetical bias, temporal bias, sensitivity of willingness to pay estimates to multi-part policy (i.e., sequencing), and the bias of a reliance on willingness to pay, relative to willingness to accept questions, when the appropriate property rights are held by the respondent. Hoehn and Randall (1987) define a 'satisfactory benefit–cost indicator' as one that does not overstate the present value of net benefits of policy. In other words, the CVM would help identify some, but not all, policies with present value of net benefits greater than zero and never falsely indicate positive present value of net benefits. Our review of the methodological challenges suggests that more methodological research is needed before we can conclude that the CVM estimates of willingness to pay are satisfactory benefit–cost indicators. If willingness to pay estimates suffer from hypothetical bias, temporal bias, or are valued independently, benefits may be overestimated. Willingness to pay estimates in these cases should be considered upper bounds in benefit–cost analysis and sensitivity analysis should be applied.

Increased attention must be paid to aggregation issues. A finely tuned sample average willingness to pay estimate inappropriately extrapolated to the population can swamp other standard problems in benefit–cost analyses. Aggregation issues do not fall under either the categories of advantages of using the CVM or methodological challenges. Aggregation issues are a concern with any benefit estimation methodology. However, the CVM relies on survey research methods that consistently lead to standard sample bias problems. The geographic extent of the market can be determined by sampling a larger geographic area than is typically considered and assessing the effect of own-price and/or distance on willingness to pay. When sample bias is a problem, standard survey research methods can be used to more accurately extrapolate sample average willingness to pay values to the population.

While CVM-derived benefit estimates abound in the literature, relatively few benefit–cost analyses using the CVM are readily available. Publication of more applied studies that place the CVM-derived willingness to pay estimates within the context of the benefit–cost analysis framework would shed some much needed light on the magnitude of the potential problems highlighted here (see, Chambers et al., 1998; Johnson and Whitehead, 2000). Policy relevant CVM research focusing on the parameters of a benefit–cost analysis would go beyond the traditional CVM research of split-sample hypothesis testing and development of new econometric estimators that reduce the variance of willingness to pay. We may find that biased willingness to pay estimates rarely lead to changes in the sign of the present value of net benefits of government policy or programs. If so, concern over statistically significant bias in willingness to pay estimates is less relevant for policy analysis. On the other hand, we may find that statistically significant bias in willingness to pay estimates may be a major concern when the CVM is implemented for benefit–cost analysis. In this case, more methodological research will be needed to make the CVM more useful for benefit–cost analysis.

In the context of the appropriateness of the CVM for natural resource damage assessment, Diamond and Hausman (1994) asked 'is some number better than no number?' Extending this question to benefit–cost analysis, we feel the answer is clearly 'yes' but 'with caution'. We feel that 'some number can be better than no number' (Blomquist and Whitehead, 1995). The inevitable alternative to the use of the CVM in benefit–cost analysis for many important policy questions is a reliance on the subjective perceptions of decision makers about the benefits of policy or an imperfect political process. For many government projects and policies the CVM is a crucial and necessary component of benefit–cost analysis.

References

Adamowicz, Wiktor, Jordan Louviere and Michael Williams (1994), 'Combining revealed and stated preference methods for valuing environmental amenities', *Journal of Environmental Economics and Management*, 271–92.

Adamowicz, Wiktor, Peter Boxall, Michael Williams and Jordan Louviere (1998), 'Stated preference approaches for measuring passive use values: choice experiments and contingent valuation', *American Journal of Agricultural Economics*, **80**, 64–75.

Blomquist, Glenn C. (2001), 'Economics of value of life', in the Economics Section edited by Orley Ashenfelter of the *International Encyclopedia of the Social and Behavioral Sciences*, edited by Neil J. Smelser and Paul B. Baltes, New York: Pergamon of Elsevier Science.

Blomquist, Glenn C. and John C. Whitehead (1995), 'Existence value, contingent valuation, and natural resources damages assessment', *Growth and Change*, **26**, 573–90.

Blumenschein, Karen, Magnus Johannesson, Glenn C. Blomquist, Bengt Liljas and Richard M. O'Conor (1997), 'Hypothetical versus real payments in vickrey auctions', *Economic Letters*, **56**, 177–80.

Blumenschein, Karen, Magnus Johannesson, Glenn C. Blomquist, Bengt Liljas and Richard M. O'Conor (1998), 'Experimental results on expressed certainty and hypothetical bias in contingent valuation', *Southern Economic Journal*, **65**, 169–77.

Blumenschein, Karen, Magnus Johannesson, Krista K. Yokoyama and Patricia R. Freeman (2001), 'Hypothetical versus real willingness to pay in the health care sector: results from a field experiment', *Journal of Health Economics*, **20**, 441–57.

Boardman, Anthony E., David H. Greenberg, Aidan R. Vining and David L. Weimer (2001), *Cost–Benefit Analysis: Concepts and Practice*, 2nd edn, Upper Saddle River, NJ: Prentice Hall.

Boyle, Kevin J., William H. Desvousges, F. Reed Johnson, Richard W. Dunford and Sara P. Hudson (1994), 'An investigation of part–whole biases in contingent-valuation studies', *Journal of Environmental Economics and Management*, **27**, 64–83.

Cameron, Trudy Ann (1992), 'Combining contingent valuation and travel cost data for the valuation of nonmarket goods', *Land Economics*, **68**, 302–17.

Cameron, Trudy Ann and Jeffrey Englin (1997), 'Welfare effects of changes in environmental quality under individual uncertainty about use', *Rand Journal of Economics*, **28**, S45–S70.

Carson, Richard T. and Robert Cameron Mitchell (1995), 'Sequencing and nesting in contingent valuation surveys', *Journal of Environmental Economics and Management*, **28**, 155–73.

Carson, Richard T., Nicholas E. Flores and W. Michael Hanemann (1998), 'Sequencing and valuing public goods', *Journal of Environmental Economics and Management*, **36**, 314–24.

Carson, Richard T., Nicholas E. Flores, Kerry M. Martin and Jennifer L. Wright (1996), 'Contingent valuation and revealed preference methodologies: comparing the estimates for quasi-public goods', *Land Economics*, **72**, 80–99.

Carson, Richard T., Theodore Groves and Mark J. Machina (2000), 'Incentive and informational properties of preference questions', Department of Economics, University of California, San Diego, February 2000.

Chambers, Catherine M., Paul E. Chambers and John C. Whitehead (1998), 'Contingent valuation of quasi-public goods: validity, reliability, and application to valuing a historic site', *Public Finance Review*, **26**, 137–54.

Champ, Patricia A., Richard C. Bishop, Thomas C. Brown and Daniel W. McCollum (1997), 'Using donation mechanisms to value nonuse benefits from public goods', *Journal of Environmental Economics and Management*, **33** (June), 151–62.

Cummings, Ronald G., Glenn W. Harrison and E. Elisabet Rutström (1995), 'Homegrown values and hypothetical surveys: is the dichotomous choice approach incentive-compatible?', *American Economic Review*, **85**, 260–6.

Cummings, Ronald G., Steven Elliot, Glenn W. Harrison and James Murphy (1997), 'Are hypothetical referenda incentive compatible?', *Journal of Political Economy*, **105**, 609–21.

Cummings, Ronald G. and Laura O. Taylor (1999), 'Unbiased value estimates for environmental goods: a cheap talk design for the contingent valuation method', *American Economic Review*, **89**, 649–65.

Dalecki, Michael G., John C. Whitehead and Glenn C. Blomquist (1993), 'Sample non-response bias and aggregate benefits in contingent valuation: an examination of early, late, and non-respondents', *Journal of Environmental Management*, **38**, 133–43.

Diamond, Peter A. and Jerry A. Hausman (1994), 'Contingent valuation: is some number better than no number?', *Journal of Economic Perspectives*, **8**, 45–64.

Edwards, Steven F. (1988), 'Option prices for groundwater protection', *Journal of Environmental Economics and Management*, **15**, 475–87.

Greenley, Douglas A., Richard G. Walsh and Robert A. Young (1981), 'Option value: empirical evidence from a case study of recreation and water quality', *Quarterly Journal of Economics*, **96**, 657–73.

Haab, Timothy C., Ju-Chin Huang and John C. Whitehead (1999), 'Are hypothetical referenda incentive compatible? A comment', *Journal of Political Economy*, **107**, 186–96.

Hanemann, W. Michael (1991), 'Willingness to pay and willingness to accept: how much can they differ?', *American Economic Review*, **81**, 635–47.

Hoehn, John P. and John B. Loomis (1993), 'Substitution effects in the valuation of multiple environmental programs', *Journal of Environmental Economics and Management*, **25**, 56–75.

Hoehn, John P. and Alan Randall (1987), 'A satisfactory benefit–cost indicator from contingent valuation', *Journal of Environmental Economics and Management*, **14**, 226–47.

Hoehn, John P. and Alan Randall (1989), 'Too many proposals pass the benefit–cost test', *American Economic Review*, **79**, 541–51.

Huang, Ju-Chin, Timothy C. Haab and John C. Whitehead (1997), 'Willingness to pay for quality improvements: should revealed and stated data be combined?', *Journal of Environmental Economics and Management*, **34**, 240–55.

Johansson, Per-Olov (1993), *Cost–benefit Analysis of Environmental Change*, Cambridge: Cambridge University Press.

Johnson, Bruce K. and John C. Whitehead (2000), 'Value of public goods from sports stadiums: the CVM approach', *Contemporary Economic Policy*, **18**, 48–59.

Kahneman, Daniel and Jack L. Knetsch (1992), 'Valuing public goods: the purchase of moral satisfaction', *Journal of Environmental Economics and Management*, **22**, 57–70.

Kahneman, Daniel, Jack L. Knetsch and Richard H. Thaler (1990), 'Experimental tests of the endowment effect and the coase theorem', *Journal of Political Economy*, **98**, 1325–50.

Kling, Catherine L. (1993), 'An assessment of the empirical magnitude of option values for environmental goods', *Environmental and Resource Economics*, **3**, 471–85.

Kolstad, Charles D. and Rolando M. Guzman (1999), 'Information and the divergence between willingness to accept and willingness to pay', *Journal of Environmental Economics and Management*, **38**, 66–80.

Kopp, Raymond J. (1992), 'Why existence value should be used in cost–benefit analysis', *Journal of Policy Analysis and Management*, **11**, 123–30.

Larson, Douglas M. and Paul R. Flacco (1992), 'Measuring option prices from market behavior', *Journal of Environmental Economics and Management*, **22**, 177–98.

Loomis, John B. (2000), 'Vertically summing public good demand curves: an empirical comparison of economic versus political jurisdictions', *Land Economics*, **76**, 312–21.

Loomis, John B., Thomas Brown, Beatrice Lucero and George Peterson (1996), 'Improving validity experiments of contingent valuation methods: results of efforts to reduce the disparity of hypothetical and actual willingness to pay', *Land Economics*, **72**, 450–61.

McFadden, Daniel (1994), 'Contingent valuation and social choice', *American Journal of Agricultural Economics*, **76**, 689–708.

Messonier, Mark L., John C. Bergstrom, Christopher M. Cornwell, R. Jeff Teasley and H. Ken Cordell (2000), 'Survey response-related biases in contingent valuation: concepts, remedies, and empirical application to valuing aquatic plant management', *American Journal of Agricultural Economics*, **83**, 438–50.

Mitchell, Robert Cameron and Richard T. Carson (1989), 'Using surveys to value public goods: the contingent valuation method', Resources for the Future, Washington, DC, 1989.

Randall, Alan and John R. Stoll (1980), 'Consumer's surplus in commodity space', *American Economic Review*, **71**, 449–57.

Randall, Alan and John P. Hoehn (1996), 'Embedding in market demand systems', *Journal of Environmental Economics and Management*, **30**, 369–80.

Rollins, Kimberly and Audrey Lyke (1998), 'The case for diminishing marginal existence values', *Journal of Environmental Economics and Management*, **36**, 324–44.

Rosenthal, Daniel H. and Robert H. Nelson (1992), 'Why existence value should not be used in cost–benefit analysis', *Journal of Policy Analysis and Management*, **11**, 116–22.

Shogren, Jason F., Y.S. Seung, J.H. Dermot, and J.B. Kliebenstein (1994), 'Resolving differences in willingness to pay and willingness to accept', *American Economic Review*, **84**, 255–70.

Smith, V. Kerry (ed.) (1984), *Environmental Policy under Reagan's Executive Order: The Role of Benefit–Cost Analysis*, Chapel Hill: The University of North Carolina Press.

Smith, V. Kerry (1993), 'Nonmarket valuation of environmental resources: an interpretative appraisal', *Land Economics*, **69**, 1–26.

Smith, V. Kerry (1999), 'Of birds and books: more on hypothetical referenda', *Journal of Political Economy*, 10–7, 197–200.

Smith, V. Kerry and William H. Desvousges (1987), 'An empirical analysis of the economic value of risk changes', *Journal of Political Economy*, **95**, 89–114.

Smith, V. Kerry and Carol Mansfield (1998), 'Buying time: real and hypothetical offers', *Journal of Environmental Economics and Management*, **36**, 209–24.

Stevens, Thomas, Nichole E. DeCoteau and Cleve E. Willis (1997), 'Sensitivity of contingent valuation to alternative payment schedules', *Land Economics*, **73**, 140–48.

Stumborg, Basil E., Kenneth A. Baerenklau and Richard C. Bishop (2001), 'Nonpoint source pollution and present values: a contingent valuation study of lake mendota', *Review of Agricultural Economics*, **23**, 120–32.

Viscusi, W. Kip and Joseph E. Aldy (2003), 'The value of a statistical life: a critical review of market estimates throughout the world', *Journal of Risk and Uncertainty*, **27**, 5–76.

Walsh, Richard G., John B. Loomis and Richard A. Gillman (1984), 'Valuing option, existence, and bequest demands for wilderness', *Land Economics*, **60**, 14–29.

Whitehead, John C. (1995), 'Willingness to pay for quality improvements: comparative statics and interpretation of contingent valuation results', *Land Economics*, **71**, 207–15.

Whitehead, John C., Peter A. Groothuis and Glenn C. Blomquist (1993), 'Testing for non-response and sample-selection bias in contingent valuation: analysis of a combination phone/mail survey', *Economics Letters*, **41**, 215–20.

Whitehead, John C., Timothy C. Haab and Ju-Chin Huang (1998), 'Part–whole bias in contingent valuation: will scope effects be detected with inexpensive survey methods?', *Southern Economic Journal*, **65**, 160–8.

Whitehead, John C., Thomas J. Hoban and William B. Clifford (1994), 'Specification bias in contingent valuation from omission of relative price variables', *Southern Economic Journal*, **60**, 995–1009.

5 Hypothetical preferences and environmental policy

Gregory Cooper

5.1 Introduction

Economists measure preferences. When these preferences are over goods traded in markets, economists can measure them by studying consumer behavior. Many environmental goods, however, are not traded in markets. To study these, economists often resort to 'hypothetical preferences'; that is, they create hypothetical markets and study consumer 'behavior' in the hypothetical scenarios. In this way economists are able to quantify the values people hold over a wide range of public environmental goods such as clean air and water, biodiversity, and a host of other environmental amenities. The process has been controversial, coming under fire internally from other economists and externally from, among others, environmental philosophers. This chapter focuses on the external criticisms. As it turns out, many of these criticisms are aimed only indirectly at the special methodology involving hypothetical preferences. Instead, they raise issue with the larger project within which the strategies of contingent valuation and conjoint analysis are embedded – an approach to public policy that takes as its central goal the measurement of preferences in the population and the deployment of resources so as to maximally satisfy those preferences. As a result, a significant part of this chapter, especially the first sections, will be devoted to a discussion of this larger project. With these broader issues clarified, the discussion then turns to the appeal to hypothetical preferences proper.

Before proceeding, two points of clarification are in order. First, I focus on the preference satisfaction approach to public policy because I believe that this model remains very influential. In 1981 President Reagan issued executive order 12 291 requiring that all new major federal regulation be supported by a cost–benefit analysis. That order reflects an approach to the rational determination of public policy, which, in my view, is still a powerful force shaping public decisions. However, I will not argue the point here. Second, I suggest, in the end, that preference satisfaction is only one among a plurality of values that should be taken into account in the development of public policy. This stance has other champions as well. Both philosophers (see e.g. Holland, 1995) and economists (see e.g. Kahn, 2005) have defended the idea. I suppose most who are concerned with the normative side of public policy formation would adopt some form of pluralism, the main difference being in the particular mix and weight of the values involved. At any rate, this chapter is directed towards those who might aspire to a greater hegemony for preference satisfaction. In a more positive vein, the chapter seeks to contribute to the important goal of clarifying the role that preferences – especially hypothetical preferences – should play in the determination of environmental policy.

5.2 Social utility

Since around the middle of the last century, public policy formation has been dominated by a particular approach that we may call the 'social utility model'. Oversimplifying, the central idea behind the model is to make preference maps and cause resources to be distributed so as to maximize the satisfaction of preferences. The rationale for the model is straightforward. As Freeman puts it, 'the basic premises [of welfare economics are] that the purpose of economic activity is to increase the well-being of the individuals who make up the society, and that each individual is the best judge of how well-off he or she is in a given situation' (Freeman, 1993: 294).

On this model, the market plays an important role, both in the aggregation of preferences and in the distribution of resources. People reveal their preferences through economic behavior. By studying consumer choices, economists make the preference maps that provide the values that drive policy choices. The invisible hand of the market is regarded as the most efficient allocative mechanism and is counted on to work its magic in the distribution of resources wherever possible. Of course, there are many examples of market failure, and various steps are taken to correct these failures.

All of this is ground well covered and I will not rehearse the familiar details. What I want to emphasize is the seductiveness of this decision-theoretic model. If probabilities can be associated with the various possible outcomes of a set of alternative decisions, and if utilities can be associated with these outcomes as well, then decision making becomes simply a matter of mathematical calculation. Of course, we have to do some hard science to get the probabilities and the measures of preferences in the population. But part of the attractiveness of the model is just that – that it is a question for science. This is especially attractive on the normative side, where value questions can be removed from the more nebulous and subjective realms of philosophy (ethics, aesthetics, etc.) and turned into questions for the social sciences, where presumably objectivity is more readily available. There is also a political attractiveness to the model in that it embodies a kind of ideal of representative democracy. Just as we tote up votes and rely on the majority to express the political will of the country, so too we tot up preferences and use these outcomes to express the normative will of the population.

The next three sections will describe a series of problems with the social utility model, as at least insofar as that model is taken to be the canonical procedure for making public policy decisions. I begin with a general difficulty that applies to any attempt to use the neoclassical tradition to supply the preference maps needed to deploy the model. I then turn to economic approaches that appeal to hypothetical preferences. Finally, I discuss a number of generic problems with the social utility model as a decision-making strategy.

5.3   The economist's dilemma

Economics is subject to a fundamental equivocation. On the one hand, it seeks to be a predictive science, enabling us to project the consequences of, among other things, public policy decisions into the future. On the other hand, it also seeks to be a normative guide to the determination of public policy. As a predictive science, it is crucial that it have an accurate picture of the values that exist in the population, whatever those values may be. In order to predict and understand individual behavior, it is important to have a clear idea of what people are motivated to do. It is important not to impute more rationality or reflection than is likely to occur in the population under study.

The situation is different when it comes to economics as a normative guide. Here it is appropriate for a kind of laundering to take place. This laundering ought to proceed along a number of dimensions. First, some preferences or desires ought not to be satisfied, simply on moral grounds. These preferences are, as the economists like to say, 'anti-social'. Second, elements of irrationality ought to be eliminated to the extent that this is possible. If we want to avoid irrationality in our public policies, then we ought to seek to eliminate irrationality in the package of goals or values that are the object of these policies. Third, though closely related to the second point, we should be interested in what Rawls (1971) calls 'considered judgments'. To the extent that our public policies are driven by the goals found in the populations they serve, those goals or values should capture what people care about upon reflection. This reflection should include, among other things, searching for patterns of inconsistency in the commitment to various kinds of values, becoming as factually informed as possible about the situations over which judgments are made and expressing a willingness to turn matters over to the judgments of experts if the situation is appropriate. In general, reflection involves engagement in the process of reason giving, both in terms of supporting one's own stance and responding to the positions of others. The two pictures of values that fuel these two conceptions of economics are distinct. The problem of equivocation occurs when the one is transferred into the other – specifically, when the values that best predict individual behavior are taken to be the values that ought to inform our search for appropriate public policies.

I suspect that what I am claiming to be a dilemma, many economists will see as no problem at all. In part this is because the neoclassical tradition in economics has operated with an abstract and theoretically ideal model of human agency. For example, preferences over bundles of goods are assumed to be complete, transitive, continuous, and convex (Sugden, 1999: 152). However there is a clear trend in economics toward the use of more realistic models of human agency, which incorporate relevant findings in psychology and sociology (stimulated in no small measure by the soul searching that has accompanied the deployment of methodologies like contingent valuation). Sunstein summarizes the situation as follows:

> In the last two decades, social scientists have learned a great deal about how people actually make decisions. Much of this work requires qualifications of rational choice models, which have dominated the social sciences, including the economic analysis of law. Those models are often wrong in the simple sense that they yield inaccurate predictions. People are not always 'rational' in the sense that economists suppose. But it does not follow that people's behavior is unpredictable, systematically irrational, random, rule-free, or elusive to social scientists. On the contrary, the qualifications can be described, used, and sometimes even modeled (Sunstein, 2000: 1).

As economic models become more faithful to the empirical phenomena they seek to predict and explain, the gulf between the two kinds of values – between economics as a positive science and economics as a normative guide to public policy – can only widen. When economists work with an image of human nature that is better informed by psychology and the social sciences then they are even further removed from the ideal of rationality that we would like to embody in our public policy.

5.4 When preferences are hypothetical

A different type of problem with the social welfare model arises when we focus specifically on environmental policy. Most environmental goods are public goods in the sense that they are not traded in markets. This poses a challenge for traditional economic methodology. How can we make preference maps if we cannot read them off economic behavior? Economists have responded to this problem with two fundamental strategies. One is to identify surrogate goods, goods that are traded in markets that can stand in for the non-market environmental goods. To the extent that the surrogate goods are sufficiently correlated with the non-market goods, we can resort to the traditional behavioral strategies. The second strategy is to resort to hypothetical preferences – primarily via the methodology of contingent valuation (CV).

The move to hypothetical preferences poses a wide range of potential problems and there exists a vast literature both on the nature of the problems and appropriate methodological responses. The hypothetical situations over which choices are to be exercised, together with relevant context, must be described and the manner in which this is done can influence the choices made. Because the choices are hypothetical, the discipline of opportunity cost is missing. There can be a temptation to strategize in constructing responses. Sometimes respondents may be motivated by considerations that are not even on the survey designers map, such as concerns about fairness. Sometimes responses embody irrational elements (from the standpoint of the respondents' self-interest), such as spitefulness. Serious questions have even been raised about whether there are values there to be measured in the first place, or whether they are constructed by the very process of measurement. An entire taxonomy has been developed to catalogue the potential pitfalls. Thus we have scope effects, framing effects, embedding effects, context effects, and so forth. These issues have been explored by much more capable hands both elsewhere in this volume and in many other places, so I will not venture forth into this terrain (for a sampling of the debate see Adamowicz, 1995; Boyle and Bergstrom, 1999; Bjornstad and Kahn, 1996; Diamond and Hausman, 1994; Fisher, 1996; and Hanemann, 1995, 1996). I want to confine my remarks to two closely related issues – what we might call the problem of disenfranchisement and (following Baron) the problem of protected values.

The first of these problems arises most dramatically in the case of individuals with lexicographic preferences. As Hanley puts it:

> if these individuals are treated as having an infinite WTAC [willingness to accept compensation] to avoid environmental losses, then this will mean that no project involving such losses will pass the CBA [cost–benefit analysis] test: this effectively disenfranchises all other citizens. More usually, therefore such responses in CVM exercises are treated as protest bids, and ignored in the CBA process. Yet this disenfranchises the lexicographic individuals (1995: 42–3).

Nor do the preferences need to be strictly lexicographic in order for the idea of protest bids to be deployed. Outliers cause problems. Either they are incorporated, skewing the results and potentially disenfranchising the majority, or they are ignored, removing the voice of those with more extreme views. Of course, calling such outliers protest bids certainly makes it easier to justify their elimination. But the extreme values may not be protests at all. CV studies often call upon respondents to make monetary judgments in very unfamiliar contexts. Furthermore, these situations may be of a type where questions of monetary compensation seem inherently wrong – for example, they may involve matters of principle. As Holland (1995: 22) points out, there is something strange about a question such as, 'How much would you pay to see hanging retained/abolished?'

Often these 'protest bids' will give expression to what Baron (2002) calls 'protected values' (PVs). They tend to be matters of principle and not amenable to monetary tradeoff. It might be tempting to argue at this point that this domain of principle is not so neatly sealed off from preference satisfaction as it might seem. People may pay lip service to all sorts of principled concerns, but the real test of value commitment is not what they say but what they do. As Baron points out, this would be to mischaracterize the situation.

> Notice that the issue here is not behavior. Surely, people who endorse PVs violate them in their behavior, but these violations do not imply that the values are irrelevant for social policy. People may want public decisions to be based on the values they hold on reflection, whatever they do in their behavior. When people learn that they have violated some value that they hold, they may regret their action rather than revising the value (Baron, 2002: 13–4).

In fact, the gulf between values and behavior may be even more dramatic. Mark Sagoff has argued that people may be genuinely schizophrenic in their lives as citizens and consumers. As he puts it, 'I support almost any political cause that . . . will defeat my consumer interests. This is because I have contempt for – although I act upon – those interests. I have an "ecology now" sticker on a car that leaks oil everywhere that it's parked' (Sagoff, 1981: 303). Sagoff's point is that we must draw a distinction between the values embodied in our consumer behavior and the values we endorse for our community. Furthermore, it is the latter not the former that ought to be ensconced in public policy. By targeting consumer preferences, the economists are modeling the wrong set of values.

Holland (1995: 29) suggests that Sagoff's criticism is overdrawn. And there is reason to believe that Sagoff would himself agree these days (see Sagoff, 1998). The primary reason for this is that the appeal to hypothetical preferences has enabled economists to cast a broader net with regard to the kinds of preferences they can seek to model. Obviously, when preferences are read off of consumer behavior, then consumer preferences are the net result. When hypothetical preferences are used, however, it becomes possible to incorporate 'non-use' values. Non-use values can take on a number of forms, such as bequest value, existence value, and so forth. According to Pearce, 'To the economist, economic value arises if someone is made to feel better off in terms of their wants and desires. The feeling of well-being from contemplating a beautiful view is therefore an economic value' (Pearce, 1992: 6). The scope of what counts as an economic value has been vastly enlarged, and this is crucial for the deployment of the social utility model.

That model requires a numerical measure of utility over possible outcomes. This economics does. But, if it only provides them for consumer preferences, then there will be an important part of the normative picture that gets left out. Enlarging the concept of economic value in this way promises to restore completeness. 'It seems, then, that the economist can respond to Sagoff's critique by denying that they are assimilating values to preferences narrowly understood, and insisting that the notion of preference with which they operate is an enlarged "technical" notion embracing anything towards which a human being may be said to be favorably disposed' (Holland, 1995: 31).

Does this help with the disenfranchisement and the problem of protected values? In the end I think the answer must be no. In defining preference in this broad way, the economist is still working with an overly simplistic model of human agency. As Holland points out, there is a great deal of heterogeneity among the values people hold. Some things we care about for consequentialist reasons and others for deontological (for example, principle-driven) reasons. Some of our values are self-interested; others are altruistic. Some desires are second order (for example, they are desires about what kinds of desires we would or would not like to have). Some of our values are fundamental; others are means values (Baron, 1996). Some are readily substitutable; for others the idea of tradeoff is virtually unthinkable, and the same can be said for the idea of pricing.

It seems to me, then, that expanding the concept of economic value to incorporate anything anyone might care about is over-reaching. That does not mean that non-use values are no use, only that we should temper our expectations about what they can deliver. Most of the problems mentioned at the beginning of this section may well be avoidable by ever-more sophisticated methodological maneuvers, but this one – call it the problem of value heterogeneity – seems to be a fundamental obstacle to the goal of developing an economic approach that will enable us to quantify the entire range of values relevant to the determination of social policy – and that does not bode well for the deployment of the social utility model as the vehicle for social decisions.

5.5 Beyond social utility

The economist's dilemma discussed above poses one sort of problem for the social utility model. Even if solved however, there would remain the problem of completeness. Most neoclassical economists would now acknowledge that at least some values would remain uncaptured. The move to hypothetical preferences and non-use values offers the promise of completeness, but we now see that this will not work either. It is time to look more directly at problems with the social utility model.

The social welfare model of public policy formation is attractive in a number of ways: it promises the rigor of quantification, the authority of democratic choice, and the prospects for turning murky questions of value into research projects in the social sciences. However, the approach is not without problems. Again, much of this is familiar ground, so I will not go into any detail but simply outline the issues that have been discussed in the literature. One set of problems concerns distributional inequities. Pareto efficiency is the normative engine behind this decision-making model, and, as is well known, Pareto efficiency does not speak to distributional patterns. A distribution of resources can be Pareto efficient despite the fact that it concentrates virtually all of the resources in the hands of a few individuals. The implication, which is widely acknowledged, is that the decision-theoretic model under discussion must be supplemented by a theory of distributive justice.

A second sort of distributional problem stems from the fact that willingness to pay depends to some degree on ability to pay. Insofar as willingness to pay is used as a measure of strength of preference, this can lead to over-representation of the values of the haves over the have-nots. A third type of distributional problem involves the notion of regulatory capture. The socio-economically disadvantaged may not have the same access to political power as the well-heeled. As a consequence, they may reap fewer of the benefits and bear a greater share of the risks associated with various kinds of regulation. This is especially true of environmental regulation, and the literature on environmental justice documents numerous cases of this phenomenon. This is not a problem with the social welfare model as such, but it is a consequence of distributional inequities that can co-exist in the face of the deployment of this model.

A further problem with the social welfare model concerns the laundering of preferences. Economists recognize that not all preferences are worthy of satisfaction. Often this point is accommodated by excluding 'anti-social' preferences. While that may seem straightforward enough, it disguises the fact that independent criteria are needed for determining which preferences are anti-social. While this may seem obvious enough in cases like a preference for child pornography, it is less clear when it comes to what we might call the normative frontiers of society. I live in Virginia. I suppose there was a time in my state when the majority of the population had a preference for slave ownership. That preference would not have been laundered out as anti-social at the time, though clearly it is viewed as such now. On the contemporary scene, some environmentalists would regard certain preferences for the use of animal products, such as fur coats or T-bone steaks, as anti-social and in need of laundering. I am not suggesting that this is so; my point is simply that laundering projects need criteria in terms of which to do the laundering. We have here once again a situation in which the social welfare model cannot handle the normative side of policy making all by itself. It needs to be supplemented with ideas, in this case primarily ethical ideas, in order to adequately capture the values that ought to be the objective of policy-making decisions.

A second area in which preferences may need a bit of massaging concerns the earlier claim by Freeman that each individual is the best judge of their well-being. There is a vast literature that challenges the idea that the satisfaction of consumer preferences will automatically lead to maximal well-being on the part of the individuals who have those preferences. Once again, we have the need for supplemental criteria, in this case paternalistic criteria, for successful deployment of the social welfare model. I will have more to say about autonomy and paternalism below.

Norton et al. (1998: 194) suggests another criterion for laundering preferences, and that is a sustainability criterion. Specifically, they make the following point: 'there may be a social interest in influencing individual preferences toward less material consumption-oriented forms of satisfaction'. In a similar vein, Perrings registers the following concern.

> The present efforts to explore the non-use value of environmental resources through contingent valuation methods (CVM) and related techniques beg the most important question that needs to be posed about our use of environmental resources: What is the value of the loss of output in production and consumption that is due to the degradation of environmental resources? This is a question that cannot be answered by considering the subjective evaluation of environmental resources by individuals with little understanding of ecosystem functions (Perrings, 1995: 64).

To some extent the problem of expertise can be alleviated through education as a part of the survey process, but even that education will have to express a point of view and in that sense is likely to stake a stand on at least mildly contested issues. The upshot is that we have yet another reason to question the 'consumer sovereignty' that lies at the heart of the social utility model.

A final problem with the preference satisfaction model is the point made, for example, by Sen (and others) that people's preferences are conditioned by their prospects (see Sen, 1987; Anderson, 1993; Shrader-Frechette, 2004; Beckley, forthcoming). A lower-caste woman in India is not likely to expect as much out of life as an upper-middle-class American. In that sense, her preferences will be less demanding (for example, more easily satisfied) – if only as a matter of psychological necessity. Should they be taken at face value, or should we take into account the way in which they have been shaped by social circumstances? Sen's point is that we have, once again, grounds for laundering.

5.6 Philosopher kings and egalitarian economists

Kopp (1993) suggests that the fundamental difference between philosophers and economists, when it comes to preference satisfaction and well-being, traces back to differing attitudes with respect to autonomy and paternalism. Specifically, economists respect the principle of autonomy by adopting the stance that people are the best judges of their own well-being. Everyone, and all of their preferences, insofar as this is possible, are placed on a par. Philosophers, on the other hand, and here he refers specifically to Thomas Scanlon, are inclined to substitute some kind of paternalistic judgment in the place of the individual's judgment. The individual is not always the best judge of her own well-being, nor is the democratic summing up of individual preferences always the best guide for the objectives of social policy.

This is, at bottom, another form of the preference laundering/consumer sovereignty issue. It is a difficult issue because there are strengths and weaknesses on both sides. On the one hand, there is the vexing issue of who gets to do the laundering, and what criteria are to be used in that process. Inability to gain widespread consensus on these issues argues in favor of respect for autonomy. And there is the further issue of freedom: people ought to have the freedom to make their own mistakes. On the other hand, there is the problem that has dogged economics from the beginning, and that is the deployment of an ideal and in many ways unrealistic picture of human nature or human psychology. People are not, in actuality, the ideal, self-interested, rational agents that economic models presuppose. Insofar as economics is being put to normative ends, it would seem to make sense to avoid incorporating these cognitive limitations into public policy. In addition, there is the point mentioned at the end of the previous section that people's preferences are conditioned by their social circumstances. Correcting for things like bounded rationality and the social conditioning of preferences would seem to make sense in developing measures of the overall value of alternative social states of affairs. These are some of the arguments on the side of paternalism.

This issue is closely connected to a second problem. I have been talking about the difficulty in articulating a well-being metric for the evaluation of social utility. But there is also the question of political legitimacy. Our public policies are designed to achieve certain social outcomes. In a liberal democracy, the outcomes that are the objective of this policy-making process ought to be decided upon through the democratic process, for example by majority rule. What gives these policy outcomes their legitimacy is the fact that everyone potentially affected has had their say in the selection of what these policy goals ought to be. Again, a kind of autonomy/paternalism issue arises. On the autonomy side, it appears that we should simply tote up the various preferences that exist in the population (typically in the form of a vote) and implement policies in pursuit of those goals that are favored by the majority. From the political perspective, it does not matter how rational or irrational these preferences are, what their origins are, and so forth. On the paternalistic side, there is the problem of the tyranny of the majority. Not all social outcomes that the majority might prefer should be on the table, and, in a constitutional democracy, it is the constitution that launders out certain of these social outcomes. Though they may ultimately be susceptible to change by the democratic process itself, these constitutional boundaries are not themselves typically up for grabs in the determination of the goals of public policy.

Thinking now of the domain of environmental policy, what is needed is an analog of these constitutional boundaries. This 'environmental constitution' would put constraints on where the pursuit of preference satisfaction (for example, the pursuit of social utility in the economists' sense) can take us (see Holland, 1995 for a similar discussion). View these constraints as a series of pre-commitments regarding what is in play and what is out of bounds in the realm of public policy regardless of the temptations of the moment – like Ulysses binding himself to the mast so as to resist the siren's song. How might we arrive at such an environmental constitution? Surely the answer must be, at least in part, that these constraints would be the outcome of a process of deliberation by those we trust, a deliberation that we have neither the time nor the expertise to engage in. These deliberators may be the philosopher kings (these days it might be more accurate to talk about scientist kings standing at least alongside the philosopher kings) that Kopp (1993) is worried about, but it is hard to see how their input can be avoided. What might it involve? Presumably, it would make reference to certain relatively uncontroversial components of well-being and to basic considerations of environmental justice; it is likely that it would also include elements that speak to our obligations to future generations and to questions of sustainability. From whence would it gain its political legitimacy? Like all constitutional commitments, it would require a super-majority for its implementation, and, given the controversial nature of environmental issues, this is likely to be the rub.

However, emphasizing constitutional pre-commitment is potentially misleading in that it disguises the deliberative nature of the political process itself. In fact, when the deliberative process gives full expression to the scope of values that shape environmental concerns we can get the effect of constraint on preference satisfaction without the explicit constitutional machinery (which in itself may be a bit of political pie-in-the-sky). Such a deliberative model of public decision making would include all of the various kinds of values relevant to environmental policy, the reasons for caring about these values, and the strategies for negotiating the inevitable tradeoffs among them. The pursuit of social utility (for example, the satisfaction of preferences even broadly construed) would find its place among the panoply of values, but it would not be the sole engine driving the process. Thus the decision-making process itself could supply significant constraint on the pursuit of subjective preference.

A useful way to think about the process of environmental decision making is in terms of what might be called the 'possible futures' model. The model has structural similarities with the social utility model. Think of it this way. Suppose we are facing a hypothetical environmental decision: we can do A or do B (see Figure 5.1).

If we do A, we will end up in one of, say, three possible futures. Call them world 1, world 2, or world 3. Each of these three worlds has a certain probability of ending up being the actual world, should we do A. And, for the sake of simplicity, suppose that the three options are mutually exclusive and exhaustive, so the probabilities sum to one. If, alternatively, we do B, we might end up, say, in one of two possible futures: call them world 4 and world 5. Again, each of these worlds has a certain probability of becoming actual, and again suppose that these probabilities sum to one. If we were deploying the social utility model, we would consult our preference maps and determine the utilities associated with each of these possible outcomes. The correct decision would then be simply a matter of maximizing expected utility.

The difference between the possible futures model and the social utility model is that we abandon the idea that we can quantify the utilities associated with these various possible futures, and thus abandon the idea that we can mathematically calculate the optimal or appropriate decision. Instead, we recognize that there are a number of normative dimensions along which each of these possible futures can be evaluated, the satisfaction of consumer preferences being just one such dimension. We might be able to consult our preference maps and determine how each of worlds 1–5 fare with respect to the satisfaction of consumer preferences, and we might even have the requisite probabilities associated with each of the possible outcomes and thus

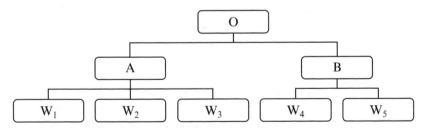

Figure 5.1   The 'possible futures' model

be able to calculate the expected utilities associated with doing A and doing B. But having that information is not dispositive in the decision situation. Instead, as I mentioned, it is just one dimension of value that plugs into the decision-making process – call it economic value. Other dimensions of value are important as well. One obvious dimension is ethical value. One or more of these possible futures might involve the serious infringement of rights or a distribution of risk or resources that involve gross inequities. Other dimensions of value would include aesthetics, issues of sustainability, ecosystem integrity, ecosystem health, the preservation of biodiversity, perhaps various kinds of cultural and/or historical values, and so forth. I do not suppose the list to be exhaustive, nor am I suggesting that some of the items on the list are not reducible to others, but I do not propose to examine these questions here.

What I am suggesting is that success at environmental decision making requires a capacity to think clearly about these various categories of value and, in particular, about the ways to negotiate the tradeoffs among them. To do this, we need for each category three things: (1) an understanding of the nature of each kind of value (for example, what is ecosystem integrity?); (2) the ability to operationalize each kind of value (for example, how would we know when our policies are actually succeeding in the pursuit of that particular value?); (3) an articulation of the reasons for caring about each kind of value (for example, what reasons can be given for the pursuit of a particular category of value?). The capacity to identify the relevant categories of value and to assess the three issues just mentioned provide the resources for engaging in a deliberative, democratic process of policy selection. We deploy these reasons in debate amongst ourselves over which of the possible futures we should seek to actualize.

Now, one might say that this is really still a matter of preferences after all – preferences over possible futures. I have no problem with viewing the matter in this way. But, if we so conceive it, we must at the same time recognize that these kinds of preferences over possible futures are not much like the consumer preferences, even the hypothetical ones, that economists seek to measure. They are preferences backed by reasons, shaped by argument and counter-argument, and so forth. In short, they are the stuff of deliberative democratic decision making – the outcome of the deployment of what Rawls (1999) calls 'public reason'.

5.7   Conclusion

Unlike some of my more extreme philosophical colleagues, I do believe that there is a place for contingent valuation studies in the overall project of articulating values to guide environmental decisions. To be sure, the approach is not without its pitfalls, and many of the early studies had serious shortcomings. However, significant methodological progress has been made. The NOAA panel guidelines are clearly a step forward. I agree with Green and Tunstall (1999) that the next round of methodological progress in contingent valuation studies will come from taking a multidisciplinary approach. Economics has a long history of operating with naïve pictures of human psychology. Whether or not this has been a serious impediment to the neo-classical tradition, it is clear that the next generation of CV analyses will have to be based on our best psychological understanding. The same can be said about the other social sciences. There is a vast body of experience in the design and implementation of social surveys here, and this knowledge should find its way in CV studies. Economists, above all, should recognize the inefficiency of re-inventing the wheel.

But contingent valuation is just one tool in the tool kit. Many of its shortcomings should be addressed, not by yet another revolution in methodological sophistication, but by alternative strategies altogether. Conjoint analysis offers some clear advantages in this respect. For example, it offers a more comprehensive picture of preferences across a range of options, and, as Green and Tunstall (1999: 243) point out, it is an iterative process that offers the opportunity for respondents to learn their preferences through practice. However, there are some problems involving the appeal to hypothetical preferences that are beyond even the reach of conjoint analysis. These problems come in two forms. One set has to do with the determination to quantify matters of value. The goal is laudatory enough – if we are going to apply the social utility model of decision making, we need measures of social utility. We then face the problem of how to handle those who are uncomfortable putting a monetary value on things they care about most deeply. This is the disenfranchise problem that was discussed above. The second set of problems has to do with the deployment of the social utility model as the operative means of making environmental decisions. Perhaps the central issue here is the issue of laundering preferences. The proper response to both sets of problems, in my view, is to move in the direction of a deliberative democratic process as the ultimate vehicle for decision making. The measures of social utility can enter into that process as one kind of reason for making policy choices, but it does not take on the role of the dominant mechanism of decision making.

Let me close by calling attention to a suggestion made by one of the most trenchant critics of CV approaches over the years. Mark Sagoff (1998) points to a 'deliberative and discursive turn' in recent CV research. One of the methodological responses the problems such as framing and embedding has been to form groups of individuals, provide relevant information, and open upon channels for dialogue. Sagoff suggests that such groups could 'function not as informants about their personal utilities but as citizen-juries reaching judgments about environmental values on the basis of argument and evidence' (Sagoff, 1998: 226). In other words, by setting up the context for their survey research in this deliberative and discursive way, environmental economists have gone a long way towards establishing the circumstances for the reasoned discussion of public environmental values described in the previous section. Of course, the economists have done this so as to get better measures of preferences. Sagoff, ever the skeptic when it comes to the relevance of preference satisfaction for environmental policy, is suggesting that they set that project to the side and focus instead on reasoned debate over conceptions of the public interest. I would like to register a point of agreement and a point of disagreement, and then end with a suggestion.

I have discussed how an appeal to hypothetical preferences allows economists to operate with a very broad notion of preference, and, correspondingly, a very broad conception of economic value – Pearce labeling the contemplation of a beautiful view an economic value is an example. Broadening the notion of preference in this way is, in effect, an attempt to get at this very debate over conceptions of the public interest, but to do so in a way that preserves the overall framework of preference satisfaction as the metric of environmental value. I suspect the ultimate motivation for doing so is to preserve the conditions for the application of the social utility model, which, as we have seen, requires the quantification of value. Insofar as this is the project, I share Sagoff's skepticism. But I do not agree that preference satisfaction is irrelevant to environmental policy. Knowledge of subjective preferences over environmental goods is an important input into the overall process of deliberation over environmental policy and it is the business of environmental economics to supply this knowledge. Thus I do not endorse Sagoff's suggestion that the measurement project be simply abandoned in favor of the deliberative one.

Finally, the suggestion: in large measure, the decades-long debate between economists and philosophers in the environmental arena has been fueled by a desire for hegemony by both sides. On the economists part this has primarily taken the form of an attempt to collapse all relevant environmental values into preferences existing in the population. On the philosophers side the project has been to recast all relevant environmental concerns as matters of morality, which can then serve as trumps over the pursuit of economic gain. The extensionist project (extending moral standing to non-human nature) has been the centerpiece of this movement and has dominated the debate in environmental ethics since its inception. Neither project strikes me as very promising. Value pluralism reigns in the environmental domain, and we would be better served by directing our efforts at becoming clear about the nature of the values involved and about how to negotiate the inevitable tradeoffs among them. Viewed in this light, Sagoff's suggestion has merit. Environmental economists are well position to contribute to the development of effective deliberative frameworks – not as an alternative to their traditional research, but as a form that this research might take.

References

Adamowicz, Vic (1995), 'Alternative valuation techniques: a comparison and movement to a synthesis', in K.G. Willis and J.T. Corkindale (eds), *Environmental Valuation*, Oxon: CAB International, pp. 144–59.

Anderson, Elizabeth (1993), *Value in Ethics and Economics*, Cambridge, MA: Harvard University Press.

Baron, Jonathan (1996), 'Rationality and invariance: response to Schuman', in David J. Bjornstad and James R. Kahn (eds), *The Contingent Valuation of Environmental Resources*, Cheltenham: Edward Elgar, pp. 145–63.

Baron, Jonathan (2002), 'Value trade-offs and the nature of utility: bias, inconsistency, protected values, and other problems', paper presented at a conference on Behavioral Economics and Neoclassical Economics, American Institute for Economic Research, Great Barrington, MA, July.

Beckley, Harlan (forthcoming), 'Human dignity in economics: can cost/benefit analysis advance respect for dignity?', *Oxford Handbook of Theological Ethics*, Oxford: Oxford University Press.

Boyle, Kevin J. and John C. Bergstrom (1999), 'Doubt, doubts, and doubters: the genesis of a new research agenda?', in Ian J. Bateman and Kenneth G. Willis (eds), *Valuing Environmental Preferences: Theory and Practice of the Contingent Valuation Method in the US, EU, and Developing Countries*, Oxford: Oxford University Press, pp. 183–206.

Bjornstad, David J. and James R. Kahn (1996), 'Characteristics of environmental resources and their relevance for measuring value', in David J. Bjornstad and James R. Kahn (eds), *The Contingent Valuation of Environmental Resources*, Cheltenham: Edward Elgar, pp. 3–15.

Diamond, Peter A. and Jerry A. Hausman (1994), 'Contingent valuation: is some number better than no number?', *Journal of Economic Perspectives*, **8**(4), 45–64.

Fischhoff, Baruch (1991), 'Value elicitation: is there anything in there?', *American Psychologist*, **46**(8), 835–47.

Fisher, Anthony C. (1996), 'The conceptual underpinnings of the contingent valuation method', in David J. Bjornstad and James R. Kahn (eds), *The Contingent Valuation of Environmental Resources*, Cheltenham: Edward Elgar, pp. 19–37.

Freeman, A. Myrick III (1983), 'The ethical basis of the economic view of the environment', in Donald VanDeVeer and Christine Pierce (eds), *The Environmental Ethics and Policy Book*, Belmont, CA: Wadsworth Publishing Co., 2nd edn, 1998, pp. 293–301.

Green, Colin and Sylvia Tunstall (1999), 'A psychological perspective', in Ian J. Bateman and Kenneth G. Willis (eds), *Valuing Environmental Preferences: Theory and Practice of the Contingent Valuation Method in the US, EU, and Developing Countries*, Oxford: Oxford University Press, 2001, pp. 207–57.

Hanemann, W. Michael (1995), 'Contingent valuation and economics', in K.G. Willis and J.T. Corkindale (eds), *Environmental Valuation*, Oxon: CAB International, pp. 79–117.

Hanemann, W. Michael (1996), 'Theory versus data in the contingent valuation debate', in David J. Bjornstad and James R. Kahn (eds), *The Contingent Valuation of Environmental Resources*, Cheltenham: Edward Elgar, pp. 38–60.

Hanley, Nick (1995), 'The role of environmental valuation in cost–benefit analysis', in K.G. Willis and J.T. Corkindale (eds), *Environmental Valuation*, Oxon: CAB International, pp. 39–55.

Holland, Alan (1995), 'The assumptions of cost–benefit analysis: a philosopher's view', in K.G. Willis and J.T. Corkindale (eds), *Environmental Valuation*, Oxon: CAB International, pp. 21–38.

Kahn, James R. (2005), *The Economic Approach to Environmental Natural Resources*, 3rd edn, US: Thomson-South-Western.

Kopp, Raymond J. (1993), 'Environmental economics: not dead but thriving', *Resources for the Future*, **111** (Spring), 7–12.

Norton, Bryan et al. (1998), 'The evolution of preferences: why "sovereign" preferences may not lead to sustainable policies and what to do about it', *Ecological Economics*, **24**, 193–211.

Pearce, D. (1992), 'Green economics', *Environmental Values*, **1**(1), 3–13.

Perrings, Charles (1995), 'Ecological and economic values', in K.G. Willis and J.T. Corkindale (eds), *Environmental Valuation*, Oxon: CAB International, pp. 56–66.

Rawls, John (1971), *A Theory of Justice*, Cambridge, MA: The Belknap Press of Harvard University Press.

Rawls, John (1999), *The Law of Peoples; with The Idea of Public Reason Revisited*, Cambridge, MA: Harvard University Press.

Sagoff, Mark (1981), 'At the Shrine of Our Lady of Fatima, or why political questions are not all economic', in Donald VanDeVeer and Christine Pierce (eds), *The Environmental Ethics and Policy Book*, Belmont, CA: Wadsworth Publishing Co., 2nd edn, 1998, pp. 301–10.

Sagoff, Mark (1998), 'Aggregation and deliberation in valuing environmental public goods: A look beyond contingent pricing', *Ecological Economics*, **24**, 213–30.

Sen, Amartya (1987), *On Ethics and Economics*, Oxford: Basil Blackwell.

Shrader-Frechette, Kristin (2002), 'Risky business: nuclear workers, ethics, and the market-efficiency argument', in Victoria Davion (ed.), *Ethics and the Environment*, Bloomington: Indiana University Press, pp. 1–23.

Sugden, Robert (1999), 'Alternatives to the neo-classical theory of choice', in Ian J. Bateman and Kenneth G. Willis (eds), *Valuing Environmental Preferences: Theory and Practice of the Contingent Valuation Method in the US, EU, and Developing Countries*, Oxford: Oxford University Press, pp. 152–80.

Sunstein, Cass R. (2000), 'Introduction', in Cass R. Sunstein (ed.), *Behavioral Law and Economics*, New York: Cambridge University Press, pp. 1–10.

6   Protest bids, commensurability, and substitution: contingent valuation and ecological economics
Brent Haddad and Richard Howarth

It is fair to say that the worth of the things we love is better measured by our unwillingness to pay for them.
Mark Sagoff, 1988: 68

6.1   Introduction

Contingent valuation (CV) surveys regularly encounter responses that are difficult to reconcile with the standard assumptions of applied welfare economics. There are many well-known explanations for such behavior. Consistent with the theory of public goods, respondents may strategically bid below their true willingness to pay (WTP) to secure a public good, if they believe that others will carry the cost of providing that good. Efforts are regularly made in survey design to enhance 'incentive compatibility' and thereby minimize strategic behavior. Mitchell and Carson (1989) express puzzlement over strategic behavior. Noting that response outliers seem to be concentrated among respondents with lower incomes and education levels, and among older and female respondents, they comment: 'Such characteristics hardly describe those of whom strategic behavior is expected' (1989: 167).[1] Of course, the theory behind CV assumes that all individuals are equally strategic in their behavior.

Another category of anomalous behavior is the embedding effect, the bête noir of CV in the eyes of the expert National Oceanic and Atmospheric Administration (NOAA) Contingent Valuation Panel (NOAA, 1993). Embedding describes a behavior in which respondents' WTP differs based on whether the object of valuation is part of a program or set of similar objects, or stands alone. If it is part of a program or set, WTP may not scale up as the proposed beneficial intervention scales up. Respondents may, for example, report a WTP to clean up five lakes that is equivalent to or only slightly higher than a WTP to clean up one lake. While diminishing marginal returns suggest that respondents should value subsequent lake clean-ups slightly less than previous ones, a consultation of one's preferences regarding clean versus polluted lakes should evoke a much higher WTP to clean five lakes as opposed to just one, assuming the environment contributes positively to preference satisfaction. Some economists suggest respondents are basing their choices on a desire to feel good about contributing to a public activity, a feeling that, once sated, requires no additional investment (e.g., Diamond and Hausman, 1994). This has been described as 'the purchase of moral satisfaction' (Kahneman and Knetsch, 1992), and labeled the 'warm glow' effect.

A large proportion of anomalous bids are categorized as protest bids. Protest bids take a number of forms: refusals to participate or dropping out of a survey, extremely low or zero bids, and extremely high or infinite bids. Protest responses often comprise 5–10 per cent of overall responses (Mitchell and Carson, 1989), but can also range to 20 per cent (Spash and Hanley, 1995) or even 50 per cent (Stevens et al., 1991). The common interpretation is that such behavior produces 'implausible' and 'illegitimate' responses for purposes of cost–benefit analysis (CBA). That is, a protest bid does not reveal how the respondent actually values the survey object in terms of his or her underlying preferences. The *ex ante* analytical response is to design surveys that minimize the presence of protest votes. In general, Carson et al. (1999: 112–13) describe the 'commodity definition problem' as one of clearly explaining what physical changes will occur if a hypothetical project proceeds. They note that changes can have multiple attributes and that respondents' beliefs and concerns about the good and its provision should be studied during the survey-development phase. The *ex post* analytical response is to consider protest bids to be outliers and to discard them. There is neither a well-established theoretical basis for discarding protest votes, nor do widely accepted protocols exist (Boyle and Bergstrom, 1999). Following removal of obvious outliers, Mitchell and Carson (1989) recommend using a 'trimmed mean' technique to estimate true mean and median WTP, given the potential existence of additional (but less obvious) outliers. This statistical approach reduces random survey and response errors. Hanemann and Kanninen (1999: 405–6) suggest a 'hot deck' procedure for imputing the value of non-answers. This procedure assumes that respondents and non-respondents within the same classification group have the same distribution of responses. A random draw from existing data supplies the missing answers. Hanemann and Kanninen warn that imputation is a 'dangerous art', since it yields a data set that does not include the same variability that would be found in a truly complete data set.

Numerous motivations can be ascribed to respondents who offer protest bids, reflecting a range of attitudes toward government (and taxes) and toward paying for public goods (Table 6.1; see also Jorgensen et al., 2000). Respondents may struggle with the choices of whether to answer, and how

Table 6.1   *Possible reasons for protest bids in contingent valuation studies involving public goods*

It is unfair to be asked to pay additional money for a public good.
Existing public money or money sources should be used.
Government already wastes too much money.
Use of this public good is a right that should not be paid for.
Collected money may not actually be used for the public good as promised.
Taxes are already high enough/too high.
Only users/polluters of a public good should pay.
The intrinsic value of the public good cannot be quantified.

Source: Jorgensen and Syme (2000), Table 2 and text.

to answer (Clark et al., 2000). But underlying issues remain: why would the same individual who does not engage in protest behavior in market transactions ('I'll offer you zero dollars for your gas-guzzling sport-utility vehicle') and in election voting ('I vote no on everything') choose to protest in a CV survey?[2]

How one understands CV protest behaviors sheds light on a number of fundamental differences between environmental economics and ecological economics, an incipient but deeply rooted alternative approach to understanding the overlapping, inter-related spheres of economy, society, and ecosystems. Environmental economics is largely concerned with balancing the costs and benefits of environmental policies to achieve economic efficiency. Ecological economics, in contrast, focuses on managing the links between economic and ecological systems to promote human well-being, social fairness, and ecological sustainability (Costanza and Folke, 1997). While cost–benefit indicators are of course useful in gauging preferences and therefore well-being, ecological economics proceeds from the assumption that management decisions often involve moral values that cannot be reduced to monetary valuation. The contingent valuation literature highlights differences between these perspectives.

This chapter takes up the question of why there should be protest behaviors in the first place, and what they tell us. Far from being illegitimate cast-offs, we believe that protest behaviors – the fact of and the reasons behind their existence – provide key insights into the valuation process. This chapter begins with a discussion of utilitarianism and contractarian liberalism as they relate to the general challenge of valuation. It then draws linkages between protest bidding, substitutability between natural and created capital, and commensurability. The chapter concludes with a discussion of research on alternative approaches to valuation that are based on discursive ethics and how they might relate to the existing practices and policy roles of CV.

6.2   Utilitarianism and contractarian liberalism

Utilitarianism is a social ethic calling for the maximization of the summed utility of all members of society. Utility can mean either pleasure-minus-pain, as in the 'greatest happiness' principle of Bentham (1789) and Mill (1863), or can be interpreted broadly in terms of cardinal indices of individual preference rankings (Sen and Williams, 1982). These two meanings of utility differ since preference rankings can involve values other than happiness. Rarely do philosophers tout utilitarianism as a 'stand-alone' ethical system for social organization. Alone, it can justify such practices as punishing innocent persons to satisfy a mob, or otherwise damaging the interests of minority groups. In critiquing utilitarianism, Brown (1998) points out the absence of protections of minority groups; the weak link between satisfaction of preferences and increased happiness; the practical inability to maximize the utility of joint undertakings when the focus is on individual utility maximization; and the problems that arise when an anthropocentric perspective on preferences, pleasure, and pain is emphasized without considering the interests of non-human sentient beings.

Utilitarianism does not point to or suggest particular complementary social institutions. This ethic can underlie such disparate systems as democracies, totalitarian states, markets, and command economies. Its framework, however, does not entail a simple concern for economic efficiency or for providing a setting in which people can pursue their individual self-interest. Instead, utilitarianism implies that income and other resources should be distributed so as to equate the marginal utility of each good across all members of society. Since the early work of John Stuart Mill (1863), utilitarians have argued for the leveling of class distinctions and economic inequalities since, by assumption, an extra unit of income provides more utility to a poor person than to a rich person.

Economists often laud the market mechanism and democratic political processes on the ground that their proper functioning tends to promote individual well-being. It should be borne in mind, however, that the notions of consumer sovereignty and democratic governance rest on moral foundations that are conceptually distinct from utilitarianism. Under contractarian liberalism (which undergirds the basic structure of the US Constitution), the role of the state is to advance and defend both the liberty and welfare of its citizens. Following the seventeenth-century insights of John Locke (1690), liberty is linked to the protection of property rights, civil rights, due process, and equal protection under the law. In this formulation, the welfare of individuals is advanced through both market transactions and democratic consent – ideally through the emergence of social consensus that government action (for example, taxation and regulation) is preferable to unrestricted freedom (Howarth and Wilson, in press). State power in the pursuit of welfare can be rationalized provided that – at least hypothetically – it gains the consent of each and every person. This would only be possible if there were 'no losers' – that is, each party is compensated for any costs they bear. Randall (1987) calls this the 'Pareto safety' criterion.

Utilitarianism and contractarian liberalism give rise to contrasting perspectives on the use of cost–benefit criteria in policy analysis. Under utilitarianism, individual preferences as revealed by WTP are a core element of utility aggregation and resource allocation. As such, utilitarians employ a monetary metric to infer preference-rankings from bidding/buying behavior. Of course, the marginal utility of income would generally differ across individuals in a society characterized by income disparities and social heterogeneity. Hence the application of utilitarianism would require that the net monetary benefits that a policy conferred on each member of society be weighted according to that individual's marginal utility of income. In practice, however, the use of welfare weights is uncommon because utility – and hence the marginal utility of income – is generally seen as unmeasurable. As such, the prevailing practice of cost–benefit analysis departs from the dictates of philosophical utilitarianism.

Under contractarian liberalism, it remains useful to employ monetary valuation techniques to evaluate the impacts of policies on the preferences and welfare of individuals. However, liberalism envisions individual members of society voluntarily relinquishing certain private rights in order to obtain more highly valued civil order and protections. This approach emphasizes rights and process, and calls for individuals to be actively engaged in decision making. Legitimacy, not welfare, is its normative goal, although a concern for individual welfare co-exists with legitimacy interests. Generally speaking, liberals distrust the notion that it is morally legitimate to impose uncompensated costs on some individuals for the greater benefit of society. Individual consent, not a concept of aggregate social welfare, is seen as the appropriate basis of social decisions.

6.3 The problem of valuation

The challenge of valuation is central to any application of cost–benefit analysis. Since the 1970s, the governments of industrialized nations – especially the United States – have become more self-conscious and methodical in this endeavor, with formal CBA growing in importance as a policy tool (Loomis, 1999). Expressed WTP is considered to be an indicator of underlying preference rankings, the satisfaction of which presumably increases well-being.[3] The aggregate satisfaction of individual preferences, considered in light of tradeoffs for other goods and services, is seen to maximize social utility. Part of the challenge is to construct 'true' preference rankings from revealed WTP. Strict rules consistent with consumer theory govern what is a valid WTP response (that is, a response from which 'true' preference rankings can be inferred). In addition to meeting rationality criteria (described in Sagoff, 1994), decision criteria must be exclusively self-referential (for example, exclude public mindedness or altruism as sources of value) in order to avoid double-counting biases.

CV is one tool that enables CBA to be extended into the environmental realm.[4] CV has generated academic interest in part because it represents the only way to measure the non-use values that are so critical to many people's conception of wilderness and species preservation. As such, CV studies often form a basis for damage awards against parties found to have despoiled natural systems (Heyde, 1995).

Yet a fundamental philosophical mismatch exists. As a matter of public policy, calls for the valuation of non-use goods emerge from a legitimacy-oriented contractarian approach to social organization. That is, the valuation process occurs as part of legislative, administrative, and judicial processes. The calls have been answered by a valuation tool (CV) through which relative measurements of individual preferences emerge from surveys of WTP for the natural system in question. The strict rules of the valuation tool are often inconsistent with contractarian social organization, which is based in part on public mindedness and altruism.

Norgaard et al. (1999) offer six dilemmas related to utilitarianism in general, each with implications for CV in particular (Table 6.2). All six dilemmas deal directly or indirectly with values and valuation processes, and involve both survey designers/investigators and respondents. Here we explore two of the six dilemmas: the multiple contexts of values and the disaggregation/reaggregation of nature problem.

6.3.1 Multiple contexts of values
Norgaard et al. point out that individuals may possess 'multiple centers of value' corresponding to the many roles in life an individual plays (parent, business owner, elected official, non-profit-organization member, etc.). Valuation decisions may emerge from any of these centers. Such decisions are incommensurable in that they cannot be ascribed to a single preference map that is consistent with the rationality requirements of consumer theory. Vatn and Bromley (1994) point out that preferences are developed or discovered as part of the act of choosing, and that this act has a moral aspect. Social norms may restrict or reject the 'commodity fiction' of a CV survey. Since the context of the choice can influence the choice,

Table 6.2   Utilitarian dilemmas and implications for contingent valuation

Dilemmas in utilitarianism	Explanation and challenge to contingent valuation
1. Distribution of rights	Environmental valuation techniques do not address how rights are distributed, inter- or intra-generationally. Challenges the 'norm' of favoring WTP over WTA in survey design.
2. Values–aggregation dilemma	To communicate with the public and with policy makers, scientists must aggregate and simplify complex data. This process embeds scientific values in the data that ultimately are presented. Challenges the objectivity of survey design.
3. Socially constructed values	Values are not objective but emerge from social processes. Values are influenced and sustained by social processes, including the policy process. Challenges the individual preference-to-policy causality chain.
4. Multiple contexts of values	One individual can express multiple and mutually inconsistent value sets depending upon the social context (e.g., consumer v. citizen). Other values are best understood at a collective, as opposed to individual, level. Challenges whether preferences identified by a single-context CV survey reflects respondents' 'true' preferences.
5. Co-evolving knowledge and values	Expanding scientific knowledge of biodiversity and other environmental topics influences societal values regarding biodiversity. Changing values in turn influence research choices. Challenges the presumed separateness of CV survey design from responses.
6. Disaggregating/ re-aggregating nature	Due to their complexity and inter-relationships, ecosystems cannot be disaggregated into component parts without loss of value. Some aspects of the human experience of nature (e.g., biodiversity, climate change) are best understood collectively, not individually. Challenges the assumption that societal well-being can be aggregated from individual preferences.

Note: Titles and order have been slightly adjusted from the original. Except for (1) above, challenges to contingent valuation are provided by the authors of this chapter.

Source: Norgaard, Scholz and Trainor (1999).

CV-imposed restrictions on possible tradeoffs can alter perceptions of value.

Sagoff (1994, see also 1998) distinguishes between what he calls 'self-regarding' and 'ideal-regarding' preferences. He argues that US environmental values emerge from Americans' 'character as a people', which cannot be measured by aggregating individual preferences (1988: 28, 55). Values regarding sentimentality, history, ideology, culture, aesthetics, and ethics emerge that are separate from values related to one's role as a consumer. Sagoff notes the consistency of his ideas with Sen's (1977: 329) use of 'commitment' as a personal value that drives 'a wedge between personal choice and personal welfare'. Ajzen et al. (1996) found that, when CV respondents did not have a strong personal interest in the survey topic, significantly different WTP figures could be elicited based on the questionner's verbal cues that prompted either an individualistic or an altruistic orientation.

Sagoff believes that attempts to find a 'combined' or inclusive set of preferences involve category errors and are bound to fail. Citizenship-based preferences are based on one's opinions on issues of public interest and impact. They are expressed as beliefs or convictions. Self-regarding preferences can be expressed as willingness to pay. An obvious awkwardness results when a CV survey asks for a WTP for a belief or conviction. Vatn and Bromley (1994) note the potential for conflict and ambivalence among respondents when such questions are asked. Ready et al. (1995) offer a bounded-rationality interpretation. They suggest that ambivalence rises as the difficulty of calculating tradeoffs between money and environmental amenity increases. Eventually, respondents may abandon their efforts at calculation and adopt simple decision rules such as conservatism (preference for the status quo) or lexicographic rules (favoring one category over another every time). What Sagoff describes as a category error, Ready et al. suggest is an individual's 'core of persistent ambivalence' – an unresolvable difficulty in identifying portions of one's indifference curve related to tradeoffs between environmental amenities and money.

A contextual issue involves the potential for foregoing utility-improving choices. From the perspective of rights-based or 'Kantian' ethics (Kant, 1785), an individual is free to maximize preference satisfaction over the set of options that are consistent with his or her moral responsibilities. A rational person places duties (expectations or requirements to which one is morally obligated) ahead of preferences. Duties are contextual: a parent may make one choice the day before her 18-year-old leaves home, and, given the same choice set the following day, make another choice.

Certain values are not effectively integrated into systems involving preferences or welfare. Consider the example of an aging woman who has one desire in life: to use her wealth to benefit impoverished children. Her interest coincides perfectly with the children's: both enjoy enhanced satisfaction (utility) when she gives her money to children's charities. The 'double-counting' argument, however, says that policy makers should actually ignore this woman's preferences since they arise from altruistic motives, a sense of duty, or moral obligation (see Milgrom, 1993). They should pit the benefits that she would obtain from personally consuming her wealth against the basic needs of the kids. This does the woman a profound disservice. It fundamentally rejects her autonomy and right to construct her own vision of the good.

6.3.2   *Dis-aggregating and re-aggregating nature*

Norgaard et al. argue that the total value of ecosystems cannot be determined using a dis-aggregation/re-aggregation technique. Dis-aggregation involves dividing an ecosystem into component parts capable of valuation (the commodity definition problem), while re-aggregation involves summing the individual values stated for the component parts. Assuming an ecosystem A can be disaggregated into component parts D, E, F, . . ., K, the commonly understood total valuation of A, V_A, is the summation of all individual (*i*) values of A's component parts:

$$V_A = \sum_{i=1}^{n} (V_{Di} + V_{Ei} + V_{Fi} + \ldots + V_{Ki}),$$

where the subscripts refer to the value that each individual attaches to each component. Norgaard et al. would argue on two counts that the correct relationship is not equality, but the left-hand side having a larger magnitude. With respect to dis-aggregation, they note the complexity of ecosystems and their inseparability without loss of function, writing that nature 'does not break in to separable phenomena with discrete consequences on isolated individuals . . .' (p. 6). That is, A can provide services (climate stabilization, disease vector control, etc.) only if all its component parts are present. Similarly, Turner (1999) describes the economy and the environment as a jointly determined system linked in a process of co-evolution and having a system-wide value related to its resilience.[5] Turner notes a 'glue' value related to the structure and functioning of a healthy ecosystem that holds everything together, as well as a 'redundancy reserve' or pool of latent species or processes that provide resilience to the system in the face of stress or shock.

Turning to the re-aggregation of individually stated values, Norgaard et al. point out that a consequentialist ethic, of which utilitarianism is one, encounters value-measurement problems when consequences (results of climate change, biodiversity loss, etc.) cannot be clearly predicted. Turner also notes this challenge, describing it as an impossibility of measuring all potential indirect use values related to ecosystems's life-support functions. In valuing biodiversity, Norgaard et al. also stress that some benefits of ecosystem services are enjoyed collectively as well as individually. Life-support functions are an example. Norgaard et al. offer the analogy of a public good problem: since collective values and certain non-market values are not captured in the re-aggregation of individual values, a summation of individual valuations of the benefits of biodiversity would be lower than its actual worth.

6.4   Substitutability, commensurability, and contingent valuation

Of the two categories from Norgaard et al. discussed above, one focuses on how humans perform the act of valuation, while the other points out the incompatibilities between ecosystem structure and function and utilitarian valuation processes. A core assumption (and one which performs a 'sorting function' between environmental economists and ecological economists) involves the extent of substitutability between natural capital and created capital. To the extent that different types of capital can substitute for each other, their value can be compared (i.e., they are commensurable). Natural capital refers to the endowment of environmental resources available to this generation. It includes the beneficial functions ('ecosystem services') and resilience of ecosystems, the low-entropy concentrations of mineral and biotic wealth, as well as the potential wealth presented by heretofore unexplored biodiversity. Created capital includes the transformations of natural capital into physical capital (machinery, factories), and technology. The substitutability assumption fits neatly into the realm of created capital: individuals can liquidate stock portfolios and purchase machinery, and then sell the machinery and re-invest in equities. The assumption weakens when one considers natural capital. While an owner of old-growth forest can harvest old-growth trees, sell them, and then invest in created capital, this is not a reversible transaction. When one considers the forest more broadly as a forest ecosystem, the substitutability assumption weakens even in the absence of old growth. That is, a third-growth forest ecosystem may be qualitatively different from a second-growth system, as: (1) the system may increasingly lose resilience with repeated logging and (2) it is unlikely that the same series of climatic events and colonizing species will occur, resulting in the same forest.

The philosophical divergence between environmental and ecological economics comes into sight over the extent to which created capital can serve as a functional equivalent to lost natural capital, providing, for example, something that is not old growth but offers equivalent benefits. The question of irreversibility in natural-capital-to-created-capital transactions takes on added importance when one considers ecosystem services provided by natural capital that are closely related to the preservation of human life, such as climate stabilization, flood mitigation, water purification, and natural controls on disease vectors. Some ecologists reject the substitutability assumption with respect to vital ecosystem services (e.g., Ehrlich and Mooney, 1983). Daily et al. (1997) believe the total value of ecosystem services provided by soils 'could only be expressed as infinite'. For other aspects of natural capital, full substitutability is occasionally possible. Examples include polio vaccines substituting for prior (moderately successful) natural controls on the spread of the polio virus, and artificial diamonds substituting for natural diamonds in industrial uses.

One can distinguish between objective and subjective aspects of substitutability (Table 6.3). Objective substitutability refers to quantitatively measurable qualities of capital. To what extent does the substitute provide equivalent tangible services and to what extent are sufficient quantities of the substitute available given the existing level of the service? The availability of created capital with high objective substitutability can reduce a society's reliance on natural capital; low objective substitutability means that the degradation or loss of the natural capital would result in a net loss of the service. High objective substitutability between natural and created capital indicates that a cardinal value ranking is theoretically feasible.

Subjective substitutability refers to qualities of capital that may or may not be quantifiable. Subjective factors involve peoples' willingness to accept the substitute. Examples of created capital with low subjective substitutability include indirect potable water reuse projects (re-introducing highly treated wastewater into aquifers or reservoirs designated for human use) and, especially in Europe, genetically modified organisms. Objective

Table 6.3   Subjective and objective dimensions in substitutability between natural and created capital: societal perspectives

		Subjective substitutability	
		High	Low
Objective substitutability	High	Polio vaccine for natural disease vector controls	Indirect potable reuse of reclaimed water for water already in reservoirs or aquifers*
	Low	Fertilizer for natural processes of soil regeneration	Tree farm for a forest with cultural or religious significance

* Indirect potable reuse of reclaimed water is the purposeful reintroduction of urban recycled water into bodies of water intended for human use.

measurements may not reveal deficiencies (or may even reveal superior qualities) in the substitutes. Yet people's perceptions of 'naturalness' or other subjective criteria may influence their preference rankings. When environmental values extend beyond the instrumental to include moral values, such as deep ecology or duties to future generations, subjective substitutability declines. To the extent that people view nature reverentially – as a source of spiritual grounding and renewal – substitution becomes a moot point. A tree farm is not a substitute for a forest imbued with religious or spiritual significance.

With respect to services that are categorically non-substitutable, Spash and Hanley (1995) discuss lexicographic preferences. If a respondent believes that an aspect of nature, such as wildlife, has an absolute right to protection, he or she may refuse any and all tradeoffs.[6] Lockwood (1998) characterizes lexicographic preferences as a form of non-compensatory ordering, since the respondent refuses to produce a value-ranking of alternatives. The respondent's indifference curve is reduced to a single point, since no tradeoffs are possible between a given quantity of wildlife and an alternative good. In this situation, responses to CV questions could range from zero to infinity WTP depending on the nature of the resulting protest. According to Spash and Hanley, roughly 25 per cent of Stevens et al.'s (1991) biodiversity CV respondents provided answers consistent with lexicographic preferences, and 23 per cent of responses to their own survey of biodiversity values evinced lexicographic preferences.

A valuation process should be able to integrate gradations of objective and subjective substitutability and their resulting gradations of incommensurability. A potential response under conditions of low or non-substitutability is that it may be a mistake even to try to establish WTP values. This leads one in the direction of applying the famous economic adage to new territory: if a market format is an acceptable environmental valuation technique to CV respondents, then a market should already exist for the good or service in question! Carson (1998, 16) notes that '(i)n principle, it is possible to construct CV survey markets . . .', and Kahneman (1986) expresses confidence that a 'proper market' can be devised that will accurately reveal respondents' preferences. Hypothetical CV markets assume the same institutional arrangements that a real market requires. Markets are sets of institutions that emerge to aid society in the allocation of scarce resources. They provide a mechanism that helps to balance the costs and benefits of different goods. Among other requirements, commensurability is critical to efficient decision making. The same reasons, including incommensurability problems, that preclude a real market from forming in a specific resource-allocation scenario suggest that broad incompatibility may exist between the goals of society and the hypothetical institutional arrangements in the survey. These reasons could block a CV survey from achieving a level of realism necessary to evince reliable quantities, while also evoking protest responses. In a similar vein, Freeman (1986, 160) notes the importance of familiarity and experience with valuation exercises, and points out that CV 'is likely to work best for those kinds of problems where we need it least . . .'. Where respondents have had experience with tradeoffs involving levels of a particular environmental good and substitutions, there is likely to be an existing valuation record to which researchers can appeal. In terms of human health and safety, the US Congress may have implicitly taken a stand against the substitutability assumption. Statutes like the Clean Air Act, the Clean Water Act, and the Endangered Species Act are based on protecting the public's right to a clean environment or to species conservation. These statutes explicitly preclude balancing costs and benefits in setting health-based standards and requiring habitat protection (Kraft, 1996). Economists tend to think that Congress was naïve or misguided in passing these laws (for example, Burtraw and Portney, 1991). Yet one could argue that these laws are based on rights-based moral reasoning and are consistent with contractarian liberalism. That is, the state through legislation has extended its fiduciary or trustee duties to include air quality, water quality, and biological conservation. While economists have sought to balance costs and benefits with the implicit assumptions that the natural capital protected by legislation can be substituted for other capital of equal or greater value, and that correct valuation is possible, Congress has focused on the definition and protection of rights.

6.5 A home for the 'warm glow' effect

The recognition by economists of non-use values some 40 years ago triggered an extensive intellectual inquiry into how they could be identified and measured (Krutilla, 1967). The development of the CV method, and the controversies it has spawned, have brought about in recent years a fortuitous collision between economics in the Marshallian tradition and economists whose work emerges in part from the older 'political economy' as practiced by Adam Smith, John Stuart Mill, and others. Environmental economists, descending through Marshall from the utilitarians, continue to explore and refine the CV method. CV's role is to provide commensurate non-use values of nature for purposes of rendering policy recommendations based on cost–benefit analysis. But to fit their findings into a utilitarianism-based social ethic, they have had to sacrifice (choose not to count) incompatible forms of value. The highest-profile valuation 'problem' involves the pejoratively labeled 'warm-glow effect'. The expert NOAA panel considers the embedding effect to be 'perhaps the most important internal argument against the reliability of the CV approach' (1993, 4607). As described above, the embedding effect is characterized by the absence of a significant scaling up of WTP in response to a series of questions that scale up a proposed beneficial intervention. Critics of the CV method suggest that respondents are not actually consulting their preferences for the beneficial intervention, but rather are specifying an amount of money they are willing to pay that is consistent with a general spirit of public mindedness,[7] thus yielding to the investors a 'warm glow'. Critics emphasize the importance of purging this effect from CV studies.

The NOAA panel and Hanemann (1994) have already pointed out, among other critiques, that the questions asked in a leading empirical example of embedding had a scale difference that may have been ecologically trivial in the eyes of respondents. But assuming such an effect actually exists, one could also argue that respondents were consulting an internal preference map or center of value that is ideal regarding or based on commitment. In this case, respondents may have been identifying the public commitment they would make to solving a common problem. Their understanding of their role in a social process of environmental governance, including the extent to which others would share a financial burden, would play a role in determining their WTP (Schkade and Payne, 1994). Many of the issues related to protest votes summarized in Table 6.1 could arise.

From the broader perspective of establishing rules for a just and prosperous society, how could one's public-policy method of valuation possibly dismiss acts of altruism, duty, or moral obligation as double-counting errors? To edit out such motivations from the ledgers of social accounting presents an inescapable moral dilemma, one that must be faced by any policy process that emerges directly from utilitarianism. Ecological economists, working from rights-based perspectives enumerated by Kant and Locke, and consistent with contractarian liberalism, are engaged in developing alternative approaches to non-use valuation. These alternatives entail group-based approaches to valuation. Their scholarship describes philosophical foundations for group-based valuation, as well as what ground rules and procedures should be utilized. O'Hara (1996), for example, advocates implementing public-policy processes based on Habermas's (1979) concept of discursive ethics. O'Hara describes discursive ethics as supporting a 'communicative process in which discourse participants share their concerns, expecting mutual acceptance and respect for their positions' (p. 97). Both Keeney et al. (1990) and McDaniels and Roessler (1998) have proposed a 'public value forum' approach to clarifying public values with respect to multidimensional public-policy decisions. Prato (1999) describes community-based collaborative decision making, while Sagoff (1998) recommends using non-CV deliberative, discursive, jury-like approaches when dealing with public-goods issues. And Norgaard et al. (1999), O'Connor and Spash (1999), and O'Connor (2000) also advocate group-based alternatives, based on participants' prior commitment to discursive ethics.

Many new questions arise from this agenda (part of what makes the collision 'fortuitous'). While valuation processes based on discursive ethics appear fit to minimize or eliminate protest behaviors, what benefits of the current CV approaches are sacrificed? What other benefits arise? Will group-based valuation be viewed as a more or less legitimate public-policy process by participants, stakeholders, and authorities? For example, Clark et al. (2000) found in post-CV survey interviews and group discussions that 25 out of 31 CV respondents felt the environmental preservation of a wetland (the subject of the CV survey) should proceed regardless of their stated WTP, and none felt that asking for individual WTP was a satisfactory approach to making decisions on nature conservation.

Folding group-based processes of valuation into the existing utilitarianism-based framework of cost–benefit analysis poses challenges on both philosophical and practical levels. While group-based valuation can theoretically capture and quantify collective values in addition to individual values (Howarth and Wilson, in press), it may not be able to yield a single WTP figure when multiple 'centers of value' are consulted and category errors exist. Non-utilitarian or hybrid approaches to social science are emerging which may or may not satisfy society's current preference for science to provide discrete answers to public-policy problems. A richer economics, more accurate though perhaps less precise, may be emerging as scholars grapple with the philosophical, ecological, and other bases of the valuation challenge.

Notes

1. Jorgensen and Syme (2000) confirm a concentration of protest votes among lower-income individuals.
2. A protest in a CV survey differs from a voter's choice to stay home on election day since a person involved in a CV survey is essentially already at the polling booth.
3. See Brekke and Howarth (2002) for a critical discussion of this assumption that focuses on the endogeneity of preferences and the role of social status in motivating economic behaviour.
4. Other environmental valuation methods include the travel-cost method, hedonic pricing, property value studies, and valuations of risks to life.
5. Resilience refers to an ecosystem's ability to absorb or respond to shock and stress without fundamentally altering function or organization.
6. In this case, the lexicographic preference is a deliberate choice, not an adaptation to one's cognitive limits, as described above.
7. These economists appear to assume that public-mindedness does not scale up in proportion to the requirement for sacrifice. This characterization leaves little room for explaining why anyone would give 'their last full measure of devotion' to any public cause.

148   *Contingent valuation and economic theory*

References

Ajzen, I., T. Brown and L. Rosenthal (1996), 'Information bias in contingent valuation: effects of personal relevance, quality of information, and motivational orientation', *Journal of Environmental Economics and Management*, **30**, 43–57.

Bentham, J. (1789), *Introduction to the Principles of Morals and Legislation*, Buffalo, NY: Prometheus (1988).

Boyle, K. and J. Bergstrom (1999), 'Doubt, doubts, and doubters: the genesis of a new research agenda?', in I. Bateman and K. Willis (eds), *Valuing Environmental Preferences*, Oxford: Oxford University Press.

Brekke, K.A. and R.B, Howarth (2002), *Status, Growth and the Environment*, Cheltenham, UK and Northampton, MA: Edward Elgar.

Brown, P. (1998), 'Toward an economics of stewardship: the case of climate', *Ecological Economics*, **26**, 11–21.

Burtraw, D. and P. Portney (1991), 'Environmental policy in the United States', in D. Helm (ed.), *Environmental Policy Towards the Environment*, Oxford: Blackwell, pp. 289–320.

Carson, R. (1998), 'Valuation of tropical rainforests: philosophical and practical issues in the use of contingent valuation', *Ecological Economics*, **24**, 15–29.

Carson, R., N. Flores and R. Mitchell (1999), 'The theory and measurement of passive-use value', in I. Bateman and K. Willis (eds), *Valuing Environmental Preferences*, Oxford: Oxford University Press.

Clark, J., J. Burgess and C. Harrison (2000), 'I struggled with this money business: respondents' perspectives on contingent valuation', *Ecological Economics*, **33**(1), 45–62.

Costanza, R. and C. Folke (1997), 'Valuing ecosystem services with efficiency, fairness, and sustainability as goals', in G. Daily (ed.), *Nature's Services: Society's Dependence on Natural Ecosystems*, Washington, DC: Island Press.

Daily, G., P. Matson and P. Vitousek (1997), 'Ecosystem services supplied by soil', in G. Daily (ed.), *Nature's Services: Society's Dependence on Natural Ecosystems*, Washington, DC: Island Press.

Diamond, P. and J. Hausman (1994), 'Contingent valuation: is some number better than no number?', *Journal of Economic Perspectives*, **8**(4), 45–64.

Ehrlich, P. and H. Mooney (1983), 'Extinction, substitution, and the ecosystem services', *BioScience* , **33**, 248–54.

Freeman, R. (1986), 'On assessing the state of the arts of the contingent valuation method of valuing environmental changes', in R. Cummings, D. Brookshire, and W. Shulze (eds), *Valuing Environmental Goods: An Assessment of the Contingent Valuation Method*, Totawa, NJ: Rowman & Allan.

Habermas, J. (1979), *Communication and the Evolution of Society*, Boston: Beacon Press.

Hanemann, W.M. (1994), 'Valuing the environment through contingent valuation', *Journal of Economic Perspectives*, **8**(4), 19–43.

Hanemann W.M. and B. Kanninen (1999), 'The statistical analysis of discrete-response CV data', in I. Bateman and K. Willis (eds), *Valuing Environmental Preferences*, Oxford: Oxford University Press.

Heyde, J. (1995), 'Is contingent valuation worth the trouble?', *Chicago Law Review*, **62**, 331–62.

Howarth, R.B. and M.A. Wilson (in press), 'A theoretical approach to deliberative valuation: aggregation by mutual consent', Land Economics.

Jorgensen, B. and G. Syme (2000), 'Protest responses and willingness to pay: attitude toward paying for stormwater pollution abatement', *Ecological Economics*, **33**, 251–65.

Jorgensen, B., M. Wilson and T. Heberlein (2001), 'Fairness in the contingent valuation of environmental public goods: attitude toward paying for environmental improvements at two levels of scope', *Ecological Economics*, **36**, 133–48.

Kahneman, D. (1986), 'Comments' in R. Cummings, D. Brookshire and W. Schulze (eds), *Valuing Environmental Goods: An Assessment of the Contingent Valuation Method*, Totawa, NJ: Rowman & Littlefield.

Kahneman, D. and J. Knetsch (1992), 'Valuing public goods: the purchase of moral satisfaction', *Journal of Environmental Economics and Management*, **22**, 57–70.

Kant, I. (1785), *The Moral Law; Kant's Groundwork for the Metaphysic of Morals*, English translation by H.J. Paton, New York: Barnes & Nobel (1967).

Keeney, R., D. Von Winterfeldt and T. Eppel (1990), 'Eliciting public values for complex policy decisions', *Management Science*, **36**(9), 1011–30.

Kraft, M. (1996), *Environmental Policy and Politics*, New York: Harper-Collins.

Krutilla, J. (1967), *Conservation Reconsidered*, Washington, DC: Resources for the Future.

Locke, J. (1690), *The Second Treatise on Civil Government*, Buffalo, NY: Prometheus (1986).

Lockwood, M. (1998), 'Integrated value assessment using paired comparisons', *Ecological Economics*, **25**, 73–87.

Loomis, J. (1999), 'Contingent valuation methodology and the US institutional framework', in I. Bateman and K. Willis (eds), *Valuing Environmental Preferences*, Oxford: Oxford University Press.

McDaniels, T. and C. Roessler (1998), 'Multiattribute elicitation of wilderness preservation benefits: a constructive approach', *Ecological Economics*, **27**, 299–312.

Milgrom, P. (1993), 'Is sympathy an economic value? Philosophy, economics, and the contingent valuation method', in J. Hausman (ed.), *Contingent Valuation: A Critical Assessment*, New York: North-Holland.

Mill, J.S. (1863), *Utilitarianism*, Oxford: Oxford University Press (1998).

Mitchell, R. and R. Carson (1989), *Using Surveys to Value Public Goods: The Contingent Valuation Method*, Washington, DC: Resources for the Future.

National Oceanic and Atmospheric Administration (1993), 'Report of the NOAA Panel on contingent valuation', *Federal Register*, **58**(10), 4601–14.

Norgaard, R., A. Scholz and S. Trainor (1999), 'Values, valuation, and valuing processes', Presented at the Symposium on Valuation of Nature and the Environment in Honor of Roefie Hueting, Royal Netherlands Academy of Arts and Sciences, Amsterdam (April 23).

O'Connor, M. (ed.) (2000), 'Social processes of environmental valuation', Special Issue of *Environmental Economics*, **34**(2).

O'Connor, M. and C. Spash (1999), 'Valuation and the environment', in R. Constanza (ed.), *Advances in Ecological Economics*, Cheltenham: Edward Elgar.

O'Hara, S. (1996), 'Discursive ethics in ecosystems valuation and environmental policy', *Ecological Economics*, **16**, 95–107.

Prato, T. (1999), 'Multiple attribute decision analysis for ecosystem management', *Ecological Economics*, **30**, 207–22.

Randall, A. (1987), *Resource Economics*, 2nd edn, Columbus, Ohio: Grid Publishing.

Ready, R., J. Whitehead and G. Blomquist (1995), 'Contingent valuation when respondents are ambivalent', *Journal of Environmental Economics and Management*, **29**, 181–96.

Sagoff, M. (1988), *The Economy of the Earth*, New York: Cambridge University Press.

Sagoff, M. (1994), 'Should preferences count?', *Land Economics*, **70**(2), 127–44.

Sagoff, M. (1998), 'Aggregation and deliberation in valuing environmental public goods: A look beyond contingent pricing', *Ecological Economics*, **24**, 213–30.

Schkade, D. and J. Payne (1994), 'How people respond to contingent valuation questions: a verbal protocol analysis of willingness to pay for an environmental regulation', *Journal of Environmental Economics and Management*, **26**, 88–109.

Sen, A. (1970), *Collective Choice and Social Welfare*, San Francisco: Holden-Day.

Sen, A. (1977), 'Rational fools: a critique of the behavioural foundations of economic theory', *Philosophy and Public Affairs*, **6**(4), 317–44.

Sen, A. and B. Williams (1982), *Utilitarianism and Beyond*, New York: Cambridge University Press.

Spash, C. and N. Hanley (1995), 'Preferences, information, and biodiversity preservation', *Ecological Economics*, **12**, 191–208.

Stevens, T., J. Echeverria, R. Glass, T. Hager and T. Moore (1991), 'Measuring the existence value of wildlife: what do CVM estimates really show?', *Land Economics*, **67**, 390–400.

Turner, R. (1999), 'The place of economic values in environmental valuation', in I. Bateman and K. Willis (eds), *Valuing Environmental Preferences*, Oxford: Oxford University Press.

Vatn, A. and D. Bromley (1994), 'Choices without prices without apologies', *Journal of Environmental Economics and Management*, **26**, 129–48.

PART II

ECONOMETRIC AND EMPIRICAL ISSUES IN CONTINGENT VALUATION

PART II

ECONOMETRIC AND EMPIRICAL ISSUES IN CONTINGENT VALUATION

7 An introduction to choice modeling for non-market valuation
Steven Stewart and James R. Kahn

7.1 Introduction

Critical to the ongoing social assessment of environmental policy is a need for estimates of individuals' values for environmental (public) goods and services relative to private goods and services. We can easily observe individuals' valuation for private goods (homes, candy bars, dry cleaning, etc.) because these goods are exchanged in markets where goods have prices and the quantities traded can be observed. In general, a private good confers benefits only to the individual consuming it (or the individual's family, friends). In contrast, public goods confer benefits (or costs) to many members of society. Public goods and services such as national parks, ecosystem services, scenic views, and weather or climate forecasts are not generally traded in markets, thus it is difficult to determine how people value them. We believe that multi-attribute elicitation mechanisms such as choice modeling offer powerful tools to analyse the values that individuals place on public goods.

While society relies on markets to make many choices about resource allocation such as whether to use a forest for timber production or housing, purchase a new car or a used one, or pursue a career as an economist or schoolteacher, many important resource allocation decisions, such as those related to environmental assets, are not captured by market transactions. However, even environmental choices involve tradeoffs. Sometimes these tradeoffs can be easily measured in dollars such as the choice between leaving water instream for species protection at the cost of lost agricultural production, while other situations involve tradeoffs that are more difficult to reconcile such as cool water habitat required by non-native rainbow trout versus warm water episodic flows required by a native minnow population. Choice models allow the researcher to qualitatively and quantitatively assess these tradeoffs. Choice models are extremely useful for multidimensional changes where varying the level of the attributes of each of the alternatives allows measurement of the individual's willingness to substitute one attribute for another. Economic values may be estimated if one of the attributes is measured in economic terms (dollars, taxes, jobs, etc.).

Section 7.2 presents a summary of the evolution of choice models and a comparison with other stated preference models. Section 7.3 provides a brief overview of random utility, the framework on which choice models are based. Section 7.4 outlines survey development issues for choice models. Section 7.5 illustrates the use of choice model data and concludes.

7.2   Stated preference techniques

7.2.1   *Stated preference models*

One class of technique that economists use to elicit individuals' values for non-market goods is known as stated preference (SP) methods. SP methods, which typically require individuals to provide responses to hypothetical questions, include the contingent valuation method, conjoint analysis, and contingent behavior models. Stated preference techniques have performed favorably in tests of tests of criterion, construct, and convergent validity over the last two decades.

The contingent valuation method (CVM) is a survey-based approach used to estimate the value of a non-market asset based on how a subject responds to a question about his/her willingness to pay or accept compensation to obtain or forego a change in the quantity or quality of the asset. In CVM, individuals are simply asked how much they would be willing to pay, (either in dollars or as a yes/no response to a provided dollar amount) to obtain an increase in quality or quantity of a public good, or how much they would be willing to accept to face a decrease in the quantity or quality of the public good. The use of CVM is written into law as a tool to measure economic loss in environmental damage cases, the Exxon Valdez oil spill being the most famous. A thorough analysis of CVM is beyond the scope of this chapter, but several discussions are provided in this book, including a chapter on the history of use of CVM (Chapter 2, Smith) and a practitioners guide to CVM (Chapter 3, Whitehead). Other chapters of this book discuss the controversy associated with CVM, including controversy about sources of bias. As Casey indicates in Chapter 16, 'Choice Modeling' has the potential to resolve many of these problems.

Conjoint analysis (CJ) is the broad term for a suite of techniques that require individuals to make comparisons across bundles of goods. Four types of conjoint surveys can be constructed. The ranking format is the most cognitively burdensome task and asks the subject to rank alternative scenarios (1, 2, . . ., 7, etc.) each with different attributes and levels from most to least desirable. Closely related to ranking is the dichotomous choice (choose one, or simply 'choice') format, in which the subject is presented with two or more scenarios and is asked to choose the scenario that is most preferred.[1]

The most widely used format outside of economics is the rating format, which requires the subject to rate the different scenarios on a bounded integer scale (1, 2, . . .,10) from very desirable to undesirable. The ratings format is useful because it captures the intensity of the individual's preferences, which gives a measure of cardinality and allows respondents to be indifferent between scenarios. Ratings differ from rankings in that ranking occurs relative to the other scenarios and ratings are independent of the alternative scenarios (Matthews et al.,1998). A fourth format is the graded-pair comparison. Subjects are asked to consider two scenarios at a time and are asked to rate the intensity of their preference for one scenario over the other.

Which format is best has yet to be proven – there is considerable evidence supporting the validity of all of the formats and some studies have shown that similar results are obtained from all of the models.[2] Which format to use depends on the researcher's output requirements and the nature of the good being examined. Both rankings and binary choice provide ordinal information. An ordinal utility scale captures the respondent's preferences if she is asked to rank the bundles. If the individual is asked to consider the intensity of her preferences for the different bundles of goods and rate them, cardinal utility may be measured.[3] Ratings and graded-pair formats provide cardinal information. The binary choice format is almost identical to dichotomous choice contingent valuation (Adamowicz et al., 1994). Both rankings and binary choice responses are easily modeled in the random utility framework that is common in the non-market valuation literature.

Perhaps because of its similarity to CVM and its transparency to day-to-day choice tasks, such as choosing goods in market situations, the choice model format has been adopted most widely by economists. Choice experiments offer cognitive transparency and a more realistic decision framework. Individuals routinely answer the question (albeit revealed through purchase decision or choices that they make): 'Given the following products, each of which has several attributes, which do you most prefer?' Choice-based conjoint can be informationally identical to contingent valuation, which is widely used to measure the non-market value of natural resources. The choice format relies upon the presentation of a choice between one or more alternatives involving changes in one or more of the alternatives' attributes. In contrast to CVM, it relies less on the information contained in the description of the scenario and more on the description of the attributes of each alternative.

Choice models uncover individuals' preferences by asking them to choose among several feasible policy options where tradeoffs are involved. Choice models ask questions in a format that may be more familiar to individuals. Individuals are asked to make choices from bundles of goods according to the level of attributes contained in each bundle. For example, individuals routinely make choices among goods that have multiple attributes such as the choice among automobiles having different colors, engines, interiors, and so on. Similarly, individuals make this type of choice when making decisions that bundle both private and public goods, such as choosing a place to live. To reiterate, in contrast to CVM, conjoint analysis does not require individuals to directly place a value on an attribute; the value is revealed by a choice, with this choice task being more representative of the choices that individuals regularly face in making decisions. In traditional CJ applications, such as the analysis of transportation or shopping center choices, the development of a provision mechanism is relatively straightforward. However, with choice modeling, inadequate attention has been paid to provision mechanisms for choice models, however Taylor et al. (2004) are making progress on the topic. In the CVM literature, there has been much discussion of provision mechanisms, which could be adapted to CJ applications with appropriate modification.

Conjoint analysis in general and choice modeling in particular is receiving increasing attention in the economics literature as well as in policy circles, particularly because of the flexibility it provides. Its use has been legitimized by NOAA's proposed habitat equivalency ruling, which arose in part due to the criticisms that CVM was subjected to during the Exxon Valdez damage assessment case (60 FR 39816).[4] In particular, NOAA recommended conjoint analysis as a tool to measure in-kind compensation for damaged natural assets.

Choice models examine individuals' preferences by asking them to consider the tradeoffs they are willing to make. In contrast to contingent valuation, which asks individuals to explicitly state their willingness to pay (or answer a take-it-or-leave-it yes/no question about a given value) for a proposed change in environmental quality, preferences in a choice model are 'revealed' as the respondent is asked to consider a series of scenarios where he must choose his most preferred outcome from a series of possible outcomes (choice sets). This allows the researcher to obtain the tradeoffs that the individual is willing to make between attributes presented in the choice sets, as well as allow the estimation of welfare.

Within the survey, the consideration of substitutes is part of the selection process. The utility or satisfaction of an alternative received by a respondent is a function of the levels of each of the alternative's attributes. Because there are multiple alternatives from which the respondent can choose, she can use the levels to judge the relative merits of each alternative. Thus the role of substitute levels is explicitly recognized. In traditional contingent valuation, the role of substitutes is relegated to a reminder sentence or two in the description of the good.

7.3   Theory

7.3.1   Random utility

Choice modeling has its theoretical basis in the household production framework (Lancaster, 1966, 1971) and random utility modeling (Thurstone, 1927; McFadden, 1974; Ben-Akiva and Lerman, 1985).

Lancaster (1966) is generally acknowledged to have laid down the foundations of the household production framework upon which choice models are based. His work showed that an individual's utility arises from consumption of goods and services and can be decomposed based on observable characteristics of those elements combined with contributions from the individual's time.

Random utility models (RUM) allow the estimation of preferences under choice situations. RUM models assume that individuals make choices among bundles of goods having various characteristics. In a well-designed study, the investigator can account for the way in which these elements influence choice behavior, but she may not be able to observe or control for all of the inputs to a decision. In the RUM framework, utility is comprised of both deterministic components that are stated by the subject or revealed by his actions and random components that are unobservable by the investigator. There are likely to be many unobservable elements for each survey participant that affect decisions. If these influences can be assumed random, a RUM framework may be appropriate.

The output of a RUM model is an estimate of the probability that an individual will select a policy alternative based on the attributes that the alternative contains. If the utility of a policy is greater than that of competing policy alternatives, the individual will choose it. The RUM framework is directly estimable from choice models.

The ultimate goal of most stated preference studies is the estimation of welfare change. The measurement of welfare changes in RUM models is similar across dichotomous choice CVM, site choice travel cost, and choice models. Following Roe et al. (1996) and Stevens et al. (1997), the utility of a management program i is given by:

$$U^i(q^i, z), \tag{7.1}$$

where the utility of program i for the individual is a function of the attributes of i, q^i, while z represents individual characteristics. While utility is an interesting measure of preferences, it is not particularly valuable because it does not reflect the tradeoffs (financial or otherwise) individuals must make in order to consume a bundle of goods. Thus we typically consider the indirect utility function, which expresses utility as a function of income and prices:

$$v^i(p^i, q^i, m, z) + \varepsilon, \tag{7.2}$$

where P represents the price of policy i, m represents income, and z represents characteristics of the individual. Then the standard random utility model can be estimated from the discrete choice conjoint data using multinomial or conditional logit:

$$\Pr(i) = \Pr\{v^i(p^i, q^i, m, z) + \varepsilon > v^0(p^0, q^0, m, z) + \varepsilon\}. \tag{7.3}$$

The probability that the program having attributes i is chosen is the probability that the indirect utility of program i plus an unobservable random error is greater than the indirect utility of program 0 and its error term.

   To estimate the welfare impacts, i.e. willingness to pay, for a change from the status quo state of the world and the chosen state, one calculates:

$$v^i(p^i, q^i, m - CV, z) + \varepsilon = v^0(p^0, q^0, m, z) + \varepsilon \tag{7.4}$$

where compensating variation (CV) is the income adjustment necessary to leave the individual as well of with bundle i as she was with bundle 0.[5] Note that personal characteristics do not vary in this utility difference model. As such, they will drop out of the welfare calculation. See Section 5 for more detail on the inclusion of socio-economic information in random utility models.

7.4   Survey design
This section serves as an introduction to some of the key issues in survey design. In-depth coverage of general survey design issues can be found in Dillman (2000) and Deaton (1997). Survey design issues specific to choice modeling are covered in Louviere et al. (2000).

7.4.1   *Use of focus groups to define the good*
In non-market valuation, the policy question usually points to the good or set of goods to be valued. However more often than not, a disconnect exists between the public's perception and the scientific understanding of the good. This imprecise mapping between the scientific descriptions of the good and the way the good is understood by the public often leads to a definition of the good as a broad package, i.e. instream flow to protect riparian habitats rather than a specific species in a habitat and the use of qualitative attribute descriptions.[6]

It is important to recognize that environmental policy researchers and the general public are likely to perceive environmental systems differently. In choice modeling, the choice of attributes is extremely important for obtaining valid and defensible welfare measures. If important attributes are omitted from the analysis, or are measured in a way that is inconsistent with the way the attributes are perceived by users, the researcher loses control over the value elicitation process.

The use of focus groups comprised of individuals drawn from the study population allows the researcher to determine which of the system's attributes are relevant for the policy changes being considered. Unless the population of interest is comprised entirely of individuals with advanced university educations, it is unlikely that attributes defined solely by the research team will represent those that are important to the study population. The research team almost certainly has a broader knowledge of the system of interest, as well as more detailed understanding of what might be scientifically appropriate measures of changes in the system. On the other hand, the study population will often have on-the-ground knowledge of the environmental system and institutions that the distant researcher does not. For valuation to be accurate, it is important to measures changes in the system as they are perceived by the study population. Focus groups allow the researcher to identify exactly how the population perceives the system and identify individual attributes for valuation. Further, the focus group allows the researcher to hone in on changes in the levels of an attribute that are salient to the survey respondent.

Several focus groups may be needed for a successful survey design. The first focus group efforts will likely identify the broad issues of the system that are important and known to members of the population. The research team can use this information to develop sets of attributes that represent different ways of describing the important levels of the system. For example, suppose the broad policy issue is valuation of instream flow in a semi-arid river system. It would be a mistake for the researcher to go directly to a survey instrument that asks individuals to place a dollar value on a specific change in instream flow (i.e. 200 cubic feet per second (cfs)) for some period of time. The first focus group might indicate that what is important is the services that flow provides, not specific flow levels (i.e. riparian habitat or the abundance and composition of vegetation, birds, fish) is important. A second focus group might reveal more detail on which birds, fish, and vegetation are important and what are meaningful metrics of those attributes and changes in those attributes.

Later focus group efforts should have the goal of synthesizing the information on which attributes are important, how changes in the attributes should be measured, which changes in the levels of attributes are both meaningful from a policy perspective and salient to respondents, as well as means of financing policy changes. This is an appropriate time to explore payment vehicles and bid designs for the survey.

7.4.2   Some issues in experiment design

The focus group process should yield an understanding of how the attributes of the system in question are perceived by the study population. Given the selection of appropriate attributes and salient ranges of attribute levels, the choice experiment can be designed. Suppose that the attributes and their levels in Table 7.1 were identified as being important.[7] A full factorial design would present every feasible combination of these attribute levels to survey respondents. Two attributes have three levels, two have two levels, and one attribute (cost) has eight levels such that a full factorial design would require $192 = (3^2 \times 2^2 \times 8^1)$ combinations.[8] These 192 combinations represent a full factorial design. Full factorial design ensures that all attribute effects are orthogonal so the effects of all variables can be considered independent (Louviere et al., 2000). Each of these combinations can be thought of as a unique policy option.[9]

Because of the cognitive burden (and likely impossibility!) of having each subject evaluate 192 policy options, the choice experiment is often designed to be estimated from a subset of the feasible combinations. This is known as a partial factorial design. Most CM examples in the environmental valuation literature have considered fractional factorial designs. Fractional factorial designs rely on the assumption that some (and possibly all) interactions between attributes are zero. Louviere et al. (2000) suggest that 70–90 per cent of variance in choice data can be explained by main effects only, while two-way interactions account for an additional 5–15 per cent. Care must be taken in the design to ensure that important interaction effects are estimable. They further suggest that a reasonable design strategy is to consider all main and two-way interactions.

Statistical procedures in programs such as SAS allow one to generate a partial factorial design, given identification of the main and important

Table 7.1   Example focus group attributes

Attribute	Attribute levels
Fish habitat	Good, fair, poor
Bird habitat	Natives, non-natives
Riparian vegetation	Cottonwood-willow, salt cedar/tamarisk, barren
Streamflow	Ephemeral, perennial
Cost	$0, $5, $10, $25, $50, $100, $200, $400

interaction effects to be identified. The partial factorial design can often be estimated using 8, 12, or 16 combinations of policy options or 'choice sets'. The number of required choice sets is dependent on the number of attributes and levels of each attribute. The number of choice sets evaluated by subjects can further be reduced by blocking the partial factorial design into smaller numbers of choice sets, say six or eight.

The number of important experimental design issues is too broad to cover here. Three excellent references on experimental design are Street and Street (1987) for a general reference on experimental design, Louviere et al. (2000) for design issues specific to choice models, and Kuffeld (2004) for detail on using SAS to design choice experiments.

7.4.3   Effects coding

Effects coding for qualitative variables is frequently used with choice models. Table 7.2 illustrates simple dummy variable and effects coding for a qualitative variable taking on three levels. For example, consider a variable that measures streamflow. Flow condition is measured as low, medium, or high. In both the dummy and effects coded cases, two variables must be created to represent the three levels. The example variables are high flow and medium flow, while low flow is excluded.

The coefficient of the excluded variable in a dummy variable treatment is correlated with any information contained in the intercept term. The coefficient for the omitted variable under effects coding is the negative of the sum of the included variable coefficients. In contrast to dummy variable coding, the coefficient on the excluded effects coded variable is uncorrelated with the intercept coefficient and is directly comparable with the coefficients of the included variables.

7.4.4   Bid design

Choosing an optimal bid design for choice models is as much art as science, While an analysis of optimal bid design for choice models is beyond the

Table 7.2   *Example coding for High flow and Medium flow variables*

Condition	Effects variable coding		Dummy variable coding	
	High flow	Medium flow	High flow	Medium flow
High	+1	0	+1	0
Medium	0	+1	0	+1
Low	−1	−1	0	0

scope of this chapter, guidelines are generally the same as those for CVM. See Boyle (1990), Kanninen (1993), Cooper (1993), or Alberini (1995) for a variety of approaches. A key issue in the design is to ensure that most of the requested bids fall close to the median WTP of the distribution. Excessive bids in the tails of the distribution tend to lead to over or under-estimates of WTP (Hannemann and Kanninen, 1988).

7.4.5   The choice experiment

The essence of the choice experiment is to have individuals choose their most preferred policy option from a set of alternative policies. An example choice set is presented in Table 7.3. In this case the individual is asked to choose from three options, each having varying levels of the attributes: agriculture-free zone, mussel recovery, sportfish, agricultural income, and cost. Note that in the example presented, Option C represents the base case, or status quo option.[10] The status quo option is the outcome assuming no new policy is implemented.

The choice model, unlike contingent valuation, asks each individual to evaluate four to eight choice sets during the survey. Each new choice set contains different combinations of attribute levels – at least one level of one attribute must change for the choice set evaluation to be meaningful.[11]

7.4.6   The pilot survey

Once the appropriate 'good' has been determined by the focus groups and the feasible attributes, attribute levels, and choice sets have been determined

Table 7.3   Example choice set

	Option A	Option B	Option C No new action
Agriculture-free zone	10 yards Clinch/ 5 yards tributaries	10 yards Clinch/ 5 yards tributaries	none
Mussel recovery	full recovery	partial recovery	continued decline
Sportfish	no change	increase	no change
Songbirds	increase	increase	no change
Agricultural income	no change	no change	no change
Cost to household ($ per year)	$50	$25	no change

using the fundamentals of experiment design, the pilot survey can be tested. Too often, public policy research surveys are constructed and implemented in the field without adequate field testing (Dillman, 2000). The number of surveys in the pilot should be sufficient to run preliminary regressions. Fortunately the choice model generates several observations for each individual, so this can usually be done with as few as 20 completed surveys.

Using the pilot survey data, the researcher should ensure that the choice design generates enough variability in responses to estimate the econometric model. It can also be helpful to determine whether specific alternatives are always chosen or rejected. Possible reasons include a bid design that is faulty or the existence of dominated alternatives in the survey design.

The pilot survey represents the initial field survey and should be regarded as an experiment in design, not as a means of collecting data to answer a policy question. Since it is an experiment, one would expect the design to be modified before achieving a final form that communicates well with the survey participants. In some cases, if the research team knows the resource and the population well, the survey will go through the testing process without change and become the final survey instrument.

7.5   Model estimation and outputs

7.5.1   Case study

The following stylized example is borrowed from a study conducted by the authors of this chapter on the value of biodiversity in riparian areas in the Clinch River Valley, USA.

7.5.2   The data

Choice data look similar to those obtained in a site choice travel cost model. Each choice set that an individual responds to generates three rows of data, one for each of the policy options in the choice set. The information contained in each row includes a binary variable taking the value of zero or one to indicate whether that option was chosen, a variable for each attribute that indicates the level of the attribute contained in the policy option presented, and variables that reflect her socio-economic characteristics.[12]

To provide a more concrete example, consider the data in Table 7.4 generated by a female, college-educated store clerk who makes $18k/year who has just completed one choice set evaluation. Assume that she chooses Option A, a policy to restrict farming on a 10-yard wide zone on the banks of the Clinch River that is financed by a $5/year/household increase in property tax. In addition, Option A provides 'partial recovery' for aquatic species and an 'increase' in sportfish, songbirds, and wildlife.[13] Assume in this instance that agriculture income does not change because the tax

Table 7.4 Example choice data

1	2 Choice (0,1)	3 Aquatic life	4 Sportfish	5 Songbird	6 Wildlife	7 AgInc	8 Tax	9 Male (1/0)	10 Educ	11 Income
Option A	1	0	1	1	1	1	$5	0	5	$18000
Option B	0	1	1	1	1	0	$25	0	5	$18000
Status quo	0	-1	0	0	0	1	$0	0	5	$18000

payment provides compensation to farmers for foregone farming in the agriculture-free zone next to the river. Option B and Option C (the status quo) were available when she made her choice, thus they must be included in the analysis even though she did not select either of them.[14]

From inspection of the data generated in a single choice set, one can see the problem with including socio-economic data in the analysis. There is variance within the attribute variables (columns 2–8), but the socio-economic variables (columns 9–11) are identical for each of the observations.

7.5.3 Model estimation

The alternative-specific constants (ASC) in a discrete-choice model, much like the constant term in a traditional binary logit model, serve to incorporate any variation in the dependent variable that is not explained by the choice set attributes or respondent characteristics. If there are $N = 3$ policy options contained in the choice sets, $N-1$ ASCs will be included in the econometric model.

Using a conditional logit specification (McFadden, 1974) we regress the choice variable (*CHOICE*) on each of the attributes presented in the choice set as well as individual characteristics interacting with either ASCs or choice set attributes. The estimated specification is identified in equation (7.5). An example of the estimation output is provided in Table 7.5. In this case, the variable *CHOICE* is regressed on the choice set attributes

Table 7.5   Conditional logit results

Variable	Coeff	Std. Error	T-stat.	P-value
SMALLZONE	0.697	0.155	4.497	0.000
BIGZONE	0.306	0.158	1.936	0.053
PARTRECOVERY	0.084	0.148	0.564	0.573
FULLRECOVERY	0.831	0.150	5.541	0.000
SPORTDECLINE	−0.727	0.179	−4.054	0.000
SPORTINCREASE	0.593	0.127	4.679	0.000
SONGINC	0.079	0.120	0.657	0.511
AGDEC	−0.157	0.069	−2.271	0.023
COST	−0.033	0.004	−8.654	0.000
ASC1	−0.771	1.288	−0.599	0.549
ASC1×EDU	0.010	0.088	0.119	0.905
O1×AGE	−0.013	0.008	−1.508	0.132
ASC1×MALE	−0.624	0.266	−2.345	0.019
O1×MOST	0.790	0.264	2.993	0.003
O1×FISH	0.256	0.250	1.024	0.306
O1×ENV	0.492	0.308	1.597	0.110

MUSSELRECOVERY, SPORTFISH, SONGBIRDS, AGINCOME, and *COST* as well as a set of alternative specific constants, *ASC*1 and *ASC*2 and interactions between the ASCs and the individual characteristics *MALE* and *EDUCATION*.

$$
\begin{aligned}
Choice = \; & ASC1 + ASC2 + \beta_1 PARTRECOVERY \\
& + \beta_2 FULLRECOVERYt + \beta_3 SPORTDECLINE \\
& + \beta_4 SPORTINCREASE + \beta_5 BIRDINCginc \\
& + \beta_6 AGDECLINE + \beta_7 COST + \beta_8 ASC1*EDUC \\
& + \beta_9 ASC2*MALE + \varepsilon
\end{aligned} \tag{7.5}
$$

The coefficients for the conditional logit model are interpreted in a manner similar to the standard multinomial logit. A positive and significant coefficient on a continuous variable indicates that individuals are more likely to choose scenarios having higher levels of the attribute. For example, the negative coefficient on *COST* indicates that individuals are less likely to choose policies having higher costs. For dummy and effects coded variables, a positive sign indicates a higher probability of choosing policies having the attribute in question. See Louviere et al. (2000) for an exposition on the use of effects coded variables.

The effects coded attribute *SPORTFISH*, which takes on the levels no change, increase, and decrease, is represented by two effects coded variables in the regression. *SPORTDECLINE*, which represents policies where sportfish decrease, and *SPORTINCREASE*, which represents policies having increased sportfish, are included in the regression, while the level no change is omitted. The negative and significant coefficient on *SPORTDE-CLINE* suggests that individuals are less likely to choose policies where sportfish are declining, while *SPORTINCREASE*, which is positive and significant, implies that policies having increased sportfish populations are more likely to be chosen.

Had the negative coefficients on *ASC*1 and *ASC*2 been significant, it would imply that individuals were less likely to choose options 1 and 2 in the choice set over the status quo alternative. The implication of a significant ASC has an interesting meaning; it implies that individuals tend to choose (or avoid choosing) alternatives for some systematic reason that is not accounted for by the choice set attributes. The authors have found negative and significant ASCs in many different policy studies, including the value of biodiversity, reservoir management, and view shed analyses, suggesting a strong bias towards the status quo.

The socio-economic variables, which do not vary across choices for an individual, must be interacted with either the ASCs or choice set attributes if they are to be incorporated in the econometric analysis. As such, they can be difficult to interpret. In the example regression, the socio-economic variables *MALE* and *EDUC* were interacted with the ASCs. The interaction terms for $ASC1 \times MALE$ and $ASC2 \times MALE$ are negative and significant, indicating that males were less likely to choose options 1 and 2 in the choice sets presented. The interaction terms for $ASC1$ and $ASC2$ and *EDUC* are not significant. One can see that such interactions may not be very useful unless the theoretical model provides clear guidance on the relationship.[15] Given a theoretical justification for the relationship, interactions between the socio-economic variable and a choice set attribute may be preferred, given the difficulty in interpretation of interactions with the ASCs.

The goodness of fit of conditional logit choice models is generally testable using tests suitable for standard logit and probit CVM models of willingness to pay. Programs such as LIMDEP, Stata, and SAS have discrete choice routines that can be used to implement the model without significant programming on the part of the user. These models will provide the McFadden ratio test and other criteria for model selection, such as Akaike's information criterion.

7.6 Using model results

7.6.1 Measures of welfare

The most common use of choice models in environmental applications is to generate estimates of the change in economic welfare due to changes in a policy that affect attributes of the system. From an economist's perspective, the value of a policy change such as a program to increase water quality is the change in the economic welfare of those affected by the quality change. The various versions of this value measure are appropriate given different specifications of property rights to the change in question, and whether the individual can readjust consumption bundles after the change. All versions of the measure calculate an individual's willingness to pay or willingness to accept to move between different indifference curves, i.e. the tradeoff she is willing to make to move from her initial level of utility to the level of utility implied by the change in water quality (or any environmental change).

The conditional logit results can be used to obtain economic surplus measures following standard techniques outlined in Hanneman (1984), Cameron (1988) and Louviere et al. (2000). The choice model indirect utility functions can be inverted to specify a willingness to pay function that measures welfare or the willingness to pay function can be estimated directly from the survey data.

The econometric specification of welfare change is:

$$WTP = -\frac{1}{\beta_{Cost}}(utility\ of\ new\ policy - status\ quo\ utility) \qquad (7.6)$$

or more formally:

$$WTP(Choice) = -[(\alpha + \beta_1 Cost + \beta_2 Attributes^1 + \beta_3 Socioecon^* + \varepsilon)_{newlevel}$$
$$- (\alpha + \beta_1 Cost + \beta_2 Attributes^0$$
$$+ \beta_3 Socioecon^* + \varepsilon)_{statusquolevel}]/\beta_{Cost} \qquad (7.7)$$

where *Socioecon* represents socio-economic characteristics interacted with choice attributes or ASCs, and the superscripts *, 1, and 0 represent mean value, with policy, and without policy.[16]

In contrast to CVM, which is constructed by design to estimate welfare for a single policy change, choice models allow the researcher to calculate welfare for a change in the level of any attribute or combination of attributes. Further, there is no limit to the number of policies that can be considered as long as the attributes of each policy fall within the range of levels of attributes considered in the choice sets.

Using the results of the regressions reported in Table 7.5 and equation (7.6) above, the compensating variation for a change from the status quo to a policy that provides partial recovery for aquatic life is $27.72, i.e. the average respondent would be willing to pay $27.72 to move from the status quo to the state of the world having partial recovery for aquatic life. For a program that leads to full recovery, the average individual would be willing to pay $38.15. We can calculate welfare changes for policy changes affecting other attributes as well; the representative individual would have to be compensated $80.15 to move from the status quo to a scenario with decreased sportfish.

7.6.2   Calculation of implicit prices

The implicit price (part-worth) is the negative of the ratio of any two of the attributes and provides the measure of tradeoffs that individuals in the sample would be willing to make between attributes that is implied by the data. Further, that tradeoff is made while holding utility constant. The implicit price, then, is the marginal rate of substitution between the two attributes, or the slope of an indifference curve.

We can take the estimated coefficients from the conditional logit regression (Table 7.5), which is used to estimate the choice model, and use them to calculate implicit prices, or part-worths, for each attribute with respect to all of the other attributes in the model.

Perhaps the most intuitive tradeoffs to illustrate are the tradeoffs between dollars and other attributes. In theory, the calculation can be made in terms of any one attribute for another. For example the implicit price of moving from the status quo level of aquatic life (continued decline) to partial recovery is:

$$implicit\ price = -\left(\frac{\beta_{PRECOV}}{\beta_{COST}}\right)$$

$$implicit\ price = -\left(\frac{0.084}{-0.033}\right)$$

$$implicit\ price = \$2.54 \tag{7.8}$$

which can be interpreted as indicating that the average respondent would give up \$2.54 to move from the status quo level of aquatic life to partial recovery of aquatic life. The implicit price of an increase from the status quo level of sportfish (no change) to an increase (*SPRTINC*) is given by:

$$implicit\ price = -\left(\frac{\beta_{SPRTINC}}{\beta_{COST}}\right)$$

$$implicit\ price = -\left(\frac{0.593}{-0.033}\right)$$

$$implicit\ price = \$17.97.$$

Other potentially useful tradeoffs can be considered as well. Typically, natural resource policies lead to different mixes of socially desirable attributes. We can look at the tradeoffs between attributes other than dollars that are acceptable to individuals in the sample as well. For example, the amount of aquatic life (non-game species) that individuals are willing to sacrifice to increase sportfish populations is given by:

$$implicit\ price\ of\ sportfish\ in\ terms\ of\ aquatic\ life = -\left(\frac{\beta_{SPRTINC}}{\beta_{AQUATICLIFE}}\right)$$

$$implicit\ price = -7.05$$

Individuals would be willing to trade 7.05 units of aquatic life (species other than sportfish) for one unit of sportfish. For such measures to be useful, the units of measure must be meaningful. In this example, the sign of the implicit price has meaning, i.e. individuals generally prefer sportfish to non-sportfish, but the magnitude does not.

Implicit prices are useful to gain insight about the importance of attributes to individuals, but they do not take into account the change in well

Table 7.6   Example choice model format: weather forecasts

Forecast attribute	Forecast 1	Forecast 2	Forecast 3
Lead time	10 days	4 days	2 days
Precipitation skill	90 per cent	80 per cent	50 per cent
Temperature skill	90 per cent	10 per cent	98 per cent
Spatial resolution	20km	5km	40km
Cost	$100	$100	$0

being, or welfare that would likely come from an increase or decrease in the level of an attribute. This is not a fault of implicit prices and the MRS concept, but merely a different way to think about tradeoffs.

7.6.3   Probability of choice
Choice models can be informative even when they are not used to obtain measures of value. Suppose, for example, that an agency is interested in determining preferences for alternative weather forecast formats for the purpose of targeting research expenditures. For example, suppose that forecasts have the attributes temperature skill, precipitation skill, lead time, and spatial resolution.[17] An extremely stylized example choice set is given in Table 7.6.

By requiring the choice of one of the presented forecasts, the CM format forces the individual to confront tradeoffs between forecast attributes. Presenting multiple sets of forecasts and observing an individual's choices allows the researcher to infer tradeoffs between forecast attributes that she is willing to accept.

Such analyses might inform the researcher that some users, say emergency managers, place more importance on skill in predicting precipitation than on other attributes, while other stakeholders such as farmers, may be interested in increases in spatial resolution so that they can have forecasts that better represent their particular plots of land. Additionally, the choice model format will allow the prediction of the ideal, or utility maximizing forecast, from those presented. Assuming that the agency has a way of determining whose needs matter most, the choice model gives a clear signal on where future research dollars should be spent.

7.7   Answering environmental policy questions with conjoint analysis
The discussion in this chapter has focused on the properties of conjoint analysis as an effective method for valuing changes in the level of environmental quality or other public goods. While the ability to efficiently estimate both direct and indirect-use values is an important advantage of

conjoint analysis in comparison to other valuation methods, there exist other important reasons why conjoint analysis should be used to inform environmental decision making.

One important advantage that arises is when people are concerned not only about ultimate outcomes, but about the process by which outcomes are generated. In other words, the characteristics of the policy that arrives at the outcome may be important as well as the level of environmental quality that is generated by the policy. Such characteristics might include the sharing of the burden of the costs of environmental improvement, payment mechanisms, community participation in the process, and impacts on the rest of the community (in addition to impacts on the individual). These characteristics can be incorporated as attributes in developing choice sets which survey respondents are then asked to evaluate. Stewart et al. (2005) establish this type of approach in their analysis of the value of preserving aquatic diversity in the Clinch River (South-west Virginia and East Tennessee). In developing their choice sets, Stewart et al. not only consider individual costs associated with environmental improvement, but also examine impacts on regional economic well-being. In addition, since area farmers could wind up paying a disproportionate share of the costs (as land in proximity of the rivers is taken out of production and cattle are fenced away from rivers), the degree of compensation farmers might receive or losses they might bear is a characteristic of alternative choice sets.

Sometimes, the policy or process is even more important than the outcome. For example, in the case of remediating a toxic waste site, there are many options for reducing the exposure of community residents. The waste can be isolated in situ, homes can be moved away from the vicinity of the site, or the waste could be removed through a variety of physical processes. Not only would each possible remediation plan have an impact on both costs and exposure, but each remediation plan could have different implications for future use of the land. In this case, all of these variables could be incorporated as characteristics of the choice set, with a variety of means of analysing the data. All three types of conjoint analysis (choice-based, ratings-based, and rankings-based) could be applied in this case. In this type of situation, ranking- or ratings-based conjoint analysis could potentially yield less ambiguous information than choice-based conjoint analysis or more traditional valuation methods. Swallow, Opaluch, and Weaver (1992) provide a good example of this type of analysis applied to the siting of noxious facilities.

A final example of the importance of conjoint analysis to policy decisions is in examining environmental decision making in the subsistence sector of developing countries. Many of the tools of environmental valuation are simply ineffective in these circumstances. For example, hedonic pricing techniques only are good estimation techniques if the assumption of perfect mobility holds. This is generally not true in developing countries in general, and particularly unlikely to be true in the subsistence sector of these societies. Similarly, for people who have very limited participation in the market economy, the type of willingness to pay question that is typically asked in contingent valuation is unlikely to be meaningful to the survey participants. Although some contingent valuation surveys have experimented with the use of time as the measure of willingness to pay (e.g. how much further would you be willing to walk to a source of clean drinking water), time has severe limitations as such a valuation metric. Time has an ultimate constraint of 24 hours to the day. If a survey respondent says that they are not willing to expend additional time, all that is known is that the value of the activity in the survey (time expenditure for clean water) is less than the value of the activity that would be sacrificed.

In a study of riberinho communities on the Rio Solimões, Casey et al. (2005) examine their willingness to be compensated to accept risk of environmental damage from the transportation of natural gas and petroleum. As part of choice sets developed in this study, these tradeoffs are examined through compensation with supply of varying amounts of diesel fuel and gasoline (for electric generators and boat motors), better access to health care, and better access to education. The study shows that these types of tradeoffs are meaningful to the people of the community, and can be used to inform a broad set of policy questions.

7.8 Conclusions

The last 50 years has seen the development of a very useful set of tools for measuring the value of environmental resources and changes in the level of environmental quality. Market approaches, revealed preference approaches (such as travel cost and hedonic pricing), and contingent valuation have made important contributions to informing environmental policy. In the last two decades, the conjoint analysis approach has seen considerable development and it has great potential as a valuation tool. Several important advantages can be articulated concerning the potential of conjoint analysis.

First, and most importantly, the nature of the choice sets that are employed in conjoint analysis generate the potential to significantly reduce some of the biases associated with contingent valuation. In particular, part–whole, embedding, sequential, and hypothetical biases are likely to be less of a problem with conjoint analysis than with contingent valuation.

Second, in addition to providing less-biased information, conjoint analysis can supply more comprehensive information to the decision-making process. The multidimensional nature of the choice sets allows for the evaluation of more complex environmental outcomes than traditional valuation methods. Not only can a set of complex outcomes be integrated into the choice sets, but characteristics of the policies used to derive these outcomes can be a part of the choice sets.

An important component of this informational advantage can be found when evaluating environmental change in developing countries. Conjoint analysis promises to be a better tool for evaluating environmental change in developing countries, particularly in the subsistence sector.

Notes

1. Making choices across bundles of goods requires effort. Individuals may first limit their choice sets by separating bundles by segregating them into 'good' and 'bad' bundles. The bad bundles receive no more attention. If only one bundle is in the good category, the individual's task is complete. If there are more than one in the 'good' category, additional effort is needed. Arguably, many consumer decision processes end here. From the good bundle, the consumer may choose one and stop his choice process. This choice or 'choose one' may mimic actual choice behavior the best, but provides the least amount of information about preferences.
2. Ben-Akiva et al. (1991) and Feather (1973) address the cognitive burden that goes with trying to differentiate between bundles of goods. Ben-Akiva found that the reliability of rankings data decreases as the scenario decreases in rank. Feather was able to illustrate that the ease of selecting ratings may reduce subjects' willingness to make detailed distinctions about the desired attributes. In a survey of parental values for children, Alwin and Krosnick (1985), Krosnick and Alwin (1988), find that ratings and rankings lead to similar aggregate measures of preferences, and there is a high correlation for the two measures for most subjects. Kalish and Nelson (1991) compare conjoint results using ratings and rankings and find little to choose between the two. The performance of the models was undifferentiated especially when trying to predict choice behavior. Elrod, Louviere, and Davey (1992) found that ratings and ratings worked equally well at predicting choice. The work of Roe et al. (1996) takes advantage of the fact that the recovery of rankings and binary choice information from ratings data are possible if one assumes that preferences are transitive. Given this the ratings format may be the most flexible of the formats to use.
3. There is considerable debate in the profession about whether cardinal utility is even measurable. The marketing research literature and the more recent literature of conjoint analysis in non-market valuation have largely been able to show that preferences recovered from ratings (cardinal utility) and rankings (ordinal utility) are similar.
4. Habitat equivalency proponents argue that the appropriate measure of damage to a natural resource, such as a wetland, is provision (or augmentation) of ecological services that substitute for the ones lost, e.g, improvement of wetlands in other areas.
5. All of the compensating, equivalent, variation, and surplus measures can be similarly calculated to correspond to the proper property right and gain/loss scenario.
6. From an ecologist's viewpoint, this may be preferred. And, given the inability for a species to live outside its native ecosystem, it may only make economic sense to value at the level that limiting factors, such as a safe minimum standard or ecosystem viability, no longer pose constraints.
7. The qualitative labels good, fair, and poor are often how scientific measures of habitat are perceived by the public. The public may not care that a certain water temperature and turbidity lead to habitat that is conducive to viable fish populations, they often just want to know whether fish populations are viable. Inclusion of natural scientists in the focus group process can help establish a link between quantitative indicators of change in the system and qualitative descriptions that the public understands.
8. The calculation is the product of levels raised to the attributes power.
9. The marketing research literature uses the term 'profile'.

10. In cases where a no choice or status quo alternative is to be included, it is not necessary to explicitly present the status quo attribute levels as in the example.
11. An exception to this is when the researcher desires to perform a consistency check by presenting the same choice set to test for consistent behavior across the choice experiment.
12. As in site choice travel cost models, the inclusion of socio-economic characteristics is somewhat contentious.
13. Clearly the value and interpretation of changes in management programs is a function of the measure of the units of these attributes. Attributes can be measured as a discontinuous change in outcome ('recovery or no recovery'), changes in a physical measure (1000 mussels per river mile) or percentage change (20 per cent recovery) among others. The key is that the metric used is understood by the participant and meaningfully represents changes that could occur.
14. Given the binary nature of the choice variable, one might attempt to analyse the data using a standard logit model. The model will likely converge, but the output is meaningless. Each yes/no response is a take it or leave it response given the availability of alternative options. If only the yes responses are included in the analysis, all information about other available scenarios is lost. It is almost certain that IIA is violated in this case.
15. In these data, we can possibly rationalize including the observed empirical relationship between the ASCs and the socio-economic variable MALE; males are often accused of resisting change from the status quo, which appears to be the case in this data set.
16. The socio-economic variables are traditionally entered at their mean levels, but can be set at the level that the researcher is interested in.
17. Skill is a measure of the accuracy of forecasts. Lead time is the interval between the forecast and the forecasted event. Spatial resolution is the spatial scale at which distinction can be made between forecast events.

References

Adamowicz, W., J. Louviere and M. Williams (1994), 'Combining revealed and stated preference methods for valuing environmental amenities', *Journal of Environmental Economics and Management*, **26**, 271–92.

Adamowicz, W., J. Swait, P. Boxall, J. Louviere and M. Williams (1997), 'Perceptions versus objective measures of environmental quality in combined revealed and stated preference models of environmental valuation', *Journal of Environmental Economics and Management*, **32**(1), 65–84.

Alberini, A. (1995), 'Optimal designs for discrete choice contingent valuation surveys: single-bound, double-bound, and bivariate models', *Journal of Environmental Economics and Management*, **28**, 287–306.

Alwin, Duane F. and Jon A. Krosnick (1985), 'The measurement of values in surveys: a comparison of ratings and rankings', *Public Opinion Quarterly*, **49**, 535–52.

Ben-Akiva, M. and S.R. Lerman (1985), *Discrete Choice Analysis: Theory and Application to Travel Demand*, Boston, MA: MIT Press.

Ben-Akiva, Moshe, Takayuki Morikawa and Fumiaki Shiroishi (1991), 'Analysis of the reliability of preference ranking data', *Journal of Business Research*, **24**, 149–64.

Bjornstad, David J. and James R. Kahn (1996), *The Contingent Valuation of Environmental Resources: Methodological Issues and Research Needs*, Cheltenham: Edward Elgar.

Bockstael, Nancy and Kenneth McConnell (2002), 'The behavioral basis of non-market valuation', in Joseph Herriges and Catherine Kling (eds), *Valuing Recreation and the Environment*, Cheltenham: Edward Elgar.

Boyle, K. (1990), 'Dichotomous choice contingent valuation questions: functional form is important', *Northeastern Journal of Agricultural and Resource Economics*, **19**, 125–31.

Boxall, Peter C., Wiktor L. Adamowicz, Joffre Swait, Michael Williams and Jordan Louviere (1996), 'A comparison of stated preference methods for environmental valuation', *Ecological Economics*, **18**, 243–53.

Cameron, T. (1988), 'A new paradigm for valuing non-market goods using referendum data: maximum likelihood estimation by censored logistic regression', *Journal of Environmental Economics and Management*, **15**(3), 355–79.

Casey, James, James R. Kahn and Alexandre Rivas (2005) (unpublished), 'Is environmental preservation a luxury good? Evidence from the Ribeirinho Communities of Amazonas', Brazil.

Cooper, J.C. (1993), 'Optimal bid selection for dichotomous contingent valuation surveys', *Journal of Environmental Economics and Management*, **24**, 25–40.

Deaton, Angus (1997), *The Analysis of Household Surveys*, Johns Hopkins for the World Bank.

Dillman, Don A. (2000), *Mail and Internet Surveys: The Tailored Design Method*, New York: Wiley.

Elrod, Terry, Jordan J. Louviere and Krishnakumar S. Davey (1992), 'An empirical comparison of ratings-based and choice-based conjoint models', *Journal of Marketing Research*, **29** (August), 368–77.

Feather, N.T. (1973), 'The measurement of values', *Journal of Psychology*, **5**, 221–31.

Freeman, A. Myrick (1993), *The Measurement of Environmental and Resource Values*, Washington, DC: Resources for the Future.

Hannemann M. and B.J. Kanninen (1998), 'The statistical analysis of discrete response contingent valuation data', in I.J. Bateman and K.G. Willis (eds), *Contingent Valuation of Environmental Practices: Assessing Theory and Practice in the USA, Europe, and Developing Countries*, Oxford: Oxford University Press.

Huber, Joel (1987), 'Conjoint analysis: how we got here and where we are', in Sawtooth Software Conference Proceedings.

Johnson, F.R., D.J. MacNair and E.E. Fries (1997), 'Ill-considered values: contingent valuation in light of evidence from multiple-response stated-preference surveys', in Britt-Marie Drottz Sjöberg (ed.), *Proceedings of the 1997 Annual Meeting of the Society for Risk-Analysis*, Stockholm: Society for Risk Analysis.

Kalish, Shlomo and Paul Nelson (1991), 'A comparison of rating, ranking and reservation price measurement in conjoint analysis', *Marketing Letters*, **2**(4), 327–35.

Kanninen, B.J. (1993), 'Design of sequential experiments for contingent valuation studies', *Journal of Environmental Economics and Management*, **25**, S-1–S-11.

Krosnick, Jon A. and Duane F. Alwin (1988), 'A test of the form-resistant correlation hypothesis', *Public Opinion Quarterly*, **52**, 526–38.

Kuffeld, Warren F. (2004), 'Marketing research methods in SAS: experimental design, choice, conjoint, and graphical techniques', available on the web at: http://support.sas.com/techsup/technote/ts694.pdf.

Lancaster, Kelvin J. (1966), 'A new approach to consumer theory', *Journal of Political Economy*, **74**, 132–56.

Lancaster, K. (1971), *Consumer Demand: A New Approach*, New York: Columbia University Press.

Loomis, J. and M. Haefele (2001), 'Improving statistical efficiency and testing robustness of conjoint marginal valuations', *American Journal of Agricultural Economics*, **83**(5), 1321–7.

Louviere, J., D. Henscher and J. Swait (2000), *Stated Choice Methods-Analysis and Application*, Cambridge: Cambridge University Press.

Louviere, J., M. Fox and W. Moore (1993), 'Cross-task validity comparisons of stated preference choice models', *Marketing Letters*, **4**(3), 205–13.

Louviere, J. and Gary J. Gaeth (1988), 'A comparison of rating and choice responses in conjoint tasks', *Proceedings of the Sawtooth Software Conference on Perceptual Mapping, Conjoint Analysis and Computer Interviewing*, 59–73.

Mackenzie, John (1993), 'A comparison of contingent preference models', *American Journal of Agricultural Economics*, **75** (August), 593–603.

McFadden, Daniel (1974), 'Conditional logit analysis of qualitative choice behavior', in P. Zarembka (ed.), *Frontiers in Econometrics*, New York: Academic Press, pp. 105–42.

Matthews, Kristy, F. Reed Johnson, Richard W. Dunford and William Desvousges (1998), 'The potential role of conjoint analysis in natural resource damage assessments', Triangle Economic Research working paper.

Morrison, Mark (2002), 'Choice modeling and tests of benefit transfer', *American Journal of Agricultural Economics*, **84**(1), 161–70.

Roe, Brian, Kevin J. Boyle and Mario F. Teisl (1996), 'Using conjoint analysis to derive estimates of compensating variation', *Journal of Environmental Economics and Management*, **31**(2), 145–159.

Stevens, T.H., Christopher Barret and Cleve Willis (1997), 'Conjoint analysis of groundwater protection programs', *Agriculture and Resource Economics Review*, October, 229–36.

Stevens, T.H., R. Belkner, D. Dennis, D. Kittredge and C. Willis (2000), 'Comparison of contingent valuation and conjoint analysis for ecosystem management', *Ecological Economics*, **32**(1), 63–74.

Stewart, Steven, James R. Kahn, Amy Wolf, Robert V. O'Neill, Victor B. Serviss, Randall Bruins and Matthew Heberling (2005), 'Valuing biodiversity in a rural valley: Clinch and Powell River Watershed', in R. Bruins and M. Heberling, *Economics and Ecological Risk Assessment: Applications to Watershed Management*, New York: CRC Press, pp. 253–90.

Swallow, Stephen K., James J. Opaluch and Thomas F. Weaver (1992), 'Siting noxious facilities: an approach that integrates technical, economic, and political considerations', *Land Economics*, **68**(3), 283–301.

Taylor, Laura, Kevin Boyle and Mark Morrison (2004), unpublished manuscript, Georgia State University.

Thurstone, Louis (1927), 'A law of comparative judgment', *Psychological Review*, **34**, 273–86.

8 Experimental methods for the testing and design of contingent valuation
*Laura O. Taylor**

8.1 Introduction

Experimental methods have increasingly become part of the economists's tool-bag, and those concerned with the elicitation of values for non-priced environmental goods are no exception. In this chapter, the ways in which experimental economics may be used to enhance our understanding of the contingent valuation method and to hopefully improve our ability to estimate values for non-priced goods are explored. Particular attention will be paid to the strengths and weaknesses of early experimental work designed to validate and improve the contingent valuation (CV) method. The interested reader should also see List and Gallet (2001), Shogren (2004), and Harrison and List (2005). Experiments are a natural tool for exploring such issues because they are a means by which an individual's economic choices may be observed, while controlling the rules, information, and institutions in which those choices are made – much as CV exercises are designed to do.

As experimental methods have been applied more frequently to non-market valuation problems, the distinction between classical laboratory experiments, field experiments, and 'choice experiments' as CV surveys are sometimes termed, is becoming increasingly blurred. In the next section of this chapter, induced-value and value-elicitation experiments are reviewed and the essential features of these experiments are contrasted to the CV method. Sections 8.3 and 8.4 focus on early experimental work designed to assess the validity of CV and to improve the conduct of CV by reducing any biases thought to be present.[1] Concluding comments are provided in Section 8.5.

8.2 The experimental method

At its heart, an experiment simply consists of a set of rules by which a participant (or participants) must abide by choices which will have actual monetary (utility) consequences. These decisions may occur in a simulated market, a strategic game, or simply as an individual choice in which the actions of other participants are irrelevant (such as in the decision to accept a lottery). Regardless of the complexity, or simplicity of an experiment, the essential element is that actual monetary transactions take place. It is this element that distinguishes an experiment from a CV exercise. Terminology such as 'choice experiments' has been applied to CV, referring to exercises in which a hypothetical survey instrument is altered in a systematic manner to determine the effects of these changes on stated valuation responses.[2] For the purposes of clarity, in this chapter, the use of the term 'experiment' will mean to apply to any exercise in which subjects make decisions involving actual monetary exchanges. Beyond this simple definition, an experiment may take any form and may be conducted in a centralized manner in which all subjects are together in a room such as a computer laboratory, a classroom, or a meeting hall. Experiments may also be decentralized, taking place through the mail, the internet, or over the phone. Regardless of the way in which the subjects are organized, it is the possibility of real monetary payments (either to them or by them) that satisfy the condition for an experiment.

First, consider the components of a classical laboratory experiment in economics. At its most basic level, a typical laboratory experiment can be thought of as consisting of two primary components: the design of an institution in which trades or economic interactions take place, and the establishment of the experimenter's control of subject preferences within this institution.[3] The design of an institution involves the explicit description of all aspects of an experiment that may substantially affect an agent's behavior – such things as property rights, rules governing exchange and payoffs (positive and negative), and information. For example, consider a simple second-price, sealed-bid auction. The rules governing exchange in this example would be as follows. Each participant submits a sealed bid to a central authority (the experimenter), who then arrays the bids from highest to lowest; the bidder with the highest bid wins the auction (is allowed to purchase the good), but he/she pays the price submitted by the bidder with the second-highest bid price. In this example, information available to each participant is limited to his/her own private value for the good being auctioned, and the rules of the auction.

Control of subject preferences within a laboratory experiment is established by the use of induced values. In any exchange environment, subjects typically are buying (or selling) 'units' of a non-descript good, which has no intrinsic value.[4] The 'induced value' of the good is established by the experimenter's commitment to redeem units of the good acquired by the buyer at a fixed dollar amount. Payoffs, or net income, for a buyer is then given by the induced value (or redemption value) of any units purchased minus the costs to the buyer of obtaining the unit. In the earlier example of the sealed bid, first-price auction, each bidder would be assigned a 'redemption value', which is the amount of money the experimenter would pay the subject should he/she win the auction and purchase the 'good'. Thus, a good with no inherent value has an induced value for each subject through the assignment of these redemption values. So, for example, a winning bidder in the sealed price auction with an induced value of $100 would receive a net payoff of $20 if the second-highest bid price was $80 (the redemption value of $100 minus the cost of acquiring the good of $80), and should not be willing to pay more than 100 tokens for the good.[5]

Smith (1982) sets out four requirements that an induced-value experimental design must include to establish control over subjects' preferences. They are:

(1) *Pay-off dominance*: rewards must be large enough to offset any subjective costs that subjects place on participation in the experiment.
(2) *Non-satiation*: subjects must prefer more of the reward medium to less.
(3) *Saliency*: the level of rewards received by subjects must be related to their decisions.
(4) *Privacy*: each subject must know only his or her own payoffs so that they do not receive any subjective value from the payoffs of other subjects.[6]

These four conditions are stated here not so much for discussion of their importance for induced-value experiments, but to provide a useful framework for comparing classical experiments to 'field experiments' as well as CV exercises.[7]

Smith (1982: 931) states that: 'Control over preferences is the most significant element distinguishing laboratory experiments from other methods of economic inquiry.' Yet a growing body of research is devoted to the conduct of 'field experiments', which specifically do *not* control preferences. Davis and Holt (1993: 32) define field experiments (or tests) as those in which some variable is directly manipulated in an otherwise naturally occurring process. Field experiments are conducted in either 'natural' economic settings or less-natural settings, perhaps even including a laboratory setting. What is common to field experiments is that they employ controlled institutions to elicit values for actual commodities that have some intrinsic value to subjects. For example, in field experiments by List (2001), List and Lucking-Reilly (2000), and List and Shogren (1998) auctions for sports cards are conducted using various auction structures. These experiments were undertaken at sites where sports cards auctions take place with a subject pool drawn from the traders who are already present at the auction site. By changing only one feature of the auction across trials, the authors could observe changes in behavior (revealed values) associated with their design changes. This is a typical use of field experiment methods.

It is important to note that field experiments, although they involve preference elicitation, not inducement, may still incorporate and satisfy conditions (1)–(4) above. Of most importance, because they involve actual transactions for real goods, field experiments are salient. Saliency, as defined above, is the feature that sets apart a field experiment from a CV exercise. Both elicit values for 'real' goods, but with field experiments, rewards (or punishments) are related to subject decisions in a transparent manner since transactions are binding (and based upon the subject's revealed values in a manner set out by the experimenter). The transparency of a relationship between decisions (revealed values) and rewards/punishments in CV, and hence the saliency of CV, is a source of much debate, however. Rather than rehash this debate, the reader is referred to Diamond and Hauseman (1994), Hanemann (1994) and Chapter 2 in this volume. What is important for our purposes is to recognize that, regardless of whether one believes CV surveys can be salient under some conditions (see, for example, Carson et al., 1999), field experiments offer a natural tool for exploring this question because of their saliency, replicability, and their potential to parallel the institutions and mechanisms commonly employed in CV surveys. A cautionary note is needed however. Because values are elicited for goods with intrinsic values to subjects (which the experimenter can never truly know) the experimenter can only observe *differences* in behavior in response to a change in the experimental parameter, and cannot make unqualified statements about divergences of revealed values from the 'true' values since these values are not known. This point is very important for field experiments designed to test the validity of the CV method, an issue taken up in some detail in the next section of this chapter.

8.3   Validity

There exists a substantial literature reporting efforts by environmental economists to assess the validity of the CV method beginning, arguably, with Knetsch and Davis (1966) and Bishop and Heberlein's (1979) seminal papers comparing values derived from the CV method with corresponding values derived from indirect methods such as the travel-cost model. Other external tests have involved comparisons of CV and hedonic values (for example, Brookshire et al., 1982 and Cummings et al., 1986). Later validation efforts moved along several distinct lines including: validation tests for internal consistency using CV surveys (for example, did CV results follows patterns expected by theory; see, for example, Diamond, 1996 and Smith and Osborne, 1996), internal consistency tests using field experiments, and comparisons of values elicited *via* CV surveys with values elicited in field experiments. It is the latter two validity efforts to which we now turn our attention.

8.3.1   Hypothetical bias

The essence of an experiment designed to assess the potential for hypo-thetical bias in CV involves posing a willingness to pay question for a specific, non-artificial good (for example, candy, calculators, strawberries, or a contribution to some environmental organization) in two distinct treat-ments. In one treatment, subjects are placed in a real market situation where they are faced with the option of purchasing or selling a good under specific conditions described to them by the experimenters. The willingness to pay (WTP) (or willingness to accept – WTA) responses obtained from these markets are then compared with those obtained from hypothetical surveys that ask subjects to report what their WTP *would be* under the conditions described in the survey. The hypothetical surveys are typically designed to mimic the real markets as closely as possible, so that only the payment con-dition (hypothetical or real) varies across treatments.[8] Using the nomen-clature established in the previous section, the real payment treatments are referred to as field experiments, while the hypothetical payment treatments are referred to as surveys.

Tests of hypothetical bias using experimental methods are seen as early as Bishop and Heberlein's (1979, 1986) work involving auctions for goose and deer hunting permits in Wisconsin and Dickie et al. (1987) sales of strawberries door to door in Laramie, Wyoming. More recent examples of experimental tests of hypothetical bias are seen in Neill et al.'s (1994) Vickery auction for art prints to students at the University of New Mexico; Cummings et al. (1995) elicitation of WTP for juicers and chocolates using a dichotomous choice question; and Loomis et al.'s (1996) use of an open-ended question to elicit WTP for art prints.[9] In each of these experiments, it is typically the case that reported WTP (WTA) for these private goods was significantly larger in hypothetical treatments as compared with the real treatments, providing evidence consistent with hypothetical bias.[10] For instance, Cummings et al. (1995) asked adult subjects (i.e. non-student sub-jects) whether or not they would be willing to pay $8 for a juicer in either a hypothetical payment treatment or a real payment treatment. Results were that in the hypothetical treatment 41 per cent of subjects said they would pay $8 for the juicer, while in the real treatment only 11 per cent said they would pay $8. Similar results were found for two other goods: chocolates and calculators. For these goods, student samples were used, and while 42 per cent of subjects said they would pay $3.50 for a box of chocolates only 8 per cent actually did at that same price. Similarly, for the calculators, 21 per cent said they would purchase the calculator for $3, but only 8 per cent actually did at that same price.

Critics of this literature argued, among other considerations, that since these experiments involve private (not public) goods, and do not involve payment institutions commonly used in CV (for example, a referendum vote), their relevance for CV is questionable (see Smith and Mansfield, 1998 and Randall, 1996). Several papers take up these challenges, eliciting WTP for public goods in both hypothetical and real treatments using elicitation and/or survey methods that are common to CV exercises. Brown et al. (1996) and Champ et al. (1997) use CV-like methods to elicit WTP to improve the natural conditions of the Grand Canyon's northern rim. Both hypothetical and real mail surveys were conducted eliciting WTP with either an open-ended or dichotomous choice question (Champ et al. only report results from dichotomous choice treatments). Both studies found evidence consistent with hypothetical bias regardless of whether the open-ended or dichotomous choice elicitation format was used. Brown and Taylor (2001) conducted in-person interviews eliciting WTP for preserving rainforest property in Costa Rica with an open-ended question in both hypothetical or real payment treatments. Again, significant evidence of hypothetical bias was found, and the size of the bias was found to differ across genders.

While the body of literature using both private and public goods to test for hypothetical bias using experimental methods, taken on a whole, indicates that hypothetical bias may be a significant issue for CV, a critical issue for these tests is whether the methodology used to elicit WTP from subjects in the real payment treatments are incentive compatible or demand-revealing.[11] If a demand-revealing mechanism is used to elicit values, then hypothetical bias tests may be conducted by comparing results from hypothetical and real payment treatments. However, if a demand-revealing mechanism is *not* used, then the real payment scenario may not be the correct benchmark to which responses from hypothetical surveys should be compared if it is judgments regarding 'validity' that are to be drawn from these comparisons. Comparisons between hypothetical and real institutions are still valid in the sense that we may observe the magnitude and directions of differences in reported WTP. But it is impossible to determine whether differences are due to biases present in the real treatment and not the hypothetical treatment – or due to biases in the hypothetical treatment that are not present in the real treatment – or some mixture of the two.

Horowitz and McConnell (2000a) highlight these issues with field experiments eliciting preferences for private goods with an open-ended elicitation method (which is not an incentive compatible elicitation mechanism) using real payment treatments only. Their results indicated that the preferences elicited for over half of their subjects were not economically plausible (i.e. subjects responses indicated that they were ignoring opportunity costs). These results are interpreted as casting 'doubt on the use of real experiments as the sole indicators of preferences or as a standard against which hypothetical surveys should be judged' (Horowitz and McConnell,

2000a: 236). Their point is well taken – judgments about the validity of hypothetical mechanisms for eliciting WTP that rely on comparisons to real mechanisms are critically dependent on the real mechanism's ability to truthfully reveal demand.[12]

This issue is particularly important in value-elicitation experiments involving public goods. If the real payment experiment is not demand revealing, then it could be the case that differences in responses between hypothetical and real valuation questions are due to *free riding* in the real payment scenario and not due to *hypothetical bias* in the hypothetical survey. In an attempt to avoid this drawback, Cummings et al. (1997), and Cummings and Taylor (1999) conduct a series of experiments using a binary choice, simple majority rule referendum as the elicitation mechanism. A binary choice referendum (for example, you may vote for candidate A or B only; or you may vote 'yes' or 'no' on a project) is incentive compatible or strategy proof when the voting rule is a simple majority rule (for example, the referendum passes if more than 50 per cent of respondents vote 'yes').[13] In this case, revealing anything other than your true preferences in an anonymous vote cannot enhance your chances of receiving your preferred outcome (see Moulin, 1988 for a formal proof). Thus, it was expected in this research that the real-referenda would provide an unbiased benchmark to which the hypothetical referenda responses could be compared.

The basic design for the real payment referendum in these studies was as follows. Subjects voted on a proposition involving contributions to a non-profit organization in New Mexico, which would provide information booklets to low-income families describing potential ground-water contamination in the area and how the families can have their well-water tested at no cost to them.[14] The proposition that subjects voted on was that each person in the group would contribute $10 to the non-profit organization to provide a certain number of booklets. If more than 50 per cent of the subjects voted yes, each subject would donate $10 to the program – regardless of whether they themselves voted yes or no. In the hypothetical payment referenda, subjects were simply asked how they *would vote* if the referendum were for real. Results from these experiments were that the percentage of subjects voting yes on the proposition was significantly higher in the hypothetical referenda as compared with the real payment referenda.[15]

While seeming to definitively test for hypothetical bias, even these experiments have a note of caution associated with them. The Gibbard–Satterthwaite theorem, as applied to these referenda, relies on the maintained hypothesis that there is no possibility for provision of the good outside the voting group. If this is not the case, then the referendum is no longer 'closed' and voters who support the project (and would vote yes in a closed referendum) may misrepresent their preferences and vote no if they feel that the good will provided by others outside the voting group. Essentially, the voters in the group may choose to free-ride off of potential providers of the public good outside the group. Thus, if one finds a higher percentage of voters voting yes in the hypothetical referenda as compared with identical real referenda, it could be due to free-riding effects in the real referenda and not hypothetical bias in the hypothetical referenda.[16] In an extension to the referendum design just described, Taylor (1998) conducted closed referenda for the same public good (the New Mexico program) and still found a higher percentage of subjects voting yes in the hypothetical referenda as compared with the real referenda, suggesting these effects may have been minimal in the aforementioned studies.

In summary, the use of 'real-world' public (or private) goods by design implies that the researcher can never know with certainty the *true* underlying preferences of the subjects over these goods. As a result, many 'validation' experiments allow, at most, only a comparison of reported values for one specific good across two variants of the same institution (hypothetical and real). Attribution of all differences across hypothetical and real institutions to hypothetical bias in these cases may be somewhat inappropriate. Indeed, research conducted by Taylor et al. (2000) suggests that perhaps hypothetical institutions are equally good at revealing values for a public good if those values are well defined. They conduct induced-value referenda in both hypothetical and real settings. They found individual responses were *not* consistent with demand revelation in both the hypothetical and real payment referenda. Interestingly, while neither mechanism appeared to be fully incentive compatible, they found no significant difference in the voting behavior across the payment treatments. In light of earlier evidence reporting significant differences in voting behavior across hypothetical and real referenda, they suggest the following:

> With respect to validating contingent valuation surveys, our results may indicate that it is not the value *elicitation* problem (i.e. formulating a vote given a value for the good), but the value *formation* problem that may be at the heart of the prevalent 'hypothetical bias' results found in previous CV validation experiments. That is, subjects may form their values for a good differently in a hypothetical market than in a market in which real money is 'on the line'. However, *given* a value has been formed, the hypothetical nature of the payment mechanism may *not* induce different revelation behavior as compared to a real payment mechanism (Taylor et al., 2001, p. 65).

8.3.2   Internal consistency
Depending on the definition of property rights, welfare changes arising from changes in the quality or quantity of public goods, should be elicited with either a WTP question or a WTA question. Classical utility-maximizing

models would suggest that, with small income effects and many available substitutes, WTP for a good should be approximately equal to the WTA to forgo consumption of the good (Willig, 1976).[17] However, estimates of WTA have repeatedly been found to be larger than estimates of WTP in CV surveys. Critics of contingent valuation view this as additional evidence that the method is inherently flawed. However, as will be discussed here, experimental tests of the proposition that WTP equals WTA do not necessarily support this conclusion.

Field experiments examining the relationship between WTP and WTA typically involve endowing a subject with a commodity, and then asking the subject their WTA compensation in return for giving up their endowment. Mean WTA responses are then compared with the mean WTP responses of subjects who are not endowed with the good, but are given the opportunity to purchase the good. It is generally the case in these experiments that a large disparity between WTP and WTA is found, even for goods with small income effects and many substitutes, such as candy bars and coffee mugs. Examples of field experiments comparing WTA and WTP responses are Knetsch and Sinden (1984) (lottery tickets, WTA/WTP ratio = 4.04); Bishop and Heberlein (1986) (goose hunting permit, WTA/WTP ratio = 4.8), Brookshire et al. (1986) (elk hunting, WTA/WTP ratio = 5.4), Kahnemann et al. (1990) (coffee mugs, WTA/WTP ratio = 2.6) and Shogren et al. (1994) (food safety, WTA/WTP > 3.5).

Horowitz and McConnell (2000b) conduct a review of 45 studies that elicit WTA and WTP and find an average WTA/WTP ratio across studies of approximately seven. Their analysis also indicates that this ratio increases the less familiar or 'ordinary' the good being valued, highlighting that, in addition to understanding the processes underlying bidding behavior, it is important for environmental and natural resource issues to link those behaviors to the type of good being valued. For example, a WTA/WTP ratio of approximately seven would imply that 'roughly speaking, that the amount of land that would be preserved if development rights were held by the general public is *seven times higher* than the amount that would be preserved if the rights were deeded to the landowner and must be purchased by the public' (Horowitz and McConnell, 2000b).

Several explanations for observed disparities between WTA and WTP have been presented and tested experimentally. Knetsch and Sinden (1984) and Kahneman, Knetsch and Thaler (KKT) (1990) suggest that endowment effects or loss aversion (Kahneman and Tversky, 1979) may be the reason for the observed differences: that individuals will offer to sell a commodity already in their possession at a higher rate than they are willing to pay for it if not in their possession. While Knetsch and Sinden did not utilize incentive-compatible mechanisms when eliciting WTP and WTA for lottery tickets,

Kahneman, Knetsch, and Thaler used a Becker–DeGroot– Marschak mechanism, which is theoretically incentive compatible, to elicit WTP and WTA for pens and coffee mugs. They still found that WTA is significantly larger than WTP and attribute this result to the presence of endowment effects.

Shogren et al. (1994) provide evidence contrary to that of KKT, however. They conduct similar experiments to KKT, but use a multiple-round second-price auction to elicit WTA or WTP from subjects. They find that WTA is significantly larger than WTP for an unfamiliar good with few substitutes (food safety), but find no significant difference between WTA and WTP for goods similar to those used by KKT. In addition, Shogren et al. (forthcoming) repeat the experiments by KKT with the Becker–DeGroot–Marshak mechanism, and compare these results to those obtained with multiple-round second price auctions and random nth price auctions. Shogren et al. argue that, if endowment effects underlie the divergences in WTP and WTA, then these effects should be present in different market conditions (for example, different auction structures) and after subjects have obtained considerable market experience. Using the same goods as KKT, Shogren et al. find that, although early rounds of each auction have significant differences in WTP and WTA, as subjects gain experience with the elicitation mechanism, the disparity between WTP and WTA is not statistically significant in any of the three market mechanisms.[18] Thus, Shogren et al. conclude that endowment effects can be rejected as the underlying behavioral phenomenon in WTA/WTP experiments.

Neilson et al. (1998) explore yet another alternative explanation for the disparities between WTA and WTP, and suggest they may arise due to uncertainty regarding either the value of the good or whether or not it will be provided. Using a Becker–DeGroot–Marshak mechanism in induced-value experiments, Neilson et al. find that the disparity between WTA and WTP is increasing with the degree of uncertainty surrounding the value of the good or its certainty of being provided. Yet, the disparity can be reduced by allowing low-cost recontracting (for example, allowing reversibility in their decisions).

Overall, the evidence from this literature seems to indicate that in one-shot bidding games (or initial rounds of multiple-round bidding games), individuals do behave in a manner consistent with the theory of endowment effects – for example, that we may expect WTA > WTP even for goods with small income effects and good substitutes. However, these effects may dissipate with multiple rounds as subjects gain experience with the elicitation mechanism. The results from these field experiments indicate that it is not necessarily a flaw of contingent valuation *per se* that WTA estimates are found to be larger than WTP, but rather the result of a behavioral phenomenon that we do not fully understand. That contingent valuation elicits similar behavior to the field experiments is a positive sign that it can elicit economic responses from subjects. However, it should be noted that evidence suggests that the disparity between WTA and WTP may be larger in CV surveys than in field experiments for the same goods. For example, Brookshire and Coursey (1987) found a WTA/WTP ratio equal to five or more in field experiments, but found a ratio closer to 75 in a contingent valuation exercise for the same good.

8.4 CV design and calibration

The previous section highlights the importance of understanding the incentive properties of any mechanism or market used to elicit values, especially if one wishes to use one mechanism as a 'benchmark' to which other mechanisms may be compared. In this section, we review methods which are used to design and improve contingent valuation surveys. Both field and laboratory experiments are proving useful in this arena as well. With field experiments, using the real payment treatment as a benchmark to which new designs for hypothetical surveys may be compared is a burgeoning literature. As will be noted, these studies vary in their success with regard to the demand revelation properties of their elicitation mechanisms. Regardless of their success, however, they are still useful examples to stimulate innovative ways of exploring the design of CV surveys. The laboratory experiments reviewed here focus on incentive properties of donation mechanisms for public goods provision. While field tests of these mechanisms are in their infancy, the laboratory literature is explored, with the hopes of stimulating new designs for field experiments.

8.4.1 Ex ante *design and* Ex post *calibration for eliminating hypothetical bias*

Several papers attempting to adjust the hypothetical elicitation instrument have relied on 'word-smithing' of one kind or another to induce subjects to provide responses to the hypothetical treatments that are not statistically different than the responses obtained in the real treatments. Loomis et al. (1994) and Neill (1995) precede the valuation question with a 'reminder' of potential budgetary substitutes. In both cases, the reminder was ineffective in reducing the differences between the hypothetical WTP responses and the real payment WTP responses. Cummings and Taylor (1999) develop a 'cheap talk' design for the contingent valuation survey in which the topic of hypothetical bias is effectively made an integral part of the survey. They first conduct hypothetical and real referenda as described earlier in Section 8.3.1 for four different public goods: a non-profit organization in New Mexico (described earlier), the Georgia Chapter of the Nature Conservancy, the Nature Conservancy's Adopt and Acre program for rainforest preservation, and a non-profit organization in Atlanta that builds public pedestrian trails. For all goods except the non-profit organization in Atlanta that builds trails, voting results indicated a significantly higher percentage of subjects voted yes in the hypothetical referenda as compared with the real referenda – evidence the author's suggest is consistent with hypothetical bias. Cummings and Taylor then introduce a cheap talk script into the hypothetical referendum design which makes the substance of hypothetical bias – why it might occur, how it affects responses to valuation questions – an integral part of the survey. For all three public goods where evidence of hypothetical bias was found, the cheap talk script was effective in inducing voting behavior in hypothetical referenda that was *not* statistically different than what was observed in the real referenda. In addition, for the fourth good, where there was no evidence of hypothetical bias in the first place, introducing the cheap talk script into the survey for this good did not 'bias downward' the votes for this good. In other words, again, the voting results for the hypothetical survey with cheap talk was not statistically different from the real (or hypothetical in this case) referenda for this good. This result was robust to changes in the experimental design as well as to small changes in the cheap talk script.

Additional support for Cummings and Taylor's cheap talk design can be found in List (forthcoming), which implements the cheap talk script in field experiments involving auctions for sports cards. List uses a second-price auction for a baseball sports card to participants in a trade show in Florida. Actual (real payment) auctions are conducted with two samples: dealers, who buy and sell the cards for a living, and 'enthusiasts', who visit the show (and may buy or sell cards while there). In addition, separate samples of enthusiasts and dealers are asked in a hypothetical survey how much they would pay for the sports card under conditions identical to those in the real auctions. List finds evidence consistent with hypothetical bias in both the dealer and enthusiast samples. In separate samples, he then introduces the cheap talk script prior to asking the hypothetical valuation question. His results indicate that the cheap talk script was ineffective in removing hypothetical bias in the dealers, but was effective in removing hypothetical bias in subjects that were just sports cards enthusiasts. These results demonstrate that cheap talk may not be effective in all settings (for example, markets for private goods and on subjects who are agent brokers that buy and sell the good for profit). However, the results for non-dealers (enthusiasts) are encouraging for the use of cheap talk in most settings where contingent valuation is applied.

In an alternative approach, Bjornstad et al. (1997) develop a 'learning design' that does not rely on word smithing, but instead gives the subjects an opportunity to learn how the hypothetical institution works, *vis-à-vis* a real payment institution. In the learning design, subjects participate in three referenda (subjects are not told how many referenda they will be participating in). The first is a hypothetical referendum to provide a real-world public good (call it good A). After tallying the votes, and announcing the results to the group, the subjects are told they are going to re-vote on the same proposition, but this time the vote will be for real – if the referendum passes in this vote, everyone will pay the amount stated in the proposition. The votes of this real referendum are tallied, and announced to the group. By participating in this sequence, subjects are able to observe how they reacted to a real referendum versus a hypothetical referendum, and are also able to observe how the overall voting results of the group was affected by the hypothetical versus real context. Finally, the subjects vote in a third referendum, which is hypothetical, and for a different real-world public good (say good B). The results from the third referendum – the hypothetical referendum for good B – are then compared with an out-of-sample referendum conducted with the same good (good B) in an experiment in which the subjects only participate in a single real referendum on good B. Results indicated that referendum votes in the hypothetical, third referendum of the learning design, were *not* significantly different than the votes in the out-of-sample real referendum. This result was robust to changes in the public good offered to the subjects.

The research described above seeks to alter the hypothetical institution so that elicited WTP is affected in a manner making it consistent with WTP obtained in real payment treatments. A second, related line of inquiry uses *ex post* calibration experiments to develop methods by which responses to hypothetical surveys may be calibrated to more accurately reflect responses that would be obtained in actual markets. Blackburn et al. (1994), Fox et al. (1998) and Harrison et al. (1999) use within-sample methods where subjects respond to hypothetical and then real valuation questions. A calibration (or statistical bias) function is then estimated, which relates the differences in responses obtained in the two treatments to subject characteristics in an attempt to 'predict' the bias. Unfortunately, as Fox et al. note, 'calibration may be commodity specific', and so applications of this type of method 'might be best restricted to more test-marketing of new private goods rather than moving immediately into the public goods arena' (p. 464).

A similar line of *ex post* calibration involves the use of respondent's certainty about their WTP to calibrate the hypothetical responses. In these experiments, hypothetical WTP questions are followed by a question asking the respondent to rank how certain they are that they would pay the amount they stated. A scale of 1 to 10 where 1 is very uncertain and 10 is very certain is usually used to elicit the respondent's level of certainty.

Champ et al. (1997) and Blumenschein et al. (1998) used dichotomous choice questions to elicit WTP and found that discrepancy between hypothetical and real responses was removed if subjects who said yes in the hypothetical survey, but then reported a certainty level less than 10, were coded as having said 'no'.

Additional studies using the uncertainty calibration approach unfortunately indicate that the calibration factor used by Champ et al. (1997) and Blumenschein et al. (1998) may be too severe. Champ and Bishop (2000) and Johannesson et al. (1998) conduct similar experiments, but find that coding only subjects with the highest level of certainty as 'yes' results in underestimates of the real response rates. For example, in the experiment conducted by Champ and Bishop, if subjects who reported a certainty level of 7 or lower (on a scale of 1 to 10, where 10 is the most certain) were re-coded with WTP equal to 0, the results from the hypothetical survey were not statistically different than those in the real payment treatment. Poe et al. (1999) find yet a different calibration factor to be appropriate. They conduct a survey of households asking WTP for a green-power pricing program using a dichotomous choice question in a provision point setting (described in the next section in more detail). A split sample design was used in which one sample of households were actually given the opportunity to sign-up for the program (at a cost of $6 per month) and the other sample were only asked if they would sign up for the program if it were available to them (at the same cost). Results indicate that coding respondents with a certainty of 5 or lower (again, on a scale of 1 to 10) as 'no' results in a proportion of yes responses in the hypothetical survey that is not distinguishable from the actual sign-up rates.

Johannesson et al. (1999) use the uncertainty follow-up question in a different manner, combining it with the statistical bias function approach discussed earlier. Subjects in their experiments were asked a hypothetical, dichotomous choice WTP question for a private good (either sun glasses or chocolates), followed by a certainty question (0 to 10 scale), and then an actual offer to purchase the good. Results indicate a significantly higher proportion of yes responses to the hypothetical WTP question as compared with the real WTP question (both in-sample, and out-of-sample tests were conducted). A bias function was then estimated for the subjects who said yes to the hypothetical WTP question. The probability of a yes response to the real offer was estimated as a function of the subject's stated level of certainty, a proxy for the cost of the good, and subject's socio-economic characteristics. Based on the estimated bias function, the probability that each subject would say yes to the real offer to purchase the good was computed. When subjects whose estimated probability of saying 'yes' to the real offer was less than 50 per cent were re-coded as 'no' responses, the proportion of 'yes' responses was not statistically different across the hypothetical and real payment question. Whether the 50 per cent cut-off level for the predicted probability of contributing used by Johannesson et al. (1999) would be robust across goods (public and private) or whether other probability cut-off levels would suffice is unclear.

Overall, each of the *ex ante* and *ex post* methods for adjusting CV surveys, or their responses, need much in the way of robustness testing before they can be confidently applied to situations in which a real payment treatment cannot be conducted for comparison. The *ex ante* methods proposed have not been tested for robustness to important design elements, and we do not understand under what conditions we may expect them to work or not work. Calibration is still too much in its infancy. Thus far, it appears that this literature points to commodity-specific calibration methods. Similar results have been reported in the marketing literature. For example, Louviere (1996: 170) observes that, 'I think it very unlikely that one simple and generalizable approach to 'adjusting' (stated preference) numbers will be found . . . differences in product awareness, learning, etc . . . necessarily imply that no one magic constant can exist across all product categories.' Unless robustness of an *ex ante* or *ex post* adjustment method is established, or at least the systematic links between adjustments (pre- or post-elicitation) and some observables are found, calibration of any sort is not likely to prove important for the conduct of CV. A calibration method that is commodity and/or context specific will always rely on the real payment treatment being conducted, thus defeating its purpose for CV.

8.4.2   Survey design

In addition to attempting to reduce or eliminate hypothetical bias, field experiments have also been used to test suppositions regarding the 'proper' design of CV surveys. For example, Cummings and Taylor (1998) evaluate the merits of developing CV surveys that are 'realistic' as a means of inducing responses to hypothetical surveys that may be more aligned with real payment surveys. 'Realistic' is meant in the sense that the survey impresses upon the subject that policy makers may see the results of the survey, and thus make decisions based on the information (and, so, actual payments may result at some point in the future). Cummings and Taylor operationalize this concept by conducting probabilistic referenda. In this design, subjects are told that, if the referendum passes, then a bingo cage, with 100 red and white balls in it would be spun to see if the referendum was binding. If a red ball was drawn from the bingo cage, then the referendum was binding and every subject would have to pay the amount stated in the proposition; if a white ball was drawn, the referendum was not binding and no payments would be made. The probability that the referendum would be binding was varied across subject groups by varying the number of red balls in the bingo cage. Results were that the probability that a referendum would be binding if it should pass had to be quite high (75 per cent chance or better) before voting results in these referendum were not statistically different than those obtained in the benchmark referenda (real payment referenda with no bingo cage).

Another survey design question involves the choice of the value elicitation format. The two most commonly used formats to elicit WTP are the dichotomous choice and the open-ended question formats. Often, CV researchers have suggested that the dichotomous choice elicitation format is preferred over an open-ended format, for various reasons including that they may reduce opportunities for strategic behavior and they are cognitively easier (Mitchell and Carson, 1989). Yet there has been much concern and debate over this recommendation, especially since empirical studies suggest that mean WTP estimates resulting from dichotomous choice questions tend to be larger than mean WTP estimates from open-ended questions (for example, Boyle et al., 1996).

Bohara et al. (1998) offer a potential behavioral explanation for why open-ended and dichotomous choice questions may result in different value revelations by subjects and then test the hypothesis using laboratory experiments. Specifically, they conjecture that information about the total cost of providing a public good, as well as the number of people who will be providing it, will significantly affect open-ended valuation responses because subjects can compute a 'fair share' cost price, but not be a significant determinant of the dichotomous choice valuation responses. To test this, they conduct a telephone CV questionnaire in which subjects were asked their WTP to help establish a trust fund to protect in-stream water flows (subjects were told it would be a one-time donation). Split samples received either an open-ended or a dichotomous choice valuation question and one of four information treatments. The information treatments varied according to whether or not the subjects were told: only the total cost of the project; only the number of people contributing; both total cost and group size; neither total cost nor group size. Laboratory experiments were also conducted with induced values, where subjects contributed to a context-free, laboratory public good. The same treatments were conducted in the laboratory as with the CV survey. The results from both the survey and the lab experiment suggest that open-ended valuation responses were sensitive to information concerning the cost of the public project and the group size, but dichotomous choice valuation responses were not. Since cost and group size information are not related to individual valuation, Bohara et al. suggest that the dichotomous choice format is preferred since it yields more consistent results across information provided.

The recommendation of Bohara et al. is in contrast to what Brown et al. (1996) suggest in their study eliciting WTP for road removal from the northern rim of the Grand Canyon. They elicit WTP in both hypothetical and real payment treatments using both open-ended and dichotomous-choice elicitation questions. Contrary to expectations, they found that the difference in mean WTP between the hypothetical and real payment treatments was smaller in the open-ended treatment as compared with the dichotomous choice treatment. Poe et al. (1999) find similar results as well in their study involving WTP questions to fund a green power pricing program. They conduct hypothetical dichotomous choice and open-ended valuation questions and compare the responses with those obtained when subjects were actually given the opportunity to sign up (the real treatment used only a dichotomous choice question). Results also indicated that the hypothetical dichotomous choice question overestimated real participation more than the hypothetical open-ended question. Yet, Poe et al. warn that it is not clear that open ended is necessarily preferred to dichotomous choice as an elicitation format. Open-ended questions appear to do a little better in terms of predicting responses in real payment situations (for example, stronger criterion validity (Mitchell and Carson, 1989)), yet results from these studies also indicate that dichotomous choice questions may perform better in terms of construct validity (which is the degree to which the responses are related to explanatory variables theory would predict to be important).

8.4.3 Contribution mechanism design

Understanding how individuals make economic choices in hypothetical surveys, as compared with real markets, can only be done in comparison with our understanding of how individuals make choices in the real markets. The study of individual rationality, and strategic interactions in markets are particularly interesting in the case of providing public goods. Many experimental investigations focus on the incentive properties of provision rules to provide these goods. A primary issue is, of course, the potential for free-riding and under-provision of the public good. Two related mechanisms for eliciting donations to a public good developed by Groves and Ledyard (1977) and Smith (1979) have desirable theoretical properties in that each individual's incentives are to fully reveal their true marginal valuation for the public good (for example, they are incentive compatible mechanisms). While these mechanisms have enjoyed some degree of success in having the efficient level of public good being provided by a group of individuals in laboratory environments (Smith, 1979 and Chen and Plott, 1996), they are complicated and not likely to be feasible for implementation in CV studies.[19]

In contrast, simple provision rules which lend themselves to CV applications, such as the voluntary contributions mechanism, are troublesome because the dominant strategy of individuals is to misrepresent their preferences (in real markets). Each individual's dominant strategy is to contribute zero to the public good, and so the non-cooperative, Nash equilibrium is for the public good not to be provided at all. Early work testing for free-riding effects in voluntary contributions to public goods, such as Bohm (1972) and Scherr and Babb (1975), elicited contributions to real-world public goods and their results suggested that free riding may not be a significant problem. These results were relied upon by many environmental economists for confidence in the CV method (see, as examples, Cummings et al., 1986; Chapter 3, and Mitchell and Carson, 1989; Chapter 7). However, most induced-value tests have found that, in general, free riding exists, but is more limited than the non-cooperative, competitive solution would suggest.

For context, consider the general design used in voluntary contribution game experiments in which subjects must choose to either contribute tokens to a group fund or keep them in their private fund. Each token that is kept in the private fund earns a private return of v. Each token that is contributed to the group returns a common value to all members of the group of z. Define y_i as the ith subject's initial endowment of tokens ($i = 1. . .n$), x_i as number of tokens the ith subject contributes to the common fund, and E as the expected total contributions of tokens to the group fund by all other $n-1$ subjects. Subject i's pay-off, p_i, is then given by:

$$p_i = v(y_i - x_i) + zx_i + zE.$$

Typically, values for v and z are set such that a social optimum (Pareto optimum) obtains with $x_i = y$ (all tokens are contributed), but free riding (no tokens contributed) is a Nash equilibrium. In other words, the group return is set low enough so that individuals find it optimal to contribute zero tokens, yet is still high enough so it is socially optimal for each individual to contribute all tokens to the group fund. For example, with $n = 5$, $y_i = 10$ for all i, $v = 10$, and $z = 3$, a Pareto optimum is for each subject to 'fully contribute' ($x_i = 10$), in which case each subject earns a payoff of 150. In a non-cooperative game however, the Nash equilibrium is zero contributions, $x_i = 0$, resulting in each subject receiving 100 tokens as their payoff.

In most experimental tests of cooperation under conditions similar to those given above, the Nash equilibrium of zero contributions (by all subjects) is almost never observed, even after as many as 60 rounds (for example, Smith and Walker, 1993; see Ledyard, 1995 and Laury and Holt, 1998 for an overview).[20] However, contributions tend to remain approximately 40–60 per cent below the optimal level (see Ledyard, 1995 for a thorough review of the voluntary contributions mechanism). Factors that have been considered as possible explanations for such observed behavior include altruism, error, reciprocity, a sense of fairness, adaptive evolutionary responses, and/or tacit cooperation (Holt and Laury, 1997, 2), although altruism and error ('noisy behavior') tend to be most often cited as the probable behavioral phenomena leading to the observed results (Ledyard, 1995, 170; Palfrey and Prisbrey, 1997, Andreoni, 1995; Goeree et al., 2000). Goeree et al. find that, under conditions where the dominant strategy is to free ride, the strongest effect on contributions is the internal or private return. Decreases in the private return, which reduces a subject's cost of contributing to the public good, are correlated with increases in contributions. Similarly, contributions are positively correlated with changes in the external rate of return, z, and with increases in the size of the group (for example, increases in the benefits others receive from a contribution), suggesting altruism is not simply of the 'warm-glow' variety.

A feature of the experiments just described is that they are all continuous public goods experiments. In other words, the size of the public good is a continuous function of allocations to the good. This design feature may have limited applicability for real-world public-good provision scenarios, such as those often described in CV surveys. It is often the case that the provision of the public good is 'lumpy' in the sense that it can only be provided in somewhat large, discreet units. Recognition of this fact has led to the design and use of public goods experiments that include one or more 'provision points'. A provision point is a minimum level of contributions that must obtain from subjects if the good is to be provided. In most experimental designs, if contributions fall short of the provision point, subject contributions are returned to them and the public good is not provided. If the provision point is met, then the public good is provided (in the amount stated).

Early experimental tests implementing the provision point mechanism (PPM) were quite promising. Bagnoli and McKee (1991) obtain results wherein the provision point (which was also the Pareto optimal level of contribution) was reached or exceeded in 85 of their 98 rounds, with the *exact* provision point attained in 53 rounds. However, a later study that replicates the Bagnoli and McKee study (Mysker et al., 1996) observed much fewer allocations at or above the provision point with almost no allocations exactly at the provision point. Performance of the PPM, in terms of reaching the provision point, has been shown to improve with designs that allow for such things as non-binding group discussions (van de Kragt et al., 1983), equal pay-offs (Dawes et al., 1986), and multiple interactions with money-back guarantees (Rapoport and Eshed-Levy, 1989). Recently, Rose et al. (1997) and Rondeau et al. (1999) conduct provision point experiments on large groups (up to 100 subjects) using a provision point, with money back guarantee and proportional rebate. Here, if contributions do not meet the provision point, subjects who contributed tokens are given their money back. If contributions meet and exceed the provision point, any excess contributions are rebated to subjects on a proportional basis. Results here indicated that aggregate contributions in small groups (of six subjects) were approximately 64 per cent of the optimal level, while in the large group (50 students), they were not statistically different than 100 per cent of the optimal level. The results for the large groups were also invariant to whether or not subjects were given information on what the provision point was, and the number of subjects in the group attempting to reach that provision point.

An extension of the PPM is to provide multiple provision points. Multiple provision point mechanisms are of interest, as many public goods have the feature that the good can only be provided if a threshold is met and then increased 'in size' only if an additional, higher provision point(s) is met. In general, efficient outcomes have been found to be even more difficult to obtain when multiple provision points are used (see, for example, Bagnoli et al., 1992; Marwell and Ames, 1979). Most recently, Chewning, Collier and Laury (1999) conducted experiments using one, two, three, and five provision points. In each of these experimental treatments, there are two equilibria: strong free riding in which no contributions are made and weak free riding in which group contributions sum to the lowest provision point (if multiple provision points are offered). The provision point was reached or exceeded in 48 of 70 rounds when the single provision point was used. When multiple provision points were used, however, contributions declined towards the weak free-riding equilibrium in early rounds and a group optimum was never reached in final rounds.

While the provision point seems to be promising as an elicitation mechanism for public goods, increasing contributions to optimal levels in some circumstances, behavioral responses to provision points are still not fully understood. For example, Rondeau et al. (1999) report results in which some subjects over-reveal their WTP for the public good, while others under-reveal their WTP (for example, free or easy ride). Although, in total, their PPM design elicits efficient aggregate contributions, it was not individually incentive compatible (for example, revealing true reservation prices for each individual). A mechanism that is demand revealing on average is useful for benefit–cost tests, but, if we are concerned with distributional issues associated with provision, it is important to identify individual demands properly.

8.5 Concluding comments
In this chapter, several areas have been explored in which experimental methodologies have particular importance for the design and improvement

of CV. An overall assessment of this literature is as follows. First, evidence suggests that CV responses probably reflect economic choices (Section 8.3.2), but that hypothetical bias is likely to be pervasive (Section 8.3.1). The issue of hypothetical bias is still a contentious one, however. Any test of theory is a simultaneous test of the theory as well as the experimental design used to test the theory. Failure of results to adhere to theoretical predictions are not necessarily a failure of theory – the anomalous results may be due to faulty experimental design. Definitive tests for hypothetical bias – tests in which demonstrably effective demand-revealing mechanisms for valuing public goods are used under varying conditions relevant for CV – are yet to be conducted. For future research, robustness tests and care in interpreting results are clear prescriptions.

Beyond just assessing the validity of contingent valuation, experimental methods may be employed in a more proactive manner and used as a tool for improving the design of CV (Section 8.4). If we do not understand how important design elements such as value elicitation mechanisms, questionnaire formats, and information sets affect value revelation and economic choices in actual markets, we have little to bring to the debate regarding the validity and/or design of CV. Experiments (induced value experiments) have a distinguished history as a tool for understanding the incentive structure associated with markets, and, more broadly, economic choice institutions. CV seeks to create these institutions in the minds of respondents. Thus, it would seem our problem as economists seeking to use the CV tool is twofold. First, we must create institutions with incentive structures that have been *demonstrated* to be effective (on whatever metric is relevant) in actual economic markets or institutions. We know that institutions matter, experiments help us understand exactly how. Second, we must establish the transferability of these incentive structures from actual markets to the 'markets in our mind'. Here, experiments are at least one-half of the equation we wish to solve. It is my hope that sufficient interest has been generated that future researchers will take up these challenges, building on the strengths and overcoming the weaknesses of the current literature.

Notes

*   The author wishes to thank Ronald Cummings, Susan Laury, and Jason Shogren for helpful comments. This work draws upon material written with Ronald Cummings and Michael McKee.
1. Because experiments are a particularly powerful tool for examining individual behaviors under various informational and market regimes, there are many experimental literatures that bear importance for CV survey design as they advance our understanding of how people form values and report them in various institutions. The interested reader may refer to Shogren (2004) for an extensive discussion of other experimental literatures that relate to the CV method such as those involving the design of incentive compatible auction mechanisms (i.e., where truth telling is a dominant strategy).

2.   This type of exercise has a long history of applications in the contingent valuation literature, which is reviewed in Chapter 2 of this volume.
3.   An extensive review of classical experiments may be found in Davis and Holt (1993), as well as Kagel and Roth (1995) and Plott and Smith (forthcoming).
4.   The use of a non-descipt, or neutral good is important so that subjects do not bring to the experiment value judgements associated with the good, which are unknown to the experimenter.
5.   Similarly, for subjects in an experiment that are sellers of units of the good, their costs are 'induced' by the experimenter who simply sets the cost the seller will incur if he/she sells a unit of the good.
6.   It should be acknowledged that even with induced-values, the researcher is not assured control over preferences. Indeed, much research examines preference components such as justice and fairness using induced-value experiments (see, for example, Forsythe et al., 1994).
7.   While precepts (1)–(4) are sufficient to provide controlled tests of theory, Smith also includes 'parallelism' as a precept for transferring laboratory results to the field ('real-world' environments). Parallelism, as important to experiments related to environmental and natural resource economics is discussed in detail by Cummings, McKee, and Taylor (1999).
8.   It should also be noted that the use of hypothetical payments is not limited to environmental economists. As early as 1948, experimental economists reported hypothetical experimental treatments (see Davis and Holt, 1993: pp. 6 and 7).
9.   Additional examples of research eliciting hypothetical and real WTP are presented in later sections of this chapter which had additional design features beyond just testing for hypothetical bias.
10. Smith and Mansfield (1998), as part of a telephone–mail–telephone contingent valuation study, asked respondents if they would be willing to participate in future surveys in return for a randomly assigned payment of between $5 and $50. A split sample was conducted in which respondents were asked this question in either a hypothetical or real-payment context. They found no significant difference across the two treatments in the WTA of the respondents to give up their time to complete a future survey.
11. Incentive compatible mechanisms or institutions are loosely defined (see Smith, 1979) as those in which a subject's dominant strategy is to fully and truthfully reveal his or her preference ordering. Gibbard (1973) and Satterthwaite (1975) independently developed the conditions under which decision rules that map individual preferences over alternatives into a single collective preference ordering for the entire group are strategy-proof, or incentive compatible. References to incentive compatible mechanisms commonly include second (or nth) price auctions, Dutch or English (clock) auctions, the Becker–DeGroot–Marshak mechanism, and the Groves–Ledyard mechanism for allocating public goods (see Davis and Holt (1993) for a comprehensive review of each of these mechanisms).
12. Of course, comparisons between hypothetical and real institutions are informative regardless of the nature of the institution if one only wishes to compare outcomes, and not make judgements about which, if either, of the instruments reveals the preferences truthfully.
13. If voters have strict preference orderings (i.e., they cannot be indifferent to the two choices) and the choice is binary, then a voting rule that is monotonic is strategy proof. Monotonicity implies a new supporter can do no harm – which is the case in a binary-choice, majority-rule referendum.
14. Cummings et al. (1997) use only the New Mexico good, while Cummings and Taylor (1999) use three other public goods in addition to the program in New Mexico.
15. Cummings and Taylor (1999) found voting results that were identical across the hypothetical and real referenda for one of their four public goods.
16. This, of course, presupposes that there are no incentives to free-ride in these hypothetical referenda (i.e., since no money payment will result from the vote in the hypothetical

referenda, why not 'tell the truth'?). I am unaware of any convincing theoretical arguments or empirical evidence that suggests this is, or is not, the case.

17. Hanemann (1991) shows that, in addition to large income effects, if there are few substitutes for the commodity, the divergence between WTP and WTA can be quite large.
18. Earlier, Coursey, Hovis and Schulze (1987) also found that, as experience with the elicitation mechanism increased, the disparity between WTA and WTP decreased.
19. For instance, in the Groves–Ledyard mechanism, subjects collectively agree how much of the public good to produce, and a central authority then returns a tax scheme to the subjects based on a modified share of the average cost of producing the public good. Subjects are then allowed to revise their decisions, and a new tax scheme is returned based upon the revised decisions. This process is repeated until an equilibrium is established and no one wishes to modify the provision rule.
20. Experimental results also seem to suggest that repetition of the contribution game has a significant impact on provision levels. Typically, positive levels of the public good are provided in early rounds (little free riding), with provision levels declining in later rounds, usually after the fifth period or so (Kim and Walker, 1984; Isaac, McCue, and Plott, 1985; Banks, Plott, and Porter, 1988). Isaac, McCue and Plott (1985, 51–2) conclude that 'Our results unambiguously demonstrate the existence of the under-provision of public goods and related "free-riding" phenomenon and thereby discredit the claims of those who assert as a general proposition that the phenomenon does not or cannot exist.'

References

Andreoni, James (1995), 'Cooperation in public goods: kindness or confusion?', *American Economic Review*, **85**, 891–904.

Bagnoli, M., S. Ben-David and M. McKee (1992), 'Voluntary provision of public goods: the multiple unit case', *Journal of Public Economics*, **47**, 85–106.

Bagnoli, M. and M. McKee (1991) 'Voluntary contribution games: efficient private provision of public goods', *Economic Inquiry*, **29**, 351–66.

Banks, Jeffrey S., Charles R. Plott and David P. Porter (1988), 'An experimental analysis of unanimity in public goods provision mechanisms', *Review of Economic Studies*, **55**, 301–22.

Bishop, R.C. and T.A. Heberlein (1979), 'Travel cost and hypothetical valuation of outdoor recreation: comparisons with an artificial market', mimeographed, University of Wisconsin, Madison.

Bishop, R.C. and T.A. Heberlein (1986), 'Does contingent valuation work?', in R. Cummings, D.S. Brookshire, and W.D. Schulze (eds), *Valuing Environmental Goods*, Savage, MD: Roman & Littlefield, chapter 9.

Bjornstad, D., R. Cummings and L. Osborne (1997), 'A learning design for reducing hypothetical bias in the contingent valuation method', *Environmental and Resource Economics*, **10**(3), 207–11.

Blackburn, McKinley, Glenn W. Harrison and Elisabeth E. Rutström (1994), 'Statistical bias functions and informative hypothetical surveys', *American Journal of Agricultural Economics*, **76**(5), 1084–88.

Blumenschein, Karen, Magnus Johannesson, Glenn C. Blomquist, Bengt Liljas and Richard M. O'Conner (1998), 'Experimental results on expressed certainty and hypothetical bias in contingent valuation', *Southern Economic Journal*, **65**, 169–77.

Bohara, Alok, M. McKee, R. Berrens, H. Jenkins-Smith, C. Silva and D. Brookshire (1998), 'Effects of total cost and group-size information on willingness to pay responses: open ended vs. dichotomous choice', *Journal of Environmental Economics and Management*, **35**, 142–63.

Bohm, Peter (1972), 'Estimating demand for public goods: an experiment', *European Economic Review*, **3**, 111–30.

Boyle, Kevin, F. Johnson, D. McCollum, W. Desvousges, R. Dunford and S. Hudson (1996), 'Valuing public goods: discrete versus continuous contingent valuation responses', *Land Economics*, **72**, 381–96.

Brookshire, David S., L. Eubanks and Alan Randall (1986), 'Estimating option price and existence values for wildlife resources', *Land Economics*, **59**, 1–15.

Brookshire, David S. and D. Coursey (1987), 'Measure the value of a public good: an empirical comparison of elicitation procedures', *American Economic Review*, **77**, 554–66.

Brookshire, David S., Philip T. Ganderton and Michael McKee (1996), 'Evolving entitlements: intervening to prevent a collective harm', *Journal of Agricultural and Resource Economics*, **21**(1), 160–73.

Brookshire, David S., Mark A. Thayer, William D. Schulze and Ralph C. d'Arge (1982), 'Valuing public goods: a comparison of survey and hedonic approaches', *American Economic Review*, **72**, 156–77.

Brown, Kelly, M. and Laura O. Taylor (2001), 'Do as you say, say as you do: evidence on gender differences in actual and stated contributions to public goods', *Journal of Economic Behavior and Organization*, forthcoming.

Brown, Thomas C., P. Champ, R.C. Bishop and D.W. McCollum (1996), 'Response formats and public good donations', *Land Economics*, **72**(1), 152–66.

Carson, Richard T., Theodore Groves and Mark J. Machina (1999), 'Incentive and informational properties of preference questions', Department of Economics working paper #0508, University of California, San Diego, June.

Champ, Patricia A. and Richard C. Bishop (2000), 'Using expressed uncertainty about contingent donations to estimate actual willingness to donate for an environmental good', working paper, Rocky Mountain Research Station, USDA Forest Service, Fort Collins, Colorado.

Champ, Patricia A., Richard C. Bishop, Thomas C. Brown and Daniel W. McCollum (1997), 'Using donation mechanisms to value nonuse benefits from public goods', *Journal of Environmental Economics and Management*, **33**, 151–62.

Chen, Yan and Charles R. Plott (1996), 'The Groves–Ledyard mechanism: an experimental study of institutional design', *Journal of Public Economics*, **59**, 335–64.

Chewning, Eugene, Maribeth Collier and Susan K. Laury (1999), 'Voluntary contributions to a multiple threshold public good', *Research in Experimental Economics*, forthcoming.

Coursey, D., J. Hovis and W.D. Schulze (1987), 'On the supposed disparity between willingness to accept and willingness to pay measures of value', *Quarterly Journal of Economics*, **102**, 679–90.

Cummings, Ronald G., D.S. Brookshire and W.S. Schulze (1986), *Valuing Environmental Goods*, Savage, MD: Rowman & Littlefield.

Cummings, Ronald G., Glenn W. Harrison and Lisa B. Rutström (1995), 'Homegrown values and hypothetical surveys: is the dichotomous choice approach incentive-compatible?', *American Economic Review*, **85**, 260–6.

Cummings, Ronald G., Steven Elliot, Glenn W. Harrison and James Murphy (1997), 'Are hypothetical referenda incentive compatible?', *Journal of Political Economics*, **105**(3), 609–21.

Cummings, Ronald G., W. Schulze, S. Gerking and D. Brookshire (1986), 'Measuring the elasticity of substitution of wages for municipal infrastructure: a comparison of the survey and wage hedonic approaches', *Journal of Environmental Economics and Management*, **13**, 269–76.

Cummings, Ronald G. and Laura O. Taylor (1998), 'Does realism matter in contingent valuation?', *Land Economics*, **74**(2), 203–15.

Cummings, Ronald G. and Laura O. Taylor (1999), Unbiased value estimates for environmental goods: a cheap talk design for the contingent valuation method', *American Economic Review*, **89**(3), 649–65.

Cummings, Ronald G., Michael McKee and Laura O. Taylor (1999), 'To whisper in the ears of princes: laboratory economic experiments and environmental policy', in T. Tietenberg, S. Gerking, and L. Gabel (eds), *Frontiers of Environmental Economics*, Cheltenham, UK: Edward Elgar.

Davis, Douglas D. and Charles A. Holt (1993), *Experimental Economics*, Princeton, NJ: Princeton University Press.

Dawes, R., J. Orbell, R. Simmons and A. van de Kragt (1986), 'Organizing groups for collective action', *American Political Science Review*, **80**, 1171–85.

Diamond, Peter (1996), 'Testing the internal consistency of contingent valuation surveys', *Journal of Environmental Economics and Management*, **30**, 337–48.

Diamond, Peter and Jerry Hausman (1994), 'Contingent valuation: is some number better than none?', *Journal of Economic Perspectives*, **8**(4), 45–64.

Dickie, M., A. Fisher and S. Gerking (1987), 'Market transactions and hypothetical demand data: a comparative study', *Journal of the American Statistical Association*, **82**, 69–75.

Forsythe, Robert, Joel Horowitz, N.E. Savin and Martin Sefton (1994), 'Fairness in simple bargaining games', *Games and Economic Behavior*, **6**, 347–69.

Fox, John, Jason Shogren, Dermot Hayes and James Kleibenstein (1998), 'CVM-X: calibrating contingent values with experimental auction markets', *American Journal of Agricultural Economics*, **80**, 455–65.

Gibbard, Allan (1973), 'Manipulation of voting schemes: a general result', *Econometrica*, **41**, 587–601.

Goeree, Jacob K., Charles A. Holt and Susan K. Laury (2000), 'Private costs and public benefits: unraveling the effects of altruism and noisy behavior', Working Paper, Department of Economics, University of Virginia, Charlottesville, Febuary.

Groves, T. and J. Ledyard (1977), 'Optimal allocation of public goods: a solution to the free rider problem', *Econometrica*, **45**(6), 783–809.

Hanemann, Michael (1991), 'Willingness to pay and willingness to accept: how much can they differ?', *American Economic Review*, **81**, 635–7.

Hanemann, Michael (1994), 'Valuing the environment through contingent valuation', *Journal of Economic Perspectives*, **8**(4), 19–44.

Hanley, N., R. Wright and V. Adamowicz (1998), 'Using choice experiments to value the environment', *Environmental and Resource Economics*, **11**, 413–28.

Harrison, Glenn W., Robert Beekman, Lloyd Brown, Leianne A. Clements, Tanga McDaniel, Sherry Odom and Melonie Williams (1999), 'Environmental damage assessment with hypothetical surveys: the calibration approach', in M. Boman, R. Brännlund, and B. Kriström (eds), *Topics in Environmental Economics*, Amsterdam: Kluwer.

Harrison, Glenn and John List (2004), 'Field experiments', *Journal of Economic Literature*, **XLII**, 1009–55.

Holt, Charles A. and Susan K. Laury (1997), 'Theoretical explanations of treatment effects in voluntary contribution games', forthcoming in C. Platt and V. Smith (eds), *Handbook of Experimental Economic Results*, New York: Elsevier Press.

Horowitz, John K. and K.E. McConnell (2000a) 'Values elicited from open-ended real experiments', *Journal of Economic Behavior and Organization*, **41**, 221–37.

Horowitz, John K. and K.E. McConnell (2000b), 'A review of WTA/WTP studies', Department of Agricultural and Resource Economics Working Paper, University of Maryland, College Park, MD.

Isaac, R. Mark, Kenneth F. McCue and Charles R. Plott (1985), 'Public goods provision in an experimental environment', *Journal of Public Economics*, **26**, 51–74.

Johannesson, Magnus, Bengt Liljas and R.M. O'Connor (1997), 'Hypothetical versus real willingness to pay: some experimental results', *Applied Economic Letters*, **4**, 149–51.

Johannesson, Magnus, Bengt Liljas and Per-Olov Johansonn (1998), 'An expeirmental comparison of dichotomous choice contingent valuation questions and real purchase decisions', *Applied Economics*, **30**, 643–47.

Johannesson, Magnus, G.C. Blomquist, K. Blumenschein, P. Johansson, B. Liljas and R. O'Conor (1999), 'Calibrated hypothetical willingness to pay responses', *Journal of Risk and Uncertainty*, **8**, 21–32.

Kagel J. and A.E. Roth (ed.) (1995), *The Handbook of Experimental Economics*, Princeton, NJ: Princeton University Press.

Kahneman, D., J. Knetsch and R.H. Thaler (1990), 'Experimental tests of the endownment effect and the coast theorem', *Journal of Political Economy*, **98**, 1325–48.

Kahneman, D. and Amos Tversky (1979), 'Prospect theory: an analysis of decision under risk', *Econometrica*, **47**, 263–91.

Kim, Oliver and Mark Walker (1984), 'The free rider problem: experimental evidence', *Public Choice*, **43**, 3–24.

Knetsch, J. and R. Davis (1979), 'Comparison of methods for recreational evaluation', in A. Kneese and S. Smith (eds), *Water Research*, Washington, DC: Resources for the Future.

Knetsch, J. and J.A. Sinden (1984), 'Willingness to pay and compensation demanded: experimental evidence of an unexpected disparity in measures of value', *Quarterly Journal of Economics*, **99**, 507–21.

Kragt, Alphons van de, John M. Orbell and Robyn M. Dawes (1983), 'The minimal contributing set as a solution to public goods problems', *American Political Science Review*, **77**, 112–22.

Laury, Susan K. and Charles A. Holt (1998), 'Voluntary provision of public goods: experimental results with interior Nash equilibria', forthcoming in C. Plott and V. Smith (eds), *Handbook of Experimental Economics Results*, New York: Elsevier Press.

Ledyard, J. (1995), 'Public goods: a survey of experimental research', in J. Kagel and A.E. Roth (eds), *The Handbook of Experimental Economics*, Princeton, NJ: Princeton University Press.

List, John (2000), 'Do explicit warnings eliminate the hypothetical bias in elicitation procedures? evidence from field auctions for sportscards', forthcoming in *American Economic Review*.

List, John A. and Craig A. Gallet (2001), 'What experimental protocol influence disparities between actual and hypothetical stated values?,' *Environmental and Resource Economics*, **20**(3), 241–54.

List, John and David Lucking-Reilly (2000), 'Demand reduction in a multi-unit auction: evidence from a sportscard field experiment', forthcoming in *American Economic Review*.

List, J. and J. Shogren (1998), 'Experimental calibration of the difference between actual and hypothetical reported valuations', *Journal of Economic Behavior and Organization*, **37**(2), 193–205.

Loomis, John, A. Gonzalez-Caban and R. Gregory (1994), 'Substitutes and budget constraints in contingent valuation', *Land Economics*, **70**(4), 499–506.

Loomis, John, T. Brown, B. Lucero and G. Peterson (1996), 'Improving validity experiments of contingent valuation methods: results of efforts to reduce the disparity of hypothetical and actual willingness to pay', *Land Economics*, **72**, 450–61.

Louviere, Jordan (1996), 'Relating stated preference measures and models to choices in real markets: calibration of CV responses', in D. Bjornstad and J.R. Kahn (eds), *The Contingent Valuation of Environmental Resources: Methodological Issues and Research Needs*, Cheltenham and Brookfield, US: Edward Elgar, pp. 167–88.

Marwell, G. and R.E. Ames (1979), 'Experiments on the provision of public goods: I: Resources, interest, group size, and the free-rider problem', *American Journal of Sociology*, **84**, 1335–60.

Mitchell, Robert C. and Richard T. Carson (1989), *Using Surveys to Value Public Goods: The Contingent Valuation Method*, Washington, DC: Johns Hopkins Press for Resources for the Future.

Moulin, Hervé (1988), *Axioms of Cooperative Decision Making*, Cambridge: Cambridge University Press.

Mysker, M., P. Olson and A. Williams (1996), 'The voluntary provision of a threshold public good: further experimental results', in R. Mark Isaac (ed.), *Research in Experimental Economics*, volume VI, London: JAI Press.

Neill, Helen (1995), 'The context for substitutes in CVM studies: some empirical observations', *Journal of Environmental Economics and Management*, **29**(3), 393–7.

Neill, H., R. Cummings, G. Harrison and T. McGuckin (with H. Neill, P. Ganderton, G. Harrison and T. McGuckin) (1994), 'Hypothetical surveys and real economic commitments', *Land Economics*, **70**(2), 145–54.

Neilson, W., M. McKee and R.P. Berrens (1998), 'WTA can exceed WTP: uncertainty as an explanation', Working Paper, Department of Economics, Texas A&M University.

Palfrey, Thomas R. and Jeffrey E. Prisbrey (1997), 'Anomalous behavior in linear public goods experiments: how much and why?', *American Economic Review*, **87**, 829–46.

Plott, Charles R. (1987), 'Dimensions of parallelism: some policy applications of experimental methods', in A.E. Roth (ed.), *Laboratory Experimentation in Economics: Six Points of View*, Cambridge: Cambridge University Press, chapter 7.

Plott, Charles R. and Vernon L. Smith (eds) (forthcoming), *Handbook of Experimental Economics Results*, New York: Elsevier Press.

Poe, Gregory, Jeremy Clark, Daniel Rondeau and William Schulze (1999), 'Can hypothetical questions predict actual participation in public programs? A contingent valuation validity test using a provision point mechanism', Working Paper, Cornell University.

Randall, Alan (1996), 'Calibration of CV responses: discussion', in D.J. Bjornstad and James R. Kahn (eds), *The Contingent Valuation of Environmental Resources*, Cheltenham, UK: Edward Elgar, 198–207.

Rapoport, A. and D. Eshed-Levy (1989), 'Provision of step-level public goods: effects of greed and fear of being gypped', *Organizational Behavior and Human Decision Processes*, **44**, 325–44.

Rondeau, Daniel, William D. Schulze and Gregory L. Poe (1999), 'Voluntary revelation of the demand for public goods using a provision point mechanism', *Journal of Public Economics*, **72**, 455–70.

Rose, S., J. Clark, G.L. Poe, D. Rondeau and W.D. Schulze (1997), 'The private provision of public goods: tests of a provision point mechanism for funding green power programs', Environmental and Resource Economics working paper no. 97–02. Cornell University.

Satterthwaite, Mark (1975), 'Strategy-proofness and Arrow's conditions: existence and correspondence theorems for voting procedures and social welfare functions', *Journal of Economic Theory*, **10**, 187–217.

Scherr, Bruce A. and Emerson M. Babb (1975), ' Pricing public goods: an experiment with two proposed pricing systems', *Public Choice*, **23**, 35–48.

Shogren, Jason (2004), 'Experimental methods and valuation', in K.G. Mäler and J. Vincent (eds), *Handbook of Environmental Economics*, Amsterdam: Elsevier.

Shogren, Jason F., S. Cho, C. Koo, J. List, C. Park, P. Palo and R. Wilhelmi (forthcoming), 'Auction mechanisms and the measurement of WTP and WTA', *Environmental and Resource Economics*.

Shogren, Jason F., S.Y. Shin, D.J. Hayes and B. Kliebenstein (1994), 'Resolving differences in willingness to pay and willingness to accept', *American Economic Review*, **84**(3), 255–70.

Smith, V. Kerry and Carol Mansfield (1998), 'Buying time: real and hypothetical offers', *Journal of Environmental Economics and Management*, **36**, 209–24.

Smith, V. Kerry and Laura L. Osborne (1996), 'Do contingent valuation estimates pass a "Scope" test?', *Journal of Environmental Economics and Management*, **31**, 287–301.

Smith, V. Kerry and Laura Osborne (1996), 'Do contingent valuation estimates pass a "Scope" test a meta analysis?', *Journal of Environmental Economics and Management*, **31**(3), 287–301.

Smith, Vernon L. (1979), 'Incentive compatible experimental processes for the provision of public goods', in V.L. Smith (ed.), *Research in Experimental Economics*, Greenwich, CT: JAI Press.

Smith, Vernon L. (1982), 'Microeconomic systems as an experimental science', *American Economic Review*, **72**(4), 923–55.

Smith, Vernon L. and J.M. Walker (1993), 'Monetary rewards and decision cost in experimental economics', *Economic Inquiry*, **31**, 245–61.

Sweeney, John W. Jr. (1973), 'An experimental investigation of the free-rider problem', *Social Science Research*, **2**, 277–92.

Taylor, Laura O. (1998), 'Incentive compatible referenda and the valuation of public goods', *Agricultural and Resource Economics Review*, **27**(2), 132–9.

Taylor, Laura O., M. McKee, S.K. Laury and R.G. Cummings (2000), 'Induced value tests of the referendum voting mechanism', manuscript, Policy Research Center, Georgia State University, Atlanta, GA.

Willig, R.D. (1976), 'Consumer surplus without apology', *American Economic Review*, **66**, 589–97.

9 Designing a contingent valuation study to estimate the benefits of the conservation reserve program on grassland bird populations[1]

Mary Clare Ahearn, Kevin J. Boyle and Daniel R. Hellerstein[2]

9.1 Introduction

Wildlife biologists have expressed concern about declining populations of grassland bird species, and loss of habitats is generally cited as the major reason for their decline. The major historical grassland area of the US is in the heartland, where agriculture dominates the landscape. Over time, farms and farm fields have been established and consolidated, leaving less undisturbed habitat. While agricultural activities may be detrimental to some species, other species may benefit from the habitat and food sources provided by agricultural lands. However, the majority of grassland bird species appear to be declining. Data from the Breeding Bird Survey, which tracks the populations of 431 species in North America, reveal that only 23 per cent (between 1966 and 1998) of grassland bird species populations increased. The comparable rate for all bird species combined indicates that 52 per cent increased (Sauer et al., 1999).

In Fiscal year 1996, the Federal government spent $6.7 billion on resource conservation and related programs affecting agriculture (USDA/ERS, 1997). The Conservation Reserve Program (CRP) is the major conservation program of the US Department of Agriculture (USDA), costing $1.8 billion in fiscal year, 1996. The CRP pays farmland owners to retire their environmentally sensitive lands from agricultural production for periods of 10 or 15 years. CRP enrollment represents about 7 per cent of the cropland in the 48 contiguous states. While more than three-quarters of all US counties have some CRP acreage, over four-fifths of the acreage is concentrated in one-fifth of the counties, which are typically located in the Midwest and plains states. Most of the CRP acres are planted to perennial grasses, which is likely to benefit grassland bird species. The Wildlife Management Institute (1994) reports that the CRP land in grasses is at least twice the size of grassland habitats in the entire national and state wildlife refuges within the continental US.

Anecdotal evidence by wildlife experts (e.g., National Audubon Society, 1994) and empirical analyses (e.g., Lauber, 1991) suggest that the CRP has helped to reduce, stop, or reverse the declines in the populations of some grassland bird species.

Initial enrollments in the CRP were prioritized according to the erodibility of the soil. As priorities of the CRP are expanded to include other environmental benefits, such as improvements in grassland bird populations, information is needed on the broader range of values the public assigns to such increases. There have been very few non-market valuation studies that have considered grassland birds. These have focused on use values such as small game and pheasant hunting (Ribaudo et al., 1990; Hansen et al., 1999). While policy issues often motivate many contingent valuation (CV) applications, the reporting of the study results more often than not focus on methodological contributions. In this chapter, we will describe an application of the CV method to valuing grassland birds to demonstrate how a CV study can be designed to address a timely policy issue. Specifically, we report on a study that was designed to provide national welfare estimates for improvements in grassland bird populations due to the implementation of the CRP.

9.2 The CRP and the Environmental Benefit Index

Following the legislated objectives of the CRP, the US Department of Agriculture (USDA) develops criteria for prioritizing land submitted for enrollment. When the CRP was established in 1985, the erodibility of land was the key environmental priority. Over time, other environmental factors, such as water quality, carried weight in the prioritization of land for enrollment. Revisions to the CRP that went into effect with the tenth sign-up in 1991 introduced the Environmental Benefits Index (EBI) to prioritize and rank landowners' offers of land for enrollment. The EBI is composed of a number of environmental indicators and points assigned to each indicator by a panel of experts for each parcel of land submitted for enrollment in the CRP (Table 9.1) (USDA, FSA, 1999).[3] Land is accepted into the CRP based on the total score on the EBI, which includes a cost component. For instance, land with a high score and a low rental bid receives the highest priority. The maximum number of points assigned to each 'factor' ranges from 25 to 100, and the points for some factors are broken down into 'subfactors'. During the 1995 sign-up for the CRP, land owners were given open access to the information on how the EBI was calculated (Osborn, 1997), thereby allowing them to purposefully increase their score by providing certain cover attributes. Contingent valuation results on the value the public places on improvements in grassland bird populations can help to inform expert assessments, which are the basis for assignment of points under the EBI's 'wildlife' factor.

*Table 9.1   Environmental Benefit Index for the Conservation Reserve
Program: sign-up period that ended 11 February 2000*

Factors	Subfactors	Points
Wildlife (0 to 100 points)	Wildlife cover habitat cover benefits	0–50
	Endangered species	0–15
	Proximity to water	0, 5, or 10
	Adjacent to protected areas	0, 5, or 10
	Wildlife enhancement	0 or 5
	Restored wetland and upland cover	0 or 10
Water quality (0 to 100 points)	Location in area designated for water quality protection	0–30
	Ground water quality benefits, based on soil type and population using groundwater for drinking	0–30
	Surface water quality benefits	0–30
	Wetland benefits	0–10
Erosion (0 to 100 points)	Erodibility Index	0–100
Enduring benefits (0 to 50 points)	Variety of practices with benefits that will be realized after the contract period ends: type of tree, wetland restoration, seeding of more than five species of grass, rare habitat restoration, shrub plantings, registered historic place, maintaining functions after CRP period, cultural resources present	0–50
Air quality benefits from reduced wind erosion (0 to 35 points)	Wind erosion impacts, including population that may be impacted	0–25
	Wind erosion soils list	0–5
	Air quality zones	0–5
State or national conservation priority area (0 or 25 points)	If at least 51 per cent of parcel is in a designated area	0–25

Table 9.1   (continued)

Factors	Subfactors	Points
Cost	Per-acre rental rate offered	Points determined after the sign-up concludes
	Request of government cost-share	0 or 10
	Per-acre rental rate offered bonus	Receives 1 point for every dollar below the maximum acceptable payment rate, not to exceed 15

Besides being useful in constructing a better EBI, the economic information being developed in this study has potential for use in *ex post* benefit–cost analyses of the CRP.[4] The most widely cited benefit–cost analysis of the CRP to date is Ribaudo et al. (1990) (see also CAST, 1995; Federal Register, 1996; US, GAO, 1993), which has been updated and enhanced by Feather et al. (1999). Both of these economic analyses include benefits of the CRP from recreational hunting and in the case of Feather et al., viewing wildlife. In terms of grassland birds, Feather et al. estimated the benefits of pheasant hunting to be $80 million per year and the benefits of wildlife viewing, which may contain values for viewing grassland birds, to be $348 million per year. The values estimated in the study reported here include more game birds than pheasants and include wildlife viewing that is specific to grassland birds.

9.3   Designing a CV study to address a specific policy application
The design of this study presented two fundamental challenges. First, most CV studies published in the journals deal with methodological issues, where the key feature is the experimental design and the policy issue takes a secondary role. In the current application, the policy issue and the experimental design were equally important, and careful design to address the policy issue requires attention to framing the valuation question that may be conveniently overlooked in methodological studies.

Secondly, the NOAA Blue Ribbon Panel (1993)[5] suggested some very stringent standards for the use of CV to estimate passive use values. While the Panel was specifically considering applications for Natural Resource Damage Assessments, they set a hurdle that many feel must be met for any

CV study of passive use values where the results will be used in policy analyses. Thus, our second challenge was to carefully consider the extent to which the study design met the Panel's proposed criteria.

These two challenges are interrelated. One of the studies (the so-called 'Exxon birds study') that prompted the formation of the NOAA Panel, found that passive use values are not sensitive to the number of birds being valued (Boyle et al., 1994; Desvousges, 1993), which compromises the usefulness of value estimates for policy analyses. This result has commonly become referred to as a lack of, or insensitivity to, scope. The NOAA Panel concluded that the burden of proof for credible CV estimates rests with the researchers, and, in particular, emphasized the importance of finding scope in CV results. Carson (1997) has argued that insensitivity to scope is 'a point readily conceded by (contingent valuation) practitioners, but . . . is generally avoidable with appropriate survey design, pretesting, and administrations' (p. 6). Thus, tests of scope are fundamental in the estimation of policy-relevant estimates of values for changes in grassland bird populations and in addressing the NOAA Panel's criterion for credible estimates of passive use values.

The survey design was developed through a series of 21 focus groups conducted over an eight-month period (April–November, 1996).[6] The following subsections discuss how we addressed the NOAA Panel's criteria for a credible survey, designed the survey to address the policy issue, and developed tests of scope.

9.3.1   *Addressing key components of the NOAA Panel criteria*

A listing of key study design features identified by the NOAA Panel, the Panel's criterion for each feature, and the specific design features for our study are listed in Table 9.2. A few of the NOAA Panel guidelines were not relevant to our study because they are specific to studies of passive use values for Natural Resource Damage Assessments and are not included in the table.[7] Our study design is generally consistent with the NOAA Panel recommendations, with three key exceptions: (1) the method of data collection, (2) conservative design, and (3) warm glow. The extensive information we conveyed to respondents could not have been accomplished with a pure telephone survey; thus, the choice was between in-person interviews and a mail survey. Our decision to use a mail survey was purely financial. Mail surveys have a low cost per observation, which allowed for larger sample sizes and more extensive testing for scope. A large national sample is much more useful for addressing national policy issues, than a sample from a small region. We followed the Dillman Total Design Method (Dillman, 1978) for mail surveys and believe the research supporting this approach is quite strong.

Table 9.2   *Selected NOAA Panel design criteria and their implementation in the grassland bird study design*

Features	NOAA guidelines	Study design features
General guidelines		
Sample type and size	Probability sampling, with guidance of a sampling statistician	Probability based (random) samples of US ($n = 2750$) and Iowa ($n = 5000$) households
Non-response	Minimize	Monetary incentives were provided to entice sample participants to respond
Data collection	Face-to-face preferable, but telephone interviews have some advantages	Mail survey was used
Interviewer effects	Pre-test for	Not applicable
Pre-testing	Careful pilot work and pretesting	21 focus groups conducted
Guidelines for value elicitation surveys		
Conservative design	Choose a design that tends to underestimate WTP	Used a multiple-bounded question that included response options of *definitely* and *probably yes*, *unsure* and *definitely* and *probably no*, and only used *definitely yes* responses as *yes* in the data analyses
Elicitation format	Willingness to pay, not willingness to accept	Willingness to pay used
Referendum format	Valuation question posed as a single-bounded yes/no vote on a referendum	Valuation question posed as a referendum vote
Accurate description of program or policy	Must be adequate and relevant	Information booklet was used to present valuation scenario in written form with numerical and graphical displays

Table 9.2   (continued)

Features	NOAA guidelines	Study design features
Pre-testing of photographs	Explore effects of photographs on subjects	Pen and ink drawings of birds were pretested in focus groups and found not to work
Substitutes	Respondents must be reminded of substitutes	Respondents were reminded, just before answering the referendum question that a *yes* vote would mean that they would have less money to spend on other environmental issues
No-answer option	Allow yes/no and no answer responses to referendum question	Respondents were allowed to say they would not pay anything and then did not answer the valuation question
Yes/no follow-ups	Follow up referendum question with open-ended questions about why the choice was made	Followed up with questions that had fixed and open-ended response options
Cross-tabulations	Include questions to help interpret valuation responses, characteristics, etc.	Included questions on income, interest in grassland birds, attitudes toward survey topic, understanding of valuation exercise, belief scenario will work and others
Checks on understanding and acceptance	Above guidelines must be met without making the survey too complex	Respondent was asked to take a true/false quiz as a measure of their comprehension of the details of the valuation scenario

Table 9.2   (continued)

Features	NOAA guidelines	Study design features
Goals for value elicitation surveys		
Alternative expenditure possibilities	Remind respondents	Same as 'substitutes' above
Deflection of transaction value	Avoid the warm-glow of giving and the dislike of big business	Warm glow not directly addressed and big business not relevant to the application
Burden of proof	Show through pretesting or other experiments that the survey does not suffer problems the above guide-lines are intended to address	Survey design included tests of scope, true/false questions to test respondents knowledge, a question asking respondents if they believed grassland bird populations would increase, and probes after the yes/no votes

With reference to point (2) above, it is not entirely clear what the Panel meant by a 'conservative design', as there are many features of the design that can influence the magnitude of welfare estimates. We used a multiple-bounded variant of a referendum question with polychotomous responses (Welsh and Bishop, 1993; Welsh and Poe, 1998). This question design is conservative in two dimensions. The multiple-bounded component, where all respondents vote on a sequence of bid amounts, appears to avoid the bid effect of single-bounded questions and provides more conservative welfare estimates (Roach et al., 2001). The polychotomous response options allow for various codings of yes/no responses so as to provide a conservative welfare estimate (Welsh and Poe, 1998).

Finally, there is no clear guidance of how warm glow (point (3)), if it even exists, can be avoided in survey design. Thus, this recommendation was not specifically addressed in the study design.

9.3.2   *Addressing the policy question*
Use value estimates for bird hunting and bird watching are available in the literature and data are available to update these estimates from at least two ongoing Federal surveys (see Feather et al., 1999). Hence, an important

objective in this study was on the development of a national estimate of passive use values for national policy analysis. The policy motivation of this study directed the study design features in a number of ways, including the identification of the study region, the use of plausible information on the changes in the bird populations, and the description of the CRP program features.

The first step was to define the study region. Because of the focus on national estimates, one sample was defined as a national, random sample of households. In addition, a random sample of households within a specific region was selected to address three questions. One question was whether people located in areas with concentrated CRP acreage care about increasing grassland bird populations. Another question was, if both samples hold non-zero values for grassland bird populations, are the regional and national value estimates comparable? Finally, we wondered if a regional sample, where respondents are likely to hold use and passive use values, would be more likely to demonstrate scope effects in value estimates.[8] The acreage in the CRP is primarily concentrated in three geographic regions, the panhandle of Texas, Iowa and the boundary areas of adjacent states, and eastern Montana through North Dakota and into northwestern Minnesota (USDA, FSA, 2000). We chose Iowa as the area from where a second sample should be drawn.

Participants in the national sample were asked to value changes in the populations of grassland birds in the greater Iowa area, west of the Mississippi River, which we referred to as the 'Central Plains Region' in the survey instrument. This area includes Iowa, northern Missouri, eastern Kansas, Nebraska and South Dakota, and southern Minnesota, which represents one of the three high density clusters of CRP acreage. Participants in the Iowa sample were asked to value changes in grassland bird populations in Iowa alone, a subset of the Central Plains Region specified for the national sample. This was done because focus groups conducted in Iowa suggested that it would be difficult to elicit values from Iowa residents for changes in grassland bird populations in Iowa and adjoining states. Specifically, all logical payment vehicles would only require Iowa residents to pay for the change and focus group respondents indicated that people in other states should also pay for the program if there were going to be effects in their states.

The next key step was to develop realistic changes in the populations of grassland birds. Lauber (1991) conducted a preliminary analysis of the effect of the CRP on bird populations using national CRP enrollment data from 1986, the first year of the program, through 1989. He found that of 102 bird species whose habitats are associated with agriculture, 31 were spatially correlated with CRP acreage. Four species showed significant, positive population increases after the introduction of the CRP (Western Meadow

Lark, Ring-necked Pheasant, Brown-headed Cowbird, and Northern Bobwhite Quail). Lauber's major advisor, Raymond O'Connor (Professor of Wildlife Ecology, University of Maine), updated the analyses using CRP data from 1986 through 1995, focusing specifically on Iowa. O'Connor identified 15 species whose populations were positively correlated with CRP acreage and eight species whose populations were negatively correlated with CRP acreage.[9]

Describing a program that will provide both positive and negative changes is not consistent with the vast majority of non-market valuation studies that consistently assume that a change is all good or all bad. Moreover, the empirical findings on changes in bird populations are not consistent with the general perspective that CRP acreage has resulted in increases in the populations of grassland birds. From an ecologist's point of view, this result is not surprising when one recognizes that any ecosystem intervention is likely to have positive and negative effects. In initial focus groups in Iowa we pretested a scenario where the populations of 15 species increased and the populations of eight species declined as a result of the CRP. We observed total scenario rejection; respondents could not deal with a scenario where some species would gain and some species would decline. This rejection was so complete, we decided to not even attempt to pretest this scenario in focus groups outside of Iowa.

Given this scenario rejection, we re-examined our use of the empirical results from Lauber and O'Connor. In particular, we questioned our reliance on a strict interpretation of the findings due, for example, to conflicting results between Lauber's and O'Connor's findings about the relationship between the population of ring-necked pheasants and CRP acreage in Iowa. In addition, O'Connor felt that his model was much less reliable on a state basis than at the national level. Some wildlife biologists dispute the quality of the data used by Lauber and O'Connor because bird counts are developed by driving along roads and creation of CRP acreage could have moved grassland birds away from the roadsides to more desirable habitat. This would have the effect of reducing counts even if populations had increased. Thus, we chose to use the model predictions as reasonable predictions of grassland bird populations and changes in the populations. But, we only valued increases in the populations of 16 species, eight whose populations had declined over the past 30 years and eight whose populations had increased over the last 30 years (Tables 9.3 and 9.4). The bird populations in Table 9.3 and 9.4 are from the survey questionnaire for the national sample. These tables were included in the information booklets that accompanied the survey instruments, along with a graphical depiction of the bird population changes. Values for the changes in the populations of all 16 species were elicited as a group rather than individually. This

Table 9.3   Species whose populations decreased over the last 30 years and proposed program enhancements

Species	Native or introduced	Permanent or migratory	Populations 30 years ago	1997 (current) populations	Populations with habitat enhancement	Percentage change due to proposal
Grasshopper Sparrow	Native	Migratory	172 000	70 000	165 000	136 per cent
Henslow's Sparrow	Native	Migratory	35 000	17 000	33 000	94 per cent
Mourning Dove	Native	Permanent	608 000	347 000	600 000	73 per cent
Eastern Kingbird	Native	Migratory	169 000	110 000	165 000	50 per cent
Northern Bobwhite Quail	Native	Permanent	562 000	423 000	542 000	28 per cent
Horned Lark	Native	Permanent	622 000	473 000	595 000	26 per cent
Dickcissel	Native	Migratory	1 294 000	1 010 000	1 237 000	22 per cent
Pheasant	Introduced	Permanent	783 000	666 000	762 000	14 per cent

Table 9.4 Species whose populations were constant or increased over the last 30 years and proposed program enhancements

Species	Native or introduced	Permanent or migratory	Populations 30 years ago	1997 (current) populations	Populations with habitat enhancement	Percentage change due to proposal
Lark Sparrow	Native	Migratory	111 000	111 000	204 000	84 per cent
Upland Sandpiper	Native	Migratory	26 000	27 000	44 000	63 per cent
Gray Partridge	Introduced	Permanent	66 000	71 000	112 000	58 per cent
Field Sparrow	Native	Migratory	169 000	169 000	248 000	47 per cent
Indigo Bunting	Native	Migratory	222 000	222 000	280 000	26 per cent
Killdeer	Native	Migratory	152 000	159 000	199 000	25 per cent
Barn Swallow	Native	Migratory	489 000	493 000	600 000	22 per cent
House Wren	Native	Migratory	233 000	238 000	285 000	20 per cent

circumvented having to determine the correct algorithm for adding the value estimates for individual species.

Another key feature was to design the valuation question so respondents would not value the CRP as a whole, but focus only on the effects on bird populations. This was accomplished by describing a program where the type of grass on CRP land would be changed to be more beneficial to birds with no change in CRP acreage. This avoided the problem that people would value a change in the amount of CRP acreage. It also avoided the problem that people would include in their value other potential benefits, such as those from the control of soil erosion.

The final issue concerned the length of the CRP contracts, which is generally ten years. Respondents were concerned that land enrolled in the CRP would return to production as soon as the contracts expired, thereby reversing the gains in grassland bird populations. While this concern has some validity, we attempted to convince respondents that much of the land enrolled in the CRP is marginal from an economic viewpoint and will remain in CRP indefinitely.

The payment vehicle for the national (Iowa) sample was a one-time increase in respondents' 1998 Federal (Iowa) income taxes. Respondents were told that the one-time payment was necessary to fund the program to change the type of grass planted on CRP lands and that it would take about five years for the bird populations to reach their new levels.

9.3.3   Tests of scope

The original study was conceived to estimate values for changes in the populations of grassland birds and the scope test is in terms of different levels of change. Different levels of change were also of interest from a policy perspective so that marginal values could be developed for differential impacts of the CRP as more or less land was enrolled. The increases in bird populations included small, medium, and large changes. The large changes, as presented in Tables 9.3 and 9.4, were based on O'Connor's best estimates of the effects of the CRP on the populations of grassland birds. The small change was 10 per cent of the large change and the medium change was 50 per cent of the large change for each species.

During the pre-testing of the survey instrument in the focus groups, it became apparent that scope may also be important in another dimension. Iowa respondents appeared to be very concerned about the presence/absence of game species. Thus, a third treatment was administered to the Iowa sample, which was a large change without the three game species in the design (partridge, pheasant, and quail).

Participants in the national and Iowa focus groups indicated a heightened interest about the presence of an endangered species. The endangered species treatment used the large change (with game birds) and respondents were told the Henslow's sparrow was endangered.[10]

The large, medium, and small changes in grassland bird populations present a scope test over the quantity of birds effects. The game bird and endangered species treatments may be viewed as a scope test in the quality dimension, since it introduces a variation in the types and status of individual species affected.

The national sample was randomly stratified into four treatment groups. The Iowa sample was randomly divided into five groups, with four groups receiving the same treatments as the national sample. The fifth group received the large change without game birds.[11]

9.4   Modeling framework

Willingness to pay (WTP) for changes in grassland bird populations is based on an additive functional form, with a normally distributed error term (ε) that represents information the analyst cannot observe:

$$WTP = X\beta + \varepsilon \qquad (9.1)$$

where . . .

$$\varepsilon = Normal\ (0,\ \sigma^2)$$
$$PROB(NO) = prob(WTP < BID) = \Phi[(BID - X\beta)/\sigma]$$

and where X is a vector of variables that represent the various treatments to investigate scope, β is a vector of parameters to be estimated, BID is a bid amount respondents are asked to vote on, and Φ designates a normal cumulative distribution function. This is a generalized statement for any given respondent and a single bid from the multiple-bounded panel of bid amounts.

The linearized model of WTP is specified as:[12]

$$X\beta = \beta_o + \beta_s\ per\ cent\Delta + \beta_{s2}\ per\ cent\Delta^2 + \beta_g G + \beta_e E + \beta_a A_j, \qquad (9.2)$$

where per centΔ is the per cent change in grassland birds, E is a dummy that equals one for the treatment that includes the endangered species, G is a dummy for treatments that include game species, and A is a vector of respondent specific characteristic.[13] If scope is present in the quantity dimension of changes in grassland populations, then β_s and/or β_{s2} would be significantly greater than 0. Scope in the quality dimension would imply that β_g and/or β_e would be significantly greater than 0. The respondent characteristics are:

Income: respondent's annual household income,
Age: respondent's age,
Male: 1 if respondent is male and 0 otherwise,
Succeed: 1 if respondent thinks bird numbers will definitely increase and 0 otherwise,
CRP access: dimension-less index that increases for living near more CRP acreage, and
Hunt view: 1 if someone in respondent's household hunts or views wildlife and 0 otherwise.

The succeed variable relates to the NOAA Panel's Burden of Proof criterion that respondents believe the valuation scenario.

The multiple-bounded question presented each study participant with 13 bid amounts to respond to, ranging from $1 to $100. A clear advantage of a multiple-bounded question over a single-bounded question is that the interval where the latent variable (WTP) lies is narrowed. By contrast, in a single-bounded question, the investigator only knows if the latent variable lies above or below a single threshold. The multiple-bounded question reveals an interval where the latent variable lies between the bids where responses switch from a yes to a no response. Given these upper and lower bounds, the likelihood function, following Welsh and Bishop (1993) is:

$$L = \sum_{i=1}^{n} \ln \left[\Phi \left(\frac{BID_i^u - X_i \beta}{\sigma} \right) - \Phi \left(\frac{BID_i^l - X_i \beta}{\sigma} \right) \right]. \tag{9.3}$$

The polychotomous instrument requires a classification of answers from five categories (ranging from 'DEFINITELY YES' to 'DEFINITELY NO') into 'YES' and 'NO'. In this analysis we treat DEFINITELY YES as YES, and all other answers as NO. This is a conservative choice, and yields smaller WTP values.[14]

9.5   Data collection

The survey implementation was carried out by the Madison, WI office of Hagler Bailly, Inc. Hagler Bailly purchased random samples of US households and Iowa households from Genesys, Inc., and administered the survey by mail with a full set of follow-up mailings as prescribed by Dillman (1978).

The national sample size was 2750 (Table 9.5). There were four different 'treatments': small change, medium change, large change, and a large change with one endangered species. All of the treatments included game bird species. The first three treatments in the national sample were administered to 750 households; the large treatment with the endangered species was administered to 500 households. This survey was administered from

Table 9.5 Design of scope treatments and sample size (number of surveys mailed)

Treatments	Changes	National sample	Iowa sample
Small change	Bird species increase by 10 per cent of the large change treatment	n = 750	n = 1500
Medium change	Bird species increase by 50 per cent of the large change treatment	n = 750	n = 750
Large change	Bird populations increase by the amounts presented in Tables 9.3 and 9.4, which were derived from wildlife models	n = 750	n = 750
Large change, with a locally endangered species	Same as large change, plus the Henslow's Sparrow designated as endangered	n = 500	n = 1000
Large change, without game species	Same as large change, except the ring-necked pheasant, gray partridge, and bob-white quail were excluded species	Not applicable	n = 750

12 May 1997 through 18 August 1997. The response rate (percentage of completed deliverable surveys) was 45 per cent.

The Iowa survey was administered in two phases. In the initial printing of the survey instruments for the Iowa sample, the printer inadvertently switched two pages in two survey versions. As the error was not detected until after the surveys were administered, Hagler Bailly re-administered part of the survey. Phase I had seven versions; five of those had a multiple-bounded CV format and two had a single-bounded format. The five multiple-bounded treatments were: a large change without game birds or endangered species, a large change with game birds and without endangered species, a large change with both game birds and endangered species, a medium change with game birds and without endangered species, and a small change with game birds and without endangered species. The two versions with the problem survey instruments were: a large change without game birds and without an endangered species and a large change with game birds and without an endangered species. The treatments of the two single-bounded CV formats were a large change and a small change, both with game birds and without an endangered species. The first phase of the Iowa survey was administered to 5000 households, but 1500 of those households received the problem survey instruments. The survey was administered between 20 June and 15 September 1997. The response rate, as a percentage of deliverable surveys, was 56 per cent.

The second phase of the Iowa survey was administered to a sample of 3500, with five versions (Table 9.5). Four of the five versions used a multiple-bounded CV format: large change without game birds or endangered species, large change with game birds and without endangered species, large with both game birds and endangered species, and a small change with game birds and without endangered species. The treatment of the single-bounded version in the second phase of Iowa data collection was a large change with game birds and without an endangered species. The second phase of the Iowa sample was administered between 9 January and 11 March 1998, with a response rate of 58 per cent. In the Iowa analyses reported here, we use all of the data from the first and second phases, except the data for the two treatments that were compromised by the printing error in the first mailing.[15] For the treatments where two sets of data were pooled, we were not able to detect any substantial significant differences in respondent characteristics or responses to the valuation questions.

We provided respondents with a monetary incentive to return the surveys.[16] For the Iowa second phase survey the response rate was only 42 per cent without a monetary incentive, but went as high as 62 per cent with a $5 incentive (Hagler Bailly, 1998). For the national sample, the response rate was only 32 per cent without a monetary incentive and went as high as 55 per cent with a $5 incentive (Hagler Bailly, 1997). The response rates reported are averages for respondents who did and did not receive monetary incentives, and we found that the incentives did not affect response to the valuation questions.

9.6 Results

Table 9.6 reports basic socioeconomic characteristics of our sample. The national sample was about the same percentage of males and the same average age as the Iowa sample, but had higher levels of educational and household income.

Both samples had heard of at least one of the grassland bird species whose populations would be increased. However, respondents in the Iowa sample were much more concerned about helping grassland birds than were respondents in the national sample, and were much more likely to be users. These results suggest that WTP may vary between the samples.

About one-third of the respondents thought the proposal would succeed in accomplishing the goal of increasing grassland bird populations, and an additional 40 per cent thought that the program may succeed. Perceptions of success were weakly correlated with the scope treatments. In the

Table 9.6   Basic descriptive statistics

	National	Iowa
Socio-economic characteristics		
Percentage male	69 per cent	67 per cent
Mean age (years)	50	52
Percentage with some college	72 per cent	64 per cent
Mean income	$52 000	$43 000
Respondents knowledge and concern for grassland birds		
Heard of any of the bird species?	91 per cent yes	96 per cent yes
Helping grassland birds is much less important than other environmental problems?	21 per cent strongly or somewhat disagree	54 per cent strongly or somewhat disagree
Anyone in household hunt?	23 per cent yes	29 per cent yes
Hunt game grassland birds?	47 per cent yes	83 per cent yes
Anyone in household watch wild birds?	55 per cent yes	64 per cent yes
Belief in scenario		
Think proposal will be successful in increasing grassland bird populations?	33 per cent definitely yes 48 per cent maybe yes	35 per cent definitely yes 46 per cent maybe yes

National survey, about 40 per cent thought the large program would succeed (46 per cent thought it may succeed), compared with 26 per cent (and 48 per cent) for the small program. The Iowa survey had similar results, with about 38 per cent (46 per cent) saying the large program would (may) succeed, and 30 per cent (46 per cent) saying the small program would (may) succeed.

As noted earlier, the survey began with a set of true/false questions to test respondent understanding of the valuation task, one of the NOAA Panel's burden of proof criteria. Overall, responses were quite similar in the national and Iowa samples, which indicates comparable understanding of the valuation task (Table 9.7). In terms of questions that relate to the scope tests, respondents did quite well with an average percentage grade in the 80s. Respondents did not do well with statements regarding whether there would be other environmental effects from the program, in addition to the increase in grassland bird populations. We observed this in the focus groups as well, in that some people are aware that different components of ecosystems are interconnected. Indeed, some respondents did not accept our attempts to partition out just the effects on grassland birds, from increasing

Table 9.7 Results of test of respondents' understanding of valuation task

Questions	Percentage true	
	National	Iowa
Grassland bird populations are lower than 30 years ago.	98	97
Without proposal, scientists expect populations of grassland bird species to remain constant at current levels.		
Small, medium, large, and large without game birds treatments.	76	77
Large with an endangered species treatment (other than the endangered Henslows sparrow).	70	67
Land in CRP will increase	32	28
Proposal will provide significant benefits in terms of soil erosion, water quality and populations of other wildlife.	66	65
It will take 20 years for grassland bird populations to reach their new levels.	19	20
The proposal will cause large increases in the populations of robins, blue jays, cardinals and red-winged blackbirds.	11	12
None of the birds affected by the proposal is endangered.		
Small, medium, large, and large without game bird treatments.	92	92
Large with an endangered species treatment.	10	15
Proposal will restore populations to levels of 30 years ago.		
Small and medium treatments	35	37
Large, large without game birds and large with an endangered species treatments.	93	80
Proposal will increase pheasant numbers.		
Small, medium, large, and large with an endangered species treatments.	87	87
Large without game bird treatments.	NA	21
Populations of all species will increase by 10 per cent or less.		
Small treatment.	89	90
Medium, large, large without game birds, and large with an endangered species treatments.	20	22

land in the CRP and other beneficial environmental effects.[17] These test results suggest that valuation estimates may be biased upward for some respondents because they are including other environmental effects. While it is desirable to partition estimates for different components of a policy change, this may be difficult to do in reality when respondents recognize underlying physical and biological interrelationships.

Moving to the valuation results, 29 per cent (26 per cent) of the respondents in the national (Iowa) sample indicated that they would not pay anything to increase grassland birds. These results are weakly correlated with scope treatments. For example, in the Iowa survey, the percentage of these 'non-participants' ranges from about 22 per cent (large with endangered) to about 27 per cent (small). However, this is not a clear tendency, as evidenced by the 28 per cent non-participation in the large treatment. The National survey has similar results, with non-participation ranging from 28 per cent (large with endangered species) to 33 per cent (small).[18]

Analysis of the valuation responses presents some mixed results with respect to scope (Table 9.8). In the national sample, sensitivity to scope does not exist for the change in the populations of grassland birds, but does exist in the quality dimension (presence of an endangered species) when respondent-specific covariates are introduced into the model. For the Iowa sample, scope exists in terms of the change in the populations of grassland birds and in the quality dimensions (absence of game birds) when covariates are not included, and only arise in terms of the population change when covariates are included. Two caveats apply here, these scope findings are unique to the imposition that scope in birds numbers is a continuous (linear, with quadratic terms) function, which is no more stringent than the assumptions imposed in market demand estimation (of adding up and symmetry). Secondly, as is true with other studies, economic theory provides little guidance as to the inclusion of covariates. We have simply chosen a parsimonious set of covariates that seemed plausible to include in the estimation, and, as noted, the scope results are sensitive to the inclusion of covariates. The only scope result which is robust to the inclusion/exclusion of covariates is the change in the populations of grassland birds for the Iowa sample.

The covariates were significant and their qualitative impact was as expected.[19] For both National and Iowa samples, INCOME is significant and positive – wealthier individuals will pay more for the program. SUCCEED is also significant and positive – individuals who believe the program will succeed will pay more. AGE, while not significant, seems to reduce WTP, while proximity to CRP lands (which might proxy for awareness and concern for the wildlife impacts of CRP lands) is positive (though not significant).

The survey questionnaire included debriefing questions to determine why respondents voted yes or no. Of the respondents who answered definitely yes to at least one of the bid amounts, 68 per cent of respondents indicated that the change in the grassland bird populations was worth the highest bid amount for which they answered definitely yes and 23 per cent indicated that they were not valuing grassland birds or were behaving strategically.[20] Of the 23 per cent, 15 per cent gave responses that suggest overstatement of value and 8 per cent gave responses that suggest understatement of value.

Table 9.8　*Estimates of coefficients in equation 2[a] (standard errors in parentheses)*

Variables	National results		Iowa results	
	Without covariates	With covariates	Without covariates	With covariates
Constant	1.855	−4.348	−0.068	−11.452*
	(1.388)	(4.184)	(2.070)	(2.920)
Percentage	0.058	0.119	0.147*	0.115*
	(0.044)	(0.118)	(0.067)	(0.069)
Percentage squared	−0.0003	−0.001	−0.0010*	−0.0008
	(0.0003)	(0.001)	(0.0006)	(0.0006)
Includes game	NA	NA	2.695*	1.990
			(1.616)	(1.679)
Includes endangered	2.614	4.949*	−0.231	−0.416
	(2.179)	(2.511)	(1.451)	(1.519)
Income		0.00004*		0.0001*
		(0.00002)		(0.00001)
Age		−0.012		−0.054
		(0.057)		(0.035)
Male		−3.985*		0.526
		(1.928)		(1.153)
Succeed		13.179*		11.322*
		(1.745)		(1.009)
CRP access		0.108		0.044
		(0.092)		(0.033)
Hunt view		6.384*		8.511*
		(1.926)		(1.383)
Bid	23.565*	23.141*	22.091*	20.811*
	(0.668)	(0.451)	(0.224)	(0.245)
N	1048	913	2377	2076
Wald Statistic	1248	3615	10839	10072

Note:　[a]Asterisks denote significance at the 10 per cent level. NA indicates that the variable is not applicable.

Less than 1 per cent indicated reasons that might be interpreted to imply invalid or protest responses. In the Iowa survey, 80 per cent indicated that the change in the population was worth the highest amount they answered definitely yes to, but 14 per cent indicated they were not valuing grassland birds or behaving strategically. Of the 14 per cent, 8 per cent likely overstated their values and 5 per cent understated their values. As with the national sample, less than 1 per cent of the Iowa respondents indicated they provided protest or invalid no responses. These results suggest that most respondents were providing truthful responses, but there were invalid yes responses that could serve to inflate value estimates. The invalid yes responses were less than 14 per cent of the people who said they would pay something in the national sample and are offset to some extent by the respondents who may have revealed understatement of their values. The comparable percentage for the Iowa sample is less than 7 per cent.

Welfare estimates range from about $10.89 to about $14.42 (Table 9.9). Even when the model coefficients support the presence of scope effects, the changes in welfare estimates are quite small across treatments. A conservative annual aggregate welfare estimate, based on the results of the small treatment is approximately $33 million (in 1998 dollars). In comparison, a recent annual aggregate estimate of the wildlife recreation benefits associated with the Conservation Reserve Program amounted to $538 million (in 1998 dollars) (Feather et al., 1999). Hence, the national non-use value of grassland birds of the Central Plains region is about 6 per cent of the major environmental use values of the CRP. Of course, CRP enhances grassland bird habitat in places other than the Central Plains and enhances the

Table 9.9   Average WTP across sample (Krinsky–Robb standard deviations in parentheses)

Treatments	National data		Iowa data	
	Without covariates	With covariates	Without covariates	With covariates
Small	10.89	12.12	10.77	11.63
	(0.97)	(1.10)	(0.54)	(0.63)
Medium	12.13	13.68	13.20	13.59
	(0.99)	(1.02)	(0.76)	(0.86)
Large	11.96	12.00	12.78	13.23
	(0.76)	(0.95)	(0.56)	(0.52)
Large with locally endangered species	13.02	14.42	12.89	13.21
	(1.06)	(1.25)	(0.83)	(0.70)
Large without game	NA	NA	13.06	13.43
			(0.66)	(0.61)

Notes: WTP is calculated using a 'censored mean':

$$E[WTP] = \Phi\,(X\beta/\sigma)\,X\beta + \phi\,(X\beta/\sigma)\,\sigma,$$

where: ϕ and Φ are the pdf and cdf of the standard normal.
$X\beta$ and σ are the unconditional mean and the standard deviation.
To estimate the standard error, a Krinsky–Robb approach was used; with 100 draws of the coefficient vector (based on the covariance matrix of the coefficients).

habitat of other wildlife, as well. The estimated $33 million should be viewed as a partial estimate of the passive value associated with agricultural conservation programs, like the CRP. So, while this estimate is not large, especially compared with the $2 billion annual cost of the program, it is not unimportant. Furthermore, the $33 million estimate provides some indication that a fuller accounting of non-use values associated with the CRP will likely be significant.

9.7 Conclusions

The purpose of this chapter was to present an example of how a CV study could be designed to address a specific public policy issue, the benefits of improved grassland bird populations due to the CRP. We attempted to design a CV instrument to address the policy issue as closely as possible using realistic data. We found that complete realism was difficult from a number of perspectives. While CV studies, and environmental valuation studies in general, typically assume that all changes have only positive effects, analyses of the effects of the CRP on grassland bird populations suggest both positive and negative effects. Such an outcome is not surprising given that any environmental intervention is unlikely to yield universally positive or negative effects. Unfortunately, respondents in early focus groups could not respond to scenarios when the populations of some bird species increased and the populations of others decreased. Moreover, some of the decreases (for example, for ring-necked pheasants) did not coincide with local wisdom of the effects of the CRP on bird populations, raising questions about the reliability of the estimates of the changes in grassland bird populations from surveys of bird counts. Based on the initial focus group results and the mixed evidence of whether the populations of some species even did decrease, we converted the valuation scenario to only encompass those species of grassland birds whose populations had increased.

The second difficulty dealt with the desire to only estimate passive use values for grassland birds, as USDA already had benefit estimates for a number of other beneficial environmental effects of the CRP. We were largely successful in decoupling the changes in grassland bird populations from valuing the CRP in general, but some respondents still thought that changes in grassland bird populations would have other positive and negative environmental effects. This outcome is not surprising given that people recognize that elements of ecosystems are interconnected and changing one element will affect other elements. Thus, some people revealed values that include more than just the changes in the populations of grassland birds. This presents a difficult situation for environmental valuation for public policy: valuing a conservation program by components interjects artificial segmentation that is difficult for a program to implement and may result in double counting when the components are combined to yield an aggregate benefit measure.

Finally, given the NOAA Panel's focus on scope, the lack of scope in the Exxon birds study and the fundamental policy issue valued here, testing for scope is key. WTP did vary somewhat with the size of the program, but the only robust result was scope in terms of changes in bird populations for the Iowa sample.

Despite these mixed results, we conclude a substantial proportion of people value increases in grassland birds at both the national level and in Iowa. Thus, if these values are excluded from a benefit–cost analysis of the CRP, this would serve to underestimate benefit estimates. This general result also suggests that land proposed for enrollment in the CRP, which enhances grassland bird habitat, should receive some weight in the EBI index.

Moving beyond this general result to use the welfare estimates in aggregate benefit calculations presents more of a dilemma. Respondents who indicated on the true/false test that the valuation scenario provides more environmental benefits than just increases in bird populations suggest that estimates of central tendency reported in Table 9.9 may be overstated, but the extent of this bias is unknown. A compounding factor is the low survey response rate, even with the monetary incentives to reply. The low response rate suggests only those people who are most interested in the survey topic responded. We would advocate a conservative approach of assigning a value of $0 to the portion of households who did not respond to the survey when computing aggregate benefit estimates.

How these estimates are used for policy purposes depends on the policy context and, in particular, how important is precision of the estimates in that context. One approach to using these estimates for benefit–cost analyses would be to use only the Iowa results, where more robust scope results were found and apply these estimates to households in areas of CRP concentrations. As we made no attempt to restrict these estimates to passive use values, USDA's estimates of use values for these households would have to be removed from aggregate benefit estimates to avoid double counting. The advantage to this approach would be that the benefit estimates would be based on the more robust Iowa results. The disadvantage to this approach would be that the aggregate benefit estimates would exclude the non-use benefits of those who do not reside in areas of CRP concentration. However, excluding values from the areas in the nation which lack concentrations of CRP land would serve to provide conservative estimates of aggregate benefits.

Another approach to using these results to develop aggregate benefit estimates would be to include a national estimate for passive use value. As this study has shown, the passive use values are likely to be quite large, and, hence, worth considering in program design and implementation. The WTP values provided by respondents outside of the areas with concentrations of CRP land could be the basis for constructing estimates of passive use value for those areas in the nation that exclude the three areas of high concentrations of CRP, or even all areas of the nation. These estimates can then be aggregated with use values estimated from travel cost approaches with little concern for double counting, to provide a more complete estimate of total benefits.

The bottom line is that designing a valuation study to address a specific policy issue is challenging and using the resulting value estimates in policy analyses is complicated. These issues do not present obstacles that prevent benefit estimation, rather they suggest that benefit estimation must proceed with care and caution and clearly indicate areas where future research can improve benefit estimation for public policies. Our results on scope point to a need for more research on applying CV to environmental goods that are distant, yet perhaps common, amenities. In addition, fruitful future research in the general area of ecosystem valuation would address the issue that we faced in this study of some respondents recognizing that a great deal of scientific complexity exists in our ecosystems. This recognition on the part of respondents tends to undermine the credibility of narrowly defined scenarios.

Notes

1. This research benefitted greatly from the contributions of our colleagues on the larger study team: Richard Bishop, Mike Welsh, Andrew Laughland, John Charbonneau, and Anna Alberini. The research was funded by the US Department of Agriculture, the US Fish and Wildlife Service, and the University of Maine Agricultural and Forest Experiment Station. The opinions expressed in this chapter do not represent the official positions of the funding agencies.
2. Senior Economist, Economic Research Service, USDA; Libra Professor of Environmental Economics, University of Maine; and Natural Resource Economist, Economic Research Service, USDA.
3. These experts consider a variety of input from specialists when assigning points to a parcel of land. The rating scheme draws on previously established indicators of priorities, such as parcels that can be associated with designated endangered species, or government protected habitat, or conservation priority areas. For example, a parcel of land will receive more points under the wildlife habitat cover benefit subfactor if the cover is one which wildlife experts believe is more beneficial to wildlife, and extra points are given under an endangered species subfactor if the cover is expected to benefit Federal and/or State Threatened and Endangered species.
4. The latest Federal Executive Order on regulatory analysis, E.O. 12866, requires that benefit–cost analyses be undertaken. OMB has identified 'best practices' for preparing economic analyses which embrace standard benefit–cost approaches and advocate for an effort to quantify all potential real benefits to society in monetary terms (OMB, 2000).
5. The latter report is the US National Oceanic and Atmospheric Administration's Blue Ribbon Panel (1993), which was commissioned in the wake of the Exxon Valdez oil spill and NOAA's need for guidance in the implementation of the Oil Pollution Act of 1990.

6. All focus groups were conducted using the facilities of market research firms in Ankenny, IA, 2 groups; Cedar Rapids, IA, 11 groups; Baltimore, MD, 4 groups; and Los Angeles, CA, 4 groups.

7. The omitted design features included: adequate time lapse from the accident, temporal averaging, steady state or interim losses, present value calculations, and advanced approval.

8. In the final surveys, 23 per cent of the national sample had someone in their household who hunted and 47 per cent of these people hunted birds (pheasant, quail, and partridge). In contrast, 29 per cent of the respondents in the Iowa sample had someone in their household who hunted and 83 per cent of these people hunted grassland birds. In addition, 55 per cent of the national sample had someone in their household who participated in viewing of wild birds, while the figure for the Iowa sample was 64 per cent. Thus, respondents in the Iowa sample have a much higher proclivity to participate in activities that might involve the bird species being valued. In addition, the distribution of the CRP acreage suggests that changes in grassland bird populations due to the CRP are not likely to affect use values for residents of areas with lower CRP land concentrations.

9. The species whose populations had increased were Red-winged Blackbird, Vesper Sparrow, Starling, Brown-headed Cowbird, Brown Thrasher, House Wren, Barn Swallow, Dickcissel, Killdeer, Gray Partridge, Eastern Kingbird, Upland Sandpiper, Mourning Dove, Eastern Phoebe, and Grasshopper Sparrow. The percentage increases ranged from 4 per cent (Red-winged Blackbird) to 132 per cent (Grasshopper Sparrow). The species whose populations declined were Eastern Bluebird, Ring-necked Pheasant, Meadowlark, Northern Bobwhite, Indigo Bunting, Horned Lake, Field Sparrow, and Lark Sparrow. The population declines ranged from −10 per cent (Eastern Bluebird) to −84 per cent (Lark Sparrow).

10. The Henslow's sparrow is actually a threatened species in Iowa, and does not have a Federal designation. No official estimates exist on the current population of Henslow's sparrow, as it is too rare to show up in the breeding bird counts on which the populations of other bird species are based. The Henslow's sparrow numbers used in the survey are purely hypothetical. In the small, medium, large, and large without game birds, the Henslow's sparrow was listed as one of the species. Only about 14 per cent of all respondents to the surveys had ever heard of the Henslow's sparrow prior to receiving the survey instrument, and this percentage is not significantly different between the national and Iowa samples.

11. The Iowa sample also had two other treatment groups that received the large and small changes, but were asked a single-bounded, dichotomous-choice question. These results are not reported in this chapter.

12. We also estimated a number of models that included dummies for each of the several variants. Although these models are more robust (they impose minimal structure on preferences), the linearized model more clearly demonstrates the effects of program size, the inclusion of game species, and the inclusion of an endangered species. More importantly, the results from the 'dummy' models were qualitatively similar, hence little is lost by using this simpler 'linearized' model (Boyle et al., 2000).

13. For the national data set, *G* cannot be included (since all scenarios include game species).

14. We also estimated models where 'PROBABLY YES' is also treated as a 'YES' answer. The scope results were qualitatively similar, though the overall level of WTP was about three times larger.

15. Note that the first phase included 1500 'single-bounded' CV instruments and the second phase included 750 single-bounded CV instruments, which we did not use in this analysis.

16. Respondents were randomly assigned one of eight monetary incentives to induce them to respond to the survey. The incentives were randomized within each of our experimental treatments so as not to affect response rates to individual treatments. The incentives were: $0, $1, two $1 bills, a $2 bill, three $1 bills, four $1 bills, five $1 bills, and one $5 bill.

17. For example, 34 per cent (36 per cent) of the National (Iowa) respondents thought that the proposed program would have other environmental effects.

18. In both surveys, about one-third of non-participants claimed that 'tax money should not be used for this proposal', with personal value reasons (such as, 'I cannot afford to support the proposal at any dollar amount') given about one-fifth of the time.
19. For both National and Iowa datasets, a Wald test on the joint significance of the covariates was highly significant: 87.2 (6 degrees of freedom, probability < 1 per cent), and 278.3 (6 degrees of freedom, probability < 1 per cent), for the National and Iowa data respectively. Also note that likelihood ratio tests of the joint significance of all parameters is large in all models (with probabilities well below 0.1 per cent).
20. Strategic respondents (about 6 per cent of all respondents who would pay something) answered '*yes*' to the following debriefing questions: 'I wanted to keep my costs down and I thought the proposal would be carried out no matter how I voted, so I only voted *definitely yes* for low dollar amounts.'

References

Boyle, Kevin J., William H. Desvousges, F. Reed Johnson, Richard W. Dunford and Sara P. Hudson (1994), 'An investigation of part–whole biases in contingent-valuation studies', *Journal of Environmental Economics and Management*, **27** (1), 64–83.

Boyle, Kevin J., Richard C. Bishop, Mary C. Ahearn, Daniel Hellerstein, Michael P. Welsh, Andrew Laughland and John Charbonneau (2000), 'Test of scope in contingent valuation studies: are the numbers for the birds?', Paper presented at the ASSA meetings, Boston, MA, 6–9 January.

Carson, Richard T. (1997), 'Contingent valuation surveys and tests of insensitivity to scope', in R.J. Kopp, W.W. Pommerehne and N. Schwarz (eds), *Determining the Value of Non-marketed Goods: Economic, Psychological, and Policy Relevant Aspects of Contingent Valuation Methods*, Boston: Kluwer Academic Publishers.

Council on Agricultural Science and Technology (1995), 'The conservation reserve: a survey of research and interest groups', Ames, IA: Pub. No. 19, July 1995.

Desvousges, William H., F. Reed Johnson, Richard W. Dunford, Kevin J. Boyle, Sara P. Hudson and K. Nicole Wilson (1993), 'Measuring natural resource damages with contingent valuation: tests of validity and reliability', in J.A. Hausman (ed.), *Contingent Valuation: A Critical Assessment*, Amsterdam: North-Holland, pp. 91–164.

Dillman, Donald A. (1978), *Mail and Telephone Surveys: The Total Design Method*, New York: Wiley.

Feather, P., D. Hellerstein and L. Hansen (1999), 'Economic valuation of environmental benefits and the targeting of conservation programs: the case of the CRP', USDA, ERS, AER No. 778.

Federal Register (1996), 'Benefit cost analysis of the conservation reserve program', 23 September, 1996. Prepared by the USDA, FSA.

Hagler Bailly Services (1997), 'Grassland bird survey: final report for national study', Hagler Bailly, Madison, WI, 24 September.

Hagler Bailly Services (1998), 'Grassland bird survey: final report for Iowa study, Phase II'. Hagler Bailly, Madison, WI, 11 June.

Hansen, LeRoy, Peather Feather and David Shank (1999), 'Valuation of agriculture's multi-site environmental impacts: an application to pheasant hunting', *Agricultural Resource Economics Review*, **28** (2), October, 199–207.

Lauber, Bruce (1991), 'Birds and the conservation reserve program: a retrospective study', Unpublished M.Sc. Thesis, University of Maine, Orono.

National Audubon Society (1994), 'Investing in wildlife: multiple benefits for America', A report based on research by Purdue University, 29 November.

NOAA Panel on Contingent Valuation (1993), Federal Register, **58** (10), 4601–14.

Office of Management and Budget (2000), 'Report to Congress on the costs and benefits of Federal Regulations', Chapter 1, www.whitehouse.gov/OMB/inforeg/chap1.html.

Osborn, T. (1997), 'New CRP criteria enhance environmental gains', *Agricultural Outlook*, October, pp. 15–18

Ribaudo, M., D. Colacicco, L. Langner, S. Piper and G. Schaible (1990), 'Natural resources and users benefit from the Conservation Reserve Program', USDA, ERS, AER No. 627, January.

Roach, B., K.J. Boyle and M. Welsh (2001), 'Testing bid design effects in multiple-bounded, contingent-valuation questions', *Land Economics*, **78** (1), 121–31.

Sauer, J.R., J.E. Hines, I. Thomas, J. Fallon and G. Gough (1999), 'The North American Breeding Bird Survey, results and analysis, 1966–98', Version 98.1, USGS, PWRC, Laurel, MD.

US Department of Agriculture, Economic Research Service (1997), 'Agricultural resources and environmental indicators, 1996–97', Washington, DC: AH No. 712, July.

US Department of Agriculture, Farm Service Agency (1999), 'Conservation reserve program sign-up 20: environmental benefits index', Fact Sheet, Washington, DC, September.

US Department of Agriculture, Farm Service Agency (2000), 'Conservation Reserve Program', Washington, DC: www.fsa.usda.gov/dafp/cepd.

US General Accounting Office (1993), 'Conservation Reserve Program: cost-effectiveness is uncertain', Report to the Chairman, Subcommittee on Agriculture, Rural Development, Food and Drug Administration, and Related Agencies, Committee on Appropriations, House of Representatives, GAO/RCED-93-132, March.

Welsh, Michael P. and Richard C. Bishop (1993), 'Multiple bounded discrete choice models', in J.C. Bergstrom (ed.), 'W-133 Benefits and costs transfer in natural resource planning: sixth interim report', Western Regional Research Publication, Department of Agricultural and Applied Economics, Athens, GA, pp. 331–52.

Welsh, Michael P. and Gregory L. Poe (1998), 'Elicitation effects in contingent valuation: comparisons to a multiple bounded discrete choice approach', *Journal of Environmental Economics and Management*, **36**, 170–85.

Wildlife Management Institute (1994), 'The Conservation Reserve Program: a wildlife conservation legacy', Washington, DC, October.

10 Modelling behaviour in dichotomous choice with Bayesian methods

Carmelo J. León[1] and Roberto León[2]

10.1 Introduction

Contingent valuation (CV) aims at valuing public or environmental goods by relying on cross-section data from a sample of individuals. The essential variables to be elicited are the willingness to pay (WTP) for the commodity and the effect of covariates which may explain individual variation. In this chapter we discuss the use of Bayesian techniques in contingent valuation. The econometric analysis of contingent valuation data sets has evolved in parallel with the advance in elicitation techniques. For instance, mean willingness to pay from the dichotomous choice model may turn out to be a non-linear function of the parameters estimated from a survival distribution. The Bayesian approach to inference differs from the classical approach in that the likelihood function of observed data is combined with some prior information on the parameters of interest, in order to derive a posterior probability measure. Thus, the parameters to be estimated are always conditional on the observed data, and can be revised as new data comes out, whereas in classical methods the data are supposed to be the result of a probability measure determined by some population parameters.

Bayesian methods can be introduced into the econometric analysis of any models for which the researcher is willing to specify a prior describing his/her beliefs about the parameters of interest before data are actually collected. In this sense, there are Bayesian models for the linear regression, logit, and probit models, which can be applied to contingent valuation data sets resulting from the open-ended or single-bounded dichotomous choice formats (e.g. Zellner, 1985; Albert and Chib, 1993; Koop and Poirier, 1993, and McCulloch and Rossi 1994). From a computational point of view, Bayesian methods offer solutions to complex problems of integration and can be useful with small samples. For instance, Araña and León (2002) showed with an example that Bayesian estimation of the single-bounded dichotomous choice model (Hanemann, 1984) can be more accurate with small samples. In addition, Fernández et al. (2004) demonstrate that Bayesian methods are capable to be implemented, using flexible distributions, within the interval type of data resulting from double-bounded

(Hanemann et al., 1991) and one-and-a-half bounded (Cooper et al., 2002) dichotomous choice methods.

Nevertheless, Bayesian techniques could also offer an interesting theoretical interpretation of individual behaviour, in the sense that economic agents could be seen as using Bayesian updating mechanisms when adopting economic decisions. This investigation is possible whenever data are available about actions before information becomes available to the agents, and after information has become available. The interest for this type of hypotheses is reflected, for instance, in the work by Viscusi (1989), who considers an individual model for the assessment of probabilities in a Bayesian framework. Empirical evidence reveals that subjects tend to overestimate small risks and underestimate large risks. This misperception could be explained because consumers hold prior beliefs about the probability that an event may occur, and update it using the stated probability as the likelihood.

From a theoretical standpoint, Bayes' theorem provides the optimal way of combining prior and sample information for a rational individual. This means that any rational individual would use Bayes' rule when updating her prior information in the light of further sample information. Thus rationality is a maintained hypothesis, which is based on a number of axioms of rational choice (Berger, 1985). There is also a learning process implicit in the updating mechanism. In contingent valuation, the individual can be seen as participating in a market for an environmental good where there is scope for learning behaviour. That is, the subject's prior valuation could be updated as she faces the elements of the constructed market. In this context, the use of a Bayesian approach does provide a sound theoretical interpretation to the learning process implicit in the evolution of a contingent valuation interview.

The application of Bayesian techniques in contingent valuation has a recent history, and has focused both on the development of estimation techniques and on modelling individual behaviour in iterative elicitation techniques. Earlier applications, focused on modelling the behavioural aspects, involved the double-bounded dichotomous choice method, which has been proved to provide gains in statistical efficiency (Hanemann et al., 1991). Since this method involves two iterated willingness to pay questions, there is scope for some kind of behaviour when moving from the first to the second question. Econometric modelling of these data has attempted to contemplate the alternative hypotheses, which might explain a potential change in behaviour. Alberini et al. (1997) capture behavioural responses taking place after the follow-up question using a structural shift term, while Herriges and Shogren (1996) consider the hypothesis of an anchoring effect. Nevertheless, the Bayesian approach allows us to model the individual's process of updating his prior value when facing a sequence of valuation questions. Hence, by assuming individuals behave rationally in constructed market scenarios, a Bayesian mechanism could be appropriate for modelling the updating process implicit in iterated elicitation methods.

In the following sections we discuss how the Bayesian approach to estimating environmental benefits can be applied to contingent valuation data sets. Section 10.2 presents some basic concepts of Bayesian statistics, and compares them with the classical approach. Section 10.3 reviews the use of Bayesian concepts in contingent valuation, both from a theoretical and from an empirical point of view. Section 10.4 presents a Bayesian model for double-bounded dichotomous choice, which combines a prior distribution from the first question with a logistic likelihood function. This model is estimated by simulation using Markov Chain Monte Carlo (MCMM) methods as explained in Section 10.5. Finally, Section 10.6 presents the conclusions and the directions for further research.

10.2   The Bayesian approach

The main difference between Bayesian and classical methods is that the former include prior beliefs in the estimation of the parameters. These prior beliefs may reflect complete uncertainty about the parameters, or can be based on past experience or information. A Bayesian statistician combines prior beliefs and the likelihood derived from the data using Bayes' theorem. A non-Bayesian statistician only considers the likelihood of the data to make inference about the unknown parameters.

Suppose one wishes to estimate a parameter θ (or vector of parameters), which can be interpreted as the mean of the compensating or equivalent surplus for a population. The prior beliefs about the parameter must be reflected in the prior distribution of θ. Let $\pi(\theta)$ be the prior distribution of θ, and $l(x|\theta)$ the likelihood of a sample data x on willingness to pay, which can be obtained from a contingent valuation survey. This likelihood function provides the probability of observing the data given the parameter θ. The updated belief about mean willingness to pay is derived from the distribution of θ after having observed the sample. Formally, following Bayes' theorem,

$$\pi(\theta|x) = \frac{l(x|\theta)\pi(\theta)}{l(\theta)},$$

where

$$l(\theta) = \int l(x|\theta)\pi(\theta)d\theta.$$

The distribution of θ given the observed sample $\pi(\theta|x)$ is the posterior distribution, i.e. the distribution after updating prior beliefs in the light of sample information. Bayesian inference is developed from studying the characteristics of this posterior distribution, which can be evaluated in some cases analytically or in other cases numerically. These characteristics include location measures such as the mean, the mode or the median, as well as dispersion measures such as the variance, standard deviation, and interquartile range. The researcher can also calculate an interval (a, b) such that the probability of the parameter θ belonging to it is $100(1 - \alpha)\%$. In the context of Bayesian statistics, these intervals are known as credible intervals. That is, given the posterior distribution $\pi(\theta|x)$, the interval (a, b) is a $100(1 - \alpha)\%$ posterior credible interval of θ if

$$\int_a^b \pi(\theta|x)\, d\theta = 1 - \alpha$$

The analogue concept in classical statistics is confidence interval. But these cannot be interpreted in the same way, since the level of confidence cannot be regarded as a probability.[1] Credible intervals are based on the probability mass obtained from the posterior distribution, i.e. they refer to the probability of mean willingness to pay lying in a particular interval.

If a point estimate of θ is needed, then it would be reasonable to give that point estimate that minimizes the expected value of the loss function. The loss function $f(\theta, \theta')$ gives the incurred loss when the real value of the parameter is θ but the researcher thinks that the value of the parameter is θ'. The expected value of the loss function is defined as

$$\int f(\theta - \theta')\pi(\theta|x)d\theta$$

If we assume that the loss function has the form $(\theta - \theta')^2$, then the point estimate that minimizes the expected loss is the posterior mean. If the loss function has the form $|\theta - \theta'|$ then the point estimate that minimizes the expected loss is the posterior median. Although the posterior mode does not minimize the expected loss for any particular loss function, it is often reported as a point estimate.

10.3   A review of previous studies

Bayesian methods have started to be used in contingent valuation for modelling individual behaviour when posed with hypothetical market scenarios. In particular, Bayes' rule has been especially useful to researchers in the econometric modelling of iterative elicitation methods, such as the dichotomous choice with follow up format.

The theoretical contribution by Crocker and Shogren (1991) was the first to postulate a Bayesian learning process for individual behaviour in contingent valuation scenarios. Consumers are assumed to behave as Bayesian statisticians who do not know their preferences completely, and learn about their utility function by choosing a particular bundle of goods and experience its utility level. Thus, the information provided by the chosen bundle is treated using Bayes' theorem. The posterior distribution will enable the consumer to choose a bundle with higher utility in future periods. This setting leads to higher willingness to pay for successive goods than in the case of perfect knowledge of the utility function. As a consequence, the amount of money that an individual would be willing to pay for a good with ambiguous utility will decrease after experiencing the good several times; that is, initial large values for willingness to pay are justified from the consumer's optimizing behaviour. The individual is willing to pay more for the good with ambiguous utility in order to know more about his own preferences. Therefore, it is not clear whether large initial values should be regarded as unreliable, since they come from an optimization process.

However, in this model consumers learn or form their posterior distribution of the utility function after observing a sample of utilities from consuming successive goods. Thus, there is no account of the learning process when subjects answer to hypothetical questions about untried goods. In this aspect, Bjornstad et al. (1997) give empirical evidence supporting that a learning setting in contingent valuation may reduce hypothetical bias. These results also suggest that the initial hypothetical values may be too high because the consumer does not know her preferences or the contingent valuation process with certainty. Thus, the value of willingness to pay that should be taken into account is the value that the consumer reports after having learnt her preferences.

The behavioural change observed in iterated elicitation methods can also be explained by competing hypotheses, instead of a possible learning process, which can also be modelled with Bayesian concepts. For instance, the answers to successive bids might be subject to anchoring or starting point effects. In this case, respondents may perceive the survey bid values as providing information, such as what 'society' or 'experts' believe these values should be. Thus their responses may be affected by the value of the first bid offered. However, bid values are not intended to have any effect on the individuals' valuation. Rather, they are designed to maximize statistical efficiency. In this context, it is the prior or unaffected beliefs of the consumer that should be the interest of the decision maker, not the posterior estimates that are artificially influenced by an optimal bid design.

Following this argument, Herriges and Shogren (1996) suggest that the individual may anchor his WTP to the initial bid offered. They model this idea by assuming that the consumer forms a revised WTP (W') after answering to the first question according to the pattern $W' = (1 - \beta)W + \beta b_1$, where b_1 is the first price offered to the individual in a double-bounded dichotomous choice format, W is the initial WTP, and β is the extent of anchoring, where $0 \leq \beta \leq 1$. Thus, with this formulation, the revised WTP is an arithmetic weighted average of the initial WTP and the bid offered in the first question. The individual will accept to pay the first bid if his initial WTP is greater than the first bid, and he will answer yes to the second question if his revised WTP (W') is greater than the second bid. It can be shown that the variance of the estimator of WTP is larger than when anchoring is not present. That is, anchoring reduces the information in the second questions, making the estimator of WTP less precise.

The assumption that the answer to the second bid price is based on a combination between the first bid offered and the prior willingness to pay can be seen as the result of the individual using Bayes' theorem in order to update their prior WTP. This is the interpretation of McLeod and Bergland (1998), which draws on an earlier paper by Viscusi (1989), and also suggested by Horowitz (1993). The model assumes that prior beliefs can be represented with a Beta distribution, which is combined with a binomial likelihood function using Bayes' theorem. Hence, individuals are assumed to combine the prior WTP and the first bid offered using Bayes' theorem, leading to $W' = (\gamma/(1 - \gamma))W + 1/(1 + \gamma)b_1$. It can be seen that this linear combination is exactly the same as the one utilized by Herriges and Shogren (1996), but with a different interpretation of the parameters defining the weights. Thus, the updating mechanism is intended to model how subjects deal with preference uncertainty in the context of successive bids offered through the double-bounded dichotomous choice elicitation method. The parameters defining the linear combination, which follow from the application of Bayes' theorem, can be interpreted as the degree of anchoring, or, in other words, as the degree to which the initial distribution is changed after the first bid is offered.[2]

However, the former approaches to deal with the change in the distribution of WTP do not utilize Bayesian methods to derive the posterior distribution of WTP. The assumption of a Bayesian updating mechanism follows from the way in which the individual combines her prior WTP and the first bid offered. As a result, the maximum likelihood approach incorporating this hypothesis does not lead to a Bayesian estimation of welfare benefits, since it fails to derive a posterior distribution for WTP from sample data. This is attempted in León and Vázquez-Polo (1998). In this paper, the researcher combines a prior distribution on the mean willingness to pay from the first dichotomous choice question with the likelihood function resulting from the full double-bounded data. The estimation of mean willingness to pay with this model approaches the estimates obtained with the single-bounded model. In addition, the case study showed that the standard double-bounded model led to similar results as the open-ended format, which is known to be subject to potential strategic bias.

Finally, it should be noted that Bayesian estimation techniques offer some advantages over classical estimation methods, and this has motivated their increasing application to CV data sets, particularly in the context of dichotomous choice modelling. First, Bayesian methods provide exact inference with small samples. Second, they can make feasible the estimation of complex and more realistic models. The recent developments of simulation techniques have enabled the estimation of posterior distributions involving complex and intractable integrals. The posterior distribution can be simulated with Markov Chain Monte Carlo (MCMC) methods, such as Metropolis–Hastings and Gibbs sampling algorithms. These methods involve generating a succession of random values that approximate the posterior distribution. These random values are used to calculate the moments of the parameters of interest. In these methods it is necessary to check for the convergence of the series of simulated values (e.g. Best et al., 1999).

MCMC algorithms are straightforward and useful examples of their application in contingent valuation can be found in Araña and León (2002) and Fernandez et al. (2004) for the single-bounded and double-bounded elicitation methods, respectively. Bayesian simulation techniques also allow for a convenient resolution of complex estimation problems, such as the estimation of mixture models, which encompass a large number of distributions. For instance, Araña and León (2004) consider a model of a mixture of normal densities, which is flexible enough to accommodate any empirical distribution as the number of components in the mixture increases. This model is shown to perform better than other flexible and semi-nonparametric approaches, particularly with small samples and under data heterogeneity. The Bayesian approach can also be useful for hypothesis testing and model comparison when there is uncertainty about the true model. León and León (2003) show that the results from the bivariate probit and double-bounded model can be combined in a Bayesian framework to obtain an estimate of WTP with smaller mean squared error. In this framework, the credible interval for WTP takes into account the uncertainty regarding the existence of anchoring effects. This is in contrast with classical maximum likelihood estimation, which reports results conditional on just one model and hence fails to take into account model uncertainty.

10.4   Modelling dichotomous choice with follow up

The Bayesian approach to inference can be suitable for modelling contingent valuation data from iterated elicitation methods, such as the double-bounded dichotomous choice format. Follow-up questions in

dichotomous choice are intended to increase the efficiency of the WTP estimates by obtaining more information about the individual's distribution.
However, posing individuals with a follow-up question may increase bias in
contingent valuation estimates. The existence of this bias is revealed by the
evidence that there is often a significant difference between the underlying
WTP in the answers to the first and second questions.[3] Since this effect is
undesirable, the researcher is more interested in estimating welfare benefits
before the change occurred, that is, the value of WTP previous to the
answers to the first question. This is the true parameter to be modelled with
a Bayesian mechanism, which incorporates information at each point of
the elicitation process.

Single-bounded and double-bounded models will yield different information about WTP if individuals do change their stated valuation after
answering the first question. These two information sets can be combined
by using Bayes' theorem in a setting where the prior distribution reflects the
more reliable information contained in the answers to the first question,
and the likelihood function follows from the answers to both questions.
This specification captures the efficiency advantage of double-bounded
results, while ameliorating the bias in WTP by using the prior information
provided from the responses to the first question.

Let the individual's WTP be a function of two components, a determin-
istic component μ and a stochastic component ε. Thus, $WTP = \mu + \sigma\varepsilon$,
where μ and σ are the mean and standard deviation of WTP in the population, respectively. Assuming that ε follows a standard logistic distribution,[4] if the individual is faced with the price A_i, then the probability of
accepting the offer is

$$\pi_i^y = \frac{\exp\left(\dfrac{\mu}{\sigma} - \dfrac{1}{\sigma}A_i\right)}{1 + \exp\left(\dfrac{\mu}{\sigma} - \dfrac{1}{\sigma}A_i\right)}$$

Therefore, the likelihood function from all sample observations is

$$l\left(x \mid \frac{\mu}{\sigma}, \frac{1}{\sigma}\right) = \prod_{i=1}^{n} \frac{\left[\exp\left(\dfrac{\mu}{\sigma} - \dfrac{1}{\sigma}A_i\right)\right]^{v_i}}{1 + \exp\left(\dfrac{\mu}{\sigma} - \dfrac{1}{\sigma}A_i\right)},$$

where v_i takes the value 1 if individual i accepted to pay A_i, and n is the
number of individuals in the sample.

Following Koop and Poirier (1993), we specify a prior distribution for μ/σ and $1/\sigma$ that

$$
\pi\left(\frac{\mu}{\sigma}, \frac{1}{\sigma}\right) = \frac{\exp\left(rn\,\frac{\mu}{2\sigma}\right)}{\displaystyle\prod_{i=1}^{n}\left[1 + \exp\left(\frac{\mu}{\sigma} - \frac{1}{\sigma}(A_i - \bar{A})\right)\right]^{r}}\frac{1}{c}
$$

belongs to the same family as the likelihood function when ε follows a logistic distribution, where $\bar{A} = \sum A_i/n$, r is a free parameter and c is the constant equal to[5]

$$
\frac{\exp\left(\frac{rn}{2}\left[\log\left(\frac{\pi_i^y}{1-\pi_i^y}\right) - \frac{A_i}{\sigma}\right]\right)}{\displaystyle\prod_{i=1}^{n}\left[1 + \exp\left[\log\left(\frac{\pi_i^y}{1-\pi_i^y}\right) + \frac{A}{\sigma}\right]\right]^{r}}\frac{1}{c}\left[\frac{1}{\pi_i^y(1-\pi_i^y)}\right]\frac{1}{\sigma^2}
$$

$$
\int_0^{\infty}\int_0^{\infty}\left[\frac{\exp\left(rn\,\frac{\mu}{2\sigma}\right)}{\displaystyle\prod_{i=1}^{n}\left[1 + \exp\left(\frac{\mu}{\sigma} - \frac{1}{\sigma}(A_i - \bar{A})\right)\right]^{r}}\right]d\frac{1}{\sigma}\,d\frac{u}{\sigma}.
$$

In the absence of prior information, the prior distribution should reflect the researcher's uncertainty about WTP. One way to determine how much information the prior distribution contains is by looking at the probability of the individual accepting to pay the offered price. It can be shown that prior (4) reaches its highest value when $1/\sigma$ is zero, independently of μ. As a result, the acceptance probability evaluated at the mode of the parameters is independent of the bid price and equals one half.[6] Hence, the researcher is uncertain about the answer of the individual for any value of the bid offered. This lack of information could not be reasonable for the extreme values of the bid vector design, but it is plausible for most of the bid prices offered in the sample.

A zero mode $1/\sigma$ also indicates that the researcher gives prior high weights to large values of the dispersion parameter. Hence, the prior distribution is not convenient for estimating σ, since it is likely to give upwardly biased results. However, it is appropriate for estimating μ because it contains little information about this parameter.

The parameter r can be interpreted by considering the prior information as arising from a fictitious sample of size n with the same bid vector design as the observed data. The maximum likelihood estimates of μ/σ and $1/\sigma$ calculated with this fictitious sample are zero. The larger r the greater is the strength of the prior relative to the data at hand. As r tends to zero, the prior distribution reduces to a uniform prior.

If a logistic distribution is assumed, this specification has the appealing property that the posterior distribution is globally concave, and therefore can be easily simulated using the rejection method (Gamerman, 1997). Further, the methods of Tierney and Kadane (1986) are particularly well-suited for approximating the posterior means of positive functions for the parameters.

If we now consider a follow up dichotomous choice question, this would give us the double-bounded format. Assuming a logistic distribution for the random component ε, the likelihood derived from the answers to both questions is,

$$l\left(l\Big|\frac{x}{\sigma},\frac{1}{\sigma}\right) = \prod_{i=1}^{n}(\pi_i^{yy})^{v_1 v_2}(\pi_i^{yn})^{v_1(1-v_2)}(\pi_i^{ny})^{(1-v_1)v_2}(\pi_i^{nn})^{(1-v_1)(1-v_2)}$$

where

$$\pi_i^{nn} = \frac{\exp\left(\dfrac{\mu}{\sigma} - \dfrac{1}{\sigma}A_i^d\right)}{1 + \exp\left(\dfrac{\mu}{\sigma} - \dfrac{1}{\sigma}A_i^d\right)}$$

$$\pi_i^{yy} = \frac{\exp\left(\dfrac{\mu}{\sigma} - \dfrac{1}{\sigma}A_i^u\right)}{1 + \exp\left(\dfrac{\mu}{\sigma} - \dfrac{1}{\sigma}A_i^u\right)}$$

$$\pi_i^{yn} = \frac{\exp\left(\dfrac{\mu}{\sigma} - \dfrac{1}{\sigma}A_i\right) - \exp\left(\dfrac{\mu}{\sigma} - \dfrac{1}{\sigma}A_i^u\right)}{\left[1 + \exp\left(\dfrac{\mu}{\sigma} - \dfrac{1}{\sigma}A_i^u\right)\right]\left[1 + \exp\left(\dfrac{\mu}{\sigma} - \dfrac{1}{\sigma}A_i\right)\right]}$$

$$\pi_i^{ny} = \frac{\exp\left(\dfrac{\mu}{\sigma} - \dfrac{1}{\sigma}A_i^d\right) - \exp\left(\dfrac{\mu}{\sigma} - \dfrac{1}{\sigma}A_i\right)}{\left[1 + \exp\left(\dfrac{\mu}{\sigma} - \dfrac{1}{\sigma}A_i\right)\right]\left[1 + \exp\left(\dfrac{\mu}{\sigma} - \dfrac{1}{\sigma}A_i^d\right)\right]}$$

where A_i is the first bid offered to individual i, A_i^u is a larger bid that is offered to the individual if she answered 'yes' to the first question, A_i^d is a smaller bid that is offered to the individual if she answered 'no' to the first question, v_1 takes the value one if the individual answered 'yes' to the first question and zero otherwise, and v_2 takes the same values but for the second question.

This likelihood function follows from the assumption that the individual does not change her willingness to pay after answering the first question. However, some studies have found evidence that the estimated mean value of WTP utilizing the answers to the first question differs from that obtained from the answers to the second question. In spite of this, little is known about the way individuals change their WTP, and there are a number of plausible hypotheses. For instance, Herriges and Shogren (1996) suggest that there are multiple forms of specifying the anchoring effect. The number of possible specifications rises when the degree of anchoring depends on the distance between the first bid price and the individual's true WTP. Each of these specifications would imply a different likelihood function. In addition, specifying the way in which individuals change their WTP conveys a loss of efficiency of the estimates, since it amounts to discarding part of the information in the second answer.[7]

Assuming that the value underlying the answers to the first question is the true value of WTP, the bias caused by a change in WTP can be reduced by giving more importance to the answers to the first question. This can be done by specifying as the prior distribution the posterior distribution of the model from the first dichotomous choice question. That is,

$$
\pi\left(\frac{\mu}{\sigma}, \frac{1}{\sigma}\right) = \prod_{i=1}^{n} \frac{\left[\exp\left(\frac{\mu}{\sigma} - \frac{1}{\sigma}A_i\right)\right]^{v_1} \exp\left(rn\frac{\mu}{2\sigma}\right)}{\left[1 + \exp\left(\frac{\mu}{\sigma} - \frac{1}{\sigma}A_i\right)\right]\left[1 + \exp\left(\frac{\mu}{\sigma} - \frac{1}{\sigma}(A_i - \bar{A})\right)\right]^r} \frac{1}{d}
$$

where d is the constant

$$
\int_0^\infty \int_0^\infty \prod_{i=1}^{n} \frac{\left[\exp\left(\frac{\mu}{\sigma} - \frac{1}{\sigma}A_i\right)\right]^{v_1} \exp\left(rn\frac{\mu}{2\sigma}\right)}{\left[1 + \exp\left(\frac{\mu}{\sigma} - \frac{1}{\sigma}A_i\right)\right]\left[1 + \exp\left(\frac{\mu}{\sigma} - \frac{1}{\sigma}(A_i - \bar{A})\right)\right]^r} d\frac{\mu}{\sigma} d\frac{1}{\sigma}
$$

The principal advantage of this Bayesian approach is that it reduces the bias caused by a change in WTP without losing the efficiency of the double-bounded models. This is because it utilizes the likelihood function from the double-bounded data in combination with the prior from the results to the first dichotomous choice question. This allows us to model statistically the process of change in the distribution of WTP, which might be explained either by an implicit learning process on behalf of the individual, or by the appearance of strategic behaviour, or by the effect of starting point bias.

10.5   Simulating the posterior distribution

The posterior distribution of the model presented in the previous section can be simulated using the algorithm proposed by Metropolis et al. (1953) and Hastings (1970). This algorithm enables simulation from a distribution by developing a succession of random values. As the number of values in the succession rises, the probability of obtaining a value belonging to an interval (a, b) is approximately the probability determined by the distribution to be simulated. In other words, once convergence is reached, the values in the succession can be considered as approximate draws from the posterior distribution.

These simulated values can be used to calculate the mean and interquartile range of the posterior distribution. For instance, the posterior mean of μ/σ is approximated by the mean of the simulated values for the parameter μ/σ. Other characteristics of the posterior distribution, such as credible intervals, can be similarly evaluated. The posterior mean of μ can be estimated by averaging the ratio of the simulated values μ/σ and $1/\sigma$. All these estimators are strongly consistent.

Convergence can be analysed by observing the properties of the simulated chain. For instance, we could discard the first D values of the simulated chain and divide the rest of the chain in several parts. If the properties of these sub-samples are similar, we can conclude that convergence is reached at least after the Dth iteration. This analysis can be reinforced by considering sub-samples from chains started at different initial values.

The model presented in the previous section was estimated using data from a contingent valuation survey conducted in the Canary Islands (Spain).[8] The posterior distribution was simulated for three different values of the parameter r (0.1, 0.5 and 0.9). For each of these values, a chain of length 20 000 was developed. The analysis of convergence, not reported here, showed that the chain did reach convergence at least after the 5000th iteration. Table 10.1 shows the characteristics of the implied posterior distribution for μ, i.e. mean WTP.

The posterior distribution appears to be symmetric. However, it is very sensitive to the value of parameter r, i.e. the parameter specifying the influence of the prior on the posterior. The value of r should be chosen according to the coherence between the prior information and the sample data. Parameter r can be chosen by looking at the predictive distribution.

That is, the prior distribution with the largest value of the predictive distribution is the prior with the information that is most similar to the information contained in the data. The predictive likelihood is defined as

$$f(y) = \int f(y|\theta)p(\theta)d\theta$$

where $f(y|\theta)$ is the likelihood function and $p(\theta)$ is the prior distribution. The predictive likelihood is the expected value of the likelihood function with respect to the prior distribution. Hence, a small value for the predictive likelihood indicates that the prior distribution contains information that is different from the information contained in the likelihood.

In the case of the simulated model, the predictive likelihood can be estimated using the simulated sample from the posterior distribution. Newton and Raftery (1994) proposed a consistent estimator. That is

$$\hat{f}(y) = \left[\frac{1}{n}\sum_{i=1}^{n} \frac{1}{l(\theta_i)} \right]^{-1},$$

where $\theta_1, \ldots, \theta_n$ are sample values from the posterior distribution and $l(\theta)$ is the likelihood function. The values of the predictive likelihood for each value of r are also presented in the last column of Table 10.1. It can be seen that the prior distribution with r equal to 0.1 contains the information less contradictory with the data.[9] Thus, the posterior results with $r = 0.1$ are preferred to produce inference on the value of the environmental good, i.e. we obtain the non-informative distribution, which contradicts the data less.

For comparison purposes, Table 10.2 reports the results from modelling single- and double-bounded logistic regressions without covariates. Mean willingness to pay is larger for single than for double-bounded. It can be seen that the Bayesian model produces a point estimate of mean WTP that is closer to the single-bounded model, but does not deviate as much from the double-bounded estimate. In addition, the credible interval for $r = 0.1$ is not as large as the confidence interval in the logistic single-bounded

Table 10.1   Characteristics of the posterior distribution of mean WTP (US dollars) and predictive likelihoods for different values of r

r	Mean	Mode	Median	80% credible intervals	Predictive likelihood
0.1	10.64	10.64	10.64	(10.36, 10.91)	0.036
0.5	9.71	9.7	9.71	(9.37, 10.06)	0.028
0.9	8.77	8.77	8.77	(8.39, 9.17)	0.022

Table 10.2   Single and double-bounded logistic mean WTP

Model	Single	Double
Mean (standard error)	11.69 (0.39)	10.34 (0.23)
80% Confidence Intervals	(11.20, 12.18)	(9.85, 10.43)
Log L	−460.51	−1042.32

model. Thus, the Bayesian approach increases efficiency with respect to the first dichotomous choice question, while modelling the change in willingness to pay in the second answer.

10.6   Conclusions

Bayesian methods are starting to be applied in contingent valuation econometric models and promise to become a successful strategy to deal with empirical data. The Bayesian approach is characterized by the utilization of prior information to be combined with the likelihood from sample observations. In this setting, inference is carried out on the parameters of interest, given the data and other parameters conditioning individual behaviour. Bayesian methods are suitable to model situations in which there is prior information available. Although CVM is conducted with the aim of valuing environmental goods in carefully designed and specific market scenarios, this does not prevent the use of prior information to improve statistical models. Further, recent developments in numerical methods are making Bayesian econometrics less dependent on the use of conjugate and convenient distributions, which provided in the past a serious limitation to represent empirical distributions.

Looking at the specific techniques conducting CVM research, there are a number of areas in which the use of Bayesian approaches may enhance the statistical and econometric analyses. First, it could be particularly useful in dealing with iterated elicitation data, where there is scope for potential biases in willingness to pay responses. Second, although this application is in an early stage of development, Bayesian approaches could provide techniques to deal with the problem of bid vector design in dichotomous choice contingent valuation. Bid vector design is a crucial step in generating dichotomous choice data, where the researcher usually disposes pre-test or past information on the distribution of WTP. Finally, as the experience and the practice of CVM increase, the information on the values of the structural parameters explaining WTP could be introduced in the econometric modelling of new data sets, with an increase in efficiency results.

In this chapter we have illustrated the application of Bayesian methods in CVM by postulating a model for double-bounded dichotomous choice data. The double-bounded elicitation method adds a follow-up dichotomous choice question to the standard single-bounded technique. This raises some problems that have left the method subject to serious criticisms. Some of these problems are derived from the scope for biased results from double-bounded data, since the individual could perceive the opportunity to behave strategically in the second question, and the second answer could be influenced by the first bid price offered.

It is clear that the strongest advantage of double-bounded is its demonstrated larger statistical efficiency. This argument is sufficient to consider other ways of modelling double-bounded data to be consistent with the competing hypotheses explaining individual behaviour when posed with a second question. This could be provided by the utilization of a Bayesian approach, where the likelihood function from double bounded is combined with the prior distribution resulting from the first dichotomous choice responses. This setting has the advantage of enhancing the interpretation of the results, while dealing with the problem of bias without reducing efficiency. It is expected that further developments in the application of Bayesian and other econometric techniques will allow researchers to disentangle the alternative hypotheses explaining the change in WTP between the first and second dichotomous choice questions.

Notes

1. In classical inference, if the model was estimated repeatedly in a large number of samples, a $(1-\alpha)\%$ confidence interval calculated for each sample would contain the parameter in $(1-\alpha)\%$ of the samples. However, once the confidence interval is calculated for a particular sample, the level of confidence cannot be interpreted as a probability.
2. Alberini et al. (1997) study three alternative hypotheses which might explain the change in WTP between the first and second dichotomous choice questions: (i) presence of random effects, (ii) structural shift between first and second questions, and (iii) heterocedasticity between and within respondents. The second hypothesis is in the same line as the hypothesis of anchoring formulated by Herriges and Shogren (1996).
3. See for instance Cameron and Quiggin (1994), Herriges and Shogren (1996), and McFadden and Leonard (1995).
4. The analysis can be easily extended to allow for the use of covariates and other statistical distributions, such as the loglogistic.
5. Note that prior (4) implies a prior for any function of $(\mu/\sigma, 1/\sigma)$. For instance, the implied prior distribution for the probability of answering yes to the first bid price (π_i^y) and the standard deviation of WTP (σ) is

$$\frac{\exp\left(\frac{rn}{2}\left[\log\left(\frac{\pi_i^y}{1-\pi_i^y}\right)-\frac{A_i}{\sigma}\right]\right)}{\prod_{i=1}^{n}\left[1+\exp\left[\log\left(\frac{\pi_i^y}{1-\pi_i^y}\right)+\frac{A}{\sigma}\right]\right]^r}\frac{1}{c}\left[\frac{1}{\pi_i^y(1-\pi_i^y)}\right]\frac{1}{\sigma^2}$$

6. In fact, the prior distribution for π_i^y and σ implied by (4) reaches its maximum when $\pi_i^y = 1/2$ and $\sigma = \infty$.

7. Alberini et al. (1997) and Herriges and Shogren (1996) show the loss in efficiency of the estimators when different explanations of the change in WTP are taken into account in the specification of the likelihood function.
8. A double-bounded dichotomous choice survey was conducted to value Teide National Park in the island of Tenerife, which contains the highest peak in Spain with 3714 mts. The survey was carried out in the summer of 1997. The interviews were conducted on-site to the visitors who had just finished their visit to the park. The random sample of 1045 respondents was reduced to 845 subjects after screening for protest and non-responses. A five bid vector design was chosen for the first dichotomous question (500, 1000, 1500, 2000, 3000 pesetas), with lower bid vector follow up (100, 500, 1000, 1500, 2000) and upper bid vector follow up (1000, 1500, 2000, 3000, 4000). The bid prices were randomly distributed across the sample. See León et al. (1998).
9. The predictive likelihood was evaluated by considering the likelihood derived from the answers to the first question as the likelihood function. The likelihood of the double-bounded model will then form part of the prior distribution. The calculations become easier by using this interpretation while the posterior distribution does not change. Since the predictive likelihoods are increased by a proportional factor, the ranking of the prior distributions will remain the same.

References

Alberini, A., B. Kanninen and R.T. Carson (1997), 'Modeling response incentive effects in dichotomous choice contingent valuation data', *Land Economics*, **73**(3), 309–24.

Albert, J.H. and S. Chib (1993), 'Bayesian analysis of binary and polychotomous response data', *Journal of the American Statistical Association*, **88**(1), 669–79.

Araña, J. and C.J. León (2002), 'Willingness to pay for health risk reduction in the context of altruism', *Health Economics*, **11**(7), 623–35.

Araña, J. and C.J. León (2004), 'Flexible mixture distribution modelling of dichotomous choice contingent valuation with heterogeneity', *Journal of Environmental Economics and Management*, forthcoming.

Best, N., M. Cowles and K. Vines (1999), 'Convergence diagnosis and output analysis software for gibbs sampling output version 0.30', MRC Biostatistics Unit, Institute of Public Health.

Berger, J.O. (1985), *Statistical Decision Theory and Bayesian Analysis*, New York: Springer-Verlag.

Bernardo, J.M. (1979), 'Reference posterior distributions for Bayesian inference (with discussion)', *Journal of the Royal Statistical Society*, Series B, **41**, 113–47.

Bjornstad, D., R. Cummings and L. Osborne (1997), 'A learning design for reducing hypothetical bias in the contingent valuation method', *Environmental and Resource Economics*, **10**, 207–21.

Cameron, T.A. and J. Quiggin (1994), 'Estimation using contingent valuation data from dichotomous choice with follow-up questionnaire', *Journal of Environmental Economics and Management*, **27**(3), 218–34.

Cooper, J.C., W.M. Hanemann and G. Signorello (2002), 'One-and-one-half-bound dichotomous choice contingent valuation', *Review of Economics and Statistics*, **84**, 742–50.

Crocker, T. and J. Shogren (1991), 'Preference learning and contingent valuation methods', in F. Dietz, F. van der Ploeg and J. van der Straaten (eds), *Environmental Policy and the Economy*, New York: Elsevier Science.

Fernández, C., C.J. León, M. Steel and F. J. Vázquez-Polo (2004), 'Bayesian analysis of interval data contingent valuation models and pricing policies', *Journal of Business Economics and Statistics*, forthcoming.

Gamerman, D. (1997), *Markov Chain Monte Carlo-Stochastic Simulation for Bayesian Inference*, Chapman & Hall.

Hanemann, W.M. (1984), 'Welfare evaluations in contingent valuation experiments with discrete responses', *American Journal of Agricultural Economics*, **66**, 103–18.

Hanemann, W.M., J. Loomis and B. Kanninen (1991), 'Statistical efficiency of the double bounded dichotomous choice contingent valuation', *American Journal of Agricultural Economics*, **73**, 1255–63.

Hastings, W.K. (1970), 'Monte Carlo sampling methods using Markov chains and their applications', *Biometrika*, **57**, 97–109.

Herriges, J. and J. Shogren (1996), 'Starting point bias in dichotomous choice valuation with follow-up questioning', *Journal of Environmental Economics and Management*, **30**, 112–31.

Horowitz, J. (1993), 'A new model of contingent valuation', *American Journal of Agricultural Economics*, **75**(5), 1268–72.

Jeffreys, A. (1961), *The Theory of Probability*, Cambridge: Cambridge University Press.

Koop, G. and D.J. Poirier (1993), 'Bayesian analysis of logit models using natural conjugate priors', *Journal of Econometrics*, **56**, 323–40.

León, C.J. and F.J. Vázquez-Polo (1998), 'A Bayesian approach to double bounded contingent valuation', *Environmental and Resource Economics*, **11**, 197–215.

Leon, C.J., F.J. Vazquez-Polo, P. Riera and N. Guerra (1998), 'Testing benefit transfer with prior information', Working Paper, Department of Applied Economic Analysis, University of Las Palmas de Gran Canaria.

León, R. and C.J. León (2003), 'Single or double bounded contingent valuation? A Bayesian test', *Scottish Journal of Political Economy*, **50**(2), 174–88.

McCulloch, R. and P.E. Rossi (1994), 'An exact likelihood analysis of the multinomial probit model', *Journal of Econometrics*, **64**, 207–40.

McFadden, D. and G. Leonard (1995), 'Issues in the contingent valuation of environmental goods: methodologies for data collection and analysis', in J.A. Hausman (ed.), *Contingent Valuation: A Critical Assessment*, Amsterdam: North-Holland.

McLeod, D.M. and O. Bergland (1998), 'Willingness-to-pay estimates using the double-bounded dichotomous-choice contingent valuation format: a test for validity and precision in a Bayesian framework', *Land Economics*, **75**(1), 115–25.

Metroprolis, N., A.W. Rosenbluth, M.N. Rosenbluth, A.H. Teller and E. Teller (1953), 'Equation of state calculations by fast computing machine', *Journal of Chemical Physics*, **21**, 1087–91.

Newton, M.A. and A.E. Raftery, (1994), 'Approximate Bayesian inference by the weighted likelihood bootstrap (with discussion)', *Journal of the Royal Statistical Society*, Series B, **56**, 3–48.

Tierney, L. and J.B. Kadane (1986), 'Accurate approximations for posterior moments and marginal densities', *Journal of the American Statistical Association*, **81**, 82–6.

Viscusi, W. (1989), 'Prospective reference theory: toward an explanation of the paradoxes', *Journal of Risk and Uncertainty*, **2**(3), 235–64.

Zellner, A. (1985), 'Bayesian econometrics', *Econometrica*, **53**, 253–69.

11 Temporal reliability in contingent valuation (with a restrictive research budget)

Paul M. Jakus, Becky Stephens and J. Mark Fly

11.1 Introduction

Information provided by contingent valuation (CV) surveys is becoming more commonly used as an input into the policy-making process. Loomis (1999), for example, outlines the degree to which numerous federal and state agencies in the United States have used WTP estimates to formulate policy decisions and options. At the same time that demand for valid and reliable willingness to pay (WTP) estimates is growing, the criteria by which a CV survey can be evaluated as 'good' have become very stringent. The NOAA Panel on Contingent Valuation (Arrow et al., 1993) set the bar very high, outlining a set of prescriptions they claimed were necessary to produce reliable and valid WTP estimates for non-use values to be used in natural resource damage litigation. These criteria make CV surveys very expensive, and also beg the question about 'quality' criteria for CV surveys intended to estimate use values for environmental commodities whose services are well known to users. If valid and reliable WTP estimates can be done relatively inexpensively, this would allow trustees to make better informed policy and management decisions.

CV surveys have often been used to estimate use values for outdoor recreation activities such as hunting and fishing. Indeed, a seminal CV article focused on hunting permits and was sponsored by the Wisconsin fish and game agency (Bishop and Heberlein, 1979). In recent years, state fish and game agencies have come under increasing pressure to incorporate human dimensions research into their management of wildlife and policy decisions affecting wildlife. Numerous state agencies now sponsor human dimensions research either within the agency itself (e.g., Oklahoma) or with university-affiliated research centers (e.g., Tennessee, Colorado, and New York). The purpose of most surveys is to monitor the activities and attitudes of hunters and anglers, and to evaluate proposed changes in species management (e.g., bag limits). However, oftentimes an agency may desire an estimate of WTP for a given management program. Whereas the agency may be willing and able to fund baseline human dimensions research, the allocated survey budget may not be adequate to fully implement and satisfy the criteria outlined by the NOAA Panel for WTP estimates to be used in litigation.[1]

This chapter reports on two survey efforts that labored under tight budget restrictions (tight, of course, by CV standards). The Tennessee Wildlife Resources Agency (TWRA) wished to have an estimate of hunters' WTP for a different form of access to lands owned by timber companies. Unfortunately, the agency could not increase the survey budget to allow for complete implementation of many recommended CV practices (focus groups, the use of visual aids, etc.). The budget constraint required survey design compromises that, *ex ante*, may or may not have been adequate to the task of providing valid and reliable WTP estimates.

The key research question of this chapter is to determine the cumulative effect of these decisions on the quality of the WTP estimate; for example, to what degree is confidence in the WTP estimate well founded? Put another way, how far can one push the methodology? To answer this question, the temporal reliability of WTP estimates for access to Public Hunting Lands in Tennessee is evaluated. Data from two random digit dial surveys conducted over a four-year interval are used. After a brief review of the literature on temporal reliability, a discussion of the survey methodology focuses on the compromises made necessary by the survey budget. Results and implications for future research follow.

11.2   The WTP function and temporal reliability

11.2.1   The WTP function

A person's WTP for a public good is dependent upon a variety of factors, and McConnell (1990) developed the variation function to show the functional relationship among those factors.[2] The compensating welfare measure associated with a change in the quantity of a public good is given by the difference in expenditure functions,

$$C_t = m(p_t, q_t^0, u_t^0) - m(p_t, q_t^1, u_t^0), \tag{11.1}$$

where C_t is the welfare measure as estimated at time t, $m(.)$ are the expenditure functions governing the income necessary to achieve utility u_t^0 at prices p_t given a change in public good level from q_t^0 (initial quantity) to q_t^1 (subsequent quantity). Substituting the indirect utility function $V(p_t, q_t^0, y_t)$ for the reference utility, McConnell denotes the difference on the right-hand side of equation (11.1) as the variation function, $s(p_t, q_t^0, q_t^1, y_t)$, where y_t is income at time t. This function defines the compensation at time t needed to hold utility constant as we change the public good from q_t^0 to q_t^1. In addition to prices, income, and the public good q, $s(.)$ more generally will include other factors believed to influence WTP such as demographics, D, so that

$s(.) = s(p_t, q_t^0, q_t^1, y_t, D_t)$. Econometric estimation of the variation function yields parameters β that reflect the parameters of the originating preference structure.

Differences in WTP over time can be traced to the differences in the value of the variation function over time. Comparing time $t = 0$ to time $t = 1$, then,

$$\Delta WTP = s(p_0, q_0^0, q_0^1, y_0, D_0; \beta_0) - s(p_1, q_1^0, q_1^1, y_1, D_1; \beta_1). \quad (11.2)$$

Temporal differences in WTP can arise from changes in any of the arguments of the variation function across time, or changes in the parameters of the variation function over time. If preferences are stable ($\beta_0 = \beta_1$) but we observe changes in, say, prices or income, then WTP should differ over time and the left-hand side of (11.2) is non-zero. This is the essence of so-called 'test–retest' experiments in which the parameters of the WTP function are estimated using the same sample of people at two points in time. This approach allows one to capture all changes in the constraints under which people make choices (i.e., prices, income, other demographic factors, as well as changes in the availability of public goods) and focus on the stability of the preference parameters β. After controlling for changes in the explanatory factors, if one concludes that $\beta_0 \neq \beta_1$, the implications are (a) preferences have changed or (b) CV is an unreliable methodology.

In the absence of test–retest samples, one must rely upon repeated cross-section samples to estimate relationships (1) and (2). This is more challenging in that the same people do not appear in each sample, so that one cannot fully control for possible changes in the explanatory variables. Whereas the test–retest methodology gives the analyst a better opportunity to net out the unobserved factors that may influence WTP but are not measured, the repeated cross-sectional approach does not permit this. For the sample collected at time $t = 1$, the analyst cannot 'go back in time', so to speak, to re-construct the set of prices, income, and the like that constrained consumption at time $t = 0$. Although the repeated sample approach is an incomplete strategy relative to the test–retest approach, one may use a variety of statistical methods to test the hypothesis of preference stability, $\beta_0 = \beta_1$.

11.2.2 *Temporal reliability*
Amongst the many recommendations made by the NOAA Panel was a recommendation that WTP estimates collected over a period of time be averaged in order to provide a stable estimate of WTP. As noted above, there are a number of reasons why WTP may change over time; for example, the true value of an environmental commodity may change as consumers gain more experience with the commodity or as they learn more about the services provided by an environmental commodity. Within the context of the

Exxon Valdez oil spill, the Panel was concerned about the timing of valuation surveys relative to the timing and publicity associated with the environmental damage incident; i.e., there might be a temporary increase in WTP in close temporal proximity to the event. This effect may fade with time as people learn more about the damage and have the chance to place it in perspective with consumption of other market and non-market goods. But concern about the reliability of CV WTP estimates over time did not originate with the NOAA Panel, and many researchers have investigated the temporal reliability of CV.

Loomis examined the temporal reliability of CV estimates in a pair of early studies (1989, 1990). Using a test–retest methodology in which the same respondents were sampled at a nine-month interval, he found that WTP to protect a hyper-saline lake were, in general, reliable over that time period. Reiling et al. used two separate samples to estimate peoples' WTP for control of black flies (1990). Respondents interviewed during the peak of the black fly season were found to have the same WTP as respondents interviewed following the season. Since the publication of the NOAA Panel report, a small number of additional studies have examined the temporal reliability of CV (Teisel et al., 1995; Downing and Ozuna, 1996; Carson et al., 1997; McConnell et al., 1998; Whitehead and Hoban, 1999; and Berrens et al., 2000). The study by McConnell et al. uses the test–retest approach, while the remainder use repeated cross-section samples. (The study by Teisel et al. uses both methods, along with pre- and post-test control groups.) The time frame between measurements of WTP ranges from the very short – a few months in the McConnell et al. and Teisel et al. studies – to longer periods of time – one or two years in the Berrens et al., Downing and Ozuna, and Carson et al. studies. Only Whitehead and Hoban have let a large amount of time pass between WTP measurements. In their study of the WTP by a general population for cleaner air and water, the CV estimates of WTP were significantly different over the five-year time period. However, after examining changes in environmental attitudes by the population, the authors conclude that the true WTP value had changed due to changes in explanatory variables. Any differences in WTP could be explained by the change in environmental attitudes by the population and the CV method had correctly measured the change in WTP.

11.3 Survey design
11.3.1 Background and the contingent commodity
Concerns about the availability of land on which Tennessee sportsmen may hunt led the TWRA to enter into arrangements with a number of large timber companies to allow public hunting on timber company lands. These lands are called Public Hunting Areas (PHAs) and, at the time of the

surveys, some 700 000 acres of timber company land was enrolled throughout the state. Timber companies were compensated for allowing access to PHAs by collecting a per acre payment from TWRA and also by collecting fees directly from hunters.[3] Hunters who purchased a permit were given access only to PHA lands of the company from which they purchased the permit. The average permit cost was about $20, allowing access to an average of 80 000 acres. Hunters were not granted access to lands held by another company unless an additional permit was purchased from that company. At the time of both surveys, approximately 12–15 per cent of Tennessee's hunters (about 40 000–50 000 hunters) used Public Hunting Areas during the course of the hunting season.

Beginning in the 1990s, timber companies informed TWRA that the administrative burden of collecting small fees from a large number of hunters was much greater than that of collecting a large fee from a single hunting group. Thus, companies had an incentive to move toward private leasing arrangements rather than allowing access to the general hunting public. Further, timber companies may have the perception that a single group would take greater care of the land when that group holds an exclusive property right to hunt the land. These two forces caused TWRA officials to become concerned that public access to PHAs was threatened.

In response to these concerns, the agency considered an alternative method by which the administrative burden on timber companies could be lessened. Under a single permit method, TWRA would offer all hunters the opportunity to purchase a single permit that would allow the purchaser to gain access to all PHAs in the state. TWRA would be responsible for collecting the payments from hunters, and then distributing the proceeds to the timber companies. Receiving a lump sum from the TWRA relieves the companies of the need to collect small payments from a large number of hunters. The agency was interested in determining how much hunters were willing to pay for the single permit.

11.3.2   Key survey design issues

The TWRA provided an adequate level of funding for analysis of most policy questions in the past, but this amount was not sufficient to fund a state-of-the-art CV study. Consequently some compromises were made. For example, the expense of conducting formal focus groups made their use impossible. Instead, CV questions were formulated using a combination of expert opinion (using TWRA personnel to help design the questions) and a series of pre-tests involving known hunters who were representative of the population. Second, the sample sizes for the various treatments in a CV study were small because the Random Digit Dial survey method (needed to achieve the primary goals of the survey) made it difficult to generate a large sample from the relatively small population of hunters in Tennessee (less than 10 per cent of the adult population). To overcome small sample sizes, an estimation method that improves the statistical properties of the WTP estimate, the so-called double-bounded estimator, was used (Hanemann, Loomis, and Kanninen, 1991; Alberini, 1995).[4] Finally, whereas telephone surveys provide a compromise between the expense of in-person surveys and cheaper mail surveys that can be subject to serious non-response problems, the policy question in this case would seem to require a map of PHA locations, something that could not be done over the phone. For example, one might wish to assure that the respondent was well-informed about the location of PHAs and have a measure of the respondent's perceived proximity to Public Hunting Areas, but the survey budget precluded the use of multiple stage telephone–mail–telephone format. Instead, we were forced to rely upon a set of secondary measures to gauge knowledge of and proximity to PHAs. For example, hunters were asked if they had hunted a PHA in the past, and zip code information was used to determine if the hunter resided in or near a county in which a PHA was located.

Prior to asking hunters about the single permit system, some introductory text provided hunters with an overview of the PHA system as it was operated at the time of the surveys. It described the average permit price and the average size of a PHA, finishing with a statement that there were approximately 700 000 acres of land in state PHAs. This text was followed by the double-bounded CV question regarding the single PHA permit method.[5]

11.3.3 Response rates

The analysis is based on two random digit dial surveys of the general population of Tennessee. The surveys were conducted in March and April of 1995 and 1999. For each survey, the RDD sampling frame began with 10 000 numbers. After removing ineligible numbers (businesses, disconnects, and fax machines), 7078 (1995) and 8529 (1999) eligible numbers remained. All phone numbers were attempted at least five times prior to being placed in the 'no contact' category. Excluding the no contact group yielded a response rate of 45.8 per cent and 33.1 per cent for 1995 and 1999, respectively. This study is concerned only with active hunters, of whom 255 were contacted in 1995 and 213 were contacted in 1999. Mean values for key variables from the two surveys are presented in Table 11.1.

11.4 Contingency analysis

Contingency analysis was conducted using the raw survey response data without covariates (Table 11.2). The second and third columns of Table 11.2 give the percentage of respondents who said they would be willing to purchase a single PHA permit at the stated price for 1995 and 1999,

Table 11.1   Mean values for key variables

Variable	1995	1999
Live in metropolitan statistical area (% yes)	43.5%	39.0%
Hunted in public hunting area last season (% yes)	17.3%	15.5%
Live near a public hunting area (% yes)	50.2%	49.3%
Access to good hunting land is a problem (% yes)	31.0%	35.7%
Years hunted (years)	21.4	25.7
Days hunted last season (days)	25.8	26.6
Observations	255	213

Table 11.2   Contingency analysis for responses to CV questions

Initial value	First CV question only			Both CV questions
	% yes to the first question 1995	% yes to the first question 1999	*P*-value for difference	*P*-value for difference
$20	45.2	76.5	0.01*	0.16
$25	60.0	56.3	0.76	0.43
$35	56.4	50.0	0.56	0.92
$50	37.8	52.8	0.20	0.39
$75	27.3	23.5	0.77	0.86
$100	30.6	35.5	0.67	0.97

respectively. The *P*-value reported in the fourth column is for the Pearson chi-square test that the proportions in 1995 and 1999 were identical. The *P*-value in the fifth column reports the Pearson chi-square test that the distributions of the four possible response combinations for any initial value (Yes–Yes, Yes–No, No–Yes, and No–No) were identical across the two years. In only one case – the $20 value for the initial question – were the responses significantly different across the two years. This suggests that the implied CV values were temporally reliable across the two years.

11.5   Double-bounded responses, using covariates

Analysis of the double-bounded CV responses follows the restricted bivariate probit model (Alberini, 1995). This model assumes that the underlying 'true' WTP remains constant across the two questions, but allows the error correlation to differ from one (a restriction of the Hanemann, Loomis, and Kanninen approach). Models were estimated for the 1995 data only, the

1999 data only, and the combined dataset. The permit prices for 1999 were adjusted for inflation by the relative change in the consumer price index between March 1995 and March 1999 so that all models are based on 1995 prices.

Hunters' WTP for access to PHAs was hypothesized to be a function of a number of variables. In addition to the permit cost (price) the sign of which should be negative, whether or not the respondent hunted in PHAs was likely to influence WTP (hunt in PHA). Although congestion effects may be present, one would anticipate that those who had already paid for a PHA permit would be willing to pay more for access to a much larger acreage (presuming that the additional acreage is relatively proximate to the hunter's residence). Thus, a positive sign on this variable was expected. Hunters who reported experiencing problems gaining access to hunting lands were hypothesized to be more likely to support the single permit program because the proposed program increased the acreage available to hunters (access is a problem).

Finally, two additional factors were believed to condition hunters' responses to the program. All else equal, proximity to a PHA may influence WTP, although it is not clear that proximity to one PHA would increase one's WTP for the expanded program (live near PHA). WTP for access to PHAs may be related to measures of a hunter's experience such as the number of years they had been hunting (years hunted), or the number of days hunted during the season (days hunted). It was not clear, a priori, what sign to anticipate on these variables, because those who have hunted for a long period of time, or very frequently during the season, may have better knowledge of alternative lands to hunt.

11.5.1   Parameter estimates

Models were estimated for each individual year (columns 2 and 3 of Table 11.3) and for both years combined (columns 4 and 5). In all models reported in Table 11.3 hunters were responsive to the price of the single permit. The two variables measuring the number of days hunted in the previous season were significant in all base models as well. The number of days hunted showed a quadratic relationship to the probability that a person would support the single permit system, all else equal. This suggests that those who hunt only a few days each season and those who hunt very often were less likely to support the single permit system than those who hunt a moderate number of days each year.

Whether or not a person lived in a metropolitan statistical area (live in MSA) was significant in three of the four models. The log of number of years that a respondent had hunted (Ln years hunted) was negatively related to the probability of support for the single permit system, but this was true

Table 11.3   Single permit system: double-bounded models

Variable	1995 only	1999 only	Both years model 1	Both years model 2
Intercept	0.130	0.089	0.077	0.084
	(0.45)[a]	(0.27)	(0.36)	(0.38)
Price	**−0.007**	**−0.014**	**−0.009**	**−0.009**
	(−2.97)	**(−3.99)**	**(−4.99)**	**(−4.79)**
Hunt in PHA	0.329	−0.061	0.176	0.177
	(1.58)	(−0.25)	(1.16)	(1.17)
Live near PHA	−0.083	0.166	0.016	0.016
	(−0.48)	(0.87)	(0.13)	(0.13)
Access is a problem	0.192	0.127	0.161	0.161
	(1.24)	(0.70)	(1.38)	(1.37)
Live in MSA	0.092	**0.412**	**0.220**	**0.221**
	(0.53)	**(2.32)**	**(1.82)**	**(1.82)**
Ln (years hunted)	−0.123	−0.120	**−0.113**	**−0.113**
	(−1.55)	(−1.23)	**(−1.85)**	**(−1.85)**
Days hunted	**0.012**	**0.021**	**0.016**	**0.016**
	(1.93)	**(2.95)**	**(3.38)**	**(3.37)**
Days hunted squared	**−8.9 × 10⁻⁵**	**−1.2 × 10⁻⁴**	**−1.0 × 10⁻⁴**	**−1.0 × 10⁻⁴**
	(−1.68)	**(−2.15)**	**(−2.61)**	**(−2.60)**
Year = 1995				−0.017
				(−0.15)
Rho	**0.318**	**0.517**	**0.400**	**0.397**
	(1.99)	**(3.11)**	**(3.56)**	**(3.48)**
Ln L	−260.96	−209.48	−473.90	−473.89
Observations	204	165	369	369
WTP	$12.92	$29.06	$22.32	$22.12
95% CI	−$20.76−$46.59[b]	$15.17−$42.94	$6.53−$38.11	$6.00−$38.24

Notes:
Coefficients in boldface are significant at α = 0.10.
[a] Number in parentheses is ratio of the coefficient to its asymptotic standard error.
[b] Confidence interval calculated using the delta method.

only in the two models using the dataset that combined both years of data. It is possible that the larger sample size, relative to the models for each individual year, resulted in efficiency gains sufficient to make this variable statistically significant. None of the remaining variables was significant at conventional statistical levels. Finally, all specifications were also estimated using income as an explanatory variable – in no case was income statistically significant.

11.5.2   Temporal reliability

Reliability is assessed by conducting likelihood ratio and Wald tests of the hypothesis that the parameters of the WTP function are identical across the two different years. The likelihood ratio test took the form $Q = -2 \times (\ln L_{combined} - (\ln L_{1995} + \ln L_{1999}))$, where Q is distributed chi-square, and the $\ln L$ are the values of the log likelihood function for the combined 1995 and 1999 datasets, respectively. The Wald test is a bit different, looking at the difference between the two estimated parameter vectors and the relative precision of the estimates by using the estimated variance covariance matrices

$$Q = (\beta_{95} - \beta_{99})' (VC_{95} + VC_{99}) (\beta_{95} - \beta_{99}),$$

where the β and VC are the estimated parameter vectors and variance–covariance matrices for the 1995 and 1999 models, and Q is a distributed chi-square. In addition to the likelihood ratio and Wald tests, the 'Both years model 2' used a dummy variable to test for changes in the intercept between the two different years.

The combined model presented in column 4 of Table 11.3 restricted the coefficients of each variable to be identical across the two years. The likelihood ratio test of the null hypothesis of parameter stability across the two years is not rejected ($Q = 6.32$ with nine degrees of freedom). Similarly, the Wald test of differences in the coefficient vector also failed to reject the null hypothesis of $\beta_{95} = \beta_{99}$, with the test statistic value $Q = 6.73$. This suggests temporal reliability of the parameters of the WTP function.

One may also compare the actual estimates of WTP across the two time periods. Changes in WTP over time can occur given changes in the parameters of the WTP function or changes in the arguments of the function. With $WTP = \beta X$, then $dWTP = (d\beta \times X) + (\beta \times dX)$. Given the finding above that $d\beta = 0$, this is equivalent to testing whether the explanatory factors, both observed and unobserved, have changed sufficiently across the time periods to influence WTP. The WTP estimates for the 1995 and 1999 models are reported at the bottom of Table 11.3. The point estimates for each year appear to be different ($12.92 and $29.06 for 1995 and 1999, respectively), but the 95 per cent confidence intervals for these estimates are relatively wide, especially for 1995. Given that each estimate is a random variable, one may use the method of convolutions to test the null hypothesis that $WTP_{95} - WTP_{99} = 0$ (Poe et al., 2005). The convolutions test fails to reject the null hypothesis at conventional significance levels, with the two-sided P-value of 0.32.

Finally, an additional test of temporal reliability is to add a dummy variable that identifies the different years and allows a shift in the intercept or allows the slopes for each coefficient to differ across the years. The 'intercept shift' model is presented in column 5 of Table 11.3. The dummy variable YEAR = 1995 was statistically insignificant, indicating that the two years do not differ with a simple change in intercept. An additional specification, not reported in Table 11.3, interacted a dummy variable for 1995 with every explanatory variable. None of the interaction terms was statistically significant, indicating temporal reliability of the estimating equation.

11.6 Conclusions

This chapter examined the temporal reliability of WTP estimates generated by a restrictive research budget. A number of compromises were made in the design and implementation phases of the study. Specifically, the survey budget precluded the use of focus groups, it prevented the use of visual aids to communicate the location and size of PHAs relative to the hunter residence, and only relatively small samples of hunters could be gleaned from the random digit dial survey method. Still, it was decided to carry through with the experiment because (1) the contingent commodity was well-known to hunters and had a long-established payment mechanism, (2) the WTP estimate would reflect only use values, and (3) estimates were needed for policy decisions.

The compromises in survey design and implementation appear to have had little impact on the temporal reliability of WTP estimates. In no case could one reject the null hypothesis that the parameter estimates were the same across both years in which the CV exercise was conducted, nor could one reject the null hypothesis that the WTP estimates were the same across both years. Some authors, however, have suggested that temporal reliability is a necessary condition for a quality CV WTP estimate, but is not sufficient to assure that the WTP estimate is valid (Desvousges et al., 1996).

Indeed, in reporting the results of these models to the sponsoring agency, a key concern was theoretical validity. The empirical results satisfied important economic criteria: namely, a negative price effect and zero income effects associated with the relatively small permit price. Where the validity of the models came into question was with respect to our 'external' knowledge of the sample (Carson et al., 2001). A reasonable assumption was to expect that those people who had hunted on PHAs to have a greater WTP than those who had not. A dummy variable capturing this effect was insignificant in all specifications. Further, the WTP point estimates from a split sample test (PHA hunters versus those who did not hunt PHAs) did not allow one to conclude that a statistically significant difference was present. The results suggest that the contingent valuation methodology was pressed to its absolute limit in this study, with serious concerns about how well respondents understood the contingent commodity being offered.

Given these shortcomings, did the study still provide information to policy makers? The short answer is 'yes'. Following discussions with agency personnel, a key conclusion of the modeling effort was that the expanded acreage provided by a single permit system would be unlikely to attract additional hunters to PHAs, at least at permit costs that would fund program administration (roughly $30 or more). The effort to design a single permit system was no longer seriously pursued. As a final postscript, the TWRA was never able to implement a fee collection system to allow access to all PHAs. In the 2000–01 hunting season, a major timber company removed over 200 000 acres from the Public Hunting Area program, preferring to lease to a limited number of individuals or hunting clubs. Even more land was removed from the program over the next several seasons, such that by 2004 only 63 000 acres remained in Public Hunting Areas, less than 10 per cent of the 1999 acreage (TWRA, 2004).

Notes

1. Harrison and Lesley (1996) make the distinction between 'gold-plated "litigation quality" surveys on the one hand and homely "research quality" surveys on the other hand.'
2. Hanemann (1999) develops an income compensation function that is closely related to McConnell's variation function.
3. TWRA remains responsible for enforcement of hunting regulations on PHAs.
4. Relative to a single-bound estimator, the double-bounded estimator provides a minimum mean squared error.
5. The text for the CV question is in Appendix A. In the survey, a second CV question was also asked about license fee increases. The order of the two CV questions was randomized, with some hunters getting the single permit question first, and the remaining hunters getting the license fee question first. Analysis indicated that the order of the question was not a statistically significant factor in peoples' responses.

References

Alberini, A. (1995), 'Efficiency v. bias of willingness-to-pay estimates: bivariate and interval-data models', *Journal of Environmental Economics and Management*, **29**(2), 169–80.

Arrow, K. et al. (1993), 'Report of the NOAA Panel on contingent valuation', *Federal Register*, **58**, 4601–14.

Berrens, R.P. et al. (2000), 'Contingent values for New Mexico instream flows: with tests of scope, group-size reminder, and temporal reliability', *Journal of Environmental Management*, **58** (January), 73–90.

Bishop, R.C. and T.A. Heberlein (1979), 'Measuring values of extra-market goods: are indirect measures biased?', *American Journal of Agricultural Economics*, **61**(5), 926–30.

Carson, R.T., N.E. Flores and N.F. Meade (2001), 'Contingent valuation: controversies and evidence', *Environmental and Resource Economics*, **19**(2), 173–210.

Carson, R.T. et al. (1997), 'Temporal reliability of estimates from contingent valuation', *Land Economics*, **73**(2), 151–63.

Desvousges, W.H., S.P. Hudson and M.C. Ruby (1996), 'Evaluating CV performance: separating the light from the heat', in J.R. Kahn and D. Bjornstad (eds), *The Contingent Valuation of Environmental Resources*, Cheltenham, UK and Northampton, MA: Edward Elgar, Chapter 7.

Downing, M. and T. Ozuna (1996), 'Testing the reliability of the benefit function transfer approach', *Journal of Environmental Economics and Management*, **30**(2), 316–22.

Haab, T. and K.E. McConnell (1997), 'Referendum models and negative willingness to pay: alternative solutions', *Journal of Environmental Economics and Management*, **32**, 251–70.

Hanemann, W.M. (1999), 'The economic theory of WTP and WTA', in I.J. Bateman and K.G. Willis (eds), *Valuing Environmental Preferences*, New York: Oxford University Press, Chapter 2.

Hanemann, W.M., J.B. Loomis and B. Kanninen (1991), 'Statistical efficiency of double bounded dichotomous choice contingent valuation', *American Journal of Agricultural Economics*, **73**, 1255–63.

Harrison, G.W. and J.C. Lesley (1996), 'Must contingent valuation surveys cost so much?', *Journal of Environmental Economics and Management*, **31**(1), 79–95.

Loomis, J.B. (1989), 'Test–retest reliability of the contingent valuation method: a comparison of general population and visitor responses', *American Journal of Agricultural Economics*, **71**(1), 76–84.

Loomis, J.B. (1990), 'Comparative reliability of the dichotomous choice and open-ended contingent valuation techniques', *Journal of Environmental Economics and Management*, **18**(1), 78–85.

Loomis, J.B. (1999), 'Contingent valuation methodology and the US institutional framework', in I.J. Bateman and K.G. Willis (eds), *Valuing Environmental Preferences*, New York: Oxford University Press.

McConnell, K.E. (1990), 'Models for referendum data: the structure of discrete choice models for contingent valuation', *Journal of Environmental Economics and Management*, **18**(1), 19–35.

McConnell, K.E., I.E. Strand and S. Valdes (1998), 'Testing temporal reliability and carry-over effect: the role of correlated responses in test–retest reliability studies', *Environmental and Resource Economics*, **12**, 357–74.

Poe, G.L., K.L. Giraud, and J.B. Loomis (2005), 'Simple computational methods for measuring the difference of empirical distributions: application to internal and external scope tests in contingent valuation', *American Journal of Agricultural Economics*, **87**(2), 353–65.

Reiling, S.D. et al. (1990), 'Temporal reliability of contingent values', *Land Economics*, **66**(2), 128–34.

Teisel, M.F. et al. (Three co-authors) (1995), 'Test–retest reliability of contingent valuation with independent sample pretest and posttest control groups', *American Journal of Agricultural Economics*, **77**(3), 613–19.

Tennessee Wildlife Resources Agency (TWRA). http://www.state.tn.us/twra/hunt001c.html (retrieved 7 November 2004.)

Whitehead, J.C. and T.J. Hoban (1999), 'Testing for temporal reliability in contingent valuation with time for changes in factors affecting demand', *Land Economics*, **75**(3), 453–65.

Appendix: text of contingent valuation questions

Introductory text

Several different timber companies own lands that are currently designated as Public Hunting Areas. To gain access to these areas, a hunter must purchase a separate permit for each area, at approximately $20 per permit. A hunter must purchase the permit in order to hunt on only one Public Hunting Area, which average about 80 000 acres each.

An alternative plan would use a single permit to gain access to all Public Hunting Areas in Tennessee – about 700 000 acres total. Only those hunters purchasing the permit would be able to hunt in Public Hunting Areas. If you were offered the opportunity to purchase a single permit for ($20 $25 $35 $50 $75 $100) would you do so?

1   Yes
0   No
98 Don't Know

(IF YES) It is possible that management expenses may be higher than expected, so the permit price may be higher. Would you be willing to pay {$40 $50 $70 $100 $150 $200} for the permit?

1   Yes
0   No
98 Don't Know

(IF NO) It is possible that management expenses may be lower than expected, so the permit price may be lower. Would you be willing to pay {$10 $12.50 $17.50 $25 $37.50 $50} for the permit?

1   Yes
0   No
98 Don't Know

(IF YES) People may say 'yes' for a variety of reasons. Why did you say 'yes'? (DNT RD)

1   Better quality hunting areas
2   Greater area to hunt
3   PHA are less crowded
98 Don't Know
97 Other (SPF): _____

(IF NO) People may say 'no' for a variety of reasons. Why did you say 'no'? (DNT RD)

1   Too expensive
2   Not worth it
3   No PHA near me
4   PHA have poor quality hunting
5   Would rather hunt elsewhere/don't hunt PHA's
6   Don't believe this would work
7   Don't want to pay additional money for this
98 Don't Know
97 Other (SPF): _____

PART III

APPLICATIONS

12 Non-market valuation on the internet
Hale W. Thurston

12.1 Introduction

Will surveys on the internet eventually be used by economists to collect data to conduct unbiased non-market valuation studies? The answer is 'yes'. Can we do this now? The answer is 'not quite'. The lure of the internet for data collection is strong: marginal cost of data collection almost nil and the electronic format lends itself to easy data handling. Furthermore, unlike other survey methods, the researcher can enhance the respondent's understanding of the good in question by showing drawings, photographs, and graphs on the survey page, or provide links to other pages where pertinent information is readily available. The survey can be designed such that the researcher can track the time a respondent spends pondering a question. The researcher can keep the respondent from looking ahead or back in the text, or, if so desired, he can 'watch' as the respondent 'flips' back a page or two and changes an answer. Virtual interviewers (of different races and gender) can be embedded in the page to read the survey questionnaire to the respondent. The possibilities are endless. The catch? No matter how elaborate the survey, the conclusions drawn by the study are constrained by the survey's sample.

Access to the internet continues to increase. The National Telecommunications and Information Administration estimated that 26.2 per cent of US households had internet access in 1999, up from 18.6 per cent in 1997, and the Pew institute puts the number at approximately 50 per cent by 2000 and 59 per cent nationally in 2002 Spooner (2003). And, while the digital gap that existed only a few years ago is narrowing, internet use is still not uniformly distributed demographically according to Rhode and Shapiro (2000), nor geographically according to Spooner (2003). In fact there is a widening gap in access corresponding to some socio-economic traits; the sample one gets from the internet is still not representative of the US population. We are not the first generation to overestimate the coverage of a new technology. Dillman (2000) reminds us of the 1936 Literary Digest phone survey that picked Landon to beat Roosevelt in the upcoming presidential elections. The survey used a large sample, but it was a sample drawn from the 35 per cent of US households that had phones at that time. The conclusions were of course biased by a sample that was not representative of the target population. Today approximately 94.1 per cent of US households have phones, and samples consisting of randomly selected phone-users are generally accepted as accurate representations of the population. There is no reason to believe that internet access will not be as widespread as phone access in the near future. However, even total access does not guarantee there are no technology-specific biases we will run across. Couper (2001) notes that the ease of data collection (or solicitation) might ultimately prove a curse. If internet users are so bombarded with requests to fill out surveys that some tune out the requests or respond based on content or appearance of the survey, samples will be biased.

This chapter addresses some of the unique possibilities and potential pitfalls of using the internet for non-market valuation. The first section outlines some internet surveys that have recently been undertaken or are ongoing, and points out the valuation methodology and any unique high-tech attributes. At the end of the first section, I focus on one of the biggest challenges facing those who want to use the internet for surveys, the problem of a biased sample. In the second section of the chapter I detail some of the technical information a practitioner should be familiar with. Section 12.3 of the chapter outlines the methodology and results from one of the first contingent valuation surveys conducted on the internet and points out some mistakes and lessons learned.

12.2   Current research

The present subject matter is changing almost daily; most of the valuation surveys using internet technology are in press or have yet to be published. What follows is an overview of some of the surveys currently or recently posted on the World Wide Web. While in some cases all but preliminary results are still unavailable, potential internet surveyors can glean something from this look at state-of-the-art methodology.

The Farmland Survey, undertaken by Mackenzie at the University of Delaware uses a conjoint/paired comparison approach to valuing protected farmland through development rights purchase. The various market and non-market benefits of farmland are explained, as is a 'Purchase of Development Rights' program that allows for farmland preservation through private acquisition and set-aside. Participants in the survey are faced with several opportunities to choose between farms of differing attributes. Farms' attributes include: size, farm type, cost of protecting the farmland, portion of the farm that is in forested land, contiguity with farmland that already is protected, prior loss of road frontage, pace of development in the area, long-run viability of local agriculture, and annual income.

The URL of the survey was http://bluehen.ags.udel.edu/survey/survey_intro.html. Computer-generated pictures illustrate the farmland choices faced by the respondent. One example is shown in Figure 12.1.

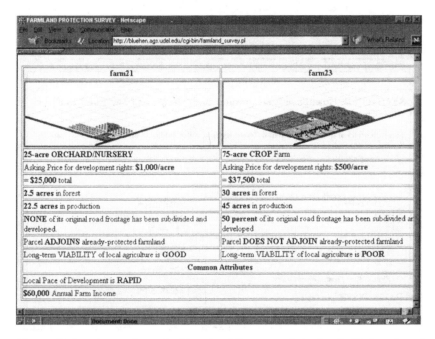

Figure 12.1   A page from the Farmland Survey website by the University of Delaware

Above the two choices is written, 'Please Select the Farm You Prefer', which the respondent does by clicking on the appropriate image.

Whitehead's ongoing survey at http://www.appstate.edu/~whiteheadjc/ Research/survey/ focuses on water quality in the Neuse and Tar-Pamlico rivers in North Carolina. Whitehead uses a take it or leave it bid question: 'Suppose a special "Neuse and Tar-Pamlico Clean Water Fund" is established by the state and funded by higher state taxes. Tax money would be put into the fund and used to pay farmers to use best management practices in the Neuse and Tar-Pamlico River Basins . . . Would you be willing to pay $50 each year in higher state taxes into the Neuse and Tar-Pamlico Clean Water Fund to improve water quality to a swimable level?'. This dichotomous choice (DC) question is followed up with an open-ended maximum willingness to pay (WTP) for the same improvement in water quality.

This survey takes advantage of several of the internet's strong points. Maps of the areas of interest are presented with hyperlinks to larger illustrations. Confusing or specialized terms can be selected to open a glossary. The 'water quality ladder', shown in Figure 12.2, is clickable so that respondents can enlarge it to view greater detail. There are links that facilitate skipping over questions that do not pertain to a given respondent (based on

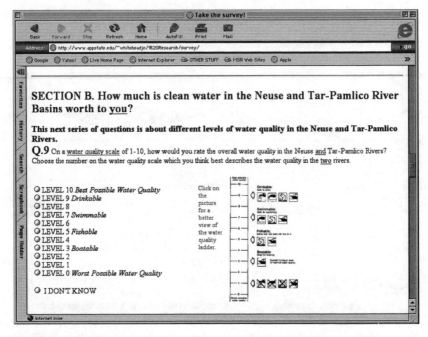

Figure 12.2   The 'water quality ladder' developed at Appalachian State Univeristy

answers to previous questions). Graphics are used to increase understanding of the environmental amenity in questions, for example a photograph illustrates a fish kill caused by non-point source pollution.

A summary of data collected through 1998 is posted at the site. Mean values of socio-demographic characteristics from an admittedly small sample (*n* = 29) characterize an average respondent that is young (year of birth 1968), wealthy ($46 550 per year), educated (15.83 years of education), male (66 per cent), and involved in environmental issues (25 per cent belonged to an environmental or conservation organization). The mean WTP to improve water quality to a swimmable level is $39.14. At the time of posting this was a test of the survey, and therefore Whitehead is not concerned with the obvious bias that would result by posting summaries of other people's answers.

Brian Griner from University of Pittsburgh presents a conjoint analysis survey at URL: http://www.pitt.edu/~griner/wqsurvey.html. The good being valued is water quality change in the Lower Allegheny watershed. The survey reads:

There are federal, state and private initiatives to improve water quality in Western Pennsylvania. These initiatives will cost the public money, either in increased

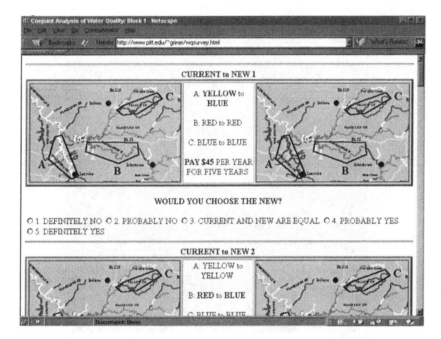

Figure 12.3   A page from the University of Pittsburgh water survey website

taxes, increased prices for goods or in private contributions. On the other hand, reductions in water quality may require some compensation to the public.

The page displays a map of the watershed with river stretch water quality denoted by color: red (severely polluted), yellow (moderately polluted), and blue (unpolluted), as shown in Figure 12.3.

Griner defines the levels of pollution in potential use terms (e.g.: fishable, not drinkable). Three of these river stretches are highlighted and become the focus of the ranking exercise to follow. Respondents are asked to accept or pay money for decrements or increments, respectively, in the river water quality of the highlighted stretches in each of eight scenarios. The survey appears to be in the draft stage, but it represents a straight-forward conjoint application on the internet.

The Global Policy Survey was perhaps the most ambitious internet survey undertaken at its time. Respondents were contacted through a network of academics at institutions worldwide and asked to fill out this survey in one of three languages. The front page is shown in Figure 12.4.

With this truly interactive survey instrument, Cameron takes advantage of the ability to change the format of the web site in real time, depending

Figure 12.4   The Global Policy survey home page

on responses. Cameron plans to address a multitude of research areas including; reasons for dropouts, relation of risk aversion to valuation, difference between perceived and actual time to completion and, of course, WTP to avoid global warming. There was also a draw for a $500 prize at each quarter of the year. The review version of the survey on-line mentions that this may be turned into a control variable by offering different prize amounts to different sample groups. At the time of press, however, the lottery portion of the survey was no longer operational. Cameron provides links to pages that offer opinions and information on global warming. The survey's address is http://climatesurvey.ucla.edu/.

Berrens et al. (2004) use data from two large internet data collection firms (detailed below) in a contingent valuation (CV) study designed to glean public perceptions about adoption of the Kyoto Protocol, and make use of some of the technology unique to the internet mode of surveying. The authors track time spent and additional effort put into the answers in the survey by respondents. By allowing respondents to access a 'vastly enhanced information menu', on the web, the authors claim the information in one of their scenarios may be the 'greatest quantity of information provided in any CV survey to date', and hypothesize there should be a difference in WTP responses. As it turns out though, the authors find that, while those who used the information had statistically significantly higher WTP values, simply having access to this additional information had no effect.

Currently, several researchers are conducting computer-assisted in-person surveys, which might translate to the internet if satisfactory contact methods are discovered. Mathews, Kask, and Rotegard look at some of these studies in their forthcoming 'Computer-assisted nonmarket valuation survey implementation: when do the benefits outweigh the costs?'. A major distinction between computer-assisted surveys and those performed entirely on the internet is the amount of oversight the interviewer has. Once the survey is posted, it has to be user friendly and user proof.

12.2.1   Sampling

The growing interest by academics, marketers, and political officials in using the internet for surveying is evident. Based on the literature, it is also apparent there is general understanding of the need for caution when generating survey samples from a medium that exhibits demographic and regional variations in use. Two relatively new companies taking advantage of the internet's popularity as a survey tool are Harris Interactive (HI) and Knowledge Networks (KN). Their sample selection processes, however, differ significantly. HI contacts web users through advertisements, and offers an incentive of 'HIpoints' – points that can be redeemed for merchandise from a catalogue. Once a user responds to one survey he is asked if he would like to become a member of Harris Poll Online. According to Chang and Krosnick (2003), 90 per cent of Harris Poll Online members come from exite.com or the marketing company Matchlogic. A panel member enters demographic information which becomes the basis on which he might be asked to participate in a given survey, and allows HI to put together a sample that matches a given population (e.g. that of the United States based on census data). Panel members are asked, via email approximately weekly if they are interested in completing a certain survey, and, if they do not log on to complete it, are reminded via email that the survey 'is still open'. Since the sample is drawn directly from internet users, one might hypothesize that the HI sample would over represent those who are more likely to have internet access: wealthy, young, white, urban males.

To avoid sampling issues associated with internet non-use, KN uses a random digit dialing (RDD) telephone contact method to identify potential respondents for their sample pool. KN offers a WebTV to people who participate in a series of surveys. WebTV equipment is sent to respondents who agree to participate and is installed by the participant with the help of a technician on the phone if necessary, and internet access with email is provided. The equipment is taken away if the potential respondent fails to participate in a given number of surveys. The KN sample will, of course, suffer from any bias inherent in RDD sample selection, and KN also excludes portions of the population living where there is no access to WebTV.

Two studies that have tackled the question of sample selection differences between HI, KN, and RDD are Chang and Krosnick (2002) and Berrens et al. (2003). Smith (2001) compares results from a KN and an in-person survey, the 2000 General Social Survey (GSS). The results are ambiguous. Chang and Krosnick (2003) compare large surveys done by HI and KN and an RDD survey conducted by the Ohio State University Center for Survey Research (CSR). These workers find that the unweighted HI poll sample did over represent educated, wealthy, white men relative to the US population and the samples of the CSR and the KN. But response quality, statistical measures of predictability of answers due to things like self-pacing, flexibility of timing, low memory burden were higher in the internet-based HI and KN over the CSR. The comparisons presented here are from the unweighted data. Weighting, the practice of using what researchers know about the population they intend to sample to weight their actual sample accordingly, is not uncommon in survey research and changes the results somewhat.

Berrens et al. (2003) compare two HI surveys with a KN and a RDD survey. These researchers find all modes to over estimate college graduates compared with the Census data and the HI to be the greatest overestimate. They note that the three internet samples under represent Hispanics and Blacks. Surprisingly they note that the incomes reported in the telephone survey are close to the US household mean, and that the internet estimates are 'substantially lower'. Interestingly the samples from the two HI surveys appear quite different. However, the authors conclude that with the appropriate weighting and under certain circumstances the internet will provide 'similar estimates of parameters' of interest to political scientists.

Smith (2001) compares the in-person GSS and the KN and notes general similarities, but some important and systematic differences. He maintains that even the 'most promising' internet survey procedure – one that, like the KN survey, uses a pre-recruited panel from the general population – produces notable differences from non-internet surveys. Smith concludes that

> Until the differences in the error structures of these different forms of surveying are better understood and can be modeled and minimized, results from the different survey modes are likely to be common and notable.

12.3   Technical information

Sampling issues will be paramount until the same population has access to the internet as the population the researcher wishes to sample. Some aspects of internet surveying, however are easier to control such as technical issues surrounding the web page itself and the manner in which data is collected.

It is important to view a web page on different screens with different settings and with different web browsers to ensure that important aspects of the survey are being seen by every potential respondent. Colors, fonts, and spacing will vary from computer screen to computer screen. Of the surveys on line to date, only Cameron mentions to respondents that they should adjust their viewers to a particular arrangement.

To successfully carry out a survey, one can write the instrument in hypertext markup language (HTML) so that it is readable as a web page. There are also many 'what you see is what you get' (WISIWYG) programs commercially available Trellian WebPAGE, VisualVision, Easy Web Editor™, WebEdit to name but a few. These programs allow the user to construct a web page without using HTML code. These programs can be expensive, and not as flexible as writing ones own code.

In the parlance of the internet, a survey instrument is of the document type 'form' (as in fill in form). While much thought must go into some of the aesthetic aspects of the survey and, as noted above, a great deal of information can be gathered by using a rather complex instrument, writing the form itself is not hard. With the help of an HTML resource guide (some are listed in the bibliography) and armed with some common conventions, even a novice can create a professional looking page. Retrieving responses to the form, however, requires a fairly complex file called a Common Gateway Interface (CGI). The CGI program is executed in real-time (unlike a web page which is static), and interfaces external applications with servers like Web Servers or Hypertext Transfer Protocol (HTTP). At most institutions, access to CGI files is restricted to only a handful of computer technicians. Since a CGI program is executable, the use of one is tantamount to opening your personal system to the world. Therefore, answers to your survey will probably be sent to your ISP, using his CGI program (which is properly fire-walled) then e-mailed on to you. With this in mind, you may want to discuss your intentions with your ISP and note beforehand how the CGI program available to you makes responses appear. The three steps above are illustrated in the following example. Figure 12.5 is the HTML script that creates a table like question number 13 in Figure 12.6. This returns submitted information classified as 'q19' in the email sent by the CGI file, as shown in Figure 12.7. Proper naming keeps the data orderly and easily exported into spreadsheets for subsequent manipulation. The specification of questions 5.f and 7.f (in Figure 12.7) denote a specific bid amount being offered in a DC contingent valuation survey.

<P>13) Please indicate the highest level of education you have completed
<font color="#8b0000"><input type="radio" name="q19" value="0">SOME HIGH SCHOOL
<input type="radio" name="q19" value="1">HIGH SCHOOL /GED
<input type="radio" name="q19" value="2">SOMECOLLEGE
<inputtype="radio"name="q19"value="3">COLLEGE   DEGREE
<input   type="radio"   name="q19" value="4">SOME   GRADUATE   SCHOOL
<input   type="radio" name="q19"   value="5">GRADUATE DEGREE
<input type="radio" name="q19" value="-99">DK/NA </p>

Figure 12.5   The HTML script used to create question 13 as shown in
Figure 12.6

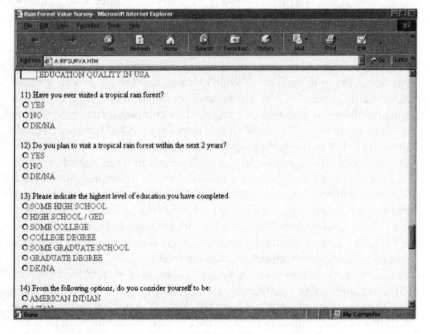

Figure 12.6   How the HTML script in Figure 12.5 *appears on screen*

Once the survey is up and running, the likelihood of it being accessed in a search (perhaps in addition to a contact method) can be increased by 'suggesting' the uniform resource locator (URL) to search engines. This is achieved rapidly and easily by filling out a form located on the given search engines home page.

Two internet-survey-related companies worth mentioning (but no endorsement is necessarily implied) include Sawtooth software and Air

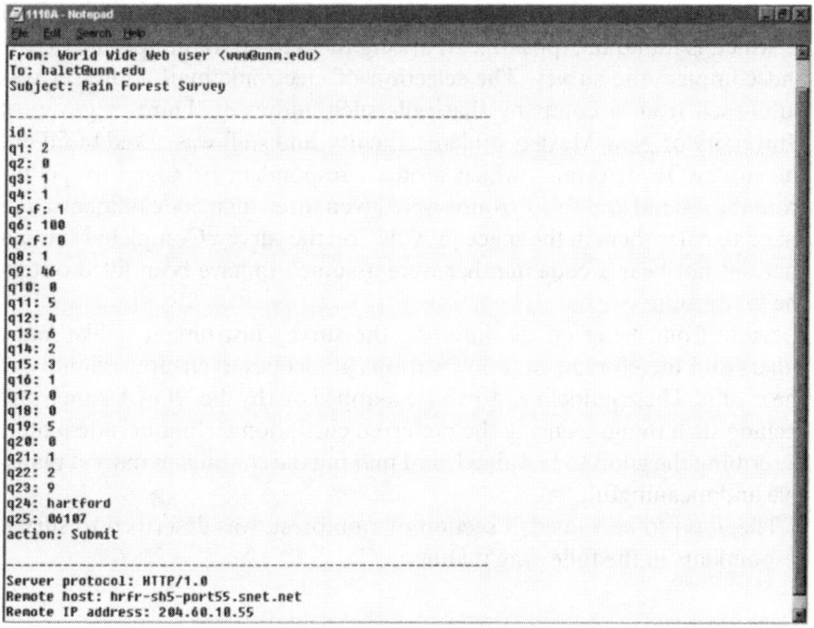

```
1118A - Notepad

From: World Wide Web user <www@unm.edu>
To: halet@unm.edu
Subject: Rain Forest Survey

-------------------------------------------------------
id:
q1: 2
q2: 0
q3: 1
q4: 1
q5.f: 1
q6: 100
q7.f: 0
q8: 1
q9: 46
q10: 0
q11: 5
q12: 4
q13: 6
q14: 2
q15: 3
q16: 1
q17: 0
q18: 0
q19: 5
q20: 0
q21: 1
q22: 2
q23: 9
q24: hartford
q25: 06107
action: Submit

-------------------------------------------------------
Server protocol: HTTP/1.0
Remote host: hrfr-sh5-port55.snet.net
Remote IP address: 204.60.18.55
```

Figure 12.7   Replies to a survey using a CGI program

Resource Specialists. The first, located at sawtoothsoftware.com is a private firm offering useful advice and web-based tools related to conjoint analysis, primarily concerned with marketing issues. Air Resource Specialists, Inc. market a software program called WinHaze that allows one to alter photos to create the effect of varying levels of air pollution. It is available at www.air-resource.com.

The following section outlines the use of the internet survey techniques in a case study.

12.4   Rain forest value survey

The survey entitled 'Rain Forest Valuation Survey' was posted on the internet.[1] It was accessible by going to its URL or by following links from the University of New Mexico Department of Economics Home Page. Three distinct groups of people completed the survey. The first group was people who came across the page as they were 'surfing the net', or searching for keywords that appear in the title of the survey or in the description of the website provided to search engines. The URL of the survey was suggested to and found on such search engines as YAHOO, Alta Vista, Lycos, Netcrawler, and SNAP. The second group of people completing the survey consisted of recipients of an unsolicited electronic mail message, the text of which is found in Appendix A, asking them to go to the specified URL and complete the survey. The selection of electronic mail addresses was purchased from a company that sells such addresses. Third, a group of University of New Mexico students, faculty, and staff was asked to fill out the survey. To determine which group a respondent belonged to, people from the second and third groups were given three-digit code numbers, and asked to enter them in the space provided on the survey. Completed surveys that did not bear a code number were assumed to have been filled out by the first group.[2]

Aside from being on the internet, the survey instrument is like many others and therefore must follow various guidelines to ensure reliability of the results. These guidelines are those mapped out by the NOAA panel, and include such things as using the preferred elicitation technique, adequately describing the good to be valued, and making the contingent market plausible and meaningful.

The good to be valued, a section of rainforest, was described to survey respondents in the following manner:

> Tropical rain forests provide many benefits. Some of these benefits are associated with harvest of timber: harvest benefits include supplying wood for construction, furniture making and paper products. In less developed countries wood from the rain forests is used for cooking and heating. Some of the benefits of the forest can be called non-harvest benefits: standing rain forests provide protection from erosion in areas where there are torrential rains. Rain forests provide habitat for up to 95 per cent of the existing plant and animal species, and approximately 25 per cent of new medicines come from tropical rain forests. The rain forest is also nearly half carbon by weight; as rain forests shrink due to deforestation, atmospheric carbon dioxide will increase; this might make global warming worse.

The choice setting, including the payment vehicle, the administrating body, and the incremental change in the good were included in the following descriptive paragraph:

> In the past, groups such as the International Monetary Fund (IMF) have set up funds in the interest of developing countries. With these funds, the principle is usually left intact, while the interest that accrues each year is used by a developing country to pay for particular development projects.
> The IMF fund would be set up to maintain approximately 10 per cent of the forested area in existence today (that would be about 220 million acres) as virgin rain forest. Currently about 5 per cent of the rain forest in the world is actually set aside into preserves. Private contribution to a fund for the preservation of rain forest would be a one-time affair, and households from all over the United States would be asked if they wanted to contribute.

The first choice question was then posed as follows:

> Would your household contribute a one-time donation of [DC AMT] to a fund such as the one described above that would enable developing countries to set up forest preserves for an additional 5 per cent of the world's rain forest?

DC AMT is a variable bid level ranging from $5 to $300.[3]

In addition to the common WTP question, this survey also included a supplemental PP follow-up question and a choice question aimed at estimating a WTA amount. The DC WTA question, which was intended to determine mean minimum WTA compensation for degradation of the same size section of rainforest, was written:

> It is possible that there are substitutes for some of the non-harvest benefits that we get from the rain forest. Perhaps, if developing countries allow the additional 5 per cent of the forest to be cut down, but charge timber companies a fee for doing so, those countries might be able to use the money from these fees to set up a fund similar to the one discussed above. This fund could be used to find substitutes for some of the benefits we get out of the rain forest.
>
> Suppose that currently there are 20 major logging firms operating in tropical rain forests. If a fund of the same size as the one above is to be set up, each of these firms would have to pay [DC WTA AMT] to be allowed to cut the 5 per cent of the rain forest that would have been protected. Do you think this is the right price to pay to be allowed to cut this additional 5 per cent of the rain forest.

DC WTA AMT was the DC AMT from the WTP question multiplied by the number of households in the United States (approximately 91 million) then divided equally among the hypothetical 20 firms.

The final component of the survey includes questions about socioeconomic and demographic characteristics. Analysis of the sample does not assuage our concerns about biases toward white, young, wealthy males.

12.4.1 *Survey data and discussion*
Completed surveys number 238. Of these, 101 respondents are college students, 107 are unsolicited, and 30 are responses to the solicitation message.[4] The average age of the survey respondent is 24 years old if contacted university students are included, and 29 years without. When the contacted student population is included, the number of male and female respondents is 123 and 107 respectively, and 64 and 67 when students are excluded. Some further sample data are summarized in Table 12.1.

In summary, the sample excluding contacted students is young, fairly wealthy with an average family income range of $30 to $50 thousand dollars (median income for the US is $29 943), is well educated (the average respondent answered that he had some years of college – median education level

Table 12.1   Characteristics of the surveyed sample

Variable	Including contacted students	Excluding contacted students
Income level		
$0–$20 000	32 per cent	23 per cent
$20 001–$30 000	12 per cent	11 per cent
$30 001–$50 000	19 per cent	21 per cent
$50 001–$75 000	16 per cent	18 per cent
$75 001–$100 000	6.6 per cent	8.4 per cent
$100 001–$125 000	4.6 per cent	3.7 per cent
$125 001–$150 000	1.5 per cent	0.93 per cent
$150 001–$200 000	1.5 per cent	2.8 per cent
Over $200 000	7.1 per cent	11 per cent
Race		
American Indian	1.8 per cent	2.4 per cent
Asian	3.1 per cent	3.2 per cent
Black	2.8 per cent	4.8 per cent
Hispanic	14 per cent	4.8 per cent
White non-Hispanic	78 per cent	85 per cent
Education		
Some high school	14 per cent	23 per cent
High school/GED	10 per cent	9.4 per cent
Some college	42 per cent	20 per cent
College degree	13 per cent	16 per cent
Some graduate school	5.3 per cent	6.3 per cent
Graduate degree	15 per cent	26 per cent
Member of environmental organization	14 per cent	21 per cent
Political ideology		
Extremely conservative	2.9 per cent	2.6 per cent
Conservative	23 per cent	18 per cent
Middle of the road	43 per cent	44 per cent
Liberal	26 per cent	27 per cent
Extremely liberal	4.8 per cent	7.8 per cent
Plan on visiting a rainforest	25 per cent	30 per cent
Have visited a rainforest	20 per cent	20 per cent

for the US is 12.4 years of school total)[5] and is slightly liberal. Respondents were also asked to rank six large-scale problems on a scale from 1 (most important) to 6 (least important). These problems were chosen because, except for two, they concern environmental issues. The two not dealing with

*Table 12.2   Mean rankings given to large-scale
problems (standard error of the
mean is given in parentheses)*

Global warming	3.37
	(0.11)
Tropical deforestation	2.94
	(0.09)
Acid rain	4.68
	(0.14)
Air/water pollution	2.66
	(0.10)
War/starvation in Africa	4.05
	(0.11)
Education quality in the USA	3.21
	(0.14)

the environment – war and starvation in Africa and educational quality in
the US – were chosen because of the scope of each problem; the former
being noticeably global from a US point of view and the latter being local.
The mean rankings for each problem are given in Table 12.2.

The low ranking (denoting high importance) of tropical deforestation is
possibly due to 'yea saying', and/or might warn us about a self-selection bias
in the sample. That is, people coming to a URL dealing with tropical deforestation might be more concerned than most about forests. However, despite
having the second lowest rating among the large-scale problems listed,
respondents reported that they were less informed about problems associated with tropical deforestation than one might imagine. On a scale from
1 (not informed) to 4 (extremely well informed) the mean response is 2.05.

For a more rigorous analysis of the data collected in the survey and to
estimate a dollar value for rainforest preservation, econometric analysis
is employed. Two LOGIT regressions, one with WTP as the dependent
variable and one with WTA as the dependent variable, were run using as
independent variables some test characteristics and some personal characteristics. WTP is the dichotomous choice payment question equaling 0 if
the respondent answers NO he is not willing to pay the given BID amount
and taking a value 1 if the answer is YES. The value of the fund if all households in the US contributed the BID mentioned for WTP is divided equally
among 20 hypothetical tropical timber-logging firms and becomes the basis
for the WTA question. This variable takes on a value 1 if the respondent
feels this figure is 'the right price' for each of the firms to pay to be allowed
to clear cut the area, or if the respondent feels it is not the right price, but

signifies with the follow-up question that the price is too high. The variable takes a value of 0 if the respondent feels the price is too low.

For analytical purposes the independent variables took on the following values: SEX takes a value of 0 if the survey respondent answers female and 1 if male. INC takes a value from 1 to 9 as reported income increases in increments from 0–$20 000 to over $200 000 per year. STUDDUM is a student dummy variable that takes the value 1 if the respondent is one of the contacted college students and 0 otherwise. IDEO ranges from 0 to 4 as respondents reported political ideology ranges from 'extremely conservative' to 'extremely liberal'. BID is a discrete variable that takes the value: 5, 25, 40, 50, 75, 100, 150, 175, 200, and 300. INFORM is a variable that takes a value 1, 2, 3, or 4, depending on whether the respondent feels he is: not informed, informed, well informed, or extremely well informed regarding tropical rain forests. GW (global warming), TD (tropical deforestation), and US (education quality in USA) are three of the ranked variables shown in Table 12.2. SHARE takes a value 0 if respondents disagree that industrial countries should share in the costs associated with slowing the rate of deforestation and 1 if the respondent agrees. The variables used in the regressions are summarized in Table 12.3.

Results of the LOGIT regressions are shown in Table 12.4.

Signs on the variables are, for the most part, as one would expect. In particular, the bid is negatively correlated with the probability of answering Yes to the WTP DC question, while SHARE, INFORM, and INC are all positive. Also as expected is the fact that the two environmental problems included in the regression GW and TD vary inversely with the WTP (the higher the respondent's WTP the more important the ecological issues), while the local large-scale problem US is positively related. It is also intuitively pleasing that the signs tend to switch when willingness to accept (WTA) is the dependent variable. From the surveyed sample, using the variation function, we estimate the mean WTP for the specified amount of rainforest preservation to be $240. Using similar methodology, we can estimate the WTA to forgo the same amount of preservation. Mean WTA is approximately $280. Rather high, but not impossible-to-believe representations of people's valuation of the non-market benefits of a section of rainforest.

12.5   Conclusions

The internet is a new powerful tool available to social scientists. Practitioners of the very popular CVM and conjoint analysis will be taking increasing advantage of the internet to reduce time spent collecting data, lower costs, and improve sample size. And with conjoint analysis, where comparative scenarios are so important, the internet provides an optimal tool for displaying pictures or descriptions of different scenarios.

Table 12.3 Definitions of variables used in the regression analysis[1]

Variable	Definition	Mean	Std. dev.
SEX	Gender of the respondent, 0 female, 1 male	0.53	0.5
INC	Value from 1 to 9 as reported income increases in increments from 0–$20,000 to over $200 000 per year	3.2	2.3
STUDDUM	Student dummy, 1 if solicited student, 0 otherwise		
IDEO	Political ideology ranked from 0 extremely conservative to 4 extremely liberal	2	0.89
BID	Take it or leave it referendum dollar amount, 5, 25, 40, 50, 75, 100, 150, 175, 200, 300	93	80
INFORM	Takes the value 1, 2, 3, or 4 depending on whether the respondent feels he is: not informed, informed, well informed, or extremely well informed regarding tropical rain forests	2.1	0.72
GW	Three of the problems ranked by	3.4	1.7
TD	respondents, global warming, tropical	2.9	1.5
US	deforestation, and educational quality in the United States	3.2	2.2
SHARE	Takes a value 0 if respondents disagree that industrial countries should share in the costs associated with slowing the rate of deforestation, and 1 if the respondent agrees	0.89	0.31
HILO	Asks those who answered NO to the WTA question if the figure is too high or too low	0.11	0.098

Note: [1]Mean and standard deviations are for the sample including the contacted student group.

However, the primary obstacle to widespread use of the internet for non-market surveys is the fact that unweighted samples are not representative of most populations normally of interest. Additionally, internet surveys are susceptible to the same instrument biases already recognized in other survey methods, and we cannot rule out the introduction of heretofore-unknown biases unique to the technology as noted above regarding over-solicitation. Parenthetically, specific to bias and conjoint analysis, Couper et al. (2003) warn that, while for some of their survey respondents the inclusion of pictures, easily done in an internet survey, added clarity,

Table 12.4 LOGIT regression results

Independent variable	Dependent variable: WTP	Dependent variable: WTA
SEX	−0.89	−0.21
	(−1.8)*	(−0.48)
INC	0.095	0.12
	0.82	(1.2)*
STUDDUM	0.11	0.88
	(0.20)	(1.6)*
IDEO	−0.46	0.18
	(−1.5)*	(0.65)
BID	−0.0097	0.0042
	(−2.8)**	(1.4)*
INFORM	0.83	0.20
	(2.2)**	(0.64)
GW	−0.37	0.23
	(−2.3)**	(1.7)*
TD	−0.35	0.16
	(−1.7)*	(0.85)
US	0.25	0.064
	(1.6)*	(0.47)
SHARE	1.2	−1.7
	(1.8)*	(−2.4)**
CONSTANT	2.3	−2.6
	(1.3)*	(−1.6)*
R^2	0.26	0.13

Notes:
t-statistics are in parentheses.
* indicates significance at the 80 per cent confidence level.
** indicates significance at the 90 per cent confidence level.

for others they may have 'reinforced a narrow interpretation of the questions meaning'.

The data collected from the Rainforest Value Survey also confirms some fears of using the internet. The sample, albeit fairly small, seems to be comprised of respondents with those characteristics one might associate with people who have access to the internet. An obvious first step toward a solution is to increase sample size, and fortunately this is easily done with an internet survey.

Other suggestions for the improvement of the present survey include: (1) a random assignment of bid level as opposed to a bi-weekly change of the bid. It is possible that some seasonal effects (especially a 'spirit of giving' during the Christmas season) biased the results of this survey.

Without a variance in the bid amount during the suspect period of time, there is no way to test for the bias. (2) Pages of the survey should not scroll, but rather page foreword only after a response is given. This keeps survey respondents from looking to future questions perhaps influencing their present answer. Evidence that this occurred in the Rainforest Value Survey includes several instances in which the respondent chose not to answer the DC question, but did answer a probability follow-up question. (3) The URL of the survey should have been made a hyperlink in the email solicitation message. This probably would have increased responses tremendously. These improvements in survey design are all fairly easily implemented: as CVM practitioners become more familiar with HTML and WYSIWYG programs, more sophisticated web pages and hence better surveys will be posted on the net. But the limiting factor remains the low percentage of households that have access to the World Wide Web.

Notes

1. The URL of the survey was: http://www.unm.edu/~econ/research/rfsurva.htm. A full copy of the text of the survey is included as Appendix B.
2. This is a risky assumption. Quite probably many people from either group 2 or 3 did not enter their password for fear of loss of anonymity.
3. Specifically, bid amounts were changed approximately every two weeks and were: (5, 20, 40, 50, 75, 100, 150, 200, 300). This range was chosen based on previous studies' results, especially Kramer and Mercer (1997).
4. This breakdown is based on the code number given on the survey. It is likely, as noted above, that of the 107 unsolicited responses several represent respondents who were solicited and did not enter a code number.
5. US Bureau of the Census (1992).

References

Berrens, R.P., Alok Bohara, Hank Jenkins Smith, Carol Silva and David Weimer (2003),'The advent of internet surveys for political research: a comparison of telephone and internet samples', *Political Analysis*, **11**(1), 1–22.
Berrens, R.P., Alok Bohara, Hank Jenkins Smith, Carol Silva and David Weimer (2004), 'Information and effort in contingent valuation surveys: application to global climate change using national internet samples', *Journal of Environmental Economics and Management*, **47**, 331–63.
Cameron, T.A. and J. Quiggen (1994), 'Estimation using contingent valuation data from a "dichotomous choice with Follow-up" Questionnaire', *Journal of Environmental Economics and Management*, **27**, 218–34.
Cameron, T.A. and M. James (1987), 'Efficient estimation methods for closed-ended contingent valuation survey data', *Review of Econometrics and Statistics*, **69**, 269–76.
Couper, Mick P. (2001), 'Web surveys: a review of issues and approaches', *Public Opinion Quarterly*, **64**(4), 464–94.
Chang, L. and J.A. Krosnick (2003), 'RDD telephone vs. internet survey methodology for studying American presidential elections: comparing sample representativeness and response quality', Paper presented at the American Political Science Association Annual Meeting, Boston, Massachusetts.
Couper, Mick P., Roger Tourangeau and Kristin Kenyon (2004), 'Picture this! Exploring visual effects in web surveys', *Public Opinion Quarterly*, **68**(Summer), 255–61.

Dillman, Don A. (2000), *Mail and Internet Surveys: The Tailored Design Method*, New York: John Wiley & Sons.

Kramer, Randall A. and D. Evan Mercer (1997), 'Valuing a global environmental good: US residents' willingness to pay to protect tropical rain forests', *Land Economics*, **73**, 196–210.

Mathews, L.G. et al. (2000), 'Computer-assisted nonmarket valuation survey implementation: when do the benefits outweigh the costs?', American Agricultural Economics Association, Tampa, Florida.

Rhode, Gregory L. and Robert Shapiro (2000), 'Falling through the net: toward digital inclusion', US Department of Commerce, Economics and Statistics Administration and National Telecommunications and Information Administration.

Smith, Tom W. (2001), 'Are representative internet surveys possible', Proceedings of Statistics Canada Symposium.

Spooner, T. (2003), 'Internet use by region in the United States: regional variation in internet use mirror differences in educational and income levels', *Pew Internet and American Life Project*, www.pewinternet.org.

Appendix A: survey solicitation message

Dear Sir or Madam:

This message regards academic research, and is not an attempt to sell anything. Your e-mail address was chosen at random.

My name is Hale Thurston, and I am a graduate student in Economics at the University of New Mexico. As part of my Ph.D. dissertation I am asking people from all over the country if they will fill out an important academic survey. The survey is an integral part of research that I am doing regarding the value different people put on the rain forest eco-system. The survey is located at

http://www.unm.edu/~econ/research/rfsurva.htm

it can also be reached via a link from the University of New Mexico, Department of Economics home-page (click on **Research**).

The survey is completely confidential, your name will never be attached to any answers you give, and it only takes about 12–15 minutes to complete.

When you reach the web-page, there is a space for a password/code number, please fill in this space with the number *___*

Your participation in this research is greatly appreciated.

If this message is unwelcome/unwanted I apologize for any inconvenience, and rest assured you will not be contacted again.

Sincerely,

Hale W. Thurston

Appendix B: text of rain forest value survey
Rain Forest Value Survey

Hello, and thank you for taking the time to come to this page. This survey takes about 15 minutes to complete. All answers are strictly confidential, and neither this page nor any of your responses will be used for any commercial purposes.

If you have questions or comments regarding this survey please contact Hale W. Thurston, Department of Economics, 1915 Roma, University of New Mexico 87131. Or contact me electronically at halet@unm.edu

If you were given a code number please enter it here. This code number doesn't identify individuals only groups.

_____

Please read the following questions about the rain forest carefully, answer truthfully, and remember there are no wrong answers. If you feel you cannot answer a question please mark the Don't Know/No Answer (DK/NA) space provided.

(1) On the following scale, please mark how informed you consider yourself regarding tropical rain forests:

EXTREMELY WELL INFORMED
WELL INFORMED
INFORMED
NOT INFORMED
DK/NA

Tropical rain forests provide many benefits. Some of these benefits are associated with harvest of timber, *harvest benefits* include supplying wood for construction, furniture making and paper products. In less developed countries wood from the rain forests is used for cooking and heating.

Some of the benefits of the forest can be called *non-harvest benefits*, standing rain forests provide protection from erosion in areas where there

---

are torrential rains. Rain forests provide habitat for up to 95 per cent of the existing plant and animal species, and approximately 25 per cent of new medicines come from tropical rain forests. The rainforest is also nearly half carbon by weight; as rain forests shrink due to deforestation, atmospheric carbon dioxide will increase, this might make global warming worse.

(2) It has been argued recently that the rate of deforestation in tropical countries is too high. Logging for timber, cutting down trees to allow for agriculture crops and clearing land for people to live, it is said is proceeding too fast. Do you think the rate of deforestation is:

TOO HIGH
JUST RIGHT
TOO LOW
DK/NA

(3) Some people argue that developing countries are forced to over-exploit the rain forest in order to meet short term development responsibilities. It has been suggested that since the rain forest provides (non-harvest) benefits on a global level, that perhaps the world community might help developing countries with money enough to take some pressure off of the rain forest (such as helping to pay some foreign debt). Do you agree that industrialized countries should share in the costs of slowing deforestation?

YES
NO
DK/NA

In the past groups such as the International Monetary Fund (IMF) have set up funds in the interest of developing countries. With these funds, the principle is usually left intact, while the interest that accrues each year is used by a developing country to pay for particular development projects.

(4) It is possible that the IMF could set up such a fund with the specific goal of preserving rain forest in a certain country. Money for the fund would come from private donations and would be taken and used for such projects as re-planting deforested areas or setting up nature preserves where no deforestation takes place. If such a fund were put up for a vote would you vote for or against it?

FOR
AGAINST
DK/NA

Different households may place different dollar values on this project. As you answer the following questions, please keep in mind that any dollars that your household spent on the rain forest could not be spent on other things, such as other environmental programs, charities, groceries or car payments. Also remember, we are not actually asking for money, just your opinion.

> The IMF fund would be set up to maintain approximately 10 per cent of the forested area in existence today (that would be about 220 million acres) as virgin rain forest. Currently about 5 per cent of the rain forest in the world is actually set aside in preserves. Private contribution to a fund for the preservation of rain forest would be a one time affair, and people from all over the United States would be asked if they wanted to contribute.

(5) Would your household contribute a one-time donation of $_____ to a fund such as the one described above that would enable developing countries to set up forest preserves for an additional 5 per cent of the world's rain forest?

YES
NO
DK/NA

(6) Suppose that next week you were contacted by an official from the organization, who requests a donation for the fund. On a scale from 0 to 100, how probable is it that you would actually contribute the $____ to the fund?

_____ per cent

> It is possible that there are substitutes for some of the non-harvest benefits that we get from the rain forest. Perhaps, if developing countries allow the additional 5 per cent of the forest to be cut down, but charge timber companies a fee for doing so, they might be able to use the money from these fees to set up a fund similar to the one discussed above. This fund could be used to find substitutes for some of the benefits we get out of the rain forest.

(7) Suppose that currently there are 20 major logging firms operating in tropical rain forests. If a fund of the same size as the one above is to be set up, each of these firms would have to pay \$_____ to be allowed to cut the 5 per cent of the rain forest that would have been protected. Do you think this is the right price to pay to be allowed to cut this additional 5 per cent of the rain forest?

YES
NO
DK/NA

(8) If your answer to number 7 was NO, do you think the price is too high or too low? (If you answered YES to number 7, please click DK/NA):

TOO HIGH
TOO LOW
DK/NA

To be able to analyse your answers, and to be able to draw conclusions from answers of others like you, please answer the questions below:

(9) What is your age (years)?

_____

(10) What is your gender?

M
F
DK/NA

(11) Please rank the following issues in order of increasing importance to you; with 1 being the most important and 6 being the least important:

_____ GLOBAL WARMING
_____ TROPICAL DEFORESTATION
_____ ACID RAIN
_____ AIR/WATER POLLUTION
_____ WAR/STARVATION IN AFRICA
_____ POOR EDUCATION IN USA

(12) Have you ever visited a tropical rain forest?

YES
NO
DK/NA

(13) Do you plan to visit a tropical rain forest within the next 2 years?

YES
NO
DK/NA

(14) Please indicate the highest level of education you have completed:

SOME HIGH SCHOOL
HIGH SCHOOL / GED
SOME COLLEGE
COLLEGE DEGREE
SOME GRADUATE SCHOOL
GRADUATE DEGREE
DK/NA

(15) From the following options, do you consider yourself to be:

AMERICAN INDIAN
ASIAN
BLACK
HISPANIC
WHITE NON-HISPANIC
DK/NA

(16) Do you belong to any environmental group?

YES
NO
DK/NA

(17) From the following scale, do you consider yourself to be politically:

EXTREMELY CONSERVATIVE
CONSERVATIVE
MIDDLE OF THE ROAD
LIBERAL

EXTREMELY LIBERAL
DK/NA

(18) From the following broad income categories, please choose the one that most closely corresponds to your income last year (1997):

$0–$20 000
$20 001–$30 000
$30 001–$50 000
$50 001–$75 000
$75 001–$100 000
$100 001–$125 000
$125 001–$150 000
$150 001–$200 000
OVER $200 000
DK/NA

(19) Approximately what is the population of the city/town you live in, or live closest to?

_____

(20) Please enter your zip code.

_____

THANK YOU
This concludes the survey. Please click the **SUBMIT** button below at this time.

Submit

Thank you very much. Your time and answers are greatly appreciated. Once again, if you have questions or comments concerning this survey please feel free to contact me, Hale W. Thurston at halet@unm.edu

13 Use of contingent values of wildlife and habitat preservation in policy and benefit–cost analyses

John B. Loomis

13.1 Introduction

A common question asked of contingent valuation practioners is, 'Do real decision makers ever use the results of such studies?' This is a tough question to answer unequivocally, and one asked of methods in many fields ranging urban traffic simulation to epidemiological studies. Given that policy decisions are (and should be) affected by many concerns besides economic efficiency (for example, distributional equity, sustainability), it is rare to be able to point to any one technique in the policy process and say it was the definitive factor. Nonetheless, the increased attention that contingent valuation surveys received after the Exxon Valdez oil spill by industry, their lawyers and mainstream economists suggests that contingent valuation must matter. Why else would Senator Slade Gorton of Washington (a pro-dam advocate) officially request that the US Army Corps of Engineers cancel its contingent valuation survey on the recreation benefits and passive use values of removing dams on the Snake River to restore salmon? However, some utility companies have begun to use contingent behavior surveys when they expect it to promote their agenda. For example, large power companies such as Idaho Power have commissioned valuation surveys to provide some balance to the unconstrained demands of state agencies for greater instream flows.

Contingent valuation can also have a more profound role in changing the nature of the policy debates. Perhaps the best example of this is in the public trust case involving water flows into Mono Lake in California. To provide water for the City of Los Angeles, the Department of Water and Power was diverting several streams that would normally flow into Mono Lake. This diversion was detrimental to fish in those streams as well as it lowered the level of Mono Lake. Because the water was being used for urban uses by people, the Department of Water and Power cast the debate in terms of '300 Fish versus 28 000 People?'. The implication was that providing water for fish in the tributary streams flowing into Mono Lake would deprive people of benefits. Besides being a counterproductive way to view the resource allocation issue, surveys of the California citizenry showed this was a false dichotomy. People cared about the fish and the Mono Lake ecosystem. Using a contingent valuation survey described below, the dollar sacrifice these people would make to provide water for fish and birds could be quantified and compared with the replacement cost of water from other sources including agricultural and municipal water conservation.

The State of California's Water Resources Control Board was sufficiently impressed with the initial household survey measuring the existence values from just knowing Mono Lake would be preserved that they required the contractor preparing the state Environmental Impact Report (EIR) to perform a far more thorough referendum style contingent valuation method (CVM) survey. The economic values from that survey were published in the EIR. These dollars of willingness to pay (WTP) to protect the Mono Lake ecosystem were counted dollar for dollar as equivalent to hydropower and water supply benefits and costs in the economic analysis of the different water allocation alternatives (Jones and Stokes Associates, 1993). In the end, the State ordered the flows into Mono Lake be increased and LA's water rights be reduced by nearly half. While air and water quality concerns were the driving force in this decision, being able to show that such water reallocations were not uneconomic probably aided in making such a dramatic change.

The purpose of this chapter is to present the economic values of wildlife resulting from contingent valuation surveys and describe how these values have been used in natural resource policy analyses (for example, environmental impact statements).

13.2 First CVM applications to recreation benefits

From its birth in 1963 in Robert Davis' dissertation at Harvard to its return in the early 1970's (Brown and Hammack, 1972), CVM was applied to value consumptive wildlife recreation such as hunting. It was soon applied to value other types of recreation as well (Randall et al., 1974). In the arena of valuing recreation, CVM found relatively rapid endorsement as an acceptable technique. In 1979, the US Water Resources Council, which set standardized benefit–cost guidelines for water-related Federal agencies such as the US Army Corps of Engineers and US Bureau of Reclamation, recommended CVM, along with the travel cost method (TCM) as the two preferred techniques for quantifying recreation benefits. With moral support from the US Department of Interior (due Robert Davis' position in the Office of Policy Analysis), joint Department of Interior and US Army Corps of Engineers, training sessions were held throughout the early 1980s to train agency economists in techniques such as TCM and CVM. In 1986, the COE issued a handbook for performing CVM studies as part of its benefit–cost manual series (Moser and Dunning, 1986). In 1986, the Houston District of the COE conducted a CVM survey to estimate the value of urban recreation as part of a flood control planning study (Hansen et al., 1990). A Sacramento District COE study (Mannesto, 1989) applied CVM to value water-based recreation at the Sacramento Delta for its benefit–cost analysis.

The US Fish and Wildlife Service uses CVM as part of its bidecennial National Survey of Fishing, Hunting and Wildlife Associated Recreation. In the 1980, 1985, 1990, and 1996 National Surveys, CVM questions have been asked to value fishing, hunting, and (starting in 1985) non-consumptive wildlife use.

The National Park Service (NPS) has commissioned or participated in several CVM studies. CVM has been used by the NPS for valuing the improvement of air-quality-related visibility at several National Parks (Rowe and Chestnut, 1983). One of the first NPS application of CVM was to the benefits of reducing congestion in the Yosemite National Park (Walsh, 1980). The proposed guidelines of OMB for Federal government benefit–cost analyses allows for the use of CVM to value a wide range of non-market effects from health to environmental amenities.

13.3   Recent application of CVM to measure passive-use values

As originally noted by Krutilla (1967) many individuals who may never go hunting, fishing, or wildlife viewing still receive some benefits from just knowing that unique wildlife exist or that salmon migrations will continue as part of the cycle of life in that region (Olsen et al., 1991). These existence values are a type of pure public good and provide benefits to millions of off-site or indirect users of the wildlife. To estimate these existence values, households would be asked to pay for protection of the species critical habitat in a contingent valuation survey. This is commonly done in the form of a CVM style referendum, where households are asked if they would vote in favor of a particular resource protection action, if it cost their household $X. The amount of $X varies across households, so that a statistical relationship can be traced out that predicts the percentage of households that would pay each amount asked. From this relationship, average willingness to pay is calculated.

Of course a serious concern with using survey respondents' statements of their willingness to pay is its susceptibility to hypothetical bias. Would they really pay the dollar amounts they agree to in the survey? In the case of recreation, from Carson et al.'s summary of dozens of comparisons of CVM derived values with those from the actual behavior-based Travel Cost Method, the answer is yes. In fact, CVM derived estimates of WTP is slightly less than those derived from the Travel Cost Method. Unfortunately when dealing with existence values the empirical evidence is less encouraging. The statements of what people would pay are often two or more times higher than actual cash payments for the same good or resource (Loomis et al., 1996; Champ et al., 1997). However, recent efforts at calibrating stated WTP using respondent certainty shows promise of allowing CVM derived WTP to be adjusted toward valid estimates (Champ et al., 1997). Specifically, Champ et al., determined that accepting only affirmative responses from those respondents that were the most certain, yielded an estimate of WTP that was nearly identical to what a separate sample actually paid in cash. Loomis and Ekstrand (1998) investigated the effect of respondent uncertainty on WTP for protection of critical habitat for the Mexican Spotted Owl. They too found that restricting affirmative responses to just those individuals that conveyed high levels of certainty in their answers, substantially reduced calculated WTP. However, treating uncertain affirmative and negative answers symmetrically actually increased WTP as compared with the standard dichotomous choice analysis. A plot of respondent certainty levels against bid showed that respondents were most uncertain when the dollar amount they were asked to pay was in the $100 to $150 range (close to the mean WTP from the dichotomous choice). Respondents were more certain of their yes responses at low bids and no responses at high bids. Incorporating respondent uncertainty appears a promising avenue for improving the validity of stated WTP amounts.

In many of the studies cited below, the public good nature of the existence values often dwarf the recreation use values and the opportunity costs of protecting water resources. For example, in the original Mono Lake CVM analysis (Loomis, 1987) even the lower-bound estimate of the benefits exceeded the cost by far more than the hypothetical bias possible in CVM (e.g., $1525 million in benefits versus $26.5 million in costs). The large benefits is partly a result of what economists call the public good nature of existence values. Small values per household of $30–150 per year when multiplied by 10 million households in California, result in substantial aggregate estimates of total benefits. Recent empirical analyses suggest that for many natural resources such as protection of salmon in the Pacific Northwest, the benefits extend nationally to nearly 100 million households (Loomis, 1996).

13.4   Policy acceptability of CVM

Besides the State of California's use of CVM and measurement of existence values not only for water resources such as Mono Lake, but also in assessing the damages of oil spills, there are numerous federal agencies that rely upon CVM. As mentioned above, the US Army Corps of Engineers and Bureau of Reclamation use CVM as recommended in the US Water Principles and Guidelines. When Congress passed the Comprehensive

Environmental Response, Compensation and Liability Act of 1980 (CERCLA), the US Department of Interior adopted CVM as a method for valuing the loss in both recreation and existence values from toxic waste sites and hazardous materials spills (US Department of Interior, 1986). The importance of using CVM to measure existence values did not go unnoticed by industry. Nonetheless, when industry challenged the use of CVM, the Court of Appeals upheld CVM and ordered the Department of Interior to broaden its use to measure existence values (what the court called passive use values), even when there was direct, on-site recreation use of the resource (State of Ohio v. US Department of Interior, 1989). Consistent with economic theory, the court interpreted that Congress intended recreation use and existence values as additive.

When Congress passed the Oil Pollution Act of 1990 in the wake of the mammoth Exxon Valdez oil spill, the responsible agency, the National Oceanic and Atmospheric Administration (NOAA) recommended CVM be used to measure both the recreation and passive use values lost due to oil spills. Given the controversy surrounding this, NOAA appointed a 'blue ribbon' panel chaired by two Nobel Laureates to assess the reliability of the CVM for measuring passive use values. In its report in 1993, the Panel concluded that carefully designed and implemented CVM studies could provide estimates of passive use/existence values that would serve as a useful starting point for administrative and judicial decisions (Arrow et al., 1993). The Panel also provided a list of criteria for CVM studies to follow. We now turn to examples of the use of CVM in several benefit–cost analyses.

13.5   Examples of CVM in policy and benefit–cost analyses

13.5.1   Threatened and endangered species
While agencies are precluded from using economic valuation information in decisions regarding listing of species as threatened or endangered (T&E), they are allowed to consider economic factors in determining the extent of critical habitat and in performing Environmental Impact Statements on critical habitat. As shown in Table 13.1, there have been about 17 T&E species that have been valued using CVM. While only some of these were originally for agency policy analyses, often times agencies draw upon these academic studies when performing their economic analysis. For example, in the US Fish and Wildlife Service's Economic Analysis of Critical Habitat designation for the Northern Spotted Owl, the agency relied upon the two northern spotted owl CVM studies shown in Table 13.1 (US Fish and Wildlife Service, 1992).

The results in Table 13.1 illustrate many features of the application of CVM to endangered fish and wildlife. First, comparing studies for the same species often illustrates sensitivity of the WTP estimates to the quantity of

Table 13.1 Summary of CVM derived economic values of rare and T&E species ($1993)

	Low value	High value	Average of studies	References
Studies reporting annual WTP				
Northern Spotted Owl	$44	$95	$70	Rubin et al. (low) Hagen et al. (high)
Mexican Spotted Owl		$40		Loomis and Ekstrand
Pacific Salmon/Steelhead	$31	$88	$60	Oslen et al.
Grizzly Bears			$46	Brookshire et al.
Whooping Cranes	$32	$50	$41	Bowker and Stoll
Red Cockaded Woodpecker	$10	$15	$13	Reaves et al.
Sea Otter			$29	Hageman
Gray Whales	$17	$32	$25	Loomis and Larson
Bald Eagles	$15	$33	$24	Boyle and Bishop (low) Stevens et al. (high)
Bighorn Sheep	$12	$30	$21	King et al. (low) Bookshire et al. (high)
Sea Turtle			$13	Whitehead
Atlantic Salmon	$7	$8	$8	Stevens et al.
Squawfish			$8	Cummings et al.
Striped Shiner		$6		Boyle and Bishop
Studies reporting lump sum WTP				
Bald Eagles	$178	$254	$216	Swanson
Humpback Whale			$173	Samples and Hollyer
Monk Seal			$120	Samples and Hollyer
Gray Wolf	$16	$118	$67	Duffield (low) USFWS (high)
Arctic Grayling			$17	Duffield and Patterson

the single species protected. For example in the Loomis and Larson (1994) gray whale study, the low value is for a 50 percent increase in whale populations as valued by non-visiting households. While not shown in Table 13.1, these households valued a 100 percent increase in the gray whale population at $19, a value that was statistically different from the 50 percent increase at the 0.01 level (Loomis and Larson, 1994: 284). The high value of $32 was for a 100 percent increase in whales valued by gray whale watchers. Viewers value for a 50 percent increase in gray whale populations was $26. This value was also significantly different from the $32 for the

100 percent increase in gray whale populations at the 0.01 level. Thus non-user households that only have existence values legitimately indicate a value lower than visitors who have recreation and option values as well as existence values. This same pattern is evident in the comparison of the relatively low value of bighorn sheep ($12) by Tucson, Arizona households (King et al., 1988) and the high option and existence values of bighorn sheep ($30) of Wyoming hunters (Brookshire et al., 1983). The active on-site user versus off-site passive user dichotomy is also the pattern evident in the salmon and wolf studies. The high salmon value ($88 for option and existence values) is for anglers and the low salmon value ($31 solely for existence values) is for non-fishing households in the Pacific Northwest (Olsen et al., 1991). Reintroduction of wolves into Yellowstone National Park (Duffield et al., 1993) has a high value of $118 for visitors and a low estimate of $16 for regional households (US Fish and Wildlife Service, 1994).

The sensitivity of CVM derived estimates of WTP to the wildlife population levels is by no means a universal finding. Desvousges et al. (1992) found insensitivity to scope for order of magnitude changes in waterfowl populations (although these changes were portrayed to respondents as being 1 percent or about 2 percent). Thus, visual aids are often needed to communicate the relative size of wildlife population changes. This was a finding from pre-testing in the Loomis and Larson (1994) whale study. Thus the authors used scaled bar charts with whale icons to make it transparent to even a mathematically challenged respondent what a 50 percent change in whale population numbers meant. The challenge of designing a scope sensitive survey becomes even more difficult if the analyst is comparing the value of one species to multiple species (which includes the original single species). It is challenging to provide information on multiple species without overloading the respondent with pages of charts and text. A further challenge is that since not all species provide equal utility to respondents, a single symbolic or charismatic species may have a value only slightly less than a bundle of species, if the other species in the bundle are viewed as less desirable (e.g., snakes, spiders, cacti). See Loomis and Ekstrand (1997) for a scope test involving different species.

Using the Bald Eagle studies we can also examine sensitivity of WTP to one-time versus annual payments. The two studies that provide annual WTP to prevent a 100 percent loss of Bald Eagles, have a low value of $15 (Boyle and Bishop, 1987) and a high value of $33 (Stevens et al., 1991). The lump sum WTP for a large increase in Bald Eagle populations yielded $178 with the open-ended WTP question format and $254 with the dichotomous choice WTP question format (Swanson, 1993). While such undesirable sensitivity to question format is common (this is the explanation of the variation in values for the Red Cockaded Woodpecker, Northern Spotted

Owl), the temporal sensitivity is more encouraging. The implied discount rate that would annualize the lump-sum WTP amounts are 6–8 percent for the Boyle and Bishop (1987) study and 13–18.5 percent for the Stevens et al. (1991) study. These are plausible discount rates and ones consistent with consumer use of credit cards.

The US Fish and Wildlife Service also requested a CVM study of the benefits of protecting critical habitat for the Mexican Spotted Owl. Such a study was completed (Loomis and Ekstrand, 1998) and forwarded to the agency for its use. The US Fish and Wildlife Service and National Park Service commissioned and included a CVM study on the economic benefits of the wolf reintroduction program in Yellowstone National Park in the agency's Environmental Impact Statement (Duffield, 1991; US Fish and Wildlife Service, 1994). This was a significant use of CVM in a very high profile and controversial natural resource decision. Duffield performed and the NPS reported in the EIS both contingent visitation estimates and existence values of the general public. This valuation information helped to provide balance to the overemphasis of locals on livestock losses. The NPS has implemented the EIS and has reintroduced wolves into Yellowstone National Park.

13.6 Use of CVM for evaluation hydropower tradeoffs
Perhaps one of the most prominent uses of CVM has been sponsored by the US Bureau of Reclamation in its evaluation of the economic effects of re-regulating the flow releases from Glen Canyon Dam. Due to the dam being upstream from Glen Canyon National Recreation Area (GCNRA) and Grand Canyon National Park (GCNP), peaking power operations at the dam were having a deleterious effect on downstream fishing and rafting. As always, the million dollar question was 'just how much is this recreation worth' as compared with market values of the peaking power. Thus the first studies carried out used CVM to quantify how the value of fishing in GCNRA and rafting in GCNP would change with more even base flows as compared with peaking power. Visitors were surveyed in the mid 1980s. The economic effects were substantial, representing changes of $2 million annually (Bishop et al., 1989). The impact of this analysis was far more than the magnitude of the values, as it helped change the perspective of discussion. Rather than recreation versus hydropower, it was now finding a release pattern that increased the economic value of all the multiple purposes. For a variety of reasons, more even flows were put in place, while the final environmental impact studies took place. Congress formalized these flows when it passed the Grand Canyon Protection Act of 1992.

In fact the impact of the recreation study was sufficient to result in one of the first, major passive-use value studies being funded by a federal agency. As it became clear that more than recreation was at stake in re-regulation of Glen Canyon dam, it also became more obvious that citizens throughout the US cared about how dam operations affected the natural resources of the Grand Canyon. In particular, people were concerned about threatened and endangered (T&E) fish, erosion, native vegetation, and birds, which were all being adversely affected by unnatural flows and lack of high spring flows. The Bureau of Reclamation funded a major passive-use value study of households throughout the US to estimate their WTP for flow regimes that would protect the natural resources in the Grand Canyon. These results showed strong support for a more natural flow regime. While it is difficult to point to any one study as definitively affecting management of Glen Canyon dam, the public support combined with concerns over T&E fish have resulted in substantial changes in the management of the dam. For example, recall the large water releases from Glen Canyon dam during the spring of 1995 to emulate the natural high spring flows.

Contingent valuation has also been used in Federal Energy Regulatory Commissions (FERC) deliberations over the level of minimum instream flow conditions to attach to 50 year operating licenses. One of the strongest indications of the difference that environmental valuation could make was in the FERC case involving whether to permit construction of a dam at Kootenai Falls in Montana. The following quote is from Dr John Duffield, who was the economist that performed the CVM analysis and presented it before the administrative law judge in the court case:

> The judge's decision turned on the aesthetics and recreation values. This is an interesting case in that not only was contingent valuation the primary method, but additionally, a compensation-demanded measure was apparently accepted as plausible. The utility appealed the judge's decision to the full Federal Energy Regulatory Commission, which upheld the rejection of the application. Our understanding is that this is one of only two or three cases where FERC has not approved an application for a major hydroelectric project. (Duffield, 1992: 314)

Idaho Power Company commissioned a CVM study of the economic benefits of alternative flow releases over Shoshone Falls on the Snake River. Their intention is to evaluate whether the gain in recreation benefits from more water passing over the falls is worth the power foregone from not running that water through the turbines. Our preliminary analysis suggests that during the summer months, triple the current minimum 50 cfs is economically efficient (Loomis and Feldman, 1995). This of course illustrates the 'double edge sword' of CVM. While it demonstrates that huge increases in minimum instream flow requests are not justified, it also suggests more than trivial increases in flows are often efficient. Thus neither environmentalists nor the utility may fully support reliance on the CVM results, as it may be viewed alternately as too little or too much.

The importance of FERC relicensing for public natural resources has resulted in a rare coordinated interagency (US Fish and Wildlife Service and US Forest Service) effort to force FERC to explicitly require environmental valuation, including CVM, in its decision making. To facilitate the use of environmental valuation in FERC relicensing, the US Fish and Wildlife Service recently commissioned a comprehensive report, which provides detailed guidance on estimating the economic value of instream flow and other water-related environmental resources (see Industrial Economics Inc. (1999) for details).

13.7   Dam removals for fishery benefits

As more and more anadromous fish species have been added to the Endangered Species list, serious consideration has been given to complete removal of dams blocking salmon migration. Not only do the dams block upstream migration of adult salmon, but the reservoir pools behind the dams substantially slow the migration of juvenile salmon to the ocean. Given the dams contribution to the decline of this symbolic species in the Pacific Northwest, there has been a groundswell of support from newspaper editors in Boise, Idaho to citizens in Washington to remove dams.

The first dams to receive a formal environmental impact analysis for removal are Elwha and Glines dams on the Elwha River on the Olympic Peninsula in Washington. These old, 200 foot dams, have no fish ladders and are in such a narrow canyon that fish ladders would be very costly and likely to be ineffective. Given the age of the dams and the fact they block migration of fish to 70 miles of pristine spawning grounds in Olympic National Park, their removal would more than triple salmon populations on the Elwha River.

However, being biologically effective is not the same as being economically effective. The cost to remove the dams and remove the 50 years of sediment build-up was estimated to cost in the neighborhood of $100–$125 million. The economist coordinating the joint National Park Service, Bureau of Reclamation and Indian Tribe economic analysis recognized that limiting the benefits of dam removal to recreational and commercial fishing benefits would likely be inadequate. The economist asked me to work with him in developing a contingent valuation survey that would estimate the existence and bequest values (benefits the current generation receives from providing salmon to future generations). The survey asked households if they would vote in favor of removing the dams and restoring the river so as to triple salmon populations (illustrated in the survey using a bar chart). The cost each household was asked to pay varied from $3 to $150. Besides surveying households in the State of Washington, households throughout the US were also surveyed.

The CVM survey was successful on a number of fronts. After two mailings, the survey response rate in Washington was quite high at 68 percent, and 55 percent for the rest of the US (a respectable return rate). The internal validity of the results were indicated by the coefficient on the dollar amount households were asked to pay, being negative and statistically significant. This means, that the higher the dollar amount the household was asked to pay, the less likely they would agree to pay. This conforms to the basic economic theory of downward-sloping demand curves. It also indicates that households considered the dollar amount they were asked to pay quite seriously. If the costs were ignored by households, the coefficient on costs would have been insignificant. The mean WTP per household ranged from $73 for Washington households (90 percent confidence interval of $60–$99) to $68 for rest of US households (90 percent confidence interval of $56–$92). Even just considering Washington residents, the $73 per household times the number of households in Washington would nearly cover the cost of removing the dams and restoring the river. Given the 86 million households in the rest of the US, national willingness to pay was in excess of a billion dollars. Thus, even if there is an upward bias to the CVM estimates of willingness to pay, the national benefits are far in excess of the costs.

These results were included in the draft and final Environmental Impact Statement (EIS) prepared by the National Park Service on dam removal (National Park Service, 1996). The recommendation in both the draft and final EIS was to remove both dams and restore the Elwha River. This is consistent with the economic analysis, although many factors contributed to the National Park Service's recommendation. The Clinton Administration included in their budget request to Congress the money to purchase the dams from the private owners, with the intent to request funds for dam removal and restoration in subsequent fiscal years. The federal government now owns the dams, and work is underway to finalize how the dams will be removed.

Two of the most controversial dam removal proposals to date are consideration of removing four dams on the Lower Snake River and removal of Glen Canyon dam. The Lower Snake River dam removal study was requested by the National Marine Fisheries Service as part of its Biological Opinion about recovering several threatened and endangered salmon in this river system. As part of the Environmental Impact Statement on dam removal, the US Army Corps of Engineers used a survey-based contingent behavior–travel cost method hybrid to measure the benefits a restored free-flowing river might provide (Loomis, 2002). This study was to originally include a CVM survey of the existence values of increasing salmon and

Table 13.2   Agency use of CVM

Agency	Recreation	Passive use value	T&E species critical habitat
Bureau of Reclamation	x	x	
Corps of Engineers	x		
Fish and Wildlife Service	x	x	x
National Park Service	x	x	x
National Oceanic and Atmospheric Admin	x	x	
State of California	x	x	
State of Colorado	x		
State of Montana	x		
State of Washington	x	x	

returning the river to a free flowing state. However, while Senator Slade Gorton of Washington was unable to stop the contingent behavior TCM recreation survey, his political pressuring of the COE did eliminate the existence value portion of the survey. The unusual meddling and pressure brought to bear on the COE to eliminate the CVM survey to estimate existence values indicates that opponents of dam removal clearly saw a large potential influence of the non-market valuation results on the final decision. Nonetheless, in place of the original survey, a benefit transfer of existing CVM and contingent ranking passive use value studies was used and results reported in the Final Environmental Impact Statement in 2002 (Corps of Engineers, 2002).

Table 13.2 summarizes federal and state agency use of CVM for three common resource issues: recreation, passive use values, and T&E species critical habitat decisions. As detailed in this chapter, there are at least five federal agencies and the State of California that have relied upon CVM-derived values or directly employed CVM surveys. The State of Colorado has relied upon CVM for estimating damages in natural resource damage assessment cases associated with old mine sites (see Ward and Duffield, 1992). The State of Montana has relied upon CVM in the valuation of hunting and fishing in Montana. The State of Washington recently commissioned a survey on the passive use values of salmon using a CVM-like technique called conjoint analysis.

Conclusion

Does contingent valuation matter? I believe a reasonable case can be made that contingent valuation results do matter in natural resources decision making. The nature of the contribution is often case specific. In some cases reviewed, the contingent valuation changed the character of the debate from being a 'people v. the environment' to one of recognizing that people care about the environment in the same way they care about cheap water or electricity. In other cases, contingent valuation helped defuse the often heard mantra that 'while we would like to protect the environment, we simply can't afford it. Protecting the environment is just too costly.' What the contingent valuation studies often show is that protecting the environment or endangered species often provides more benefits than the value of commodities foregone. Finally, in the Elwha example, contingent valuation was used to estimate the benefits to society as a whole from salmon restoration. Viewing salmon restoration narrowly, as increased commercial fishing revenues or even sport fishing benefits, would reflect just a fraction of the public benefits from increasing salmon populations.

What is the value of contingent valuation? The value lies in providing a more complete accounting of all of the benefits and costs to all of the people, not just visitors or users of the resource. Contingent valuation studies of the general public can make possible a 'dollar democracy' in which every citizen's voice is heard through their benefits and costs, regardless of how small they are per person. Valuation studies have the potential to provide an effective way to diminish the often bemoaned role of 'special interests' in the current policy process. For this reason alone, contingent valuation studies might be worth their weight in gold.

References

Arrow, Kenneth, Robert Solow, Paul Portney, Edward Leamer, Roy Radner and Howard Schuman (1993), 'Report of the NOAA Panel on contingent valuation', *Federal Register*, **58**(10), 4602–14.

Bishop, R., C. Brown, M. Welsh and K. Boyle (1989), 'Grand Canyon and Glen Canyon Dam Operations: an economic evaluation. in W-133 benefits and costs in natural resources planning', Interim Report No. 2, K. Boyle and T. Heekin (eds), Dept of Agricultural and Resource Economics, University of Maine, Orono.

Bowker, J.M. and John R. Stoll (1988), 'Use of dichotomous choice nonmarket methods to value the Whooping Crane resource', *American Journal Agricultural Economics*, **70**(2), 372–81.

Boyle, K. and R. Bishop (1987), 'Valuing wildlife in benefit–cost analysis: a case study involving endangered species', *Water Resources Research*, **23**(5), 943–50.

Brookshire, David S., Larry S. Eubanks and Alan Randall (1983), 'Estimating option prices and existence values for wildlife resources', *Land Economics*, **59**(1), 1–15.

Brown, Gardner and Judd Hammack (1972), 'A preliminary investigation of migratory waterfowl', in J. Krutilla (ed.), *Natural Environments: Studies in Theoretical and Applied Analysis*, Washington, DC: Resources for the Future.

Carson, R., N. Flores, K. Martin and J. Wright (1996), 'Contingent valuation and revealed preference methodologies', *Land Economics*, **72**(1), 80–99.

Champ, P., R. Bishop, T. Brown and D. McCollum (1997), 'Using donation mechanisms to value nonuse benefits from public goods', *Journal of Environmental Economics and Management*, **33**(3), 151–62.

Corps of Engineers (2002), 'Final Lower Snake River juvenile salmon migration feasibility report and environmental impact statement on the Lower Snake River', Walla Walla District, Walla Walla, WA.

Cummings, R.G., P.T. Ganderton and T. McGuckin (1994), 'Substitution effects in CVM values', *American Journal of Agricultural Economics*, **76**(2), 205–14.

Desvousges, W., R. Johnson, R. Dunford, K. Boyle, S. Hudson and K. Wilson (1992), 'Measuring nonuse damages using contingent valuation', Research Triangle Institute, North Carolina.

Duffield, John (1991), 'Existence and nonconsumptive values for wildlife: application to wolf recovery in Yellowstone National Park', in Cathy Kling, compiler, 'Benefits and costs in natural resources planning', Fourth Interim Report, Department of Agricultural Economics, University of California, Davis, CA.

Duffield, John (1992), 'Contingent valuation: issues and applications', in K. Ward and J. Duffield, *Natural Resource Damages: Law and Economics*, New York: John Wiley & Sons.

Duffield, John (1992), 'An economic analysis of wolf recovery in Yellowstone: Park visitor attitudes and values in wolves for Yellowstone?', J. Varley and W. Brewster (eds), National Park Service, Yellowstone National Park.

Duffield, John and David A. Patterson (1992), 'Field testing existence values: comparison of hypothetical and cash transaction values', Benefits and Costs in Natural Resource Planning, Fifth Interim Report. W-133 Western Regional Research Publication.

Hageman, Rhonda (1985), 'Valuing marine mammal populations: benefit valuations in a multi-species ecosystem', Administrative Report LJ-85-22, Southwest Fisheries Center, National Marine Fisheries Service, P.O. Box 271, La Jolla, CA 90238.

Hagen, Daniel, James Vincent and Patrick Welle (1992), 'Benefits of preserving old-growth forests and the Spotted Owl', *Contemporary Policy Issues*, **10** (April), 13–25.

Hansen, William, Alan Mills, John Stoll, Roger Freeman and Carol Hankamer (1990), 'A case study application of the contingent valution method for estimating urban recreation use and benefits', IWR Report No. 90-R-11, Institute for Water Resources, US Army Corps of Engineers, Fort Belvoir, VA.

Industrial Economics Inc. (1999), 'Economic analysis for hydropower project relicensing: guidance and methods', Report prepared for US Fish and Wildlife Service, Washington, DC.

Jones and Stokes Associates (1993), 'Draft environmental impact report for the review of the Mono Basin Water Rights of the City of Los Angeles', Prepared for California State Water Resources Control Board, Division of Water Rights, Sacramento, CA.

King, David A., Deborah J. Flynn and William W. Shaw (1988), 'Total and existence values of a herd of desert bighorn sheep', Benefits and Costs in Natural Resource Planning, Interim Report, Western Regional Research Publication W-133.

Krutilla, John (1967), 'Conservation reconsidered', *American Economic Review*, **57**, 787–96.

Loomis, J. (1987), 'Balancing public trust resources of Mono Lake and Los Angeles' water right: an economic approach', *Water Resources Research*, **23**(8), 1449–56.

Loomis, J. (1996), 'Measuring the benefits of removing dams and restoring the Elwha River: results of a contingent valuation survey', *Water Resources Research*, **32**(2), 441–7.

Loomis, J. (2002), 'Quantifying recreation use values from removing dams and restoring free-flowing rivers: a contingent behavior travel cost model for the Lower Snake River', *Water Resources Research*, **38**(6), 1029–36.

Loomis, J. and E. Ekstrand (1997), 'Economic benefits of critical habitat for the Mexican Spotted Owl: A scope test using a multiple-bounded contingent valuation survey', *Journal of Agricultural and Resource Economics*, **22**(2), 356–66.

Loomis, J. and E. Ekstrand (1998), 'Alternative approaches for incorporating respondent uncertainty when estimating willingness to pay: the case of the Mexican Spotted Owl', *Ecological Economics*, **27**(1), 29–41.

Loomis, J. and M. Feldman (1995), 'An economic approach to giving "equal consideration" to environmental values in FERC hydropower relicensing', *Rivers*, **5**(2), 96–108.

Loomis, J. and Douglas Larson (1994), 'Total economic values of increasing Gray Whale populations: results from a contingent valuation survey of visitors and households', *Marine Resource Economics*, (9), 275–86.

Loomis, J., T. Brown, B. Lucero and G. Peterson (1996), 'Improving validity experiments of contingent valuation methods: efforts to reduce the disparity of hypothetical and actual willingness to pay', *Land Economics*, **72**(4), 450–61.

Mannesto, Greg (1989), 'Comparative evaluation of respondent behavior in mail and in-person contingent valuation method surveys', Ph.D. dissertation, Graduate Group in Ecology, University of California, Davis.

Moser, David and Mark Dunning (1986), 'A guide for using the contingent valuation methodology in recreation studies', National Economic Development Procedures Manual – Recreation Vol 2, IWR Report 86-R-5. Institute for Water Resources, US Army Corps of Engineers, Fort Belvoir, VA.

National Park Service (1996), 'Elwha River ecosystem restoration implementation', Final Environmental Impact Statement, Denver Service Center, Denver, CO.

Olsen, D., J. Richards and D. Scott (1991), 'Existence and sport values for double the size of Columbia River Basin salmon and steelhead runs', *Rivers*, **2**(1), 44–56.

Randall, A., B. Ives and C. Eastman (1974), 'Bidding games for valuation of aesthetic environmental improvements', *Journal of Environmental Economics and Management*, **1**, 132–49.

Reaves, D.W., R.A. Kramer and T.P. Holmes (1994), 'Valuing the endangered red-cockaded woodpecker and its habitat: a comparison of contingent valuation elicitation techniques and a test for embedding', AAEA meetings paper.

Rowe, R. and L. Chestnut (1983), *Managing Air Quality and Scenic Resources at National Parks and Wilderness Areas*, Boulder, CO: Westview Press.

Rubin, J., G. Helfand and J. Loomis (1991), 'A benefit–cost analysis of the Northern Spotted Owl', *Journal of Forestry*, **89**(12), 25–30.

Samples, K.C. and J.R. Hollyer (1989), 'Contingent valuation of wildlife resources in the presence of substitutes and complement', in R.L. Johnson and G.V. Johnson (eds), *Economic Valuation of Natural Resources: Issues, Theory and Application*, Boulder, CO: Westview Press.

State of Ohio v. US Department of Interior (1989), US District Court of Appeals (for the District of Columbia), Case number 86-15755, 14 July 1989.

Stevens, T., J. Echeverria, R. Glass, T. Hager and T. More (1991), 'Measuring the existence value of wildlife: what do CVM estimates really show?', *Land Economics*, **67**(4), 390–400.

Swanson, C. (1993), 'Economics of non-game management: bald eagles on the Skagit River Bald Eagle Natural Area', Washington. Ph.D. Dissertation, Department of Agricultural Economics, Ohio State University.

US Fish and Wildlife Service (1992), 'Economic analysis of critical habitat designation effects for the Northern Spotted Owl', Washington, DC.

US Fish and Wildlife Service (1994), 'The reintroduction of Gray Wolves to Yellowstone National Park and Central Idaho', Final Environmental Impact Statement. Helena, MT.

US Department of Interior (1986), 'Natural resource damage assessments: final rule', *Federal Register*, **51**(4), 27674–753.

US National and Oceanic and Atmospheric Administration (1996), 'Oil pollution act damage assessments: final rule', *Federal Register*, **61**(4), 439–510.

US Water Resources Council (1979), 'Procedures for evaluation of national economic development (NED) benefits and costs in water resources planning: final rule', *Federal Register*, **44**(242), 72892–976.

US Water Resources Council (1983), 'Economic and environmental principles and guidelines for water and related land resources implementation studies', US Government Printing Office, Washington, DC.

Walsh, R. (1980), 'An economic evaluation of the general management plan for Yosemite National Park', Water Resources Research Institute, Colorado State University, Fort Collins, CO.

Ward, K. and J. Duffield (1992), *Natural Resource Damages: Law and Economics*, New York: John Wiley & Sons.

14 Valuing wildlife at risk from exotic invaders in Yellowstone Lake

Todd L. Cherry, Jason F. Shogren,
Peter Frykblom and John A. List

14.1 Introduction

In 1994, an angler caught a lake trout (Salvelinus namaycush) in Yellowstone Lake, Yellowstone National Park, Wyoming. Judging by the size of the trout, and from subsequent data provided by the US Fish and Wildlife Service, biologists now believe that someone must have illegally planted lake trout in the lake some five years earlier. They blame humans for the introduction because natural movement of this non-native species into Yellowstone Lake is improbable. Based on catch and mortality rates, biologists now estimate that thousands, maybe tens of thousands, of lake trout of several age classes, some capable of spawning, live in Yellowstone Lake (Kaeding et al., 1995). Yellowstone Lake is a prime spot for lake trout to flourish, because they thrive in the cold, deep water. But the problem is that Yellowstone Lake is the last premier inland cutthroat trout fishery in North America. And after years of working to restore the native Yellowstone cutthroat trout (oncorhynchus clarki bouvieri) population back to viable levels, lake trout are putting the last cutthroat stronghold at risk. Experts have concluded that the lake trout population is likely to expand and cause a serious decline in the cutthroat population. If left unchecked, some biologists have predicted that these voracious exotic species could reduce the catchable-size cutthroat population to 250 000–500 000 from 2.5 million within the near future (Kaeding et al., 1995).

Lake trout eat cutthroat, but they do not replace them in the food chain. And, as if putting native cutthroats at risk is not bad enough, lake trout also put another popular species at risk – the grizzly bear (Ursus arctos), currently listed under the US Endangered Species Act as endangered since 1975 (see Anderson, 1998). Grizzly bears feed on cutthroat in over half of the 124 tributary streams when the trout spawn. For example, researchers observed an adult female grizzly harvest an average of 100 fish per day for ten days (Schullery and Varley, 1995). Lake trout do not replace cutthroat in the food chain because they spawn in the cobble and rubble in the lake, far from any predators' reach. Approximately 40 other birds and mammals also depend on cutthroat trout for food – including the bald eagle (Haleaeetus leucocephalus) and the osprey (Pandion haliatus).

The reduction in risks to wildlife is a priority in Yellowstone National Park (see Figure 14.1) given that wildlife viewing has been estimated to be the 'single most important activity' for over 90 per cent of park visitors (Varley and Schullery, 1995). Park officials have attempted to protect cutthroat by netting lake trout. Netters have removed half the lake trout from Yellowstone Lake, catching the trout that reach known spawning grounds in the West Thumb region of the Lake. Netting has kept the foreign species from spawning in any large numbers in the lake. The analysis suggests that, while the netting program of the park has cut into the lake trout population, netting may have to continue indefinitely, and at great expense. The reduction in the catch of lake trout is good, but it could lead to future questions about the value of continuing the netting program (Casper Star-Tribune, 1999).

The risk to Yellowstone cutthroat and grizzly bears is one example of a growing issue in species protection – species put at risk from exotic invaders. Organisms that move beyond their traditional natural range can have undesirable ecological and economic consequences. Scientists have documented numerous examples of exotic plant and animals causing unacceptable damages, both monetary and non-monetary. Exotic deer and livestock, for instance, have altered the structure and composition of native vegetation in the Nahuel Huapi National Park in Argentina (Veblen et al., 1992). Nile perch released into Africa's Lake Victoria have caused mass extinction of native fish, and induced water quality problems. Field bindweed is estimated to cause over $40 million in crop damages in Kansas every year (FICMNEW, 1998). Zebra mussels in the Great Lakes have led to serious biotic and abiotic effects, e.g. greatly diminished phytoplantkton biomass and biofouling of man-made structures (MacIsaac, 1996).

Understanding the economic value of reducing these risks to wildlife remains a key part of any wildlife management strategy. This chapter explores how economists have and continue to use the contingent valuation method (CVM) to measure the value of reduced risks to endangered species. Endangered species, such as the grizzly bear in Yellowstone, provide many services to society – ranging from aesthetic value to basic life support to new genetic material for pharmaceutical purposes. These species provide a broad set of valuable services, many of which remain unpriced by the market. Because these public services are rarely bought and sold on the auction block, they never enter into private markets and remain unpriced by the public sector. Because wildlife does not stay within the confines of either public or private property, many people enjoy the benefits or suffer the costs without compensation paid or received.

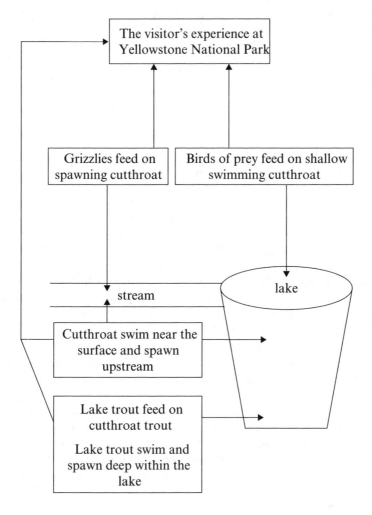

Figure 14.1   Diagram of species at risk in Yellowstone Lake

Some people find the gains from endangered species protection so obvious that benefits need not be measured. The essential ecological services are so valuable that the benefits of species preservation will always exceed the benefits of development (see, for example, Roughgarden, 1995). To others, however, the benefits of species protection do not obviously outweigh the benefits of development. Epstein (1995: 278) illustrates this view stating:

Some people believe that it is important to develop nature to the full, to overcome poverty and to ensure prosperity; others believe that nature should be left
in its original condition to the extent that is possible, even if it means a cutback
in overall standards of living. It is not within the power of either side to convert
the doubters to the opposite position, and coercive systems of regulation are the
worst possible way to achieve uniform social outcomes in the face of social
disagreement. The interconnectedness of what goes on in one place and what
goes on in another cannot be presumed on some dubious theory of necessary
physical linkages for all events.

These people desire a pecuniary estimate of the potential benefits of endangered species protection. Valuing endangered species is a challenge, however,
given the problems of assigning economic value to goods that most people
never directly use, and the method – contingent valuation – used to estimate
these values. Most economists now acknowledge that people might have
preferences about protecting species and related services they will rarely ever,
if at all, see or use (Krutilla, 1967). The main point of contention relates to
linking a monetary value to these preferences. The primary tool for estimating use and non-use values is contingent valuation, which is essentially a
public opinion survey that uses a sequence of questions to obtain a monetary
value from stated preferences. The method is highly contentious, because a
number of potential biases have been identified, the importance of which is
the subject of conceptual and empirical debate.

Despite the analytical difficulties associated with measuring the social
value that should be placed on preserving each species, determining at least
a plausible range for these values is essential if we are to make judgments
about the benefits of preservation. The remainder of this chapter proceeds
as follows. Section 14.2 follows the thread of earlier CVM efforts to value
the protection of endangered species. Section 14.3 describes our case study,
survey methods, empirical techniques, and empirical results. Section 14.4
concludes and discusses some important caveats to the general CVM literature for endangered species.

14.2   Previous work

We now briefly focus on one critical thread in species valuation, whether it
is more appropriate to value species in isolation or as part of a system that
includes their habitat. This discussion is placed in context by examining
a select group of CVM surveys concerning endangered species. We highlight methods used in these analyses to place our empirical estimates into
perspective, and to provide the reader with references on the current state of
the art. A common thread through many CVM studies is that they tend to
focus only on one species, usually a charismatic megavertebrate. In doing so,
these studies do not address important ecological complementarities, since

higher profile species may depend on the existence of other lower profile species, which may be an important link in biodiversity. Additionally, megavertebrate may be keystone species, which means their elimination could cause general system change. Nevertheless, we note that an implicit value of other components of the ecosystem, such as plants and lower profile animals, could be retrieved when valuing one species near the top of the food chain (see Crocker and Tschirhart, 1992). The interested reader should also consult the survey of CVM species studies in Loomis and White (1996).

The estimation of anthropocentric values of endangered and threatened species has typically been carried out using a willingness to pay (WTP) approach. Although one could argue that the public owns the species and should be justly compensated for its extinction, the adopted measure of choice has been WTP (Just et al., 1982). Using a WTP measure of value within a CVM survey, researchers have estimated a range of WTP for individual species as low as $6 for a striped shiner and as high as $95 for the northern spotted owl (Loomis and White, 1996).

Within this large range of values lies some interesting CVM studies that vary by geography and method. For example, when Langford et al. (1998) examined a single species (Mediterranean monk seal (Monachus-monachus)), they used a multivariate binomial-log normal mixture model to develop a bid function whose level was determined by socio-demographic variables such as income, gender, age, and education. Amongst other findings, Langford et al. (1998) show that Greek households place a non-trivial dollar value on preserving the monk seals. Although the Langford et al. (1998) study uses an interesting empirical method to derive values, it is similar in nature to the majority of other CVM surveys in that it relies on the anthropocentric valuation model which elicits one species' value, rather than examining the linkages of certain species and examining the entire habitat.

In contrast, Carson et al. (1994) and Walsh et al. (1985) use a more integrated valuation approach by examining multiple species. Carson et al. (1994) estimate the value for speeding up recovery of four species in California (bald eagle, peregrin falcon, kelp bass, white croaker), and find from a dichotomous choice survey that the mean individual is willing to pay around $63 in a one-time lump sum tax to expedite the recovery process. Walsh et al. (1985) examined 26 species in Colorado using an open-ended CVM survey and found that Colorado residents were willing to pay $58 as a one-time lump sum tax to protect the 26 species.

Along similar lines, Jakobsson and Dragun (1996) conducted a mail survey to residents of Victoria in Australia concerning their WTP to avoid either a decline in a number of endangered species (flora and fauna) or the loss of Leadbeater's possum. The aggregate mean estimates for protection of flora and fauna in dollars (per year) are as follows:

Aggregate estimate based on the minimum WTP per household: $160 million ($118 per household).
Aggregate estimate based on the maximum WTP per household: $386 million ($284 per household).
Aggregate estimate based on minimum WTP per individual: 40 million ($118 per individual).
Aggregate estimate based on maximum WTP per individual: $821 million ($284 per individual).

The aggregate mean estimates for protection of Leadbeater's possum in dollars (per year) are as follows:

Household minimum $39.7 million ($29.2 per household).
Household maximum $103 million ($75.6 per household).
Individual minimum $84.4 million ($29.19 per individual).
Individual maximum $218 million ($75.6 per individual).

The results show that the value expressed for the conservation of the Leadbeater's possum is less than those values for the conservation of endangered flora and fauna in general, suggesting that respondent's value one individual endangered species significantly less than a collection of endangered species, which is consistent with intuition.

These three studies have advantages over previous CVM efforts in that they consider the valuation of multiple species, rather than a species in isolation. The approach of Watts-Reaves et al. (2000) is another advance in this direction, as they value both species and the habitat that supports them. They use a three-way treatment design to value the red-cockaded woodpecker and the restoration of its habitat following a natural disaster, which could be viewed as a much more holistic approach than previous efforts. Valuing both the species and its habitat allows Watts-Reaves et al. (2000) to measure benefits for more than one individual species, and also provides an indication of the merit of estimating benefits within a habitat-based evaluation. Overall, Watts-Reaves et al. (2000) find that across each treatment all mean WTP values to preserve the woodpecker and restore its habitat are statistically different from zero and that the value distributions are centered around $10.

Overall, the reported estimates above, and in other reviews, suggest people say they will pay a non-trivial dollar value to preserve and protect endangered species, whether individually or in aggregate. More importantly, the literature is moving toward a more thorough recognition of the complementarity and substitution effects across species and habitat that can critically matter when valuing a species. In our view, this trend will continue, and in what follows we carry out a CVM study that links endangered species by examining preservation values for an ecosystem put at risk from exotic invaders.

14.3   Wildlife at risk in Yellowstone Lake: the survey and findings

We now return to the case of the exotic invader in Yellowstone Lake. Surveys were distributed in person to visitors of Yellowstone and Teton National Parks in Jackson Hole, Wyoming.[1] Respondents had approximately 40 days to return the surveys.[2] We chose the intercept approach because we are interested in visitor attitudes on the lake trout problem.

The survey had four sections: background, perception, valuation, and demographic. The background section contained the following passage to inform the respondent, with a short and thorough explanation, of the cause and potential effects of Lake trout being present in Yellowstone Lake:

> Lake trout were found in Yellowstone Lake in July of 1994. Lake trout are a non-native fish species to Yellowstone Lake and are predators of the lake's native and popular fish species – Cutthroat trout. Cutthroat are not only a popular species for fishermen, but are also a main food source for natural predators such as Osprey, White Pelicans and Grizzly Bears. Unlike Cutthroat, Lake trout swim too deep for birds to prey on them and do not spawn upstream where bears can feed on them. Lake trout, in essence, consume Cutthroat without replacing them in the food chain.
>
> Potential impacts from the presence of Lake trout in Yellowstone Lake are great. Left unchecked, Lake trout will flourish and greatly diminish or eliminate the native Cutthroat trout population. The impacts on the ecosystem will not end with the reduced numbers of Cutthroat. Ospreys, White Pelicans and Grizzly Bears will see an important food source diminish, and as a result, the numbers of these species will be diminished.
>
> While fishermen will feel the impact of reduced numbers of Cutthroat trout, all visitors will experience reduced chances of seeing certain birds of prey and Grizzly Bears. So the presence of Lake trout may not only have a great impact on the Yellowstone Lake ecosystem but also the experience of visitors to this area. This survey will contribute to determining the best course of action for managing this problem. Your participation is crucial for this research effort to succeed.

The perception section elicited the views of the respondent concerning the potential impacts of the exotic species in Yellowstone Lake, including how the possible changes would influence their decision to visit the park. Table 14.1 presents the perceptions and attitudes of respondents. With half of respondents (50.4 per cent) indicating no familiarity with the lake trout

Table 14.1   Visitor perceptions of the lake trout issue

Question/answer	Percent of sample
How familiar were you with this problem?	
Well Informed	14.8
Moderately Informed	22.4
Barely Informed	12.4
Not Informed at All	50.4
How serious do you consider this problem?	
Very Serious	48.0
Moderately Serious	30.0
Barely Serious	11.6
Not a Problem at All	3.6
No Opinion	8.0
Do you expect to visit YNP to view wildlife in the future?	
Definitely Will	45.7
Probably Will	33.9
I Don't Know	15.0
Probably Will Not	4.7
Definitely Will Not	0.8
Do you expect to visit YNP to fish in the future?	
Definitely Will	12.3
Probably Will	15.5
I Don't Know	13.1
Probably Will Not	30.6
Definitely Will Not	28.6
Would a decreased chance of catching cutthroat trout affect your decision to visit YNP?	
Yes	12.7
No	87.3
Would a decreased chance of viewing birds of prey affect your decision to visit YNP?	
Yes	39.5
No	60.5
Would a decreased chance of viewing grizzly bears affect your decision to visit YNP?	
Yes	54.3
No	45.7
Would a decreased chance of catching lake trout affect your decision to visit YNP?	
Yes	3.6
No	96.4

problem, the clarity and accuracy of the description of the issue becomes vital. Subsequent responses, in addition to general feedback, indicate participants understood the explanation of the problem. Nearly 80 per cent of our respondents agreed that the lake trout problem was either very serious (48 per cent) or moderately serious (30 per cent), and responses were broadly consistent regarding the expected benefits and costs of visiting Yellowstone.

As Table 14.1 reports, respondents generally indicated that future visits would revolve around viewing wildlife rather than fishing within the park. This non-fishing slant corresponds to the lack of influence that decreased numbers of cutthroat trout would have on future decisions to visit the park. Conversely, responders indicate that the subsequent effects of the reduced cutthroat populations on the abundance of wildlife would influence future visitation decisions. As a final consistency check, responders indicated that decreased lake trout numbers would have no significant impact on future decisions to visit the park. As such, even though responders were generally unfamiliar with the lake trout issue, their perceptions and preferences regarding the problem were internally consistent for each question.

In the Valuation section, we use a two-step process following Kriström's (1997) spike model. The spike model allows for a non-zero probability of zero willingness to pay. First, the respondent is asked to accept or reject the scenario of paying a sum of money A. The scenario is represented as the change $z^0 \rightarrow z^1$, where z^0 denotes a scenario with less biodiversity, while z^1 denotes a scenario with a sustained biodiversity. The willingness to pay (WTP) to sustain current biodiversity is defined as:

$$v(y - WTP, z^1) = v(y, z^0),$$

where $v(y, z)$ is the respondent's indirect utility function and y is income. The probability that an amount A is at least as high as the respondent's WTP is:

$$\Pr(WTP \leq A) = F_{wtp}(A),$$

where $F_{wtp}(A)$ is a continuous non-decreasing function. The functional form of WTP is assumed to be:

$$F_{wtp}(A) = \begin{cases} 0 & \text{if } A < 0 \\ p & \text{if } A = 0 \\ G_{wtp}(A) & \text{if } A > 0, \end{cases}$$

where $p \in (0,1)$ and G_{wtp} is a continuous and increasing function such that $G_{wtp}(0) = p$ and $\lim_{A \to \infty} G_{wtp}(A) = 1$.

Second, the respondent was asked whether she was willing to pay anything at all to ensure the baseline level of preservation, that is:

$$S_i = 1 \text{ if } WTP > 0 \text{ (0 otherwise).}$$

T_i indicates whether the respondent was willing to pay the suggested price:

$$T_i = 1 \text{ if } WTP \geq A \text{ (0 otherwise).}$$

The log likelihood for the sample is then equal to:

$$l = \Sigma S_i T_i \ln[1 - F_{wtp}(A)] + S_i(1 - T_i) \ln[F_{wtp}(A) - F_{wtp}(0)]$$
$$+ (1 - S_i) \ln[F_{wtp}(0)].$$

Following Hanemann (1984), in the assumption of a linear utility function:

$$v(k, y; z) = \alpha_k + \beta y + \gamma's \quad \beta > 0, k = 0, 1$$

where α and β are coefficients, y denotes income, γ is a vector of coefficients, and s denotes a vector of socio-economic and demographic characteristics gives:

$$\Delta v = (\alpha_1 - \alpha_0) - \beta A,$$

where Δv denotes an approximation of the utility change. Using a logistic distribution G_{wtp} we have:

$$G_{wtp} = \frac{1}{1 + \exp(-\Delta v)}.$$

Maximizing the log likelihood function, Kriström (1997) finds mean WTP:

$$E(WTP) = \int_0^\infty (1 - F_{wtp}(A))dA = -\frac{1}{\beta}\ln(a + \exp(\alpha_1 - \alpha_0)).$$

The variance was computed using the Gauss approximation described in the LIMDEP (1992) manual, p. 156.

Under Kriström's (1997) framework, the Valuation section initially established a hypothetical payment mechanism with the following market construct:

Suppose a special 'Yellowstone Lake Preservation Fund' is established by the National Park Service. Money from the Trust would be used to fund a program to manage the Lake Trout problem in Yellowstone Lake. With the program, the Cutthroat Trout will likely remain a viable species in the lake and other species that depend on the presence of Cutthroat will also likely remain at natural levels in the surrounding ecosystem. Without the program, Cutthroat will likely disappear and other species will diminish in numbers from the ecosystem. In sum, the Yellowstone Lake ecosystem will likely continue its natural existence with the program and will likely be significantly altered without the program.

The following question was posed to determine whether the respondent had a positive willingness to pay for the preservation fund:

If you did not answer yes, would you be willing to contribute any amount of money each year to the 'Yellowstone Lake Preservation Fund' in order to support the program?

1 YES
2 NO

If respondents indicated a positive willingness to pay, they were asked the following discrete choice (DC) question:

Suppose that a $X contribution from each United States household each year would be needed to support and fund the preservation program. Would you be willing to contribute $X each year to the 'Yellowstone Lake Preservation Fund' in order to support the program?

1 YES
2 DON'T KNOW
3 NO

Three DC bids X ($5, $15 and $30) were randomly distributed among the sampled individuals. The bids were chosen to provide sufficient information about the tails of the empirical survival distribution. In our survey, 60 per cent of the respondents were willing to pay a positive amount for preservation. The large number of respondents unwilling to pay a positive amount shows the importance of using a distribution that allows for a zero WTP. Popular distributional assumptions such as log-logistic, log normal, or Weibull imply that all respondents have a positive WTP. Use of such an assumption may, therefore, result in a biased benefit estimate.

Finally, the Demographic section obtained respondent and household characteristics. The responses provided additional regressors for the valuation function estimates, which also allow consistency tests for our data. Demographic information is indicative of our unique target population of national park visitors – 56 per cent of respondents were male with an average age of 46.7 years. While only 10 per cent of the respondents lived alone, 60 per cent of the represented households had no children. As expected, the targeted sample had relatively high education and income levels with nearly 70 per cent of the sample having four years or more of college education and 53 per cent earning more than $50 000 annually.

Two hundred and eighty-four of the 496 distributed surveys were returned within 30 days. The response rate of 57.3 per cent arose amid conflicting pressures: (1) the rate is higher due to the non-inclusion of the people who refused to take a survey (sometimes with emphasis) and the potential of greater interest by the selected sample and (2) the rate is lower due to the inability to use follow-up measures that often significantly increase the sample size. Of the 284 returned surveys, 28 (5.6 per cent) failed to respond to the WTP question; thereby eliminating them from the sample. Sixty-eight, or 13.7 per cent, responded 'do not know' to the WTP question and were coded as negative responses for estimation. Finally, the sample was trimmed further due to respondents not completing questions related to our regressors, such as age, income, gender, etc. The final sample included 238 observations.

Table 14.2 presents the estimated value function. Coefficient estimates generally follow intuition as well as previous results. For example, income and fishing interest regressors have positive coefficients that are significant at conventional levels. Furthermore, men tend to have higher values than women, and respondents that consider the cut-throat problem 'very serious' also place considerably higher values on the Yellowstone Lake ecosystem than their peers. Although these effects are only significant at the $p < 0.19$ level using a one-sided alternative, they are suggestive of underlying preference patterns. In order to estimate aggregate values, we compute a mean WTP equal to $11.16 (s.d. = $3.25). This value estimate is significantly

Table 14.2   Estimated value function

Variable	Coefficient	Standard error	P-value
Intercept	0.39982	0.22244	0.07226
Bid	−0.08178	0.02090	0.00009
Income	0.54343	0.16176	0.00078
Age	−0.01254	0.01303	0.33615
Kids	−0.03724	0.02110	0.84377
Gender	0.30234	0.33989	0.37371
Fisherman	−1.27290	0.52608	0.01554
Serious: very	0.09033	0.71488	0.32902
moderately	−0.69778	0.71488	0.32902
not at all	0.01425	0.62734	0.99819
no opinion	1.96560	1.43620	0.17114

Note: For a definition of the variables used, see the Appendix of this chapter.

different from zero at conventional levels and suggests the average park visitor will pay about $11 per year to fund a program to help protect the Yellowstone Lake ecosystem, which includes cutthroats, eagles, and grizzly bears.

The aggregate value estimate is enlightening when placed into a management context. Park officials recently extended the current management scheme of deep netting that has decreased the lake trout population by 50 per cent since 1996. In addition, officials substantially increased funding of deep netting to $1 million over the next four years. The annual cost of $250 000 includes a commercial grade vessel and a crew solely dedicated to the thinning of lake trout numbers. Distributing the annual cost over the estimated three million visitors in calendar year 2000 would entail each person paying about nine cents – less than 1 per cent of the estimated $11 mean. In fact, collecting the estimated WTP from 1 per cent of the visitors, akin to only charging visitors from an average July day (about a $20 entrance fee per vehicle), would cover the costs associated with the deep netting program. Our results indicate that visitor benefits clearly outweigh the cost of current policy.

14.5 Conclusion and caveats

This chapter provides new value estimates of the willingness to pay to protect the Yellowstone Lake ecosystem from lake trout – an exotic invader that puts other key native species at risk, namely the threatened Yellowstone cutthroat and the endangered grizzly bear. Using data collected from visitors at Yellowstone and Teton National Parks in Jackson Hole, Wyoming, our estimates using Kriström's (1997) spike model suggest the average person states that he will pay about $11 to help fund a program to manage the lake trout problem. These computed benefits are found to substantially exceed the costs of protecting Yellowstone Lake through a managed strategy of gill netting lake trout.

We conclude by highlighting some open questions in CVM, both in our study and in the current state of the art. First, a piecemeal species-by-species approach most likely will overestimate economic benefits. To illustrate, if one summed the stated preferences from various endangered species surveys in Loomis and White (1996) as a crude measure of benefits, the average person was willing to pay about $1000 to protect 18 different species. Multiplying $1000 by the number of US households, suggest that we would be willing to pay over 1 per cent of GDP to preserve less than 2 per cent of the endangered species. Many will find these values to be high; others might not (Smith, 1993; Brown and Shogren, 1998).

Second, critics also complain that hypothetical surveys elicit surrogate preferences for species protection in general, rather than for the specific species in question. Rather a person's stated willingness to pay acts as surrogate measure of general preferences toward the environment – a 'warm glow' effect. That is, eliciting existence values with a CVM survey provides respondents with a chance to state their general preferences toward the entire gamut of endangered species, not just for the specific species in question. This is often the first, if not only, occasion a person has been asked to reveal a public opinion on the environment, and, as such, the value revealed may reflect his or her overall desire to save the environment. For example, Hoehn and Loomis (1993) find that independent aggregation of the benefits of only two programs overstates their total benefits by 27 per cent, the overstatement with three programs is 54 per cent.

The exchange between Kahneman and Knetsch (1992) and Smith (1992) illustrates this issue. Kahneman and Knetsch observed that the average person's willingness to pay to clean up one lake in Ontario was about the same as his willingness to pay to clean up all the lakes in the province. They cite this as evidence that people are not responding to the specific good, but rather to the idea of contributing to environmental preservation in general – the warm glow. Smith questioned this view, arguing that incremental willingness to pay should diminish with the amount of the good already available, and that the evidence is therefore consistent with economic theory.

But other reports support the warm glow argument; Desvousges et al. (1992) find evidence that the average willingness to pay to prevent 2000 birds from dying in oil-filled ponds was about the same as the value to prevent 20 000 or 200 000 birds from dying. After examining numerous CVM studies on all types of environmental resources, Arrow et al. (1993) note the bimodal distribution of benefit estimates – zero or a positive benefit around $30 to $50. This finding suggests these values serve a function similar to charitable contributions (Brown and Shogren, 1998). In another example, McClelland et al. (1992) found that up to one-half of the reported values for a specific environmental charge can be attributed to surrogate values. The fraction appears to depend on the contextual information provided in the survey.

Finally, most people are unfamiliar with the services provided by endangered species. A recent survey suggested that over 70 per cent of Scottish citizens were completely unfamiliar with the meaning of biodiversity (Hanley and Spash, 1993), and there is little reason to expect substantially more knowledge in the United States (Coursey, 2000). These three issues suggest that the future of estimating the benefits of endangered species protection will remain elusive and contentious, and that more research is needed to reduce the lack of confidence in estimates of this type of public good.

Notes

1. The entrance into Yellowstone and Teton National Park are the same so we treat the visitors in the two adjacent parks as the same.
2. Distribution covered three days while the closing date was fixed. Some respondents (2.2 per cent) chose to complete the survey on site.

References

Anderson, S. (1998), 'The evolution and use of the Endangered Species Act', in J. Shogren (ed.), *Private Property and the Endangered Species Act. Protecting Habitats, Saving Homes*, Austin, TX: University of Texas Press.

Arrow, K., R. Solow, P. Portney, E. Leamer, R. Radner and H. Schuman (1993), 'Report of the NOAA panel on contingent valuation', Photocopy, Resources for the Future, Washington, DC.

Brown, G. Jr. and J. Shogren (1998), 'Economics of the Endangered Species Act', *Journal of Economic Perspectives*, **12**, 3–20.

Carson, R., W.M. Hanemann, R.J. Kopp, J.A. Krosnick, R.C. Mitchell, S. Presser, P.A. Ruud and V.K. Smith (1994), 'Prospective interim lost use value due to DDT and PCB contamination in the southern California bight', report to National Oceanic and Atmospheric Administration.

Coursey, D. (2000), 'The panitae of environmental value estimates', in J. Shogren and J. Tschirhart (eds), *Endangered Species Protection in the United States: Biological Needs, Political Realities, Economic Choices*, New York: Cambridge University Press.

Crocker, T. and J. Tschirhart (1992), 'Ecosystems, externalities, and economics', *Environmental and Resource Economics*, **2**, 551–67.

Desvousges, W., F.R. Johnson, R. Dunford, K. Boyle, S. Hudson and K. Wilson (1992), 'Measuring natural resource damages with contingent valuation: tests of validity and reliability', Research Triangle Institute, NC.

Epstein, R. (1995), *Simple Rules for a Complex World*, Cambridge, MA: Harvard University Press.

Federal Interagency Committee for the Management of Noxious and Exotic Weeds (FICMNEW) (1998), *Invasive Plants: Changing the Landscape of America, Fact Book*, Washington, DC.

Haneman, M.W. (1984), 'Welfare evaluations in contingent valuation experiments with discrete responses', *American Journal of Agricultural Economics*, **66**, 332–41.

Hanley, N. and C. Spash (1993), 'The value of biodiversity in British forests', Report to the Scottish Forestry Commission, University of Sterling, Scotland.

Hoehn, J. and J. Loomis (1993), 'Substitution effects in the valuation of multiple environmental programs', *Journal of Environmental Economics and Management*, **25**, 56–75.

Jakobsson, K.M. and A.K. Dragun (1996), *Contingent Valuation and Endangered Species: Methodological Issues and Applications*, Cheltenham, UK and Lyme, NH: Edward Elgar; distributed by American International Distribution Corporation, Williston, VT, pp. xxiii, 269.

Just, R., D. Hueth and A. Schmitz (1982), *Applied Welfare Economics and Public Policy*, New Jersey: Prentice-Hall.

Kaeding, L., G. Boltz and D. Carty (1995), 'Lake trout discovered in Yellowstone Lake', in J. Varley and P. Schullery (eds), 'The Yellowstone Lake crisis: confronting a lake trout invasion', A Report to the Director of the National Park Service, Yellowstone Center for Resources, National Park Service, Yellowstone National Park, Wyoming, pp. 4–11.

Kahneman, D. and J. Knetsch (1992), 'Valuing public goods: the purchase of moral satisfaction', *Journal of Environmental Economics and Management*, **22**, 57–70.

Kriström, B. (1997), 'Spike models in contingent valuation', *American Journal of Agricultural Economics*, **79**, 1013–23.

Krutilla, J. (1967), 'Conservation reconsidered', *American Economic Review*, **57**, 787–96.

Langford, I.H., A. Kontogianni, M.S. Skourtos, S. Georgiou and I.J. Bateman (1998), 'Multivariate mixed models for open-ended contingent valuation data: willingness to pay for conservation of monk seals', *Environmental and Resource Economics*, **12**, 443–56.

Loomis J.B. and D.S. White (1996), 'Economic benefits of rare and endangered species: summary and meta-analysis', *Ecological Economics*, **18**(3), 197–206.

LIMDEP 6.0 (1992), Econometric Software, Inc, Bellport, NY.

MacIsaac, H. (1996), 'Potential abiotic and biotic impacts of zebra mussels on the inland waters of North America', *American Zoology*, **36**, 287–99.

McClelland, W., W. Schulze, J. Lazo, D. Walurang, J. Doyle, S. Eliot and J. Irwin (1992), 'Methods for measuring non-use values: a contingent valuation study of groundwater cleanup', Center for Economic Analysis, Boulder, CO.

Roughgarden, J. (1995), 'Can economics protect biodiversity?', in T. Swanson (ed.), *The Economics and Ecology of Biodiversity Decline*, Cambridge: Cambridge University Press, pp. 149–54.

Schullery, P. and J. Varley (1995), 'Cutthroat trout and the Yellowstone Lake ecosystem', in J. Varley and P. Schullery (eds), 'The Yellowstone Lake crisis: confronting a lake trout invasion', A Report to the Director of the National Park Service, Yellowstone Center for Resources, National Park Service, Yellowstone National Park, Wyoming, pp. 12–21.

Smith, V.K. (1992), 'Arbitrary values, good causes, and premature verdicts', *Journal of Environmental Economics and Management*, **22**, 71–89.

Smith, V.K. (1993), 'Rethinking the rithmetic of damage assessment', *Journal of Policy Analysis and Management*, **12**, 589–95.

Varley, J. and P. Schullery (1995), 'Socioeconomic values associated with the Yellowstone Lake cutthroat troat', in J. Varley and P. Schullery (eds), 'The Yellowstone Lake crisis: confronting a lake trout invasion', A Report to the Director of the National Park Service, Yellowstone Center for Resources, National Park Service, Yellowstone National Park, Wyoming, pp. 22–7.

Veblen, T., M. Mermoz, C. Martin and T. Kitzberger (1992), 'Ecological impacts of introduced animals in Nahuel Huapi National Park, Argentina', *Conservation Biology*, **6**, 71–83.

Walsh R., R.D. Bjonback, T.D. Rosenthal and R. Aiken (1985), 'Public benefits of programs to protect endangered wildlife', in Colorado Symposium on Issues and Technology in the Management of Impacted Western Wildlife, Thorne Ecological Institute, Glenwood Springs, CO.

Watts-Reaves D., R.K. Kramer and T.P. Holmes (2000), 'Does question format matter? Valuing an endangered species', working paper, Virginia Tech University.

Appendix A

Bid: The DC bid given to the respondent
Kids: Number of children in household
Gender: 1 – male, 0 – female
Age: Years
Income   1 – less than $20 000
          2 – 20 001 to 30 000
          3 – 30 001 to 40 000
          4 – 40 001 to 50 000
          5 – 50 001 or more

Fisherman: What are the chances that you will visit YNP in the future with a purpose of fishing for species such as the Cutthroat Trout?

   1. Definitely will
   2. Probably will

3. Don't know
4. Probably will not
5. Definitely will not
Coded as 1 if any of the two first alternatives were chosen, otherwise coded as a zero.

Serious: How serious do you consider the consequences of having non-native Lake Trout in Yellowstone Lake? (coded as 1 if selected)
1. Very
2. Moderately
3. Barely
4. Not a problem at all
5. I have no opinion at all

15 The demand for insecticide-treated mosquito nets: evidence from Africa
Christine Poulos, Maureen Cropper,
Julian Lampietti, Dale Whittington and
Mitiku Haile

15.1 Introduction

Brouwer and Koopmanschap (2000) discuss the differences between what they call the 'welfarist' and 'extra-welfarist' perspectives on economic evaluations of health interventions. The 'welfarist approach', characterized by Harrington and Portney (1987) and Berger et al. (1994), aims to embed evaluations in welfare economics. The 'extra-welfarist' approach, characterized by Cuyler (1991) and Williams (1993), aims to help decision makers maximize health from a given budget by 'replacing utility with health as the outcome of interest for evaluation' (Brouwer and Koopmanschap, 2000: 444). While Brouwer and Koopmanschap take aim at the controversial assumptions underlying welfarist evaluations, this study shows that welfarist approaches convey information about individual behavior, which has implications for both health outcomes and health budgets.

This study bridges the gap between welfarist and extra-welfarist perspectives by estimating a household demand for insecticide-treated bednets (ITNs) that allows policy makers to balance the goal of cost recovery against the desire to guarantee that a certain fraction of the population receives protection from malaria and other vector-borne diseases. ITNs have helped to reduce the incidence of malaria and other vector-borne illness in various parts of Africa (Binka et al., 1997), but their use as a health intervention raises an important policy question: should ITNs be provided privately or publicly? If they were sold privately, how many bednets would be purchased (at various prices)? This information would help public health agents balance the goals of cost recovery – which is necessary for a program to be self-sustaining – against the arguments for government subsidization of the program because of the externalities associated with the control of infectious disease.

We estimate the demand for bednets based on a survey of over 250 households in Tigray, an agricultural area characterized by seasonal, unstable malaria in the north of Ethiopia. At the time of our study, bednets were essentially unknown to households in Tigray as a method of treating malaria.[1] The Tigray Region Malaria Control Department was considering ITNs as an intervention to decrease the risk of malaria and other diseases.

To measure the demand for bednets, we asked the household head (or spouse) how many bednets he or she would purchase if they were available. This modified stated preference method asked respondents to choose the quantity of goods they would purchase at a given price, rather than their willingness to pay for a fixed quantity of good. This modification permits estimation of the household demand for bednets. Given the supply price of ITNs, the demand curve can be used to calculate the subsidy necessary to guarantee that a certain fraction of the population is protected, assuming the bednets are sold as private goods.

The demand curve can also be used to calculate the benefits of such a program if bednets are provided free of charge. While this is not a Hicksian compensated benefit measure, the area under the bednet demand curve between 0 and $n/2$ bednets (each bednet protects at least two people) approximates the compensating variation associated with purchasing n bednets.

The plan of the chapter is as follows. The household demand for bednets is derived in Section 15.2 by combining the health production model of Grossman (1972) with Becker's (1981) benevolent dictator model. Our modified stated preference method is described. Count regression models, in which the number of bednets purchased is constrained to be less than or equal to one-half family size, are used for the econometric representation of bednet demand. Section 15.3 describes the region where our survey was conducted, the status of malaria in the region, and our sample's experience with malaria. Section 15.4 contains estimates of the demand for bednets and uses the demand curve to estimate the benefits of a bednet distribution program. Section 15.5 discusses the extent to which results from Tigray can be generalized to other parts of Africa.

15.2 Theoretical model and study methodology

This section develops a model of ITN demand that combines Becker's (1981) benevolent dictator model and Grossman's (1972) health production model.[2] Becker assumes that a single individual, such as a head of household or their spouse, makes the consumption choices for the entire household. We assume that the decision maker's utility depends on the amount of a numeraire that each family member consumes (X_i), on each person's leisure time (L_i), and on the amount of time each family member is ill with malaria (S_i). Utility also depends on taste variables such as the decision maker's education, age, and gender (Z) that affect the weight he or she places on children's versus adults' consumption and of health versus other goods. Assuming n family members, utility is given by

$$U = u(X_1, \ldots, X_n, L_1, \ldots, L_n, S_1, \ldots, S_n, Z). \qquad (15.1)$$

The time each family member is ill with malaria (S_i) is, in turn, a function of preventive care, such as ITNs (A_i), and treatment, such as chloroquine (M_i). How effective these inputs are depends on individual health characteristics (H_i) and, in the case of malaria, on the prevalence of mosquitoes (endemicity), E.

$$S_i = s(A_i, M_i, H_i, E). \qquad (15.2)$$

The amounts of preventive care, medical care and other goods each person consumes are constrained by the household's budget

$$\sum_{i=1}^{n} I_i + \sum_{i=1}^{n} w_i(T - L_i - S_i) = \sum_{i=1}^{n} X_i + p_a \sum_{i=1}^{n} A_i + p_m \sum_{i=1}^{n} M_i, \qquad (15.3)$$

where $\sum_{i=1}^{n} I_i$ is non-earned income, w_i is the wage of family member i and $\sum_{i=1}^{n} w_i(T - L_i - S_i)$ is earned income. (T is total time available to each household member.) The sum of these must equal household expenditures on consumption (the price of which is 1), use of bednets (with price p_a), and treatment (with price p_m).

The decision maker selects values of X, L, A, and M to maximize household utility subject to the budget constraint and to the health production functions. This yields a household demand function for ITNs, where A^* is the number of ITNs chosen by the decision maker

$$A^* = g(I, \mathbf{w}, p_a, p_m, \mathbf{Z}, \mathbf{H}, E). \qquad (15.4)$$

This function indicates that demand for ITNs depends on household non-earned income, a vector of wages for each household member, as well as the prices of ITNs and mitigating health care, characteristics of the decision maker, baseline health of each individual, and the prevalence of the malaria vector.

The discrete nature of bednets suggests that equation (15.4) be estimated using a count data model, such as the Poisson. Since at least two people can sleep under each bednet, purchasing more than $n/2$ bednets cannot increase welfare. We estimate a truncated Poisson model which imposes the constraint that the household never purchases more than $n/2$ ITNs.

The count data were collected using a modified stated preference method in which the respondent was asked if he would purchase one or more ITNs at one of five randomly assigned prices. If the respondent answered 'yes', he was asked how many ITNs would be purchased. While this method is different than most stated preference applications, which value a fixed, exogenous quantity of the good, some prior studies have made use of data on quantities chosen by respondents. These studies fall into two categories. The first are travel cost models that estimate count regression models using data on revealed demand for recreation trips (see, Loomis et al., 2000). The second combines revealed demand with stated preference data in a joint estimation of revealed and stated preference models (see, for example, Cameron, 1992; Englin and Cameron, 1996; Jakus, 1994). Most of these applications are found in the travel cost literature.

Only one other study, to our knowledge, has asked respondents to choose quantities in a stated preference approach. Niklitschek and Leon (1996) measure stated preferences for an exogenous environmental quality improvement and stated, rather than revealed, demand for beach trips. They jointly estimate a discrete choice model and a linear travel cost model to measure household preferences for water quality improvements. Their results are used to determine beach user fees that maximize aggregate recreational benefits.

Like Niklitschek and Leon, our study will rely on stated or intended demand, but it will not implement a joint estimation. Also, recognizing the discrete nature of the data, we use count regression models to estimate a Marshallian demand function. The WTP measure from the estimated Marshallian demand function is not a Hicksian benefit measure. Willig (1976) demonstrates that, if the area to the left of the Marshallian demand function is approximately 5 per cent of money income, then the Hicksian benefit measure and the Marshallian benefit measure are within a few per cent of each other.[3]

15.3 Study site and research design

The data used to estimate the demand for ITNs were collected in 1997 in Tigray, a province in northern Ethiopia. The main activity in Tigray is subsistence farming; however, the low productivity of the soil and lack of adequate rainfall have resulted in chronic food shortages.

The climate in most of Tigray is marginally 'suitable' for malaria, meaning that malaria may follow strong seasonal cycles with great inter-annual variation (Ghebreyesus et al., 1996; MARA, 2001). In areas with this transmission pattern, malaria affects adults and children equally. Microdams, which have been constructed in Tigray to provide water for crops, have exacerbated malaria by providing a breeding ground for mosquitoes.

Approximately 900 households in 18 villages were surveyed to assess the demand for malaria prevention and to compute the medical costs and productivity losses associated with the disease.[4] The head of household or their spouse was asked to identify the symptoms associated with malaria and was asked how the disease was transmitted and how it could be prevented and treated. Respondents who were familiar with the disease were asked to describe their family's experience with malaria during the last two years.[5] This included a detailed description of the respondent's most recent malaria episode, as well as the most recent malaria episode experienced by a teenager or child in the family. These descriptions included information about treatment, treatment costs, lost work time, caretakers' time, and intra-household labor substitution.

Approximately one-third of respondents (279) living in six of the villages were asked whether they would purchase one or more ITNs for members of their family if ITNs were to become available. The bednet scenario coupled an explanation of how using a bednet reduces the probability of contracting malaria with an actual demonstration of a double-size polyester bednet impregnated with 1 per cent Deltamethrin. Respondents were then presented with information about annual re-impregnation of an ITN over its four-year expected life and were told that they could spread payments for the bednets over four months. After being reminded that other measures could be taken to prevent malaria, such as draining standing water and/or taking medicine as prophylaxis, the respondent was asked if he would purchase one or more ITNs at one of five randomly assigned prices. (Prices ranged from US$1 to US$16 per bednet.) The highest price is based on an estimate of the charge that would be needed for full cost recovery of an imported ITN. If the respondent answered 'yes', he was asked how many ITNs would be purchased. The survey ended with questions about the family's socio-economic circumstances, including education, occupation, income, assets, and housing construction. Table 15.1 shows the sample means.

Table 15.1   Means and standard deviations of variables

Variable	N	Mean	Std. Dev.	Min	Max
Log income (thousand Birr)	279	1.97	1.23	−4	4
Missing wage (1 if no wage)	279	0.39	0.49	0	1
Number of teenagers	279	0.56	0.78	0	4
Number of children	279	1.74	1.33	0	5
Household cost of illness (Birr)	279	22.26	16.45	0	97
Married (1 if married)	279	0.70	0.46	0	1
Gender (1 if female)	279	0.66	0.47	0	1
Read (1 if read easily)	279	0.53	0.50	0	1
Age (years)	279	41.04	15.04	16	80
Alt (hundred meters)	279	16.51	1.89	12	19
Household size	279	4.53	2.03	1	12

The remaining two-thirds of respondents (569) were asked whether they would purchase one or more hypothetical malaria vaccines for members of their family, if such a vaccine were to become available. These responses are analysed in Cropper et al. (1999, 2004).

15.3.1   Malaria in Tigray

Our survey was conducted in villages where malaria follows a seasonal pattern, with peak transmission occurring just before harvest (i.e., after the rainy season) and, to a lesser extent, during the rainy season. Government malaria control activities include spraying in outbreak areas, encouraging communities to drain ditches of standing water, and training volunteer community health workers to recognize and treat malaria with chloroquine.

Seventy-eight per cent of the 848 respondents in our sample said that they had been ill with malaria at some time in their lives, with 58 per cent reporting at least one episode of malaria in the last two years.[6] Fifty-three per cent of respondents said that at least one other adult in the household had experienced malaria in the last two years, and 49 per cent of respondents said that at least one child or teenager in the family had experienced the disease within the last two years.

15.3.2   Cost of illness estimates

The costs of illness (COI) measure the out of pocket expenditures[7] plus the productivity losses (proxied by lost wages)[8] associated with an episode of malaria. The COI associated with an average episode, depending on productivity assumptions, ranges from US$7 to US$24 for an adult and US$7 to US$12 for a child.[9] If we compute the COI for each household and average this value across all households (including those with no malaria), the annual per household COI ranges from US$31 (assuming productivity losses of US$1 per day) to US$9 (assuming productivity losses of US$0.5 per day).

These results are comparable with most of the other published COI estimates from areas like Ethiopia that face an unstable, seasonal malaria transmission pattern. Other studies' estimates range from US$3 in Pakistan (Kahn, 1966) to US$16 in Sri Lanka (Konradsen et al., 1997), and US$18 in Chad (Sauerborn et al., 1991). (The estimates from Pakistan are likely an underestimate because the data on the number of cases and the costs per case are taken from national statistics on the formal health care sector.)[10]

To place these numbers in context, we computed household income as the sum of the value of agricultural output, off-farm earnings, and the annualized value of farm animals. Average income is US$220 per household per year, implying that as much as 14 per cent of income is lost to malaria annually. This figure does not include the cost of activities that are undertaken to prevent the disease.[11]

15.4   Empirical analysis of ITN demand
15.4.1   Description of responses
Table 15.2 shows the number of bednets households which said they would purchase at each price. Quantity demanded is clearly sensitive to price: the percentage of households who declined to purchase nets increases from 19 per cent at a price of US$1 to 63 per cent at a price of US$16. The percentage of families who said they would buy two or more nets also declines monotonically as price rises. A rise in price from US$1 to US$3 and from US$3 to US$6, however, increases the percentage of families purchasing one net. Families who would buy two nets at a lower price would buy only one net at higher prices.

One reason for analysing bednet demand is to predict the number of households who would purchase bednets at various prices. For example, Table 15.2 can be used to predict the fraction of households who would buy a bednet at a price that would permit cost recovery. It can also be used to determine what price would induce a desired fraction of households to purchase nets. Figure 15.1 illustrates the number of bednets that would be purchased in a village of 200 households, assuming that these households have the same characteristics as those in our sample (e.g., average household size is five). At a price of US$6 per net, for example, 166 nets would be purchased. Calculating the number of people in the village who would be covered at this price requires an assumption about the number of people who sleep under a net. If this is two, then one-third of the population of the village would sleep under insecticide-treated nets at a price of US$6 per net.

15.4.2   Estimation of household demand functions for bednets
Count data models are appropriate in this case, since households buy a non-negative integer quantity of bednets. Table 15.3 presents estimates of Poisson, Negative Binomial, and Truncated Poisson models of the demand for bednets. The Truncated Poisson model imposes on the Poisson model the constraint that a household will never purchase more than $n/2$ bednets.

Table 15.2   Number of bednets purchased by price

Price (1997 US$)	0 nets	1 net	2 nets	3 or more nets
1	19%	21%	43%	17%
3	22%	33%	32%	13%
6	41%	37%	20%	2%
10	52%	23%	19%	6%
16	63%	25%	11%	2%

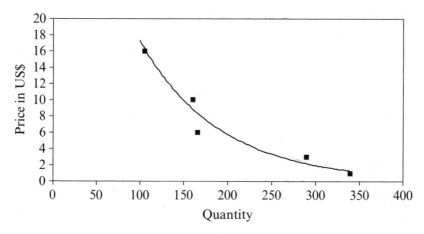

*Figure 15.1   Demand for bednets in 200 household villages in Tigray,
Ethiopia*

The theoretical model described in Section 15.2 suggests that the number
of vaccines purchased should depend on vaccine price, household income,
and family size. It might also depend on family composition, i.e. on the
number of adults, children, and teenagers in the family, and on the characteristics of the respondent – gender, age, marital status, and education –
which may influence his taste for health-related goods. We measure education by whether the respondent can read a newspaper. Income, which enters
the demand function in log form, is made up of three components: annual
gross crop income, the annualized value of livestock holdings, and reported
annual off-farm wages. Since 28 per cent of observations on off-farm wages
are missing, we replace missing values with zero and then include a 'missing
wage' dummy variable, equal to one if off-farm income is not reported.

The demand for the vaccine should also depend on the incidence of
malaria in the area and on family members' susceptibilities to the disease.
We proxy malaria incidence by village altitude. We proxy household susceptibility to malaria with a variable that measures past experience with the
disease. Specifically, we sum the number of malaria episodes that members
of the household experienced during the last two years, weighting each
episode by the average age-specific cost of treatment. This is the household's direct COI. Household size is measured by a series of dummy variables, because the number of bednets respondents say they will purchase
does not increase linearly with household size.

The only variables whose coefficients are significantly different from
zero are price, income, and age of the respondent. Price is strongly
significant in all three models. Income is marginally significant in the

Table 15.3   Parameter estimates for bednet models (n =279)

Variable	Poisson	Negative binomial	Truncated poisson
Price	−0.014[a]	−0.014[a]	−0.016[a]
(Birr)	0.002	0.002	0.003
Log household income	0.093[b]	0.093[b]	0.097
(thousands of Birr)	0.059	0.059	0.075
Missing wage	0.019	0.019	0.265
(1 if no wage)	0.188	0.188	−0.132
Number of teenagers	0.116	0.117	0.118
(number)	0.109	0.109	0.147
Number of children	0.044	0.044	0.032
(number)	0.099	0.099	0.142
Household dir. cost of illness	−0.005	−0.005	−0.006
(Birr)	0.005	0.005	0.006
Married	0.045	0.045	0.022
(1 if married)	0.195	0.195	0.271
Gender	0.012	0.012	0.009
(1 if female)	0.146	0.146	0.213
Read	0.022	0.022	−0.010
(1 if read easily)	0.160	0.160	0.224
Age	−0.010[a]	−0.010[a]	−0.012
(years)	0.005	0.005	0.008
Altitude	0.067	0.067	0.082
(hundreds of meters)	0.038	0.038	0.049
Intercept	−0.541	−0.541	0.461
	0.844	0.846	1.116
Lnα		−17.323	

Notes: Dichotomous variables for household size and enumerators are reported in the Appendix. Standard errors in small font.
[a] Significant at the 5 per cent level.
[b] Significant at the 10 per cent level.

Poisson and Negative Binomial models, as is respondent age. The income elasticity of demand for bednets is low: a 10 per cent increase in income increases the demand for bednets by only 1 per cent. Older respondents have lower demand than younger respondents do.

The lack of significance of so many explanatory variables in these models is due in part to small sample size (279 households). Nevertheless, we believe Table 15.3 indicates that we probably have accurate estimates of the impact of price on the purchase of bednets, which is most likely the variable of greatest policy significance.

Table 15.4   Goodness of fit criteria for bednets

	Actual	Poisson	Negative binomial	Truncated poisson
Log likelihood	N/A	−322.30	322.30	−311.75
Mean $Y|\mathbf{X}$	1.07	1.07	1.07	1.09
Variance of $Y|\mathbf{X}$	1.63	0.56	0.56	0.57
$Y >$ (household size)/2	0%	2%	2%	0%
Frequency				
0	39%	54%	54%	52%
1	28%	37%	37%	38%
2	25%	8%	8%	8%
3	6%	1%	1%	1%
4	0%	0%	0%	0%
5	0%	0%	0%	0%
6 or more	1%	0%	0%	0%

Table 15.4 compares the performance of the three models in predicting within-sample behavior. A likelihood ratio test fails to reject the null hypothesis that the data follow a Poisson distribution. Since the Poisson model is a special case of the Negative Binomial model and the Truncated Poisson model, it is not surprising that the three models produce similar results. All models over-predict the number of households purchasing zero bednets or one bednet and underpredict the number of households purchasing two or more bednets. This suggests that, for purposes of predicting bednet purchases, it is better to rely on the raw data in Table 15.2.

15.4.3   Willingness to pay for bednets

Our estimates of bednet demand can also be used to compute the household's total willingness to pay for a given number of nets. To illustrate, suppose that a donor were to provide enough bednets to protect all persons in a village. What are the economic benefits of such a program? The value to a household of owning x nets (its total WTP for the nets) is the area under its demand curve between 0 and x nets. Thus, the value of the program would be the sum of each household's total WTP for the nets it received. Assuming that each household received $n/2$ nets, mean and median household WTP for bednets are given in Table 15.5.[12]

These benefit estimates are difficult to compare with the other two benefit estimates measured in this study: COI and WTP for a hypothetical malaria vaccine. While WTP for ITNs lie in the range of annual household COI associated with malaria, these values are difficult to compare because COI indicates the benefits of eliminating malaria for one year, while ITNs

Table 15.5   Willingness to pay for bednets in US$ (n =279)

	Poisson	Negative binomial	Truncated poisson
Willingness to pay			
Mean	20	20	22
Median	18	18	19
Standard deviation	11	11	13
Minimum	3	3	1
Maximum	74	74	95

reduce, but do not eliminate, risk for four years. Average household WTP for a hypothetical malaria vaccine that is 100 per cent effective for one year is estimated to be US$36 per year (Cropper et al., 2004). Thus, mean WTP for ITNs (US$22 for Truncated Poisson) is 60 per cent of mean WTP for vaccines. The difference between these estimates may be partially explained by the fact that, although bednets are a durable good with a four year expected lifetime, they provide only partial protection against malaria. Moreover, they require some effort to use.[13]

15.4.4   Policy implications of the results

These results can assist decision makers seeking to maximize health given a fixed budget by illustrating the tradeoff between public expenditures and bednet coverage. It has been estimated that the supply price of an ITN is about US$16. At this price, however, 63 per cent of households in Tigray would buy no bednets. Figure 15.1 plots the number of ITNs purchased at each of our sample prices, and connects these points. The figure shows that only 200 persons in a village of 200 households (1000 persons) would be protected by bednets. At a price of US$1, about 340 bednets are sold and 680 persons (68 per cent of the population of the village) would sleep under a bednet. Since the revenue from selling 100 bednets at US$100 per ITN is almost four times as great as the revenue from selling 340 bednets at US$1 per ITN, there is clearly a tradeoff between coverage and profit maximization, were ITNs to be sold as private goods. Indeed, our estimates of demand for ITNs imply that the possibility of distributing the bednets through the private sector is slim.

  These results are due to a relatively steep demand curve – implying that, as the price of ITNs fall, the number purchased increases, but gradually. Households' mean WTP for $n/2$ bednets as a percentage of income (8 per cent) is twice as large as intended bednet expenditures as a percentage of income (4 per cent or less). The policy implications of this result are that, while the benefits from allocating resources to bednets are large, it will be difficult to achieve significant market penetration unless the price is subsidized.

To compute the private benefits of free ITNs, we compute the consumer surplus that each household would receive if it were given x bednets. This is approximated by the area under the household's demand function between 0 and $n/2$ bednets. The average annual household benefits from bednets are US\$20–22. Summing these benefits over the 279 households in our sample yields total annual benefits of US\$5580–6138. The costs of this program to the public health agency would equal the number of bednets provided (i.e., one-half of the number of people protected, since ITNs protect at least two people) times the subsidy per bednet. If the subsidy is set so that the price per bednet is about US\$9 or less, then the program yields positive net benefits.

15.5   Conclusions and generalizability of the results

This chapter illustrates how the results of a welfare economic study can assist decision makers seeking to maximize health given a fixed budget. The study is one of the first to use a stated preference method asking respondents to choose the quantities of good that they would demand. Typically, stated preference methods measure respondents' preferences for a fixed quantity of a good. The modified stated preference approach permits straightforward estimation of the market demand function.

Our estimates of the household demand for ITNs have three policy implications. First, the estimated ITN demand curve is such that, even at low prices, many households would not purchase bednets. For example, at a price of US\$1, one-fifth of all households in Tigray would purchase no bednets. Second, there is a sharp trade-off between cost recovery and assuring that a significant fraction of the population receives protection from bednets. Third, the shape of the demand curve implies that, even though few bednets are purchased, consumer surplus from bednets is high. This implies that the net benefits from donor-sponsored bednet distribution could be positive, even though few households would privately purchase ITNs.

To what extent are these results likely to apply in other parts of Africa? Malaria is a disease that varies widely in its incidence and in its pattern of transmission. In many parts of Africa, malaria is endemic: transmission is perennial and most adults experience at least one episode of the disease each year. In these areas morbidity and mortality from malaria are highest among groups having low immunity, such as infants and children. In areas where malaria follows an unstable, seasonal transmission pattern, such as Tigray, the working age population suffers more episodes of malaria relative to perennial transmission, and the income losses due to malaria are greater. For these reasons, one must be cautious in transferring results from Ethiopia to the rest of sub-Saharan Africa.

Notes

Christine Poulos, Research Triangle Institute, 3040 Cornwallis Road, Research Triangle Park, North Carolina, 27709, email: cpoulos@rti.org. Maureen Cropper, The World Bank and Professor of Economics, University of Maryland-College Park. Julian Lampietti, The World Bank. Dale Whittington, Professor of Environmental Sciences and Engineering and City and Regional Planning, University of North Carolina at Chapel Hill. Mitiku Haile Dean, Mekelle University College, Mekelle, Ethiopia.
This investigation received financial support from the UNDP/World Bank/WHO Special Programme for Research and Training in Tropical Disease. The authors would like to thank Melba Gomes for comments and Bill Evans for providing the SAS code used to estimate the multivariate model. Carol Jenkins conducted the initial ethnographic survey. The field work would not have been possible without the help of Kristin Komives, Zarai, Amare, Gebremedhin, Gebremichael and the members of the enumeration teams. Special thanks are also due to Tedros Ghebreyesus and the Tigray Malaria Control Office and to staff at University College Mekelle.

1. In response to the question, 'What are the best ways to avoid getting malaria?', only four respondents mentioned sleeping under a bednet (either unimpregnated or impregnated).
2. Our model ignores risk of death from malaria, which, in Tigray, is low relative to risk of death from other causes. In Tigray, eight persons out of every 10 000 die each year from malaria (Ethiopian Ministry of Health, 1996). By contrast, risk of death from other causes is 160 per 10 000 people.
3. There is a distinction between (1) the economic value of an exogenous change in malaria exposure (e.g., vector control program) that causes a risk reduction equivalent to the risk reduction achieved by the ITN and (2) the economic value of the risk reduction achieved by the ITN. The former can be measured by the change in expenditure on a private good that is a pure substitute for malaria exposure (i.e., the area *under* the price and to the left of quantity). However, this substitution method is invalid for non-marginal changes in exposure (Freeman, 1993). The latter, which is measured in this study, is the area *above* the price and to the left of quantity.
4. A detailed description of the project and its results may be found in Cropper et al. (2004).
5. Of 889 respondents who received our questionnaire, 41 were not familiar with malaria. These households were dropped from the sample.
6. These figures measure self-reported malaria. Only 164 respondents said that they had ever had their malaria diagnosed with a blood test.
7. These include the costs of medicine, fees paid to health care providers, and the costs of traveling to health care providers.
8. The total number of workdays lost by all family members during a malaria episode equals the number of workdays lost by the patient, plus the number of days other family members stopped their normal activities to take care of the sick patient, minus the number of days other family members substitute for the sick patient at work. The net number of workdays lost to the family is, on average, 21 days for an adult episode of malaria, 26 days for a teenager's episode of malaria, and 12 days for a child's episode of malaria.
   To compute the average private cost of an episode of malaria, workdays lost must be valued and added to the private costs of treatment. A workday lost by an adult is valued at the daily wage of an unskilled laborer (US$1). Teenagers are assumed to be half as productive as adults, and children half as productive as teenagers.
9. At the time of the study, US$1 = Birr 6.3.
10. See Hammer (1993), Gomes (1993), and Mills (1991) for thorough reviews of COI due to malaria.
11. Eighty-four per cent of respondents (712/848) said that they drained areas near their home of standing water to prevent malaria transmission. Seven per cent of respondents took chloroquine prophylactically.

12. When not an integer, $n/2$ was rounded down to the nearest integer.
13. Mills (1998) reviews studies of both expenditures and WTP for other preventive goods. These values are also difficult to compare to our ITN results because preventive goods offer various levels of risk reduction and durations of effectiveness.

References

Becker, G., (1981), 'Altruism in the family and selfishness in the market place', *Economica*, **48** (189), 1–15.

Berger, M., G. Blomquist, D. Kenkel and G. Tolley (1994), 'Framework for valuing health risks', in Tolley et al. (eds), *Valuing Health for Policy: An Economic Approach*, Chicago: The University of Chicago Press.

Binka, F., O. Nensah and A. Mills (1997), 'The cost effectiveness of ermethrin impregnated bednets in preventing child mortality in Kassena-Nankana district of northern Ghana', *Health Policy*, **41**, 229–39.

Brouwer, W. and M. Koopmanschap (2000), 'On the economic foundations of CEA: Ladies and gentleman, take your positions!', *Journal of Health Economics*, **19**, 439–59.

Cameron, T.A. (1992), 'Combining contingent valuation and travel cost data for the valuation of nonmarket goods', *Land Economics*, **68** (3), 302–17.

Cropper, M., J. Lampietti, C. Poulos, H. Mitiku and D. Whittington (1999), 'The value of preventing malaria in Tigray, Ethiopia', Report to the World Health Organization.

Cropper, M.H. Mitiku, J. Lampietti, C. Poulos and D. Whittington (2004), 'The demand for a malaria vaccine: evidence from Ehiopia', *Journal of Development Economics*, **75**, 303–18.

Cuyler, A. (1991), 'The normative economics of health care finance and provision', in A. McGuire, P. Fenn and K. Mayhew (eds.), *Providing Health Care: The Economics of Alternative Systems of Finance and Delivery*, Oxford: Oxford University Press.

Englin, J. and T. Cameron (1996), 'Augmenting travel cost models with contingent behavior data', *Environmental and Resource Economics*, **7**, 133–47.

Ethiopia Ministry of Health (1996), 'Burden of Disease', *Ethiopia Social Sector Study Report*, September.

Freeman. A. (1993), *The Measurement of Environmental and Resource Values: Theory and Practice*, Washington, DC: Resources for the Future.

Ghebreyesus, T., T. Alemayehu, A. Bosman, K. Witten and A. Teklehaimanot (1996), 'Community participation in malaria control in Tigray region Ethiopia', *Acta Tropica*, **61**, 145–56.

Gomes, M. (1993), 'Economic and demographic research on malaria: a review of the evidence', *Social Science and Medicine*, **37**, 1093–108.

Grossman, M. (1972), 'On the concept of health capital and the demand for health', *Journal of Political Economy*, **80**(2), 223–55.

Hammer, J. (1993), 'The economics of malaria control', *The World Bank Research Observer*, **8**, 1–22.

Harrington, W. and P. Portney (1987), 'Valuing the benefits of health and safety regulations', *Journal of Urban Economics*, **22**(1), 101–12.

Jakus, P. (1994), 'Averting behavior in the presence of public spillovers: household control of nuisance pests', *Land Economics*, **70**, 273–85.

Khan, M.J. (1966), 'Estimate of economic loss due to Malaria in West Pakistan', *Pakistan Journal of Health*, **16**, 187–93.

Konradsen, F., W. Van Der Hoek, P.H. Amerasinghe and F.P. Amerasinghe (1997), 'Measuring the economic cost of malaria to households in Sri Lanka', *American Journal of Tropical Medicine and Hygiene*, **56**, 656–60.

Loomis, J., S. Yorizane and D. Larson (2000), 'Testing significance of multi-destination and multi-purpose trip effects in a travel cost method demand model for whale watching trips', *Agricultural and Resource Economics*, **29**, 183–91.

MARA (Mapping Malaria Risk in Africa) Project (2001), Updated 7 May, http://www.mara.org.za, accessed 14 October 2001.

Mills, A. (1991), 'The economics of malaria control', in G. Targett (ed.), *Malaria: Waiting for the Vaccine*, Chichester: John Wiley & Sons.

Mills, A. (1998), 'Operational research on the economics of insecticide-treated mosquito nets: lessons of experience', *Annals of Tropical Medicine and Parasitology*, **92** (4), 435–47.

Niklitschek, M. and J. Leon (1996), 'Combining intended demand and yes/no responses in the estimation of contingent valuation models', *Journal of Environmental Economics and Management*, **31**, 387–402.

Sauerborn, R., D.S. Shepard, M.B. Ettling, U. Brinkmann, A. Nougtara and H.J. Diesfeld (1991), 'Estimating the direct and indirect economic costs of malaria in a rural district of Burkina Faso', *Tropical Medicine and Parasitology*, **42**, 219–23.

Williams, A. (1993), 'Cost–benefit analysis: applied welfare economics or general decision aid', in A. Williams and E. Giardina (eds.), *Efficiency in the Public Sector*, Cheltenham: Edward Elgar.

Willig, R. (1976), 'Consumer's surplus without apology', *American Economic Review*, **66**, 589.

Appendix

Table A1   Household size and enumerator effects for bednet models

Variable	Poisson	Negative binomial	Truncated poisson
DIhh_2	−0.227	−0.227	−0.971
	0.446	0.447	0.732
DIhh_3	0.230	0.230	−0.626
	0.442	0.443	0.709
DIhh_4	−0.239	−0.239	−1.256
	0.482	0.483	0.733
DIhh_5	0.101	0.101	−0.914
	0.523	0.523	0.794
DIhh_6	0.367	0.367	−0.628
	0.563	0.563	0.866
DIhh_7	0.296	0.296	−0.714
	0.641	0.641	0.959
DIhh_8	0.110	0.110	−0.876
	0.732	0.730	1.089
DIhh_9	0.885	0.885	−0.039
	0.802	0.802	1.192
Iname_2	−0.203	−0.203	−0.202
	0.319	0.319	0.409
Iname_3	0.500b	0.500b	0.588b
	0.278	0.277	0.347
Iname_8	0.126	0.126	0.126
	0.302	0.302	0.373
Iname_9	0.430	0.430	0.439
	0.303	0.304	0.386
Iname_10	−0.064	−0.064	−0.123
	0.331	0.332	0.430

Table A1 (continued)

Variable	Poisson	Negative binomial	Truncated Poisson
Iname_12	−0.784a	−0.784b	−0.838a
	0.368	0.367	0.408
Iname_13	−0.059	−0.059	−0.090
	0.333	0.333	0.460
Iname_14	0.412	0.412b	0.512
	0.266	0.266	0.337
Iname_16	−0.916a	−0.916a	−1.052a
	0.408	0.407	0.463
Iname_18	−0.135	−0.135	−0.185
	0.336	0.337	0.405
Iname_19	−0.032	−0.032	−0.091
	0.305	0.305	0.445

Notes:
Standard errors in small font.
[a] Significant at the 5 per cent level.
[b] Significant at the 10 per cent level.

16 Choice modeling of farmer preferences for agroforestry systems in Calakmul, Mexico
James F. Casey

16.1 Introduction

To this point we have heard plenty about the Contingent Valuation Method (CVM); its uses, benefits, different implementation strategies and its importance for policy. But, what about alternatives to CVM? Are there any? Why might we want an alternative? We may want an alternative for several reasons. First, Kahn, in (Prato, 1998) criticizes contingent valuation as being too narrow and only allowing for single attribute valuation. Second, as Opaluch and Swallow (1993) points out, it is easy to develop 'scores' for systems by simply using the coefficients on individual attributes and multiplying by a specific level of the attribute. Finally, CVM estimates may be biased upwards because of 'yea-saying' and a lack of consideration for substitutes (Stevens et al., 1997). An alternative to CVM is choice modeling (CM). Originally termed conjoint analysis and now commonly referred to as attribute-based methods (Holmes and Adamowicz, 2003) or choice experiments (Shrestha and Alavalapati, 2004), CM is now the most common alternative to CV for valuing non-market goods and services.

The rest of the chapter will answer two simple questions: (1) What is choice modeling?, and (2) How does one conduct a choice modeling experiment? The emphasis of this chapter is on question number 2 and a case study is used in order to illustrate how to conduct an actual choice modeling experiment. In combination with the chapter by Stewart and Kahn, this will allow the reader of the book to have a good understanding of the application of choice modeling to valuation problems.

16.2 What is choice modeling?

Choice modeling experiments are most common in the marketing and applied decision research literature (Adamowicz et al., 1994), yet the case for their use in economic analysis has been presented by McFadden (1974) in Adamowicz et al. (1994). Developments in the past 20 years by Louviere and Hensher (1983) and Louviere and Woodworth (1983) allow for choice experiments that meet the necessary and sufficient conditions to satisfy the statistical requirements of multinomial logit (MNL) choice models (Louviere, 1988). These discrete choice experiments provide the respondent with several different products or services and simply ask the respondent to identify the most-preferred alternative in the choice set. Unlike traditional rank-order or rating methods, this method does not require any assumptions to be made about order or cardinality of measurement (Louviere, 1988). A more important advantage of discrete choice modeling is that one can estimate choice models directly from choice data, and thus avoid the potentially unrealistic *ad hoc* assumptions about choice behavior that are implied by rating and/or ranking a single choice (Louviere, 1988). Additionally, the inclusion of a 'no choice' option, together with an opportunity cost attribute allows for estimates of conditional and absolute value (Rolfe et al., 2000). These value estimates can then be used to derive Hicksian welfare measures (McConnell, 1995).

16.2.1 Theoretical foundation for CM

The CM technique has a theoretical foundation in the random utility model (RUM). The RUM describes the utility associated with a given choice as being comprised of a systematic component and a stochastic component. The systematic component is observable to the researcher and the stochastic component is known only to the individual (Rolfe et al., 2000). Utility can be described by the following equation

$$Uij = Vij + eij \tag{16.1}$$

The observable component (Vij), can be disaggregated further into the attributes of the relevant good (Zij) and the characteristics of the individual (Si).

$$Uij = V(Zij, Si) + eij \tag{16.2}$$

The choice among alternatives is a function of the probability that utility associated with one alternative is higher than other alternatives in the given choice set (Rolfe et al., 2000)

$$P = \text{Prob } Vij + eij > Vih + eih; \text{ for all } h \text{ in the}$$
$$\text{choice set}, j \neq h \tag{16.3}$$

Assuming the utility function follows a linear path in the parameters and that the error terms are gumbel distributed leads to the convenient closed-form solution, the multinomial logit (MNL) (McFadden, 1974).

$$P = \exp(\lambda Vij)/\Sigma \exp(\lambda Vih) \text{ for all } h \text{ in the choice set} \tag{16.4}$$

The MNL model generates results for a conditional indirect utility function of the following form:

$$Vij = \lambda(B + B1Z1 + B2Z2 + BnZn + BaSa + BbSb + BmSj), \quad (16.5)$$

where $B1$ to Bn and Ba to Bm are the vector of coefficients attached to the vector of attributes Z and individual characteristics S. Welfare estimates can be derived using the following formula:

$$CS = -1/\alpha \, (\ln \Sigma \exp Vi0 - \ln \Sigma \exp Vi1), \quad (16.6)$$

where CS is the compensating surplus welfare measure and α is the marginal utility of income (Rolfe et al., 2000). Now, the marginal value of any change within a single attribute can be represented by the ratio of coefficients for equation (16.5) and (16.6) reduces to:

$$W = -1(Ba/B\$) \quad (16.7)$$

$B\$$ is the coefficient on the price variable. This is the part-worth, which effectively is the marginal rate of substitution between income change and the attribute in question. These theoretical underpinnings are also discussed in the chapter by Stewart and Kahn. Most recently, applications of CM have been used to estimate the non-use values of rainforest in Australia (Rolfe et al., 2000), improvements in water quality (Farber et al., 2000), preferences for forest management (Holmes and Adamowicz, 2003), and the environmental benefits of silvopasture practices (Shrestha and Alavalapati, 2004). Choice modeling experiments are particularly useful for valuing environmental commodities, as environmental programs may have several features and it is quite useful to divide the program into its different components to assess people's willingness to pay for each program attribute (Johnson et al., 1995). The same is true for agroforestry systems.

16.3   How to conduct a CM experiment

In order to illustrate the usefulness of CM, a case study is presented based on a project conducted in rural Mexico aimed at valuing the multiple attributes of agroforestry systems. Agroforestry systems are composed of many different components and provide numerous benefits, some market and some non-market. It is useful to know how farmers perceive the benefits of each of the components, which may be things such as shade for animals, soil fertility, watershed control, risk spreading, labor flexibility, or windbreaks. Choice modeling has the advantage of permitting the valuation of both the agroforestry system as a whole and the various attributes of the system. The technique allows respondents to evaluate tradeoffs among multiple attributes, encouraging respondent introspection, and facilitates consistency checks on response patterns (Johnson et al., 1995).

The experimental design phase of any choice modeling experiment is perhaps the most important element of the study. The importance of experimental design cannot be overstated. Opaluch and Swallow (1993) emphasizes this, stating that, 'If the experiment is not well-thought out from the beginning and precision is not taken in designing the survey instrument, then the information will be useless to the researcher.' There are several stages to this process, summarized in the following 4 steps:

1. Pre-information stage.
2. Designing and testing the choice experiments.
3. Pre-testing the survey instrument.
4. Implementation of the survey.

16.3.1   Pre-information stage

If the overall objective is to analyse potential agroforestry systems for their adoption potential and their value, or worth, as production strategies, it is important to develop systems that not only address physical problems of production, but do so in such a way that farmers will actually consider implementing them within an overall production strategy. Numerous agro-forestry projects have failed simply due to the lack of attention to the socio-economics of the situation. Hence, it is important to understand the existing social, economic, and ecological conditions in the area under question. To this end, relevant background material should be obtained and synthesized. A thorough secondary data retrieval and assessment at the beginning of the process will enhance the overall quality, uniformity, and efficiency of the evaluation (Mercer, 1993). This alone, however, is not sufficient and local land-use professionals as well as the farmers themselves needed to be included in this process.

Therefore, key informant interviews and focus groups need to be conducted with local agricultural and forestry extension people. In addition to this, focus groups and informal interviews with farmers are highly recommended at this stage of the process in order to determine if local extension people and farmers view local problems the same way.

To this end, it was necessary to develop a list of key questions for debate in the focus groups. In this study, the list consisted of the following questions to prompt some insightful debate with both farmers and technical experts (see Table 16.1).

Lack of water resources, lack of transportation, pestilence, lack of technical training, and the rigidity of tree delivery from local nurseries were

Table 16.1   Questions for local farmers and extension agents

---
1. What are the main limits to production?
2. What are some ideas to improve production?
3. What things should be considered when implementing a new system?
4. How can agroforestry address questions 1–3?

---

some of the problems identified by both farmers and technical experts. When exploring and considering the implementation of new and/or additional production systems some of the key variables identified were: meeting self-consumption needs, consistent production over time (i.e. minimizing variance in output), and immediate returns to labor (i.e. high discounting by farmers). Farmers saw agroforestry as a way to diversify outputs and combine short-term returns (i.e. crops) with long-term investment such as timber-producing trees.

16.3.2   Designing and testing the choice experiment
The focus groups provided a cumulative list of what I considered to be the most important characteristics for evaluation by the farmers. This yielded 17 potential attributes for farmers to evaluate as components of an agroforestry system. The attributes were categorized as (1) essential, (2) secondary, and (3) non-essential. This allowed the research team to choose more efficiently which attributes to include in the initial testing of the conjoint question. Table 16.2 lists these attributes and their rating.

This list was then narrowed to the following eight attributes: labor, time for production, value of production, non-market benefits, flexibility in planting, weeding schedule, pest control, and the price of wood. The next step required combining these attributes into potential agroforestry systems. This was done using the Breton–Clark conjoint design software. Fractional factorial designs were used to construct sets of choices. The use of orthogonal fractional designs ensures that each of the separate alternatives is independent across sets (Louviere and Woodworth, 1983). A result is that, the odds of choosing alternative A in relation to alternative B is constant regardless of what other alternatives are present. It has been shown that a $2N$ factorial design can be used to put N choice alternatives into choice sets such that the parameters of MNL models, estimated from choices made in response to the design, will be near optimal in statistical efficiency (Louviere and Woodworth, 1983). Also, Louviere and Woodworth (1983) note that orthogonal main effects designs ensure independence across all alternatives. That is, the attributes of agroforestry system A will be independent of those in system B, as long as the design is orthogonal.

Table 16.2   Preliminary attributes for
agroforestry systems

Attribute importance	
Labor	Essential
Time for Production	Essential
Value of Production	Essential
Non-market benefits	Essential
Flexibility of Planting	Essential
Weeding Schedule	Essential
Pest Control	Essential
Price of Wood	Secondary
Capital Accumulation	Non-essential
Investment of Excess Labor	Non-essential
Technical Assistance	Essential
Location of Trees	Non-essential
Additions to System	Non-essential
Planting Densities	Essential
Overall Goal of System	Non-essential
Place of Establishment	Non-essential
Types of Products	Essential

16.3.3   Pre-testing

Once a list of potential systems was developed, the next step was to determine if the systems made sense to the farmers. At this point, the survey was ready for testing. Our survey consisted of 36 total questions and was broken into five sections. Section 1 contains general socio-economic questions. Section 2 is concerned with farming activities in general. Section 3 asks the producer about tree planting activities. Section 4 is the conjoint experiment, and section 5 concludes with a contingent valuation question and closing comments. The survey instrument was specifically designed to facilitate thinking about production strategies from the general to the specific, with final emphasis on planting trees on farms. This is the appropriate time in the development of the survey to answer such pertinent questions as: (1) Do the farmers understand the question? (2) How many attributes can be included in each system? (3) How many choices will each farmer make before becoming tired and disinterested? (4) How do farmers seem to make their choices; do they consider the whole system or do they focus on one or two characteristics?

At this stage, I discovered: (1) the farmers did understand the question; (2) eight attributes seemed to be a lot of information to evaluate at once, so we narrowed this to five attributes; (3) seven or eight choices appeared

Table 16.3   Attributes and levels for choice modeling survey

Attribute	Level 1	Level 2	Level 3
Labor Requirement	Low	Medium	High
Technical Assistance	One year	Three years	Five years
Forest Conservation	No impact	Improved in future	Worse in future
Plant Availability	Work in nursery	Pay for delivery	Look in forest
Products from System	Timber and crops	Fruit, timber and crops	Timber only

to be the limit for the farmers (initially 15 were tried). The literature pertaining to this question says up to 20 choices can be made, but in this particular context of interviewing primarily illiterate farmers, 20 choices could not even be considered. And (4) the farmers seemed to consider the entire system and to not just focus on one all-important attribute.

16.3.4   Implementation

In the choice modeling experiment, the five attributes listed in Table 16.3 were combined at varying levels to create the hypothetical agroforestry systems. For example, a system may include the following attributes: three years of technical assistance, the farmer must pay for seedlings, the system will increase forest cover in the future, and the farmer will produce fruit, timber and crops (see Figure 16.1).

The total population for sampling consists of all the communities participating in CONSEJO, which is the regional council for development in Calakmul. Considerations at this point revolved around the basic question

Please Choose System A or B

A	B
medium	Low
3 years assistance	1 years assistance
pay for seedlings	work in nursery
increase forest cover	the forest will be the same
produce fruit, timber and crops	produce timber and crops

Figure 16.1   Example of choice question

of whether it is more important to cover a larger area and less people in each community, or to concentrate on fewer communities and more people in each one. This decision should depend on local circumstances and the resources available to your survey team. The survey was conducted in a minimum of 20 per cent of the communities and a minimum of 20 per cent of the population in each community were interviewed. Ejidos were randomly selected from two strata. One strata consisted of ejidos in the northwest region and the other in the southeast. The rationale here is that there is more rainfall to the southeast, and rainfall should impact the choice of a production system. Also, within each ejido, a completely random sample of individuals to interview was selected from the ejido register in each community. All of this took place from August 1997 to January 1997.

16.4 Estimation of models and results

Since the dependent variable in a choice modeling experiment only takes on discrete values, i.e. 1 or 0, an OLS estimating procedure is inappropriate (MacKenzie, 1990). Therefore, the choice of an agroforestry system is estimated as a logistic regression. The equation estimated is:

$$\text{Choice} = \text{alpha} + b(\text{labor}) + b(\text{assistance}) + b(\text{prod 1}) + b(\text{prod 2}) + b(\text{plant 1}) + b(\text{plant 2}) + b(\text{cons 1}) + b(\text{cons 2}) \quad (16.8)$$

In the above equation, labor is the number of days to implement the agroforestry system. Assistance is the number of years for which you will receive technical assistance. Prod 1 is a system that produces timber and crops. Prod 2 is a system that produces fruit, timber, and crops. Plant 1 means the farmer will work in a nursery in order to obtain seedlings. Plant 2 represents the system whereby the farmer must pay for the delivery of seedlings. Cons 1 is the variable for keeping the environment the same, and Cons 2 represents improving the environment.

16.4.1 Results

Two simple models that include only the attribute levels and a full model that also includes socio-economic variables are estimated. The first simple model includes (labor) and (assist) as continuous variables and the second simple model includes them as discrete variables. Therefore, I will refer to the models as: (1) simple-continuous (SC), (2) simple-discrete (SD), and (3) full. Most attributes in the model are statistically significant at conventional levels and signs are as expected except for the labor variable. Unfortunately, the probability that an individual will choose a particular system increases with increasing labor costs[1].

Needless to say, this was not expected and precludes the development of welfare estimates. In spite of this, however, alternatives can still be ranked based on the part-worths. Again, the part-worths relate how important each attribute level is relative to the others. This allows for comparison between individual levels of attributes and the derivation of scores for agroforestry systems, based on combinations of individual attribute levels. Even though I am unable to derive welfare estimates, useful comparative information can still be derived. Referring to equation (16.7), the marginal tradeoff between two attribute levels can be examined, as each of the coefficients represents the 'part-worth' (Louviere, 1988) of that level of the attribute. For example, if the coefficient on A is 0.5 and the coefficient on B is 0.25, then A is 'worth' twice as much as B (see Table 16.4).

Table 16.4   Logistic regression results

Variable	Simple discrete Coef.	Simple continuous Coef.	Full model Coef.
Constant	-1.38***	-1.91***	-2.41***
	(0.138)	(0.174)	(0.311)
LABOR	–	0.006**	0.006**
		(0.003)	(0.002)
High	0.211*	–	–
	(0.128)		
Low	-0.08	–	–
	(0.106)		
ASSIST	–	0.117***	0.118***
		(0.032)	(0.032)
1 year	-0.223**	–	–
	(0.114)		
5 years	0.227**	–	–
	(0.111)		
Prod 1	0.207	0.241**	0.246**
	(0.122)	(0.121)	(0.121)
Prod 2	0.571***	0.602***	0.609***
	(0.107)	(0.107)	(0.107)
Plant 1	0.555***	0.552***	0.557***
	(0.106)	(0.106)	(0.106)
Plant 2	0.119	0.171	0.172
	(0.122)	(0.121)	(0.121)
Cons 1	0.297**	0.288***	0.289***
	(0.122)	(0.122)	(0.122)
Cons 2	0.825***	0.822***	0.829***
	(0.109)	(0.108)	(0.109)

Table 16.4   (continued)

	Simple discrete	Simple continuous	Full model
Forestry experience	–	–	0.152
			(0.068)
Farm hectares	–	–	0.007
			(0.003)
Age	–	–	0.004
			(0.004)
Number of children	–	–	−0.029
			(0.019)
Years on lot	–	–	0.013
			(0.008)
Forest area	–	–	−0.006
			(0.004)
Tree planting	–	–	−0.015
			(0.018)
Education	–	–	−0.042
			(0.069)
Previous experience	–	–	−0.098
			(0.071)
Honey cultivators	–	–	−0.288
			(0.234)
Participation	–	–	0.098
			(0.099)
Harvesting trees	–	–	−0.145
			(0.136)
$N =$	2182	2168	2168
Chi2 (10)	158.33	(8)161.27	(20)181.65
Log Likelihood	1379.6	1369.4	1359.2

The simple-discrete model allows for a fuller inspection of the labor and technical assistance variables. Using the missing dummy variable as a baseline, it is possible to determine if there are significant differences in preferences for the other levels of the attribute.

In the full model, the two additional variables that influence the choice decision are the amount of forestry experience and the total area of the farm. Both of these variables are positively related to choosing an agroforestry system. The rest of the socio-economic variables hypothesized to influence the choice decision are not significantly different from zero.

Farmers exhibit negative utility for working five or ten days (LOW) and positive utility for working 40 or 50 days (HIGH). The difference between

Table 16.5   Marginal value of labor

Labor	Part-worth
Low	−0.08
Medium	0.00
High	0.211

Table 16.6   Marginal value of forest conservation

Environment	Part-worth
Worse	0.00
Same	0.297
Better	0.825

LOW and MEDIUM (20 or 30 days) is not significant, but farmers do exhibit significant differences in their preference for HIGH v. MEDIUM. Again, it is possible that farmers interpreted this variable as a 'quality' or 'output' attribute, and not the cost of the agroforestry system (see Table 16.5).

An especially interesting and important result is the part-worth of the environment attribute. Improving the environment, described in the experiment as increasing forest cover (BETTER), is the most important attribute level of all those included in the model. And, the result is robust across all three specifications. Farmer preferences for improving forest cover (BETTER) compared with keeping the environment the same (SAME) are almost four times as strong, and both of these options are significantly preferred to the option of reducing forest cover (WORSE).

All technical assistance coefficients are significant at the 0.05 level. From a policy perspective this is an important variable. There is a significant difference between receiving one of technical assistance and the baseline of three years. Not surprisingly three years is preferred to one, and five years is preferred to three.

As expected, more product diversity is better. There is no significant difference between timber only and timber and crops, but the option of all three products is preferred to the others. Since the timber only option and the timber with crops option are not significantly different, yet the addition of fruit to the system is significantly preferred, we can interpret this as a strong preference for fruit trees as part of an agroforestry system. This result makes intuitive sense, because fruit trees provide a relatively rapid return, whereas timber trees are a longer-term investment.

Table 16.7   Marginal value of
              technical assistance

Technical assistance	Part-worth
1 year	– 0.223
3 years	0.00
5 years	0.227

Table 16.8   Marginal value of production

Products	Part-worth
Timber & Crops	0.207
Fruit, Timber & Crops	0.571
Timber	0.000

Table 16.9   Marginal value of plant
              availability

Plant availability	Part-worth
Work in nursery	0.555
Pay for delivery	0.119
Collect from forest	0.000

In terms of plant availability, the most preferred option is to work in a nursery and receive seedlings. Again, from a policy perspective, this is important and valuable information. This result supports the on-going efforts in the Yucatan aimed at developing small nurseries.

16.4.2   Concluding the case study

In order to address concerns related to the behavior of subsistence farmers with respect to their use of agroforestry, a CM experiment was used in order to access the importance of five characteristics of agroforestry systems. These characteristics were (1) cost, (2) conservation of forest resources, (3) method of obtaining seedlings, (4) years of technical assistance, and (5) diversity of outputs. CM was chosen in order to address issues concerning multiple attributes, substitution, and the development of reliable 'scores' (Opaluch, 1993). The initial attempt to derive welfare estimates was thwarted due to problems with the cost characteristic, but all other characteristics are still useful and comparisons can still be made between all the other attribute levels. This is important, because, if a CV study had been conducted, we would have been left without any useful information because of the confusion with the cost variable.

Not all is lost with a CM study and perhaps this is one of the greatest benefits of CM. The time and effort that went into the experiment still provides useful information pertaining to the relative value of system attributes. Although these values are not absolute values, they are comparable and allow for policy choices to be determined based on actual tradeoffs, such as working for seedlings versus paying for them, or receiving three years of technical assistance versus five years. Again, we do not have a willingness to pay estimate for having a nursery or receiving three years of assistance, but we know a nursery is preferred to the alternative of paying for seedlings and five years of assistance is preferable to three.

16.5   Conclusion

The primary purpose of this chapter was to introduce an alternative to the contingent valuation method and provide a step-by-step guide on how to conduct a choice modeling experiment. If the reader is interested in a fuller account, the history and development of choice modeling can be found in Holmes and Adamowicz (2003).

In the end, there is no panacea for dealing with the limitations of non-market valuation. However, CM as an alternative to CVM has the added ability to model more complex choice decisions and to frame choices consistent with real-life decisions. Additionally, as this case study pointed out, all is not lost with the CM experiment if there is confusion with the 'cost' variable. It is still possible to gain information about trade-offs, but without the welfare measures associated with these preferences. Choice modeling and the contingent valuation method should not be seen as substitutes, rather they should be viewed as potential complements for enhancing our understanding of preferences not borne out in markets. Ultimately it is up to the researcher to determine what preference elicitation method to use and how to implement it in the field.

Note

1. I hypothesize that farmers interpreted the cost variable as a 'quality/output' variable. They may have interpreted more work-days as more output or higher quality for the system. The only way to test this hypothesis will be to return to Calakmul and re-interview each farmer.

References

Adamowicz, W., J. Louviere and M. Williams (1994), 'Combining revealed and stated preference methods for valuing environmental amenities', *Journal of Environmental Economics and Management*, **26**, 271–92.

Carlsson, Fredrik, Peter Frykblom and Carolina Liljenstolpe (2003), 'Valuing wetland attributes: an application of choice experiments', *Ecological Economics*, **47**, 95–103.

Farber, Stephen and Brian Griner (2000), 'Valuing watershed quality improvements using conjoint analysis', *Ecological Economics*, **34**.

Holmes, Thomas P. and Wiktor L. Adamowicz (2003), *Attribute-based methods: A Primer on Non-Market Valuation*, P. Champ, T. Brown and K. Boyle (eds), Dordrecht, The Netherlands: Kluwer Academic Publishers.

Johnson, F.R. and W.H. Desvousges (1995), 'Conjoint analysis of individual and aggregate environmental preferences', TER Technical Working Paper No. T-9502.

Louviere, J.J. (1988), *Analyzing Decision Making: Metric Conjoint Analysis*, Newbury, CA: Sage Publications.

Louviere, J.J. (1988), 'Conjoint analysis modeling of stated preferences', *Journal of Transport Economics and Policy*, January, 93–119.

Louviere, J.J. and D.A. Hensher (1983), 'Using discrete choice models with experimental design data to forecast consumer demand for a unique cultural event', *Journal of Consumer Research*, **10**.

Louviere, J. and G. Woodworth (1983), 'Design and analysis of simulated consumer choice or allocation experiments: an approach based on aggregate data', *Journal of Marketing research*, **20**, November.

McConnell, K.E (1995), 'Consumer surplus from discrete choice models', *Journal of Environmental Economics and Management*, **29**, 263–70.

McFadden, D. (1974), 'Conditional logit analysis of qualitative choice behavior', in P. Zarembka (ed.), *Frontiers in Econometrics*, New York: Academic Press.

Mercer, D.E. (1993), 'A framework for analyzing the socio-economic impacts of agroforestry projects', FPEI working paper No. 52.

Opaluch, James and Stephen Swallow (1993), 'Evaluating impacts from noxious facilities: including public preferences in current siting mechanisms', *Journal of Environmental Economics and Management*, **24**(1).

Prato, Tony (1998), *Natural Resource and Environmental Economics*, Ames, Iowa: The Iowa State University Press.

Rolfe, John, Jeff Barnett and Jordan Louviere (2000), 'Choice modeling and its potential application to tropical rainforest preservation', *Ecological Economics*, **35**.

Shrestha, Ram K. and Janaki R.R. Alavalapati (2004), 'Valuing environmental benefits of silvopasture practice: a case study of the Lake Okeechobee watershed in Florida', *Ecological Economics*, **49**, 349–59.

Stevens, Thomas H., Christopher Barrett and Cleve E. Willis (1997), 'Conjoint analysis of groundwater protection programs', *Agricultural and Resource Economics Review*.

17 The use of contingent valuation in developing countries: a quantitative analysis
Dan Biller, Karoline Rogge and Giovanni Ruta[1]

17.1 Introduction

The past three decades have witnessed an expansion in academic and professional journals, of economic valuation methods of public goods, public bads and externalities, especially those targeting environmental problems. Despite significant improvements in the understanding of economic values and methods to measure them in the presence of market failures, economic valuation is yet to reach policy making, and even projects, with the same level of success as in academia. While advancements in environmental laws and regulations design and implementation, law suits, other environmental policy instruments and priority setting exercises suggest that techniques to assess the economic value of environmental issues would be in high demand, environmental policy makers and project managers, who could in principle be major users of economic valuation, are often resistant. At the policy, planning, program, and project level, economic valuation in broad terms, and more specifically the contingent valuation method, are viewed with suspicion. Several explanations for the skepticism are given but tend to fall into three broad categories: (1) The advantages of undertaking economic valuation are unclear; (2) there are many environmental issues that cannot be 'monetized' or have a price tag placed upon them; and (3) economic valuation, especially CV, is difficult to do and costly to undertake.

Items (1) and (2) have been addressed in detail in the literature. While these items are also discussed in this chapter, item (3) is its main focus. The chapter is divided into six sections. The following section clarifies the advantages on undertaking economic valuation, briefly discusses different forms of values and provides a rationale for carrying out a simple quantitative analysis to study the motivation to engage in contingent valuation (CV) studies in developing countries. While data availability is limited, the third section describes in detail the available data against different clustering frameworks directly linked to environmental issues. The fourth section presents an initial statistical analysis, which indicates that CV can be particularly useful for middle-income countries. Through a logit model, the fifth section analyses the choice of CV study *vis-à-vis* the perceived environmental priorities of countries. Finally, the last section presents the concluding remarks.

17.2 Rationale

Economic valuation methods of public goods, public bads, and externalities have dominated much of the research agenda on environmental economics over the past 30 years. The level of acceptance of different methods varies, but none has generated as much controversy as CV methods. Questions about CV span from theoretical to empirical, and, while controversial and perhaps because of it, CV has been quite successful in reaching academic journals.

Many developed and developing countries have environmental impact assessment (EIA) laws and regulations, requiring the analysis of project alternatives. In some countries, these regulations are often well established, dating back to the 1970s and early 1980s and serve as the basis for environmental policy. Some countries are incorporating strategic environmental assessments (SEA) into their laws and regulations, which are specifically designed to target policies, plans, and programs. Yet, with few exceptions, economic valuation seldom plays a role in environmental policy making and in the analysis of environmental impacts of projects.

To a certain extent, this situation is replicated in multilateral organizations. For example, the World Bank's Operational Policy (OP) 10.04 on economic evaluation of investment operations and Bank Procedure (BP) 10.04 set out the requirements for investment projects economic analysis. BP 10.04 specifies that the economic evaluation of projects integrates financial, institutional, technical, sociological, and environmental considerations. Yet, other World Bank documents recognize the difficulties associated with economic valuation of public goods, public bads, and externalities and its use is still limited regardless of the fact that a need has been underscored for over a decade (Silva and Pagiola, 2003).

Economic valuation is often believed to have powers that it neither has nor claims to have. In fact, while providing an estimate of value where there is a market failure, this estimate is often only a subset of the total economic value. Alternatively, environmental policy makers are often quick to dismiss estimations due to associated uncertainties and necessary caveats. Yet, both sides miss some key benefits of undertaking economic valuation of market failures, especially those related to the environment. The main purpose of valuation as related to environmental policy making is to foster better decision making. Economic valuation assists in priority setting by providing systematic and consistent approaches to policy problems. It facilitates the choice among alternatives in a manner that approximates the maximum social welfare, which is a key aspect of policy making. Moreover, economic valuation methods provide a consistent approach to the estimation of the level of policy instruments focusing on addressing market failures. Identifying and calculating the values facilitate capturing the related benefits by providing information that is relevant to the interested parties. This should be an integral part of policies, plans, programs, and projects at the design, appraisal, implementation, and evaluation phases (OECD, 2002; OECD, 2003; Waller-Hunter and Biller, 2001).

The argument that there are many environmental issues that cannot be 'monetized' or have a 'price tag' placed upon them implies a different set of values that economic valuation is unable to capture. In essence, this set of values does not conform to the concept of total economic value that has been widely discussed in the environmental economics literature.[2] This different value system has been specially underscored on issues related to biodiversity, and may have important policy considerations as stated in OECD (2002):

> While much of the conservation literature debates the economic and the non-economic approaches, the more relevant issue is what questions the different approaches are best suited to answering. If the issue is awareness raising, all approaches are probably relevant: arguments that appeal to some people will not appeal to others. If the issue is one of choosing between losses of biodiversity in order to make gains in other areas, the economic approach is potentially very useful, but so is an informed participatory debate in which economic aspects are one ingredient. Some values, however, do not lend themselves easily to making choices. Notions of 'intrinsic value', 'primary value' and 'spiritual value', for example, would all be relevant to awareness raising, but may not assist in making choices that necessarily involve sacrifices. In some contexts the primacy of these non-economic values will simply make the consideration of economic opportunity costs appear irrelevant.
>
> . . . A distinction between intrinsic and anthropocentric approaches can frequently be detected in debates about resource allocation. Those who believe that biodiversity has an intrinsic value – a value 'in itself' and independent of human valuation – will want to argue that it cannot be traded against notions of resource cost because: (a) intrinsic value cannot be measured; and, (b) cost is an anthropocentric concept which cannot be compared to intrinsic value. Those who accept that all decisions about conservation involve costs may prefer to see the benefits of conservation brought directly into comparison with those costs; a view that underlies the economic approach.
>
> Perhaps the most useful point that can be made is that the different approaches need to be articulated clearly and then applied to the questions that are likely to be relevant in terms of policy decisions.

While the use of economic valuation in environmental policy making and project analysis is still relatively incipient, there are signs indicating that policy makers and project managers are becoming less resistant to its use of economic valuation. While indicating that there is substantial scope for growth, a recent review of the World Bank portfolio found that the use of environmental valuation has increased from one project in 162 in the last decade to as many as one third of the projects in recent years (Silva and Pagiola, 2003). Even in important international fora addressing biodiversity, the use of economic valuation in environmental policy making is being stimulated. For example, via Decision IV/10, the Conference of the Parties (COP) to the Convention on Biological Diversity (CBD) acknowledges that 'economic valuation of biodiversity and biological resources is an important tool for well-targeted and calibrated economic incentive measures', and encourages the Parties to 'take into account economic, social, cultural, and ethical valuation in the development of relevant incentive measures' (UNEP, 1998).

Resistance to economic valuation, especially CV, also comes from the claim that it is difficult to do and costly to undertake. Yet, stated preference methods in general and CV in particular are necessary in estimating non-use values. Given the controversies surrounding CV, the US National Oceanic and Atmospheric Administration (NOAA) convened an expert panel that offered a set of guidelines on the CV process. The recommendations focus on a set of guidelines that should be followed if CV is to provide information about non-use values of sufficient quality to pass scrutiny linked to legal compensation for environmental damage (Arrow et al., 1993). These guidelines are now covering all CV studies. They include:

- Use personal interviews
- Use a willingness to pay (WTP) measure rather than willingness to accept compensation (WTA)
- Use a dichotomous choice format
- Adequately pre-test the survey instrument
- Carefully pre-test any photographs used
- Use an accurate scenario description
- Favor a conservative design (more likely to under rather than over-estimate WTP)
- Deflect warm glows (overstatement of WTP to appear generous)
- Check temporal consistency of results
- Use a representative sample (rather than a convenience sample)
- Remind respondents of undamaged substitutes
- Remind respondents of budget constraints
- Provide a no answer or don't know options
- Include follow-up questions to the valuation question
- Cross-tabulate the results
- Check respondents understanding.

OECD (2002) indicates that:

> CVM [Method] is likely to be most reliable for valuing environmental gains, particularly when familiar goods are considered, such as local recreational amenities . . . The most reliable studies (i.e. those that have passed the most stringent validity tests and avoided severe 'embedding' whereby values are not sensitive to the quantity of the good being offered) appear to have been those that have valued high profile species or elements that are familiar to respondents. In other cases, the need to provide information to elicit reliable values is a limit to both CVM and other attribute based choice models.

While cost estimates to apply the NOAA guidelines or even to undertake any CV study are likely to be site and country specific, the guidelines implicitly indicate that CV studies are labor intensive and more importantly dependent on skilled labor. This suggests that CV may indeed be costly and difficult to undertake, restricting its potential use in environmental policy and indicating that the concern voiced by environmental policy makers and project managers is justified. This would be particularly severe in developing countries, where traditionally there is a shortage of skilled human capital even if existing unskilled labor tends to be abundant.

On the other hand, several developing countries have made significant progress in improving the skills of its labor force by investing in education. In addition, awareness of environmental problems has increased throughout the world. While it is difficult to capture costs or undertake CV studies in specific countries and data on tertiary education is often lacking, the changes aforementioned could be captured through other data such as income. In addition, one would expect that the research agenda reflects the environmental concerns existing in the countries, especially if one is targeting developing countries where overall financial and human capital constraints diminish the likelihood that economic research focuses on theory as opposed to policy. A recent survey and very comprehensive study provides the necessary data to provide a quantitative analysis of the use of CV in developing countries. This study is arguably the most complete compilation of CV studies from around the world and provides a unique opportunity to undertake a simple analysis of the motivation behind CV use in developing countries and its possible links to environmental policy making.

17.3 Summary statistics
Based on Carson (forthcoming)[3] and its 5571 references, we identified 250 country-specific CV studies undertaken in 73 different developing countries.[4] Figure 17.1 shows that only 16 of these countries contributed to 57 per cent of the CV studies, namely 143 studies. According to the *World Development Indicators* (2005), of these 16 countries, seven are low

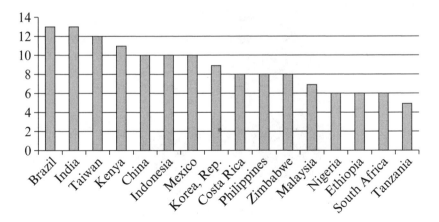

Figure 17.1   Developing countries with largest number of CV studies

income (LI) economies (gross national income (GNI) per capita of $766 or less in 2002), four lower middle income (LMI) (GNI per capita above $766 up to $3035), three upper middle income (UMI) (GNI per capita within $3035 to $3385) and two high income (HI) economies (GNI per capita of $9076 or more). In Section 2 we discuss if income can explain the number of studies.

Figure 17.2 shows that 71 per cent of the 250 contingent valuation studies address environmental issues. Of these 177 studies, 102 analysed the so-called green issues – natural resource management (41 per cent of all studies); that is, renewable and non-renewable natural resources, biodiversity, ecosystem services, and recreation. About one third of the studies, namely 75 studies, address brown issues, such as the pollution of air, water, soil, or coastal areas.

We can further break down the types of green studies as done in Figure 17.3. The majority of green studies are motivated by tourism or recreational concerns (56 per cent of all green studies, or 58 studies). About a third of green studies, or 36 studies, address numerous typical green issues, such as the management of forest and fish resources, the valuation of ecosystems and biodiversity. Six out of the 16 studies examining agricultural values were related to green issues, such as aesthetic landscape, making up 6 per cent of all green studies.

Brown studies (Figure 17.4) most often address water and sanitation (38 per cent of all brown studies, that is, 28 studies), while another third of brown studies address a variety of air, water, soil, and coastal pollution problems (35 per cent, or 26 studies). Health concerns are also important subject of analysis (12 per cent of all brown studies, or nine studies).

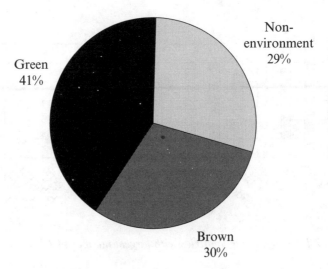

*Figure 17.2   Environmental v. non-environmental CV studies in developing
countries (*N = 250*)*

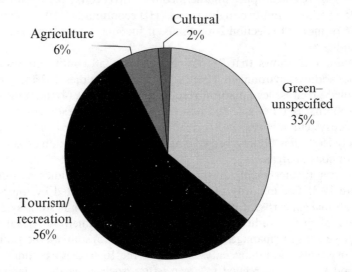

*Figure 17.3   Break down of green studies (*N = 102*)*

Most of the 73 CV studies that are neither addressing green nor brown
issues examine willingness to pay (WTP) for infrastructure investments such
as better water supply; that is, 40 per cent of all non-environmental studies,
or 28 studies fall into a subsection of water and sanitation (Figure 17.5).

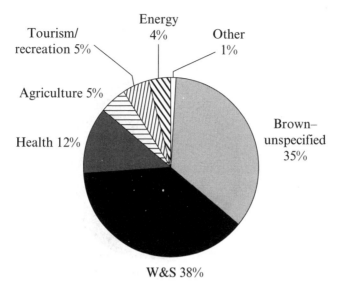

Figure 17.4   Break down of brown studies (N = 75)

As these studies are dealing with infrastructure investments for water supply (a service), we excluded them from environmentally related studies. With almost one third of all non-environmental CV studies, health concerns play a major role as well (28 per cent, or 23 studies). The remainder of the non-environmental studies is divided between agriculture (six studies), the analysis of willingness to pay for cultural values and the preservation of cultural heritage (five studies), housing (five studies), transport (three studies), energy sector (two studies), and others (three studies).

Another way of looking at these data is to distinguish between income and geographical location. We have grouped the 73 developing countries into four income categories according to the *World Development Indicators* (World Bank, 2005): low income (LI), lower middle income (LMI), upper middle income (UMI), and high income (HI). Figure 17.6 provides insights into the distribution of the type of CV studies (environmental, green or brown, non-environmental) with regard to the income group. While non-environmentally related CV studies are the first priority for low-income economies, followed by green and then brown studies, all higher-income groups had the smallest number of studies in non-environmental subject matters. For lower-middle-income economies, the trend is reversed: ranking highest are brown studies, followed by green, and then non-environmental studies. However, disregarding the income category, when adding green and brown studies, the majority of CV studies are environmental ones.

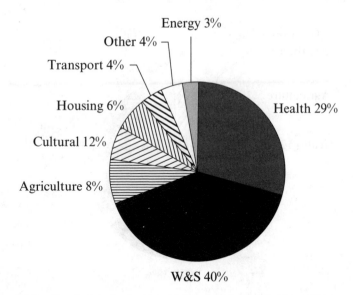

*Figure 17.5   Break down of non-environmental studies (*N *= 73)*

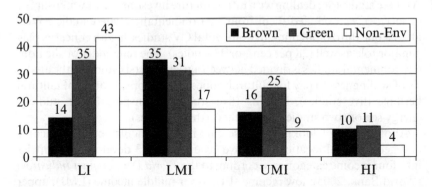

Figure 17.6   Number and type of CV studies per income group

With regard to the geographical location, we divided the 73 developing countries into groups loosely related to the five World Bank regions, namely Sub-Saharan Africa (AFR), East Asia and Pacific (EAP), Europe and Central Asia (ECA), Latin America and Caribbean (LAR), Middle East and North Africa (MNA), and South Asia (SAR). We include a sixth category ('Other'), other countries that are either higher-income non-borrowing or are not World Bank members. The appendix contains the

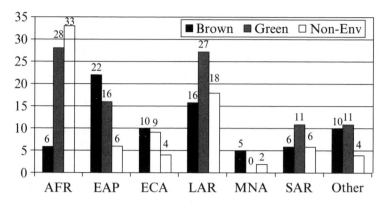

Figure 17.7   Number and type of CV studies per World Bank region

countries according to the above classification. Figure 17.7 shows the distribution of CV studies across regions.[5]

17.4   The triggers of contingent valuation research

Figure 17.1 shows very large discrepancies between countries in terms of number of CV studies conducted. Here the concern is with regard to what determines the number of studies in a given country. We test the hypothesis that income per capita and population are relevant variables affecting the number of CV studies performed. Regression results are shown in Table 17.1.

The regression shows that population is positively related to the frequency of the studies: bigger countries perform more studies than smaller ones. The results also show that both income per capita and income per capita squared are significant at the 5 per cent level. Countries with higher per capita income tend to have more CV studies but only up to a certain point. After a certain level of income the model predicts that the number of CV studies actually decreases. This is shown by the negative coefficient for the square of income per capita.

Figure 17.8 shows a scatter plot of the number of studies against per capita income. We fitted a quadratic line to the data so that the 'inverted U-shaped curve' can be represented. Applying the parameters to a hypothetical country, the number of CV studies performed would increase up to a per capita income of about US$11 000 and decrease after that level. Care should be taken with this result as our sample only has three countries with per capita income higher than US$11 000.

This result tends to back the hypothesis that CV studies are likely to be mostly undertaken in countries that have sufficient skilled human capital but labor costs and other costs are not yet high. For poorer countries, the

Table 17.1   Regression results: Studies = a0 + a1 pop + a2 gnipc + a3 gnipc2 + error

					Number of obs	67
					F(3, 63)	10.39
					Prob > F	0
					R-squared	0.3309
					Adj R-squared	0.2991
					Root MSE	2.7588
studies	Coef.	Std. Err.	t	P>t	[95% Conf.	Interval]
pop	9.02E-09	1.72e-09	5.250	0	5.59E-09	1.25E-08
gnipc	0.000594	0.0002301	2.581	0.012	0.0001341	0.0010538
gnipc2	−2.52E-08	1.05e-08	−2.389	0.02	−4.62E-08	−4.12E-09
_cons	1.906632	0.5504124	3.464	0.001	0.8067207	3.006543

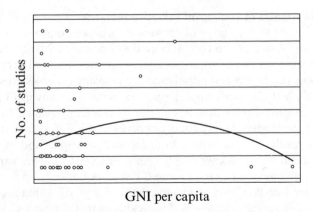

Figure 17.8   An environmental Kuznets curve for CV studies

lack of skilled labor probably precludes CV studies being undertaken in a cost effective manner (labor and capital to undertake it would often be 'imported'). Alternatively, for richer countries, while skilled labor and other inputs are available, they tend to be costly.

Another interpretation of the result is that as countries get richer they can benefit more from valuation studies for decision making or policy advice. At higher levels of income, cost of skilled labor may kick in and diminish the demand for CV studies. In other words, the demand for CV studies grows with income but alternative more cost-effective decision-making tools may become more attractive at higher level of incomes.

In general, the result illustrated in Figure 17.8 implicitly indicates that CV studies have a particular role to play in environmental policy making in middle-income countries, where the appropriate combination of policy need and national inputs is likely to be found.

17.5 The determinants of study types

We divided environmental studies between green studies, measuring WTP for natural resources, and brown studies, focusing on pollution problems. In order to test the hypothesis that study type (i.e. green v. brown) reflects a country's specific environment agenda, we used a logit model.

In particular, our model tests whether the probability of a green versus brown study depends on the following country characteristics: (a) income per capita; (b) urban population, as per cent of total; (c) threatened birds, number; (d) threatened plants, number; (e) PM_{10}[6] damages, as percentage of GNI; (f) water access, as percentage of population; (g) sanitation access, as percentage of population. In particular, the threatened birds and plants variables capture the level of stress on natural habitats and ecosystems (a green problem). A third biodiversity variable, 'threatened mammal', was excluded as it was highly correlated with the other two. The PM_{10} damages, water and sanitation access variables, capture the importance of pollution issues (a brown problem).

The dependent variable is a discrete variable that takes the value of 1 if a study refers to a green issue and takes a value of 0 if the study refers to a brown issue. The model thus measures the relationship between the occurrence of certain country characteristics and the probability of having in that country a CV study dealing with green issues rather than brown issues. The choice of explanatory variables is linked to assumptions about the factors that are likely to justify a CV study by the country or by international researchers. The availability of information has been a practical constraint to having a larger set of variables.

The results are shown in Table 17.2.

We tested the null hypothesis that all coefficients are zero and we could reject the null hypothesis at the 1 per cent significance level. The chosen specification is useful in answering two key questions:

1. Is the probability of green (rather than brown) studies linked to per capita income?
2. Does the type of studies undertaken reflect country specific environmental problems?

Table 17.2   Logit model estimation: logit green gnipc urban birds plants
            PM_{10} *dam water sanit*

Logit estimates			Number of obs		=	137
			LR chi2(7)		=	29.24
			Prob > chi2		=	0.0001
Log likelihood = −79.0216			Pseudo R2		=	0.1561
Green	Coef.	Std. Err.	z	$P > z$	[95% Conf. Interval]	
gnipc	0.000381	0.000139	2.744	0.006	0.000109	0.000654
Urban	−0.0185	0.017327	−1.067	0.286	−0.05246	0.015465
birds	−0.01739	0.0128	−1.359	0.174	−0.04248	0.007694
plants	0.008921	0.00361	2.471	0.013	0.001845	0.015997
PM_{10} dam	−1.52613	0.745272	−2.048	0.041	−2.98684	−0.06543
water	−0.03195	0.018559	−1.721	0.085	−0.06832	0.004429
sanit	−0.00683	0.011908	−0.574	0.566	−0.03017	0.016507
_cons	3.573882	1.362426	2.623	0.009	0.903576	6.244187

To answer the first question, we focus on the parameter for income per capita (variable 'gnipc'). The estimation shows that richer countries are more likely to have green CV studies performed. The coefficient is significant at the 1 per cent level, but is small. Its interpretation is that for a $100 increase in income per capita, the odd-ratio Prob (Green)/Prob (Brown) increases by 0.04 per cent.

The second question can be answered looking at the other parameters. Here we assume that the chosen explanatory variables are a representation of the relative importance of green versus brown issues. Alternatively, the explanatory variables are a proxi for country-specific environmental priorities. While the coefficients on urban population, birds, access to sanitation are not significant, the estimation shows a number of important facts. The level of PM_{10} damage costs is negatively related to the probability of a green study (or, in equivalent form, PM_{10} damage costs are positively related with the probability of a brown study). This coefficient is significant at the 5 per cent level, and an increase in PM_{10} damage costs by 1 per cent of GNI causes the odd-ratio Prob (Green)/Prob (Brown) to increase by 1.5 per cent. The 'threatened plants' variable is significant at the 5 per cent level, even if the coefficient is low. Finally, the coefficient for 'access to water' is negative and significant at the 10 per cent level. As specified, the model seems to imply that an increase in water access increases the probability of brown studies *vis-à-vis* green studies. However, there is no clear reason to expect such a result. A brown valuation study is intended to measure willingness to pay to avoid pollution problems. Attention to pollution problems should be lower the less the population is exposed to it (everything else kept constant). Having more access to water supply may either diminish exposure to polluted water, thus reducing attention towards brown studies (hence implying a positive coefficient in our logit model), or be neutral to exposure to polluted water (no clear sign of the coefficient).

The country characteristics show mixed performance in predicting the research interests of CV studies. This evidence should be taken cautiously and revised once a better set of explanatory variables is available. On the other hand, the results raise concern about the fact that reasons not related to countries' environmental problems may be at play in the selection of study types. This could be driven for example by the ear-marking of available international funding and other factors to address issues that may not form the countries' priorities. Nonetheless, such a statement is speculative and its confirmation depends on future research.

17.6   Concluding remarks

This chapter discussed the lack of reach of economic valuation methods in general and CV in particular in environmental policy making and in the analysis of environmental impacts of projects. In the past three decades, CV has been very successful in academic research, providing the basis for numerous papers published in a number of professional journals. Yet, its use in environmental policy making and project analysis have been particularly slow in developing countries. Given methodological progress and a better understanding of economic valuation methods, this trend appears to be changing.

CV has faced steep resistance in environmental policy making for reasons that usually fall within three categories: lack of clarity and understanding of the potentials of economic valuation and specifically contingent valuation; matter of principle; and concerns related to the difficulties and costs associated with economic valuation. Economic valuation serves at least three purposes. It fosters better decision making by assisting in priority setting through the provision of systematic and consistent approaches to policy problems; thereby, facilitating the act of choosing among alternatives in a manner that approximates the maximum social welfare. It provides a consistent approach to the estimation of the level of policy instruments targeting market failures, and it facilitates capturing environmental benefits and costs by providing information that is relevant to the interested parties. Even if environmental policy makers are not comfortable with economic values and their valuation methods, it is likely that in most cases economic and non-economic values can be used as complements rather than substitutes, as long as the goals being targeted are clear.

The point raised regarding the difficulties and costs often associated with economic valuation in general and CV in particular is more difficult to address, but it is in essence empirical. While data availability is limited, our simple model provided some interesting insights. If one follows the NOAA guidelines for undertaking CV, it is likely that the study will be highly dependent on the availability of skilled labor and some capital. These inputs can be costly both at low-income levels and at high-income levels, which partly explains the lack of CV studies in low- and high-income developing countries. Alternatively, middle-income countries that have capital and skilled labor without yet experiencing high input costs could be particularly suited for increasing their use of CV in environmental policy making and implementation.

The analysis also shows that, as countries become richer, they become more concerned with natural resource management issues. This may reflect the importance richer populations give to amenities typically enjoyed through tourism for example. Nonetheless, regarding the choice of CV study topic, country characteristics, and hence perceived environmental priorities, show mixed results. While this could be explained by data limitations, it may also indicate that factors other than country environmental priorities drive the CV agenda.

Notes

1. Senior authorship is not assigned, and the findings, interpretations, and conclusions expressed in this chapter do not necessarily reflect the views of the Executive Directors of The World Bank, the governments they represent, and Fraunhofer ISI. The World Bank does not guarantee the accuracy of the data included in this work. The authors are especially grateful to Prof. Richard Carson for providing them with his comprehensive contingent valuation bibliography upon which this quantitative research is based. It is expected to be published in March 2005 under the title 'Contingent Valuation: A Comprehensive Bibliography and History'. The authors also wish to acknowledge the comments from Prof. James Kahn. None of those cited bears any responsibility for the contents of this document, which is entirely the responsibility of its authors.
2. Total economic value is defined as use values (direct, indirect, and option/quasi option values) plus non-use values (bequest and existence values). Through this framework, it is possible to associate different methods (e.g. revealed-preference approaches, stated-preference approaches) to the values these are attempting to estimate. There is a vast literature on this topic. For a recent attempt to bring this conceptual framework closer to policy making, see OECD (2001 and 2002).
3. A major challenge in building our sample was not only to identify a number of studies large enough but also to identify a good reference source for it. Carson (forthcoming) is timely in that it is the most recent survey on the subject, analysing CV studies on a broad range of applications. We only included in the sample those studies that contain a practical application of CV as a valuation tool. Other studies analyse theoretical issues related to the methodology and the estimators, without focusing on any particular example, or review previous work. We did not include these studies in the data set.
4. By comparison, we identified 922 distinct CV studies in 21 different developed countries. Over all, the United States is an outlier in the data set as most CV studies were undertaken in the country.

5. It should be noted that the number of countries belonging to the World Bank and classified using these acronyms are greater than the number in our data set, since not all World Bank members have CV studies in the data set. The Republic of Korea and Singapore are members of the World Bank, but Taiwan though geographically in the EAP area is not a member. Cuba and Curacao are under LAC in our list but are not members of the World Bank. Hong Kong, Netherlands Antilles (Curacao is in fact part of the Netherlands Antilles but has a separate CV study), Puerto Rico though geographically located in the EAP or LAC areas have special status. Since we are interested in a combination of different variables, we chose not to use the exact same classification of the World Bank.
6. PM_{10} refers to particulate matter smaller than 10 microns in diameter, thus capable of reaching deeply into the respiratory system.

References

Arrow, K., R. Solow, P. Portney, E. Leamer, R. Radner and H. Schuman (1993), 'Report of the NOAA Panel on contingent valuation', *Federal Register*, **58** (10), 4602–14.
Biller, Dan (1998), 'Environmental impact assessment: the Brazilian experience', The World Congress of Environmental and Resource Economists, Venice, Italy, June.
Carson, R. (forthcoming), *Contingent Valuation: A Comprehensive Bibliography and History*, Cheltenham: Edward Elgar.
OECD (2001), *Valuation of Biodiversity Benefits: Selected Studies*, Paris.
OECD (2002), *Handbook of Biodiversity Valuation: A Guide for Policy-makers*, Paris.
OECD (2003), *Harnessing Markets for Biodiversity: Towards Conservation and Sustainable Use*, Paris.
Silva, P. and S. Pagiola (2003), 'A review of the valuation of environmental costs and benefits in World Bank Projects', Paper no. 94, Environmental Economic Series (December 2003), Washington, DC.
The World Bank (2005), *World Development Indicators 2005*, Washington, DC.
UNEP (1998), 'A programme for change: decisions from the fourth meeting of the conference of the Parties to the Convention on Biological Diversity', United Nations.
Waller-Hunter, J. and D. Biller (2001), 'Valuing ecosystems – a key prerequisite for the sustainable management of natural resources', proceedings of the 5th International Conference on the Environmental Management of Enclosed Coastal Seas, November.

Appendix: *World Bank Regions*

AFR Sub-Saharan Africa

Angola, Benin, Botswana, Burkina Faso, Burundi, Cameroon, Cape Verde, Central African Republic, Chad, Comoros, Democratic Republic of Congo, Republic of Congo, Cote d'Ivoire, Equatorial Guinea, Eritrea, Ethiopia, Gabon, Gambia, Ghana, Guinea, Guinea-Bissau, Kenya, Lesotho, Liberia, Madagascar, Malawi, Mali, Mauritania, Mauritius, Mozambique, Namibia, Niger, Nigeria, Rwanda, Sao Tome and Principe, Senegal, Seychelles, Sierra Leone, Somalia, South Africa, Sudan, Swaziland, Tanzania, Togo, Uganda, Zambia, and Zimbabwe.

EAP East Asia and Pacific
Cambodia, China, Fiji, Indonesia, Kiribati,
Democratic People's Republic of Korea,
Republic of Korea, Lao Peoples' Democratic
Republic, Malaysia, Marshall Islands, Federated
States of Micronesia, Mongolia, Myanmar,
Palau, Papua New Guinea, Philippines, Samoa,
Solomon Islands, Thailand, Timor-Leste, Tonga,
Vanuatu, and Vietnam.

ECA Europe and Central Asia
Albania, Armenia, Azerbaijan, Belarus, Bosnia-
Herzegovina, Bulgaria, Croatia, Czech
Republic, Estonia, Georgia, Hungary,
Kazakhstan, Kyrgyz Republic, Latvia,
Lithuania, Macedonia, Moldova, Poland,
Romania, Russian Federation, Serbia and
Montenegro, Slovak Republic, Slovenia,
Tajikistan, Turkey, Turkmenistan, Ukraine, and
Uzbekistan.

LCR Latin America and Caribbean
Antigua and Barbuda, Argentina, Belize,
Bolivia, Brazil, Chile, Colombia, Costa Rica,
Dominica, Dominican Republic, Ecuador, El
Salvador, Grenada, Guatemala, Guyana, Haiti,
Honduras, Jamaica, Mexico, Nicaragua,
Panama, Paraguay, Peru, St. Kitts and Nevis,
St. Lucia, St. Vincent and the Grenadines, Trinidad
and Tobago, Uruguay, and Venezuela.

MNA Middle East and North Africa
Algeria, Bahrain, Djibouti, Arab Republic of
Egypt, Islamic Republic of Iran, Iraq, Israel,
Jordan, Kuwait, Lebanon, Libya, Morocco,
Oman, Saudi Arabia, Arab Republic of Syria,
Tunisia, United Arab Emirates, West Bank and
Gaza, Republic of Yemen.

SAR South Asia
Afghanistan, Bangladesh, Bhutan, India,
Maldives, Nepal, Pakistan, Sri Lanka.

18 Combining stated-choice and stated-frequency data with observed behavior to value NRDA compensable damages: Green Bay, PCBs, and Fish Consumption Advisories

William S. Breffle, Edward R. Morey, Robert D. Rowe and Donald M. Waldman*

18.1 Introduction

The chapter uses a case study to demonstrate the use of stated-choice and stated-preference (i.e., contingent behavior) questions, combined with data on actual choices, to estimate compensable damages in a Natural Resource Damage Assessment (NRDA).[1] We summarize the stages in a NRDA, including survey design and implementation, data collection and analysis, model development and estimation, and damage calculations.

Simply put, a stated-choice question presents an individual with a number of alternatives, each described in terms of the levels of their common set of characteristics, and asks the individual to state his preferred alternative. Stated-choice techniques are used in marketing, transportation, and economic research to value products, environmental resources, and changes in transportation modes as a function of their characteristics.

Under Federal law responsible parties are liable for the damages to natural resources caused by the release of hazardous substances in accordance with the regulations at 43 CFR §11.81–11.84. Some of the major NRDAs in the last decade include US versus Exxon (Carson et al., 1992), Montana versus ARCO (Morey et al., 2002b), and the southern California bight (Carson et al., 1994).

A component of the first two of these assessments was estimating the damages to recreational users from the injuries. Such damages are deemed recreational use values (damages) and are measured in terms of willingness to pay (WTP) by users for the absence of injuries plus WTP by non-users that would be users in the absence of injuries. Use benefits that can only be experienced by being in proximity to the resource are typically considered easier to estimate than passive use benefits, because use damages partially exhibit themselves in terms of behavioral changes.[2] In this application, we only estimate a component of use damages.

Our method combines methods identified as acceptable in the DOI regulations [43 CFR §11.83(c)]. Choice-based methods are explicitly identified (as conjoint methods) in the NOAA NRDA regulations for use in valuing and scaling injuries and restoration (15 CFR part 990, preamble Appendix B, part G). In addition to estimating damages, stated-choice questions are a promising technique for making the determination of in-kind compensation and restoration, because in addition to monetizing damages, choice questions investigate how individuals make resource-to-resource tradeoffs. For this reason, stated-choice questions can be attractive to those who have no desire to estimate damages in monetary terms.

Estimating damages is essentially the task of estimating the target population's preferences for the resource in both its injured and non-injured state. One can gather information about preferences by observing choices, or by asking individuals about the choices they would make in hypothetical situations. Choice questions are a stated-preference (SP) technique for estimating preferences because the respondent is asked to state something about his preferences.[3] The same is true for stated-frequency questions. In contrast, revealed preference (RP) techniques observe an individual's actual choices in the market or other arenas, and inferences are made about the individual's preferences based on those observed choices. The emphasis here is on the use of SP techniques combined with RP techniques. SP techniques are often required because damages often cannot be estimated using only observed behavior. This is because resources similar to the injured resource, but without injuries, often do not currently exist. We present an example of how to ask and analyse stated-choice questions.

The application estimates compensable damages to anglers from fish consumption advisories caused by PCB contamination in Green Bay and the Lower Fox River of Wisconsin (Figure 18.1). PCBs, a hazardous substance under CERCLA, were released into the Lower Fox River of Wisconsin by local paper companies (Sullivan et al., 1983; WDNR, 1998; Stratus Consulting, 1999), primarily between the late 1950s and the mid-1970s. Interestingly, the PCB contamination resulted, in part, from the recycling of paper. Through time, PCBs have been and continue to be redistributed into the sediments and natural resources of the Lower Fox River and the Bay of Green Bay.

Through the food chain process, PCBs bio-accumulate in fish and wildlife. As a result of elevated PCB concentrations in fish, in 1976 the Wisconsin Department of Health and Human Services first issued fish consumption advisories (FCAs) for sport-caught fish in the Wisconsin waters of Green Bay, and in 1977 Michigan first issued FCAs for the Michigan

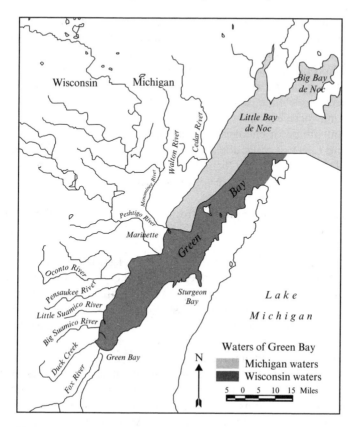

Figure 18.1   Area of the Wisconsin PCB contamination

waters of Green Bay (Stratus Consulting, 1999). These FCAs for the waters of Green Bay continue today, although the specifics of the FCAs have varied through time. Even with significant removal of PCB contaminated sediment, the FCAs may continue for 100 years or more (Velleux and Endicott, 1994; WDNR, 1997).

Damage estimates generated by inputting primary data into a statistical model, which we do here, need to be supported by independent research and answers to attitudinal questions. Solicited opinions and attitudes help to determine the site characteristics important to the population, providing support for the statistical estimates of damages. In our case, there is also abundant literature demonstrating that FCAs damage anglers, in that anglers change where and how often they fish, change what they fish for and what they keep, change how they prepare and cook the fish they catch, and experience reduced enjoyment of the fishing experience.[4] A number of studies have estimated the damages associated with FCAs, but none specifically for Green Bay FCAs.[5] They indicate that such damages can be substantial. In addition to estimating the damages associated with Green Bay FCAs, our model estimates the benefits associated with increases in catch rates, so can be used to determine how much catch rates would have to increase to compensate the anglers for the presence of the FCA. Supporting these estimates, there are hundreds of articles that estimate significant values for changes in catch rates. Some that apply to the Great Lakes and Green Bay include Samples and Bishop (1985), Milliman et al. (1992), Lyke (1993), and Chen et al. (1999). If in-kind compensation is chosen for remediation or restoration, increased catch rates is a likely candidate for such compensation.

Recreational fishing damages from FCAs can be classified into the following four categories:

1. Reduced enjoyment from current Green Bay fishing days. Current Green Bay anglers may experience reduced enjoyment from their days at the site because of concerns about health safety and displeasure with catching contaminated fish. These concerns can result in changes in fishing locations within the waters of Green Bay, changes in target species type and size, and changes in behavior regarding keeping, preparing, and consuming fish.
2. Losses by Green Bay anglers from fishing at substitute sites. Because of FCAs, anglers who fish the waters of Green Bay may substitute some of their fishing days from the waters of Green Bay to other fishing sites that, in the absence of FCAs in the waters of Green Bay, would be less preferred sites.
3. Losses by Green Bay anglers who take fewer total fishing days. Because of FCAs, anglers who fish the waters of Green Bay may take fewer total fishing days than they would in the absence of injuries. For example, an angler may still take the same number of days to other sites, but take fewer days to the waters of Green Bay to avoid the FCAs.
4. Losses by other anglers and non-anglers. Because of FCAs, some anglers may completely forego fishing the waters of Green Bay. Other individuals who would fish the waters of Green Bay if it did not have FCAs may completely forego fishing.

The approach employed here estimates the damages in a conservative fashion: the damage estimates include categories 1, 2, and 3, but not category 4.

The primary focus of the assessment is to estimate open-water recreational fishing damages for the population of anglers who purchase

Wisconsin fishing licenses in eight Wisconsin counties near Green Bay and who are active in Green Bay fishing. We will refer to this group as our target population. Data collection focuses on the Wisconsin waters of Green Bay, because PCB loadings and the resultant FCAs are more severe for the Wisconsin waters of Green Bay than for the Michigan waters of Green Bay, and because the recreational fishing activity in the Wisconsin waters of Green Bay is much larger than in the Michigan waters of Green Bay. Anglers in the target population account for the vast majority of anglers and fishing days in the Wisconsin waters of Green Bay. Data collection focuses on open-water fishing (i.e., non-ice fishing) because it accounts for almost 90 per cent of all fishing on the waters of Green Bay.

The model combines data on actual fishing activities under current conditions (for example, days fishing in the Wisconsin waters of Green Bay) with data on how anglers would be willing to tradeoff changes in fishing characteristics (including catch rates, FCAs, and costs), and data on how many days anglers would fish Green Bay under alternative conditions. From the estimated model one can derive an estimate of WTP per Green Bay fishing day and per choice occasion for the absence of Green Bay FCAs. These latter WTP estimates, when multiplied by the assumed number of choice occasions for the anglers in our target population, are used to obtain estimates of the use damages to anglers from the PCB contamination.

The rest of the chapter is organized as follows. Section 2 briefly describes the survey, sampling plan, and data collection effort. Section 3 summarizes the characteristics and attitudes of Green Bay anglers, and Section 4 considers the stated-choice and stated-frequency questions in more detail. Section 5 outlines the combined revealed and stated preference model of Green Bay fishing days. Section 6 reports estimates of 1998 damages, and Section 7 concludes.

18.2   Primary data collection

A three-step procedure was used to collect data from a random sample of individuals in the target population. First, a random sample of anglers was drawn from lists of 1997 license holders in the county courthouses in the eight counties near the Bay of Green Bay: Brown, Door, Kewaunee, Manitowoc, Marinette, Oconto, Outagamie, and Winnebago. This population includes residents of these counties, as well as residents of other Wisconsin counties, and non-residents who purchased their Wisconsin fishing licenses in these eight counties. We chose this target population for two reasons: most Green Bay fishing days are by these anglers, and fishing license data in Wisconsin are stored only in county court houses on records that cannot be removed, making it expensive to obtain a random sample of all Wisconsin license holders who fish Green Bay.

Second, a telephone survey was completed in late 1998 and early 1999. From the courthouse sample, the telephone numbers were obtained and a telephone contact was attempted with 4597 anglers; 3190 anglers completed the telephone survey for a 69 per cent response rate. The telephone survey collects data from all anglers on the number of total days fished in 1998, how many days were in the waters of Green Bay, and on attitudes about actions to improve fishing. Anglers who had participated in open-water fishing in the Wisconsin waters of Green Bay in 1998 (the target population) were recruited for a follow-up mail survey: 92 per cent of the open-water Green Bay anglers agreed to participate in the mail survey (the third and final step). Of the 820 anglers mailed in the survey, 647 (79 per cent) completed and returned the survey. In terms of the socio-economic information collected during the phone survey, the Green Bay anglers who completed the mail survey do not differ significantly from those who did not.

The core of the mail survey is a series of eight choice questions used to assess damages for reductions in enjoyment for current open-water fishing days in the Wisconsin waters of Green Bay. Figure 18.2 is an example. In each question, respondents are provided two alternatives (A and B), each with different levels of fishing characteristics for the waters of Green Bay, and asked to choose whether alternative A or alternative B is preferred. Fishing characteristics include catch rates and FCA levels for yellow perch, trout and salmon, walleye, and smallmouth bass; and an angler's share of the daily launch fee.

After each choice pair, the following follow-up question about the expected number of days the angler would visit the preferred site was asked:

> How often would you fish the waters of Green Bay if it had the conditions described by the alternative you just chose (A or B)? Your answer could depend on a number of factors:
>> How many days you typically fish in a year and how many of those days are spent fishing the waters of Green Bay.
>> How much you enjoy fishing the waters of Green Bay compared to other places you might fish.
>> How far you live from Green Bay compared to other places you might fish.
>> The cost of fishing the waters of Green Bay compared to other places you might fish.
>> Whether you think the conditions for the waters of Green Bay in the alternative you just chose are better, worse, or about the same as current conditions.

	Alternative A	Alternative B
If you were going to fish the waters of Green Bay, would you prefer to fish the waters of Green Bay under Alternative A or Alternative B? *Check one box in the last row*		
Yellow Perch		
Average catch rate for a typical angler	40 minutes per perch	30 minutes per perch
Fish consumption advisory...	No more than one meal per week	No more than one meal per week
Trout and Salmon		
Average catch rate for a typical angler	2 hours per trout/salmon	2 hours per trout/salmon
Fish consumption advisory...	Do not eat	No more than one meal per month
Walleye		
Average catch rate for a typical angler	8 hours per walleye	4 hours per walleye
Fish consumption advisory...	Do not eat	No more than one meal per month
Smallmouth bass		
Average catch rate for a typical angler	2 hours per bass	2 hours per bass
Fish consumption advisory...	No more than one meal per month	Unlimited consumption
Your share of the daily launch fee	Free	$3
Check the box for the alternative you prefer	☐	☐

Figure 18.2 Example choice question

The more you fish the waters of Green Bay the less time you will have for fishing elsewhere.

Excluding ice fishing, how many days, on average, would you fish the waters of Green Bay in a typical year if the conditions on the waters of Green Bay were those described in the alternative you chose? Fill in the blank.

———— days fishing the waters of Green Bay in a typical year.

This follow-up question allows for the estimation of damages associated with substituting days from the waters of Green Bay to other fishing sites or activities because of FCAs.

The survey also asked a number of attitudinal questions about Green Bay and its characteristics, and collected socio-economic data about the angler's household and the number of fishing days since the angler was surveyed by phone.

18.3   Green Bay angler profile

Eighty-five per cent of the anglers active in the Wisconsin waters of Green Bay had heard or have read about the FCAs, and, in general, the anglers' perceptions of the specific advisory levels (i.e., how often one could eat fish of each species) are consistent with the published FCAs. Seventy-seven per cent of the anglers identify behavioral responses to the FCAs in the Wisconsin waters of Green Bay, with 30 per cent of active anglers reporting they spend fewer days fishing the Wisconsin waters of Green Bay because of the FCAs. Over half the anglers have changed the species or size of fish they keep to eat, and over half have changed the way the fish they keep are cleaned, prepared, or cooked.

When asked to rate the importance of different enhancement activities, such as cleaning up PCBs so that FCAs could be removed, increasing the catch rates, or adding parks or boat launches, anglers identify PCB cleanup as more important than any other option. Further, when asked how bothered they are about different FCA levels on a one-to-five scale, the means for all FCA levels are greater than three, and increase with the severity of FCAs. That is, damages are a function of the scope of the injuries.

While anglers indicated that increasing catch rates is not as important as removing PCBs, not surprisingly, catching fish is an important part of fishing. For example, when anglers were asked to rate from one to five the importance of increasing catch rates in Green Bay, 68.5 per cent responded with a three or higher.

18.4   The Green Bay stated choice questions

Consider presenting a current Green Bay angler with the following simple choice pair: Green Bay with a $5 launch fee and an average catch rate of one fish per hour, versus Green Bay with an $8 launch fee and an average catch rate of one fish every 30 minutes. If an angler chooses the second alternative (higher cost and catch rate), and assuming his choice represents his preferences, his WTP per Green Bay fishing day for the doubled catch rate is at least $3. If the angler chooses the first alternative, the WTP is less than $3. Many different choice pairs can be generated by varying the launch fee and catch rates. For example, if there are three launch fees and four catch rates, there are 12 possible alternatives and 66 possible pairs. If site characteristics include cost, catch rate, and FCA level, choice pairs can determine how an angler would trade off less stringent FCAs at the site for higher cost, better catch rates for higher cost, or better catch rates for more stringent FCAs.

After each Green Bay choice question, the follow up question gives the angler the opportunity to indicate whether he considers the chosen Green Bay alternative better or worse than current conditions. For example, an angler could choose an alternative and then report he would fish Green Bay less, or even zero times, if the conditions were as in the chosen alternative.

SP data has some distinct advantages. Morikawa et al. (1990) states, 'for example, since SP data are collected in a fully controlled "experimental" environment, such data has the following advantages in contrast with RP data that are generated in natural experiments: (1) they can elicit preferences for non-existing alternatives; (2) the choice set is pre-specified; (3) collinearity among attributes can be avoided; and (4) range of attribute values can be extended.' Researchers estimating the value of environmental goods are often valuing a good or condition that does not currently exist, for example, Green Bay absent PCB contamination and FCAs. In addition, because SP data allow the researcher to control more variables and because there are more unknowns influencing the decisions in RP data, the SP data often contain less noise and measurement error (Louviere, 1996).

We combine the SP data with data on observed fishing days under current conditions, allowing the amount of noise in the SP data to differ from the amount of noise in the RP data.[6] SP and RP data provide different information about anglers' preferences, so combining them into an integrated model leads to better estimates of those preferences.

There is the incentive to make choices consistent with one's preferences, if the choices have consequences. The anglers who took our survey, current Green Bay anglers, have knowledge of the resource and its PCB injuries, care about those injuries, and felt that their answers to the choice questions would be examined by policy makers.

With choice questions, it is important to include as characteristics all the significant characteristics of the injured resource including the characteristic(s) that are impacted by the injuries, but the total list of included characteristics must be small. In recent environmental applications the number has ranged from two to nine; Morey et al. (2002c) has two and Johnson and Desvousges (1997) have nine.

If a number of different Green Bays existed that differed only in terms of their FCA levels, one could determine how anglers value different FCA levels by observing how fishing days are allocated among these different sites, but such a natural experiment does not exist. Lake Michigan has similar FCAs for PCBs, but it is a much larger water body that generally requires larger boats to fish and has varying fish species from the waters of

Green Bay. The inland lakes are much smaller and do not suffer from PCB contamination; many have FCAs, but not for PCBs.

18.4.1   Choice set characteristics

As indicated in Figure 18.2, each Green Bay alternative was described to respondents in terms of nine characteristics: a launch fee; the average amount of time necessary to catch a fish (catch time) for each of the four species (yellow perch, trout/salmon, walleye, and smallmouth bass); and an FCA level for each of the four species.

We include catch times (the reciprocal of catch rates) and costs in our characteristics set because a large body of recreational fishing literature has shown consistently that these are important characteristics of site choice. Further, catch times are included to support any subsequent computation of damages from reduced catch times and to compute benefits from increased catch rates if such a program is part of a restoration package.[7] We include FCAs as a key feature of the damages caused by the PCB contamination and because recent literature demonstrates the importance of FCAs to recreational fishing. Our focus groups, pre-tests, and the attitudinal questions on the mail survey all confirm the importance of these characteristics.

For reductions in PCB levels, the FCAs for all species will decrease or remain the same (depending on the change in PCB levels); they will not move in opposite directions. This is reflected in the design of our FCA characteristics. We define nine FCA levels covering the FCA for each of our four species of interest. Level 1 indicates PCB levels are sufficiently low such that all species may be eaten in unlimited quantities; there is no health risk from consumption. Level 9 is the most restrictive: trout/salmon, walleye, and bass should not be eaten, and a perch meal should be consumed once a month at most. In general, the stringency of FCAs for particular species increases or stays the same moving from lower to higher levels, with two exceptions.[8]

The actual FCAs for the waters of Green Bay vary by fish size and location, whereas our nine FCA levels do not. Taking account of variations due to location and size, the least restrictive advisories in 1998, by species, were once a week for perch, and once a month for trout/salmon, bass, and walleye. This corresponds to our Level 4, which is a conservative representation of the current FCA conditions in the Wisconsin waters of Green Bay for each of the four species.

The cost characteristics used to describe each Green Bay alternative is the 'share of the daily launch fee'. For angling trips that did not involve a boat, respondents were told twice they should 'think of the daily boat launch fee as a fee you would have to pay to fish the waters of Green Bay', so the cost variable in the choice question has a meaning to all respondents.[9] This presentation strategy was tested in the pre-tests and found to be accepted in a manner consistent with the design of the choice questions. For each Green Bay alternative, the launch fee took one of nine levels: free, $2, $3, $5, $7, $9, $10, $12, or $15, which includes fees that are lower than and higher than the current average fee.[10]

Supporting recreational facilities, such as more boat launches, picnic tables, and walking trails, are not included as characteristics in the choice questions because anglers in the focus groups, pre-tests, and the attitudinal questions on the mail survey indicated relatively little concern about changes in these site characteristics.[11] We concluded that addressing recreational facilities would not improve the damage assessment, but would complicate survey design and the cognitive burden for respondents. Therefore, our model is not capable of determining compensation in terms of improvements in recreational facilities (parks, picnic benches, boat ramps, etc.), which are types of restoration alternatives often proposed by potentially responsible parties (PRPs).

The Green Bay choice pairs do not ask the individuals where they would fish if they had the choice between different sites, but whether they would prefer to fish the same site under conditions A or B; that is, the choice-pair questions ask anglers to choose which Green Bay they would prefer, not how often they would go.[12] Given this, the answers to the choice pairs can be used to estimate how much anglers would prefer a Green Bay fishing day with no FCAs to fishing Green Bay under current conditions, but cannot, by themselves, be used to determine how often an angler would fish Green Bay under different conditions and the related values for changes in site visits.[13]

Given the number of characteristics and the levels they can take, there are 1620 possible Green Bay alternatives and a large number of possible pairs. Eighty of these pairs were chosen so that there would be sufficient independent variation in the levels of the six different characteristics to identify the influence of each.[14]

The 160 members of the set were randomly divided into 80 pairs, which in turn were randomly allocated among ten versions of the survey instrument. None of the simple correlations between the characteristics in the 160 alternatives is significantly different from zero, indicating independent variation among the characteristics.

18.4.2   Evaluation of choices across alternatives

Overall, the anglers' choices are very consistent with the characteristics they rate as important in other survey questions and with their reported preferences such as species target preference. Only 138 (2.7 per cent) of the choice pairs were left unanswered. This is consistent with our finding from the focus groups and pre-tests that most anglers found the survey interesting and the choice tasks reasonable. Remember that we surveyed only current Green Bay anglers. In 40.5 per cent of sample pairs, anglers chose the more costly alternative, which indicates that Green Bay anglers are willing to pay for better Green Bay conditions.

For most anglers, their chosen alternatives indicate consistent preferences across the choices; that is, the criteria on which they base the pair-wise choices appear to stem from stable preferences. The pair-wise choices are also consistent with anglers' answers to other questions in the survey. In practice we do not expect every choice for all anglers to be perfectly consistent, which the method and statistical evaluation are designed to accommodate through the random element in angler choices. In reviewing each angler's responses for consistency, only a few anglers in our sample made choices that may indicate that their choices were based on something other than their preferences, such as always choosing the first or second alternative in each of the eight choices. For example, only eight anglers (1.2 per cent) always chose the first or second alternative, and it is still possible those alternatives were always their preferred ones.

After the angler answered the eight choice pairs, the next survey question inquired about the importance of each of the Green Bay characteristics in making the pair-wise choices. FCAs for perch and walleye and perch catch rates arc the three characteristics considered to be the most important in choosing among the pairs. This is to be expected as perch is a frequently targeted and frequently caught species on Green Bay, and fishing activity in Green Bay for walleye has been rapidly growing. The choices of anglers who indicate that they typically target a particular species demonstrate that catch time and FCA for that species is more important than catch times and FCAs for other species.

Choices vary by anglers as a function of target species. In addition, women rate the FCAs more important and catch time less important than do men. This is not surprising since consumption of PCB-contaminated fish by pregnant women can affect a child's development.[15] Anglers with higher education levels generally have lower mean importance ratings, as do anglers with higher income levels. Anglers who fished 15 or more days on the open waters of Green Bay in 1998 have the same or slightly higher importance ratings for all characteristics than those who fished less than five days.

In general, anglers' intentions are consistent with their actual pair-wise choices; anglers who report catch as very important tend to choose alternatives with higher catch rates than those who view rate catch as unimportant, and anglers who report FCAs as important tend to choose alternatives with less stringent FCA levels.

18.4.3   The expected days follow-up question to each choice pair
As noted in Section 18.2, after each choice pair, the angler was asked:

> How often would you fish the waters of Green Bay if it had the conditions described by the alternative you just chose (A or B)?

The answers to these expected days follow-up questions, along with the number of days the angler fished Green Bay in 1998, will be used to estimate how the number of fishing days in Green Bay would change if there were a change in its characteristics. One would expect that, for some anglers, an improvement in conditions would lead to an increase in fishing days.

The question also gives the angler the ability to express possible displeasure with the chosen alternative by reporting that he would reduce or stop fishing Green Bay entirely if it had the conditions of the chosen alternative, for example, if the respondent feels the chosen alternative is inferior to Green Bay under current conditions. That is, the respondent has the ability to 'just say no'.[16] Alternatively, if the respondent feels the chosen alternative is superior to Green Bay under current conditions, he has the option of saying he will fish Green Bay more. The angler also can report that he would continue to fish Green Bay his current number of days.

When presented with a pair where both alternatives are unappealing, and with no way to express displeasure with these options, some individuals either may not respond out of protest or may not respond due to an inability to identify the preferred alternative. To avoid such possibilities some authors have advocated a third 'opt-out' alternative, such as 'would not fish' or 'would fish elsewhere'.[17] Our expected days question plays the role of such a third alternative, while avoiding one of its disadvantages: giving the respondent an easy way to avoid difficult choices. Choosing will be difficult when the angler is almost indifferent between the two sets of Green Bay characteristics. However, if the individual makes these choices, he reveals the rate at which he is willing to trade off site characteristics. There is no fundamental reason individuals cannot choose between alternatives they dislike, or between options both better than the status quo, and such choices provide valuable information about preferences.

In 69.9 per cent of the answered expected days questions, anglers report a number of Green Bay fishing days greater than their current 1998 numbers. If 1998 is assumed to be a typical year and a base for comparison, these responses indicate that anglers feel the preferred alternative in the pair is better than the status quo. In 8.0 per cent of the answered questions, anglers report their current number of Green Bay fishing days. In 22.1 per cent, anglers report an expected number of Green Bay fishing days less than their current numbers, indicating anglers feel the alternatives in the pair are inferior to current conditions. Eighty-five of the anglers (13 per cent) provide an answer of zero days to Green Bay in response to at least one of their Green Bay alternative choices; that is, they say they would not fish if the conditions were as described in that pair. Zero fishing days was reported for just over 4 per cent of the follow up questions.

On average, the number of expected days is higher when site quality is better. For all nine characteristics, the mean level for higher-than-current expected days is better than or the same as the mean level for lower-than-current expected days. There were 222 respondents (34 per cent) who did not vary their expected days responses throughout the eight pair questions. This is consistent with many of the comments in the focus groups about time constraints, entrenched fishing patterns, and dependencies on fishing partners. It is also consistent with the responses to Question 11 of the mail survey, where 68 per cent of the anglers indicated they had not reduced the number of days spent fishing Green Bay in response to FCAs.

That an angler does not change his or her number of fishing days in response to the change in environmental characteristics does not indicate that he or she would not benefit from an improvement in FCAs or catch rates. If conditions are improved, constraints can keep the angler from increasing fishing days, but each day fished will be enjoyed more. If conditions worsen, the angler still might prefer fishing Green Bay to doing something else, he just prefers it less. When the quality of a product is improved or its price is decreased, many consumers do not buy more of it, but they do get greater benefits from the amount they purchase. Also, if a product's quality decreases or price increases, many consumers will not purchase less in the short run. Sixty-six per cent of the anglers did vary their answers to the expected days questions over the eight pairs, indicating that, for the majority of anglers, the number of days they fish Green Bay will vary as a function of changes in the characteristics of Green Bay, even in the short run.

18.5   A combined revealed and stated preference model of Green Bay fishing days

The model is estimated using all of the SP and RP data: (1) anglers' preferred alternatives from the eight Green Bay choice pairs, (2) the expected number of Green Bay fishing days to be spent at the preferred Green Bay alternatives from the eight follow-up questions to the choice pairs, and (3) the number of days each angler fishes Green Bay under current conditions. While different types of data provide information about behavior and tradeoffs, the relative strength of RP data is in predicting trip-taking behavior, and the relative strength of SP data is in determining the rates at which the angler is willing to trade off site characteristics.

The choice data use as their foundation a probit model; it assumes the utility one receives from a commodity is a function of the characteristics of the commodity plus an additive, normally distributed, random component. There are two commodities: a Green Bay fishing day and a composite of all other alternatives, so two conditional indirect utility functions are specified and estimated. The random components associated with the three data types are allowed to differ and to be correlated.

Each angler i's chosen alternative in each stated-choice pair j is assumed to be a draw from a Bernoulli distribution whose parameter is the probability, P_{ij}, that the utility from the chosen alternative is greater than the utility from the other Green Bay alternative. It is a function of the attributes of the two alternatives.

The answer to each follow-up question on the number of days to be spent at the preferred Green Bay alternative, n_{ij}, is assumed to be a draw from a binomial distribution, where the number of trials is the angler's total number of choice occasions, n_i, and the parameter is the probability, P_{ij}^0, the utility from the chosen alternative is greater than some other non-Green Bay alternative, conditional upon the preferred Green Bay alternative being chosen. This conditional probability is a function of the attributes of both Green Bay alternatives, and the attributes of the 'other alternatives'. The total number of choice occasions for all anglers is assumed to be 50; very few anglers spent more than 50 days fishing Green Bay.

An angler's observed number of days to Green Bay under current conditions, is assumed to be a draw from a binomial distribution, where the number of trials is the angler's total number of choice occasions and the parameter is the probability, P_i^G, that the utility from Green Bay under current conditions is greater than the utility from doing something else. The likelihood function is:

$$L = \prod_{i=1}^{647} \left[\binom{n_i}{n_i^G} (P_i^G)^{n_i^G} (1 - P_i^G)^{n_i - n_i^G} \prod_{j=1}^{8} \binom{n_i}{n_{ij}} (P_{ij}^0)^{n_{ij}} (1 - P_{ij}^0)^{n_i - n_{ij}} P_{ij} \right].$$

More details are presented in Breffle et al. (1999). The maximum likelihood estimates are consistent, even if random components are correlated across pairs. If the additional assumption is made for each individual that the random components are independent across pairs, then the estimates are also asymptotically efficient.

The model is designed to be a complete demand system in that it explains the angler's allocation of choice occasions between Green Bay and all other activities, including fishing all other sites. That is, the model is designed to predict how an angler's total number of Green Bay fishing days might change if Green Bay conditions are changed.

   The utility an angler receives from a day of fishing Green Bay is assumed to be a function of costs (which include the opportunity cost of travel time, plus monetary expenses including travel costs and any launch fee); the catch times for four different species groups: trout/salmon, perch, walleye, and bass; and the level of FCAs (which can be one of nine levels, including no FCAs). The deterministic component of utility for Green Bay is assumed to be the same across data types; only the structure of the stochastic component is allowed to vary.

   Data on trip costs and the characteristics of other sites could not be collected; there are hundreds of alternative sites. Because of this, the utility from other activities is assumed to be a function of angler characteristics plus a stochastic random component that varies across anglers. These characteristics include gender, age, whether the angler owns a boat or is retired, and whether Lake Michigan is a relatively cheap substitute.

   The signs of the estimated parameters indicate anglers are worse off as catch times increase, as FCAs increase, and as costs increase. The FCA parameter estimates show that, as the severity of FCAs increases, so does the damage, but not necessarily in a linear fashion. Retired anglers, male anglers, and anglers who own boats are likely to fish Green Bay more; younger anglers and anglers with Lake Michigan as a cheap substitute fish Green Bay less often. All of the parameter estimates are statistically significant and, in addition, have small confidence intervals. The model correctly predicts 72 per cent of the 5038 choice pairs.

   The model can predict how changes in FCAs (or other Green Bay characteristics such as catch time) will affect the number of fishing days spent at Green Bay versus other activities. With the elimination of FCAs in Green Bay, the number of Green Bay days would increase by about 2 per cent.

18.6   Estimates of 1998 damages

From the estimated model, one can derive an estimate of the compensating variation per Green Bay fishing day associated with the elimination or reduction of the FCAs, and an estimate of the expected compensating variation for the elimination or reduction of the Green Bay FCAs. The first is just the estimated change in the utility from a Green Bay fishing day, converted into dollars by dividing it by the estimated marginal utility of money.[18]

   Our estimate of WTP per Green Bay fishing day for the absence of FCAs (FCA level 4 to level 1) is $7.71 for 1998.[19] This value is a dollar estimate of the reduced enjoyment for a Green Bay fishing day because of the FCAs; that is, what a Green Bay angler would pay per Green Bay fishing day to eliminate the need for FCAs. $7.71 is 10 per cent of the average of current expenditures per Green Bay fishing day ($74.32). This value is also within the range of per-day estimates for FCAs reported in the valuation literature discussed previously. One could also offset the current damages from the FCAs with improved catch rather than money. The model estimates indicate that, to do this, catch rates for all four species would have to more than double.[20]

Our estimate of the average annual expected compensating variation for the elimination of the Green Bay FCAs is $111.[21] It is what a Green Bay angler would pay per year to eliminate the need for Green Bay FCAs. It takes account of the fact that the angler might increase the number of fishing days to Green Bay in the absence of Green Bay FCAs. The 95 per cent confidence interval on the $111 estimate is $96 to $128. Based on an earlier version of this model submitted a few years ago, the yearly damage claim for Green Bay was $2.67 million with a confidence interval of $2.13 million to $3.22 million.

18.7   Concluding remarks

The FCAs currently affect more than 255 000 Green Bay fishing days per year, and more days in past years. They reduce the enjoyment of these 255 000 fishing days, and cause fishing days to be allocated to other sites and other activities when they would have been to Green Bay in the absence of PCB contamination.

The value of recreational fishing losses (damages) estimated here is consistent with the literature on recreational fishing impacts and damages from FCAs. About three-quarters of those anglers who continue to fish the Wisconsin waters of Green Bay report behavioral responses to the FCAs, and other anglers report no longer fishing the waters of Green Bay due to FCAs, all of which are comparable to other studies about FCAs on the Great Lakes.

The intent has been to provide to those involved in the process of NRDA litigation an example of how the answers to stated-preference choice and frequency questions can be combined with revealed-preference data to better estimate the damages from PCB contamination.

Notes

*   William S. Breffle, Managing Economist, Stratus Consulting, 1881 Ninth St. Suite 201, Boulder, CO 80302. bbreffle@stratusconsulting.com (http://stratusconsulting.com).
   Edward R. Morey, Professor, Department of Economics, University of Colorado, Boulder, CO 80309-0256. edward.morey@colorado.edu (www.colorado.edu/Economics/morey/).
   Robert D. Rowe, President, Stratus Consulting, Boulder, CO. browe@stratusconsulting.com (http://stratusconsulting.com/).
   Donald M. Waldman, Professor, Department of Economics, University of Colorado, Boulder, CO 80309-0256. donald.waldman@colorado.edu.
   The authors have been doing Natural Resource Damage Assessment for over ten years, with the help of many people. This work has benefitted greatly from comments and suggestions by Vic Adamowicz, David Allen, Robert Baumgartner, Rich Bishop,

388   *Applications*

Don Dillman, David Layton, Pam Rathbun, Paul Ruud, V. Kerry Smith, Roger Tourangeau, Michael Welsh, and Sonya Wytinck.

1. The assessment, Breffle et al. (1999), can be downloaded at (www.colorado.edu/ Economics/morey/).
2. Passive use benefits are benefits one can receive without being at or near the site. For example, an individual might benefit from knowing that salmon are prospering in the Columbia River basin even though he has no intention of viewing, catching, or eating them. Passive use damages are the loss of such passive use benefits.
3. Choice questions are increasingly used to estimate the value of environmental goods. See, Adamowicz (1994, 1997), Layton and Brown (1998), Magat et al. (1988), Morey et al. (1997, 2002a,b and c), Morey and Rossmann (2003), Ruby et al. (1998), Swait et al. (1998), Viscusi et al. (1991), and Mathews et al. (1997), which is a NRDA application.
4. See, for example, Fiore et al. (1989), West et al. (1989), Connelly et al. (1990), Silverman (1990), Connelly et al. (1992), Vena (1992), Knuth et al. (1993), West et al. (1993), Knuth (1996), and Hutchinson (1999).
5. See, for example, the random-utility models of Herriges et al. (1999), Chen and Cosslett (1998), Lyke (1993), Montgomery and Needelman (1997), Hauber and Parsons (1998), Jakus et al. (1997 and 1998), and Parsons et al. (1999).
6. Combining SP and RP data is widely supported. See, for example, McFadden (1986), Ben-Akiva and Morikawa (1990), Morikawa et al. (1990), Cameron (1992), Louviere (1992), Hensher and Bradley (1993), Adamowicz et al. (1994, 1997), Ben-Akiva et al. (1994), Swait et al. (1994), Morikawa et al. (1991), Louviere (1996), Kling (1997), and Mathews et al. (1997).

   Like all data on preferences (including actual choices (RP data)), the responses to choice questions may contain biases or random errors. The random errors are a component of the statistical model. Choosing can be difficult if the individual is almost indifferent between two alternatives. If each respondent is asked to answer a number of choice questions, there can be both learning and fatigue. Respondents can become frustrated if they dislike all of the available alternatives, and they may have no incentive for sufficient introspection to determine their preferred alternative. In addition there can be a bias towards the status quo, the respondent might ignore his constraints, and the respondent might behave strategically.
7. For each Green Bay alternative, the perch catch time took one of five levels: every 10, 20, 30, 40, or 60 minutes. For the other species, catch time took one of six levels: a fish every hour, every two hours, four hours, six hours, eight hours, or every 12 hours. In Green Bay, perch take less time to catch than other sport fish. These ranges were chosen on the basis of historical Wisconsin Department of Natural Resources (WDNR) catch data and feedback from anglers during pre-testing, and were chosen to include catch characteristics that are both better and worse than Green Bay conditions in recent years prior to the 1998 survey. The long-run averages (1986–1998) are 31 minutes per perch, 7.8 hours per trout/salmon, 6.9 hours per walleye, and 5.0 hours per bass. Average catch time has increased dramatically in recent years.

   Mail survey respondents were asked what they felt were the current average catch times (for all anglers, not just themselves) on the Green Bay waters. The means of the responses indicate that anglers have perceptions about average catch times that are consistent with the WDNR data for perch, but are substantially shorter than the WDNR data for other species. This might be because the respondents overestimate what other anglers catch, are optimistic, are better anglers than most, or because their perceptions correspond to long-run averages.
8. Note that in the presentation of the pairs (see Figure 18.2), the FCAs in each of the alternatives are reported by species, but because they are based on nine aggregate levels they do not vary in unrealistic ways by species across the alternatives. This design and presentation of the FCA characteristics account for the fact that the FCAs are correlated across species through their underlying cause, PCB contamination, but take into account the fact that FCAs vary by species, and that different anglers might be interested in different species. Perceived FCAs and actual FCAs are generally consistent.

9. Most Green Bay fishing is by boat.
10. We collected launch fee data for 37 launches. Fifty-one per cent of these sites charged $3.00 to launch a boat; the average was $2.84, and the range was $0.00 to $7.00. In the mail survey (Q38), anglers were asked, 'Approximately what do you think is the average daily boat launch fee for the waters of Green Bay?' The mean of the angler estimates is $4.41, the median is $4.00, and the mode is $3.00. The cost range in the choice questions is broader than actually observed to allow for higher cost tradeoffs with less stringent FCAs and higher catch rates. This range was determined from the focus groups and pre-tests and spans the partial range of cost differentials anglers indicated were acceptable for changes in FCAs and catch rates.
11. For example, in focus groups anglers were asked: 'What was the most important factor in your decisions when you first decided to fish Green Bay? What two or three factors contribute most to your enjoyment of fishing trips to Green Bay? What two or three factors detract most from your enjoyment of fishing trips on the waters of Green Bay? If you could change anything about fishing on the waters of Green Bay, what would you change?' Only one angler mentioned launch facilities and no anglers mentioned other facilities. Pre-test anglers also rated enhanced facilities for fishing in the waters of Green Bay, and, as in the final survey, recreational facilities were always rated much lower than catch times and FCAs.
12. In contrast, one could develop choice pairs where there are two or more sites available and ask which site the individual would visit. Examples include Magat et al. (1988), Viscusi et al. (1991), Adamowicz et al. (1994, 1997), Mathews et al. (1997), Ruby et al. (1998), and Morey et al. (2002a). Choice studies such as this one that ask the individual to choose over different 'states' include Johnson et al. (1995), Adamowicz et al. (1996), Roe et al. (1996), Johnson and Desvousges (1997), Morey et al. (1997 and 2002c), Morey and Rossmann (2003), Stevens et al. (1997), Layton and Brown (1998), and Swait et al. (1998).
13. Many studies use only choice questions to estimate preferences. In these cases, one must be sure that the choice questions provide everything one needs to know about preferences, including how behavior would change if site characteristics change. In this assessment, the choice questions are only one component of the data.
14. The experimental design for the choice study was accomplished using the conjoint design software of Bretton Clark (1990).
15. A typical result in the risk literature is that women are more risk averse than men (see, for example, Slovic, 1987).
16. If the angler does not like the alternatives, he also has the option of not choosing from that pair (this happened in less than 3 per cent of the pairs). In addition, 172 (3.3 per cent) of the expected days follow-up questions were unanswered. Ten anglers (1.5 per cent) left all eight of these follow-up questions blank, and 53 respondents (8.2 per cent) left one or more of them blank. Blanks on the follow-up questions were assumed to contain no information about the individual's preferences; they were not interpreted as responses of zero days.
17. With questions involving a choice of moose hunting site, Adamowicz et al. (1997) included as a third alternative, 'Neither site A nor site B. I will NOT go moose hunting.' Along with two water-based recreational sites Adamowicz et al. (1994) included as a third alternative, 'Any other nonwater related recreational activity or stay at home.' With choice pairs over mountain bike sites, Morey et al. (2002a) included no 'opt-out' alternative other than the option of not answering a choice pair. Through focus groups and the survey, they found respondents able and willing to answer most of the pairs. Ruby et al. (1998) investigated the inclusion and form of 'opt-out' alternatives, and found that the form of the 'opt-out' can matter.
18. Note that, since for this calculation there is just one alternative in each state of the world, one obtains an estimate of the compensating variation per Green Bay fishing day rather than, as is typical, an estimate of the expected value of this compensating variation.
19. For more on the difference between WTP per day and per fishing day see Morey (1994).
20. Note that increasing catch rates by this amount would not compensate the anglers for past damages.

21. The stated-frequency data, when compared with use under current conditions (the RP data), indicate that anglers may be overly optimistic in stating how much they would fish under various Green Bay conditions. If the model is calibrated so that the predicted mean number of fishing days to Green Bay under current conditions is exactly equal to the observed mean in the RP data, the expected annual compensating variation falls from $111 to $76.

References

Adamowicz, W., J. Louviere and M. Williams. (1994), 'Combining revealed and stated preference methods for valuing environmental amenities', *Journal of Environmental Economics and Management*, **26**, 271–92.

Adamowicz, W.L., J. Swait, P. Boxall, J. Louviere and M. Williams (1997), 'Perceptions versus objective measures of environmental quality in combined revealed and stated preference models of environmental valuation', *Journal of Environmental Economics and Management*, **32**, 65–84.

Ben-Akiva, M. and T. Morikawa (1990), 'Estimation of travel demand models from multiple data sources', in M. Koshi (ed.), *Transportation and Traffic Theory*, New York: Elsevier, pp. 461–76.

Ben-Akiva, M., M. Bradley, T. Morikawa, J. Benjamin, T. Novak, H. Oppewal and V. Rao (1994), 'Combining revealed and stated preference data', *Marketing Letters*, **5**(4), 335–50.

Breffle, W.S., E.R. Morey, R. Rowe and D.M. Waldman (1999), 'Recreational fishing damages for fish consumption advisories in the waters of Green Bay', Prepared by Stratus Consulting for US Fish & Wildlife Service, US Department of the Interior, and US Department of Justice, Boulder, Co.

Bretton Clark (1990), 'Conjoint designer Version 3', 89 Headquarters Plaza, North Tower, 14th Floor, Morristown, NJ 07960; (201) 993-3135 (phone), (201) 993-1757 (fax).

Cameron, T.A. (1992), 'Combining contingent valuation and travel cost data for the valuation of nonmarket goods', *Land Economics*, **68**(3), 302–17.

Carson, R.T., R.C. Mitchell, W.M. Hanemann, R.J. Kopp, S. Presser and P.A. Ruud (1992), 'A contingent valuation study of lost passive use values resulting from the Exxon Valdez oil spill', prepared for the Attorney General of the State of Alaska.

Carson, R.T., W.M. Hanemann, R.J. Kopp, J.A. Krosnick, R.C. Mitchell, S. Presser, P.A. Ruud and V.K. Smith (1994), 'Prospective interim lost use value due to DDT and PCB contamination in the Southern California Bight – Volume I', prepared by Natural Resource Damage Assessment, Inc., for the National Oceanic and Atmospheric Administration, 30 September, 248.

Chen, H.Z. and S.R. Cosslett (1998), 'Environmental quality preference and benefit estimation in multinomial probit models: a simulation approach', *American Journal of Agricultural Economics*, **80**, 512–20.

Chen, H.Z., F. Lupi and J.P. Hoehn (1999), 'An empirical assessment of multinomial probit and logit models for recreational demand', in J.A. Herriges and C.L. Kling (eds), *Valuing Recreation and the Environment*, Cheltenham, UK and Northampton, MA: Edward Elgar, pp. 65–120.

Connelly, N.A., T.L. Brown and B.A. Knuth (1990), 'New York Statewide Angler Survey 1988', prepared by the New York State Department of Environmental Conservation, Division of Fish and Wildlife, Albany, April.

Connelly, N.A., B.A. Knuth and C.A. Bisogni (1992), 'Effects of the health advisory and advisory changes on fishing habits and fish consumption in New York sport fisheries', Report for New York Sea Grant Institute Project No. R/FHD-2-PD.

Fiore, B.J., H.A. Anderson, L.P. Hanrahan, L.J. Olson and W.C. Sonzogni (1989), 'Sport fish consumption and body burden levels of chlorinated hydrocarbons: a study of Wisconsin anglers', *Archives of Environmental Health*, **4**(2), 82–8.

Hauber, A.B. and G.R. Parsons (1998), 'The effect of nesting structure specification on welfare estimation in a random utility model of recreation demand: an application to the demand for recreation fishing', Working Paper No. 98-11, University of Delaware, College of Business and Economics, Department of Economics, Newark.

Hensher, D.A. and M. Bradley (1993), 'Using stated choice data to enrich revealed preference discrete choice models,' *Marketing Letters*, **4**, 139–52.

Herriges, J.A., C.L. Kling and D.J. Phaneuf (1999), 'Corner solution models of recreation demand: a comparison of competing frameworks', in J.A. Herriges and C.L. Kling (eds), *Valuing Recreation and the Environment*, Cheltenham, UK and Northampton, MA: Edward Elgar, pp. 163–97.

Hutchison, R. (1999), 'Impacts of PCB contamination on subsistence fishing in the Lower Fox River', prepared for Stratus Consulting and USFWS, January.

Jakus, P.M., D. Dadakas and J.M. Fly (1998), 'Fish consumption advisories: incorporating angler-specific knowledge, habits, and catch rates in a site choice model', *American Journal of Agricultural Economics*, **80**(5), 1019–24.

Jakus, P.M., M. Downing, M.S. Bevelhimer and J.M. Fly (1997), 'Do sportfish consumption advisories affect reservoir anglers' site choice?', *Agricultural and Resource Economic Review*, October, 196–204.

Johnson, F.R. and W.H. Desvousges (1997), 'Estimating stated preferences with rated-pair data: environmental, health, and employment effects of energy programs', *Journal of Environmental Economics and Management*, **34**, 79–99.

Johnson, F.R., W.H. Desvousges, E.E. Fries and L.L. Wood (1995), 'Conjoint analysis of individual and aggregate environmental preferences', Triangle Economic Research Technical Working Paper No. T-9502.

Kling, C.L. (1997), 'An evaluation of the gains from combining travel cost and contingent valuation data to value nonmarket goods', *Land Economics*, **73**, 428–37.

Knuth, B. (1996), 'Who heeds fish consumption advisories?', *The Information Exchange*, **5**, 1–5.

Knuth, B.A., N.A. Connelly and M.A. Shapiro (1993), 'Angler attitudes and behavior associated with Ohio River health advisories', Human Dimensions Research Unit, Department of Natural Resources, New York State College of Agriculture and Life Sciences, A Statutory College of the State University, Fernow Hall, Cornell University, Ithaca.

Layton, D. and G. Brown (1998), 'Heterogeneous preferences regarding global climate change', presented at NOAA Applications of Stated Preference Methods to Resource Compensation Workshop, Washington, DC.

Louviere, J.J. (1992), 'Experimental choice analysis: introduction and overview', *Journal of Business Research*, **24**, 89–95.

Louviere, J.J. (1996), 'Combining revealed and stated preference data: the rescaling revolution', prepared for the AERE Workshop: Tahoe City, CA, 2–4 June.

Lyke, A.J. (1993), 'Discrete choice models to value changes in environmental quality: a great Lakes Case Study', thesis presented to the University of Wisconsin-Madison.

Magat, W.A., W.K. Viscusi and J. Huber (1988), 'Paired comparison and contingent valuation approaches to morbidity risk valuation', *Journal of Environmental Economics and Management*, **15**, 395–411.

Mathews, K.E., W.H. Desvousges, F.R. Johnson and M.C. Ruby (1997), 'Using economic models to inform restoration decisions: The Lavaca Bay, Texas Experience', TER technical report prepared for presentation at the Conference on Restoration of Lost Human Uses of the Environment, Washington, DC, 7–8 May.

McFadden, D. (1986), 'The choice theory approach to market research', *Marketing Science*, **5**(4), 275–97.

McFadden, D. (1996), 'Why is natural resource damage assessment so hard?', Hibbard Lecture, Agricultural and Resource Economics, University of Wisconsin, Madison (May).

Milliman, S.R., B.L. Johnson, R.C. Bishop and K.J. Boyle (1992), 'The bioeconomics of resource rehabilitation: a commercial sport analysis for a Great Lakes fishery', *Land Economics*, **68**(2), 191–210.

Montgomery, M. and M. Needelman (1997), 'The welfare effects of toxic contamination in freshwater fish', *Land Economics*, **73**(2), 211–23.

Morey, E.R., T. Buchanan and D.M. Waldman (2002a), 'Estimating the benefits and costs to mountain bikers of changes in trail characteristics, access fees, and site closures:

choice experiments and benefits transfers', *Journal of Environmental Management*, **64**(4), 411–22.

Morey, E.R., W.S. Breffle, R.D. Rowe and D.M. Waldman (2002b), 'Estimating recreational trout fishing damages in Montana's Clark Fork River basin: a summary of a natural resource damage assessment', *Journal of Environmental Management*, **66**, 159–70.

Morey, E.R., K.G. Rossmann, L. Chestnut and S. Ragland (2002c), 'Modeling and estimating E[WTP] for reducing acid deposition injuries to cultural resources: using choice experiments in a group setting to estimate passive-use values', in S. Narvud and R. Ready (eds), *Valuing Cultural Heritage*, Cheltenham, UK and Northhampton, MA: Edward Elgar.

Morey, E.R., K.G. Rossmann, L. Chestnut and S. Ragland (1997), 'Valuing acid deposition injuries to cultural resources', prepared by Stratus Consulting for National Acid Precipitation Assessment Program.

Morey, E.R. and K.G. Rossmann (2003), 'Using stated-preference questions to investigate variations in willingness to pay for preserving marble monuments: classic heterogeneity, random parameters, and mixture models', *Journal of Cultural Economics*, **27**(3/4), 215–29.

Morikawa T., M. Ben-Akiva and D. McFadden (1990), 'Incorporating psychometric data in econometric travel demand models', prepared for the Banff Invitational Symposium on Consumer Decision Making and Choice Behavior.

Morikawa T., M. Ben-Akiva and K. Yamada (1991), 'Forecasting intercity rail ridership using revealed preference and stated preference data', *Transportation Research Record*, **1328**, 30–5.

Parsons, G.R., P.M. Jakus and T. Thomasi (1999), 'A comparison of welfare estimates from four models for linking seasonal recreational trips to multinomial logit models of site choice', University of Delaware Working Paper (April).

Roe, B., K.J. Boyle and M.F. Teisl (1996), 'Using conjoint analysis to derive estimates of compensating variation', *Journal of Environmental Economics and Management*, **31**, 145–50.

Ruby, M.C., F.R. Johnson and K.E. Mathews (1998), 'Just Say "No": assessing opt-out options in a discrete-choice stated-preferences survey of anglers', TER Working Paper T-9801.

Samples, K.C. and R.C. Bishop (1985), 'Estimating the value of variations in anglers' success rates: an application of the multiple-site travel cost method', *Marine Resources Research*, **2**(1), 55–74.

Silverman, W.M. (1990), 'Michigan's sport fish consumption advisory: a study in risk communication', a thesis submitted in partial fulfillment of the requirements for the degree of Master of Science (Natural Resources), University of Michigan.

Slovic, P. (1987), 'Perception of risk', *Science*, **236**, 281–5.

Stevens, T.H., C. Barrett and C.E. Willis (1997), 'Conjoint analysis of groundwater protection programs', *Agricultural and Resource Economics Review* (October), 229–36.

Stratus Consulting (1999), 'Injuries to fishery resources, Lower Fox River/Green Bay Natural Resource Damage Assessment', prepared for US Fish and Wildlife Service, US Department of the Interior, US Department of Justice, 8 November.

Sullivan, J., J. Delfino, C. Buelow and T. Sheffy (1983), 'Polychlorinated biphenyls in the fish and sediment of the Lower Fox River', Wisconsin, *Bulletin of Environmental Contamination and Toxicology*, **30**, 58–64.

Swait, J., W. Adamowicz and J. Louviere (1998), 'Attribute-based stated choice methods for resource compensation: an application to oil spill damage assessment', prepared for presentation at the Natural Resources Trustee Workshop on Applications of Stated Preference Methods to Resource Compensation, Washington, DC, 1–2 June.

Swait, J., J. Louviere and M. Williams (1994), 'A sequential approach to exploiting the combined strengths of SP and RP data: application to freight shipper choice', *Transportation*, **21**, 135–52.

Velleux, M. and D. Endicott (1994), 'Development of a mass balance model for estimating PCB export from the Lower Fox River to Green Bay', *Journal of Great Lakes Research*, **84**(2), 416–34.

Vena, J.E. (1992), 'Risk, perception, reproductive health risk and consumption of contaminated fish in a cohort of New York State anglers', New York State Angler Study Year One Progress Report.

Viscusi, W.K., W.A. Magat and J. Huber (1991), 'Pricing environmental health risks: survey assessments of risk–risk and risk–dollar trade-offs for chronic bronchitis', *Journal of Environmental Economics and Management*, **21**, 32–51.

WDNR (1997), 'Polychlorinated Biphenyl (PCB) contaminated sediment in the Lower Fox River: modeling analysis of selective sediment remediation', Wisconsin Department of Natural Resources Bureau of Watershed Management PUBL-WT-482-97.

WDNR (1998), 'Fox River and Green Bay PCB Fate and Transport Model Evaluations', Technical Memorandum 2d: Compilation and Estimation of Historical Discharges of Total Suspended Solids and PCB from Fox River Point Sources, Draft, 3 June.

West, P.C., J.M. Fly, R. Marans and F. Larkin (1989), 'Michigan Sport Angler Fish Consumption Study', Natural Resource Sociology Research Lab Technical Report No. 1, University of Michigan.

West, P.C., J.M. Fly, R. Marans, F. Larkin and D. Rosenblatt (1993), '1991–92 Michigan Sport Angler Fish Consumption Study', Natural Resource Sociology Research Lab Technical Report No. 6, University of Michigan.

19 Public preferences toward environmental risks: the case of trihalomethanes*

Richard T. Carson and Robert Cameron Mitchell

19.1 Introduction

This chapter presents the results of an in-depth study conducted in Herrin, a small Illinois town with a population of about 10 000 people.[1] Our study focused on the issue of the benefits of a town installing a carbon filtration system to remove trihalomethanes (THMs) from its drinking water system. The removal of THMs from drinking water has long been a controversial issue and the class of chemicals has a number of properties that make them an interesting topic for those interested in risk analysis. We examine the public's preferences toward a proposed policy that would reduce the level of THMs in the town's drinking water supply. The process of explaining the key characteristics of the risks associated with THMs and the policy decision whether to reduce that risk are explored in the context of a contingent valuation (CV) survey designed to measure willingness to pay (WTP) to implement the policy. A variety of tests are conducted to assess the properties of the WTP estimates for use in policy decisions.

THMs are a class of chemicals created during the process of chlorinating drinking water (Culp, 1984). They have been consistently shown to be carcinogenic but represent a low-level risk (Culp, 1984; Attias et al., 1995). In November 1979 the US Environmental Protection Agency (EPA) under the 1974 Safe Drinking Water Act set an interim Maximum Contaminant Level (MCL) for total trihalomethanes (THMs) of 0.10 mg/l as an annual average (44 FR 68624). To put the risk from THMs in perspective, chlorinated water containing THMs are estimated to kill between two and 100 people per year in the United States, largely through increased incident of urinary tract cancer. The latency period associated with this class of carcinogens is thought to be in the 20–30-year range. THMs in chlorinated water present a very low level of risk to drinking water consumers. The risk from not chlorinating the water is dramatically higher and much more immediate, since the chlorine kills biological contaminants. Removal of THMs from drinking water is a relatively straightforward matter that involves passing the water over some type of activated carbon filter. The major public policy discussion on this issue is whether small towns should be exempt from meeting the US EPA THM standard. At present, the interim THM standard only applies to municipal water systems (surface water and/or ground water) serving at least 10 000 people that add a disinfectant to the drinking water during any part of the treatment process. Small towns pose an interesting policy tradeoff question with respect to THMs due to the sharply rising per capita cost of carbon filtration as population decreases. Other drinking water contaminants such as arsenic pose a similar size of place versus per capita cost tradeoff.

We consider these issues in the context of designing a survey to elicit maximum WTP for a reduction in THMs. The key survey design question involves how to communicate low-level risks to respondents. The literature on risk perception contains many examples of the difficulty lay people have in grasping just how low many risks are (e.g., Davies, Covello, and Allen, 1986; Fisher, Pavolva, and Covello, 1991; Rimer and Nevel, 1999). Placing the risk communication exercise in the context of a CV survey allows us to judge the success of the exercise by comparing our findings with a set of well-defined economic predictions.

19.2   Preliminary risk communication research

We chose Herrin, and two of its neighbors where some of the survey development work was conducted, Carbondale and Marion, because their water systems had exceeded the THM standard several times in the past three years. As required by the EPA, the water systems sent their customers an offical notice reporting this event. In the course of designing the questionnaire, we conducted four focus groups followed by a series of in-depth interviews over a six month time period to gain insight into the difficulties local residents might have in understanding the risks posed by excess THMs and how we might design the survey instrument's scenario to accurately communicate these risk levels. Among our findings and design decisions were the following:

- Despite receiving a notice that their water system had exceeded the EPA standard for THMs, the focus group participants were mostly unaware of the notice and of THMs and their risks. When they considered THMs, they tended to confuse them with other drinking water risks, especially those from PCB contamination that had been an issue in a nearby city several years earlier. To deal with the low level of knowledge about THMs, we included basic information in the survey instrument about THMs and the risks they pose and highlighted the distinction between THMs and PCBs in several places in the questionnaire.
- Focus group participants tended to place a higher value on collective drinking water improvements than on improvements taken by

individual consumers such as the purchase of bottled water or the installation of under-the-sink purification devices. Spontaneous comments by respondents in our in-depth interviews clearly indicated that many citizens hold a strong preference for collective improvements because they value knowing that their fellow townspeople will also be protected.[2] In our survey we measure the value of collective drinking water improvements.

- Participants were sensitive to how local authorities treat a risk like that posed by excess THMs. On the one hand, they are generally skeptical about assurances from the local authorities that the drinking water is 'safe'; on the other hand, they believed strongly that, if there really was a serious problem with their drinking water, the authorities and especially the local press would publicize the seriousness of the situation. This default assumption required us to specify how local authorities viewed the risks posed by the levels of excess THMs in our scenarios. We modeled this information on the actual assurances the relevant authorities had given at the time of the local THM excess risk notifications.[3] It also turned out to be important to set up the divergence in views between the US EPA and state and local agencies as a way of justifying the need for public input on the issue. It was necessary to explain the concept of the US EPA maximum contaminant level (MCL) and the fact that THM levels below the MCL were not risk free, only less risky. We described the risk reductions in terms of bringing an existing THM risk down to the MCL risk level.

- The focus group participants found it difficult to grasp the nature of mortality risks and how a contaminant can affect them. We adopted the following approach to communicate this information: The first part of our scenario described the concept of a 'basic' risk everyone faces of dying, which gets greater as people get older. We used the example of how life insurance premiums increase with age. We then introduced the concept of what we called 'extra' or 'special' risks to which some people are exposed and others are not, and described the magnitude of the extra risk as that which a Hollywood stuntman, a police officer, and someone taking a single airline flight is exposed to. In an attempt to acquaint people with the concept of the monetary value of risk reductions, the scenario said that someone who is a stuntman would have to pay a large extra premium for life insurance on top of his or her basic premium.

- Not surprisingly, it was hard for focus group participants to grasp how 'low' a low-level risk was. We used several examples of low-level risks to help communicate this concept. One was the risk of dying in the crash of a scheduled US airliner flight. Another was the risk of being killed by lightning. In the scenario we told the respondents that out of two million people who die in the US from all causes, lightning kills only 116. We said people would only have to pay five cents for a $100 000 life insurance policy against being killed by lightning in any given year because this type of death is so infrequent.

- We found that casting various risks in terms of the risk of smoking cigarettes helped our pre-test subjects to grasp the relative magnitude of low-level risks. We calculated that the risk of being killed when taking a single airliner trip was equivalent to the extra risk caused by the lifetime consumption of two cigarettes, and that the extra risk of being a stuntman was equivalent to smoking 33 000 cigarettes in a lifetime. The use of cigarette equivalence for the risk from excess THM also had the effect of emphasizing its low-level carcinogenic nature and 20–30-year latency period.[4]

- As we expected, people found it difficult to judge whether a particular risk improvement was large or small when it was described solely in numerical terms, such as annual deaths per 100 000 people. They wanted information about how this risk compared with other risks. We developed several risk communication techniques to overcome this problem, the most important of which is a risk ladder. A great deal of our instrument development work was spent testing various types of risk ladders.

- The focus group participants had difficulty understanding the first type of risk ladder we tested, a Smith–Desvousges type ladder, which used a logarithmic scale to locate the number of people who die annually from various causes or activities (Smith and Desvousges, 1987). Smith and Desvousges used this ladder as a visual aid to communicate the risk from hazardous wastes in a CV study. The large range of different types of risk levels on their ladder – from the annual risk of stuntmen dying (2 per cent) to the 0.005 per cent deaths per year due to floods – and their use of a single scale to represent the full range of risks from high to low made it difficult for them to squeeze the ladder into a single page small enough for the interviewers to use comfortably in the field. Their solution to this problem was to use a logarithmic scale and to show breaks in the ladder between the different risk intervals.[5] We concluded their risk ladder was not satisfactory for our purposes because their scale did not clearly describe the range of low level risk (below 1.0 in 100 000) comparisons we wished to show and because many focus group participants found it difficult to understand logarithmic scale.

- Tests of an alternative risk ladder in our in-depth interviewers were favorable. The new ladder continues to use annual mortality per

100 000 people to depict risk levels and to use risk examples as anchors. The most important ways it differs from the Smith–Desvousges risk ladder are: (1) it uses an equal interval rather than a logarithmic scale and (2) it employs the device of magnifying the very lowest portions of the ladder to facilitate the portrayal of the very small risk reductions we asked our respondents to value. Respondents are first shown a base ladder for the full range of risk levels between 0 annual deaths per 100 000 to 1000 deaths per 100 000 people. The yearly chance of death faced by people in several age ranges is listed on the left and five examples of 'extra' risks on the right. After acquainting the respondent with the information on the base ladder, the interviewer unfolds a second page that is displayed on the right, next to the base ladder. This page shows two successive expansions of the risk levels at the bottom of the base ladder. The first sub-ladder expands the 0–25 mortality rate segment of the base ladder approximately 19 times and the second expands the 0–1 mortality rate of the first sub-ladder by an equivalent amount. The annual extra risk of dying per 100 000 people is shown on the sub-ladders for 13 occupations or situations.[6]

● The choice of which comparative risks to display on a risk ladder obviously plays an important role in framing the THM risks for the respondents.[7] We experimented with various types of risks to find the ones respondents found most meaningful to compare with the THM risk improvements. For example, we added the risk of dying in an auto accident because people asked where this would be placed on the ladder and dropped several recreational risk examples (such as dying while hand gliding) because focus group participants regarded voluntary risks such as these as irrelevant to the risks imposed on drinking water users.

Figure 19.1 shows a black and white version of our final risk ladder. We used a color-coded version of this ladder in the field to underscore the different risk ranges.

19.3   Structure of the survey instrument

We can best summarize the risk communication portion of our scenario by listing the relevant topics in the sequence they are presented to the respondent: (1) Explanation of the relationship of 'extra' risk to 'basic' risk; (2) examples of low level risks; (3) the distinction between voluntary and involuntary extra risk; (4) application of a number of cigarettes per lifetime metric to the risk examples discussed earlier in the scenario; (5) explanation

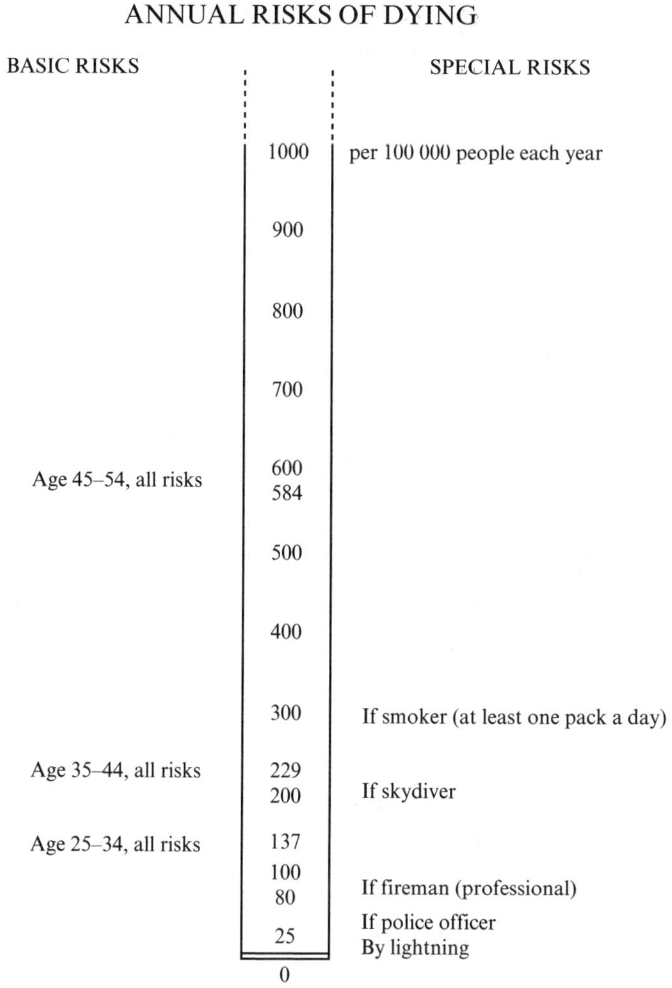

ANNUAL RISKS OF DYING

BASIC RISKS   SPECIAL RISKS

	1000	per 100 000 people each year
	900	
	800	
	700	
Age 45–54, all risks	600 584	
	500	
	400	
	300	If smoker (at least one pack a day)
Age 35–44, all risks	229 200	If skydiver
Age 25–34, all risks	137 100 80	If fireman (professional)
	25	If police officer By lightning
	0	

Figure 19.1a   Risk ladder (upper part)

of our risk ladder; and (6) description of how THMs are created in drinking water, the risk they pose at the US EPA maximum contaminant level, and where this risk is located on the risk ladder.

After telling respondents about THMs and how THMs could be reduced, we informed them that any reduction would require an increase in their water bill to pay for a drinking water filtration bond issue. They are told Herrin could get one of three different risk reduction programs, A–C, by installing different levels of carbon filtration technology on the town's

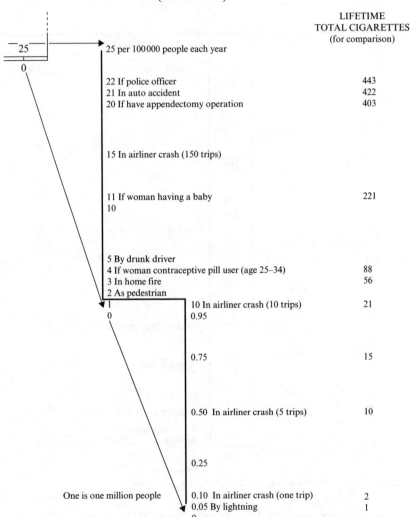

LOWER LEVEL RISKS
(ANNUAL)

Figure 19.1b   Risk ladder (lower part)

water treatment plant, each of which would bring the town's existing THM risk down to the US EPA MCL risk level. The respondents are shown a risk ladder on which the size of the risk reduction offered by each program is labeled A, B, and C.

At this point in the interview, respondents are asked about their willingness to pay for the reduction in risk from THMs. They are first asked whether they would potentially be prepared to vote in favor of taxing themselves to reduce THMs in their drinking water. If the answer is no, the respondent is recorded as being willing to pay $0.[8] If the answer is yes, the respondent is asked to value THM risk improvements by stating the maximum amount his or her household water bill could be increased and have the respondent still favor installing the carbon filtration system for each of three THM risk improvements, where C = smallest, B = middle, and A = largest.

We varied the size and sequence of the risk improvements. First we randomly assigned respondents to one of two sets of risk improvements (A or B) with the largest risk reduction in the A set being smaller than the smallest risk reduction in the B set. Second, within treatments A and B there was a further random assignment that varied the order in which the levels were presented. Thus, there are four subsamples (A1, A2, B1, and B2). Table 19.1 displays the properties of the experimental design used in terms of these four subsamples. This design allows us to test whether respondent WTP estimates are sensitive to: (1) the magnitude of risk levels they are asked to value, (2) the order in which the particular risk reduction levels are asked, and (3) the interaction between the magnitude of the risk levels and question order. Our design allows for both out-of-sample and within-sample tests of the sensitivity of the WTP estimates to the magnitude of the risk reduction valued.

Card B11 shown in Figure 19.2 displays the visual representation used for the 2.43×10^{-5} risk reduction, which was the first risk reduction one of the subsamples of respondents was asked about. This card shows the change in initial (FROM) to subsequent levels (TO) if the program was implemented as well as the actual magnitude of the change. In order to give the respondents the most meaningful context for making their risk valuation judgments, the respondent is shown a card which describes each risk reduction in terms of: (1) the absolute change in THM levels, (2) the general risk of dying per 100 000, and (3) the cigarette equivalent consumption which in this case is a reduction from 65 cigarettes in a lifetime to 11. Each respondent is shown similar cards for the other two risk reductions the respondent was asked about.

Our THM survey instrument uses an open-ended elicitation format. The open-ended format is not incentive compatible in the sense that truthful preference revelation is not always an optimal strategy (Hoehn and Randall, 1987) and, further, valuation questions concerning multiple levels of a public good where only one level of the good can be supplied are also known not to be incentive compatible (Carson, Groves, and Machina, 1999).[9] It is not possible to examine the first type of strategic behavior in

Table 19.1   Experimental design for tests of metric bias and question
order effects

Valuation question order	Smaller risk changes	Larger risk changes
1-2-3	Version A1	Version B1
	0.04/0.43/1.33	2.43/4.43/8.93
2-1-3	Version A2	Version B2
	0.04/0.43/1.33	4.43/2.43/8.93

	B to A	
<u>REFERENDUM PASSES</u> **<u>CHANGE IF</u>**	<u>From</u>	<u>To</u>
Level of THMs ppm 0.45 parts per million	0.55	0.10
General risk of dying per 100 000 2.43 per 100 000	3.0	0.57
General risk equivalent in total lifetime cigarettes 54	65	11

<u>Conditions:</u>   1. THMs only source of contamination
2. Reduced only to EPA standard
3. Authorities say risk level not high enough to worry about

Figure 19.2   Card B-11

the context of this study, but it is possible to look at the issue of the strategic incentives that follow from asking respondents multiple questions about different levels of the same good as long as we are prepared to assume that the valuation for the good should be a smooth continuous monotonic function of the quantity of the good. Under this condition, respondents should increase (or decrease) the value of the largest risk they are asked to value relative to the smallest, in order to encourage the risk-reduction agency to either supply more or less risk reduction. We formally test this proposition in the construct validity section below.

Another component of our scenario design is the use of a water utility bill as the payment vehicle. We find respondents accepted this vehicle as realistic because of its close tie to the actual problem. We ask for willingness to pay in annual payments that has the desirable property of conveying the idea that the filtration system, once installed, would continue to be operated.

After the valuation questions are asked, the survey instrument probes respondent motives for why they answered the valuation questions in the way they did. These are followed by questions measuring attitudinal and behavioral information and demographic characteristics. Respondents are also given the opportunity to revise their WTP amounts.

19.4   Sensitivity of WTP estimates to risk reduction magnitude and question order

The issue of the sensitivity of WTP estimates to the magnitude of the good being valued has been the subject of considerable debate in the literature (Mitchell and Carson, 1989; Kahneman and Knetsch, 1992; Arrow et al., 1993; Carson, 1997). Mitchell and Carson (1989) originally referred to this issue as 'metric bias' and note that it occurs in the context of risk reductions when respondents treat the risk reductions asked about in an ordinal manner rather than considering the actual magnitude of the risk reductions asked about. Contingent valuation estimates of WTP for risk reductions have in several instances been shown to be insensitive to the magnitude of the risk reduction being valued (Beattie et al., 1998; Hammitt and Graham, 1999). Such results have the obvious and troubling implication that WTP estimates obtained by a contingent valuation survey are not reliable enough to be used by policy makers.

Several reasons have been advanced to explain why WTP estimates for a given level of risk reduction vary from study to study (Kahneman and Knetsch, 1992; Baron and Greene, 1996; Fetherstonhaugh et al., 1997). One is that the initial risk communication exercise was improperly designed. Since the WTP questions depend crucially on the success of the initial risk communication exercise, its failure should translate into CV responses that do not have the expected economic properties. In this regard, low-level risk, and, particularly, differences in low-level long-term environmental risks are well known for being very difficult to effectively communicate (Fischhoff, 1990).[10] Further, our examination of the existing literature suggests that most of the troublesome cases appear in surveys where the risk reduction policy is briefly explained and the risk reduction is presented in quantitative terms with little additional context. Problems seem to be concentrated in telephone surveys where it is not possible to use visual aids. To help overcome these difficulties, we used in-person interviews with an extensive oral presentation coupled with visual aids describing both low-level risks in general and the specific THM risks that were the main focus of the CV exercise.

The major competing explanation emphasizes the inherent cognitive difficulty of understanding low-level risks and of placing monetary values on environmental amenities. The psychological heuristics and biases literature that predicts a lack of sensitivity to the quantity of the good being valued emphasizes the role framing effects have on human risk judgments. One of these is that the order in which risk-reduction goods are valued will affect how respondents value the goods (Moore, 1999), even when respondents are warned that they will be asked to value several risk improvements. In contrast, the standard economic framework does not predict an order effect if the entire sequence is known in advance of asking the first question. The experimental design adopted above allows us to investigate both of these predictions from the psychology literature.

19.5   Survey administration
The sampling frame for the survey was defined as all households within the Herrin city limits. Households are chosen using a two-stage process. At the first stage, 250 household addresses are chosen at random from the phonebook. At the second stage, the dwelling unit located two dwelling units to the right of the initially chosen dwelling unit is designated to be interviewed.[11] This procedure ensured that houses without telephones have a chance of being included in the sample. At the household level, the interviewer enumerates all household members over 18 who have financial responsibility in the household in the sense that they 'have or share responsibility for deciding the household budget and for paying housing, food and other expenses'. Where multiple household members meet the financial responsibility criteria, the person to be interviewed is chosen according to a selection table. Interviewers received two days of training during which they conducted several practice interviews. There are 237 completed interviews out of 286 attempted interviews for a response rate of 83 per cent. The survey instrument took a little over 30 minutes on average to administer.

19.6   Empirical results
The basic empirical results from our study are presented in Table 19.2. We provide five summary statistics for each of the six risk levels valued: (a) the percentage giving a zero response, (b) median WTP, (c) mean WTP, (d) the 5 per cent α-trimmed mean[12] (labeled 'α[mean]' in Table 19.2), and (e) a 'corrected' mean WTP (labeled 'C[mean]' in Table 19.2) derived after dropping the 11 cases where the interviewer's evaluation clearly indicated that the respondent did not understand the scenario and/or it was clear that the respondent had given the same large WTP ($60 or greater) response to two or more of the risk reductions. Almost all of these cases are among those

Table 19.2 Household WTP higher water bills for THM risk reductions

Version/From/To/Change	Annual deaths per 100000	THM risk improvement reductions (ppm)				
		Per cent zero	Median	Mean	α[Mean]	C[Mean]
Version A (N = 121)						
A1: 0.11/0.10/0.01	(0.04)	87 per cent		$0	$3.78	$1.13 $2.86
				(±$2.76)	(±$1.41)*	(±$1.82)
A2: 0.18/0.10/0.08	(0.43)	66	0	11.37	8.30	9.19
				(±4.33)	(±3.72)	(±3.37)
A3: 0.33/0.10/0.23	(1.33)	42	17	23.73	18.99	20.49
				(±7.37)	(±6.35)	(±5.20)
Version B (N = 117)						
B1: 0.55/0.10/0.45	(2.43)	58 per cent		0	15.23	12.70 11.79
				(±4.64)	(±4.25)	(±3.38)
B2: 0.90/0.10/0.80	(4.43)	39	20	26.25	23.08	23.51
				(±8.99)	(±5.78)	(±5.39)
B3: 1.65/0.10/1.55	(8.93)	20	36	44.27	42.32	42.68
				(±7.22)	(±7.98)	(±7.32)

Note: *Ninety-five per cent confidence intervals in parentheses.

effectively dropped when we apply the α-trimmed mean procedure to the data.[13] All WTP amounts are in 1985 dollars.

A casual examination of the results in Table 19.2 suggests that the WTP estimates for the two risk reduction subsamples – A and B – generally increase as the magnitude of the risk reductions increases, although not monotonically so. The WTP amount for the largest risk reduction valued (1.33) by those receiving Treatment A is greater than the smallest risk valued by those receiving Treatment B (2.43). We consider this issue at more length in the construct validity section below.

A simple comparison of the lowest Treatment A and Treatment B risk values rejects the null hypothesis of no difference in WTP at the $p < 0.01$ level for both the corrected and uncorrected datasets. The same result occurs when the values of the middle and largest risks for Versions A and B are compared. In each case the lower absolute value for the risk improvement receives a lower WTP value at the 0.01 level. These results reject the metric bias hypothesis.

The test can be made more rigorous by controlling for the order in which the WTP questions were posed and for a possible interaction between treatment and order effects. Table 19.3 shows the results of the relevant analysis of variance (ANOVA) tests using the corrected data. These results show that there continues to be a consistent version effect (Treatment A versus Treatment B) across all three of the amounts asked, thereby rejecting the metric bias hypothesis at $p < 0.001$ in each case. In contrast, none of the order effect tests even begin to approach traditional levels of statistical significance. The tests involving an interaction effect between treatment version and order are never significant at the $p = 0.10$ level. Similar conclusions are drawn from ANOVA estimates based upon the uncorrected dataset.

Further, evidence in favor of rejecting the hypothesis of a lack of sensitivity to the absolute magnitude of the risk can be seen in the percentage of zero WTP responses received for the smallest and largest risks valued in the two treatments. For the smallest risk, 87 per cent of respondents gave a zero WTP amount for the Treatment A risk of 0.04 annual deaths per 1000, while 58 per cent of respondents gave a zero WTP amount for the smallest Treatment B risk of 2.43 annual deaths per 1000, with the difference being significant at the $p < 0.01$ level. For the largest risk, 42 per cent of the Treatment A respondents gave a zero WTP to 1.33 annual deaths per 1000, while only 20 per cent of the Treatment B respondents gave a zero WTP amount for the largest risk of 8.93 annual deaths per 1000, with the difference also being significant at the $p < 0.01$ level.

Table 19.3   Tests for metric bias and question order effects

---

Metric test:
H0: Ordinal ranking – Amount A_i = Amount B_i, i = 1, 2, 3
H1: Cardinal ranking/scope sensitivity – Amount A_i < Amount B_i, i = 1, 2, 3

Order effect test:
H0: No question order bias – order 1, 2, 3 = order 2, 1, 3
H1: Question order bias – order 1, 2, 3 ≠ order 2, 1, 3

Interaction test:
H0: No interaction effect
$A_i - B_i$ for order 1, 2, 3 = $A_i - B_i$ for order 2, 1, 3
H1: Interaction effect
$A_i - B_i$ for order 1, 2, 3 = $A_i - B_i$ for order 2, 1, 3

Analysis of variance results (N = 230)

Amount 1	VERAB	F = 21.93	P < 0.0001
	ORDER	F = 0.09	P = −0.7641
	ORDER*VERAB	F = 2.29	P = 0.1319
Amount 2	VERAB	F = 19.90	P < 0.0001
	ORDER	F = 0.41	P = 0.5243
	ORDER*VERAB	F = 2.05	P = 0.1537
Amount 3	VERAB	F = 20.74	P < 0.0001
	ORDER	F = 0.04	P = 0.8478
	ORDER*VERAB	F = 0.48	P = 0.4886

VERAB = Treatments A and B
ORDER = Treatments 1 (1, 2, 3) and 2 (2, 1, 3)
ORDER*VERAB = Interaction between treatments A and B and 1 and 2

19.7   Construct validity

We looked at construct validity in two different ways. The first compares our results with theoretical predictions; the second evaluates whether our WTP estimates are systematically related to variables that a priori one would expect to be predictive of the magnitude of the WTP amounts given.

The economic literature on risk (e.g., Jones-Lee, 1974, 1976) poses two straightforward predictions.[14] The first is that WTP should increase with increases in the magnitude of the risk reduction ($\partial WTP/\partial\delta > 0$). The second is the rate of increase in WTP should be declining with increases in risk reductions ($\partial^2 WTP/\partial\delta^2 < 0$). Both of these predictions can be examined by examining the following regression models that were fitted to the α-trimmed mean or corrected mean WTP amounts from Table 19.2.[15] There are six observations in these regression equations, one from each treatment, following the common biometrics practice of fitting the dose response models to the relevant summary statistic from each treatment group.[16]

Starting with the α-trimmed mean estimates, which tend to drop out a group of respondents who gave the same WTP response, either low ($0) or high, for all three risk levels, one estimates the model:

$$\log(\text{WTP}) = 2.3520 + 0.6298 * \log(\delta), \qquad (19.1)$$
$$(16.98) \quad (8.08)$$

where t-statistics are in parentheses and the adjusted R^2 is 0.928. This model fits significantly better than a linear model and avoids the problem in any linear model with a positive constant term of suggesting a positive WTP for a zero reduction in risk.

Because the installation of a particular filtration level will only provide one risk improvement, economic theory suggests strategic behavior may be optimal in which WTP for the largest risk will be over or understated depending upon the respondent's ideal risk-cost combination. We construct a position variable POS, which equals -1 for the smallest risk, 0 for the second largest risk, and 1 for the largest risk that a respondent was asked to value. This variable allows for symmetric deviations in the valuation model estimated in (19.1) based upon the relative magnitude of the particular risk in the set of risks the agent was asked to value. The estimated regression model including this variable is:

$$\log(\text{WTP}) = 2.364 + 0.5380 * \log(\delta) + 0.3600 * \text{POS}, \qquad (19.2)$$
$$(31.87) \quad (10.74) \qquad (3.31)$$

where the adjusted R^2 is now 0.979 and the estimate of σ from the regression is 0.181. This model represents a clear improvement over the model presented in equation (19.1) suggesting that agent WTP for a particular risk was influenced not only by the actual magnitude of the risk, δ, but also by its relative position in the set of three risks.

It is possible to allow for a non-symmetric effect with respect to POS by allowing the lowest risk valued and the highest risk valued to have different coefficients. The F-test for the sum of these two coefficients being zero is 0.668 ($p = 0.499$). This test suggests that the hypothesis of symmetric response to POS cannot be rejected.

Turning now to the corrected mean WTP data from Table 19.2, the estimated model is:

$$\log(\text{WTP}) = 2.5508 + 0.4593 * \log(\delta), \qquad (19.3)$$
$$(19.60) \quad (6.27)$$

where the adjusted R^2 is 0.885. Again the log–log model fits substantially better than does a linear model.

The regression model fit for the corrected mean WTP data with the POS variable is:

$$\log(\text{WTP}) = 2.5635 + 0.3630^* \log(\delta) + 0.3778^*\text{POS}, \qquad (19.4)$$
$$(120.23) \quad (25.23) \qquad\qquad (12.10)$$

where the adjusted R^2 is now 0.998 and the estimate of σ is 0.052. Again this model represents a clear improvement over its counterpart (19.3) without the POS variable. The F-test for allowing POS having a different low and high effect is 0.040 ($p = 0.860$).

We use equations (19.2) and (19.4) with POS set equal to zero in order to derive our WTP estimates and in turn to make our estimates of the statistical value of life (SVL). In using these equations it is necessary to add back in a function of σ to obtain consistent estimates under the assumption of normality of the error term (Goldberger, 1968). For equation (19.4), the appropriate formula is given by

$$E(\text{WTP}) = \text{EXP}[2.5635 + 0.3778^* \log(\delta) + (0.052)^2/2], \qquad (19.5)$$

where 2.5635 and 0.3778 were the regression model coefficients and 0.052 was the estimate of σ. Consistent estimates from equation (19.2) can be obtained in a similar fashion. Figure 19.3 displays estimated WTP from equation (19.2) and (19.4) as a function of the magnitude of the risk reduction valued.

Our empirical results suggest a significant premium for the largest risk reduction the respondent is offered. After correcting for this premium associated with the largest offered risk reduction, it is not possible to reject the hypothesis that the WTP amounts for all six of the risk reductions are drawn from a single smooth continuous underlying risk–WTP function, where the log of WTP increases linearly in terms of the log of risk reduction. The log–log functional form is consistent with economic theory underlying the valuation of risk reductions. It is also interesting to note that the log–log functional form is commonly used in dose–response experiments. Further we note that a dose–response relationship between WTP and the magnitude of risk reduction is a good analogy in terms of summarizing the results. This is done in a simple figure that traces out how the percentage willing to pay a particular increase in their household water bill decreases as the size of the water bill increases.

The results from both equations (19.1) and (19.2) are consistent with the two predictions of economic theory that $\partial\text{WTP}/\partial\delta > 0$ and $\partial^2\text{WTP}/\partial\delta^2 < 0$. These results are robust to using either the raw mean WTP estimates or the

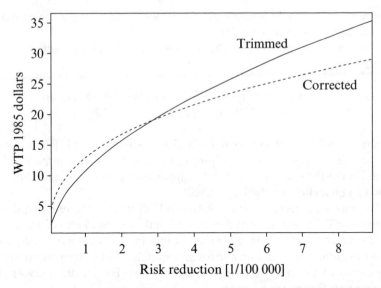

Figure 19.3   Household WTP for .04 to 8.93 in a 100 000 risk reductions

α-trimmed mean estimates as the dependent variable. Support for the $\partial WTP/\partial\delta > 0$ proposition is not sensitive to the functional form we used, while support for the $\partial^2 WTP/\partial\delta^2 < 0$ proposition, which concerns the curvature of the function, comes from comparing the fit of a linear specification with that of the log–log specification in equations (19.1) and (19.2). The linear specification clearly provides an inferior fit to the data. A quadratic model in δ provides a similar fit to the log–log model and also suggests acceptance of the declining marginal utility ($\partial^2 WTP/\partial\delta^2 < 0$) hypothesis. This declining marginal utility for risk reductions may have strong policy implications. We discuss the implications of these findings in a later section of this chapter.

Our empirical results are all consistent with several other tests that economic theory suggests concerning how WTP amounts should change with changes in risk levels. Construct validity is examined by regressing log(WTP) or the probability of a non-zero WTP response on several covariates that a priori should have particular signs. After controlling for the size of the risk reduction, we find that household size is significantly related to the probability of a non-zero WTP response. Conditional on giving a positive WTP response, we find that the log of income is a highly significant ($p < 0.001$) predictor of log(WTP) as was a rating (prior to the main CV scenario) of the harm done from chemical contaminants in Herrin's drinking water. Respondents over 55 are willing to pay substantially less than

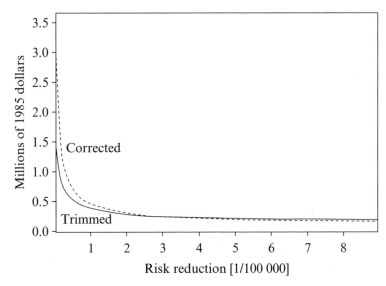

Figure 19.4   Value of a statistical life for 0.04 to 8.93 in a 100 000 risk reductions

those under 55, where the 55-year-old threshold was chosen in reference to the 20–30 year latency period of cancer from THM exposure. Household size had a significant positive effect on the probability of providing a non-zero WTP amount.

19.8   Value of a statistical life
The expectation of the statistical value of life (SVL) can be calculated by $E(SVL[\delta^*]) = (100\,000/\delta^*)(WTP[\delta^*]/2.86)$, where δ^* is the risk reduction of interest, $1/\delta^*$ provides the appropriate scale factor aggregation factor when multiplied by 100 000, $WTP[\delta^*]$ is the predicted household WTP for δ^*, and 2.86 is the estimate of the average household size from our survey. In Table 19.4 we present our estimates for the six risk reductions for both the α-trimmed mean estimates from equation (19.2) and the corrected mean equation (19.4).[17] Figure 19.4 is a graph of the estimated SVL functions using both equations (19.2) and (19.4) over the entire range of risk reductions considered, 0.04 (in 100 000) to 8.93. Figure 19.5 graphs the function after dropping the values of the smallest and largest risk reductions. This makes it possible to observe more details about the shape of the WTP function over its central range

From Table 19.4, someone familiar with the SVL literature (e.g., Cropper and Freeman, 1991) will immediately note that our estimates are on the low

412   *Applications*

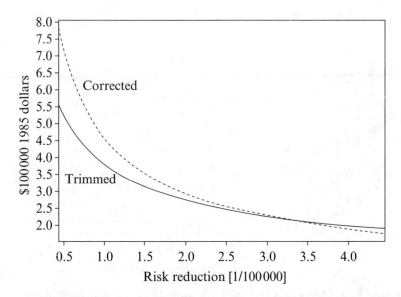

Figure 19.5   Value of a statistical life for 0.43 to 4.43 in a 100 000 risk reductions

Table 19.4   Value of a statistical life in millions of 1985 dollars

Risk reduction (δ)	Equation (2) (α-trimmed means)	Equation (4) Corrected mean
0.04	1.672	3.527
0.43	0.558	0.777
1.33	0.331	0.378
2.43	0.251	0.258
4.43	0.190	0.176
8.93	0.137	0.113

side of the range of SVL estimates in the literature. Almost all of the other estimates, however, are obtained by looking at current accident rates. That our estimates should be lower than most of the other SVL estimates in the literature is consistent with economic theory's predictions for respondents who discount their WTP for the risk reduction due to the risk's 20–30-year latency period.

After we discount our statistical life value estimates using a range of (exponential) discount rates typically used in the literature, our statistical life value estimates are well within the range commonly found in the literature

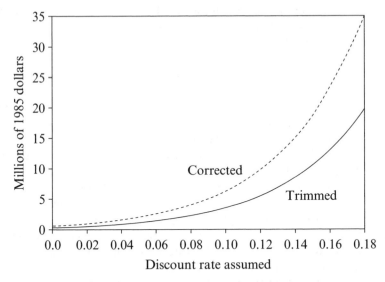

Figure 19.6   Implied values of a current statistical life assuming a 25 year latency and a 1 in 100 000 risk reduction

for WTP to avoid current period fatal accidents. Figure 19.6 displays the implied value for a current statistical life for a 25-year latency period and discount rates ranging from 0 per cent to the common consumer credit card rate of 18 per cent.

19.9   Discussion

THMs represent the quintessential type of environmental risk that confront government regulators. They involve a very low-level risk with a long latency period that is imposed upon the public as a side effect of a government action to provide a public good, in this case the reduction of harmful biological contaminants by chlorinating drinking water. Any MCL short of totally eliminating THMs from drinking water is not completely safe. There are clear economies of scale in installing equipment to bring THMs to the MCL that lead to pressure to exempt small producers. A non-federal agency must implement the technical remedy. In this particular case, our results suggest that installing public provided activated carbon filtration systems whose only benefit is to reduce THM levels to the standard is not likely to be welfare improving for Herrin.

Our CV survey appears to have worked well in this situation in the sense that: (a) most people were able to answer the WTP questions; (b) the amounts provided generally seem reasonable, if not on the low side, given the existing literature on SVL; (c) all predictions from economic theory with respect to risk (which our study was designed to test) were confirmed; and (d) the WTP amounts are systematically related to other factors such as income, age, and household size in the direction that one would expect.

Problematic with both the open-ended format used in this study and the asking of multiple questions are the incentives for strategic behavior. While the first cannot be tested for here, our empirical results, with respect to the very significant effect of the position variable (POS) in equations (19.2) and (19.4), are consistent with such behavior. We have attempted to undo the strategic behavior by setting the POS variable to equal zero in calculating WTP estimates for different risks levels. This is the conservative choice relative to setting POS equal to one, which might be justified if one thought that all of the open-ended WTP responses are biased downward, which often appears to be the case. Interestingly, while we find strong support for the presence of strategic behavior, which is predicted by economic theory, we find no evidence in support of the order effects predicted by some of the psychological literature on framing effects.

Even though we have strongly rejected the null hypothesis put forth that agents in CV studies are insensitive to the quantitative magnitudes of the good that they are asked to value, an issue that naturally arises is whether the magnitude of the differences in our WTP estimates are correct. Over small enough changes in risk, one would expect the change in WTP to increase at almost a linear rate in terms of increases in risk reductions (Machina, 1995). According to expected utility theory, if we assume that income effects are sufficiently small and available income sufficiently large, we would expect this approximate linearity to hold over a fairly large range (Weinstein, Shepard, and Pliskin, 1980; Hammitt and Graham, 1999).

Compared with most studies of risk values, our set of risk reductions both cover a much wider range – almost three orders of magnitude (0.04×10^{-5} to 8.93×10^{-5}) – and value smaller risks more than do most studies. For the larger risk reductions we examine, our results show an approximately linear relationship between WTP and the size of the risk reductions. For the smaller risk reductions, however, marginal WTP declines considerably over the range of risk reductions we examined.[18] There is an important policy implication of this finding – for the same number of statistical lives saved, the benefits of government actions to reduce very small risks over very large numbers of people are considerably greater than the benefits of actions that reduce large risks over a much smaller number of people.

There is another factor, however, which works in a different direction. As the size of the risk reduction being valued decreases, the number of respondents who give the corner solution of a zero WTP increases. This can be formally examined by stacking the observations in Table 19.2 and then

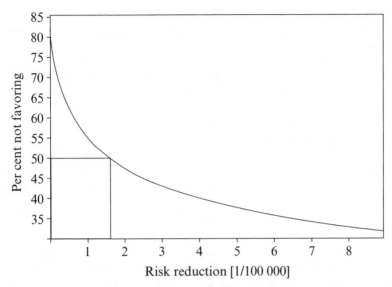

Figure 19.7   Opposition to program by magnitude of risk reduction

fitting a logistic regression model to the probability of providing a zero WTP response as a function of the risk reduction asked about. Again, as we saw earlier, using log(δ) provides a substantially better fit than δ. The fit is also improved by adding the POS variable, which suggests that some of the strategic behavior is coming through saying 'no' to risk reduction levels other than the highest level offered. The results from this model are:

$$\text{logit(prob. of \$0 WTP)} = 0.2047 - 0.4358* \log(\delta) - 0.4717*\text{POS},$$
$$(2.38) \qquad\quad (-7.05) \quad (-4.13) \qquad (19.7)$$

where the (McFadden) pseudo R-square is 0.179. Figure 19.7 shows a graph of this relationship and suggests that a THM risk reduction would have to be larger than 1 in 100 000 in order to gain majority approval. This suggests the possibility of considerable divergence between political support for a program to reduce very low-level risks and the economic value of such a plan. The lower the risk level, the lower the percentage of people who would vote for a further reduction and the higher the expected value of each life saved.

19.10   Concluding remarks
There is abundant evidence that people have difficulties with making decisions about low-level risks in their daily lives. The task of the CV survey designer would be much easier if the objective were simply to predict how

the public would vote on a policy issue, if offered the opportunity. In that case, the survey designer would only need to incorporate into the wording of the survey instrument the likely information set the voters will have available to them when they vote. The key difficulty in using CV to estimate WTP for risk reductions is not describing the reduction in the CV instrument but ensuring that respondents actually comprehend the size of the risk reduction by an effective method of communicating this information. The results of this chapter suggest that it is possible to effectively communicate risk levels to respondents even at low risk levels but replicating our success will likely be neither quick nor inexpensive. A careful program of pre-testing would be necessary along with use of the expensive in-person survey mode.

There has been surprisingly little work on the properties of different communication devices in the context of a CV survey (e.g., Loomis and duVair, 1993).[19] Much of the focus of this chapter has been on the development of a risk communication device for a low-level environmental risk with a long latency period. Our risk ladder with its cigarette equivalence scale combines properties of a Smith and Desvousges (1987) type risk ladder with risk communications devices that put the risk reduction in the context of a meaningful risk scale. It would be interesting to see how our hybrid risk ladder fares compared with other risk communication devices given its apparent success here. One encouraging recent paper by Corso, Hammitt, and Graham (2000) compares three different risk communication devices in the context of a CV survey using risks that are larger and fall in a more narrow range than those used in this study. With the first risk communication device, WTP estimates were effectively insensitive to the magnitude of the risk. The WTP estimates for the second device showed some sensitivity, and the WTP estimates for the third increased almost linearly as the magnitude of the risk reduction increased. This third device should be tested with lower-level risks such as the ones used in this study.

Additional research is also needed to determine how people discount risks over different time horizons as a wide range of estimates is obtained by assuming a wide range of different plausible discount rates. Horowitz and Carson (1990) provide a method for examining this issue. Cropper and Portney (1990) use it to look at a number of important policy issues involving discounting and find indications of non-exponential discounting over very long time horizons. In the specific context of this study it would be useful to know whether exponential discounting is a reasonable approximation over the 20–30 year latency period used and what a reasonable approximation to the discount rate for long term cancer risks is.

We suspect the reality is that people value different types of risks differently (Horowitz and Carson, 1991), that risk reductions of different magnitudes for the same risk suggests different SVL numbers, and that people do not use simple exponential discounting when they value risks with long latency periods. While such results would not be inconsistent with economic theory, they substantially complicate the situation for a policy analyst who is trying to determine whether the net benefits of a government action to help reduce risks are positive. The always-harried analyst would like to have a single SVL number and discount rate to use in an exponential manner. The empirical question is how much such a simple view of the world diverges from how people actually value risks. If divergences are large, can they be quantified in such a way that some easy to use function can be developed to replace a single SVL number and discount rate?

Notes

*   We gratefully acknowledge financial support from the US Environmental Protection Agency (Cooperative Agreement CR810466-01-6) in undertaking some of the work reported here. The views expressed here, however, are solely those of the authors. Earlier versions of this chapter were presented at meetings of the Society for Risk Analysis and the Association for Public Policy Analysis and Management. We thank Anna Alberini, Maureen Cropper and George Parsons for helpful comments on earlier versions of this chapter.

1.   For Herrin's official web page see http://www.VillageProfile.com/illinois/herrin/index.html.

2.   This suggests that purchases of household filtration devices would not be fully reflective of the full range of relevant benefits for a policy that would involve collective provision of the risk improvement.

3.   In each of the three communities we studied, the local authorities consistently downplayed the danger posed by the excess THMs. Our findings in this study are contingent on this scenario element as we believe that, if our scenario had stated that the state and local authorities urged voters to support a referendum to raise water rates to cover the cost of reducing THMs, respondents might have been willing to pay significantly more money for the same risk reductions.

4.   Neither of us are experts in risk analysis, therefore our translation of risk levels reported in the literature to the various risk levels we use in our survey should not be viewed as authoritative in any respect. We believe the risk comparisons we present to the respondents are sufficiently accurate for our purposes and that the substitution of more accurate estimates would not substantially change our findings. We also believe there is a need for an authoritative catalog of risk levels quantified in easy-to-understand metrics, such as cigarette equivalents.

5.   Smith and Desvousges augmented their ladder with pie charts to show the low-level risk changes from controlling hazardous wastes they asked their respondents to value. In our view, however, the use of separate pie charts to show low-level risk changes separates them from the important context provided by the risk ladder. Smith and Desvousges also attempted the difficult task of trying to convey separate probabilities for the risk of exposure and the risk of mortality if exposed. We did not face this issue in this study (which is typical of many environmental risks) because all households were exposed to THM via their household water supply.

6.   We pre-tested our ladder by using it in a series of in-depth interviews using our draft instrument. Respondents appeared to have much less trouble understanding the risk comparisons displayed on our ladder than they did with the Smith–Desvousges ladder. The interviewers reported that many respondents expressed considerable interest in the risk information presented in this fashion.

7. That context influences risk perception is well documented in the experimental literature on risk perception (e.g., Kahneman, Slovic, and Tversky, 1982). The inevitability of this phenomenon and the potential magnitude of these effects place a burden on the researcher to justify the context he or she uses. The context we used was intended to minimize potential sources of bias and to be policy relevant.

8. Note that this approach makes estimated aggregate WTP more conservative since some respondents will have a strategic incentive to answer no on the basis of their perception of the expected cost of the filtration system if their actual WTP is less than that expected cost. Respondents who were asked what the cost of the program would be were told they would later have a chance to state the maximum they were prepared to vote in favor of. We considered the option asking respondents how they would vote if the cost of the program was $0, but found that this was an implausible question for many respondents.

9. Other possible elicitation formats such as multinomial choice or a sequence of binary choices provide different, and often, harder to analyse incentives for strategic behavior than do open-ended type formats in the context of multiple levels of the same public good. Those elicitation formats further require one to specify the cost structure of the different risk reduction levels, which should influence the respondent's optimal response strategies. The ideal elicitation framework, asking each respondent a single binary discrete choice question about a single risk reduction was well beyond the budget constraint for this project, given the need for lengthy in-person interviews.

10. Risk communication failures are, of course, not limited to surveys. People often do not behave in the (economically) expected manner in actual market choices involving risk.

11. In a few instances, our locational shift resulted in more than one dwelling unit meeting the shift qualification. This increased the number of sampled dwelling units from 250 to 286. Further details on the sampling plan and its execution can be found in (Mitchell and Carson, 1986).

12. A 5 per cent α-trimmed mean is calculated by first dropping the lowest and highest 5 per cent of the observations and then calculating mean WTP based upon the remaining 90 per cent of the observations. The median is a 50 per cent trimmed mean.

13. Seven per cent of the sample provided the same positive WTP response for two or more of the risk levels they were asked about. Most of the respondents dropped in the corrected sample are elderly or have low educational levels.

14. There are two other standard predictions. The first of these has to do with WTP increasing with increases in income. We look at this prediction later in the chapter. The second is that the WTP for a fixed risk reduction should increase with the level of baseline risk. Smith and Desvousges (1987) look at this prediction in the context of a CV survey and fail to find support for the hypothesis with respondents appearing to ignore the randomly assigned baseline risks. This may be the rational response from a respondent's perspective, and, as such, this hypothesis may be difficult to test in a survey context.

15. Many of the respondents dropped by these two approaches whose pattern of responses suggests a failure to distinguish between risk levels are elderly and less well educated. The δ-trimmed mean effectively drops almost all of the respondents who give the same positive WTP amount for all three risk levels as well as a subset of those providing $0 for all three risk levels. The process of adjusting the mean estimate by removing a small number of cases where the interviewers indicated substantial problems with understanding the question picks up a subset of these cases.

16. Results from fitting models to the individual data produce qualitatively similar results but with, as should be expected, much lower R-squares. Some difficulties arise with the use of individual data in that the log of zero is undefined and usual correction approaches of taking the log of zero plus a small positive amount conceptually go against the possibility that some agents are at a corner solution. A standard Tobit model has the undesirable property of implying that some agents have negative latent WTP values. Some type of spike mixture model along the lines suggested by Werner (1999), which took account of the correlation structure between the three responses given by each agent, would likely be appropriate if our interest was in fitting the individual data

including covariates. Here, we are principally concerned with the aggregate value of a statistical life function and our approach is more transparent.

17. Note that these estimates are conservative in the sense that they set POS = 0. Using POS = 1 might be a better alternative in terms of making a correction for strategic behavior if one believes that open-ended CV WTP estimates are biased downward.

18. We are not the first to observe this effect. Blomquist (1982) appears to have been the first researcher to note that the studies (mostly using hedonic pricing) valuing smaller risk changes tend to have higher SVL estimates than those valuing larger risk changes. This empirical regularity has continued to hold in both revealed preference and CV studies.

19. There has been some work in the risk communications literature (e.g., Sandman, Weinstein, and Miller, 1994), on trying to find risk communication devices that adequately conveyed changes in small risks, although again less than we would have expected.

References

Arrow, K., R. Solow, P.R. Portney, E.E. Leamer, R. Radner and H. Schuman (1993), 'Report of the NOAA Panel on Contingent Valuation', *Federal Register*, **58**, 4601–14.

Attias, L.A. Contu, A. Loizzo and M. Massiglia (1995), 'Trihalomethanes in drinking water and cancer – risk assessment and integrated evaluation of available data in animals and humans', *Science of the Total Environment*, **171**, 61–8.

Baron, Jonathan and Joshu Greene (1996), 'Determinants of insensitivity to quantity in valuation of public goods: contribution, warm glow, budget constraints, availability, and prominence', *Journal of Experimental Psychology: Applied*, **2**, 107–25.

Beattie, J., J. Covey, P. Dolan, L. Hopkins, M. Jones-Lee, N. Pidgeon, A. Robinson and A. Spencer (1998), 'On the contingent valuation of safety and the safety of contingent valuation: Part I – caveat investigator', *Journal of Risk and Uncertainty*, **17**, 5–25.

Blomquist, G. (1982), 'Estimating the value of life and safety: recent developments', in M.W. Jones-Lee (ed.), *The Value of Life and Safety*, Amsterdam: North-Holland.

Carson, R.T. (1997), 'Contingent valuation surveys and tests of insensitivity to scope', in R.J. Kopp, W. Pommerhene and N. Schwartz (eds), *Determining the Value of Non-Marketed Goods: Economic, Psychological, and Policy Relevant Aspects of Contingent Valuation Methods*, Boston: Kluwer.

Carson, R.T., T. Groves and M. Machina (1999), 'Incentive and informational properties of preferences questions', Plenary Address, European Association of Environmental and Resource Economists, Compatibility Issues in Stated Preference Surveys, Oslo, Norway, June.

Culp, Gordon (ed.) (1984), *Trihalomethane Reduction in Drinking Water*, Park Ridge, NJ: Noyes Publications.

Corso, P.S., J.K. Hammitt and J.D. Graham (2000), 'Evaluating the effects of visual aids on willingness to pay for reductions in mortality risks', paper presented at the annual meeting of the Association of Environmental and Resource Economists, January.

Cropper, Maureen L. and A. Myrick Freeman (1991), 'Environmental health effects', in John B. Braden and Charles D. Kolstad (eds), *Measuring the Demand for Environmental Quality*, Amsterdam: North-Holland.

Cropper, Maureen L. and Paul R. Portney (1990), 'Discounting and the evaluation of lifesaving programs', *Journal of Risk and Uncertainty*, **3**, 369–79.

Davies, Clarence, Vincent T. Covello and Frederick W. Allen (eds) (1986), 'Risk communication', Proceedings of the National Conference on Risk Communications, Conservation Foundation, Washington, DC.

Fetherstonhaugh, D., P. Slovic, S.M. Johnson and J. Friedrich (1997), 'Insensitivity to the value of human life: a study of psychophysical numbing', *Journal of Risk and Uncertainty*, **14**, 283–300.

Fischhoff, Baruch (1990), 'Understanding long term environmental risks', *Journal of Risk and Uncertainty*, **3**, 315–30.

Fisher, Ann, Maria Pavolva and Vincent Covello (eds) (1991), 'Evaluation and effective risk communications workshop proceedings', US Environmental Protection Agency, Washington, DC.

Goldberger, A.A. (1968), 'The interpretation and estimation of Cobb–Douglas functions', *Econometrica*, **36**, 464–72.

Hammitt, J.K. and J.D. Graham (1999), 'Willingness to pay for health protection: inadequate sensitivity to probability?', *Journal of Risk and Uncertainty*, **18**, 33–62.

Hoehn, John P. and Alan Randall (1987), 'A satisfactory benefit cost indicator from contingent valuation', *Journal of Environmental Economics and Management*, **14**, 226–47.

Horowitz, J.K. and R.T. Carson (1991), 'A classification tree for predicting consumer preferences for risk reduction', *American Journal of Agricultural Economics*, **73**, 1416–21.

Horowitz, J.K and R.T. Carson (1990), 'Discounting statistical lives', *Journal of Risk and Uncertainty*, **3**, 403–13.

Jones-Lee, Michael W. (1974), 'The value of changes in probability of death or injury', *Journal of Political Economy*, **82**, 835–49.

Jones-Lee, Michael W. (1976), *The Value of Life: An Economic Analysis*, Chicago: University of Chicago Press.

Kahneman, Daniel, Paul Slovic and Amos Tversky (eds) (1982), *Judgement Under Uncertainity: Heuristics and Biases*, Cambridge: Cambridge University Press.

Kahneman, D. and J.L. Knetsch (1992), 'Valuing public goods: the purchase of moral satisfaction', *Journal of Environmental Economics and Management*, **22**, 57–70.

Loomis, J.B. and P.H. duVair (1993), 'Evaluating the effect of alternative risk communication devices on willingness to pay: results from a dichotomous choice contingent valuation experiment', *Land Economics*, **69**, 287–98.

Machina, M.J. (1995), 'Non-expected utility and the robustness of the classical insurance paradigm', *Geneva Papers on Risk and Insurance Theory*, **20**, 9–50.

Mitchell, Robert Cameron and Richard T. Carson (1986), 'Valuing drinking water risk reductions using the contingent valuation method: a methodological study of risks from THM and Giardia', Report to the US Environmental Protection Agency, May.

Mitchell, R.C. and R.T. Carson (1989), 'Using surveys to value public goods: the contingent valuation method', Baltimore: John Hopkins University Press.

Moore, Don A. (1999), 'Order effects in preference judgments: evidence for context dependence in the generation of preferences', *Organizational Behavior and Human Decision Processes*, **78**, 146–65.

Rimer, Barbara and Paul Van Nevel (eds) (1999), 'Cancer risk communications: what we know and what we need to learn', National Cancer Institute, Bethesda, MD.

Sandman, P.M., N.D. Weinstien and P. Miller (1994), 'High risk or low: how location on a "risk ladder" affects perceived risk', *Risk Analysis*, **14**, 35–45.

Smith, V. Kerry and William H. Desvousges (1987), 'An empirical analysis of the economic value of risk changes', *Journal of Political Economy*, **95**, 89–114.

Weinstein, M.C., D.S. Shepard and J.S. Pliskin (1980), 'The economic value of changing mortality probabilities: a decision-theoretic approach', *Quarterly Journal of Economics*, **44**, 373–93.

Werner, M. (1999), 'Allowing for zeros in dichotomous-choice contingent-valuation models', *Journal of Business and Economic Statistics*, **17**, 479–86.

20 Conclusions
Anna Alberini and James R. Kahn

The process of writing a concluding chapter for a book that explores a wide range of issues is a daunting task. Each specific chapter generates a conclusion or set of conclusions, but the individual conclusions do not directly aggregate into a specific set of results that provide a directed roadmap for valuation. The process is further complicated by the fact that, even though we have had 50 years of experience with contingent valuation and other stated preference approaches, contingent valuation remains a controversial method of determining the value of non-market goods. Consequently the use of these value estimates in cost–benefit analysis or other decision-making processes remains controversial.

One thing that has been made quite clear by the chapters in this book, is that substantial progress has been made in developing and implementing the contingent valuation method to produce value estimates in which people have more confidence. This progress includes econometric advances, developments in the writing of survey questions, the development of a better understanding of biases, and the ability to limit or bound the bias in value estimates, the development of tests of the validity of valuation estimates, how to use internet to implement contingent valuation, implementing contingent valuation on a limited budget, the development of related techniques such as conjoint analysis, and the application of contingent valuation to non-market valuation in developing countries, particularly in the subsistence or informal sector of developing countries. Although significant progress has been made in these areas, developmental research must continue if contingent valuation is to have a significant future role in measuring the economic efficiency implications of alternative states of the world associated with different policy outcomes. This is particularly true in the large developing countries such as China, India, Brazil, and Mexico, where non-market valuation is just emerging as a tool to help inform the decision-making process.

The authors of the various chapters of this book have done an excellent job in summarizing the progress made in each of these areas, making their own important and original contributions to dealing with these issues, and making recommendations about the directions in which future research may have the most promise. While work on the issues listed in the previous paragraph must continue to progress, they are not the only direction in which contingent valuation and stated preference methods in general must be extended. While these methods are helping to refine the results from contingent valuation studies in terms of the quality and validity of their estimates, new pathways must be followed as well. In particular, it is important to broaden the type of problem to which stated preference methods can help contribute.

Stated preference and revealed preference valuation methods were developed to measure incremental changes in environmental quality. If one examines the type of problems that were investigated in the early literature, they are problems such as changes in water quality at a site or set of sites, changes in air quality, whether a particular environmental resource should be impacted by a development project such as the erection of a dam, or measuring the value of a particular species. Tests of validity, measurement of biases and related issues have generally been conducted for this type of incremental change, as more broadly defined change is less conducive to these types of tests. For example, it is very difficult to construct a test where actual and hypothetical willingness to pay is measured for system-wide environmental changes such as the degradation of the planet's oceans or global climate change. The advances that have been made in the valuation methods as applied to incremental change do not necessarily hold in the context of more broadly defined environmental change, particularly system-wide environmental change. Additional research needs to be focused on improving the way we achieve the measurement of the value of system-wide change so we begin to approach the same confidence in value estimates that we have developed for incremental change over the last several decades.

Another way in which it is important to extend valuation methodologies is further developing their suitability for alternative decision-making paradigms. We tend to think about contingent valuation as providing inputs to cost–benefit analysis and measuring the economic efficiency of alternative policies that generate improvements or allow degradation in environmental quality. While this is, and will continue to be, an important aid to decision making, alternative decision-making criteria and alternative assessment paradigms are becoming increasingly important in the decision-making process. For example, in addition to economic efficiency, decision-making criteria that are viewed as important in environmental decision-making include equity, sustainability, environmental stewardship, ethical considerations, environmental justice, and ecosystem integrity. Contingent valuation and related methods can contribute more to the policy formation process if they can be adapted to provide more information than simple benefit estimates. Since stated preference models measure people's willingness to make tradeoffs, these models can be used to measure the willingness to trade-off increments in the level of one decision-making criteria for another.[1] In other words, how can valuation methods contribute to decision-making mechanisms other than benefit–cost analysis?

There are many different assessment mechanisms that focus on incorporating multiple decision-making criteria. This concluding chapter will focus on two alternative paradigms that attempt to integrate a suite of decision making criteria into the assessment process, including both social and ecological values. These are termed 'ecosystem-based management' and 'ecological services management', respectively.

Brussard et al. (1998), Yaffee (1999), Grumbine (1997), and others discuss the ecosystem-based management approach of managing our natural resources. A common thread of the discussion is that the models evaluate ecological regimes, focusing on characteristics such as ecological integrity (which is in itself, a set of characteristics), humans embedded in nature, adaptive management, inter-agency cooperation, and the importance of human values and behavior.

As currently construed, ecosystem management does not have a strong basis upon which to integrate the social and economic values into decision making. The orientation is to focus on the ecosystem as a unit and to guide policy so that the sustainability of the ecosystem is ensured. Instead of managing the ecosystem component by component, the integrated system is managed as a whole. However, there are many possible paths that are sustainable though which the ecosystem could be guided by encouraging or restraining different types of human activity. Although ecosystem management specifies goals, unfortunately there is not a well-defined process for choosing among the alternative paths, weighting the various goals, or otherwise assessing the relative merits of each path. An example of this is a middle Atlantic river system, that contains healthy populations of two introduced species, smallmouth bass and rainbow trout. Managing for rainbow trout would reduce smallmouth bass populations, managing for smallmouth bass would reduce trout populations, and managing to promote abundance of either of these two species might reduce populations of rare smaller fish, such as shiners or darters. How does one chose the characteristics of the ecosystem among multiple stable equilibrium states?

Contingent valuation can aid in this process, but it involves a dramatic increase in the dimensionality of the contingent valuation question. The ecosystem must be described to the respondent in terms of its individual components and the system itself. Moreover, this characterization must have both a spatial and temporal dimensionality. Contingent valuation or conjoint analysis surveys must be further developed to incorporate this characterization and dimensionality in a manner that is comprehensible to the survey respondent.

The second approach to alternative decision-making mechanisms that is used as an example in this chapter, is ecosystem service-based management (ESM). ESM focuses on managing the flow of services from an ecosystem, rather than managing the state of the ecosystem as defined by levels of ecosystem characteristics.[2]

Ecosystem service management has been defined by Farber et al. (2005, p. 1) as a process that chooses among alternative states of the world, based on how choices affect the flow of ecological services and how changes in the flow of ecological services affect human well-being.

Although the characteristics of the ecosystem obviously are related to an ecosystem's ability to produce services, managing to stabilize a level of characteristics is different than managing to provide flows of ecological services. More importantly, specifying the management problems as a choice among the alternative flows of ecological services may be more conducive to a valuation process than choosing among alternative levels of ecosystem characteristics.

However, as indicated above, there are additional complexities associated with the valuation of alternative flows of ecological services. For example, if the value of the level of a particular ecological service is a function of the levels of alternative ecological services, then the valuation process must estimate the value of multidimensional arrays of ecological services, not independent levels of ecological services. In addition, the flows of ecological services have both temporal and spatial distributions, further complicating the valuation process.

From the point of view of further development of contingent valuation and related stated preference techniques, it is critically important that the methodologies develop along these more multidimensional lines. However, the more complex the valuation process, the more likely are the problems associated with potential issues such as hypothetical bias, part-whole biases, and embedding. The lines of inquiry that have made so much progress with regard to these valuation issues need to be further developed by extending the research to valuation studies with more complex dimensionality.

Although contingent valuation and related techniques have not 'arrived' in the sense that they give indisputable evidence of the societal consequences of environmental change, they are far along the development path. Advances that have been documented in the chapters of this book and in other sources have greatly increased the ability to use valuation estimates in the decision-making process. Currently, they more than adequately inform certain types of decisions, and with further development can contribute to informing the very complex decisions we will face in the coming years.

Notes

1. See Ervin, Kahn and Livingston (2003) for a discussion of decision-making criteria.
2. See Farber et al. 2005.

References

Brussard, P.F. et al. (1998), 'Ecosystem management: what is it really?', *Landscape and Urban Planning*, **40**(1–3), 9–20.

Farber, S. et al. (forthcoming), 'Linking ecology and economics for ecosystem management: a services-based approach with illlustrations from LTER sites', *Bioscience*.

Grumbine, R.E. (1997), 'Reflections on "what is ecosystem management?"', *Conservation Biology*, **11**(1), 41–7.

Yaffee, Steven L. (1999), 'Three faces of ecosystem management', *Conservation Biology*, **13**(4), 713–25.

Index